Compton's
Encyclopedia
and Fact-Index

Compton's Encyclopedia

and Fact-Index

A—Anhui
pages 1-420

THE UNIVERSITY OF CHICAGO
COMPTON'S ENCYCLOPEDIA IS PUBLISHED WITH THE EDITORIAL ADVICE
OF THE FACULTIES OF THE UNIVERSITY OF CHICAGO

"Let knowledge grow from more to more and thus be human life enriched"

EDITOR'S PREFACE

The first edition of Compton's Encyclopedia—an eight-volume home and school reference work—was published in 1922. For its day it was unique. It was, for example, the first *pictured* encyclopedia—that is, the first to use photographs and drawings right on the same pages with the text they illustrated. Its Fact-Index was the first index to contain not merely page references to the text but also short, complete articles called Fact Entries. Compton's was also one of the first encyclopedias, if not the first, to maintain a large, permanent editorial staff so that continuous growth and revision of the set would occur each year.

On the title page of that first edition of Compton's there was the following statement:

> To inspire ambition, to stimulate the imagination, to
> provide the inquiring mind with accurate information
> told in an interesting style, and thus lead into broader
> fields of knowledge—such is the purpose of this work.

For more than half a century Compton's has never lost sight of its original purpose. It has continued to be an innovative, forward-looking reference work for young people. Compton editors have consistently maintained the encyclopedia at the highest level of quality. This has been accomplished through the efforts of dedicated editorial and art staffs working with outstanding specialists as contributors and consultants, professional advisory groups for areas of special interest, and panels of experts in special fields of knowledge.

Each edition of Compton's uses the most recent advances in the graphic arts, from papermaking to color printing. Each retains the unique features of earlier editions and by revision and expansion keeps them up-to-date in fact and in spirit.

EDITORIAL CONSULTANTS AND CONTRIBUTORS

GIORGIO ABETTI, HON. C.B.E., D.SC.
SUN
Professor of Astronomy, University of Florence; formerly director, Arcetri Observatory; past president, Italian Astronomical Society, International Committee for Study of Solar and Terrestrial Relationships; author, 'The Sun', 'Solar Research', 'The Exploration of the Universe'.

CLIFFORD ROSE ADAMS, A.B., A.M., PH.D.
FAMILY; MARRIAGE
Professor Emeritus of Psychology, School of Education, Pennsylvania State University; author, 'How to Pick a Mate', 'Making Marriage Work', etc.

CHARLES ANDERSON ALDRICH, M.D.
BABY CARE
Late Professor of Pediatrics, Mayo Foundation Graduate School, University of Minnesota; coauthor, 'Cultivating the Child's Appetite', 'Babies Are Human Beings'.

HAROLD B. ALLEN, B.A., M.A., PH.D.
LANGUAGE
Professor Emeritus of English and Linguistics, University of Minnesota; past president, National Council of Teachers of English; Teachers of English to Speakers of Other Languages, American Dialect Society.

SAMUEL ALLEN, B.A., M.A.
CARTOONS; MOTION PICTURES
Formerly staff editor, Compton's Encyclopedia; senior editor, Society for Visual Education; writer of numerous documentary films, including 'Jacques Lipchitz: Sculptor', 'What Is a Community?'; coauthor, Emmy award-winning 'The Giants and the Common Men'.

CLIFFORD J. ALLUM
AIRPLANE MODELS
Formerly Technical Director, Academy of Model Aeronautics; editor, 'Model Aviation'.

BOWER ALY, B.S., A.M., PH.D.
PUBLIC SPEAKING
Professor of Speech, University of Oregon; coauthor, 'Fundamentals of Speaking'.

AMERICAN FOREST INSTITUTE
LUMBER

A. W. ANDERSON, B.S.
FISH TECHNOLOGY
Formerly Chief Branch of Commercial Fisheries, U. S. Fish and Wildlife Service, Department of the Interior; author of many technical articles on fish.

JOHN F. ANDERSON, B.A., M.S. IN L.S.
LIBRARIES
City Librarian, San Francisco Public Library; formerly Director, Tucson Public Library, and President, Arizona State Library Association; contributor to 'American Libraries', 'Library Journal', and 'Wilson Library Bulletin'.

JEAN M. ARBO
ART
Graduate, The Chicago Academy of Fine Arts, The Art Institute of Chicago; art editor and illustrator of children's books.

LESTER ASHEIM, B.S., B.L.S., M.A., PH.D. (L.S.)
LIBRARIES
Professor, Graduate Library School, University of Chicago; formerly director, International Relations Office, and Office of Library Education, American Library Association; books include 'The Humanities and the Library' and 'Librarianship in the Developing Countries'.

MAX BACHRACH
FUR INDUSTRY
Late fur consultant and lecturer; author, 'Fur', 'Selling Furs Successfully', 'The Fur Digest'.

HERBERT B. BAIN, B.A.
MEAT; MEAT INDUSTRY
Director of Public Relations, American Meat Institute.

AUGUSTA BAKER, B.S. IN ED., B.S. IN L.S.
BIBLIOGRAPHIES; LIBRARIES; LITERATURE FOR CHILDREN
Coordinator, Children's Services, New York Public Library; storytelling specialist; awarded 1966 Parents' Magazine medal for outstanding service to nation's children; editor, 'The Talking Tree', 'The Golden Lynx', 'The Black Experience in Children's Books'.

MARTIN S. BANDER, B.S.
HOSPITALS
Director of News and Public Affairs, Massachusetts General Hospital, Boston; formerly Medical Writer, 'Herald-Traveler', Boston, and Education Editor, 'Woonsocket Call', Woonsocket, R. I.

CHRISTIAAN NEETHLING BARNARD, M.D., M.MED., PH.D., F.A.C.S., F.A.C.C., D.SC. (HON. CAUSA)
SURGERY
Honorary Professor of Surgical Sciences, University of Cape Town, South Africa; recipient of international acclaim, honors, and awards; coauthor, 'The Surgery of the Common Congenital Cardiac Malformation' and 'One Life', and author, 'Heart Attack— You Don't Have to Die'.

ANN BARZEL, PH.B.
BALLET, DANCE
Writer and critic; editorial staff, 'Dance Magazine'; contributor to 'Dance Index' and 'Dance Encyclopedia'.

W. W. BAUER, M.D.
ANATOMY; HEALTH
Late Consultant to the Director of the Division of Environmental Medicine, American Medical Association.

ROBERT F. BEATTIE, B.A.
SKIING
President, World Wide Ski Corporation; formerly director of skiing activities, University of Colorado; coach, U.S. ski team, 1964 Olympics.

ROBERT O. BEATTY, B.S., M.S.
FISHING
Formerly Conservation Director, Izaak Walton League of America, Inc.; editor, 'Outdoor America'.

ERNEST W. BECK, B.S., M.A.
ANATOMY; FROG, ANATOMY OF
Formerly Art Director, G. D. Searle & Company; free-lance medical illustrator; artist-author; 'Textbook of Physiology'.

JOAN BECK, B.S., M.S.
ETIQUETTE
Daily Features Editor, Chicago Tribune; author, 'How to Raise a Brighter Child' and 'Is My Baby All Right?'.

FRANCES OBERHOLTZER BELSEY, A.B.
SOCIAL STUDIES: GEOGRAPHY
Formerly Social Studies Supervisor and staff writer, Compton's Encyclopedia; manuscript editor, 'Journal of the American Medical Association'.

STEPHEN VINCENT BENÉT, M.A.
POETRY
Late author, 'John Brown's Body' (Pulitzer prize, 1929), 'Johnny Pye and the Fool Killer', 'Western Star' (Pulitzer prize, 1944).

WILLIAM ROSE BENÉT, M.A., LITT.D.
BIOGRAPHIES
Late contributing editor, 'Saturday Review of Literature'; editor, 'Poems for Youth', 'The Dust Which Is God' (Pulitzer prize, 1942).

ROBERT J. BENFORD, M.D.
ANTIBIOTICS; DRUGS
Formerly Director of Medical Relations, Pharmaceutical Manufacturers Association, Washington, D. C.

ADAM S. BENNION, M.A., PH.D.
MORMONS
Late Superintendent, Latter-day Saints' School; member, Latter-day Saints' General Board of Education; author, 'What It Means to Be a Mormon'.

F. LEE BENNS, A.M., PH.D., LITT.D., F.R.H.S.
MODERN HISTORY
Late Professor of History, Indiana University.

MICHAEL BERGER
JAPAN
Correspondent, 'Stars and Stripes' (Tokyo), 'San Francisco Chronicle'.

REBECCA T. BINGHAM, M.L.S., M.A.
LIBRARIES
Director of Library Media Service, Louisville Public Schools; Councilor, American Library Association; Editor, Kentucky Association of School Librarians' 'Bulletin'.

KENNETH BOLDT, B.S.
AEROSPACE FUELS
Research Associate, Union Research Center, Union Oil Company of California.

ROGER W. BOLZ, M.E.
AUTOMATION
Management consultant on automation; formerly editor, 'Automation'; author, 'Production Processes'.

FRED E. BOND
PHOTOGRAPHY
Color photographer and author; fellow, Photographic Society of America; received 1956 La Belle award for contributions to color photography.

JACK BOOKBINDER, B.S., M.F.A.
THE ARTS; SCULPTURE
Director, Division of Art Education, Philadelphia Public Schools; lecturer, Pennsylvania Academy of Fine Arts; paintings and lithographs in many collections; author, 'Invitation to the Arts'.

CHRISTY BORTH
AUTOMOBILE; AUTOMOBILE INDUSTRY
Formerly Assistant Managing Director, Automobile Manufacturers Association; author, 'Masters of Mass Production', 'True Steel', 'Pioneers of Plenty'.

ELEANOR BOYKIN, A.B.
CONVERSATION; LETTER WRITING
Journalist and lecturer: formerly Secretary of Public Relations Committee, National Council of Teachers of English.

LILLIAN MOORE BRADSHAW, B.A., B.S. IN L.S.
LIBRARIES
Director, Dallas Public Library; formerly Adult Librarian, Enoch Pratt Free Library, Baltimore, Md., and President, American Library Association; Member, Board of Consultants, 'Library Journal'; contributor to 'American Libraries', 'Library Journal', and 'Wilson Library Bulletin'.

FRANK B. BRADY
AIRPLANE INSTRUMENTS
Director, Airport Equipment Program, General Precision Equipment Corporation.

STANLEY H. BRAMS
AUTOMOBILE CAREERS
Publisher, 'Labor Trends'.

JAMES H. BREASTED, A.M., PH.D., LL.D.
ARCHAEOLOGY
Late Professor of Egyptology, Oriental History; director, Oriental Institute, University of Chicago.

CHARLES K. BRIGHTBILL, B.A., M.A.
GAMES; PARKS AND PLAYGROUNDS
Late Head, Department of Recreation, University of Illinois; chairman, National Recreation Policies Committee; president, American Recreation Society; National Director of Recreation, Veterans Administration; author, 'Community Recreation', etc.

CALVIN CHARLES BROWN, B.S., CH.E.
METALS AND ALLOYS
Chief Control Metallurgist, Open Hearth and Blooming Mills, Inland Steel Company; formerly instructor in Metallurgy and Statistics, Purdue University.

ROBERT G. BROWN
TELEMETRY
Member, Executive Committee, National Telemetering Conference; coauthor, 'Analysis and Design of Feedback Control Systems', 'Servomechanism Analysis'.

W. NORMAN BROWN, A.B., PH.D.
PAKISTAN
Professor Emeritus of Sanskrit and formerly Chairman of the South Asia Regional Studies Department, University of Pennsylvania; editor, 'India, Pakistan, Ceylon'.

REV. PATRICK WILLIAM BROWNE, S.T.D., PH.D.
PAPACY; MONASTICISM
Late Editor, 'Catholic Historical Review'.

LEO J. BRUECKNER, B.A., M.A., PH.D.
ARITHMETIC
Late Professor of Education, University of Minnesota; coauthor of widely used arithmetic textbooks.

LESLIE A. BRYAN, PH.D., LL.B.
AIRPLANE; AVIATION METEOROLOGY
Director Emeritus, Institute of Aviation, University of Illinois; author and aviation consultant; colonel, U. S. Air Force Reserve (retired).

HELEN BUCKLER, A.B.
CAMP FIRE GIRLS
Formerly Associate Director, National Public Relations Division, Camp Fire Girls, Inc.

JOHN W. BUNN, B.S.
BASKETBALL
Formerly Basketball Coach, Colorado State College; author, 'Basketball Techniques and Team Play'.

EDWARD M. L. BURCHARD, B.A., M.A., PH.D.
PSYCHOANALYSIS
Professor of Psychology, Queens College; member, Low Cost Psychoanalytic Service, William Alanson White Institute of Psychiatry, New York; president, Society of Projective Techniques, 1951–52.

JOHN ANGUS BURRELL, A.B.
BIOGRAPHIES
Late Associate Professor of English, Columbia University; coauthor, 'Dead Reckoning in Fiction', 'Adventure or Experience', 'Modern Fiction'.

J. S. BUTZ, JR., B.S., AE.E.
AIRPLANE FLIGHT CONTROLS; AIRPLANE FLIGHT THEORY
Formerly Engineering Editor, 'Aviation Week and Space Technology'.

ROBERT L. CALVERT
BOY SCOUTS OF AMERICA
National Director, Planning and Communications Group, Boy Scouts of America.

HENRY C. CAMPBELL, B.A., B.L.S., M.A.
LIBRARIES
Chief Librarian, Toronto Public Libraries, Ontario, Canada; formerly Head, Section for Bibliography and Documentation, and Clearing House for Libraries, UNESCO; books include 'Handbook on the International Exchange of Publications', 'Metropolitan Public Library Planning Throughout the World', and 'Canadian Libraries'.

R. MILTON CARLETON, PH.D.
GARDENS
Garden Editor,'Chicago Today'; formerly director of research, Vaughan Garden Research Center, Chicago, Ill.; director, Men's Garden Clubs of America; author and coauthor of many books and articles on gardening.

CARL CARMER, M.A., LITT.D., L.H.D.
AMERICAN FOLKLORE
Author and folklorist; vice-president, New York State Folklore Society; author, 'America Sings', 'Listen for a Lonesome Drum', 'My Kind of Country'.

LEON CARNOVSKY, A.B., PH.D.
BIOGRAPHIES
Professor Emeritus of Library Science, Graduate Library School, University of Chicago.

SID CATO
BUS
Vice-President, Public Relations, The Greyhound Corporation.

W. LINWOOD CHASE, A.B., A.M., PH.D.
HISTORY
Formerly Professor of Education, Boston University; president, National Council for the Social Studies.

CARL M. CHRISTENSON
AIRPLANE SAFETY
Vice-President, Safety and Industry Affairs, United Air Lines, Inc.

BYONG-UK CHUNG, B.A.
KOREA
Professor of Korean Literature, Seoul National University; formerly chairman, Society of Korean Language and Literature; author, 'A Complete Collection of Sijo Poetry'.

EVERT B. CLARK
AEROSPACE INDUSTRY
Formerly Space Technology Editor, 'Aviation Week and Space Technology'.

DAVID H. CLIFT, B.S., B.S. IN L.S.
LIBRARIES
Executive Director Emeritus, American Library Association; formerly Associate Librarian, Yale University, and Assistant to Director of Libraries, Columbia University; received Joseph W. Lippincott Award for Notable Achievement in Librarianship; Honorary Trustee, American Library in Paris.

CHARLES N. COFER, A.B., A.M., PH.D.
PERSONALITY
Professor of Psychology, Pennsylvania State University; coauthor, 'Motivation: Theory and Research'.

EMMA COHN, B.A., M.L.S.
LIBRARIES; LITERATURE
Assistant Coordinator, Young Adult
Services, New York Public Library;
chairman, Audio-Visual Committee,
Young Adult Services Division,
International Federation of Library
Associations; editor, 'Films for
Young Adults'.

CYRIL L. COMAR, PH.D.
BIOPHYSICS
Professor of Physical Biology and Head
of the Department, New York State
Veterinary College at Cornell University.

**CARLETON S. COON, A.B., A.M.,
PH.D.**
MAN
Research Curator of Anthropology,
University of Pennsylvania Museum;
author, 'The Story of Man', 'The Origin
of Races', 'The Living Races of Man'.

**JOHN NIESSINK COOPER, A.B.,
PH.D.**
PHYSICS
Professor of Physics, Naval
Postgraduate School, Monterey, Calif.;
formerly research physicist, Manhattan
Project, University of California.

**MARGARET NOURSE COUGHLAN,
B.A., M.L.S.**
STORYTELLING
Senior Reference Librarian and
Bibliographer, Children's Book
Section, Library of Congress; formerly
teacher of children's literature,
Trinity College, Washington, D. C.

ARNOLD H. CRANE, LL.B.
PHOTOGRAPHY
Attorney; instructor in History of
Photography, Columbia College;
critic and book reviewer in
photography, 'Chicago Daily News';
author, lecturer, collector.

ROBERT I. CRANE, B.A., M.A., PH.D.
INDIA
Formerly Professor of History, Duke
University; member of Policy
Committee, Research Center on
Economic Development and Cultural
Change, University of Chicago.

**JOHN D. CUNNINGHAM, A.A.,
B.A., M.A., ED.D.**
SCIENCES BIBLIOGRAPHY
Professor of Biology, Keene State
College; formerly director of
biological development, Science
Curriculum Improvement Study,
University of California at Berkeley;
author, 'Winds and Weather';
'Health Science'; 'Investigating the
Biosphere', etc.

NICHOLAS P. CUSHNER, S.J., PH.D.
PHILIPPINES
Assistant Professor of History, Ateneo
de Manila University, the Philippines;
fellow of the Royal Historical Society
(London); member, Conference on
Latin American History; author, 'Spain
in the Philippines'.

**RUBEN SANTOS CUYUGAN, PH.B.,
A.M., PH.D.**
PHILIPPINES
Professor of Sociology and Director,
Asian Center, University of the
Philippines; formerly president,
Philippine Sociological Society;
contributor to professional journals.

ALICE DALGLIESH, B.S., A.M.
BIOGRAPHIES
Formerly Editor of Books for Younger
Readers, Charles Scribner's Sons;
instructor in Literature for Children,
Teachers College, Columbia University;
author, 'A Book for Jennifer' and other
books for children.

JAMES HENRY DAUGHERTY
BIOGRAPHIES
Author and illustrator, 'Daniel Boone'
(Newbery medal, 1940), 'Abraham
Lincoln', 'Poor Richard', 'Andy and the
Lion'; illustrator of many books for
children.

MARGUERITE DE ANGELI
NURSERY RHYMES; MOTHER GOOSE
Illustrator and author of children's
books.

JOHN J. DE BOER, A.B., A.M., PH.D.
REPORT WRITING
Late Professor of Education, University
of Illinois.

JOHN L. DE JONG
BANK
Late Associate Director, News Bureau,
American Bankers Association.

VINE DELORIA, JR.
AMERICAN INDIANS
Author, 'Custer Died for Your Sins: an
Indian Manifesto', 'The War Between
the Redskins and the Feds', 'We Talk,
You Listen'; formerly executive
director, National Council of American
Indians.

NICHOLAS DeWITT, B.A., M.A., PH.D.
RUSSIA; RUSSIAN HISTORY
Professor of Economics, Indiana
University; formerly associate, Russian
Research Center, Harvard University;
member, Compton's Encyclopedia
Editorial Advisory Committee.

LEON T. DICKINSON, PH.D.
AMERICAN LITERATURE
Professor of English and formerly
Chairman, Department of English,
University of Missouri.

W. E. DOHERTY, JR.
GLIDER
Sales Manager, Commercial Aircraft,
Schweizer Aircraft Corporation;
director, Soaring School, Elmira, N. Y.

**RICHARD M. DOUGHERTY, B.S.,
MLS., PH.D.**
LIBRARIES
University Librarian, University of
California, Berkeley; formerly
Associate Director of Libraries,
University of Colorado, and professor
of Library Science, Syracuse University;
Member, Editorial Board, 'Journal of
Library Automation', and editor,
'College and Research Libraries';
books include 'Scientific Management
of Library Operations'.

MAX DRESDEN, PH.D.
ENERGY
Professor, Department of Physics,
State University of New York at Stony
Brook; visiting senior scientist,
Brookhaven National Laboratory;
consultant, Argonne National
Laboratory.

LUCY E. DRISCOLL, M.A.
FACTORS
Assistant Superintendent, Cook County
(Illinois) Schools.

DOROTHY DRUMMOND, B.A., M.A.
SOUTH AMERICA
Coauthor, 'The World Today: Its
Patterns and Cultures'; teacher of
geography; formerly assistant editor,
'Focus'.

RUTH SAWYER DURAND, B.S.
STORYTELLING
Late professional storyteller and
author, 'The Way of the Storyteller',
'Roller Skates', 'Journey Cake, Ho!',
'Joy to the World'; received Newbery
medal, 1937; Regina medal, 1965;
Laura Ingalls Wilder medal, 1965.

PETER DUUS, A.B., M.A., PH.D.
JAPAN
Associate Professor of History,
Claremont Graduate School; author,
'Party Rivalry and Political Change in
Taisho Japan', 'Feudalism in Japan'.

MERLIN K. DUVAL, M.D.
MEDICINE
Vice-President for Health Sciences,
University of Arizona; formerly Assistant
Secretary for Health and Scientific
Affairs, Department of Health,
Education, and Welfare, Washington,
D.C.

E. J. DYKSTERHUIS, PH.D.
ECOLOGY
Professor of Range Science, College
of Agriculture, Texas A & M University.

JEANETTE EATON, A.B., A.M.
BIOGRAPHIES
Late author, 'That Lively Man, Ben
Franklin', 'Young Lafayette', 'Gandhi:
Fighter Without a Sword', etc.

RICHARD EDGREN, PH.D.
BIOLOGY
Formerly Endocrinologist, Division of
Biological Research, G. D. Searle &
Company.

**MARGARET A. EDWARDS, A.B.,
A.M., B.S. IN L.S.**
LITERATURE; READING
Formerly Coordinator of Work with
Young Adults, Enoch Pratt Free
Library, Baltimore, Md.; past
president, Maryland Library
Association; author, 'The Fair Garden
and the Swarm of Beasts'.

DAVID I. EGGENBERGER, B.S.
MILITARY SUBJECTS
Editor in Chief, Professional and
Reference Books, McGraw-Hill Book
Company; author, 'Flags of the U.S.A.',
'A Dictionary of Battles'.

FRANK S. ENDICOTT, B.A., M.A., PH.D.
GUIDANCE
Formerly Director of Placement and
Professor of Education, Northwestern
University; member, Compton's
Encyclopedia Editorial Advisory
Committee.

SHIRLEY H. ENGLE, B.S., M.S., ED.D.
SOCIAL STUDIES
Professor of Education, Indiana
University at Bloomington; past
president, National Council for the
Social Studies; author, editor.

EARLE ERNST, PH.D.
JAPAN; KOREA; PHILIPPINES
Senior Professor and Chairman,
Department of Drama and Theatre,
University of Hawaii; author,
'Japanese Theatre in Highlight',
'Kabuki Theatre'.

EVAN EVANS, A.B., A.M., LL.D.
AVIATION
Formerly Executive Director, National
Aerospace Education Council;
contributor to professional magazines.

PAUL L. EVANS, B.S.
TENNESSEE VALLEY AUTHORITY
Director of Information, Tennessee
Valley Authority; formerly professor of
journalism, Ohio Wesleyan University.

JOHN D. EYRE, B.A., M.A., PH.D.
JAPAN; KOREA
Professor of Geography, University of
North Carolina; author of periodical
literature on the economic and urban
geography of Japan.

DELMER STATER FAHRNEY, B.S., M.S.
GUIDED MISSILES
Rear Admiral, U. S. Navy (retired);
pioneer work in guided missiles and
pilotless aircraft.

LEONARD V. FARLEY
CIRCUS
Museum Librarian, Hertzberg Circus
Collection, San Antonio (Tex.) Public
Library; Historian, Circus Fans
Association of America.

LEO FAY, B.S., M.A., PH.D.
READING
Professor of Education and Director,
Reading Center, Indiana University at
Bloomington; member, Compton's
Encyclopedia Editorial Advisory
Committee.

**IRWIN K. FEINSTEIN, B.S., M.A.,
PH.D.**
MATHEMATICS ARTICLES
Professor of Mathematics, University of
Illinois at Chicago; chairman,
Committee on the Strengthening of the
Teaching of Mathematics; past
chairman, Commission on the
Mathematics Preparation of Teachers
of Elementary School Mathematics;
author of mathematics textbooks.

DANIEL J. FELDMAN, A.B., M.D.
DISEASE
Adj. Professor, University of California,
Irvine, College of Medicine; formerly
director, Standford Medical Center
Rehabilitation Service, and staff
member, Institute of Rehabilitation and
Medicine, New York University School
of Medicine.

CARROLL LANE FENTON, B.S., PH.D.
LIFE; PREHISTORIC LIFE
Late Assistant Professor of Physical
Sciences, University of Buffalo;
geologist, Rutgers University and New
Jersey State Museum.

SARA I. FENWICK, B.A., M.A.
LIBRARIES; LITERATURE ARTICLES
Professor, Graduate Library School,
University of Chicago; past president,
American Association of School
Librarians; president, Children's
Services Division, American Library
Association.

C. B. FERGUSSON, M.A. (OXON.)
CANADA
Assistant Archivist for Nova Scotia;
author, 'The Establishment of Negroes
in Nova Scotia'.

**RAYMOND FIELDING, B.A., M.A.,
PH.D.**
MOTION PICTURES
Professor, Department of Radio-TV-
Film, School of Communications,
Temple University; vice-president,
International Congress of Schools of
Cinema and Television; governor,
Information Film Producers
Association; author, 'A Technological
History of Motion Pictures and
Television'; writer, director, producer of
numerous films, television and radio
programs.

LESTER E. FISHER, D.V.M.
ZOOLOGY; VETERINARY MEDICINE
Director, Lincoln Park Zoo, Chicago,
Ill.

CLARENCE M. FLATEN, PH.D.
NATURE STUDY
Supervisor of Photography and Science
Film Writer-Photographer-Editor,
Audio-Visual Center and Associate
Professor in AV Communications and
Educational Media, School of
Education, Indiana University.

**WOLFGANG B. FLEISCHMANN,
A.B., A.M., PH.D.**
LITERATURE
Professor of Comparative Literature
and Dean, School of Humanities,
Montclair State College; general
editor, Encyclopedia of World
Literature in the 20th Century'.

JOHN M. FOGG, JR., B.S., PH.D.
PLANT LIFE
Director, Barnes Arboretum; formerly
professor of botany, University of
Pennsylvania; author, 'Weeds of Lawn
and Garden'.

GENEVIEVE FOSTER, B.A.
BIOGRAPHIES
Author and illustrator, 'George
Washington's World', 'Abraham
Lincoln's World', 'Augustus Caesar's
World,' 'George Washington: an
Initial Biography', etc.

RICHARD B. FRANKEL, B.S., PH.D.
MAGNETS AND MAGNETISM
Research Staff Member, National
Magnet Laboratory, Massachusetts
Institute of Technology.

HYMAN GABAI, B.A., M.A., PH.D.
ALGEBRA; MATHEMATICS;
NUMERATION SYSTEMS AND
NUMBERS
Associate Professor of Mathematics,
York College (N. Y.); formerly member,
University of Illinois Committee on
School Mathematics, Urbana.

**ROBERT G. GALLAGHER, B.S., M.S.,
SC.D.**
INFORMATION THEORY
Professor of Electrical Engineering,
Massachusetts Institute of
Technology; past chairman, Institute
of Electrical and Electronic Engineers
Group on Information Theory; author,
'Information Theory and Reliable
Communication'.

**ALFRED B. GARRETT, B.S., M.S.,
PH.D.**
CHEMISTRY
Vice-President for Research and
formerly Chairman, Department of
Chemistry, The Ohio State University;
coauthor, 'Essentials of Chemistry',
etc.

**ROBERT MALCOLM GAY, A.B., A.M.,
LITT.D.**
SHAKESPEARE
Late Professor of English, Simmons
College; author, 'Reading and
Writing'; editor, Anthony Trollope's
'The Warden,' etc.

IGNACE JAY GELB, PH.D.
ALPHABET; BABYLONIA AND
ASSYRIA; WRITING
Professor of Assyriology, University of
Chicago; member, Société Asiatique,
Finnish Oriental Society; author
'Hittite Hieroglyphs' 3v., 'Study of
Writing'; editor, 'Chicago Assyrian
Dictionary'.

JACK A. GERTZ
AIRPORTS; AIR TRAFFIC CONTROL
Formerly Chief, Office of Public
Affairs, Federal Aviation
Administration.

WRIGHT D. GIFFORD, JR., B.S., M.S.
PARACHUTE
Engineering Office Manager, Pioneer
Parachute Company.

JAMES E. GILLEY, B.S.
COAL; MINES AND MINING
Mining engineer, U.S. Bureau of Mines,
Department of the Interior.

NORTON S. GINSBURG, PH.D.
SOUTHEAST ASIA
Professor of Geography, University of
Chicago; author, 'Atlas of Economic
Development'.

ANNA M. GORMAN, PH.D.
HOME ECONOMICS
Professor and Specialist, Home
Economics Education, Center for
Vocational and Technical Education,
The Ohio State University.

HERB GRAFFIS
GOLF
Formerly Editor, 'Golfdom', and
President, Golf Writers' Association of
America; coauthor, 'Better Golf Through
Practice'.

STEPHEN V. GRANCSAY
ARMOR
Curator Emeritus of Arms and Armor,
Metropolitan Museum of Art, New York;
author, 'The Armor of Galiot de
Genouilhac', etc.

DAVID E. GREEN, PH.D.
BIOCHEMISTRY
Professor and Codirector, Institute for Enzyme Research, University of Wisconsin; fellow, National Academy of Sciences, American Academy of Arts and Sciences; author, 'Molecular Insights into the Living Process'.

EMERSON GREENAWAY, B.S., A.B. IN L.S., LITT.D., L.H.D.
LIBRARIES
Formerly Director, Free Library of Philadelphia, and Enoch Pratt Free Library of Baltimore, Md.

WALTON E. GRUNDY, B.S., M.S., PH.D.
BACTERIA; VACCINES
Manager, Microbiology Department, Corporate Research Division, Abbott Laboratories.

ROY B. HACKMAN, B.A., M.A., PH.D.
STATISTICS; VOCATIONS
Professor of Psychology and Director of Vocational and Educational Guidance Clinic, Department of Counselor Education and Counseling Psychology, Temple University.

PYONG-CHOON HAHM, B.A., J.D.
KOREA
Professor of Law, Yonsei University; author, 'The Korean Political Tradition and Law'.

DEAN WRIGHT HALLIWELL, B.A., M.A., B.L.S.
LIBRARIES
University Librarian, University of Victoria, B.C.; formerly assistant librarian, University of Saskatchewan, Coordinator of Reference Services, Cuyahoga County Public Library, Cleveland, Ohio, and president, Canadian Library Association, Canadian Association of College and University Librarians, and British Columbia Library Association; editor, 'Saskatchewan Library Association Bulletin'.

NORMAN D. HAM, B.A.SC., S.M., AE.E.
AUTOGIRO
Associate Professor, Department of Aeronautics and Astronautics, Massachusetts Institute of Technology.

WILFRID D. HAMBLY, D.SC.
RACES OF MANKIND
Late Curator, African Ethnology, Field Museum of Natural History, Chicago; author, 'Source Book for African Anthropology', etc.

KARL C. HAMNER, PH.D.
BIOLOGICAL CLOCKS
Professor of Botany and Plant Physiology, University of California at Los Angeles.

PAUL ROBERT HANNA, B.A., M.A., PH.D.
SPELLING
Formerly Lee Jackson Professor of Childhood Education and Director of Stanford International Developmental Education Center, Stanford University; consultant, U. S. Office of Education; author, 'Spelling: Structures and Strategies'.

RT. REV. MSGR. JOHN H. HARRINGTON, D.L.S.
VATICAN CITY
Editor in Chief, Catholic Encyclopedia for School and Home; formerly librarian, St. Joseph's Seminary (Yonkers, N. Y.).

SHARON HARRIS, B.A., M.A.
DRESS DESIGN
Fashion designer; guest fashion design critic, The Art Institute of Chicago; received 1969 Gold Coast Fashion award.

VIRGINIA HAVILAND, B.A.
STORYTELLING
Head, Children's Book Section, Library of Congress; past president, National Children's Library Association; past chairman of various committees, American Library Association; author, Favorite Fairy Tales series and other books for children and adults.

ROBERT SELPH HENRY, A.B., LL.B., HON. LITT.D.
CONFEDERATE STATES OF AMERICA; RAILROADS
Late railway executive; author, 'The Story of the Confederacy', etc.

WILLIAM E. HENTHORN, PH.D.
KOREA
Assistant Professor, Department of Oriental Studies, Princeton University; author, 'A History of Korea'.

WILLIAM V. HENZEY
AVIATION REGULATION
Lecturer, Air Transport Management; director, International Air Research, School of Foreign Service, Georgetown University; formerly consultant, Air Transport Association of America.

PHILIP HERSHKOVITZ, B.S., M.S.
MONKEYS
Research Curator, Division of Mammals, Field Museum of Natural History, Chicago.

ALBERT R. HIBBS, B.S., M.S., PH.D.
EARTH; GEOLOGY
Senior Staff Scientist, Jet Propulsion Laboratory; California Institute of Technology; coauthor, 'The Earth-Space Sciences'; editorial board member, 'Planetary and Space Science', 'Space Science Reviews', and 'Icarus'; host and director of numerous radio and television programs, including 'Exploring'.

ROBERT D. HILL, D.SC.
ISOTOPES
Formerly Professor of Physics, University of Illinois; author, 'Tracking Down Particles'; coauthor, 'Manual of Vacuum Practice'.

YOSHIO HIYAMA, PH.D.
JAPAN
Professor Emeritus of Marine Biology, Tokyo University; author, 'An Outline of Marine Biology'.

ALFRED ERNEST HOBBS, B.A., M.A.
CANADA
Head of Department of Social Studies, Northern Vocational School, Toronto, Ont.; associate editor, 'World Affairs'.

ARLINE GERSON HOLDEN, B.A., M.A.
GEOGRAPHY
Formerly Reference Librarian, American Geographical Society; contributor to geographical publications in Europe and United States.

RUDOLPH HOLLMAN
OCEAN WAVES AND TIDES
Formerly Associate Research Scientist, Department of Meteorology and Oceanography, New York University.

RUTH HOLMAN, B.A., M.A.
RUGS AND CARPETS
Formerly on the staff of the Carpet and Rug Institute.

JACOB C. HOLPER, A.B., M.A., PH.D.
VACCINES
Director of Research and Development, Courtland Scientific Products Division; Abbott Laboratories.

JEAN HOLZWORTH, A.B., D.V.M.
CAT
Clinical Staff, Angell Memorial Animal Hospital, Boston, Mass.; member, American Veterinary Association, American College of Veterinary Internists, and Massachusetts Veterinary Association.

F. LOUIS HOOVER, B.S., A.M., D.ED.
DESIGN
Professor of Art and Director of Art Education, Illinois State University; formerly editor, 'Arts and Activities'; author, 'Art Activities for the Very Young'.

PHILIP S. HOPKINS
AIRPLANE HISTORY
Formerly Director, National Air Museum, Smithsonian Institution.

MARILYN J. HORN, B.S., M.S., PH.D.
CLOTHING
Professor and Director of Research and Graduate Study, School of Home Economics, University of Nevada; author, 'The Second Skin: an Interdisciplinary Study of Clothing'.

MARION HORTON, A.B., B.L.S.
LITERARY BIOGRAPHIES; BIBLIOGRAPHIES
Formerly Visiting Professor, School of Library Science, University of Southern California.

JOHN H. HOWARD, B.S., M.S.
CALCULATING MACHINES
Late Associate Director of Research, Burroughs Corporation; computers chairman, Institute of Radio Engineers.

FRANK W. HUBBARD, A.B., A.M., PH.D.
SAFETY
Formerly Director of Research, National Education Association.

CLARK HUBBS, A.B., PH.D.
EVOLUTION
Professor of Zoology, University of Texas at Austin; president, Texas Academy of Science.

GEORGE R. HUGHES, PH.D.
ANCIENT EGYPT
Director and Professor of Egyptology, Oriental Institute of the University of Chicago.

ERLING M. HUNT, A.M., PH.D.
HISTORY
Formerly Professor of History and
Head of the Department of Teaching
of Social Science, Teachers College,
Columbia University; editor, 'Social
Education' and 'Social Studies';
coauthor, 'The World History'.

**ELIZABETH B. HURLOCK, A.B., M.A.,
PH.D.**
CHILD DEVELOPMENT
Formerly Associate in Psychology, The
Graduate School, University of
Pennsylvania; Child Training Editor,
'Today's Health'; author, 'Child
Development', 'Child Growth and
Development', etc.

JOHN E. JACOBS, PH.D.
BIOENGINEERING
Professor of Science Engineering and
Executive Director, Biomedical
Engineering Center, Northwestern
University; founder, The Biomedical
Engineering Society; coauthor,
'Biomedical Engineering'.

LEWIS JACOBS
MOTION PICTURES
Film maker, writer, critic, teacher;
author, 'The Rise of the American
Film'; editor, 'The Emergence of Film
Art', 'Introduction to the Art of the
Movies', 'The Movies as Medium', 'The
Documentary Tradition'.

STEPHEN W. JACOBS, PH.D.
SHELTER
Professor of Architecture, Cornell
University; past president, Pacific
Section of the Society of Architectural
Historians; contributing author, 'The
History, Theory, and Criticism of
Architecture'.

MARSH JEANNERET, B.A.
CANADIAN HISTORY
Director, University of Toronto Press;
author, 'Story of Canada', 'From
Cartier to Champlain'.

ROBERT I. JOHNSON, A.B.
MOON; NEBULAE; PLANETS
Director, Kansas City (Mo.) Museum of
History and Science; formerly director,
Adler Planetarium and Astronomical
Museum, Chicago, Ill.; author,
'Astronomy—Our Solar System and
Beyond'.

**WILLIAM CUMMING JOHNSON, JR.,
B.S., E.E.**
BALLOON
Engineering specialist, Goodyear
Aircraft Corporation.

ARTHUR FREDERICK JONES
DOG
Formerly Editor in Chief, 'Pure-Bred
Dogs-American Kennel Gazette';
'Complete Dog Book', 'Dogs in Color',
etc.; author, 'Care and Training of
Dogs'.

SEYMOUR JONES
ART
Late art editor for various reference
works, including Compton's
Encyclopedia.

SARA C. JOYNER, A.B., M.A.
THE ARTS
Late Professor of Art, Department of
Art, University of Georgia, and
Supervisor of Art Education, State
Department of Education, Richmond,
Va.; author, 'Art and the Child', 'Report
in Primary Colors', etc.

EDMUND JOSEPH JURICA, PH.D.
PLANT AND ANIMAL DISEASES
Professor of Zoology and Chemistry,
St. Procopius College, Lisle, Ill.

HILARY STANISLAUS JURICA, PH.D.
PLANT AND ANIMAL DISEASES
Late Professor of Botany and Head of
the Department of Biology, St.
Procopius College, Lisle, Ill.

N. B. JUSTER, B.S. IN CH.E.
PROPERTIES OF IRON AND STEEL
Superintendent, Technical Service
Department, Quality Control, Inland
Steel Company, Chicago, Ill.

HANS H. KANNEGIESSER
BERLIN; GERMANY
Production Manager, Velhagen &
Klasing, West Berlin, Germany.

**MELVIN E. KAZECK, B.A., M.S.,
PH.D.**
CLIMATE
Professor and Chairman, Earth
Sciences, Southern Illinois University;
author, 'Climate Laboratory Manual',
'Weather Workbook'.

JAMES A. KEELER
AUTOMOBILE MODELS
Formerly Member, Research and
Development Department, Revell,
Incorporated; builder of prizewinning
models; contributor, 'Rod and Custom
Magazine'.

**MAHMOUD R. KHATER, B.A., M.A.,
PH.D.**
MODERN EGYPT
Professor of Education, University of
Cairo, Cairo, Egypt.

THOMAS KILLIP, A.B., M.D.
DISEASE
Professor, Cardiovascular Medicine,
Cornell Medical College, and Chief of
Cardiology and Attending Physician,
The New York Hospital.

JUN-YOP KIM, M.A., PH.D.
KOREA
Professor of History and Director,
Asiatic Research Center, Korea
University; chairman, Society of
Chinese Studies in Korea; author,
'Modern History of China'.

KYUNG-SUNG KIM, M.A.
KOREA
Professor of Geography and Chairman
of Geography Department, Seoul
National University; secretary, Korea
Geographical Union for International
Geographical Union; author, 'Human
Geography'.

ROBERT E. KINGERY, B.S.
HOBBIES
Coordinator, Community Relations
Service, Dayton and Montgomery
County Public Library; formerly special
assistant to the director, New York
Public Library; author, 'How-to-do-it
Books: a Selected Guide'.

**ALBERT MONTGOMERY KLIGMAN,
B.S., M.D., PH.D.**
DISEASE
Professor of Dermatology, Hospital of
the University of Pennsylvania,
Philadelphia; author, 'Textbook on
Dermatology', 'A Manual of Cutaneous
Medicine', 'Allergic Contact Dermatitis
in the Guinea Pig'.

CARL F. KLINCK, B.A., M.A., PH.D.
CANADIAN LITERATURE
Professor of Canadian Literature,
University of Western Ontario, London,
Ont.

ROYCE H. KNAPP, B.S., A.M., ED.D.
CITIZENSHIP
Regents Professor, Teachers College,
University of Nebraska; formerly
member, executive board, National
Council for the Social Studies;
director, the Nebraska Citizenship
project; American Legion's Boys' State
programs on citizenship.

JOHN A. KNAUSS, B.S., M.A., PH.D.
OCEANOGRAPHY
Dean, Graduate School of
Oceanography, Narragansett Marine
Laboratory, University of Rhode Island.

FRED B. KNIFFEN, PH.D.
SHELTER
Boyd Professor Emeritus, Department
of Geography and Anthropology,
Louisiana State University; past
honorary president, Association of
American Geographers; coauthor,
'Culture Worlds'.

**LORENTZ BENNETT KNOUFF, A.B.,
J.D., LL.M.**
POTTERY AND PORCELAIN
Formerly Associate Editor, 'Corpus
Juris'; member, English Ceramic Circle.

CLYDE F. KOHN, B.A., M.A., PH.D.
ARGENTINA; ASIA; AUSTRALIA;
GEOGRAPHY; LATITUDE AND
LONGITUDE; MAPS AND GLOBES
Chairman, Department of Geography,
University of Iowa; lecturer; coauthor,
'The World Today: Its Patterns and
Cultures', etc.; member, Compton's
Encyclopedia Editorial Advisory
Committee.

DALE C. KRAUSE, B.S., M.S., PH.D.
OCEANOGRAPHY
Formerly Assistant Professor, Graduate
School of Oceanography, Narragansett
Marine Laboratory, University of
Rhode Island.

IRVING B. KRAVIS, PH.D.
ECONOMICS
Professor of Economics, University of
Pennsylvania.

KAREL V. KUCHAR, C.SC., R.N.D.
UNIVERSE
Assistant Professor, Joseph Henry
Laboratories, Princeton University;
author, 'Foundations of the General
Theory of Relativity' (in Czech).

GERARD P. KUIPER, B.SC., PH.D.
ASTRONOMY, SOLAR SYSTEM
Director, Lunar and Planetary
Laboratory, University of Arizona;
Rittenhouse Medal, Kepler Gold
Medal of the American Association
for the Advancement of Science;
editor, 'The Solar System', 4v., 'Stars
and Stellar Systems', 9v.

ANN M. LALLY, B.A., M.A., PH.D.
THE ARTS
District Superintendent, Chicago
Public Schools; lecturer, De Paul
University; member, Editorial Advisory
Board, Junior Arts and Activities;
formerly Director of Art, Chicago
Public Schools; author, 'The
Development of Personal Security
Through Art', etc.

ALBERT M. LANE, B.S.
HORSE
Extension Livestock Specialist,
University of Arizona; contributor to
'Range Research Methods', 'Horses
and Horsemanship', etc.

GRACE LANGDON, B.SC., M.A., PH.D.
TOYS
Late Child Development Consultant
for American Toy Institute; instructor,
Arizona State University; coauthor,
'These Well-Adjusted Children', 'The
Discipline of Well-Adjusted Children';
columnist.

GLENN C. LANGE, B.S.J., M.S.J., M.B.A.
UNITED STATES AIR FORCE
ACADEMY; LAUNDRY
Lieutenant Colonel, USAF Reserve;
Air Force Academy Liaison Officer;
formerly public relations and editorial
manager, American Institute of
Laundering; instructor, University of
Detroit, Chicago Evening Junior
Colleges.

MARION F. LANSING, A.B., A.M.
AMERICAN COLONIAL LIFE
Author, 'America in the World',
'Makers of America', 'Great Moments in
Freedom', and many other historical
books for girls and boys.

JAMES LAVER, B.A., B.LITT., C.B.E., F.R.S.A., F.R.S.L.
DRESS
Formerly Keeper of Prints, Drawings,
and Paintings, Victoria and Albert
Museum, London, England; author,
'Taste and Fashion', 'Style in Costume',
'The Shape of Things: Dress',
'Modesty in Dress'.

STEPHEN BUTLER LEACOCK, PH.D., LITT.D., LL.D., D.C.L.
BIOGRAPHIES
Late Professor, McGill University;
author, 'Elements of Political Science',
'Literary Lapses', 'Nonsense Novels',
'Charles Dickens', etc.

KWANG-RIN LEE, M.A.,
KOREA
Professor of History, Sogang
University; author, 'A Study on the
History of Enlightenment in Korea'.

ROBERT WARD LEEPER, A.B., M.A., PH.D.
EMOTION
Professor of Psychology, University of
Oregon; author, 'Lewin's Topological
and Vector Psychology', 'Psychology of
Personality'.

BERNARD S. LEIBEL, M.A., B.SC., M.D.
DISEASE
Associate Professor, Banting and Best
Medical Research Department, Clinical
Associate, Faculty of Medicine,
University of Toronto, and Director at
Large, Canadian Diabetic Association;
author, 'Insulin', 'On the Nature and
Treatment of Diabetes'.

ROBERT A. LEVY, B.S., M.A., PH.D.
CRYSTALS; SOLIDS; SOLID STATE
PHYSICS
Author, 'Principles of Solid State
Physics'.

WILLY LEY
GUIDED MISSILES; ROCKETS
Late writer, lecturer, and consultant in
field of rockets and space travel;
author, 'Rockets, Missiles, and Men in
Space', 'Conquest of Space', 'Beyond
the Solar System'; coauthor, 'Lands
Beyond'.

LI, CHOH HAO, PH.D.
HORMONES
Professor of Biochemistry and
Experimental Endocrinology and
Director, Hormone Research
Laboratory, University of California;
received Lasker Award for Basic
Medical Research, American Medical
Association Scientific Achievement
Award, American Cancer Society
National Award.

C. C. LINGARD, M.A., PH.D.
CANADIAN STATISTICS
Formerly Director, Information
Services Division, Dominion Bureau
of Statistics, Ottawa, Ont.; editor,
'Canada Year Book'; author,
'Territorial Government of Canada',
'Canada and World Affairs'.

JOSEPH A. LIVINGSTON, A.B.
STOCKS AND BONDS
Financial Editor, 'Philadelphia Bulletin';
syndicated financial columnist;
economist, 'Business Week'.

ROBERT M. LOEBELSON, B.A.
AIRPLANE PILOT AND CREW;
AIRPLANE POWER PLANTS;
AIRPLANE PROPELLER; HELICOPTER;
JET PROPULSION
President, Aerospace Communications;
formerly military-industry editor,
'Space/Aeronautics Magazine';
Washington editor, 'Business/
Commercial Aviation Magazine';
president, Aviation/Writers
Association.

ROBERT LONG, B.A., A.M., PH.D.
LATIN AMERICA
Professor of Geography, Department
of Geography, University of
Tennessee; coauthor, 'An Introduction
to World Geography'.

JOHN G. LORENZ, B.S., B.L.S., M.S.
LIBRARIES
Deputy Librarian, Library of Congress,
Washington, D. C.; formerly director,
Division of Library Service and
Education Facilities, United States
Office of Education; chairman, Foreign
Newspapers and Microfilm
Commission, Association of Research
Libraries, and member, Executive
Committees, National Book Council,
and United States National
Commission for the International
Federation for Documentation.

JOHN F. LOOSBROCK, PH.B.
UNITED STATES AIR FORCE
Editor, 'Air Force Magazine and Space
Digest'; lecturer and author.

JEAN E. LOWRIE, A.B., B.S. IN L.S., M.A., PH.D.
LIBRARIES
Director, School of Librarianship,
Western Michigan University,
Kalamazoo; formerly editor, 'School
Libraries', and president, International
Association of School Librarians and
American Association of School
Librarians; author, 'Elementary School
Libraries'.

NOLA LUXFORD, O.B.E.
NEW ZEALAND
Roving correspondent, New Zealand;
free-lance writer for 'Baltimore News'
and other newspapers; president,
New Zealand Society of North
America.

JOHN LYMAN, B.S., M.S., PH.D.
SHIP AND SHIPPING
Formerly Oceanographic Coordinator,
U. S. Bureau of Commercial Fisheries.

HOLLIS R. LYNCH, PH.D.
AMERICAN NEGROES
Professor of History and Director of the
Institute of African Studies, Columbia
University; author, 'Edward Wilmot
Blyden: Pan-Negro Patriot, 1832–1912'.

IRINA B-M LYNCH, PH.D.
RUSSIAN LITERATURE
Associate Professor of Russian and
Chairman of the Department of
Russian, Wellesley College.

JUSTIN McCARTHY
COAL; MINES AND MINING
Editor, 'UMWA Journal'; formerly
director, United Mine Workers News
Bureau.

HARRY M. McDONALD, B.S., M.A.
AGRICULTURE
Formerly Supervisor of Vocational
Agricultural Education, Maryland
State Department of Education.

WILLIAM M. McKINNEY, PH.D.
MAPS AND GLOBES
Professor of Geography, Wisconsin
State University at Stevens Point;
contributor to textbooks and
professional journals.

GEORGE W. McLELLAN, B.A.
GLASS
Coordinator, Technical Information
Service, Corning Glass Works.

DONALD B. MacMILLAN, A.M., SC.D., F.R.G.S.
ARCTIC REGIONS; POLAR
EXPLORATION
Late explorer, lecturer; Professor of
Anthropology, Bowdoin College; leader
of many Arctic expeditions; author,
'Four Years in the White North', etc.

RUSSELL B. McNEILL, A.B., M.B.A.
INDUSTRIAL SYSTEMS
Vice-President of Administration,
Houdaille Industries, Inc.; formerly
manager, Production and Devices
group, Rand Corporation; faculty of
Harvard Graduate School of Business
Administration.

WALTER MacPEEK
BOY SCOUTS OF AMERICA
Formerly Assistant Director, Editorial
Service, Boy Scouts of America.

VICENTE MALIWANAG, LITT.B.
PHILIPPINES
Manila Bureau Manager, United Press
International; member, National Press
Club of the Philippines and Manila
Overseas Press Club.

TONY MARCH
UNITED STATES ARMY
Editor, 'Army Times'.

JANE N. MARSHALL, A.B., M.A.
AEROSPACE CAREERS
Formerly Editor, 'Skylights' and other
publications of the National Aerospace
Education Council.

THOMAS H. W. MARTIN, B.A., D.PAED.
CANADA
President, Associated Programmers
of Canada, Ltd.; formerly lecturer on
Instructional Techniques and
Practices, College of Education,
University of Toronto; chairman,
Social Studies Curriculum Committee
for Toronto.

EDWARD J. MARUSKA
CAT
Director, Zoological Society of
Cincinnati, Ohio; member, American
Association of Zoological Parks and
Aquariums, and Wild Animal
Propagation Trust.

HAROLD M. MAYER, B.S., M.S., PH.D.
TRANSPORTATION
University Professor of Geography,
Kent State University; chairman,
Ports and Cargo Systems Committee,
Maritime Transportation Research
Board; formerly director of research,
Chicago Plan Commission; author,
'The Port of Chicago and the St.
Lawrence Seaway'.

MILTON MAYER
PEACE MOVEMENTS
Professor of English, University of
Massachusetts, Professor of the
Humanities, Windham College, and
consultant for The Great Books
Foundation and The Center for the
Study of Democratic Institutions; books
include 'They Thought They Were Free',
'What Can a Man Do!', 'The Art of the
Impossible'.

FREDERIC G. MELCHER
LITERARY AWARDS
Late Chairman of the Board of R. R.
Bowker Company, publishers of
'Publishers' Weekly' and 'Library
Journal'; founder of Newbery and
Caldecott medals; honorary life
member of the American Library
Association.

W. C. MENTZER
AIRPLANE AIRFRAME
Late Vice-President, Engineering,
United Air Lines, Inc.

RAY O. MERTES, B.S., M.A.
AIRLINES
Late Director, School and College
Service, Public Relations Division,
United Air Lines, Inc.; member,
executive board, National Aviation
Education Council; consultant to U. S.
Armed Forces Institute.

HARRY MILGROM, PH.D.
ATOM
Formerly Supervisor, Elementary
Science, Board of Education of New
York City.

MARION E. MILLER, B.A., M.A.
THE ARTS
Late Director of Art Education, Denver
Public Schools; formerly president,
Department of Art Education, National
Education Association; member, Art
Committee, Motion Picture Commission,
American Council on Education;
member, Educational Staff,
Metropolitan Museum of Art.

JOHN H. MILSUM, PH.D.
BIOENGINEERING
Abitibi Professor of Control Engineering
and Director, Biomedical Engineering
Unit, McGill University; coeditor,
'Biomedical Engineering Systems'.

JIM MITCHELL
HUNTING
Formerly Editor, 'Hunting and Fishing';
Outdoor Editor, 'Chicago Daily News'.

GEORGE J. MOHR, B.S., M.D.
BABY CARE
Late Clinical Professor of Psychiatry,
University of Illinois College of
Medicine; director, Pittsburgh Child
Guidance Center; clinical director,
Institute for Juvenile Research,
Chicago; member, American Academy
of Pediatrics, American
Psychoanalytic Association.

D. BRUCE MONTGOMERY, B.A., B.S., M.S.
MAGNETS AND MAGNETISM
Group Leader, National Magnet
Laboratory, Massachusetts Institute
of Technology.

RICHARD MOODY, M.A.
THEATER
Professor of Speech and Director of
University Theatre, Indiana University.

PERCY A. MORRIS
SHELLS
Late Chief Preparator in Invertebrate
Paleontology and Assistant in
Conchology, Peabody Museum of
Natural History, Yale University; author,
'What Shell Is That?', 'Field Guide
to the Shells', etc.

W. MORRIS
UNITED STATES MARINE CORPS
Colonel, U. S. Marine Corps.

ROBERT L. MORTON, B.S., A.M., PH.D.
ARITHMETIC
Professor of Education, Ohio
University; formerly professor of
Mathematics; coauthor of arithmetic
textbooks; author, 'Teaching Children
Arithmetic', etc.

W. L. MORTON, LITT.B., M.A.
CANADA
Formerly Professor of Canadian
History and Chairman of the
Department of History, University of
Manitoba, Winnipeg; editor, 'The
Voice of Dafoe'; author, 'The
Progressive Party in Canada'.

JOHN MULHOLLAND
MAGIC
Late Editor, 'The Sphinx'; lecturer on
magic; author, 'Quicker Than the Eye',
'Story of Magic', etc.

NORMAN LESLIE MUNN, A.M., PH.D.
PSYCHOLOGY
Formerly Professor of Psychology and
Head, Department of Psychology,
Bowdoin College; author, 'An
Introduction to Animal Psychology',
'Psychological Development', etc.

ROBERT CUSHMAN MURPHY, PH.B., A.M., D.SC.
BIRDS
Late Chairman, Department of Birds,
American Museum of Natural History;
formerly president, National Audubon
Society; author, 'Oceanic Birds of
South America', etc.

ARTHUR WILFORD NAGLER, A.M., TH.D., D.D.
CHURCH HISTORY
Formerly Professor of Church History,
Garrett Biblical Institute.

EVELYN STEFANSSON NEF
NORTHMEN
Editor in Chief, Delacorte Great
Explorer Series; formerly librarian,
Stefansson Polar Library; author,
'Here Is Alaska', 'Here Is the Far
North'.

FRANK NELICK, PH.D.
ENGLISH LITERATURE
Professor of English, University
of Kansas.

JOHN J. NELLIGAN
POLICE
Late Captain, Head of Special
Investigation Section, Traffic Division,
Chicago Police Department.

ELIZABETH NESBITT, B.A., M.A., B.S. IN L.S.
FOLKTALES
Formerly Associate Dean, Library
School, Carnegie Institute of
Technology.

CURTIS PUTNAM NETTELS, PH.D.
AMERICAN HISTORY
Professor of American History, Cornell
University; member, editorial board,
'A History of American Economic Life',
'Journal of Economic History'.

OTTO NEURATH, PH.D.
VISUAL EDUCATION
Late Director, International Foundation for Visual Education; editor in chief, International Encyclopedia of Unified Science; author, 'International Picture Language'.

M. B. NEUWORTH
COAL-TAR PRODUCTS
Manager, Organic Research, Consolidation Coal Company, Inc.

ALLAN NEVINS, A.M., LITT.D., LL.D.
AMERICAN HISTORY; FRANKLIN D. ROOSEVELT
Late Professor of American History, Columbia University; Chief Public Affairs Officer, American Embassy, London; Harmsworth Professor of American History, 1940-41, Oxford University; professor of American History, Cornell University; author, 'Grover Cleveland' (Pulitzer prize, 1933), 'Hamilton Fish' (Pulitzer prize, 1937), 'A Brief History of the United States', 'Ordeal of the Union' (Scribner prize, 1946).

T. ERNEST NEWLAND, A.B., A.M., PH.D.
INTELLIGENCE TESTS; MENTAL DEFICIENCY; EXCEPTIONAL CHILDREN
Professor of Educational Psychology, University of Illinois.

YOSHIYUKI NODA, PH.D.
JAPAN
Professor of Comparative Law, Tokyo University; author, 'The History and Concept of Law.'

ROBERT J. NORRISH, B.S.
LIVESTOCK
Official, International Live Stock Exposition, International Dairy Show, International Kennel Club Dog Show, Chicago.

DELBERT OBERTEUFFER, A.B., A.M., PH.D.
HEALTH EDUCATION AND PHYSICAL EDUCATION
Professor Emeritus of Physical Education, The Ohio State University.

JAMES F. O'CONNOR, B.S., M.S.
WEATHER
Chief, Extended Forecast Branch, National Meteorological Center, Suitland, Md.; author, 'Practical Methods of Weather Analysis and Prognosis'.

HANS L. OESTREICHER, PH.D.,
BIONICS
Chief, Mathematics and Analysis Branch, Aerospace Medical Research Laboratories, Wright-Patterson Air Force Base; author of numerous technical papers relating to bionic engineering.

KAZUO OKOCHI, PH.D.
JAPAN
Professor Emeritus of Economics and Past President, Tokyo University; member, Japan Academy; author, 'Basic Problems of Social Policy', 'On Education'.

LESLIE E. ORGEL, M.A., PH.D.
EVOLUTION
Resident Fellow, The Salk Institute; fellow of the Royal Society; author, 'Ligand-Field Theory'.

ALI OTHMAN, M.A.
MOHAMMEDANISM
Liaison Officer, Arab Information Center, New York; formerly headmaster, Amiriah High School, Palestine; fellow, Ford Foundation, for study of "Authority and Public Consensus in Islam."

JACQUELINE OVERTON
BIOGRAPHIES
Late Librarian, Children's Library, Robert Bacon Memorial, Westbury, N. Y.; author, 'Life of Robert Louis Stevenson for Boys and Girls', etc.

THOMAS PARK, S.B., PH.D.
INSECTS
Professor of Biology, University of Chicago.

WALTER G. PATTON, A.B.
AUTOMOBILE BODIES AND ACCESSORIES; AUTOMOBILE CHASSIS; AUTOMOBILE POWER PLANT; AUTOMOBILE POWER TRAIN
Formerly Technical Writer, Society of Automotive Engineers, Inc.; engineering editor, 'SAE Journal'.

J. J. PEYTON
UNITED STATES ARMY
Captain, U. S. Army.

VELMA PHILLIPS, PH.B., A.M., PH.D.
FOOD
Formerly Professor of Home Management and Family Finance, San Fernando Valley State College; formerly dean, College of Home Economics, Washington State University.

WILLARD J. PIERSON, JR., B.S., PH.D.
OCEAN WAVES AND TIDES
Professor of Oceanography, Department of Meteorology and Oceanography, New York University.

ALBERT PILTZ, A.B., M.ED., D.ED.
SCIENCE
Professor of Science Education, Johns Hopkins University.

JOHN H. POMEROY, PH.D.
PHYSICAL SCIENCE ARTICLES
Assistant Director, Lunar Sample Program, National Aeronautics and Space Administration; formerly senior editor for physical sciences, Encyclopaedia Britannica; author, 'Science', 'Nuclear Terms'.

ALTON W. POTTER, B.S., M.B.A., LL.B.
LEGAL TERMS
Member (inactive), State Bar of Michigan; Chicago, Illinois State, and American Bar associations.

PITMAN B. POTTER, A.M., PH.D.
POLITICAL SCIENCE
Formerly Dean, Graduate Division, American University, Beirut; professor of International Organization, Graduate Institute of International Studies, Geneva; author, 'An Introduction to the Study of International Organization', 'International Civics', etc.

DAVID M. PRATT, B.A., A.M., PH.D.
OCEANOGRAPHY
Professor, Graduate School of Oceanography, Narragansett Marine Laboratory, University of Rhode Island.

SIDNEY L. PRESSEY, PH.D.
TEACHING MACHINES
Formerly Professor of Psychology, College of Education, The Ohio State University.

KARL H. PRIBAM, M.D.
BRAIN
Professor of Psychiatry and Psychology, Stanford University; president, International Neuropsychological Society; author, 'Languages of the Brain', etc.

DONALDA PUTNAM, B.S. IN L.S., M.A.
CANADA
Formerly Extension Librarian, Provincial Library, Regina, Saskatchewan.

GEORGE I. QUIMBY, A.B., M.A.
AMERICAN INDIANS
Curator of Ethnology, Thomas Burke Memorial Washington State Museum, and Professor of Anthropology, University of Washington; formerly Curator of North American Archaeology and Ethnology, Field Museum of Natural History, Chicago.

ROBERT J. QUINN
FIRE DEPARTMENT
Fire Commissioner, Chicago Fire Department.

STANLEY RACHESKY, B.S., M.S.
INSECTICIDES
Area adviser on pesticides, Extension Entomologist, University of Illinois; Executive Secretary, Illinois Pest Control Association.

BURTON RASCOE
BIOGRAPHIES
Late literary and drama critic; author, 'Theodore Dreiser', 'Titans of Literature', 'Prometheans', etc.

WILLIAM M. RASSCHAERT, ED.D.
SCIENCE
Formerly Supervisor of Research, Department of Instructional Research, Detroit Public Schools.

DAVID W. REED, PH.D.
GRAMMAR ARTICLES
Professor of Linguistics, Northwestern University; formerly Fulbright lecturer, Rockefeller fellow; founding editor, 'Language Learning'.

HAIM REINGOLD, A.B., M.A., PH.D.
CALCULUS
Professor and Chairman, Department of Mathematics, Illinois Institute of Technology.

ROBERT RIENOW, A.B., M.A., PH.D.
INTERNATIONAL RELATIONS; UNITED STATES GOVERNMENT
Professor of Political Science, State University College for Teachers, Albany, N. Y.; author.

ALICE SANDERSON RIVOIRE, B.S., M.S.
COOKING
Assistant to Director, National Equipment Service, Girl Scouts of the U.S.A.

DAVID M. ROBB, PH.D.
ARCHITECTURE
Chairman, Department of Art History,
University of Pennsylvania.

**HOWARD ROBINSON, A.B., A.M.,
PH.D., LL.D.**
ENGLISH HISTORY
Lecturer on History, University of
Queensland, Brisbane, Australia;
emeritus head of department and dean
of College of Liberal Arts, Oberlin
College.

JOHN W. ROBSON, B.A., M.S., PH.D.
COLOR
Associate Professor of Physics,
University of Arizona.

**FORD A. ROCKWELL, B.A., B.S.
IN L.S.**
PIRATES
Librarian, Wichita City Library;
instructor in Public Library
Administration, Emporia State
Teachers College.

JOHN RODERICK
JAPAN; KOREA
Foreign correspondent.

E. J. ROLAND, ADMIRAL
UNITED STATES COAST GUARD
Commandant, U. S. Coast Guard.

WILLIAM D. ROMEY, PH.D.
EARTH SCIENCE ARTICLES
Director, Earth Science Curriculum
Project, National Science Foundation.

CARLOS P. ROMULO, A.B., M.A.
PHILIPPINES
Secretary, Department of Foreign
Affairs, Republic of Philippines;
formerly president, United Nations
General Assembly; Philippine
ambassador to the United States;
president, University of the Philippines;
author, 'Mission to Asia: the Dialogue
Begins', 'Crusade in Asia', etc.

KENNETH ROSE, B.A., M.A.
ADDITION; DIVISION; GEOMETRY;
MULTIPLICATION; SUBTRACTION
Instructor, Academy of the New
Church, Bryn Athyn, Pa.; writer,
lecturer, and consultant.

CHARLES A. SANDERS, M.D.
HOSPITALS
General Director, Massachusetts
General Hospital, Boston, and
Associate Professor of Medicine,
Harvard Medical School; member,
American Federation for Clinical
Research, American College of
Physicians, and American Society for
Clinical Investigation.

**EULALIE STEINMETZ ROSS, A.B.,
B.L.S.**
BIBLIOGRAPHIES
Director of Work with Children, Public
Library of Cincinnati and Hamilton
County; compiler, fourth edition of
'Stories: a List of Stories to Tell and
to Read Aloud'.

NEIL P. RUZIC, B.S.J.
INTERNATIONAL GEOPHYSICAL YEAR
Editor and Publisher, 'Industrial
Research Magazine'.

JOSÉ J. SARMIENTO, M.D.
ANESTHETICS
Staff Anesthesiologist, St. James
Hospital, Chicago Heights, Ill.

FRANCES CLARKE SAYERS
BIOGRAPHIES; MYTHOLOGY;
READING
Specialist in children's literature
and formerly Superintendent of Work
with Children, New York Public Library;
formerly lecturer on Children's
Literature, English Department, and
lecturer, Library Work with Children,
School of Library Service, University
of California at Los Angeles; received
Lippincott award, 1965, Clarence Day
award, 1966; author, 'Anthology of
Children's Literature', 'Summoned by
Books', many children's books.

DAVID R. SCHINK, B.A., M.S., PH.D.
OCEANOGRAPHY
Assistant Research Professor, Graduate
School of Oceanography, Narragansett
Marine Laboratory, University of
Rhode Island.

F. WAGNER SCHLESINGER, PH.B.
RELATIVITY
Formerly Director, Adler Planetarium,
Chicago; director, Fels Planetarium,
Philadelphia.

PAUL J. SCHMIDT, B.S., M.S., M.D.
BLOOD
Chief, Blood Bank Department,
Clinical Center, National Institute of
Health, Bethesda, Md., and Clinical
Professor of Pathology, Schools of
Medicine and Dentistry, Georgetown
University; member, American Society
of Hematology, International Society
of Blood Transfusion, and College of
American Pathologists.

WILBUR SCHRAMM, A.B., A.M., PH.D.
COMMUNICATION BY WRITING
Director, Department of
Communication and Journalism,
Institute for Communication Research,
Stanford University; author.

BRIAN B. SCHWARTZ, PH.D.
MAGNETS AND MAGNETISM
Group Leader, Theoretical Physics
Group, National Magnet Laboratory,
Massachusetts Institute of Technology.

**ALBERT H. SCHWICHTENBERG,
M.D.**
AEROSPACE MEDICINE
Head, Department of Aerospace
Medicine, Lovelace Foundation for
Medical Education and Research;
member, American Board of Preventive
Medicine; fellow, Aerospace Medical
Association; formerly Command
Surgeon, Air Defense Command;
Brigadier General (retired), U. S. Air
Force (Medical Corps).

**PAUL BIGELOW SEARS, A.M.,
PH.D., SC.D., LL.D.**
LAND USE
Professor Emeritus of Conservation,
Yale University; author, 'Deserts on
the March', 'This Is Our World', etc.

MARGARET CABELL SELF
HORSE
Founder and formerly Commandant,
New Canaan Mounted Troop, an
institution for the training of riding
instructors; author, 'The Horseman's
Encyclopedia', 'Horsemastership', etc.

JACK SEWELL, M.A.
JAPAN; KOREA; PHILIPPINES
Curator of Oriental Art, The Art
Institute of Chicago; member, Board
of Directors, Chicago Chapter, Japan-
America Society; contributor to
scholarly publications.

**HAROLD G. SHANE, B.ED., M.A.,
PH.D., F.I.A.L.**
EDUCATION
University Professor of Education,
Indiana University at Bloomington;
formerly dean, School of Education,
Indiana University; superintendent of
schools, Winnetka, Ill.; author or
coauthor of 90 books and more than
200 articles.

MITCHELL R. SHARPE
SPACE TRAVEL
Science writer, rocket historian,
lecturer; author, 'Living in Space: the
Environment of the Astronaut', 'Yuri
Gagarin, First Man in Space'; coauthor,
'Basic Astronautics', 'Applied
Astronautics'.

ALBERT E. SHAW, E.E., PH.D.
ELECTRON PHYSICS
Industrial Consultant; formerly senior
physicist, Argonne National Laboratory;
assistant professor, Physics
Department, University of Chicago.

PHILIP A. SHELLEY, PH.D.
GERMAN LITERATURE
Professor of German and Comparative
Literature, Pennsylvania State
University; coauthor, 'An Outline
History of German Literature'.

**LOUIS SHORES, A.B., B.S. IN L.S.,
PH.D.**
REFERENCE BOOKS
Dean Emeritus, Library School, Florida
State University; author, 'Basic
Reference Sources'.

**MARY E. SILVERTHORN, B.A., B.S.
IN L.S., A.M.**
BIBLIOGRAPHIES
Professor Emeritus, University of
Toronto, Faculty of Library Science.

PARKE H. SIMER, M.D., PH.D.
ANATOMY
Late Professor of Anatomy, University
of Illinois College of Medicine.

**GEORGE EATON SIMPSON, B.S.,
M.A., PH.D.**
SOCIOLOGY
Professor of Sociology and
Anthropology, Oberlin College; author,
'The Negro in the Philadelphia Press';
coauthor, 'Racial and Cultural
Minorities'.

**GEORGE GAYLORD SIMPSON,
PH.B., PH.D., SC.D.**
HORSE
Professor of Geology, University of
Arizona; past president, Society of
Vertebrate Paleontology, Society for
the Study of Evolution, American
Society of Zoologists; author, 'Major
Features of Evolution', 'Principles of
Animal Taxonomy', etc.

GUILLERMO V. SISON, PH.B.
PHILIPPINES
Assistant Secretary for Press and
Public Information, Department of
Foreign Affairs, Philippines;
journalist and poet.

CARL B. SMITH, B.A., M.A., PH.D.
LANGUAGE ARTS; PHONICS
Associate Professor of Education and
Director, Measurement and
Evaluation Center in Reading
Education, Indiana University; author,
'Interrelated Language Arts
Instruction', 'Correcting Reading
Problems in the Classroom'.

GRACE SANDS SMITH, B.A., M.A.
THE ARTS
Director of Art Education, Houston
Public Schools; instructor in Art
Education, University of Houston; past
president, Texas Art Educators
Association; regional chairman,
Scholastic Art Awards.

HERBERT A. SMITH, B.S., M.A., PH.D.
CONSERVATION; SCIENCE
Associate Dean for Teacher Education,
Colorado State University; member,
Compton's Encyclopedia Editorial
Advisory Committee.

**WALLACE F. SMITH, B.A., M.A.,
PH.D.**
HOUSING
Associate Professor of Business
Administration and Chairman of the
Center for Real Estate and Urban
Economics, University of California at
Berkeley; author, 'Housing—The
Social and Economic Elements';
consultant on housing.

**WHITNEY SMITH, JR., A.B., A.M.,
PH.D.**
FLAGS
Director, Flag Research Center;
Assistant Professor of Political
Economy, Boston University; editor,
'The Flag Bulletin'; president, North
American Vexillological Association;
secretary-general, International
Federation of Vexillological
Associations; author, 'The Bibliography
of Flags of Foreign Nations', 'The Flag
Book of the United States'.

SMITHSONIAN INSTITUTION
AIRPLANE HISTORY
National Air Museum staff.

ROBERT SNEDIGAR
SNAKES
Late Curator of Reptiles, Amphibians,
and Invertebrates, Chicago
Zoological Park, Brookfield, Ill.; author,
'Our Small Native Animals', 'Life in the
Forest'.

FRED D. SNYDER, B.A.
UNITED STATES NAVY
Commander, U. S. Navy.

JUNE SOCHEN, B.A., M.A., PH.D.
WOMEN AND WOMEN'S RIGHTS
Associate Professor of History,
Northeastern Illinois State College;
editor, 'The New Feminism in Twentieth
Century America'.

**FRANK ENGLAND SORENSON, M.A.,
PH.D.**
BRAZIL; INTERNATIONAL
COOPERATION
Professor Emeritus of Educational
Administration and Secondary
Education, University of Nebraska;
Director of Education, Foreign
Service Technicians staff of the
Technical Cooperation Administration
of the U. S. Department of State;
coauthor, Our Neighbors series of
elementary geographies; U. S. staff
member, UNESCO Seminar for
Teaching Geography.

COOPER SPEAKS, A.B., M.A., PH.D.
GUSTAV MAHLER
Critic, 'Opera News Magazine' and
'Opera Magazine'; formerly associate
professor, Defiance College, assistant
professor, University of Houston, and
instructor, Duke University.

LAWRENCE D. STEEFEL, A.B., PH.D.
WORLD WAR I
Formerly Professor of History,
University of Minnesota; author, 'The
Schleswig-Holstein Question'.

JACK E. STEELE, M.D.
BIONICS
Formerly Assistant Chief,
Mathematics and Analysis Branch,
Aerospace Medical Research
Laboratories, Wright-Patterson Air
Force Base; coiner of the term *bionics;*
author of numerous publications on
bionic engineering.

**VILHJALMUR STEFANSSON, A.B.,
A.M., PH.D., LL.D., L.H.D.**
BIOGRAPHIES
Late anthropologist, geographer, Arctic
explorer; author, 'My Life with the
Eskimo', 'The Friendly Arctic', etc.

**WALLACE E. STEGNER, A.B., A.M.,
PH.D.**
CREATIVE WRITING
Professor of English, Stanford
University; editor, compiler, and
contributor; author of numerous
books; awarded Guggenheim
Fellowship 1950, 1952, 1959.

RALPH STEIN
AUTOMOBILE RACING AND RALLIES
Formerly Automobile Editor, 'This Week
Magazine'; author, 'The Treasury of
the Automobile'.

DAVID J. STEINBERG, PH.D.
PHILIPPINES
Associate Professor of Southeast Asian
History, University of Michigan; author,
'Philippine Collaboration in World War
II'; coauthor, 'Southeast Asia in World
War II'.

**DAVID BARNARD STEINMAN, B.S.,
A.M., PH.D., C.E., SC.D., D.ENG.,
D.SC.ENG., LL.D., F.R.S.A.**
BRIDGE
Late consulting engineer and
bridgebuilder; author, 'Bridges and
Their Builders', 'Famous Bridges of the
World', 'Suspension Bridges', etc.

**ELWYN FRANKLIN STERLING, A.B.,
A.M., PH.D.**
FRENCH LITERATURE
Professor and Chairman, Department
of Romance Languages and Literature,
Colgate University.

KURT STERN, M.D.
ALLERGY
Formerly Professor of Pathology,
University of Illinois College of
Medicine.

CHARLES F. STEVENS, M.D., PH.D.
NERVES
Professor of Physiology, University of
Washington, Seattle; author,
'Neurophysiology: a Primer'.

MARTIN DELAWAY STEVERS, PH.B.
SCIENCE
Formerly Managing Editor, Compton's
Encyclopedia; author, 'Steel Trails',
'Sea Lanes', etc.

**ARNOLD A. STRASSENBURG, B.S.,
M.S., PH.D.**
PHYSICAL SCIENCE ARTICLES
Professor of Physics, State University
of New York at Stony Brook; director,
Division on Education and Manpower,
American Institute of Physics.

MERVIN K. STRICKLER, B.SC., PH.D.
CIVIL AVIATION
Chief, Aviation Education Programs
Division, Office of General Aviation
Affairs, Federal Aviation Administration.

STERLING STUCKEY, B.A., M.A.
RECONSTRUCTION PERIOD
Formerly Instructor in American
History, Northwestern University and
University of Illinois; past chairman,
The Amistad Society; coeditor, 'Afro-
American History Series'.

**FELIX STUNGEVICIUS, B.A., M.A.,
M.B.A.**
URUGUAY
Consul of Uruguay, Chicago; president
International Language
Communications Center; formerly
lecturer in Political Science,
Northwestern University; vice-
president, Pan American Board of
Education.

JAMES O. SWAIN, B.A., M.A., PH.D.
LATIN AMERICAN LITERATURE;
SPANISH LITERATURE
Professor of Romance Languages,
University of Tennessee; formerly
executive secretary, Spanish Honor
Society, Sigma Delta Pi.

THOMAS L. SWIHART, PH.D.
ASTRONOMY
Professor of Astronomy, University of
Arizona; author, 'Astrophysics and
Stellar Astronomy', 'Basic Physics of
Stellar Atmospheres'.

GEORGE W. TAYLOR, PH.D.
LABOR
Professor of Labor Relations, Wharton
School, University of Pennsylvania;
formerly chairman, National War Labor
Board and National Wage Stabilization
Board; president, Industrial Relations
Research Association.

HERBERT J. TAYLOR
YUKON
Territorial Secretary, Government of
the Yukon Territory, Canada.

JOHN J. TEAL, JR., B.S., M.A.
MUSK-OX
Research Professor of Animal Husbandry and Human Ecology, University of Alaska; president, Institute of Northern Agricultural Research, Huntington Center, Vt.

NEGLEY K. TEETERS, B.SC., M.A., PH.D.
PRISONS
Late Professor Emeritus of Sociology, Temple University; author, 'The Cradle of the Penitentiary'.

JOHN H. THOMAS, PH.D.
ENVIRONMENTAL POLLUTION
Associate Professor of Biological Sciences and Curator of Dudley Herbarium, Stanford University; curator of botany, California Academy of Sciences; editor, California Botanical Society journal, 'Madrono'; author of books and periodical literature in biology.

LEWIS H. THOMAS, M.A.
CANADA
Formerly Professor of History, University of Saskatchewan, Regina Campus.

MARY P. THOMAS
COAL
Formerly Educational Assistant, Education Division of the National Coal Association; author of articles on coal.

WILLIAM C. THOMAS, JR., M.D.
DISEASE
Professor of Medicine, College of Medicine, University of Florida, and Associate Chief of Staff for Research, Veterans Administration Hospital, Gainesville, Fla.; member, Endocrine Society, and formerly on the editorial board, 'Journal of Clinical Endocrinology and Metabolism'.

CAPTAIN ROBERT THOMSON
SALVATION ARMY
Editor in Chief, National Publications Office, Salvation Army.

GLADYS TIPTON, B.F.A., M.S. IN MUS., D.ED.
MUSIC
Professor of Music Education, Teachers College, Columbia University; author, 'RCA Basic Record Library for Elementary Schools', 'Adventures in Music'.

ETHEL TOBACH, B.A., M.A., PH.D.
ANIMAL BEHAVIOR
Curator, Department of Animal Behavior, American Museum of Natural History; member, New York Academy of Science, Animal Behavior Society; author or coauthor of numerous research papers on animal behavior.

THEODORE W. TORREY, A.B., M.A., PH.D.
EMBRYOLOGY
Professor and formerly Chairman, Department of Zoology, Indiana University; author, 'Morphogenesis of the Vertebrates'; research papers on embryology and histology.

JOHN W. TURRENTINE, M.S., PH.D.
AGRICULTURAL CHEMISTRY
Late Chairman, American Potash Institute, Inc.; in charge of potash investigations, U. S. Department of Agriculture.

ROGER A. VAN BEVER, M.S.
SCIENCE
Supervisor, Elementary Science, Detroit Public Schools.

RUPERT BAYLESS VANCE, A.M., PH.D., LL.D.
POPULATION
Professor of Sociology, University of North Carolina; past president, American Sociological Society, Population Association of America; author, 'Human Geography of the South', 'All These People', etc.

EUGENE VAN CLEEF, S.B., PH.D.
GEOGRAPHICAL NAMES
Professor of Geography, The Ohio State University; author, 'The Story of the Weather', 'Finland, the Republic Farthest North', 'Trade Centers and Trade Routes'.

T. R. VAN DELLEN, M.D.
DISEASE
Syndicated Medical Columnist, Chicago Tribune-New York News Syndicate, and Associate Professor of Medicine, Northwestern University Medical School, Chicago, Ill.

CARL VAN DOREN, A.B., PH.D.
BIOGRAPHIES
Late Associate in English, Columbia University; formerly managing editor, 'Cambridge History of American Literature'; author, 'Contemporary American Novelists', 'James Branch Cabell', 'Sinclair Lewis', 'American Literature', 'Benjamin Franklin' (Pulitzer prize, 1939).

HENRY VAN ENGEN, A.B., M.A., PH.D.
HIGH-SCHOOL MATHEMATICS
Head of Department of Mathematics, Iowa State Teachers College; coauthor, 'Numbers in Action', 'Numbers We See'.

JAMES T. VEEDER, B.S., M.A.
4-H CLUBS
Head, Information and Publications Services, National 4-H Service Committee.

ROBERT WILLIAM VERDI, B.A.
HOCKEY, ICE
Hockey Writer, 'Chicago Tribune', Managing Editor, 'Hockey Digest', and member, Board of Directors, Professional Hockey Writers Association.

HOWARD P. VINCENT, PH.D.
LITERATURE
Professor of English and American Literature, Kent State University; formerly chairman, Department of Language, Literature, and Philosophy, Illinois Institute of Technology; author, 'The Trying-Out of Moby-Dick'; general editor, 'Collected Works of Herman Melville'.

DONALD A. WALKER, PH.D.
MATTER
Associate Professor of Physics, State University of New York at New Paltz.

PETER WARD
CANADIAN ARMED FORCES
Broadcaster, writer, Director of the National Press Gallery; formerly Ottawa correspondent and defense specialist, 'The Telegram' (Toronto); recipient, 1968 Southam Fellowship at University of Toronto; Lieutenant, Canadian Reserves (naval).

P. V. H. WEEMS
NAVIGATION; SHIP'S LOG
Captain, U. S. Navy (retired); conducted first class in Space Navigation at U. S. Naval Academy; designer of navigation devices; founder of Weems System of Navigation, Inc.; codeveloper, 'Air Almanac'; National Geographic Society La Gorce Medal, 1968; author, 'Air Navigation', 'Star Altitude Curves', 'Line of Position Book'.

VERNON I. WEIHE, B.SC. IN E.E.
AVIATION NAVIGATION
Director, Air Traffic Control and Navigation Programs, General Precision, Inc.; staff consultant, Air Transport Association of America; fellow, Institute of Radio Engineers.

MARY ALICE WELLER, B.A., M.A., PH.D.
PLAY
Associate Professor of Early Childhood Education, Slippery Rock State College, Slippery Rock, Pa.

DANIEL S. WENTZ II, B.A.
AEROSPACE RESEARCH AND DEVELOPMENT; WIND TUNNEL
Information Officer, Ames Research Center, National Aeronautics and Space Administration; associate member, Aviation/Space Writers Association; writer and reporter in fields of aeronautical and space activities.

FREDERICK L. WERNSTEDT, B.A., M.A., PH.D.
PHILIPPINES
Professor of Geography, Pennsylvania State University; coauthor, 'The Philippine Island World'.

JOHN H. WHITE, JR.
AUTOMOBILE HISTORY
Chairman, Department of Industries, and Curator of Transportation, National Museum of History and Technology, Smithsonian Institution.

EUGENE WHITMORE
CLOWNS
Writer, editor, and reporter; formerly editor, 'American Business Magazine'; first managing editor, 'Sales Management Magazine'; author, books on sales, advertising, and personnel management and magazine articles on clowns, circuses, and railroads.

FARIDA A. WILEY
NATURAL SCIENCE
Lecturer, Department of Education, and formerly Director of Field and Laboratory Courses in Natural Science and Conservation, American Museum of Natural History; field instructor in Ecology, National Audubon Society Camp of Maine; author, 'Ferns of Northeastern United States'.

HOW TO USE
COMPTON'S ENCYCLOPEDIA

There is an enormous amount of information, in both text and illustrations, in Compton's , and all of it has been made quickly and conveniently available to you. There is a unique Fact-Index in the back of each volume. These indexes are also combined and provided in a single volume (Volume 26). Within articles are certain features to help you. These include Previews, Cross-References, Fact-Finders, Fact Summaries, Fact Tables, and Bibliographies.

FACT-INDEX

Always consult the Fact-Index first. You may have to go no further. For example, you might only want to know when Sir Winston Churchill was born or died. These facts are given right in the Fact-Index as are hundreds of thousands of other facts about the people, places, things, and concepts that are listed alphabetically. If you need more, the Fact-Index tells you where to look in Compton's. You will be directed not only to a major article on Churchill, but also to articles that tell you about him in relation to major events in his life, honors accorded him, his hobbies, and more.

The Fact-Index also contains a number of useful tables. If you are looking up Baseball, for example, because you want to know what teams won the pennant or the World Series in specific years, you will find the information in the Fact-Index under Baseball in a table called "Baseball Pennant and World Series Winners."

In short, the Fact-Index is both a source of information in its own right and a guide to the information in all the rest of Compton's. So, if there is a single most important thing to know about how to use Compton's it is— **Always consult the Fact-Index first.**

ARTICLES

Compton's articles contain a number of features to help you get more out of them and the rest of the encyclopedia. Some long articles have Previews. Each of these is a miniature table of contents that can send you directly to the part of the article that contains any particular information you want. Cross-References within articles tell you where else in Compton's to find additional information on various specific aspects of the subject you are reading about. Long articles may also have Fact Finders, which are lists of Compton's articles related to the one being read. Some articles contain Fact Summaries or Fact Tables. These are lists of details and facts about the subject you have looked up. Many articles end with Bibliographies. There are two types. One simply mentions in the last paragraph a few good books on the subject you have looked up. The other lists a larger number of books at the end of the article.

Compton's has been written for those who want to read just for the fun of it as well as for those who need a convenient and reliable source of information. This has been achieved through the careful writing and editing of talented and conscientious contributors and staff members who know that knowledge can "come alive" when it is presented clearly, concisely, and creatively. What young students have always known and scholars have often forgotten is that information presented in an interesting way is always read the most eagerly and remembered the most easily. It is no longer "fashionable" to present even the most learned and technical articles as though they can only properly impart their information if they are dry, dull, and stilted.

Encyclopedias should not be exceptions. So with respect to readability Compton's is glad to be "in style." Compton's readers will be glad of it too.

PHOTOS: Row 1: (left) U.S. Air Force; (center right) UPI. Row 2: (left) TWA Ambassador; (far right) Salvador Dali—UNICEF. Row 3: (far left and center right) E.P.A., Inc./EB Inc. Row 4: (far left) NASA; (center left) R.C. Hunt—EB Inc. Row 5: (center right) E.P.A., Inc./EB Inc.

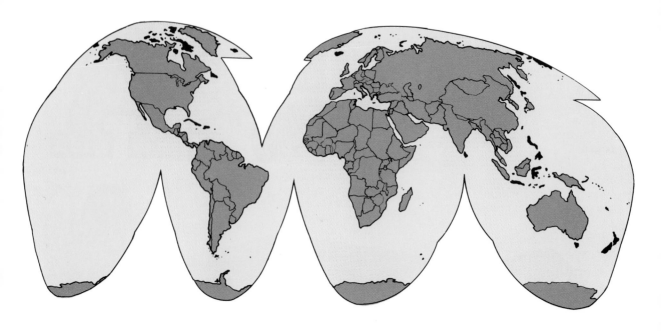

HERE AND THERE IN VOLUME 1

From the A-1 satellite to the zygote cell, thousands of subjects are gathered together in Compton's Encyclopedia and Fact-Index. Organized alphabetically, they are drawn from every field of knowledge. Readers who want to explore their favorite fields in this volume can use this subject-area outline. While it may serve as a study guide, a specialized learning experience, or simply a key for browsing, it is not a complete table of contents.

EXPLORING VOLUME 1

Federal Aviation Administration, Great Lakes Region
Public Relations Office

What has created the green stain in this thermal pool? 283.

How does the tail assembly of an airplane compare to the feathers on an arrow? 184.

Which nut-bearing tree belongs to the rose family? 314.

Name the organs most commonly found in the digestive systems of animals. 389.

What is the advantage of contour tillage on a farm? 135.

Name the seven divisions of aerospace. 67 illustration.

How does the crocodile differ
from the alligator? 310.

Why is Acapulco called the "Riviera of Mexico"? 15.

Where is the longest mountain chain in the world? 409.

Where is the snow-capped mountain that was depicted in
an Ernest Hemingway story? 94.

LeRoy F. Grannis

What is "sky surfing"? 65.

Where is the highest waterfall in the world? 414.

What heavyweight champion, barred from boxing and stripped of his title for four years, came back to become the only three-time titleholder? 306.

What are grab joints? 384.

What is the difference between general and local anesthetics? 412–13.

Where have women fought as soldiers for their countries? 323–4.

Name the Oscar-winning writer who began his career by selling jokes to columnists for a dime. 309.

What country has no national monetary unit? 410.

Who were the first Africans to put the sounds of their language in writing? 121.

What is the most serious form of drug abuse? 276.

Why was a Nigerian novelist nicknamed "Dictionary"? 18.

Who became a nun after her secret marriage to her teacher, a French philosopher, was exposed? 8–9.

Why was the Hindu temple Angkor Wat transformed into a Buddhist shrine? 416.

Who was the polar explorer who died in an attempt to rescue another explorer in the Arctic? 382.

What environmental changes have increased the life span of certain laboratory animals? 127.

Why must amphibians live near water? 379.

What major trading port is located on a lagoon rather than on the sea? 9.

Which European country had obtained the largest holdings in the New World by the end of the 17th century? 331, 334 map.

What is New Journalism? 361.

What role did ice play in the development of the roller coaster? 383.

How does a pardon differ from amnesty? 373.

How did the ancient Chinese use "oracle bones"? 406.

Which internationally acclaimed architect worked in close collaboration with each of his wives? 3.

How many bones are there in the human skeleton? 390.

How many hours of solo flying are required for a civilian pilot's license? 197.

What was "Seward's icebox"? 246.

About how long is a newly hatched alligator? 311.

How much of the Territory of Alaska was owned by the United States government? 244.

Name the two emperors who agreed in 1807 to divide the world between them. 278.

What simple experiment will prove that fire uses oxygen? 146 illustration.

What are some requirements for airline flight attendants? 198.

Which 15th-century Italian artist designed a batlike flying machine? 200 illustration.

Who were the "forty immortals"? 14.

Why did Richard Allen build his own church? 308.

How does the aardwolf ward off attacks? 3.

Why was a statue to the boll weevil erected in Alabama? 226 illustration.

What poem, written by Oliver Wendell Holmes, saved the frigate *Constitution* from demolition? 347.

What is the philosophers' stone? 273.

How does a pilot get an airplane under control when it stalls? 191, 192 illustration.

What goddess dressed her son as a girl to keep him from fighting in the Trojan War? 18.

How is alcohol denatured? 275.

Which bird has the greatest wingspread? 260.

What are the most primitive forms of plant life? 283. Of animal life? 374.

Why is it said that the early fliers flew "by the seat of their pants"? 193.

What was the Line of Demarcation? 330.

How did a fly whisk change the history of Algeria? 306.

What sport may have given rise to the myth of the Minotaur? 62.

Which famous author of children's books took an active part in the woman's suffrage movement? 277.

What American statesman was the son of one president and the grandson of another? 39 chart.

According to tradition, what sight caused Emperor Otto III to close the tomb of Charlemagne? 2.

Why and how are airplanes stacked? 217 illustration.

What is the origin of the expression "Achilles' heel," meaning vulnerable point? 18.

Why is Alabama called the Yellowhammer State? 222.

What are the differences between a configuration, a mock-up, and a prototype? 68.

Does the century plant bloom only after it is 100 years of age? 124.

What national historic site in Quincy, Mass., was the home of two presidents of the United States? 37 illustration.

What famous battle was won because of the effectiveness of the longbow against heavily armored knights? 125.

What small plateau was the site of the best temples and statues of the ancient Greeks? 23.

What was the birthplace of the aerospace industry? 67, 72 illustration.

What kinds of fuels are used in jet engines? 74.

What statesman served in the House of Representatives after completing a term as president of the United States? 37.

What large animal escapes from its enemies by digging underground? 3.

Which chemical element is the most plentiful metal in the Earth's crust? 321.

Name the woman who helped establish the world's first Juvenile Court. 40.

What city is the rubber capital of the world? 221.

The letter A

probably started as a picture sign of an oxhead, as in Egyptian hiero-glyphic writing (1) and in a very early Semitic writing used about 1500 B.C. on the Sinai Peninsula (2). About 1000 B.C., in Byblos and other Phoenician and Canaanite centers, the sign was given a linear form (3), the source of all later forms. In the Semitic languages this sign was called *aleph,* meaning "ox."

The Greeks had no use for the *aleph* sound, the glottal stop, so they used the sign for the vowel "a." They also changed its name to *alpha.* They used several forms of the sign, including the ancestor of the English capital A (4). The Romans took this sign over into Latin, and it is the source of the English form. The English small "a" first took shape in Greek handwriting in a form (5) similar to the present English capital letter. In about the 4th century A.D. this was given a circular shape with a projection (6). This shape was the parent of both the English hand-written character (7) and the printed small "a" (8).

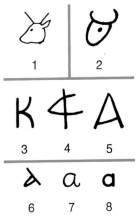

AACHEN, West Germany. The most important gateway in and out of West Germany, Aachen, or Aix-la-Chapelle, is located close to the point where the borders of The Netherlands, Belgium, and West Germany meet. The ancient city dates back to the days of the Romans, who built luxurious bathhouses around the local hot sulfur springs.

Charlemagne, the first Holy Roman emperor, is generally believed to have been born in Aachen. He started building the famous cathedral in 796. He made the city the center of European culture and the capital of his dominions north of the Alps. Because of his fondness for the city, he exempted its citizens from military service and taxation and even from imprisonment. The great emperor died there in 814 and was buried in a chapel attached to the cathedral. (*See also* Charlemagne.)

After his death Norman invaders partially destroyed the cathedral, but it was restored by Emperor Otto III in 983. According to tradition, Otto opened Charlemagne's tomb and, to his amazement and terror, saw the body sitting upright in a huge marble chair, clothed in white robes, holding a scepter and wearing a crown. Frightened by the sight, Otto had the tomb closed. It remained untouched until it was reopened by Barbarossa 160 years later. He removed the chair, crown, and scepter. They were used in the coronation ceremonies of 32 succeeding

The rotunda of the Elisenbrunnen, a spa, is shown with Aachen's cathedral in the background. The cathedral, known for its two distinctive architectural styles, contains the tomb of the emperor Charlemagne.

Lufthansa-Archiv

Holy Roman emperors. The ceremonies were held in the old Rathaus, or Town Hall.

In the 14th century, Aachen, then an important member of the Hanseatic League, controlled the territory between the Meuse and the Rhine rivers. Three treaties of Aix-la-Chapelle were signed at congresses of European powers held there. The first (1668) ended the War of Devolution between France and Spain. The second (1748) decided peace terms for the War of the Austrian Succession. The objective of the third (1818) was to bring order out of the chaotic conditions that followed the Napoleonic Wars.

After this period, Aachen lost all political and military significance. Then, toward the close of the 19th century, the development of rich coal deposits in the nearby hills transformed the city into an important industrial and railroad center. Soon many kinds of iron and steel products and textiles, glass, and leather were manufactured.

The city's peaceful commercial role changed in 1914, when the Germans launched from Aachen their surprise attack on Belgium at the beginning of World War I. Again, in 1940, it was one of the vantage points from which Nazi armies overran Belgium and Holland in World War II. Its strategic position as Germany's most westerly city, as well as its network of highways and railway lines, made it in turn a target for attack by the Allies at the start of their victorious march into Germany in 1944. Adolph Hitler signed a "death sentence" for the city by sending a "no surrender" order to the troops that were defending it. Aachen was finally captured by United States Army divisions on Oct. 21, 1944, after a savage battering by American artillery. Charlemagne's cathedral, from which his relics had been removed to safety, was one of the few buildings still standing. Although badly damaged, it has been restored.

After the war Aachen began rebuilding its industries and soon regained its rank as a railway and manufacturing center. Important research and educational facilities have developed there as well. (*See also* Germany.) Population (1979 census), 307,654.

AALTO, Alvar (1898–1976). Although Alvar Aalto worked as an architect, designer, and urban planner mostly in his native Finland, he won international acclaim. His work included houses, hospitals, churches, and factories as well as comprehensive plans for cultural, civic, and administrative centers. Inspired by the Finnish landscape, Aalto integrated shapes and materials with the natural environment, giving careful attention to human values—how people would live and work in his structures. His work features the use of natural light.

Hugo Alvar Henrik Aalto was born in Kuortane in west-central Finland on Feb. 3, 1898. He studied at the Helsinki University of Technology, leaving in 1917 to participate in Finland's struggle for independence from Russia; he returned and was graduated in 1921. He married a fellow student, Aino Marsia, who collaborated with him on much of his work.

Aalto created a distinctive style with his design (1927) for the white-walled municipal library, built 1930–35 at Viipuri in eastern Finland (now Vyborg, U.S.S.R.). Here he broke with the European functional school, which emphasized straight-lined regularity, by designing an irregular and complexly divided interior space with a sensuous use of wood that became typical of much of his later work. In the late 1930's Aalto won international attention with his Finnish pavilions at the world's fairs in Paris and New York City. Included were examples of his bent laminated-wood furniture, designed for factory production, that was to have a major influence on 20th-century furniture design.

GEKS

Alvar Aalto's town hall group used such traditional Finnish materials as red brick, wood, and copper.

In the 1940's Aalto was a visiting professor of architecture at the Massachusetts Institute of Technology, where he designed Baker House, a dormitory with a brick serpentine wall allowing views up and down the Charles River. His wife died in 1949, and in 1952 Aalto married another architect, Elissa Mäkiniemi, who also became his collaborator. Although Aalto worked closely with each of his wives and with relatively small staffs throughout his career, his designs reflected his own ideas, and every detail received personal attention.

A characteristic work of Aalto's mature period is the town hall group built at Säynätsalo, near his birthplace, during the early 1950's. The group includes municipal offices, a council chamber, and a library set around an elevated courtyard from which views of forests and lakes can be seen. The buildings are of brick and timber that are rough in texture, but they show Aalto's usual fineness of detail.

When he later resumed his use of white walls, he worked with surfaces of marble rather than reinforced concrete. A notable example was to be one of his last works, a new cultural center for Helsinki, overlooking Lake Töölö. Of the planned opera house, concert hall, museum, and library, only the concert hall (1967–71) was completed before his death on May 11, 1976, in Helsinki.

AARDVARK. The aardvark, or "earth pig," is one of Africa's strangest animals. Its thick body is thinly covered with stiff hair. Its back is arched. The animal's strong legs are short and stumpy. Its head has huge donkeylike ears, a long snout, and drooping eyelids with long lashes. Its naked tail tapers to a point from a thick base.

The Boer settlers in South Africa, who found this odd mammal rooting about at dusk among termite mounds, gave it the name aardvark. In Dutch the word means "earth pig." The animal is also called "ant bear." Aardvarks live throughout Africa south of the Sahara wherever they can find their favorite food of termites. They feed by night and sleep in underground burrows by day. They have powerful front legs, armed with four strong claws on each forefoot. With these claws they tear open termite mounds that man can break into only with a pickax. They escape from enemies by digging underground. Their tough skin protects them from the bites of soldier termites. Since the females bear only one offspring a year, aardvarks are not common.

There are two species. The Cape aardvark lives in southeastern and western Africa. The northern, or Ethiopian, aardvark is found in central and eastern Africa. Aardvarks are classified in an order by themselves, the Tubulidentata, meaning "tube-toothed." The tubular teeth are without enamel or roots. The scientific name of the Cape aardvark is *Orycteropus capensis;* of the northern aardvark, *O. aethiopicus.*

AARDWOLF. The shy aardwolf, or "earth wolf," is related to the hyena. It lives in open sandy plains and brush country across southern Africa from Somalia on the east to Angola on the west. It derives its Dutch name from its habit of digging a burrow in the earth. Unlike the hyena, it is mild and timid. Its weak jaws and small teeth are adapted to feeding on termites and other insects and on well-rotted carrion. It hunts by night.

The animal has large, erect ears, a pointed muzzle, and a short, bushy tail. Its long, coarse fur is light gray or buff in color with dark brown stripes. Along its sloping back is an erect mane of long hairs. From scent glands under its tail it can emit an evil-smelling fluid as a means of warding off an attack. The female aardwolf bears a litter of two to four pups in the late fall.

Aardwolves belong to the family Hyaenidae. Their scientific name is *Proteles cristatus.*

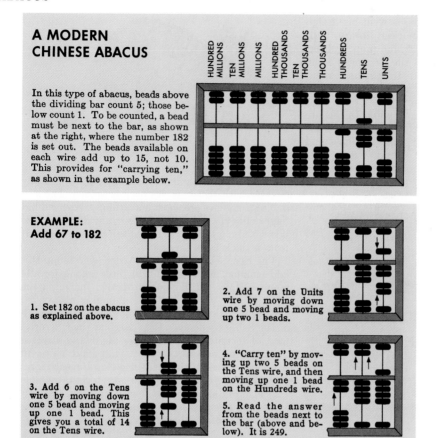

A MODERN CHINESE ABACUS

In this type of abacus, beads above the dividing bar count 5; those below count 1. To be counted, a bead must be next to the bar, as shown at the right, where the number 182 is set out. The beads available on each wire add up to 15, not 10. This provides for "carrying ten," as shown in the example below.

HUNDRED MILLIONS | TEN MILLIONS | MILLIONS | HUNDRED THOUSANDS | TEN THOUSANDS | THOUSANDS | HUNDREDS | TENS | UNITS

EXAMPLE: Add 67 to 182

1. Set 182 on the abacus as explained above.

2. Add 7 on the Units wire by moving down one 5 bead and moving up two 1 beads.

3. Add 6 on the Tens wire by moving down one 5 bead and moving up one 1 bead. This gives you a total of 14 on the Tens wire.

4. "Carry ten" by moving up two 5 beads on the Tens wire, and then moving up one 1 bead on the Hundreds wire.

5. Read the answer from the beads next to the bar (above and below). It is 249.

ABACUS. Before the Hindu-Arabic numeration system was used, people counted, added, and subtracted with an abacus. (The name comes from the Greek word *abax*, meaning "board" or "calculating table.") The Greeks and Romans used pebbles or metal disks as counters. They moved these on marked boards to work out problems. Later the counters were strung on wires mounted in a frame.

People used this device instead of working out their problems in writing because they could not "carry ten" conveniently with their cumbersome system of writing numbers. The Roman numeral system, in which letters represent numbers, was dominant in Europe for nearly 2,000 years. However, even simple addition of Roman numerals—for example, XIII (13) plus LXIX (69)—was difficult.

The ancient Egyptians, Hindus, and Chinese also used the abacus. The introduction of the Hindu-Arabic system of numeration, with the use of zero as a number, made written calculations easier, and the abacus passed out of use in Europe. However, people in the Orient, the Soviet Union, and the Middle East still use it—particularly in business.

The early abacus had ten counters to a wire. The modern form has a dividing bar. Counters above the bar count five; those below, one. It is unnecessary to handle counters larger than five in value.

ABADAN, Iran. One of the traditional centers in the Middle East for the refining of petroleum and the shipment of petroleum products is Abadan. Pipelines connect the city to oil fields in both southwestern and northern Iran. The city is located 33 miles (53 kilometers) from the Persian Gulf on an island in the Shatt al 'Arab, a stream formed by the junction of the Tigris and Euphrates rivers.

The Abadan area was acquired by Persia in a treaty with Turkey in 1847. The island was a barren mud flat with only a few groves of date palms. The city's development dates from 1909, when it became the site of the huge oil refinery erected by the Anglo-Persian Oil Company, nationalized in 1951 as the National Iranian Oil Company. In 1981, during severe border warfare between Iran and Iraq, much of the city of Abadan and the entire refinery complex were left in ruins by systematic Iraqi bombardments.

Included in the refinery complex had been several well-built compounds for the oil company's staff, which stood in sharp contrast to the lively local bazaar and poor housing quarters for immigrants. (*See also* Iran.) Population (1976 census), 296,081.

John Abbott was prime minister of Canada from 1891 to 1892. He was 71 when he resigned.

The Public Archives of Canada

ABBOTT, John (1821–1893). "I hate politics," Sir John Abbott once wrote. "I hate notoriety, public meetings . . . everything that is apparently the necessary incident of politics—except doing public work to the best of my ability." Abbott's long life of public service to Canada was climaxed in 1891 when, as leader of the Conservative party, he succeeded Sir John A. Macdonald as prime minister of Canada (*see* Macdonald).

John Joseph Caldwell Abbott was born on March 12, 1821, in St. Andrews, in the county of Argenteuil, Lower Canada (now Quebec). He was the eldest son of the Rev. Joseph Abbott and Harriet Bradford Abbott. He received his early education in St. Andrews and in Montreal, then entered McGill University. He took his law degree in 1847. In 1849 he married Mary Bethune. They had six children.

Abbott was named queen's counsel in 1862. He served as counsel for the Canadian Pacific Railway from 1880 to 1887, when he became a director. For several years he was dean of the Faculty of Law at McGill University. He held the office of mayor of Montreal from 1887 to 1889.

One of Abbott's first political acts was to sign, in 1849, an annexation manifesto that favored the union of Canada with the United States. The union movement, brought on by a business depression, lasted only a short time. In 1859 Abbott was elected to the Legislative Assembly of Canada.

As legal adviser to Hugh Allan, one of the builders of the Canadian Pacific Railway, Abbott was implicated in the Pacific Scandal of 1873. One of his confidential clerks furnished the evidence that brought about the fall of the Macdonald government in that year and the defeat of Abbott in the elections of 1874. In 1881 Abbott was returned to the House of Commons, and in 1887 he was appointed to the Dominion Senate. Upon the death of Macdonald in 1891, Abbott was a compromise choice for prime minister.

Abbott was 70 years of age and in declining health when he became prime minister. During his short term of office he accomplished a major revision of the jury law. He drafted an act that is the basis of Canadian law on insolvency today.

On Dec. 5, 1892, Abbott resigned as prime minister because of ill health. That same year he was made a knight commander of the Order of St. Michael and St. George. He died in Montreal on Oct. 30, 1893.

ABBREVIATION. A shortened form of a word or group of words used in writing to save time and space is called an abbreviation. Some abbreviations are also used in speaking.

Abbreviations often consist of the first letter of a word, or each important word in a group, written as a capital followed by a period. For example, P.O. stands for post office and C.O.D. for collect (or cash) on delivery. Sometimes an abbreviation is printed as a small letter and period, as in b. for born and m. for married. The same abbreviation may be used for different words; for example, m. may also stand for masculine or meter. The reader usually can determine the correct word from the context.

Other letters of a word may be added, as in ms. for manuscript and ft. for foot. Initial letters or syllables sometimes form a new word, as NATO (North Atlantic Treaty Organization) or OPEC (Organization of Petroleum Exporting Countries). Such abbreviations, called acronyms, are not followed by periods. Letters in abbreviations may be doubled for the plural form, as in ll. for lines and pp. for pages. For certain frequently used abbreviations small capital letters are usually used instead of large capitals, as in A.D., B.C., A.M., and P.M.

Abbreviations are most often used for common words such as the names of days, months, and states. Long words and phrases are often abbreviated such as Lieut. for Lieutenant and R.F.D. for Rural Free Delivery. Academic degrees and titles are usually abbreviated, as in D.D. for Doctor of Divinity and H.R.H. for His (or Her) Royal Highness. In modern business Co. is used for Company, Inc. for Incorporated, and Ltd. for Limited.

In most Latin phrases in common use, only the first letter of each word is used, as in *n.b.* for *nota bene* ("notice well") and *i.e.* for *id est* ("that is"). An exception is *etc.* for *et cetera* ("and others").

Ancient monuments and manuscripts show that humans began to abbreviate words soon after alphabetic writing became general. In the United States abbreviations have long been widely used. OK and C.O.D., for example, date from the 19th century. With the steady increase in federal government agencies, people began to refer to the long official names by their initials. The FHA, for Federal Housing Administration, and NASA (which is also an acronym), for National Aeronautics and Space Administration, have become household words. They are usually written without periods. (For abbreviations of chemical elements, *see* Periodic Table.)

Abbreviations

A

a.—acre; ampere; anode.
A—angstrom unit.
AAA—American Automobile Association.
AAU—Amateur Athletic Union.
A.B.—*Artium Baccalaureus*, Bachelor of Arts.
ABA—American Bar Association.
AC, A.C.—alternating current.
accel.—*accelerando*, with increasing rapidity (music).
acct—account.
A.D.—*anno Domini*, in the year of our Lord.
ADC—aid to dependent children; aide-de-camp.
ad lib.—*ad libitum*, at pleasure.
Adm.—Admiral.
AEC—Atomic Energy Commission.
AFAM—Ancient Free and Accepted Masons.
AFL-CIO—American Federation of Labor-Congress of Industrial Organizations.
AID—Agency for International Development.
Ala.—Alabama.
Alta.—Alberta.
a.m.—*ante meridiem*, before noon; *Artium Magister*, Master of Arts; amplitude modulation.
AMA—American Medical Association.
amu—atomic mass unit.
anon—anonymous.
AP—Associated Press.
Apr.—April.
apt.—apartment.
aq—*aqua*, water.
Ariz.—Arizona.
Ark.—Arkansas.
ASCAP—American Society of Composers, Authors and Publishers.
assn—association.
asst—assistant.
Aug.—August.
AV—Authorized Version (of the Bible).
av—average; avoirdupois.
Ave.—Avenue.
AWOL—absent without leave (military).
awu—relative atomic weight unit.

B

B.A.—*Baccalaureus Artium*, Bachelor of Arts.
Bart., Bt.—Baronet.
BBC—British Broadcasting Corporation.
bbl.—barrel; barrels.
B.C.—before Christ; British Columbia.
B.C.E.—Bachelor of Civil Engineering.
B.C.L.—Bachelor of Civil Law.
B.D.—*Baccalaureus Divinitatis*, Bachelor of Divinity.
B.D.S.—Bachelor of Dental Surgery.
BeV—billion electron volts.
bk—bank; book.
B.L.—*Baccalaureus Legum*, Bachelor of Laws.
bldg—building.
B.Lit.—*Baccalaureus Literarum*, Bachelor of Literature.
blvd.—boulevard.
B.M.—*Baccalaureus Medicinae*, Bachelor of Medicine.
B.M.E.—Bachelor of Mining Engineering.
BMEWS—Ballistic Missile Early Warning System.
B.Mus.—*Baccalaureus Musicae*, Bachelor of Music.
B.Phil.—*Baccalaureus Philosophiae*, Bachelor of Philosophy.
BPOE—Benevolent and Protective Order of Elks.
Br—British

Brig. Gen.—Brigadier General.
bros—brothers.
B.S., B.Sc.—*Baccalaureus Scientiae*, Bachelor of Science.
Btu—British thermal unit.
bu.—bushel; bushels.

C

c—carat; cent; circa; copyright.
C—Celsius.
cal—calendar; calorie.
Calif.—California.
Can.—Canada.
CARE—Cooperative for American Relief Everywhere.
cc—cubic centimeters.
CC—carbon copy.
CCC—Commodity Credit Corporation.
C.C.F.—Cooperative Commonwealth Federation.
cf.—*confer*, compare.
ch, or chap—chapter.
CIA—Central Intelligence Agency.
cm.—centimeter.
c/o—care of.
Co., co.—company; county.
CO, C.O.—Commanding Officer.
COD—cash on delivery; collect on delivery.
Col.—Colonel; Colossians.
Colo.—Colorado.
Comdr.—Commander.
Commo.—Commodore.
Conn.—Connecticut.
CORE—Congress of Racial Equality.
Corp.—Corporal; Corporation.
cp—compare; coupon.
C.P.A.—Certified Public Accountant.
cr—cathode ray; credit.
cresc.—*crescendo*, gradual increase of tone (music).
CST—central standard time.
cts.—cents.
cu.—cubic.
cwt.—hundredweight.
C.Z.—Canal Zone.

D

d.—*denarius*, a penny.
D—Democrat.
DAR—Daughters of the American Revolution.
D.C.—*da capo*, from the beginning (music); District of Columbia.
DC, D.C., d.c.—direct current.
D.C.L.—Doctor of Canon Law; Doctor of Civil Law.
D.D.—*Divinitatis Doctor*, Doctor of Divinity.
D.D.S.—Doctor of Dental Surgery.
Del.—Delaware.
D.Eng.—Doctor of Engineering.
dept.—department.
DEW—Distant Early Warning.
dim.—*diminuendo*, gradual decrease of tone (music).
dist—district.
D.Lit., D. Litt.—Doctor of Literature; Doctor of Letters.
dm.—decimeter.
D.M.D.—*Doctor of Dental Medicine*.
D.Mus.—*Doctor Musicae*, Doctor of Music.
DNA—deoxyribonucleic acid.
do.—*ditto*, the same.
D.O.—Doctor of Osteopathy.
doz.—dozen.
Dr.—Doctor.
D.S., D.Sc.—Doctor of Science.
DSC—Distinguished Service Cross.
DSM—Distinguished Service Medal.
DSO—Distinguished Service Order.
DST—daylight saving time.
D.V.M.—Doctor of Veterinary Medicine.
dwt.—deadweight ton; pennyweight

E

e., E, or E.—east.
ed—edition; editor; education.
EE—electrical engineer.
EEC—European Economic Community.
EEG—electroencephalogram.
EFTA—European Free Trade Association.
e.g.—*exempli gratia*, for example.
EKG—electrocardiogram.
E.M.F.—electromotive force.
Ens.—Ensign.
esp—especially.
Esq.—Esquire.
est—established.
et al.—*et alibi*, and elsewhere; *et alii*, and others.
etc.—*et cetera*, and so on.
et seq.—*et sequens*, and the following; *et sequentes, et sequentia*, and those that follow.

F

f—*forte*, loud.
f.—franc (French money); following (page).
F—Fahrenheit.
FA—field artillery.
FAA—Federal Aviation Administration.
FBI—Federal Bureau of Investigation.
FCC—Federal Communications Commission.
Feb.—February.
fed—federal; federation.
ff—folios; following (pages).
ff—*fortissimo*, very loud (music).
FHA—Federal Housing Administration.
fl.—flourished.
Fla.—Florida.
FM—frequency modulation.
FOB—free on board.
FOE—Fraternal Order of Eagles.
FRCP—Fellow of Royal College of Physicians.
FRCS—Fellow of Royal College of Surgeons.
FRGS—Fellow of Royal Geographical Society.
Fri.—Friday.
FRS—Fellow of the Royal Society; Federal Reserve System.
ft.—feet; foot; fort.

G

g.—gram; gravity.
Ga.—Georgia.
gal.—gallon; gallons.
GAR—Grand Army of the Republic.
GATT—General Agreement on Tariffs and Trade.
gcd—greatest common divisor.
GCT—Greenwich civil time.
Gen.—General; Genesis.
GMT—Greenwich mean time.
GNP—gross national product.
G.O.P.—Grand Old Party (Republican party, U. S.).
Gov.—Governor.
govt—government.

H

H.M.S.—His (or Her) Majesty's Ship (or Service).
Hon.—Honorable.
hon.—honorary.
hp—horsepower.
hq—headquarters.
hr.—hour.
HR—House of Representatives.
hwy—highway.

I

I.—Island, Isle.
ib., ibid.—*ibidem*, in the same place.
ICBM—intercontinental ballistic missile.
I.C.C.—Interstate Commerce Commission.
id.—*idem*, the same.
ID—identification.

i.e.—*id est*, that is.
IHS—symbol meaning Jesus, formed by a contraction of Greek letters.
Ill.—Illinois.
illus—illustrated.
in.—inch; inches.
inc.—incorporated; inclusive.
Ind.—Indiana.
I.N.R.I.—*Iesus Nazarenus, Rex Iudaeorum*, Jesus of Nazareth, King of the Jews.
intl—international.
IOOF—Independent Order of Odd Fellows.
IOU, I.O.U.—I owe you.
IQ—intelligence quotient.
IRS—Internal Revenue Service.
ITO—International Trade Organization.
IWW, I.W.W.—Industrial Workers of the World.

J

Jan.—January.
J.C.D.—*Juris Civilis Doctor*, Doctor of Civil Law.
J.D.—*Jurum Doctor*, Doctor of Law.
jg—junior grade.
JP—justice of the peace.
Jr.—Junior.
J.U.D.—*Juris Utriusque Doctor*, Doctor of both Civil and Canon Law.

K

K—Kelvin (scale).
Kan., Kans.—Kansas.
kg.—kilogram.
kl.—kiloliter.
km.—kilometer (km²—square kilometer).
KP—kitchen police.
kt—karat; knight.
kw.—kilowatt.
kw-hr—kilowatt-hour.
Ky.—Kentucky.

L

l.—liter.
La.—Louisiana.
L.A.—Los Angeles.
Lab.—Labrador.
lat—latitude.
lb.—*libra*, pound.
lc—lower case (type).
LCD—lowest common denominator.
LCM—least common multiple.
L.I.—Long Island.
Lieut., Lt.—Lieutenant.
Lit.B.—*Literarum Baccalaureus*, Bachelor of Literature.
Lit. D., Litt. D.—*Literarum Doctor*, Doctor of Literature; Doctor of Letters.
LL.B.—*Legum Baccalaureus*, Bachelor of Laws.
LL.D.—*Legum Doctor*, Doctor of Laws.
LL.M.—*Legum Magister*, Master of Laws.
loc. cit.—*loco citato*, in the place cited.
log—logarithm.
long—longitude.
ltd—limited.

M

m.—*meridies*, noon; meter.
M.—Mach; monsieur.
M.A.—*Magister Artium*, Master of Arts.
Ma.E.—Master of Engineering.
Maj.—Major.
Man.—Manitoba.
Mar.—March.
Mass.—Massachusetts.
M.B.—*Medicinae Baccalaureus*, Bachelor of Medicine.
M.C.—*Magister Chirurgiae*, Master of Surgery; Master of Ceremonies; Member of Congress.
M.C.E.—Master of Civil Engineering.

M.D.—*Medicinae Doctor*, Doctor of Medicine.
Md.—Maryland.
M.D.S.—Master of Dental Surgery.
mdse—merchandise.
Me.—Maine.
M.E.—Mining (or Mechanical) Engineer.
Messrs.—*Messieurs*, Gentlemen, Sirs.
MeV—million electron volts.
mf—*mezzo forte*, moderately loud (music).
mfg—manufacturing.
mg.—milligram.
Mgr., or Msgr.—Monsignor.
mi.—mile.
Mich.—Michigan.
Minn.—Minnesota.
misc—miscellaneous.
Miss.—Mississippi.
Mlle.—Mademoiselle.
MM.—Messieurs.
mm.—millimeter (mm², square millimeter; mm³, cubic millimeter).
Mme.—Madame.
Mo.—Missouri.
mo.—month.
Mon.—Monday.
Mont.—Montana.
MP, M.P.—Member of Parliament; military police.
mph—miles per hour.
M.S., M.Sc.—Master of Science.
MS—manuscript (plural, MSS).
Mt.—Mount, Mountain.
Mus.B.—*Musicae Baccalaureus*, Bachelor of Music.
Mus.D.—*Musicae Doctor*, Doctor of Music.

N

n., N, or N.—north.
NAACP—National Association for the Advancement of Colored People.
NASA—National Aeronautics and Space Administration.
NATO—North Atlantic Treaty Organization.
N.B.—New Brunswick.
N.B., n.b.—*nota bene*, note well.
NBC—National Broadcasting Company.
N.C.—North Carolina.
NCAA—National Collegiate Athletic Association.
NCO—noncommissioned officer.
n.d., ND—no date (of publication).
N.D., N. Dak.—North Dakota.
N.E.—New England.
Neb., Nebr.—Nebraska.
nem. con.—*nemine contradicente*, "no one contradicting," unanimously.
Nev.—Nevada.
Newf., Nfld.—Newfoundland.
NG—national guard; no good.
N.H.—New Hampshire.
N.J.—New Jersey.
N.M., N.Mex.—New Mexico.
No.—*numero*, number.
non seq.—*non sequitur*, it does not follow.
Nov.—November.
NP—notary public.
N.S.—Nova Scotia.
N.S.W.—New South Wales.
NT., N.T.—New Testament.
N.W.T.—Northwest Territories.
N.Y.—New York.

O

OAS—Organization of American States.
ob.—*obiit*, died.
OCS—officer candidate school.
Oct.—October.
OK, okay—all right (slang).
Okla.—Oklahoma.
Ont.—Ontario.
o.p.—out of print.
op. cit.—*opere citato*, in the work cited.
Ore.—Oregon.
OT—Old Testament.
oz.—ounce.

P

—page; *piano*, soft (music) .
Pa., Penn., or Penna.—Pennsylvania.
par—paragraph.
PAU—Pan American Union.
PC—Privy Council; Privy Councilor.
pd—paid.
Pd.M.—Master of Pedagogy.
P.E.I.—Prince Edward Island.
pf, pfd—preferred.
p.f.—*piu forte*, a little louder (music).
pfc—private first class.
Phar.D.—Doctor of Pharmacy.
Ph.B.—*Philosophiae Baccalaureus*, Bachelor of Philosophy.
Ph.D.—*Philosophiae Doctor*, Doctor of Philosophy.
Ph.G.—Graduate in Pharmacy.
Phila.—Philadelphia.
P.I.—Philippine Islands.
pk.—peck.
pkg—package.
pkwy—parkway.
p.m.—*post meridiem*, after noon.
PO—Post Office.
pp—pages; *pianissimo*, very soft (music).
P.P., p.p.—parcel post.
P.P.C.—*pour prendre congé*, to take leave.
ppd—postpaid; prepaid.
P.R.—Puerto Rico.
prof.—professor.
PS—*post scriptum*, postscript; public school.
pt.—point; port; part; pint.
PTA—Parent-Teacher Association.
pvt.—private.

Q

Q.E.D.—*quod erat demonstrandum*, which was to be shown.
Q.E.F.—*quod erat faciendum*, which was to be done.
QMG, Q.M.G.—Quartermaster General.
qt.—quart.
qu, ques—question.
Que.—Quebec.
q.v.—*quod vide*, which see.

R

R—Republican.
R.—*regina*, queen; *rex*, king.
RA—royal academy.
RAF—Royal Air Force.
RAM—Royal Academy of Music.
RCAF—Royal Canadian Air Force.
RCMP—Royal Canadian Mounted Police.
RCN—Royal Canadian Navy.
re—reference; regarding.
Rep—Representative.
Rev.—Revelation; Reverend.
RFD—Rural Free Delivery.
R.I.—Rhode Island.
RIP—*Requiescat in pace*, May he rest in peace.
rit., ritard.—*ritardando*, gradually slower (music).
riten.—*ritenuto*, retarding (music).
RMS—Royal Mail Steamship (or Service).
RN—registered nurse; Royal Navy.
ROTC—Reserve Officers Training Corps.
rpm—revolutions per minute.
RR—railroad; rural route.
R.S.F.S.R.—Russian Soviet Federated Socialist Republic.
R.S.V.P.—*Répondez, s'il vous platt*, Answer, if you please.
ry—railway.

S

s.—*solidus*, a shilling (English money).
s., S, or S.—south.
SAC—Strategic Air Command.

SAR—Sons of the American Revolution.
Sask.—Saskatchewan.
Sat.—Saturday.
S.B.—Bachelor of Science.
sc.—*scilicet*, that is to say.
S.C.—South Carolina.
Sc.B.—*Scientiae Baccalaureus*, Bachelor of Science.
Sc.D.—*Scientiae Doctor*, Doctor of Science.
S.D., S. Dak.—South Dakota.
SEATO—Southeast Asia Treaty Organization.
SEC—Securities and Exchange Commission.
sec, secy—secretary.
Sen.—Senator.
Sept.—September.
seq.—*sequentia*, the following.
s.g.—specific gravity.
sgd.—signed.
Sgt., Sergt.—Sergeant.
SHAPE—Supreme Headquarters, Allied Powers, Europe.
SJ—Society of Jesus (Jesuits).
SOP—standard operating procedure.
SPCA—Society for the Prevention of Cruelty to Animals.
SPCC—Society for the Prevention of Cruelty to Children.
sp. gr.—specific gravity.
S.P.Q.R.—*Senatus Populusque Romanus*, the Roman Senate and People.
sq.—square.
Sr.—Senior.
SRO—standing room only.
SRS—*Societatis Regiae Socius*, Fellow of the Royal Society.
SS—steamship.
SSR, S.S.R.—Soviet Socialist Republic.
St.—Saint; Strait; Street.
S.T.B.—*Sacrae Theologiae Baccalaureus*, Bachelor of Sacred Theology.
S.T.D.—*Sacrae Theologiae Doctor*, Doctor of Sacred Theology.
S.T.P.—*Sacrae Theologiae Professor*, Professor of Sacred Theology.
Sun.—Sunday.
Supt.—Superintendent.

T

t.—teaspoon; ton.
TB—tuberculosis.
tb., tbs., tbsp.—tablespoon.
Tenn.—Tennessee.
Tex.—Texas.
Thur.—Thursday.
tp.—township.
Tues., Tue.—Tuesday.
TV—television.
TVA—Tennessee Valley Authority.

U

UAR—United Arab Republic.
UEL—United Empire Loyalist.
UFO—Unidentified Flying Object.
uhf—ultrahigh frequency.
UK—United Kingdom (of Great Britain and Northern Ireland).
UN—United Nations.
UNESCO—United Nations Educational, Scientific, and Cultural Organization.
UNICEF—United Nations Children's Fund.
univ.—university.
UPI—United Press International.
U.S.—United States.
U.S.A.—United States Army; United States of America.
USAF—United States Air Force.
USIA—United States Information Agency.
USMC, U.S.M.C.—United States Marine Corps.

USN, U.S.N.—United States Navy.
U.S.P.—United States Pharmacopeia.
USS, U.S.S.—United States Ship; United States Steamer.
U.S.S.R.—Union of Soviet Socialist Republics.

V

v—verse.
Va.—Virginia.
VC—Victoria Cross.
Ven.—Venerable.
V.I.—Virgin Islands.
viz.—*videlicet*, namely.
vol.—volume.
VP—vice-president.
vs.—*versus*, against.
V.S.—Veterinary Surgeon.
Vt.—Vermont.

W

w., W, or W.—west.
WAC—Women's Army Corps.
WAF—Women in the Air Force, U.S.
Wash.—Washington.
WCTU—Woman's Christian Temperance Union.
Wed.—Wednesday.
WHO—World Health Organization.
whsle—wholesale.
Wis., Wisc.—Wisconsin.
WRNS—Women's Royal Naval Service.
wt.—weight.
W. Va.—West Virginia.
Wyo., Wy.—Wyoming.

X

xd—without dividend.
Xing—crossing.
XL—extra large.
Xmas—Christmas.

Y

yd.—yard.
YMCA—Young Men's Christian Association.
yr.—year.
Y.T.—Yukon Territory.
YWCA—Young Women's Christian Association.

Symbols

+—add; plus.
&—and.
*—asterisk (refer to footnote).
@—at; each.
¢—cents.
©—copyright.
°—degrees (temperature, arc).
÷—divide.
$—dollars.
=—equals.
≏—equivalent.
♀—female.
∞—infinity.
>—is greater than.
<—is less than.
♂—male.
'—minutes (time, arc); feet.
×—multiplied by.
≠—not equal to.
#—number; pounds; space.
¶—paragraph.
∥—parallel.
%—percent.
⊥—perpendicular.
£—pound sterling.
:—the ratio of.
℞—recipe; take.
®—registered trademark.
∟—right angle to.
"—seconds (time, arc); inches.
§—section.
/—shillings.
——subtract; minus.
∴—therefore.

7

ABDICATION *see* table in FACT-INDEX.

ABDUL-JABBAR, Kareem (born 1947). His extraordinary height of seven feet two inches combined with extraordinary skills enabled Kareem Abdul-Jabbar to become one of the greatest United States basketball players.

Abdul-Jabbar was born April 16, 1947, in New York City. His name at birth was Lew Alcindor. While at college he changed his name as a result of having come under the influence of Malcolm X, a well-known leader of the Black Muslims (followers of the religion of Islam).

As a high school basketball player, Abdul-Jabbar led his team to a four-year record of 95 wins and 6 losses and scored 2,067 points, a New York City record. He received more than 100 offers of college scholarships and chose the University of California at Los Angeles (UCLA). He enrolled there in 1965 and led UCLA to three consecutive National Collegiate Athletic Association (NCAA) championships. Abdul-Jabbar was chosen collegiate All-American three times, with a record field-goal percentage of .641.

Upon graduation from UCLA he was the leading draft choice for the professional teams and was soon claimed by the Milwaukee Bucks. At center position he continued to play spectacularly, winning the distinction of being rookie of the year in 1970 after his first season. In 1975 Abdul-Jabbar was traded to the Los Angeles Lakers. In 1980 he was awarded, for the sixth time, the Podolof Cup, presented annually to the most valuable player in the National Basketball Association (NBA). He helped the Lakers win the NBA championship in 1980 and 1982. In 1983 he became the second NBA player to score more than 30,000 career points, and in 1984 became the NBA's all-time field-goal scoring leader.

ABEL, Niels Henrik (1802–1829). The Norwegian mathematician Niels Henrik Abel made a remarkable series of contributions to science but was not fully recognized during his short lifetime. He is known for his work with integral equations, mathematical expressions that are used to compute the area beneath a curve. Integral equations have broad practical application in surveying and engineering. Abel also investigated the field of elliptic functions. (An ellipse is an oval with special properties.)

Niels Henrik Abel was born on Aug. 5, 1802, on the island of Finnøy, near Stavanger, Norway, the son of an impoverished minister. Abel was an unremarkable student until his 15th year, when his school hired Bernt Holmboe to teach mathematics. Holmboe recognized Abel's talent at once and enthusiastically encouraged him. The pupil soon surpassed his teacher.

Abel's father died in 1820, leaving the family almost without funds. When he entered the University of Oslo the following year, Abel was supported by several admiring professors who contributed to his upkeep from their salaries and invited him to their homes for meals. For four years he remained at the

university, studying independently much of the time and writing papers on mathematics.

Traveling to Berlin in 1825, Abel met August Crelle, a German engineer with an intense interest in mathematics, who was then starting a mathematical journal. Crelle published many papers by Abel.

A visit to Paris in 1826 failed to win Abel recognition from prominent French mathematicians. He prepared a long paper for presentation to the Academy of Sciences, but the professors responsible for evaluating this work simply ignored it. Disappointed, Abel returned to Berlin and then went home to Oslo where he had debts, no job, and no prospects.

Things brightened a year later when Abel secured some temporary university teaching work and unexpectedly found himself in competition with a young German mathematician, Karl G. J. Jacobi, who was also investigating elliptic functions. For a time, both men were racing to publish their discoveries first.

By this time Abel had gained a considerable reputation in European mathematical circles, and several attempts were made to find him a suitable professorship. But in the fall of 1828 his health, which had begun to fail in Berlin, deteriorated seriously. A holiday Christmas trip in an open sled contributed to his decline. He died at Froland, Norway, on April 6, 1829, from an advanced case of tuberculosis. He was 26 years old. Ironically, a university appointment in Berlin had just been announced for him. In 1830 Abel and Jacobi were awarded the Grand Prix of the French Academy. Bernt Holmboe published the first edition of Abel's works in 1839.

ABELARD, Peter (1079–1142). Of all the teachers in the cathedral school that was the forerunner of the University of Paris, Peter Abelard was the favorite. The eldest son of a minor lord in Brittany, he had forsaken the life of a noble to be a scholar. He had studied in Paris and had soon surpassed his teacher. At the age of 22 he became a master and teacher.

He was skilled in theology, but he was especially brilliant in logic. Students flocked to hear him, and learned men everywhere read handwritten copies of his book 'Sic et Non' (Yes and No). The book was so named for its "Yes" and "No" answers from the teachings of the Church Fathers to such questions as:

Is God one, or no?

Are the flesh and blood of Christ in very truth and essence present in the sacrament of the altar, or no?

Then came a love affair with a pupil, the brilliant Héloïse, who was 22 years younger than Abelard. Because marriage would interfere with his career, the lovers were married secretly. Their secret was discovered, however, and they were forced to part.

Abelard's habit of challenging his colleagues irritated them, and they attacked his doctrines, particularly his thesis that nothing should be accepted unless it could be proved. They claimed that religious faith should come first. Bernard of Clairvaux (later St. Bernard), his most bitter opponent, finally convinced the church to condemn a number of his teach-

A miniature portrait of Abelard with Héloïse was done by Jean de Meun in the 14th century.

ings. Abelard then retired to the Benedictine monastery at Cluny. The noble character of Héloïse, who for some 40 years was a nun, is shown in her letters to Abelard. Abelard died in 1142. When Héloïse died, in 1164, she was buried at his side.

ABERDEEN, Scotland. The chief commercial and fishing seaport of northern Scotland is the city of Aberdeen. It is a district of the Grampiam Region and the largest city in northeastern Scotland.

Aberdeen is situated on the North Sea coast, between the River Don, to the north, and the Dee, to the south. The mouths of the two rivers are about 2 miles (3 kilometers) apart. The Don is spanned by the 14th-century Bridge of Balgownie (Auld Brig o' Don), and the Dee by the 16th-century Bridge of Dee.

Aberdeen is called the Granite City because nearly all its buildings are made of the pale granite that is quarried nearby. The square solid buildings that line Union Street, in the New City, date chiefly from the 19th century. Marischal College, perhaps the world's largest granite building, was begun in 1844. It has many kinds of spires and pinnacles, each topped with a small gilt flag.

To the north are the narrow, twisting streets of the Old Town. Here many buildings date from the 16th century or earlier. Some are considerably older. For example, the plain stone cathedral, St. Machar's, was begun in the 14th century. King's College, founded in 1494, joined with Marischal College in 1860 to form the University of Aberdeen. Other institutions of higher education include commercial and trade colleges as well as colleges of agriculture, fisheries, soil, and animal nutrition.

Since the North Sea oil boom of the 1970's, Aberdeen has become the hub of the North Sea oil industry and a major supply center for North Sea oil platforms. The business boom financed the construction of housing, offices, and schools. Revenues of the port of Aberdeen increased fifteenfold during the years of the early 1970's.

Aberdeen's original and main harbor has been continually improved, enlarged, and modernized. In addition to the important fishing industry, other industries are chemicals, fertilizers, papermaking, tanning, machinery manufacturing, shipbuilding, granite quarrying, and curing and canning of the abundant fish catch. (*See also* Scotland.) Population (1981 census), 203,612.

ABIDJAN, Ivory Coast. The capital and largest city of the Ivory Coast, Abidjan has the unusual feature of being a major trading port that is located on a lagoon rather than on the sea. Separated from the Gulf of Guinea and the Atlantic Ocean by the Vridi-Plage sandbar, this deepwater port was opened to the sea in 1950 by the Vridi Canal. The city quickly became the financial center of French-speaking West Africa.

Abidjan was a village in 1898 and became a town in 1903 when work was begun on a railway to Upper Volta. Abidjan succeeded Bingerville as capital of the French Ivory Coast colony in 1934 and remained the capital after the country's independence in 1960. In 1958 the first of two bridges was built to link the administrative and business districts on the mainland with Petit-Bassam Island, the city's industrial area. Abidjan's international airport is located at Port-Bouët, a municipality on the sandbar.

The modern, bustling port of Abidjan exports such varied products as coffee, cocoa, timber, bananas, pineapples, manganese, and various types of fish. The tuna catch amounts to several thousand tons each year. In addition, city factories produce soap, matches, and a wide range of metal products, including furniture, automobiles, and air-conditioning and refrigerating units.

The Abidjan radio station broadcasts mostly in French. However, it also uses English and eight local African languages in its news bulletins and in educational broadcasting. A television station broadcasts in French for several hours each day.

The Abidjan museum is a rich storehouse for more than 20,000 pieces of traditional Ivorian art. The city also has a national library, agricultural and scientific research institutes, several educational facilities, and a university founded in 1964. Just north of the city is a magnificent tropical rain forest called Parc National du Banco. Population (1975 census), 685,800.

ABOLITIONIST MOVEMENT. Beginning about the time of the American Revolution, 1775 to 1783, there arose in western Europe and the United States a movement to abolish the institution of slavery and the slave trade that supported it. Advocates of this movement were called abolitionists.

From the 16th to the 19th century some 15 million Africans were kidnapped and shipped across the Atlantic Ocean to the Americas. They were sold as laborers on the sugar and cotton plantations of South and North America and the islands of the Caribbean Sea (*see* Slavery). In the late 1600's Quaker and Mennonite Christians in the British colonies of North America were protesting slavery on religious grounds. Nevertheless, the institution of slavery continued to expand in North America. This was especially true in the Southern colonies.

By the late 1700's ideas on slavery were changing. An intellectual movement in Europe, the Enlightenment, had made strong arguments in favor of the rights of man. The leaders of the American Revolution had issued a Declaration of Independence in 1776. This document also enunciated a belief in the equality of all human beings. In 1789 the French Revolution began, and its basic document was the Declaration of the Rights of Man and of the Citizen. There was a gradual but steady increase in opposition to keeping human beings as private property.

The first formal organization to emerge in the abolitionist movement was the Abolition Society, founded in 1787 in England. Its leaders were Thomas Clarkson and William Wilberforce. The society's first success came in 1807 when Britain abolished the slave trade with its colonies. When slavery itself showed no signs of disappearing, the Anti-Slavery Society was founded in Britain in 1823 under the leadership of Thomas Fowell Buxton, a member of Parliament. In 1833 Parliament finally passed a law abolishing slavery in all British colonies.

Slavery had been written into the United States Constitution in 1787, but a provision had also been made to abolish the slave trade. This was done in 1807. Unfortunately it coincided with a reinvigorated cotton economy in the South. From that time on, the North and South grew more and more different, both economically and in social attitudes.

Between 1800 and 1830 the antislavery movement in the North looked for ways to eventually eliminate slavery from the United States. One popular plan was to colonize Liberia, in Africa, as a refuge for former slaves. This experiment was a failure.

While advocates of the movement never gave up hope of gradually doing away with slavery, there emerged suddenly in 1831 a much more strident form of abolitionism. It called for the immediate outlawing of slavery. The most notable leader of this movement was William Lloyd Garrison, the founder, in 1833, of the American Anti-Slavery Society. On Jan. 1, 1831, Garrison had published the first issue of his newspaper, the *Liberator*, calling for immediate emancipation of all slaves in the United States. This was the most extreme of abolitionist positions and it never gained a large following in the North. But the zeal with which Garrison and his associates pursued their cause gave them a great deal of both influence and notoriety.

Abolitionists under Garrison's leadership spoke out against slavery throughout the North. They urged the secession of the North from the Union, arranged boycotts of goods shipped from the South, and established an Underground Railroad to help slaves escape to the North and to Canada.

For 30 years the American Anti-Slavery Society was a powerful but divisive influence in the United States. It never had the support of a majority of Northerners. Most did not like its extremism; they were aware that the Constitution left it to the states to decide about slavery, and they did not want to see the Union divided. And even though the Northern states had abolished slavery between 1777 and 1804, Northern whites did not want a large black population living in their midst.

One thing the North would not permit was the extension of slavery into new states and territories. It was this issue that eventually led to the election of Abraham Lincoln as president, the secession of the South from the Union, and the Civil War. After the war slavery was abolished by the 13th Amendment to the Constitution (*see* U.S. Constitution, subhead "Amendments after the Civil War").

Although the institution of slavery did not exist in the nations of western Europe, it did exist in their colonies. The French were the first to outlaw slavery in all their territories. In 1794 the revolutionary government freed all French slaves. Bloody uprisings in Haiti a few years later led Napoleon I, the emperor of France, to reestablish slavery there in 1802. By 1819 the French slave trade was outlawed, and in 1848 slavery was banned for good in all French colonies.

In Latin America slavery was abolished gradually, on a country-by-country basis. In Chile the first antislavery law was passed as early as 1811. The slave trade was abolished and children born of slaves were freed. However, adult slaves were not emancipated until 1823. In Venezuela abolition was also gradual, primarily because the government did not want to pay slaveholders all at once for the loss of their human property. Freed slaves were forced, as compensation, to work for former owners for a number of years. Slavery finally ended in South America in 1888 with the passage of an antislavery law in Brazil.

The removal of slavery from the entire Western Hemisphere could not occur until all trading in slaves was abolished. With this in mind, the British and Foreign Anti-Slavery Society was founded in England in 1839. By 1862 international treaties allowing the right to search ocean vessels had been signed by most Western nations, including the United States. Within a few years the slave trade was destroyed.

ABORIGINE. From prehistoric times to the present there have been many mass migrations of people throughout the world (*see* Migration of People). In some few isolated locations, however, certain tribal or ethnic groups have lived without migrating for many thousands of years. Such people are called aborigines, from the Latin phrase *ab origine*, meaning "from the beginning." Aboriginal peoples lived in areas remote from other cultures, and their existence became known to the rest of the world only when outsiders intruded upon their territories.

Some anthropologists in the 20th century question whether aborigines have always lived in the locations

Douglass Baglin

An aboriginal artist works on a painting on a sheet of bark. Such paintings are traditional in several areas.

where they have been found in modern times. It is possible that some aborigines did migrate, but in a period so remote in time that there is no record of their migration. In the case of the Indians of the Americas, for instance, it is generally accepted that their ancestors came to the Western Hemisphere by way of the Bering Strait between Siberia and Alaska many thousands of years ago (*see* Indians, American).

In the 20th century there are few regions of the world where aboriginal cultures have not been encroached upon by outsiders. Stone Age cultures exist in the jungles of South America and on the island of New Guinea. The Negritos, a pygmy-like people of Malaysia and the Philippines, live in the mountainous interiors and have succeeded in preserving their primitive ways of life without much interference.

In Africa the Bushmen (or Khoisan tribes) of the Kalahari Desert have lost most of their territory to other tribes or to European settlers. The nomadic Hottentot culture of southern Africa has virtually disappeared. The Pygmies (or Mbuti peoples) of Zaire are nomadic hunters and gatherers. They have managed to preserve their identity, but they maintain close contact with neighboring Bantu tribes. This has resulted in the loss of their Pygmy languages, and they speak the language of the non-Pygmy group to which they are most closely attached. (*See also* Africa, section on Peoples.)

On Hokkaido, the large northern island of Japan, live a people called the Ainu, who were originally distinct physically from the surrounding Mongoloid population. Over the centuries the processes of cultural assimilation and intermarriage have almost eliminated their distinctive characteristics. They now resemble the Japanese in appearance and use the Japanese language.

By virtue of their name, the Australian Aboriginals (or Aborigines, as they are also called) are probably the best known of aboriginal societies. At the time of the first European settlement about 200 years ago, the Aboriginals occupied all of Australia and the

island of Tasmania. The estimate of the 18th-century population is 300,000, comprising more than 500 tribes. In the 1980's there were about 160,000.

Most anthropologists and archaeologists believe that the Aboriginals migrated to Australia and Tasmania about 40,000 years ago. They probably originated in mainland Southeast Asia and may have reached Australia by way of a now-submerged land shelf that connected the continent with New Guinea. Others may have arrived in Australia by chance as the result of sea voyages.

Since the arrival of European settlers in Australia, the traditional Aboriginal way of life has been considerably modified. Only in the most remote areas do they still maintain a semblance of their tribal life (*see* Australia, subhead "The Aborigines").

ABORTION. The loss of a fetus, or unborn offspring, before it is developed enough to live on its own outside the womb is called abortion. It can be spontaneous, often referred to as miscarriage, or it can be intentionally caused, or induced. Induced abortion is regarded as a moral issue in some cultures. In others it is seen as a perfectly acceptable method of birth control. In the United States more than a million induced abortions are performed each year.

Abortion is a relatively simple procedure when done during the first three months of pregnancy by a trained medical worker. After the 13th week of pregnancy, abortion is done only in rare instances because of the danger to the woman's life. Before abortions became legal in the United States in 1971, many were performed illegally and in an unskilled way. This caused many deaths from infection and bleeding. It also caused much sterility, the permanent inability to have a child.

The usual technique of abortion is to insert a metal or plastic tube into the uterus (womb) through its opening, the cervix. A spoon shape at the end of the tube is used to scrape the developing pregnancy from the walls of the uterus. A suction machine at the other end of the tube removes this from the uterus. This is called a vacuum aspiration and is done in a hospital or other medical facility while the patient is under a general anesthetic.

After the 13th week of pregnancy, abortion must be performed in another way. An abortificant (a substance such as salt water) is injected into the uterus. This causes labor to begin within a few hours and the contents of the uterus to be delivered, or expelled.

Abortion as a form of birth control (*see* Birth Control; Bioethics) is practiced in countries such as the Soviet Union and Japan and in eastern Europe. In the United States abortion was made legal in 1971 over the objections of some groups, the Roman Catholic Church in particular. Those opposed to abortion feel it is the taking of a human life. Those in favor of legalized abortion cite overpopulation, the problems of unwanted children, and the dangers of illegal abortion. For further reading, see the current edition of 'The Merck Manual'.

ABRAHAM. One of the major figures in the history of religion is Abraham. He is considered the father of faith for the religions of Judaism, Christianity, and Islam. He is also called a patriarch, a term derived from the Greek words for father and beginning. Applied to Abraham, the term patriarch thus means that he is considered a founding father of the nation of Israel. There were two other patriarchs in the tradition of Israel: Isaac and Jacob, the son and the grandson of Abraham.

What is known about Abraham and the other patriarchs is found only in Genesis, the first book of the Bible. The dates of his life are uncertain, for the book of Genesis tells what happened in the early history of Israel, but it does not tell when the events occurred. A large number of Biblical scholars have concluded that Abraham must have lived sometime between 2,000 B.C. and 1,600 B.C. Since there are no other historical records concerning Abraham, the evidence about the dates is derived from careful studies of the text of Genesis. Based on such factors as place-names, names of peoples and nations, and legal and social practices described, a great number of scholars have concluded that the narration of Genesis is authentic.

Genesis states that Abraham was a native of the region of Ur in southern Mesopotamia (*see* Mesopotamia). He was probably the head of a large clan of people who lived a seminomadic existence; they lived near the city of Ur, but moved around within a limited area in search of grazing grounds for their herds. For some reason the clan moved north and settled near Haran. It was at Haran that a call from God came to Abraham, telling him to leave his homeland and go to a new location that God would show him.

In addition to the command to move, God made Abraham a promise: "I will make you into a great nation." This arrangement that God made with Abraham—command and promise contingent upon Abraham's obedience—is called a covenant. In popular parlance, one might say that God made a deal with Abraham: if Abraham would obey the command, God would keep the promise.

God made many other covenants, or agreements, with the nation of Israel, but the first covenant was the one made with Abraham. It was to this covenant that Israel owed its origin as a nation and in which it saw a special relation to God.

Abraham kept his part of the bargain. He and his clan—probably several hundred people, along with herds of animals—left Haran and traveled through Syria to Palestine. This was to be Israel's promised land for all time to come.

Once Abraham and his clan were settled in Palestine, God renewed his covenant and promised that He would give Abraham descendants. Because Abraham was already quite old, he and his wife, Sarah, were doubtful that they would ever have a child. So Abraham had a son, Ishmael, by Sarah's slave, Hagar. After Ishmael was born, Sarah had a son, Isaac. This son, according to Genesis, was to be the heir through whom the covenant would be continued.

'The Sacrifice of Isaac', a painting, depicts an angel stopping Abraham from slaying his son Isaac. God had ordered him to do so as a test of his faith.

Late in life, after Sarah had died, Abraham married a woman named Keturah and with her had many children. These other children were rewarded with an inheritance when they grew up and were then sent away from Palestine to live elsewhere. Isaac alone inherited the promised land. After Isaac's death, the land went to his son, Jacob—whose name was changed by God to Israel. Abraham died at the age of 175. He was buried next to his wife Sarah.

The story of Abraham, as told in Genesis, has three main themes: the call of God, the promise of God, and Abraham's obedience. These themes, the heart of the covenant, are reiterated throughout the Old Testament. The covenant was reaffirmed with Isaac and Jacob. Because of it, Israel as a nation saw itself in a special relationship with God: Israelites were the people of the God of Abraham. In later centuries whenever Israel was disobedient to God's laws, He would remind the nation of the covenant with Abraham and threaten it with the loss of the special covenant relationship if the people did not mend their ways. Israel came to see in the covenant a promise that God would guarantee it a perpetual national homeland. He would also raise Israel to a preeminent status among the nations of the world.

In the New Testament Abraham is highly revered as the father of faith in God, but there is a different view of his significance. He is considered to be the father of all who believe in God, whether belonging to Israel or not. He is not looked upon as the guarantor of any permanent, earthly kingdom. The promises made to Abraham are understood by Christians to have been fulfilled in Jesus Christ, and the followers of Jesus are called the new Israel. St. Paul devotes a whole chapter in one of his letters (Rom. iv) to explaining the significance of Abraham for Christians.

The religion of Islam also holds Abraham in high regard. Islamic tradition states that Abraham, assisted by his son Ishmael, built the Kaaba, the small shrine in the center of the Great Mosque in Mecca, Saudi Arabia (*see* Islam). For followers of Islam, the Kaaba is the most sacred place on Earth.

ABRASIVE. Modern industry depends on abrasives; the hard, sharp, and rough substances used to rub and wear away softer, less resistant surfaces. Without them it would be impossible to make machine parts that fit precisely together, and there would be no automobiles, airplanes, spacecraft, home appliances, or machine tools.

Abrasives include the grit in household cleansing powder, coated forms such as emery boards and sandpaper, honing stones for knife sharpening, and grinding wheels. Numerous substances such as silicon carbide and diamonds that are used in industry to shape and polish are also abrasives.

Abrasives are referred to in the Bible and are depicted in Egyptian drawings and Roman statuary. During the 13th century, the Chinese made a crude kind of sandpaper from crushed seashells, natural gum, and parchment. The first modern industrial grinding wheel was devised in 1873 to win a bet for a pitcher of beer. In 1955 diamonds (not of gem quality) were first used as abrasives.

Characteristics and Types

Hardness and toughness are important characteristics in determining the usefulness of an abrasive. For example, an abrasive must be harder than the material it grinds. Common abrasives range from soft, such as talc, to very hard, such as diamonds. Toughness determines an abrasive's useful life. The ideal abrasive grain resharpens itself in use by breakdown of its dulled cutting edge to expose another cutting edge within.

Artificial abrasives are more popular than natural types today because their grains are made uniform, leading to a more even friction, allowing more precise control of the grinding process. Abrasive materials may be used loose with a buffing wheel, mixed with a liquid binder to make an abrasive polish, stuck to paper or cloth, or bonded into a solid body such as a grinding wheel.

Natural Abrasives

Because it is the hardest of all substances, diamond is a particularly good abrasive. Industry crushes diamonds that are unsuitable for jewelry into various sizes for use in grinding wheels, polishing powders, abrasive belts, and polishing disks.

Corundum, a naturally occurring form of aluminum oxide, is used primarily to polish and grind glass. Emery, another form of aluminum oxide, is found in nature as small crystals embedded in iron oxide. It is most often used in emerycloth sandpaper and emery boards for filing fingernails.

Garnet is noted for its toughness. When its cutting edges wear down they fracture in a way that creates sharp new edges. There are seven known forms of garnet. They are widely used, particularly for coated abrasive products in the woodworking, leather, and shoe industries.

Flint, or flint quartz, is the abrasive most commonly used to make sandpaper. It is mined, crushed, and bonded to paper or cloth. Quartz, the major ingredient of sandstone, is largely responsible for the abrasive qualities of sandstone. Quartz, by itself in the form of sand, is used for sandblasting. Pumice, the cooled and hardened frothy part of volcanic lava, is a familiar mild abrasive used in polishing metals, furniture finishing, and in scouring powders and soaps.

Manufactured Abrasives

Important manufactured abrasives are those that are often called super abrasives. They include silicon carbide, aluminum oxide, cubic boron nitride, and synthetic diamond.

Silicon carbide and aluminum oxide crystals are both made in electric furnaces, the former from pure silica sand and carbon in the form of coke at temperatures up to 2480° C (4500° F), and the latter from bauxite ore at heat in excess of 1090° C (2000° F). The abrasive qualities of silicon carbide depend on the type of raw materials used and the way the furnace is operated. The chemical composition and crystalline structure of the aluminum oxide, and hence the abrasive properties of a particular batch, will vary depending upon the length of time (one to seven days) it is given to cool.

Cubic boron nitride is second only to diamonds in hardness. It is a combination of boron and nitrogen made under high pressure. It is noted for its strong crystals with sharp points and clearly defined edges.

Synthetic diamond is made by placing graphite under intense pressure. With current technology, the crystalline structure of synthetic diamond and cubic boron nitride, and hence their ultimate properties as abrasives, can be controlled during manufacture.

Other manufactured abrasives include glass beads and metal shot. Both are often blasted at machines and other objects to clean them. Steel wool, which is made by combing steel wire, is a common and widely used cleaning and surface-finishing material.

Manufacture of Abrasive Products

Almost all abrasives are crushed to a specific particle size before being used to make a product. These sizes vary from diameters of about 6 millimeters (¼ inch) to about one tenth the thickness of a human hair. The crushing method, because it affects crystal strength, also helps determine the possible uses for the resulting abrasive.

Most grinding wheels are made by combining abrasives and a bonding material; placing this mixture in slightly oversize steel molds; firing it, or bringing it to very high temperatures, in a kiln; and then cutting to precise final size. Different types of wheels are produced by varying the abrasive, binder, and firing temperature. Sandpapers are made by coating paper or cloth with a coat of adhesive, a coat of abrasive, and another coat of adhesive.

ABSTRACT ART *see* PAINTING; SCULPTURE.

ABYSSINIA *see* ETHIOPIA.

ACADEMY. Before the time of Plato ambitious young Athenians depended for their higher education upon the Sophists. The Sophists were traveling lecturers who went from city to city giving instruction in oratory and philosophy. They were always sure to find an audience in one of the three great public gymnasiums in the suburbs of Athens, where young men trained for athletic contests.

When Plato returned to Athens from his travels, about 387 B.C., he settled in a house near a gymnasium called the Academy, about a mile northwest of the city walls. He organized a college with a definite membership which met sometimes in the walks of the Academy and sometimes in his own house or garden (see Plato). Other philosophers followed his example in choosing a fixed place for their lectures and discussions. Aristotle, a pupil of Plato, set up his school in the Lyceum, a gymnasium east of the city.

The names associated with these Greek schools and discussion groups have been carried down to present times with a wide variety of meanings. The Germans, for example, use the word gymnasium not for a place for athletic exercises but for a secondary school. In France lycée is a secondary school. In the United States lyceum once meant a group that met for lectures and discussion. Today it refers to a program of planned lectures and concerts.

The word academy is used in England and America for many private secondary schools and for institutions where special training is provided, such as riding academies and military or naval academies. It is used in a more general way in several languages for learned societies formed to promote knowledge and culture or to advance some particular art or science.

Of these learned societies the most famous is the French Academy, an association of literary men established by Cardinal Richelieu in 1635. Four years later its members began work on a dictionary. Since new words had to be approved by them before being accepted as good usage, they exercised careful control over the French language. On the death of an academician the remaining members voted on his replacement. Election to this group of "forty immortals" came to be regarded the highest honor a French writer could receive. The French Academy later became associated with four other academies—of Inscriptions and the Humanities, of the Sciences, of Fine Arts, and of Ethics and Political Science—to form the Institute of France. The Academy of Fine Arts is best known for its school, the Ecole des Beaux-Arts.

Another great modern academy is England's Royal Academy of Arts, devoted to painting, sculpture, and architecture. Its membership also is limited to 40. When an artist is elected he presents to the Academy a specimen of his work, called his diploma work, and receives a diploma signed by the sovereign.

The oldest academy of this sort in the United States is the National Academy of Design, which conducts a school of design in New York City. It was founded in 1825 and incorporated under its present name in 1828. Its membership is limited to 250.

The American Academy of Arts and Letters was founded in 1904 and incorporated under an act of Congress in 1916. Its membership is limited to 50.

ACADIA. The French were the first Europeans to explore the St. Lawrence River and settle in Canada. To protect the entrance to the great river they needed to hold also the region around the Gulf of St. Lawrence.  They gave the name *Acadie* (in English, Acadia) to the land south of the Gulf. It included what is now Nova Scotia and New Brunswick.

In 1605 the French built a fort, Port Royal, at the mouth of the Annapolis River (see Nova Scotia). By 1668 a few dozen French families had settled in the beautiful Annapolis Valley. Instead of clearing the forest, they built dikes on the low-lying land and transformed the marshes into rich meadows.

Because of its geographical position, Acadia at once became involved in the long struggle between the British and French for possession of the North American continent. In 1621 James I of England granted all Acadia to Sir William Alexander, who renamed it Nova Scotia. Time after time Port Royal was conquered by the English and retaken by the French. The Acadians took no part in the wars. They also lived in peace with the friendly Micmac Indians.

The final struggle for North America began in 1754 (see French and Indian War). The English were in control of Acadia when the war started. The Acadians were French in language and customs. The English feared that French priests would persuade the Acadians and Indians to enter the war.

In 1755 the English authorities in Acadia demanded that each Acadian take an oath of allegiance to England. All who refused were deported. About 6,000 were shipped to English colonies along the Atlantic coast, from Massachusetts to South Carolina. Some made their way to Louisiana to live with the French settlers there. Their descendants are called Cajuns, many of whom still speak a French dialect. Others went back to Acadia.

In 1847 Henry Wadsworth Longfellow published his popular poem 'Evangeline', which tells of the wanderings of two lovers who were separated when the Acadians were deported by the English. Evangeline, the heroine, and her lover, Gabriel, lived in the village of Grand Pré. On the day that they were celebrating their betrothal, the English summoned all the men of Grand Pré to the church. After being held prisoner for five days, they were herded on to ships. That night the English burned their houses and barns. The next day Evangeline was exiled.

Evangeline spent the rest of her life wandering in search of her lover. Finally she became a sister of mercy in Philadelphia, Pa. There, in an almshouse, she found Gabriel as he was dying. A statue of Evangeline stands in a memorial park in Grand Pré.

ACAPULCO, Mexico. A popular resort city, the port of Acapulco is located in Guerrero state in southwestern Mexico. Situated on a deep semicircular bay, it has the best harbor on Mexico's Pacific coast and is one of the finest natural anchorages in the world.

The harbor was discovered by Hernando Cortez in 1531, and a settlement was founded in 1550. Acapulco was designated a city in 1599, becoming a main depot for Spanish colonial ships traveling between Mexico and the Orient. Eventually it became a port of call for steamship lines between Panama and San Francisco.

Acapulco's harbor is a major export point for coffee and sugar, as well as other Mexican products. Local industry is limited to the manufacture of woven sombreros, shellwork, confectionery, and other tourist-based products.

The town lies on a narrow strip of land between the bay and steep mountains that surround it. From May to November the climate is hot and humid, but from December through April it is warm and pleasant. This comfortable climate, along with luxury hotels, excellent beaches, and deep-sea fishing, has earned Acapulco its nickname of "Riviera of Mexico," after the famous French resort area.

More than a half million visitors arrive in Acapulco every year. The cliff divers who leap into the waves of a cove are a major tourist attraction. A summer school for foreigners, founded in 1955, offers courses on Mexican arts and archaeology. The city's only structure of historical significance is the Fort of San Diego, which houses a regional museum. Originally built in 1616, it was destroyed by an earthquake in 1776 and eventually restored.

No railroads connect to the city, but frequent air service and a link to the Mexico City-Cuernavaca highway make Acapulco easily accessible. Population (1978 estimate), 421,088. (For map, see Mexico.)

ACCOUNTING. Every organization needs some way of keeping accounts—that is, of recording what it spends and receives. The person who does this is called a bookkeeper. Bookkeeping is part of a larger field, accounting. People who work as accountants prepare financial statements, study an organization's costs, calculate its taxes, and provide other information to help in making business decisions.

Underlying all bookkeeping is the simple T account, so named because it resembles the letter T. It shows that money flows either in or out. The T account records this on the two sides of a perpendicular, as shown in Fig. 1. The example shows that $94 has been taken in and $27 has been paid out. The difference of $67 (called the balance on hand) is added to the out side of the account to make both totals the same. Writing in an account's balance, or balancing it, may be done whenever it is desirable to know whether the ins exceed the outs, or vice versa.

Assets and Liabilities

Opening a cash account is only the first step in establishing a bookkeeping system. A home, car, personal and household belongings, insurance, bonds— all these plus actual money make up a person's total worth. These possessions are called assets. Each one has a value that can be expressed in terms of money.

(IN)	**CASH**	(OUT)
$75		$12
19		15
		$27
		Bal. 67
$94		$94
Bal. $67		

Fig. 1. T Account

Most people also have certain debts, or liabilities, such as a mortgage, insurance premiums, and charge accounts. Liabilities must be recorded as well as assets. When the total value of one's assets is greater than the total value of one's liabilities, a person is said to be solvent; that is, in possession of more money (and property that can be converted into money) than is owed to others. A person's net worth is the difference between total assets and total liabilities.

Businesses and other organizations must have accounting systems in order to know whether or not they are operating profitably. A company's total assets include its cash, buildings, equipment, and accounts receivable (money owed by its customers). The company's assets must be weighed against its liabilities—accounts payable (money owed to its creditors), loans, and salaries.

The basic types of accounts are: (1) an asset account, such as a cash account; and (2) a liability account, or account of indebtedness, such as accounts payable. A typical asset account is shown in Fig. 2. There the received and paid entries are made on opposite pages of the account book. The sums received are written on the left-hand page under the heading Received. All money paid out is written under the heading Paid on the right-hand page. Often the account is contained on just one page. The received column is labeled "Dr.," and items in that column are called debits. The paid column is labeled "Cr.," and items there are credits.

A liability account, or account of indebtedness, is shown in Fig. 3. The name of the person or firm to whom the money is owed (Selby & Co.) appears on the lines above the account. The items representing the druggist's debt are entered on the right side. The money paid is entered on the left side. Murphy's account with Selby & Co. shows that on November 8 he purchased merchandise costing $976.45. Two days after placing his order he received the goods and paid cash, thereby closing the account temporarily until his next order.

Double Entry Bookkeeping

In any exchange of money, goods, or services, more than one person is involved. Thus there must be two

15

RECEIVED				PAID		
Nov. 6	Mrs. Daniels paid bill	$ 8	75	Nov. 1	Rent	$1,500	00
" 17	Dr. Jones paid on acct.	95	00	" 10	Selby & Co. (for merchandise)	1,376	45
" 30	Drug sales (month)	1,927	69	" 15	Light & telephone bills	982	78
	Soda fountain sales (month)	1,376	15	" 30	Salaries of delivery boys	960	00
	Prescriptions (month)	1,294	80		Salaries of fountain clerks	875	00
	Magazines & newspapers (month)	779	45		Salary of drug clerk	680	00
	Candy & tobacco sales (month)	1,280	65		Balance on hand	388	26
	Total	$6,762	49		Total	$6,762	49
Dec. 1	Balance on hand	$388	26				

Fig. 2. Cash Account, Murphy's Drugstore

parts to every transaction. In order to make a complete bookkeeping record of a transaction, entries must be made in two different accounts to keep the ins and outs balanced.

For example, Fig. 2 shows that Daniels paid her bill on November 6. In addition to recording payment in his cash account, Murphy also records it in another account—an account receivable in which he lists all her charge purchases. Thus his record of this transaction is complete. He has noted that he received a certain sum of money (by the debit to the cash account) and where he obtained the money (by the credit to Daniels' account receivable).

This is called double entry bookkeeping. Double entry does not mean that the same transaction is entered twice but that both parts of the transaction are recorded. All entries in one account must be offset by entries in another account or accounts.

The simplest set of double entry books consists of a journal (see Fig. 4) and a ledger (see Fig. 5). When a transaction takes place the bookkeeper first enters it in the journal. Transactions are entered as they occur. The bookkeeper regularly transfers the information in the journal to the various accounts, which are kept in the ledger. This is known as posting. Fig. 5 shows the results of the posting procedure. Murphy made entries in his journal (Fig. 4) as the transactions took place. Then he posted those entries in the appropriate accounts in his ledger (Fig. 5).

These bookkeeping procedures furnish the information necessary to prepare three types of statements that show the financial condition of an individual or a business. They are the trial balance, the profit and loss statement, and the balance sheet. These statements usually are prepared at the end of a specified period, such as the calendar month, quarter year, or other desired interval. The trial balance is a list of debit and credit balances found in all accounts. The total of the debits must equal the total of the credits. Disagreement between totals shows there is an error (or errors) in the records.

The profit and loss statement tells whether the individual or business has made a profit for the period. In its simplest form the profit and loss statement looks like this:

Sales..	$21,473
Less: Cost of Goods Sold....................	15,840
Gross Profit	5,633
Less: Expenses.....................................	1,748
Net Profit or Loss..................................	$ 3,885

The balance sheet is a list of all the assets and liabilities on the date of the statement. The amount by which the total assets exceed total liabilities is known as the net worth.

Computers in Accounting

Electronic data processing (EDP) systems are widely used in bookkeeping and accounting. Informa-

SELBY & CO.

DR.				CR.		
Nov. 10	Cash	$976	45	Nov. 8	Merchandise Purchases:	$976	45
					1 gross rubber gloves		
					1 doz. thermometers		
					1 doz. bathroom scales		
					1 gross First Aid kits		
					3 doz. heating pads		
					4 doz. syringes		
		$976	45			$976	45

Fig. 3. Account Payable, Murphy's Drugstore

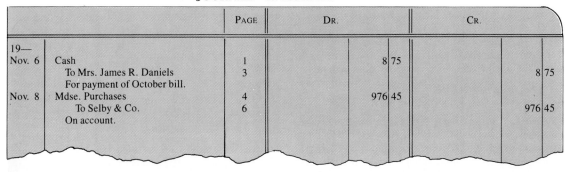

	PAGE	DR.		CR.	
19— Nov. 6 Cash	1	8	75		
To Mrs. James R. Daniels	3			8	75
For payment of October bill.					
Nov. 8 Mdse. Purchases	4	976	45		
To Selby & Co.	6			976	45
On account.					

Fig. 4. Journal Entries, Murphy's Drugstore

LEDGER—R. MURPHY

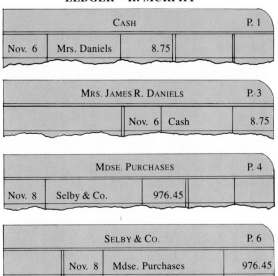

Fig. 5. Account Entries, Murphy's Drugstore

tion such as amounts, names, and account numbers is recorded on punched cards or on magnetic tape. The system performs tasks such as posting to ledger accounts, computing account balances, preparing payrolls, and printing financial statements. An EDP system operates with great speed and in a few moments can do the work of a whole roomful of clerks and typists. It usually includes several elements. A central processing unit (computer) stores information, reads the instructions, and makes computations. Various input devices such as tape readers, punched card readers, and keyboard terminals prepare information and feed it to the computer. Output devices such as display panels and printers take information out of the computer so that it can be read or distributed. The system cannot make mistakes so long as the proper information is fed into it. Most "computer errors" are actually human errors made by people who enter the wrong data.

Accounting as a Career

Accountants and bookkeepers work for business firms, government agencies, and many other organizations. Certified public, or chartered, accountants are licensed by the state to provide accounting services to clients for a fee. They must pass a difficult examination to receive their certificates. The work of a certified public accountant (CPA) consists primarily of auditing the accounts of organizations to determine whether their financial statements are fair and reliable. CPA's also advise businesses and private individuals on income tax questions. Business firms and banks employ their own accountants to supervise their accounts and prepare financial statements. Certain government agencies such as the Internal Revenue Service and the Securities and Exchange Commission employ large numbers of accountants.

ACCRA, Ghana. Located on the Gulf of Guinea, Accra is the capital and largest city of Ghana. It is a blend of modern and traditional West African customs and architecture.

Originally settled in 1482 by members of the Ga tribe, the area eventually became the site of three coastal villages. Their growth, encouraged by trade, resulted in the formation of the city of Accra in 1877. That same year Accra became the capital of the British Gold Coast colony, as Ghana was known before independence in 1957. Accra was systematically planned and laid out between 1920 and 1930, and from that time its population grew rapidly.

The central business district contains the head offices of all of the large banks in the country, the major trading firms (mostly foreign owned), vast open markets, the Supreme Court and Parliament buildings, and the Accra Central Library. Government ministries and the City Council buildings are in another area, the administrative district. Vehicle assembly plants, garment factories, and various kinds of workshops are located in what are called industrial estate areas. Scattered throughout the capital are hospitals and clinics, numerous nightclubs and hotels, schools, and churches. Accra also houses the national archives, the national museum, and the Ghana Academy of Arts and Sciences.

The city is connected directly by rail inland to Kumasi, as well as to the port of Tema, 17 miles (27 kilometers) to the east. Tema has taken over Accra's port function both as a harbor for shipping and as a base for fishing. Kotoka International Airport at

Accra is Ghana's major airport and the base for the national airline, Ghana Airways.

As Ghana's communications center, Accra is the headquarters of the Ghana Broadcasting System studios, radio and television services, and the major newspapers. (*See also* Ghana.) Population (1980 estimate), 998,772.

ACHEBE, Chinua (born 1930). His richly African stories recreate the old ways of Nigeria's Ibo people and the intrusion of Western customs upon their traditional values. Chinua Achebe was Nigeria's first world-famous novelist.

The fifth of six children of Isaiah and Janet Achebe, Chinua Achebe was born in Nigeria on Nov. 16, 1930. His father was a teacher with the Church Missionary Society. When Chinua was five, his father retired, and the family moved to their ancestral village of Ogidi, into a "modern" house of earth walls and sheet metal roof.

Chinua Achebe

When Chinua was 12, he left home to live with an older brother, John, who taught at a school in Nekede, some 60 miles away. In those days, that was a long journey by truck, and Chinua got swollen feet from walking the last six miles to his destination. He eventually earned a scholarship to Government College, a secondary school in Umuahia. He also became something of a hero to the people of his village, acquiring the nickname "Dictionary" for his knowledge of English. On another scholarship Achebe was educated in English at the newly founded University College at Ibadan (now University of Ibadan).

After a short time as a teacher, Achebe became producer for the Nigerian Broadcasting Corporation in Lagos in 1954. 'Things Fall Apart' (1958) was Achebe's first—and probably best—novel, about a tragic hero in an Africa torn between the old order and the new. For his contribution to African litera-

ture, Achebe was awarded the Margaret Wong Memorial Prize in 1959, the first of his many literary awards. 'No Longer at Ease' (1960) was a sequel to his first novel, continuing the story of the same family. In 1961 Achebe became the first director of external broadcasting in Nigeria for the British Broadcasting Corporation. That same year he married Christine Chinwe Okoli. They had two daughters and two sons.

'The Sacrificial Egg', a collection of Achebe's short stories, was published in 1962. His 'Arrow of God' (1964) was a dramatic novel of ancestral village life under British administration in the 1920's. It was followed by a children's book, 'Chike and the River' (1966), and 'A Man of the People' (1966), a political satire of African independence. During the country-wide persecution of Ibo in 1966, Achebe was forced to leave Lagos for eastern Nigeria, the Ibo heartland later called Biafra. He took an active part in the Biafran struggle for independence.

In 1971 Achebe was director of African studies at the University of Nigeria and edited *Okike*, a Nigerian literary journal. After lecturing at American universities from 1971 to 1976, Achebe returned to the University of Nigeria. He has also published books of poems—'Beware Soul Brother' (1971) and 'Christmas in Biafra' (1973)—and a critical book of essays, 'Morning Yet on Creation Day' (1975).

ACHILLES Among the Greeks who fought against Troy, the one considered the bravest was Achilles. His mother was the goddess Thetis, a sea nymph or Nereid. His father was Peleus, king of Thessaly and a grandson of Zeus, the lord of heaven. It was at the wedding feast of Thetis and Peleus that the goddess Eris (Discord) hurled among the guests a golden apple that was to cause the Trojan War.

Soon after the birth of Achilles, Thetis tried to outwit the Fates, who had foretold that war would cut down her son in his prime. So that no weapon might ever wound him, she dipped her baby in the black waters of the Styx, a river that flowed around the underworld. Only the heel by which she held him was untouched by the magic waters, and this was the only part of his body that could be wounded. This is the source of the expression "Achilles' heel," meaning a vulnerable point.

When the Trojan War began, Achilles' mother, fearing that the decree of the Fates would prove true, dressed him as a girl and hid him among the maidens at the court of the king of Scyros. The trick did not succeed. Odysseus, the shrewdest of the Greeks, went to the court disguised as a peddler. When he had spread his wares before the girls, a sudden trumpet blast was sounded. The girls screamed and fled, but Achilles betrayed his sex by seizing a sword and spear from the peddler's stock.

Achilles joined the battle and took command of his father's men, the Myrmidons. They set an example of bravery for the other Greeks. Then he quarreled with Agamemnon, the leader of the Greeks, over a captive whom he loved. When she was taken from him, he withdrew his followers from the fight and sulked in his tent. As a result the Greek armies were driven back to their ships by the Trojans.

At last, moved by the plight of the Greeks, Achilles entrusted his men and his armor to Patroclus, his best friend. Thus, when Patroclus led the Myrmidons into battle, the Trojans mistook him for Achilles and fled in panic. Patroclus, however, was killed by Hector, the leader of the Trojans. Achilles' armor became the prize of Hector.

Angered and stricken by grief, Achilles vowed to kill Hector. Meanwhile, his mother hastened to Olympus to beg a new suit of armor from Hephaestus, god of the forge. Clad in his new armor, Achilles again went into battle. He slew many Trojans, and the rest—except for Hector—fled within their city. The story of how Achilles killed Hector is related in the article Hector.

Although the Trojans had now lost their leader, they were able to continue fighting with the help of other nations. Achilles broke the strength of these allies by killing Memnon, prince of the Ethiopians, and Penthesilea, queen of the Amazons (see Amazon).

Achilles was now weary of war and, moreover, had fallen in love with Polyxena, sister of Hector. To win her in marriage he consented to ask the Greeks to make peace. He was in the temple arranging for the marriage when Hector's brother, Paris, shot him with a poisoned arrow in the only vulnerable part of his body—the heel.

ACID RAIN. When fossil fuels such as coal and petroleum products are burned, they emit oxides of sulfur, carbon, and nitrogen into the air (see Oxygen). These oxides combine with moisture in the air to form sulfuric acid, carbonic acid, and nitric acid. When it rains or snows, these acids are brought to Earth in what is called acid rain.

During the course of the 20th century, the acidity of the air and acid rain have come to be recognized as a leading threat to the stability and quality of the Earth's environment. Most of this acidity is produced in the industrialized nations of the Northern Hemisphere—the United States, Canada, Japan, the Soviet Union, and the countries of Western Europe.

The effects of acid rain can be devastating to many forms of life, including human life. Its effects can be most vividly seen, however, in lakes, rivers, and streams. Acidity in water kills virtually all life forms—fishes, frogs, bacteria, and algae, to name a few. By the early 1980's tens of thousands of lakes had been killed by acid rain. The problem has been severest in Norway, Sweden, and Canada.

The threat posed by acid rain is not limited by geographical boundaries, for prevailing winds carry the pollutants around the globe. Nor is the problem limited to the natural environment. Structures made of stone, metal, and cement have also been damaged or destroyed. Some of the world's great monuments, including the cathedrals of Europe and the Colosseum in Rome, have shown signs of deterioration caused by acid rain and the burning of fossil fuels.

Scientists use what is called the pH factor to measure the acidity or alkalinity of liquid solutions (see Acids and Bases). On a scale from 0 to 14, 0 represents the highest level of acid and 14 the most basic or alkaline. A solution of distilled water containing neither acids nor alkalies, or bases, is designated 7, or neutral. If the pH level of rain falls below 5.5, the rain is considered acidic. By the early 1980's, rainfalls in the eastern United States and in Western Europe often ranged from 4.0 to 4.5.

The cost of preventing millions of tons of pollutants from getting into the atmosphere each year is great. In the United States alone, industrial companies would have to spend billions of dollars on such equipment as burners, filters, and chemical and washing devices to neutralize dangerous wastes. The cost in damage to the environment and human life is estimated to be much greater, however, because the damage may be irreversible. Up to 500,000 lakes in North America alone may be destroyed before the end of the 20th century if acid rain is not controlled.

ACIDS AND BASES. Each of the two groups of chemical compounds called acids and bases has many different members that react together to produce entirely new products. Acids, bases, and the products of their reactions are vital to many life processes and are valuable to industry.

An acid is defined as a substance containing hydrogen that dissociates (breaks up) in water to produce hydrogen ions. It may also be defined as a compound in which the hydrogen can be replaced by a metal. The other part of the compound is called the acid radical. For example, in sulfuric acid (H_2SO_4) one atom of sulfur and four of oxygen form the acid radical that is joined to two atoms of hydrogen.

A typical metal-acid reaction occurs when zinc is placed in a solution of sulfuric acid. Hydrogen is released as a gas, and zinc unites with the acid radical to form zinc sulfate:

$$H_2SO_4 + Zn \rightarrow ZnSO_4 + H_2$$

The strongest acids are the mineral, or inorganic, acids. These include sulfuric acid, nitric acid, and hydrochloric acid. More important to life are hundreds of weaker organic acids. These include acetic acid (in vinegar), citric acid (in lemons), lactic acid (in sour milk), and the amino acids (in proteins).

A base is a substance containing the hydroxide ion, OH^-, or the hydroxyl group, OH, which dissociates in water as the hydroxide ion, OH^-. Basic solutions have a characteristic brackish taste. The hydroxides of metals are metal compounds that have the hydroxyl group, and they are bases. Hydroxides of the metals lithium, sodium, potassium, rubidium, and cesium have the special name of alkalies. The hydroxides of beryllium, magnesium, calcium, strontium, and barium are called alkaline earths. A basic solution is also called an alkaline solution.

These descriptions help explain why acids and bases react so readily with each other. An acid has hydrogen to exchange for a metal, and a base has a metal to exchange for hydrogen. When the two react, the exchange takes place. These reactions or exchanges are sometimes violent. Acids and bases react to form compounds that are called salts. The reaction of sodium hydroxide and sulfuric acid produces a salt, sodium sulfate (Na_2SO_4), and water:

$$2NaOH + H_2SO_4 \rightarrow Na_2SO_4 + 2H_2O$$

Another typical acid-base reaction is that between calcium hydroxide and phosphoric acid to produce calcium phosphate and water:

$$3Ca(OH)_2 + 2H_3PO_4 \rightarrow Ca_3(PO_4)_2 + 6H_2O$$

Acids and bases react freely in aqueous (water) solutions. It is said that when an acid dissociates, it forms an acid radical and a hydrogen ion. Actually, the hydrogen ion (H^+) does not exist in large concentrations in the aqueous solution. Instead, the hydrogen ion attaches itself to a water molecule to form the hydronium ion, H_3O^+. It is customary, however, to simplify reaction equations by using the symbol for the hydrogen ion, H^+. When a base dissociates, it produces a hydroxide ion (OH^-) with a negative charge and a metal ion with a positive charge. The hydrogen ion and the hydroxide ion combine to form a molecule of water. The negative acid radical and the positive metal ion can then form a salt.

Acids and bases can cause many organic substances to change color. For example, if lemon juice is added to tea, the tea becomes lighter in color. This occurs because the acid in the lemon juice changes the color of a substance in the tea from dark brown to light brown. The reaction can be reversed by adding an alkaline substance, such as baking soda ($NaHCO_3$), to the tea. This addition restores the original color. A substance that changes color when an acid or base is added to it is called an indicator.

Litmus paper is a common indicator. It turns red in an acid solution and blue in a basic solution. A solution that gives litmus paper a color midway between red and blue is called a neutral solution. This is a solution that contains hydrogen ions and hydroxide ions in equal amounts. Thus, a solution with an excess of hydrogen ions is an acid solution. A solution with an excess of hydroxide ions is a basic solution.

Pure water is a neutral solution. It ionizes slightly and releases an equal number of hydrogen and hydroxide ions. The concentration of these ions has been measured and found to be 1×10^{-7}. Instead of saying that the hydrogen ion concentration in pure water is 1×10^{-7}, it is customary to say that the pH of water is 7. The pH is the logarithm of the reciprocal of the hydrogen ion concentration. It is written:

$$p\text{H} = \log \frac{1}{[H^+]}$$

Since water has a pH of 7 and is neutral, solutions with pH less than 7 are acid, and solutions with pH greater than 7 are basic.

ACNE. When the pores of the skin become clogged with oily, fatty material and become inflamed, a skin condition called acne results. The problem is common among adolescents, particularly boys. Untreated acne can cause permanent scarring on the face, neck, and back. An occasional pimple on the face is different from acne that is inflamed and can become infected. Acne forms whiteheads (closed pimples) and blackheads (open pimples), which release free fatty acids (FFA) into the tissues and cause the characteristic inflammation.

Characteristics

Acne usually begins at puberty (see Adolescence), when adult levels of male hormones (androgens) cause changes both in the size of the skin glands and in the amount of oil produced by them. Most acne is worse in the winter and improves in the summer, probably because of the helpful effects of increased sunlight on the skin. Most acne is mild and disappears at the end of the teen years, but deep, infected acne can result in severe scarring.

Sometimes adolescents who have acne become embarrassed and begin avoiding social contacts because of their appearance. If this happens, it is important to seek counseling as well as medical treatment. There is no known connection between acne and diet, athletics, or sexual activity.

Control

Mild acne can be controlled by washing with mild soap several times a day, by opening pimples after they have come to a head, and by not picking at pimples that are healing. Acne medication containing vitamin A acid, benzoyl peroxide, or sulfur-resorcinol should be used twice a day. Cosmetics or lotions containing oil should not be used.

More serious acne requires the help of a physician to prevent spread and scarring. An antibiotic such as tetracycline (see Antibiotic) will often be prescribed for use over a long period of time. Opening and draining of deep infected pustules is also done by the physician. In girls, when acne appears to come and go with the menstrual cycle, a birth control pill containing synthetic female hormones sometimes can cure acne. For further reading, see 'The Merck Manual'.

ACONCAGUA. The highest mountain in South America and in the entire Western Hemisphere is the extinct volcanic peak Aconcagua. It towers in the southern Andes in Argentina near the Chilean border. Its height is 22,831 feet (6,959 meters). This is more than 2,500 feet (700 meters) higher than Mount McKinley, which is the highest peak in North America. The upper slopes of the mountain are continuously covered with snow. The peak of Aconcagua was first scaled in 1897.

A river in Chile as well as Aconcagua Province of Chile are named for the mountain. The province is a large producer of fruit and tobacco and is famed for its wines and cattle. (See also Andes.)

ACOUSTICS

ACOUSTICS. What do these seemingly unrelated experts have in common: the scientist studying the transmission of sound under water, the physician using ultrasonics to study the condition of an unborn child, the engineer developing techniques for quieting a noisy truck or providing good listening conditions for a concert hall, and the audiologist evaluating the hearing of a patient? All are involved in the interdisciplinary science called acoustics, a science that deals with the production, control, transmission, reception, and effects of sound. Lindsay's wheel of acoustics, shown in Fig. 1, indicates that acoustics has applications in the life sciences, the earth sciences, engineering, and the arts.

Noise Control Model

In today's world, the acoustical engineer is called upon to study such everyday problems as the reduction of noises produced by truck tires, garbage disposals, microwave ovens, office copying machines, and dentists' drills. In attempting to solve these problems, the engineer often utilizes noise control models. The models include the sources of the noise, how the noise is transmitted to the receivers, and the identity of the receivers. In controlling a noise problem, the acoustician may elect to reduce the noise generated by the sources, to modify the path that is traveled by the noise (such as by installing a partial barrier), or to protect the receivers (by providing hearing protection devices, for example).

Architectural Acoustics

An area of acoustics that is often misunderstood is that of architectural acoustics. It is generally appreciated that good acoustics are important in the design of concert halls, radio and television studios, and structures for similar purposes. When, however, it comes to designing classrooms, shopping center malls, pay telephone installations, apartment complexes, or general home and office environments, acoustical considerations are often neglected. Those involved in planning areas to be used by people should consider a host of factors, including the intended use of the area, the types of people who will use it, and many others. Failure to consider principles of good acoustics during the initial design and construction of an area usually results in environments where individuals cannot function optimally. Correcting a bad acoustical design after the completion of a project often costs many times more than having done the job correctly in the first place. Examples of noise sources, treatment options, and acoustic radiation characteristics necessary to provide proper acoustics for a structure are shown in Fig. 2.

LINDSAY'S WHEEL OF ACOUSTICS

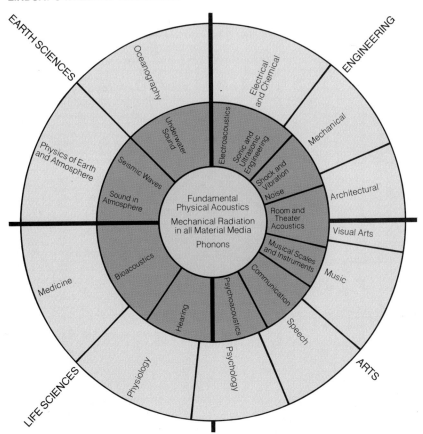

Fig. 1. Lindsay's Wheel of Acoustics illustrates that the science of acoustics has applications in various fields, including many in the life sciences, earth sciences, engineering, and the arts.

From *Journal of the Acoustical Society of America*, with the permission of R. Bruce Lindsay

Ultrasonics

Acoustic signals are often used to detect objects inside solid matter, such as impurities in metals, or objects hidden under liquids, such as those submerged in an ocean. Such detection and identification of objects hidden from the eye is one application of ultrasonics. Ultrasonic waves, or sounds at a pitch much higher than can be heard by the human ear, are also of major importance in medicine. They are used to study internal organs, assess the condition of an unborn child, and detect foreign objects for removal from the body. The instruments used both send out waves and receive those reflected by an object encountered. This technique is also utilized in submarines to locate objects in the ocean, such as other submarines, and by engineers in designing robots for undersea detection work.

Stress Testing

Another application of acoustic technology concerns the nondestructive evaluation of critical components of machinery. The continuous reliability of materials in, for instance, jet engines, automotive gas turbines, or nuclear steam generators is critical both from safety and from performance standpoints. To ensure reliable performance, it is necessary to utilize techniques that allow the evaluation of the components while the systems are in actual use. One such technique utilizes acoustic emissions produced by components as they are stressed during the operation of the equipment. As a turbine blade, shaft, or other component is strained, it produces its own characteristic acoustic signature pattern that may be used for identification purposes. (The procedure is similar to that of using voice patterns for the purpose of identifying individuals.) If the component begins to fail, its acoustic signature will change. The detection of such a change may serve as a warning for the replacement of the component before it causes failure of the entire piece of equipment.

Communication

The areas of speech and hearing are also part of the field of acoustics. When one walks beside a busy road and something unusual happens, for instance, the first indication may come from hearing a different or sudden sound. This ability to perceive acoustical warnings from a specific direction is essential for survival. The ability to communicate by spoken language is unique to mankind, but it is often taken for granted. How often each day is this ability utilized? How many times a day does one pick up the telephone to obtain information about an assignment, to make a date, or to check on a new motion picture? The individual placing the phone call, the telephone system that transmits the spoken information, the environments where the caller and receiver are each located, and the individual on the receiving end all form a complex system. Acoustical scientists are deeply involved in studying this system in attempting to improve communication. (*See also* Sound.)

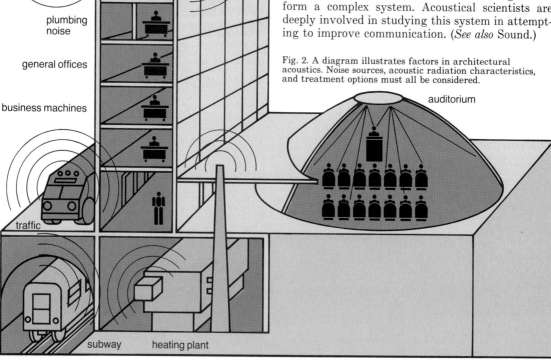

Fig. 2. A diagram illustrates factors in architectural acoustics. Noise sources, acoustic radiation characteristics, and treatment options must all be considered.

ACROPOLIS. More than 2,300 years ago, in the Age of Pericles, the Greeks created the most beautiful temples and statues in the ancient world from white marble. The best of these stood upon the Acropolis, a small plateau in the heart of Athens.

An oblong mass of rock, the Acropolis looks very much like a pedestal. It rises abruptly above the city. The top, almost flat, covers less than eight acres (three hectares). Ten miles (16 kilometers) northeast is Mount Pentelicus, which supplied the white Pentelic marble for the temples and the statues.

The earliest people of Athens, perhaps 4,000 years ago, walled in the Acropolis as a kind of fort. Here their first kings ruled, and here in later years were the chief shrines of Athena (*see* Athena).

More than 2,500 years ago, the goddess' shrines began to rise. Only 90 years later, the Lacedaemonians found the Acropolis covered with marble temples and dwellings. They destroyed the dwellings, but they paused in awe and silence before the temples and left them unharmed.

In 480 B.C., the Persians burned or smashed everything on the Acropolis and killed its defenders, but within 13 years Themistocles and Cimon had rebuilt the walls and cleared away the ruins. In 447 B.C., the statesman Pericles placed the sculptor Phidias in charge of restoring the Acropolis (*see* Pericles). Several years before, Phidias had erected on the Acropolis a large bronze statue of Athena Promachus (*see* Athena). In 447 B.C. Phidias began to build a shrine to her. This Doric temple, called the Parthenon (dwelling of the maiden) was opened in 438 B.C. It was 228 feet (70 meters) long, 101 feet (31 meters) wide, and 65 feet (20 meters) high.

On the western pediment of the new temple stood statues of Athena and Poseidon. Relief carvings, 92 in all, studded the outside. Along the portico, between the temple's outside columns and its walls, was a frieze. It extended around the top of the walls, 39 feet (12 meters) above the portico floor, and was 524 feet (160 meters) long, and 3 feet 3½ inches (1 meter)

wide. Its 350 people and 125 horses represented the Panathenaic procession that carried a new gown to Athena each year.

In the temple was a statue of Athena Parthenos, 40 feet (12 meters) tall. Its body was of ivory, its dress of gold. Its right hand held a statue of Nike, goddess of victory, and its left hand rested upon a large shield. From 437 to 432 B.C. a majestic gate, the Propylaea, was erected at the west end of the Acropolis. The Temple of Athena Nike was finished about 410 B.C. The Erechtheum, built from 421 to 407 B.C., was named for Erechtheus, foster son of Athena and king of Athens. Six marble statues, 7½ feet (2 meters) tall, served as pillars on its Porch of the Maidens.

By the 5th century A.D. the Byzantines had carried to Constantinople the statues of Athena Promachos and Athena Parthenos and had made the Parthenon a Christian church. Ten centuries later the Turks made it a mosque. In 1687, under attack by the Venetians, the Turks stored gunpowder in the mosque. Struck by a cannonball, it exploded, killing 300 men. The roof, walls, and 16 columns lay in ruin.

In 1801 Lord Elgin, British ambassador to Turkey, got permission to remove "a few blocks of stone with inscriptions and figures." Actually he almost stripped the Parthenon of its frieze, pediment, sculptures, and relief carvings. He took a frieze from the Athena Nike temple, which the Turks had torn down in 1687. From the Erechtheum he took a marble maiden and a pillar of the eastern portico. In 1816 these Elgin marbles went to the British Museum.

Freed from Turkey in 1829, Greece began to redeem the ruins. The Athena Nike temple was rebuilt in 1835 and 1836. The Acropolis Museum (opened 1878) was built north of the Parthenon. In the 20th century the American School of Classical Studies rebuilt part of the Erechtheum, wrecked by war and storms. The Propylaea, in ruins since 1645, has been partly repaired. Some fallen pillars have been restored in the Parthenon, but it is still empty and roofless. It suffered further damage in World War II.

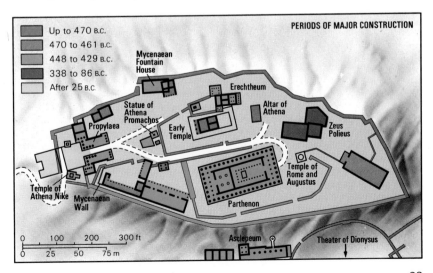

The plan of the Acropolis in Athens, Greece, is quite elaborate. It was carried out over hundreds of years.

Adapted from 'Westermann Grosser Atlas zur Weltgeschichte': Georg Westermann Verlag, Braunschweig

ACTING. Imagine a person with all the desires and fears, thoughts and actions that make a man or a woman. Acting is becoming that imaginary person. Whether the character, or role, that the actor creates is based on someone who really lived, a playwright's concept, or a legendary being, that creation comes to life through the art of acting. Acting is an ability to react, to respond to imaginary situations and feelings. The purpose of this ancient profession is, as Shakespeare has Hamlet say, "to hold, as 'twere, the mirror up to Nature, to show . . . the very age and body of the Time, his form and pressure."

It is the audience that sees itself in the mirror of acting. Acting is a process of two-way communication between actor and audience. The reflection may be realistic, as the audience sees its own social behavior; the reflection may be a funny or critical exaggeration; or the audience may see a picture of its mind—of the way it thinks—or a fantastic projection of its fears and desires—of the way it feels.

Acting makes use of two kinds of physical skills: movement and voice. Either may dominate. Body movement is highly developed in Far Eastern acting traditions, while the voice has ruled in Western cultures. If either voice or movement takes over completely, the activity is usually not called acting but dance, perhaps, or singing. But neither ballerinas nor operatic singers can reach the top of their professions without being able to act.

Tradition and Technique

In one sense there is no technique of acting; that is, when the actor is on the stage or in front of a camera, there should be no thought of technique. The actor attempts simply to be there. Technique in acting has to do with getting ready to act. There are two basic requirements: developing the necessary physical, external skills and freeing the internal emotional life, the actor's "inspiration."

The physical skills needed by actors have been understood since ancient times. They are a well-developed body and voice, ability to imitate other people's gestures and mannerisms, and mastery of the physical or vocal abilities required by the type of theater for which the actor is preparing.

Before the 20th century, the inner emotional training of actors was not thought about in a systematic way. Young actors developed a "feel" for the art by watching older, more experienced performers, but the creation of emotional truth on stage was largely thought of as a problem of imitation.

Konstantin S. Stanislavsky, a Russian director and actor, believed that actors in realistic plays should "incarnate" their roles, should live the parts. He decided that a technique was needed that would guide the actor and create a "favorable condition for the appearance of inspiration." His system does not consist of a fixed set of rules but of practical approaches to the physical and mental preparation of the actor and to the creation of a character. Some important aspects of the Stanislavsky system are (a)

learning to relax and to avoid distraction; (b) developing the imagination and the ability to memorize sensory details (tastes, smells, and so on) of past emotions in order to recreate those emotions on stage; and (c) developing a naiveté, a belief in the imagined truth of the stage (he called this the magic or creative "if"). In the rehearsal process the actor thinks of being the character to be played. The most important questions become "What do I want, and why?"

Stanislavsky's system was taken to the United States, where it was taught and then transformed by Lee Strasberg and others into method acting, often called simply "the method." The method is sophisticated in psychological terms but has been criticized for emphasizing the "inner life" of the actor at the expense of total development.

An alternative to Stanislavsky-based technique is that practiced in epic theater, developed by the German playwright and director Bertolt Brecht (*see* Brecht). The Brechtian actor does not attempt to inhabit the role but to remain outside it, to comment on it. The difficulty of understanding this concept led Brecht to give the example of a street scene. The actor is compared to an eyewitness of a traffic accident demonstrating to bystanders how it took place. The witness does not want to entertain the bystanders but simply to tell them what happened. Only enough information is given about the "characters"—the driver of the car, the pedestrian who was struck—for the bystanders to understand the essential action. If the demonstrator is too skillful, if he creates a dramatic illusion for the bystanders, then he fails. They will applaud him instead of thinking about what happened. For Brecht, character does not determine action, as in Stanislavsky's view. Rather the action reveals the characters, who are viewed as being able to change and to learn.

The Polish director Jerzy Grotowski has made the most extensive investigation of acting technique since Stanislavsky. His theater laboratory in Opole and later in Wroclaw, Poland, was active from 1959 through the early 1970's. He reduced the theater to bare essentials: the actors and an audience. His aim was for the actor to make a "total gift of himself" to the audience. Grotowski's actors underwent intense physical discipline. Those who saw the performances were impressed by the actors' strength, control, and concentration as they attempted to give physical form to intense states of mind. Grotowski saw his method not as a collection of skills but as a removal of blocks or resistances in the actor.

Another technique that has become important is improvisation. In the United States, Viola Spolin has taught it through creating gamelike exercises. The actor has certain given conditions to respond to and a goal. In performance, improvisation becomes a collaborative art of spontaneous theatrical creation.

Theory

There have been numerous philosophical efforts to define the nature of acting, but none of these has been

Members of the company of the Moscow Art Theater listen to Anton P. Chekhov read his play 'The Seagull', in which they appeared in 1899. The founders of the company, Vladimir I. Nimirovich-Danchenko and Konstantin S. Stanislavsky, are shown, respectively, standing at far left and sitting at the table on the Russian master's right.

able to arrive at a satisfying theory of acting without developing some scientific understanding of the sources of human behavior. Practical contributions to acting theory in the 20th century have come mainly from psychology, though speculation has also drawn on the fields of anthropological research, linguistics, and other disciplines.

Stanislavsky borrowed from late 19th-century French psychology the concept of emotional memory, recreating past emotions on stage by recalling the sense details that surrounded the original experience. This became the centerpiece of method acting. In the late 1940's, when the Actors' Studio, home of the method, was founded in New York City, Gestalt psychology was just becoming fashionable (see Psychology). The concepts behind many method exercises are in line with Gestalt ideas about how emotion is experienced and remembered.

Social psychology has contributed much to the understanding of what happens in the complex interaction between actor and audience. The concept of "role-playing" in everyday life has broadened the possibilities for actors in the creation of their own performing material.

A major influence on 20th-century acting emanates from the writings of the French actor and director Antonin Artaud. He conceived of the actor as an "athlete of the heart," giving physical expression to dreams, obsessions, the nonrational side of human beings. Although Artaud produced no convincing examples of his theories, experiments during the 1960's by Grotowski and the British director Peter Brook have shown some of the potential value that may lie in Artaud's thought.

Kinesics, the science of communication through body movement, has made it possible to analyze the meanings of gestures in daily life, how the body's movements have psychological significance. The development of kinesics may create the potential for the very subtle art of psychological mime.

Style

Personal style in acting is the imprint of the actor's art and personality on the roles that he or she creates. Style can also be the "look" associated with the work of a particular acting company.

A third type is historical style, which is based on approaching a play through study of the period in which it originated. The aim of historically stylized acting is to give the audience an illusion of authenticity. This is a relatively recent phenomenon in the English-speaking theater, dating only from the late 18th century. Shakespeare's theater made no attempt at historical accuracy in acting or staging.

The emphasis on historical style is characteristic of a "conservatory" approach to theater in which acting is seen mainly as a process for interpreting great dramatic literature of the past. The danger in playing styles is that they may remain empty shells with no believable life inside the characters.

History

Acting is an ephemeral art: once the performance is over, there is nothing left but the memory of it. There is no history, no documentation or record of acting itself before the end of the 19th century except for the written recollections of those who saw it. Acting masterpieces are known only by hearsay. It is as if all of Rembrandt's paintings had disappeared and only the recollections of one of his admirers remained.

The origins of acting are in the act of remembering. Acting may have begun as early as 4000 B.C. when Egyptian actor-priests worshiped the memory of the dead. The first nonreligious professional acting may possibly have developed in China. Players there kept alive the memory of the triumph of the current emperor's ancestors over the former dynasty. Acting has remained an art of remembering to the present day, when actors rely on their memories of emotions and sense experiences to perform a reenactment of those feelings on stage.

The great periods of acting are those in which actors were valued highly by their contemporary society or by some part of it. Greek acting developed from the reciting and singing of poetic texts and from ritual dances honoring Dionysus, the god of wine and fertility. The first actor, tradition says, was Thespis, who introduced to Athens in about 560 B.C. impersonation—pretending to be another person. Early actors developed acting with a mask in order to portray several characters in one play. Through mime—stylized gestures indicating the characters' emotions—they made the body express what the face, hidden by a mask, could not. Even though masks may have been designed to amplify the voice, the ability to be heard in the large outdoor theaters must have required intensive vocal training.

The Romans derived their theater from that of the Greeks and further developed the emphasis on voice. The Roman art of oratory, or public speaking, much valued because of its use in politics and law, was often compared to acting; rules for orators have continued to influence actors. Actors in Rome were slaves, and the theater was viewed principally as entertainment. Acting as showmanship flourished as the virtuosity and beauty of an individual were emphasized.

Side by side with the "high," or serious, acting tradition of the Greeks was a "low," or comical, type. Little is known about it except that it was very physical, relied on crude jokes and situations, and was apparently popular. Although serious professional acting declined along with the Roman Empire and was suppressed by the church in the Middle Ages, this "low" acting, practiced by wandering minstrels or mimes, helped to keep the spirit of acting alive.

Modern professional acting in the West began in Italy during the early 16th century. There troupes of actors performed the *commedia dell'arte* (*see* Theater, subhead "The Commedia dell'Arte"). Actors practiced improvisation, inventing words and actions to flesh out plot outlines called scenarios. Actors learned to work with each other, creating an ensemble, though the emphasis remained on an individual actor's skills and cleverness. A feature of *commedia* is the *lazzi* (probably from *le azioni*, Italian for "the actions"), short sections of comic business, stunts, and witty comments. The characters that appear in *commedia* are stock social types such as young lovers, a pompous old man, and Harlequin, the mischievous troublemaker who is often a servant.

In Elizabethan drama of the late 16th and early 17th centuries in England, actors faced the problem of portraying not types but individuals. The characters of Shakespeare demand an understanding by the actor of the motives, the psychology that determines the action. Elizabethan acting was probably not "realistic" in the modern sense. The emphasis was still on admirable vocal delivery and choice of gestures appropriate to the poet's words. The Elizabethan legacy of portraying people with complex emotions was gradually enriched by a series of brilliant English and continental actors. In the 18th century these included John Philip Kemble, his sister Sarah Siddons, and David Garrick. In the 19th century Edmund Kean, Ellen Terry, and Henry Irving dominated the stage in England, and François Talma and Sarah Bernhardt did so in France. Their contribution lies not so much in technique as in creating a living tradition, an intangible heritage of accomplishment passed from one generation to the next.

The story of 20th-century acting may be summed up as the attempt to rediscover an "inner truth" in

A Greek actor holds a tragic mask and wears a short chiton (the basic male garment of ancient Greece) and high boots. The painting is from a late 4th-century B.C. vase.

Martin von Wagner—Museum der Universität, Würzburg

SOME THEATRICAL PERSONALITIES

Some prominent persons are not included below because they are covered in the main text of this article or in other articles in Compton's Encyclopedia (*see* Fact-Index).

Barrault, Jean-Louis (born 1910). French actor, director, and manager who in 1946 formed the Renaud-Barrault Company with his wife, Madeleine Renaud. He developed new techniques in pantomime and was recognized as an accomplished satirical performer.

Booth, Edwin Thomas (1833–93). One of the first great American actors who is remembered as one of the finest performers of Shakespeare's Hamlet. Born into a family of actors, he was the brother of the actor John Wilkes Booth, who assassinated Abraham Lincoln.

Brando, Marlon (born 1924). American film star, considered one of the most powerful actors in the history of cinema. His most notable films include 'A Streetcar Named Desire', 'On the Waterfront', 'The Godfather', and 'Last Tango in Paris'. He was awarded two Oscars for best actor.

Burbage, Richard (1567–1619). English actor known as the first performer to play Shakespeare's Richard III, Othello, Romeo, Hamlet, Henry V, and Lear. He excelled in tragedy, performing in works by John Webster and Thomas Kyd as well as his close associate William Shakespeare.

Campbell, Mrs. Patrick (1865–1940). English actress who was one of the greatest theatrical stars of her generation. She was known for her startling beauty and wit. George Bernard Shaw wrote the part of Eliza Doolittle in 'Pygmalion' for her.

Chaplin, Charlie (1889–1977). English star of the motion-picture industry. His extraordinary gift for comedy and pathos made him the best known actor of silent films. He was knighted in 1975.

Coquelin, Constant (1841–1909). French actor who was best known for his portrayal of Cyrano de Bergerac. He received critical acclaim for outstanding performances in Molière's comic roles.

Cornell, Katharine (1898–1974). American actress best known for her performance of Elizabeth Moulton Barrett in 'The Barretts of Wimpole Street'. She married producer Guthrie McClintic, and he produced and she starred in numerous productions, most notably 'Antony and Cleopatra', 'The Dark Is Light Enough', and 'Romeo and Juliet'.

Duse, Eleonora (1859–1924). Italian actress considered one of the greatest performers of tragedy. She was especially successful in the plays of Émile Zola and Henrik Ibsen.

Forrest, Edwin (1806–72). First native-born theatrical star in the United States, he is remembered for his passionate renderings of Shakespeare's tragic heroes. King Lear was considered his greatest role.

Gielgud, John (born 1904). Versatile British actor, director, and manager considered one of the foremost figures in 20th-century theater. At his best in Shakespeare, especially Hamlet, he has played a variety of roles, including many in motion pictures. He was knighted in 1953.

Hayes, Helen (born 1900). American actress widely acclaimed for both stage and cinema performances. Known for her dedication to the social services, she was voted Woman of the Year in 1974 by the United Service Organization. She won Academy awards for 'The Sin of Madelon Claudet' and 'Airport'.

Hepburn, Katharine (born 1909). American actress who has starred both on the stage and in motion pictures. She won critical acclaim in stage productions of 'A Month in the Country', 'The Philadelphia Story', and 'As You Like It'. She entered films in 1932, winning Academy awards for 'Morning Glory', 'Guess Who's Coming to Dinner', 'A Lion in Winter', and 'On Golden Pond'.

Jefferson, Joseph (1829–1905). Member of a family of actors of English origin, he is best remembered for his role as Rip Van Winkle in a production he did with Dion Boucicault. As a comedian he was known for character delineation.

Keaton, Buster (1895–1966). American actor noted as the master of pantomime comedy in silent films. Keaton immortalized the theme of man versus establishment in his early films such as 'The General', 'Cops', and 'The Boat'.

Laughton, Charles (1899–1962). Actor famous on the British stage and later in Hollywood. He won an Academy award for his role in 'The Private Life of Henry VIII'. Other memorable film performances were 'Mutiny on the Bounty', 'Hunchback of Notre Dame', and 'Rembrandt'.

Lecouvreur, Adrienne (1692–1730). French actress whose extraordinary beauty and charm became legendary. With the actor-dramatist Marc-Antoine Legrand as her mentor, she made her debut at the Comédie-Française in 1717 and became a popular success.

Lunt, Alfred (1893–1977) and **Fontanne, Lynn** (1887–1983). American actor and actress who were one of the greatest Broadway teams in history. Married in 1922, they appeared opposite one another in 27 plays.

Nazimova, Alla (1879–1945). Russian actress best known for her performances of Henrik Ibsen's heroines. After touring Europe and the United States with a Russian company, she settled in New York City.

Olivier, Laurence (born 1907). British actor, producer, and director who is perhaps the most eminent theatrical figure of the 20th century. He has performed brilliantly in both classical and modern drama, light comedy as well as tragedy, and has played all the major Shakespeare heroes. A significant contribution was bringing Shakespeare to the screen. He was knighted in 1947 and elevated to the peerage in 1970.

Pickford, Mary (1893–1979). American actress in silent films who was Hollywood's first female superstar. She was best known for her portrayal of young girls and was long called "America's sweetheart." With Douglas Fairbanks, Charlie Chaplin, and D. W. Griffith she founded United Artists. She won an Academy award for 'Coquette', her first talking film.

Rachel (1821–58). French actress considered one of the great performers of tragedy. She is best remembered for her performance in Jean Racine's 'Phèdre'.

Robeson, Paul (1898–1976). American black actor and singer. Known for his performances in Eugene O'Neill's plays, particularly as Brutus in 'The Emperor Jones', and his singing of 'Ol' Man River' in 'Show Boat', he played Othello in the longest recorded run of a Shakespearean play.

Salvini, Tommaso (1829–1915). Italian actor who won international recognition for his portrayal of great tragic heroes. He was best known for the role of Shakespeare's Othello.

Talma, François Joseph (1763–1826). French actor noted for excellence in the classical roles of tragedy. He initiated reforms in the costuming of French classical plays, adopting designs that were more historically accurate. In 1799 he assisted Napoleon in drawing up a new constitution for the Comédie-Française.

Terry, Ellen (1847–1928). English actress known for her partnership with Henry Irving. As his leading lady at the Lyceum Theatre, she played the major Shakespearean heroines, including Ophelia, Portia, Desdemona, and Lady Macbeth. She was made Dame of the British Empire in 1925.

Vakhtangov, Eugene (1883–1922). Russian actor, producer, and director who created nonrealistic methods of theater production. His best known production was 'Turandot'. He was associated with the Moscow Art Theater and was a pupil and friend of Konstantin Stanislavsky.

Zeami Motokiyo (1363–1443) and **Kan-ami Kiyotsugu** (1333–84). Zeami was the greatest playwright and theorist of the Japanese No theater. He and his father, Kan-ami, were the creators of No drama in its present form.

An actor in a 17th-century masque wears a costume by Lodovico Burnacini (probably for the Harlequin character).

performance. The form that truth takes, however, depends on different and sometimes contradictory perceptions of essential human nature. Superior acting has continued on the basis of strong national theatrical traditions; this is especially true of acting in Great Britain. The popular theatrical traditions of minstrelsy, variety, and vaudeville culminated in the United States with a group of brilliant actors whose work blossomed in early motion pictures, including W. C. Fields and Will Rogers. But great changes in acting have been brought about by individuals and companies committed to a way of approaching acting that is based on psychological and political ideas current in 20th-century artistic thought.

Stanislavsky provides a kind of bridge between the old traditional acting and the new psychological approach. His system enabled the Moscow Art Theater (which he directed) to achieve ensemble productions, especially in the plays of Anton Chekhov, in which the actors functioned as an organic, living unit. Brecht founded the Berliner Ensemble in East Germany after World War II. This "epic theater" group produced a series of brilliant productions in the 1950's, including Brecht's 'The Days of the Commune', 'The Resistible Rise of Arturo Ui', and 'Coriolan', an adaptation of Shakespeare's 'Coriolanus'.

Innovations in 20th-century American acting resulted from revolts against what was seen as the commercialism and spiritual emptiness of "show business." The Group Theater of the 1930's believed in acting as a means of promoting social change. The Group Theatre included Strasberg, Stella Adler, and others who created method acting from Stanislavsky's system.

Viola Spolin's son, Paul Sills, co-founded in 1956 the Compass Players in Chicago, a group that be-

came known as Second City. This was the first professional improvisational theater company in the United States. In the 1960's, Sills created Story Theatre, improvisational theater in which actors narrated and acted out folktales and legends.

During the 1950's and 1960's, there was a continuous movement away from the big business of commercial theater, as typified by New York City's Broadway theater district. Actors moved "off-Broadway" and then "off-off-Broadway" along with productions to escape the need to show a profit. At the same time, many regional theaters offered opportunities for acting "the repertoire," the established body of great dramatic literature. University theaters provided extensive training programs and facilities. Dinner theaters staged small-scale productions.

New developments in acting have continued to emerge from the work of individuals and small groups operating outside the commercial theater. From 1963 until the mid-1970's, the off-off-Broadway Open Theatre directed by Joseph Chaikin was active. This group developed scripts collectively and set a standard for collaboration in acting.

In the early 1970's, "art performance" began to be significant. The performers filled a vacuum left by mainstream acting, which concerns itself with interpretation of dramatic literature. These performers created their own acting material and examined the nature of acting itself in a critical and creative way. (*See also* Drama; Theater.)

ACTION. A United States agency that combines several volunteer programs, ACTION offers the young and the elderly opportunities to be of service at home and abroad. The independent agency was created in 1971 to consolidate the efforts of programs organized under various federal departments.

The major programs in the ACTION agency include the Volunteers in Service to America (VISTA), Foster Grandparent Program, Retired Senior Volunteer Program (RSVP), Senior Companion Program, and Vietnam Veterans Leadership Program (VVLP). Until 1982 the Peace Corps was also part of ACTION (*see* Peace Corps).

Other ACTION programs include the Young Volunteers in ACTION (YVA), Income Consumer Counseling, and Drug Abuse Prevention Program. The Urban Crime Prevention Program (UCPP) is coadministered by ACTION and the Law Enforcement Assistance Administration. Three interagency agreements are administered by ACTION: the Community Energy Project (Department of Energy), Refugee Resettlement Program (Department of Health and Human Services), and Youth Employment Service (Department of Labor).

ACTION develops demonstration projects as test models for future agency programming or for adoption by private concerns or state and local governments. Major areas of concern are drug abuse prevention, runaway youth, and literacy. ACTION has an information support center that serves as a communication link for state and local volunteer centers.

ACUPUNCTURE

ACUPUNCTURE. A system of Oriental medicine, acupuncture has been practiced for about 5,000 years. It is used primarily for the relief of pain, but also for modifying certain body functions in diseased states.

Acupuncture is administered by the insertion of hair-thin needles through particular spots in the skin (acupuncture points) into neuroreceptors in underlying muscles. They are then stimulated either by gentle twirling, by heat, or by stimulation with a weak electrical current. Acupuncture points also can be stimulated by pressure, ultrasound, and certain wavelengths of light.

Modern Research

Modern research has demonstrated that the effectiveness of acupuncture results from the stimulation and transmission of impulses from the acupuncture point along the peripheral nerve into the spinal cord and brain, causing the release there of chemical substances known as endorphins and enkephalins. Exactly how these substances and other neurotransmitter systems react to relieve pain and regulate certain physiological functions remains a mystery.

Although still regarded legally in the United States as an experimental medical procedure, acupuncture has been used extensively in research projects in hospitals and medical centers throughout Asia, Europe, and North and South America for the relief of pain during and after dental procedures, some surgical operations, and obstetrical deliveries and to control blood pressure, relieve muscle spasm and arthritic pain, and alleviate symptoms associated with withdrawal from drug addiction, appetite control, and many other conditions. In some people and in certain medical conditions, it is not always effective. At one time it was believed that acupuncture was related in some way to hypnosis, but extensive experiments in animals undergoing surgery in veterinary hospitals has disproven that assumption.

Ancient Theory

It has been difficult for modern physicians to accept acupuncture as an effective procedure for the treatment of certain conditions. This is primarily because of the elaborate systems of fanciful theories that were developed 2,000 to 3,000 years ago by the early practitioners of acupuncture to explain its mechanisms of action. For example, the ancient Chinese designated the master force that associates, coordinates, regulates, and controls the fundamental activities of different organs in the body as vital energy, or *ch'i*. Modern science teaches that the nervous system and various chemical and hormonal substances (neurotransmitters) perform the functions that the ancients attributed to *ch'i*.

Ancient theorists also held that positive and negative forces in the body, called yin and yang, could be kept in balance by acupuncture, promoting health and controlling disease. They believed that *ch'i* flowed through the body along a system of channels, or meridians, on which more than 500 acupuncture

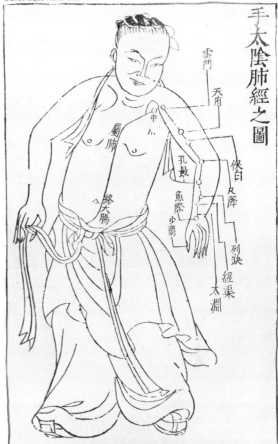

The figure from a Chinese manuscript shows acupuncture points for the insertion of needles.

points were located and that, when *ch'i* was in balance, both physical and emotional health resulted. Modern scientific studies have failed to demonstrate an anatomic meridian system. They have shown, however, that acupuncture points are more richly supplied with nerve endings than the surrounding skin areas. In certain abnormal conditions of disease, the electric resistance of particular acupuncture points is altered, indicating the specific points where the needles should be inserted for treatment.

Modern Revival

In 1972 acupuncture received great publicity, particularly in the United States, as an indirect result of President Richard M. Nixon's trip to China. A *New York Times* correspondent, who had accompanied Nixon, reported on the successful relief provided by acupuncture for pain after his emergency appendectomy. Since that time many United States physicians and dentists have been trained to administer acupuncture in courses authorized by state governments, and modern research is revealing more and more of the physiological basis for its effects. In the early 1980's, 19 states had laws or regulations governing the practice of acupuncture.

The Courtauld Institute of Art in London was built from 1775 to 1777 by the Adam brothers for the Countess of Home.

ADAM, Robert (1728–92). "Movement," claimed Robert Adam, "is meant to express the rise and fall, the advance and recess, [and] other diversity of form ... to add greatly to the picturesque" character of the whole. Thus the Scottish-born architect, acclaimed as one of the greatest 18th-century British architects, described a key element of his work.

Stressing innovation and detail as well, Adam created a new style of interior decoration that influenced English interior and furniture design. He also developed and used new concepts in London street design and created his own individual style of picturesque castle building.

The son of William Adam, then Scotland's foremost architect, Robert Adam was born in Kirkcaldy on July 3, 1728. Among his seven brothers and sisters, John and James were eventually to work with their illustrious brother. The Adam family moved to Edinburgh shortly after Robert's birth. He attended Edinburgh College (now the University of Edinburgh) from 1743 to 1745, when he became his father's apprentice and assistant.

When William Adam died in 1748, his post as master mason passed to his oldest son, John, who then formed a partnership with Robert. The brothers prospered. Among other commissions they built Fort George in the Moray Firth near Inverness and designed the interior of the Earl of Hopetoun's house.

Robert traveled to Italy with Charles Hope, the earl's younger brother, in 1754–58. There he came into contact with the latest architectural theories in Rome and received instruction in perspective and drawing from Charles-Louis Clerisseau, a French architect and draftsman. Robert's visit to the ruins of the Roman Emperor Diocletian's palace in Spalatro (now Split, Yugoslavia) gave him material for a book, 'Ruins of the Palace of the Emperor Diocletian at Spalatro in Dalmatia' (1764).

Establishing his architectural service in London, Robert Adam soon became well known. He began to develop the Adam style, with its lightness and free use of classical elements. He designed the columned screen in front of the Admiralty in Whitehall (1760). After he became one of the king's architects in 1761, he built or designed the interiors of many homes, including Landsdowne House and others at Harewood, Yorkshire, and Croome Court, Worcestershire. In 1762 he was engaged to redesign the interior of Syon House, Middlesex. Adam combined both Ionic and Doric Greek architectural forms in designs for the Royal Society of Arts building (1772–74).

Robert's brother James became his partner in 1763. Looking for larger projects, the brothers in 1768 leased land along the Thames River for a speculative housing development. Called the Adelphi, the project had several terraces of houses featuring the Adam style, but the venture failed. In 1773 the brothers speculated—again unsuccessfully—in a group of stuccoed terraces in Portland Place, London.

Three London houses, all built in the 1770s, represent the Adams' mature style. No. 20, St. James's Square (1772–74), was built for Sir Watkin Williams-Wynn; Derby House in Grosvenor Square (1773–74), for the Earl of Derby; and No. 20, Portman Square (1775–77), for the Countess of Home (now the Courtauld Institute of Art).

By 1780 the Adam brothers' popularity began to decline, but they continued to write a three-volume analysis of their creations, 'The Works in Architecture of Robert and James Adam' (published in 1773, 1779, and 1822). Robert Adam designed and built a number of romantic neo-Gothic castles, most of them dating from the 1780s, including the Castle Culzean in Ayrshire for the earls of Cassilis (1777–90). Robert also built the Register House, Edinburgh (1772–92), and designed the University of Edinburgh (1789). He died on March 3, 1792, in London.

ADAMS, Ansel (1902–84). The American photographer Ansel Adams was well known for his dramatic pictures of Western landscapes. He was a pioneer in the movement to preserve the wilderness and one of the first to promote photography as an art form.

Ansel Adams was born in San Francisco, Calif., on Feb. 20, 1902. Originally a student of music, he took photographs only as a hobby until 1927. In that year he published his first portfolio, 'Parmellian Prints of the High Sierras'. (Parmellian refers to the texture of mountain surfaces.) The style was pictorialist, similar to that of impressionist painting with its soft, misty images rather than detailed likenesses.

In 1930 Adams adopted the straight photography style of the United States photographer Paul Strand, whose photographs emphasized tones and sharp detail. Two years later, with another photographer, Adams formed Group f/64, an association of photographers who used large cameras and small apertures (lens openings) to capture an infinite variety of light and texture. Contact prints were rich in detail and

The photograph entitled 'Mount Williamson—Clearing Storm' was taken by Ansel Adams in 1944.

Ansel Adams

brilliant in showing tonal differences; subjects were portrayed in the most vivid way. Adams soon became one of the outstanding technicians in the history of photography. In 1935 he published 'Making a Photograph', the first of many books that he produced on photographic technique.

In 1941 Adams began making photomurals for the United States Department of the Interior. Their large scale forced him to master techniques for photographing the light and space of immense landscapes. He developed what he called the zone system, a method of determining beforehand, for each part of the scene, what the final tone would be.

Throughout his career Adams worked to increase public acceptance of photography as a fine art. He felt that an artist's final product was really no different from an artistically created photograph, intended to be preserved and respected. In 1940 he helped found the world's first museum collection of photographs at the Museum of Modern Art in New York City. In 1946 he established, at the California School of Fine Arts in San Francisco, the first academic department to teach photography as a profession.

From the time of his adolescence, Adams had a serious interest in preserving the environment. From 1936 he was a director of the Sierra Club, a group founded in 1892 to preserve the scenic beauty of particular areas in the United States. Many of Adams' books are pleas for the preservation of nature: 'My Camera in the National Parks' (1950), 'This Is the American Earth' (1960), and 'Photographs of the Southwest' (1976). Adams also published some general photographic anthologies, including 'Ansel Adams: Images, 1923–1974' (1974) and 'The Portfolios of Ansel Adams' (1977).

ADAMS, Henry (1838–1918). During his life Henry Adams was known chiefly as a historian and as a member of a great American family (*see* Adams Family). After his death he was recognized as a major figure in American literature. His fame rests mainly on two books: 'The Education of Henry Adams' and 'Mont-Saint-Michel and Chartres'.

Henry Adams was born on Feb. 16, 1838, in Boston, Mass. As a child, he said, he felt he really belonged to Quincy, Mass., where his grandfather, John Quincy Adams, lived. His grandfather and his great-grandfather, John Adams, had been presidents of the United States. His father was Charles Francis Adams, a noted statesman.

After graduating from Harvard (1858), Henry Adams studied in Germany and made the grand tour of Europe. From 1861 to 1868 he was in London serving as secretary to his father, who was minister to Great Britain. From 1870 to 1877 he taught medieval history at Harvard and edited the *North American Review.* He married Marian Hooper in 1872. In 1877 they moved to Washington, D.C. In 1891 Adams completed his nine-volume 'History of the United States During the Administrations of Thomas Jefferson and James Madison'.

Grieved by his wife's death in 1885, Adams spent many of his later years traveling throughout the world. The cathedrals in France awakened his interest in the spirit of the 12th century. In 1904 he had printed privately a limited edition of 'Mont-Saint-Michel and Chartres' to give to his friends. Two years later he gave them privately printed copies of 'The Education of Henry Adams'. This book was not published until after his death. Adams died March 27, 1918, in Washington, D.C.

JOHN ADAMS—

2nd President of

the United States

ADAMS, John (1735–1826; president 1797–1801). The second president of the United States was John Adams, lawyer and diplomat. Adams' public career lasted more than 35 years. He was second only to George Washington in making a place for the young United States among the nations of the world. In his devotion to our country he was second to none.

Adams was a Federalist. He, like other Federalists, believed in a strong central government. However, he was independent and decided issues for himself in the interests of his country and often against the interests of his party. Adams was defeated for a second term as president because he defied party power to act for the nation's good.

Massachusetts Boy and Man

John Adams was born Oct. 19, 1735, in Braintree (now Quincy), Mass. He was the eldest of three sons, children of John and Susanna Boylston Adams. Young John attended a "dame" school and later went to the Free Latin School. He was handy around cattle and horses, helping with the milking and feeding. He was handy in the kitchen too, building fires and cleaning up. In summer he went down to the bay to watch the sailing ships come in. In winter he skated on the frozen creeks. He flew homemade kites, collected birds' eggs, and always had a whittling knife in hand.

When he entered Harvard College, he intended to become a minister. By the time he was graduated, he had given up the idea. He taught school until he could make up his mind about his future. Adams taught in Worcester, Mass., about 60 miles west of Boston. After a year he began to study law under James Putnam, the town's leading lawyer. He kept on teaching and spent his after-school hours in Putnam's office.

Two years later he was admitted to the bar and settled in Braintree to practice. When he was 29 he married Abigail Smith, a minister's daughter. She was

John Adams

JOHN ADAMS' ADMINISTRATION
1797–1801

X Y Z Affair and naval war
with France (1798–1800)

Alien and Sedition laws passed (1798)

Kentucky and Virginia
nullification resolutions

Death of Washington (1799)

Capital moved from Philadelphia
to Washington, D.C. (1800)

Federalist party split

Adams defeated for re-election

John Marshall made Chief Justice
of Supreme Court (1801)

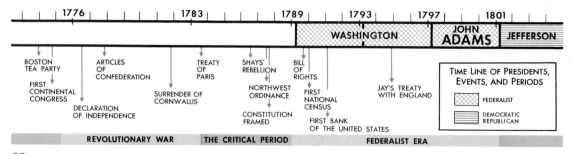

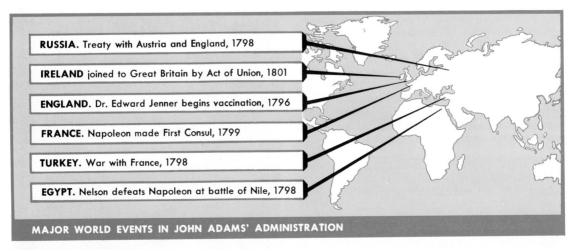

only 20, but she had schooled herself well in politics and literature (*see* White House, sections "Hostesses of the White House" and "Children in the White House"). They had four children: Abigail, John Quincy, Charles, and Thomas (*see* Adams, John Quincy).

Revolutionary War Service

Adams' first political post came when he was appointed one of the town attorneys to argue the legality of the Stamp Act (*see* Stamp Act). He also defended a British officer and seven enlisted men who fired on a rioting Boston mob. Five Bostonians were killed in the fracas, soon known as the Boston Mas-

sacre. Adams secured the outright acquittal of six men. The other two, convicted of manslaughter, were branded on the thumbs and released. Despite the unpopularity of the British, Adams was admired for his courage in defending them.

In 1774 Adams was elected a delegate to the Continental Congress. There he met other delegates and learned how they felt about the government of the American Colonies. The next year, at the second meeting, these feelings and beliefs grew into a declaration of war. It was Adams, a Massachusetts man, who nominated George Washington of Virginia as commanding general of the Continental army.

Drafting the Declaration of Independence, in Philadelphia in 1776, are, left to right, Benjamin Franklin, Thomas Jefferson, Robert R. Livingston, John Adams, and Roger Sherman.

John Singleton Copley, famous American artist, painted this portrait of John Adams (right) as American envoy to England. It shows Adams in middle age, serving his new nation with zeal.

In 1777 Adams was made commissioner to France, serving with Benjamin Franklin and Arthur Lee. Soon he was authorized to work out treaties of peace and commerce with Britain. Britain was not ready to make peace, so Adams went to Holland to raise money for America. He was successful. Holland and France were the only countries to recognize the United States as an independent nation before the war's end. After peace with England finally came, Adams was appointed minister to the Court of St. James's.

Vice-President and President

Adams returned to be elected vice-president under George Washington. In 1792 Washington and Adams were reelected.

Political parties arose under Washington. Adams and Alexander Hamilton became leaders of the Federalist party (*see* Hamilton, Alexander). They were opposed to Thomas Jefferson and his Democratic-Republican party (*see* Jefferson). In 1797 Adams became president, with Jefferson as vice-president.

Despite Adams' great ability and patriotism, he was never popular. He was often vain and blunt. He was charged with wanting to confine power to "the rich, the well-born, and the able." He did not get along well with Hamilton, and as a result the party was hopelessly split. There was increasing friction between Adams and France. The four years of Adams' presidency made up a stormy period in American history.

In 1798 the country supported Adams as he defied the French. Their demands for bribes led the American envoy to declare "Millions for defense, but not one cent for tribute" (*see* 'XYZ' Affair).

Peace with France was made in 1800, but taxation to support the war had brought complications. In Pennsylvania John Fries had led a rebellion against taxes. He and others were convicted of treason. The Federalists cried for their execution, but Adams pardoned them. The Federalists also pressed the tyrannical Alien and Sedition laws over Adams' objections

Bettmann Archive

This portrait of John Adams in retirement was painted by Samuel F. B. Morse, later to win fame for his telegraph invention but then well known as a portrait painter.

(*see* Alien and Sedition Acts). The Virginia and Kentucky legislatures passed resolutions asking other states to join in declaring the laws illegal.

In the election of 1800 Jefferson received 73 electoral votes to Adams' 65. Adams renewed his friendship with Jefferson, and they wrote to each other often. Adams died July 4, 1826, on the 50th anniversary of American independence. Jefferson died the same day, a few hours earlier. Adams, not knowing this, murmured as he died, "Thomas Jefferson still lives."

BIBLIOGRAPHY FOR JOHN ADAMS

Brown, R. A. The Presidency of John Adams (Regents, 1975).
Butterfield, L. H. and others, eds. The Book of Abigail and John: Selected Letters of the Adams Family, 1762–1784 (Harvard Univ. Press, 1975).
Fredman, L. E. and Kurland, Gerald. John Adams, American Revolutionary Leader and President (SamHar, 1973).
Smith, Page. John Adams, 2 vols. (Doubleday, 1962).
Stone, Irving. Those Who Love (Doubleday, 1965).

John Adams was born in 1735 in Braintree (now Quincy), Mass., in the house at the left. His son John Quincy Adams was born in 1767 in the house at the right.

Brown Brothers

JOHN QUINCY ADAMS—
6th President of
the United States

ADAMS, John Quincy (1767–1848; president 1825–1829). Son of the second president of the United States, John Quincy Adams was the sixth president. His whole adult life was devoted to his country's service. Diplomat, senator, president—these posts were only steps on the road to greatness. His best years in public office came after his presidency, when he was elected to the House of Representatives. He served for 17 years, above party politics and concerned only for his country's good.

Until after his presidency, Adams was always respected, sometimes admired, but rarely liked. Then public attitude toward him slowly changed. People around him and finally the whole nation began to see the honesty and devotion beneath his crusty surface. As elder statesman he received the affection that was never his before.

Boyhood in Politics

John Quincy Adams was born July 11, 1767, in Braintree (now Quincy), Mass. He was the second of four children—a girl and three boys. From infancy, young John saw history being made. Often he was taken to Boston Common to see the hated British soldiers parade. He heard his father tell about the Boston Massacre and the Boston Tea Party just after they happened. During the Revolution he saw the fires of Charlestown and heard the noise of Bunker Hill.

In 1778 John Quincy went with his diplomat father to France and later to Holland. When he was 14 he accompanied Francis Dana, commissioner to Russia, to the St. Petersburg court. He served as secretary and French interpreter. After a 14-month stay he traveled alone in Europe.

In 1785 John Adams was appointed minister to Great Britain. John Quincy went home alone to attend Harvard College. His college days were busy and happy. He debated often, saw much of his friends,

and practiced on his flute. He was graduated at 20.

Clearly, the lifework for Adams was law. He entered the office of Theophilus Parsons (later chief justice of Massachusetts), studied for three years, and was admitted to the bar. Clients were few at first, so he occupied his time by writing political articles, signing them with such names as Publicola, Marcellus, Columbus, and Barneveld. President Washington read the articles and appointed Adams minister to Holland in 1794. He was then only 27 years old.

Service Abroad and at Home

With his brother Thomas, Adams sailed for Europe. From Holland he reported on conditions during the French occupation. Back in London, he met Louisa Catherine Johnson, daughter of the American consul. She was a high-spirited girl, brilliant and sensitive. They were married July 26, 1797. (*See also* White

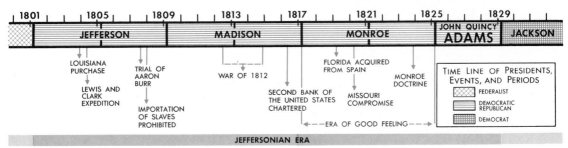

35

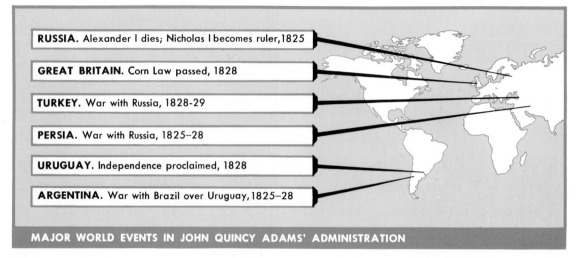

RUSSIA. Alexander I dies; Nicholas I becomes ruler,1825

GREAT BRITAIN. Corn Law passed, 1828

TURKEY. War with Russia, 1828-29

PERSIA. War with Russia, 1825–28

URUGUAY. Independence proclaimed, 1828

ARGENTINA. War with Brazil over Uruguay,1825–28

MAJOR WORLD EVENTS IN JOHN QUINCY ADAMS' ADMINISTRATION

House, section "Hostesses of the White House.")

Adams took his bride to Berlin, where he served as minister to the Prussian court. He worked out a treaty, read much, and traveled with his wife through Germany. Their first child, George Washington Adams, was born in Berlin in 1801. The same year they returned to Boston and Adams' law practice.

Senator and Diplomat

He was soon back in politics, first in the Massachusetts State Senate, then in 1803 in the United States Senate. At once he was drawn into the fight over the government of the newly acquired Louisiana Territory. Adams fought unsuccessfully to give the new land a democratic form of government.

The Federalist party was against him. Its members hated him for supporting the Democratic-Republican action against the British attack on the American frigate *Chesapeake*. Adams also supported Jefferson's embargo policy. Yet he remained independent, neither Federalist nor wholly Democratic-Republican. In 1808 he resigned from the Senate and went home to practice law.

In Washington and Boston society Adams was stiff and ill at ease. He had no skill at small talk. With his family and close friends, however, he was easy and sociable. He liked to read aloud before small groups. Children loved him and he them. During these

---

JOHN QUINCY ADAMS' ADMINISTRATION
1825–1829
Clay appointed secretary of state
Erie Canal completed (1825)
Early efforts toward
Pan American co-operation
Bunker Hill monument erected
Steam railway construction begun
Tariff becomes a burning issue
(1828)
Beginning of Democratic and
Whig parties
Adams defeated for re-election
by rising power of West

---

years his sons John and Charles Francis were born. (*See also* White House, section "Children in the White House".)

In 1809 President Madison appointed him minister to Russia. Adams saw Napoleon invade Russia and followed the news of his disastrous retreat from Moscow. At the close of the War of 1812 he was named to the commission which was to work out a peace with Britain. The commission met with the British at Ghent, Belgium, and in four months hammered out the Treaty of Ghent. The terms were generally favorable to America (*see* War of 1812).

From 1815 to 1817 Adams served as minister to Great Britain. The Adamses lived quietly in a country house in Ealing, in London, and sent their sons to English schools. Adams worked hard to strengthen the peace between Britain and the United States.

President Monroe appointed Adams secretary of state in 1817. His first important task was to defend Andrew Jackson in his supposedly unlawful raid of Spanish-held Florida. He won the administration to his view and quieted Spain and Britain. Next he induced Spain to cede Florida to the United States. He fought for the Missouri Compromise and helped write the Monroe Doctrine (*see* Missouri Compromise; Monroe Doctrine).

Sixth President

In 1824 Adams was one of four candidates for the presidency. The others were Andrew Jackson, W. H. Crawford, and Henry Clay. Jackson received the most electoral votes, but not a plurality. Adams was second. The election was turned over to the House of Representatives, and Adams won. He was accused of bargaining with Clay, and Jackson used the accusation with telling effect in the 1828 campaign.

Quarrels between Jackson's supporters (who later formed the Democratic party) and those of Adams (who became Whigs) were intense. The Democrats blocked every bill started by Adams. The South was beginning to unite against him. He hated slavery, wanted a high tariff, and worked for internal improve-

Three Lions, Inc. Brown Brothers

A house (left), built in 1731 in Quincy, Mass., was the home of generations of Adamses, including John Adams and John Quincy Adams, from 1787 to 1927. It is now a national historical site. Near the end of his career, John Quincy Adams posed for a daguerreotype (right).

ments—all against Southern interests. Few positive measures were enacted in Adams' administration.

In 1828 Jackson's followers set up a tariff bill, called the Tariff of Abominations, intending to defeat it. This would be a way to discredit Adams and help defeat him in the 1828 election. To their astonishment the bill passed and was signed by Adams.

While he was in office Adams lived quietly. He rose about 5:00 A.M. and in summer went for a swim in the Potomac. Then he read his Bible and wrote in his diary. After breakfast he met with his Cabinet. He ate dinner in company, received visitors, and read a good deal. In the late afternoon he walked or rode his horse and played billiards with his sons. In the election of 1828 he lost to Andrew Jackson, who had 178 electoral votes to Adams' 83.

Adams retired—permanently, he thought. His retirement was brief. In 1831 he was elected to the House of Representatives and held his seat until his death in 1848. Asked if he felt lowered by becoming a representative after having been president, he replied, "No person could be degraded by serving the people as a representative. . . . Nor, in my opinion, would an ex-president . . . be degraded by serving as a selectman . . . if elected thereto by the people."

At once Adams was appointed chairman of the Committee on Manufactures. He fought for the tariff against the Southern forces, already drifting toward secession. The Southerners placed a "gag rule" on petitions relating to slavery. Adams fought the gag rule until its repeal in 1844. He stood almost alone against Andrew Jackson's war on the Bank of the United States (see Bank of the United States). In the 27th Congress Adams was made chairman of the House Committee on Foreign Affairs.

Adams won the title of Old Man Eloquent—not for his skill as a speaker but for the vast amount of information in his talks. In old age he made a poor appearance. He was short, fat, and bald; his voice was shrill and disagreeable. Yet his rugged honesty and patriotism were plain for all to see.

In 1847 Adams suffered a stroke in Boston and a second one a year later in the House of Representatives in Washington. He died Feb. 23, 1848.

Bibliography for John Quincy Adams

Armbruster, Maxim The Presidents of the United States and Their Administrations from Washington to the Present, rev. ed. (Horizon, 1981).

Beard, C. A. The Presidents in American History, 10th rev. ed. (Messner, 1977).

Hecht, M. B. John Quincy Adams (Macmillan, 1972) o.p.

Morse, J. T., Jr. John Quincy Adams (Chelsea House, 1981).

Shepherd, Jack. Cannibals of the Heart: a Personal Biography of Louisa Catherine and John Quincy Adams (McGraw, 1981).

ADAMS, Samuel (1722–1803). One of the firebrands of the American Revolution was Sam Adams. He helped to start it and helped to keep it going—by speeches, newspaper articles, and behind-the-scene maneuvers. He combined great ideals with shrewd politics, and he worked hard to help America change from a British colony into an independent nation.

Samuel Adams was born Sept. 27, 1722, in Boston, Mass. His father was a well-to-do brewer and active in politics himself. Samuel was one of 12 children. The boy attended Boston Grammar School, and in 1736 he entered Harvard College. He was graduated in 1740. Three years later he went back and studied for a Master of Arts degree. He was already thinking of revolution, for he chose as his thesis subject: "Whether it be lawful to resist the Supreme Magistrate, if the Commonwealth cannot otherwise be preserved."

Adams had little inclination for the brewery business he inherited from his father and ran into debt. His first wife died, leaving two children. His second

A portrait of Samuel Adams was painted about 1770 or 1772 by the American artist John Singleton Copley.

wife practiced strict economy and gratefully accepted food and clothing from her neighbors. Adams devoted himself to public affairs. As a member of the Caucus, a political group that met in an attic, he learned the arts of the politician.

Adams' influence was due largely to his skill as a writer and to his passionate faith in the cause he served. In 1764 he was chosen to write Boston's protest against England's proposed Stamp Act. In 1765 he was elected to the Massachusetts colonial assembly and became the leader of opposition to the British government. In local politics he was called "the man of the town meeting." He brought about the creation in Boston in 1772 of a "committee of correspondence" to rouse public opinion. Other New England towns followed Boston's lead. Adams' famous "circular letter" appealed to all the colonies to join in action against the crown. In 1773 Adams presided over the mass meeting that gave the signal for the Boston Tea Party. (*See also* Revolution, American.)

As a delegate to the First and the Second Continental Congress, Adams fought for colonial independence. For his first trip to Philadelphia, one friend gave him money and another outfitted him with clothes. About this time his friends also built him a new barn and repaired his house.

Adams signed the Declaration of Independence and, in 1788, secured the ratification of the Constitution by Massachusetts, although he was at first opposed to the document. In 1794 he was elected governor of his state. He died Oct. 2, 1803.

Samuel Adams was related to the prominent Adams family (*see* Adams Family). His grandfather was a brother of the grandfather of John Adams, second president of the United States.

ADAMS FAMILY. "The achievements of the individual Adamses are dazzling in their brilliance, gripping in their drama," wrote American historian Daniel J. Boorstin. Through four generations the Adams family made important contributions to United States history and culture. John Adams (1735–1826) became the second president of the United States (*see* Adams, John). John Adams' wife, Abigail Smith Adams (1744–1818), became known for her public spirit and her distinguished letters. John Adams' son, John Quincy Adams (1767–1848), a diplomat and legislator, served as the sixth president of the United States (*see* Adams, John Quincy).

The remainder of the Adams family history is largely a chronicle of the lives of Charles Francis Adams, a son of John Quincy, and his four brilliant sons: John Quincy Adams II, Charles Francis Adams, Jr., Henry Adams, and Brooks Adams. All four sons attended Harvard College.

Charles Francis Adams (1807–1886). The last member of the Adams family to hold an elective office in the national government, Charles Francis was elected to Congress in 1858 and 1860. He became more famous for his work as United States minister in London during the American Civil War. Partly because of his efforts, Britain did not recognize the Confederacy as an independent nation.

Charles Francis Adams was born on Aug. 18, 1807, in Boston. A lawyer, he took up politics and journalism and served in the Massachusetts state legislature (1840–45). He edited most of his father's diary, 'Memoirs of John Quincy Adams' (12 vols., 1874–77). He died in Boston on Nov. 21, 1886.

John Quincy Adams II (1833–1894). Also a lawyer, John Quincy II was more interested in politics than the law. He represented the town of Quincy, Mass., in the state legislature (1867–71), twice running unsuccessfully for the office of governor (1867 and 1871). After the American Civil War he changed political parties, becoming a Democrat.

John Quincy Adams II was born in Boston on Sept. 22, 1833. He died on Aug. 14, 1894.

Charles Francis Adams, Jr. (1835–1915). Against his father's wishes, Charles Francis, Jr., fought in the American Civil War. He became known as an economist, historian, journalist, and railroad authority. His book 'Chapters of the Erie and Other Essays' (1871), written with his brother Henry, exposed railroad industry abuses and influenced later federal railroad legislation. From 1878 to 1890 he served as president of the Union Pacific Railroad.

Charles Francis Adams, Jr., was born in Boston on May 27, 1835. His other writings included 'The Life of Richard Henry Dana' (1890), 'Emancipation of the Voter' (1894), and his 'Autobiography' (1916). He died in Washington, D.C., on March 20, 1915.

Henry Adams (1838–1918). The third son of Charles Francis Adams was a journalist and a leading American historian (*see* Adams, Henry).

Brooks Adams (1848–1927). Educated for the law, Brooks preferred to study, travel, and write. A be-

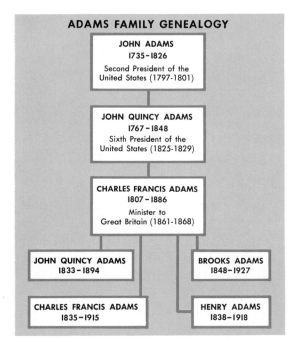

ADAMS FAMILY GENEALOGY

JOHN ADAMS
1735-1826
Second President of the
United States (1797-1801)

JOHN QUINCY ADAMS
1767-1848
Sixth President of the
United States (1825-1829)

CHARLES FRANCIS ADAMS
1807-1886
Minister to
Great Britain (1861-1868)

JOHN QUINCY ADAMS
1833-1894

BROOKS ADAMS
1848-1927

CHARLES FRANCIS ADAMS
1835-1915

HENRY ADAMS
1838-1918

liever in evolution (*see* Evolution), the theory of biological change from simple to complex life forms, Brooks developed theories that occupied him most of his life: that history moves in cycles, that all nations move through patterned stages, and that history is a science. He published his first book, 'The Emancipation of Massachusetts', in 1887.

Brooks Adams was born in Quincy on June 24, 1848. He went to England with his parents in 1861 and studied in English schools. He wrote a pamphlet, 'The Gold Standard' (1894). His best known book, 'The Law of Civilization and Decay' (1895), is a summary of Adams' view that all nations must eventually decay and die. Brooks Adams died in Boston on Feb. 13, 1927.

ADAPTATION. Certain animals and plants develop characteristics that help them cope better than others of their species with their environment. This natural biological process is called adaptation. Among the superior traits developed through adaptation are those that may help in obtaining food or shelter, in providing protection, and in producing and protecting offspring. The better adapted organisms then tend to thrive, reproduce, and pass their heritable variations along to their progeny better than do those without the superior characteristics. This is called natural selection. It results in the evolution of more and more organisms that are better fitted to their environments.

Each living thing is adapted to its mode of life in a general way, but each is adapted especially to its own distinct niche. A plant, for example, depends upon its roots to anchor itself and to absorb water and inorganic chemicals. It depends upon its green leaves for photosynthesis, the process of using the sun's energy

to manufacture food from inorganic chemicals. These are general adaptations, common to most plants. In addition, there are special adaptations that only certain species of plants possess. The mistletoe, for example, is a parasitic plant; it lacks true roots but lives with its rootlike haustoria buried in the branches of a tree. It depends upon the tree to anchor itself and to absorb water and inorganic chemicals. In order to survive, the mistletoe must establish its parasitic relationship with a suitable tree. The mistletoe is also dependent upon an insect to pollinate its flowers, and a bird to disseminate its seeds by eating the berries and depositing its droppings containing the seeds onto the branches of appropriate trees.

Many animals have adaptations that help them elude their predators. Some insects are camouflaged by their body color or shape, and many resemble a leaf or a twig. The coats of deer are colored to blend with the surroundings. Their behavior, too, is adaptive: they have the ability to remain absolutely still when an enemy is near. These adaptations arose from the natural selection of heritable variations.

Organisms have a great variety of ways of adapting. They may adapt in their structure, function, and genetics; in their locomotion or dispersal for defense and attack; in their reproduction and development; and in other respects. Favorable adaptations may involve migration for survival under certain conditions of temperature, for example. An organism may create its own environment, as do warm-blooded mammals, which have the ability to adjust body heat precisely to maintain their ideal temperature despite changing weather. Adaptations to temporary situations may be reversible, as when humans become suntanned during the summer or in tropical climates.

Usually adaptations are an advantage, but sometimes an organism is so well adapted to a particular environment that, if conditions change, it finds it difficult or impossible to readapt to the new conditions. The huia bird of New Zealand, for example, depended upon a close collaboration between male and female: the male chiseled holes in decaying wood with its stout beak, and the female reached in with her long, slender beak to capture grubs. When New Zealand was deforested, these birds could no longer feed in their accustomed way and soon became extinct.

A fawn gains protection against predators from its ability to remain still and from its dappled coat that blends into the background.
Leonard Lee Rue III

ADDAMS, Jane (1860–1935). An early concern for the living conditions of 19th-century factory workers led Jane Addams to pioneer in social work. She brought cultural and day-care programs to the poor, sought justice for immigrants and blacks, championed labor reform, supported women's suffrage, and helped train other social workers.

Jane Addams was born Sept. 6, 1860, in Cedarville, Ill. Her father, John Huy Addams, was a wealthy miller, a state senator, and a friend of Abraham Lincoln. Jane was the youngest of five children. From infancy she suffered from a slight spinal curvature. After graduation from Rockford Seminary (now Rockford College) in Illinois, her health failed, and for two years she was an invalid.

In 1883 she went abroad to travel and study. The hunger and misery she found in the great European cities impressed her more than their famous museums or historic relics. A childhood resolve to live among the poor was confirmed by a stay at Toynbee Hall in London, the first social settlement in the world (*see* Social Settlements).

In the fall of 1889 she settled with a school friend, Ellen Gates Starr, in a shabby old mansion on the near West Side of Chicago among tenements and sweatshops. Their neighbors—people of a dozen races—called the place "the old Hull house" after its builder, Charles Hull. So Hull House was adopted as the name for what was to become the most famous social settlement in the United States.

At first the neighbors were suspicious and unfriendly, but they soon saw that Addams' friendliness was sincere and practical. A kindergarten and a day nursery were started. Wealthy people, university professors, students, and business executives contributed time and money to Hull House.

Hull House fed the hungry, nursed the sick, and guided the bewildered immigrant and the wayward child. Addams became a garbage inspector so she could get the filthy streets cleaned up. She campaigned against the sweatshops and corrupt politicians. She and her associates at Hull House helped pass the first factory legislation in Illinois and establish in Chicago the world's first Juvenile Court.

Addams became one of the most deeply loved and famous Americans of her time. Universities honored her with degrees. Visitors from all over the world came to see her at Hull House. Crowds in many countries heard her talk simply about her work.

During World War I Addams faced bitter criticism when she urged that the issues that led to war be settled by negotiation rather than by bloodshed. After the war she continued to spread her ideals as president of the Women's International League for Peace and Freedom. In 1931 she was awarded the Nobel Peace prize jointly with Dr. Nicholas Murray Butler.

For 46 years Addams managed the settlement. At the time of her death it had expanded to cover a city block, with buildings centered around a courtyard. Starr had been forced by ill health to retire six years before Addams' death.

Wide World

In spite of illness and advancing age, Jane Addams continued to work at her Hull House settlement for 46 years. She never lost her love of helping immigrants, working people, and especially children.

In 1961 plans were laid to tear down Hull House to make room for a Chicago campus of the University of Illinois. Despite worldwide protests the properties were sold in 1963. The original building, however, was preserved as a memorial to Jane Addams. Hull House settlement work has continued in new locations in Chicago.

Addams' best known writings are 'Democracy and Social Ethics' (1902); 'Newer Ideals of Peace' (1907); 'The Spirit of Youth and the City Streets' (1909); 'Twenty Years at Hull-House' (1910); 'A New Conscience and an Ancient Evil' (1911); 'The Second Twenty Years at Hull-House' (1930).

ADDIS ABABA, Ethiopia. The highest city in Africa, Addis Ababa is located 8,000 feet (2,438 meters) above sea level. It is the capital and economic center of Ethiopia. The city lies on a well-watered plateau at the country's geographical center and has grown haphazardly among more than 90 square miles (230 square kilometers) of forested hills and valleys. Modern Addis Ababa stands out in contrast to a largely poor and underdeveloped country.

The city was founded in 1887 by the empress Taita and her husband Emperor Menelik II. As the population increased, the city experienced shortages of the firewood that was necessary for survival in the cool mountain climate. As a remedy, the city imported several varieties of fast-growing eucalyptus trees from Australia in 1905. The trees spread, creating a forest cover throughout the city.

In 1917 a railway was built between Addis Ababa

and Djibouti to connect the isolated inland city to the Indian Ocean. As the capital of Italian East Africa from 1935 to 1941, Addis Ababa had some of the features of a modern town, but rapid development did not really begin until the 1960's, when the number of housing units in the city doubled. New construction included high-rise office and apartment buildings, luxury villas, and low-cost housing projects.

Although Addis Ababa is the hub of Ethiopia's transportation system, only the major roads are paved, and these are mostly in commercial areas. Most residential areas have only bumpy cobblestone streets or muddy dirt paths. Only main roads have official names, and there are no addresses because of the twisted street patterns. Vehicles move slowly because they are impeded by heavy pedestrian and domestic-animal traffic.

Addis Ababa is Ethiopia's main distribution center for agricultural and consumer goods. Products manufactured in the city for the local market include textiles, shoes, food, beverages, wood products, plastics, and chemical products. Most of Ethiopia's export and import trade goes through Addis Ababa on its way to or from the ports of Djibouti and Aseb.

Ethiopia's government ministries are located in Addis Ababa, as are the houses of parliament and the headquarters of international organizations. Nearby are the city's showplaces—the imperial palaces and the imperial dens, where dozens of lions live.

Elementary and secondary schools in the city are mostly government-operated. However there are also many private, mission, and Eastern Orthodox church schools. Addis Ababa University, formerly Haile Selassie I University, was established in 1961. The city has a government-owned radio station and television station. The latter has broadcasts both in Amharic, the official language, and in English. The Ministry of Information publishes two daily newspapers—one Amharic, one English. Addis Ababa's most popular spectator sport is soccer. Major matches are played at Haile Selassie I Stadium. (*See also* Ethiopia.) Population (1980 estimate), 1,277,159.

ADDISON, Joseph (1672–1719). Among the famous London coffeehouses that sprang up in the early 18th century, "Button's" holds a high place in the history of English literature. It was a favorite meeting place for the poet and essayist Joseph Addison and four or five companions who enjoyed leisurely discussions.

Addison, the leading spirit of this group, was a gentleman of culture. Except for his last few years, which were marked by literary and political quarrels, his life was tranquil and pleasant. He was born at Milston, Wiltshire, where his father was rector. He spent a studious youth and entered Oxford University. There he became known for the charm of his verse. After touring Europe, he entered politics as a Whig. The publication of his poem 'The Campaign', celebrating the victory at Blenheim, won him much popular and political favor. From then on Addison held many offices, the most important being that of

secretary of state for Ireland in 1717, a difficult job that he kept for only one year.

It is not, however, for his statesmanship or for his poetry or for his tragedy 'Cato', so famous in their day, that Addison is mainly remembered. It was rather in his essays that he reached his highest powers.

A school friend of Addison's, Sir Richard Steele, sensed that the growing sociability of the times, as shown by the popularity of the coffeehouses, had prepared the way for a paper that would discuss news, politics, and society. So in 1709 he inaugurated such a journal, *The Tatler*. Addison soon became a contributor. After *The Tatler* was discontinued in 1711, he and Steele started another paper, *The Spectator*. This combination of editors was ideal. Steele, an Irishman, was brilliant, impulsive, and had many ideas. Addison was of a calmer temperament and could develop gracefully the ideas and characters suggested by Steele. *The Spectator* contained no news, but only light, often gently satirical essays. Imaginary members of the Spectator Club discussed all kinds of subjects, from training young ladies in the use of fans to the appreciation of Milton. The leading member of the club was the courteous, well-loved Sir Roger de Coverley, a cultured country gentleman.

Addison's style has always been greatly praised. Samuel Johnson wrote: "Whoever wishes to attain an English style, familiar but not coarse, and elegant but not ostentatious, must give his days and nights to the study of Addison."

ADELAIDE, Australia. The capital of the state of South Australia and the fourth largest city in Australia is Adelaide. It had the first municipal government on the continent, in 1840.

A city since 1919, Adelaide is in the southeastern part of Australia, near the middle of the eastern side of the Gulf St. Vincent. The city lies on a coastal lowland with the Mount Lofty Ranges to the east. Adelaide is bounded on all sides by parklands that separate it from its surrounding suburbs.

Adelaide was designed by the first South Australian surveyor general, Col. William Light, shortly after the colony was founded in 1836. It was named for Queen Adelaide, the wife of King William IV.

The city is laid out in two square sections, north and south, separated by the Torrens River. The southern half of Adelaide has become its principal business center. The northern section is residential.

The Torrens River, dammed and made into a lake, adds to the charm of the city. The main thoroughfare, King William Street, runs north and south, intersecting Victoria Square.

There are many fine buildings in Adelaide, including the Anglican Cathedral of St. Peter, the Roman Catholic Cathedral of St. Francis Xavier, government buildings, and the State War Memorial, dedi-

Australian Information Service

Adelaide City Bridge and the spires of St. Peter's Anglican Cathedral are seen in this view from Elder Park on the banks of the River Torrens.

cated to South Australians who died in World War I. South Australia's Houses of Parliament are built of locally hewn granite and marble.

The University of Adelaide (founded 1874) and the South Australian Museum are other points of interest. Adelaide College of the Arts and Education was established in 1979. The Adelaide Festival of Arts, introduced in 1960, was the first international celebration of its kind to be held in Australia. The Adelaide Festival Centre, completed in 1980, is a multipurpose performing arts complex.

The fertility of the surrounding plains, easy access to the Murray lowlands to the east and southeast, and the presence of mineral deposits in the nearby hills all contributed to the city's growth. Its factories produce automobile parts, machinery, textiles, and chemicals. A center for rail, sea, air, and road transportation, it also has harbor facilities at Port Adelaide, 7 miles (11 kilometers) northwest.

The climate is pleasant. Winters are short, wet, and cool; summers are long, dry, and hot. Freezing temperatures seldom occur in Adelaide. The average annual rainfall is 21 inches (530 millimeters). (See also Australia.) Population, including suburbs (1979 estimate), 933,300.

ADEN, People's Democratic Republic of Yemen. The port of Aden lies on the southern tip of the Arabian Peninsula on the Gulf of Aden, overlooking the southern entrance to the Red Sea and the Suez Canal. Aden is the national capital of the People's Democratic  Republic of Yemen (formerly the People's Republic of Southern Yemen). It was the capital of the state of Aden until Southern Yemen, formed in 1967, absorbed the state.

Aden is one of the hottest places on earth. It lies in the center of an extinct volcano on one of the two small peninsulas that enclose Aden Bay, its harbor.

Aden was a British naval base for 128 years. It was occupied by the British in 1839 to safeguard their Red Sea trade route to India from pirates. In 1937 the city and the surrounding British-held territory became a British crown colony. After the Suez crisis of 1956, it became Britain's chief Middle Eastern military base (see Suez Canal). Aden became partially self-governing in 1962 and was incorporated in the Federation of South Arabia, a group of about 20 tribal districts under British sovereignty, in 1963. As independence for the federation approached, two rival nationalist groups struggled for control of Aden. After British forces withdrew, Aden became part of the independent republic in late 1967. It was made the national capital in 1968.

The contemporary city has three sections—the old commercial quarter, the business section, and the harbor area. Its economy is based almost entirely on its position as a commercial center for nearby states of the Arabian peninsula and as a refueling stop for ships. It was a free port until 1970.

In 1953 an oil refinery was built at Little Aden, on the western side of the bay. The city has some small industries, including light manufacturing, evaporation of seawater to obtain marine salt, and boatbuilding. There is an international airport nearby.(See also Yemen, People's Democratic Republic of.) Population (1980 estimate), 343,000.

ADENAUER, Konrad (1876–1967). After World War II Germany lay in ruins. To Konrad Adenauer belongs much of the credit for raising West Germany to a position of economic prosperity and making it a respected free-world ally.

Konrad Adenauer was born on Jan. 5, 1876, in Cologne, Germany. He was one of four children. His father, Konrad, was a law clerk. The Adenauers were a pious Roman Catholic family. Young Konrad attended St. Aposteln Gymnasium in Cologne and the universities of Freiburg, Munich, and Bonn. He was graduated with a law degree. Married twice, he had four sons and three daughters.

Adenauer was elected deputy mayor of Cologne in 1906, senior deputy mayor in 1911, and lord high mayor in 1917, a post he held for 16 years. From 1917 to 1933 he was also a member of the provincial diet and a representative in the Prussian State Council, of which he became president in 1928.

When the Nazis came to power in 1933, Adenauer was stripped of all his political positions. He was imprisoned in 1934 and again in 1944. After the war he helped organize a new party, the Christian Democratic Union. In 1948 he became president of the parliamentary council to draft a constitution for West Germany. In 1949 he became West Germany's first chancellor. In 1961 he was reelected to his fourth consecutive term. He retired as chancellor in October 1963. He died near Bonn on April 19, 1967.

ADHESIVE

ADHESIVE. Any substance that is able to hold two materials together by its natural adhesion is an adhesive. Glue, mucilage, paste, cement, and epoxy are all forms of adhesive. Some adhesives occur in nature or are made easily from plant or animal materials. Others are made from synthetic materials. Adhesives can provide fastening in some cases where mechanical fasteners, such as nails, staples, or clamps might work poorly or not at all. The great variety of adhesives have a wide range of uses, from holding stamps on envelopes to holding heat-dissipating tiles to the exterior of a space shuttle.

Nature of Adhesives

Adhesives hold materials together by flowing into every nook and crevice, however small, of the materials' surfaces. The surfaces must be clean to allow the adhesive to "wet" each surface properly. Most adhesives are liquid or at least tacky. A few adhesives are powders or solids, and these depend on heat and pressure to liquify and flow. An adhesive creates a close bond between the surface molecules of the materials it holds together. The closer the two surfaces fit together, the stronger the bond, so a thin adhesive bond is stronger than a thick one.

One advantage of adhesives is that they easily bond particles, fibers, and films that would be difficult or impossible to bond by any other means. Examples of these are the abrasives on sandpaper; the glass, nylon, and polyester fibers in many automobile tires; the particles of wood in particle board; and the coatings on certain types of paper, such as those used in glossy magazines.

Another advantage of adhesives is that they distribute structural stresses more widely, allowing stronger, lighter construction than is otherwise possible. For example, if a sheet of paper is tacked to a wall, pulling on the paper places stress only where the tacks go through it, and the paper tears easily. If the sheet is glued to the wall, pulling on it places stress over the entire glued area, and the paper is harder to remove. This principle is applied in making aircraft and other industrial products.

Most adhesives provide a barrier to moisture, keeping it out when used in construction, such as housing, and keeping it in when used for food packaging, such as milk cartons. In addition, adhesives are often considerably faster and cheaper to use than are mechanical fasteners.

Adhesives also have shortcomings. Adhesive bonds cannot be easily tested without weakening or destroying them. Adhesive bonds also cannot be easily disassembled. Surfaces must be carefully prepared to ensure adhesion. Some adhesives require long periods of heat and pressure to set.

Types and Uses

The two main types of adhesives are natural and synthetic. Natural adhesives come from a variety of animal and vegetable sources. Synthetic adhesives are compounded from simple chemicals.

A major type of natural adhesive is animal glue. The animal glues are made from collagen, a protein found in skin, bone, and sinew. Since ancient times animal glue has been used in woodworking and now it is also used in making books, sandpaper, and certain gummed tapes. Today it is often supplemented with, or replaced by, synthetic glues. Casein glue, made from milk, is from an animal source but it is not a true animal glue. It is more moisture resistant, however, than is true animal glue.

Vegetable glues are made from starches and dextrins extracted from corn, potatoes, rice, or wheat. These glues are used mostly in paper products, primarily because they are inexpensive and have little strength or moisture resistance. Although natural gums and resins also come from vegetable sources, they are not considered vegetable glues. They form a separate group of adhesives that are widely used in the building industry and in rubber cements for bonding paper, leather, and rubber. Many of these types of adhesive are now mixed with synthetic rubber compounds or even replaced entirely by them. Both natural and synthetic rubber are used as adhesives in pressure-sensitive tapes, such as masking and cellophane tapes.

Synthetic adhesives fall into two distinct groups: thermoplastic adhesives and thermosetting adhesives. The thermoplastic adhesives can be softened any number of times by heating. Upon cooling, they once again adhere. The thermosetting adhesives undergo an irreversible chemical change when they harden. After setting, these adhesives retain their strength and do not soften when heated.

The most widely used thermoplastics are the vinyl resin adhesives. Certain vinyls have replaced most of the natural adhesives in woodworking uses because the synthetics are more resistant to moisture and harden faster. Polyvinyl acetate, for example, is commonly used in household white glue. Other thermoplastics include cellulose derivatives, which are used in wood and paper manufacture, and acrylics, the most transparent of synthetic adhesives.

Among the major types of thermosetting adhesives are the epoxies, which are used widely by themselves and also mixed with other adhesives. Epoxies are usually hardened by adding a catalyst. The adhesive then undergoes a chemical reaction, hardening with little or no contraction. Some epoxies need heat to complete hardening, but unlike thermoplastics, reheating will not soften the epoxy. Epoxies are widely used in aircraft and electronics because of their strength and electrical insulation properties. They are also used as coatings and as laminates in manufacturing plastic pipes and tanks.

Also included among the thermosetting adhesives are the polyester adhesives, which are used in fiber glass structures such as some automobile bodies, boats, luggage, and structural panels. Thermosetting phenolic adhesives can be used as liquids that harden when their solvent evaporates, or as solid sheets that bond under pressure and heat. Phenolics are hard and

A technician fits gap spacers between tiles held by adhesive to the space shuttle Columbia's nose landing-gear door.

rapid drying and provide good adhesion for wood and other porous materials. They are commonly used in plywood manufacture.

Urea adhesives—thermosetting adhesives made by combining urea and formaldehyde—are also used to make plywood and in other woodworking, but do not work well on metal and glass. Although urea-formaldehyde has been banned in home insulation, its use is not considered dangerous in adhesives. The polyurethane adhesives adhere well to all materials, porous and nonporous. They are used in bonding fabrics, foams, and rubberlike materials. There are other synthetic, thermosetting adhesive groups including such varieties as the melamines, the resorcinols, the silicones, and the polyimides.

History

Natural adhesives have been in use since ancient times, particularly animal glue, casein glue, and adhesives made from plant resins. Beeswax and pitch were used as adhesives for centuries. Some 3,300 years ago, the ancient Egyptians used animal glue to build furniture, covering it with fine ornamental wood veneers, ivory, and ebony. Such furniture has been found in ancient tombs, the glue still holding after all of that time. The Egyptians also used adhesives for other purposes. Papyrus, which was used before paper was invented, was made with a flour paste. Eggs, gum arabic, and other plant resins were used as binders for paints. In the Middle Ages, egg white was used to glue gold leaf to parchment for illuminated manuscripts.

The adhesives known to the ancients were largely unchanged by later craftsmen until the 19th century, when rubber cements and pyroxylin cements (made from nitrocellulose) were introduced. The development of synthetic adhesives in the 20th century resulted in a wide variety of new types and kinds of adhesives, made for almost every purpose.

44

ADIRONDACK MOUNTAINS. The Adirondack wilderness in northeastern New York State is one of the great playgrounds of the United States. It is a region of wild beauty, covering about 5,000 square miles (12,950 square kilometers). Rugged mountain scenery, good hunting and fishing, and skiing and other winter sports bring hundreds of thousands of visitors each year to the Adirondack Forest Preserve, more than 2 million acres (800,000 hectares) in area.

Although they are sometimes considered part of the Appalachian chain, the Adirondack Mountains belong geologically to the Laurentian Plateau (Canadian Shield) of Canada, from which they are separated by the St. Lawrence River (see Laurentian Plateau). They form the watershed between the St. Lawrence River and the Hudson River.

The peaks of the Adirondacks are scattered singly or in small groups. The highest is Mount Marcy, which is 5,344 feet (1,629 meters) high, and 41 others rise 4,000 feet (1,200 meters) or more. Major rivers in the area are the Grass, Oswegatchie, Raquette, Salmon, Ausable, Hudson, and Sacandaga.

Rounded hillocks, high mountain lakes, and deep valleys reflect the work of ancient glaciers. Swift streams have made narrow, rugged cuts in the bedrock, which is largely crystalline limestone and granite. The area has deposits of iron and graphite.

Fine highways make all parts of the region accessible. One road leads to the top of Whiteface Mountain (4,867 feet; 1,483 meters). This peak stands at the head of Lake Placid, the site of a famous winter resort. Lake Placid was also the site of the 13th Winter Olympic Games in February 1980.

The Adirondack area is heavily forested and abounds in wildlife. This fact, combined with the pleasant summer climate and heavy winter snows, has contributed to the Adirondacks' popularity with tourists. (See also New York.)

Whiteface Mountain rises beyond the Ausable River, which is one of several rivers in the Adirondack region.

ADLER, Alfred (1870–1937). The founder of individual psychology was an Austrian psychiatrist named Alfred Adler. He developed a flexible and supportive psychotherapy to direct emotionally disabled people with inferiority feelings toward maturity and social usefulness. His theories influenced educators and many other psychologists and psychiatrists.

Alfred Adler was born on Feb. 7, 1870, in a suburb of Vienna. Throughout his life his strong awareness of social problems was a principal motivation in his work. Even as a young physician (M.D., University of Vienna medical school, 1895), he stressed consideration of his patients in relation to their total environment. In 1902 Adler became closely associated with the originator of psychoanalysis, Sigmund Freud, but irreconcilable differences came between them: Adler believed that a person's motives are primarily social, not sexual. In 1911 he broke with Freud and founded his own school and journal.

In 1921 Adler established the first child-guidance clinic in Vienna. Soon, about 30 more of these clinics under his direction were opened. Adler went to the United States in 1926 and became visiting professor at Columbia University in New York City in 1927. Five years later, in 1932, he joined the faculty of the Long Island College of Medicine.

In Adler's view, the striving for perfection or success may become a striving for superiority in order to overcompensate for feelings of inferiority. One's opinion of oneself and of the world influences all one's psychological processes. The individual cannot be considered apart from society. Mankind's social interest is an innate aptitude that must be developed. The individual is unique, and one's personality structure, including a particular goal and ways of striving for it, makes up one's life-style. Although the life-style is more or less outside the person's awareness, all specific drives or emotions are subordinated to it.

Adler believed that life-style is formed in early childhood, important factors being birth order, physical inferiority, and neglect or pampering. Mental health is characterized by social interest, reason, and being able to get outside of oneself. Mental disorder is represented by feelings of inferiority, a self-centered concern for safety, and a desire for superiority or power over others.

Adler saw psychotherapy, in which physician and patient discuss problems as equals, as encouraging sound human relationships and strengthening social interest. Insights into the patient's mistakes in his or her life-style are brought out through the interpretation of early recollections and dreams.

Adler's early writings were largely theoretical. His later works, such as 'Understanding Human Nature' (1927) and 'What Life Should Mean to You' (1931), were, however, directed to the general reader. Two works that describe his views are 'The Individual Psychology of Alfred Adler' (1956) and 'Superiority and Social Interest' (1964).

Adler died on May 28, 1937, in Aberdeen, Scotland, while on a lecture tour. (*See also* Psychiatry.)

ADLER, Mortimer J. (born 1902). As author, teacher, philosopher, educator, editor, and encyclopaedist, Mortimer Jerome Adler has had an important influence on American intellectual life during the 20th century. He has written many books and helped to design several monumental publications, including the 15th Edition of 'Encyclopaedia Britannica', but perhaps his most important contribution has been his unending efforts to reform American education and to revive the spirit of liberal studies in the schools.

Adler was born in New York City on December 27, 1902. As a youth he manifested precocious intellectual powers, devouring the collected works of such philosophers as Plato, Aristotle, William James, and John Dewey at an early age and insisting stubbornly on equal devotion from his teachers to the classic thought and writings of the West. After gaining a Ph.D. from Columbia University in 1928, he moved to the University of Chicago where he taught the philosophy of law from 1930 to 1952 and supported the reforming efforts of President R. M. Hutchins. Adler also began his lifetime of service to Britannica, producing (with Hutchins) the 54-volume 'Great Books of the Western World' (1952) whose famous 'Syntopicon' Adler planned and edited. In 1952 he established the Institute for Philosophical Research, first in San Francisco and later in Chicago, and for it produced a number of philosophical works, including 'The Idea of Freedom' (2 vols., 1958–61), 'The Conditions of Philosophy' (1965), 'The Time of Our Lives' (1970), 'Aristotle for Everybody' (1978), 'How to Think About God' (1980), and 'How to Speak and How to Listen' (1983). His best-selling work, 'How to Read a Book', first appeared in 1940 and was revised with the assistance of Charles Van Doren in 1972. His autobiography, 'Philosopher at Large', was published in 1977.

In 1950 Adler was instrumental in the founding of the Aspen Institute for Humanistic Studies at Aspen, Colo. One aspect of the institute's 'agenda was the Aspen Executive Program, inaugurated in 1951. Based on a reading list devised by Adler, the seminars for business executives proved to be a unique and popular experiment in adult education.

In his later years Adler, at the head of the so-called Paideia Group, produced a series of books and papers

Mortimer J. Adler

on the reform of education in America, most notably 'The Paideia Proposal' (1982). The group's main thesis is that education in a democracy must be excellent not only for some but for all students, and that no less than universal liberal education is required by the democratic ideal and the democratic promise. In practice this ideal will be only partially attained, but if the Paideia Group's proposals are taken seriously, Adler's efforts and zeal are likely to be rewarded by major improvements.

ADMINISTRATIVE LAW. The executive branches of government, from the local to the national level, are empowered to administer laws for the welfare of society. To accomplish this end, agencies, departments, bureaus, and commissions are set up as part of an executive branch. These administrative bodies are created by legislative bodies to carry out a wide variety of functions both on behalf of government and for the public. These functions include the overseeing of education, traffic control, tax collecting, defense, highway and bridge construction, quality control of consumer goods, slum clearance, and public transportation, among others.

Administrative bodies are empowered by legislatures with the authority to do their work. Their power may be allocated in two ways: specific statutory directions that tell an agency exactly how it shall operate, or discretionary authorization that allows an agency to devise its own regulations. In many cases, it is a mixture of the two. The term administrative law has come to mean both the regulations that govern the internal operation of an agency or department and the procedures it may use in the performance of its tasks.

The powers that agencies have are called delegated powers; they do not originate in the constitution of a nation as do the powers of the legislature, courts, and executive branch. Because the powers are delegated, or granted, they must be subject to some check by a higher authority so that agencies do not exercise their power in a way that would be detrimental to the public good. The process by which the activities of agencies are checked and controlled by the courts is called judicial review.

Judicial review inquires into the legal competence of public agencies, the validity of their regulations, and the fairness and adequacy of their procedures. If, for instance, a government department decided to build a new highway through a city, citizens could sue the government to stop the project until all environmental issues had been considered. A court or tribunal would then have the task of deciding the validity of the case.

In the United States the court systems exercise the power of judicial review, and they have far-reaching authority in doing so. In the 20th century much of the adjudication of disputes has also been done by tribunals, federal agencies with a large measure of independence from the executive branch. Among these agencies are the Securities and Exchange Commis-

sion, the Interstate Commerce Commission, the National Labor Relations Board, and the Civil Aeronautics Board.

Other countries have different systems of judicial review. In Great Britain special tribunals ensure that public agencies carry out the intentions of Parliament. In France the courts are forbidden to oversee public agencies; the job is done by a Council of State. The French system has been adopted by other nations, including Belgium, Italy, Portugal, Spain, Greece, Egypt, and Turkey. West Germany has an administrative court system and a Federal Administrative Court that acts as a court of appeals.

In the Soviet Union and other Communist nations there is no clear definition of the powers of public agencies. Each agency is assumed to have unlimited power to run its own affairs, subject to the power of higher agencies or organs of government. There is in the Soviet system an institution called the Procuracy to oversee all administration, but it does not have the power of a court and cannot make binding decisions. The work of the procurators is entirely subject to the authority of the Supreme Soviet, the governing body of the nation.

ADOBE. A Spanish word for sun-dried clay bricks, adobe also refers to structures built from such bricks or to the clay soil from which the bricks are made. The use of adobe dates back thousands of years in several parts of the world, especially in areas with arid or semi-arid climates.

Adobe bricks are usually made by wetting a quantity of suitable soil and allowing it to stand for a day or more in order to soften. Then a small amount of straw, or another fibrous material, is added to the soil. These materials are mixed with a hoe and then trampled upon with bare feet. Then the adobe is poured into simple lumber or sheet metal molds that have four sides and are open at the top and bottom. The bricks are laid out to dry in the sun and are turned from day to day so that they dry evenly. Then they are stacked up under cover until needed. The

Adobe ovens in Taos, New Mexico, are built on a solid cement foundation so they cannot be damaged by groundwater.

Adolescents usually prefer to be with friends rather than family. Sharing music or sports with peers becomes much more enjoyable than engaging in these activities with family members.

© Jean-Claude Lejeune

bricks vary in size—in width and length as well as thickness—depending on their intended use. In the brick-making industry, assembly-line techniques are also used to manufacture adobe bricks.

In dry climates, adobe is an excellent building material. With proper care and construction, adobe structures may last for centuries. Adobe is inexpensive and can be produced in abundance in regions where there is clay soil. The art of building with adobe was undoubtedly brought to Spain from northern Africa and then to the New World by the Spanish. American Indians in the southwestern United States built walls by hand manipulation of the pliable clay into courses, or layers, allowing each course to dry before adding each subsequent layer.

Adobe structures have remarkable insulation properties, allowing their interiors to stay evenly warm in winter and cool in summer. To protect them against heavy or frequent rains, adobe walls are usually built on solid waterproof foundations of stone or concrete. This prevents the action of groundwater from causing any disintegration of the lower layers, which are set in a mortar of the same material. These bricks are finished with a coat of adobe, or sometimes with lime or cement plaster.

ADOLESCENCE. The process of changing from a child into an adult is called adolescence. During the period of change young people mature physically, begin to take responsibility for themselves, and start to deal with the world on their own. For most young people, adolescence is a time in which pleasure and excitement are mixed with confusion and frustration. Adolescence begins at puberty, sometime between the ages of 11 and 14, and continues for approximately six to ten years.

Puberty marks the beginning of adult levels of hormone production. This causes the growth of almost every part of the body, including the sexual and reproductive organs. All cultures acknowledge and celebrate puberty in some way, from the Christian confirmation and Jewish bar mitzvah to a great many rituals of primitive cultures. In societies where all

able people are required to work, the young male or female moves from puberty directly into adulthood, so adolescence as Westerners know it does not exist. In Western culture the "teenager" (a word invented only in the 1950's) runs into problems created by the culture itself. During these years young people are expected to accomplish several goals. They must learn to separate from the family and to stand on their own; they develop a strong sense of identification as a male or female; education is expected to be mostly completed; and a way of making a living must be thought about or found.

Physical Changes

Rapid changes in body size and shape are the most obvious signs of approaching adolescence. These changes begin before puberty and differ for boys and girls and from one person to another. During puberty acne, a skin condition (see Acne), often develops.

Girls begin the "growth spurt" between the ages of 10 and 12, about two years earlier than do boys. By the time they are 14, most girls have reached their adult height. About three fourths of the way through this rapid growth a girl reaches menarche, the first menstrual period, and is soon able to become pregnant. Breasts and body hair begin to grow a year or so before menarche.

The physical development of boys follows a different timetable and can be quite different for each. The growth spurt generally begins at about age $12\frac{1}{2}$ and continues through the 16th year. Body hair and deepening of the voice also occur during these years.

In both sexes the reproductive (sexual) organs gradually reach their adult sizes and functions during the first two thirds of adolescence. These changes are caused by the flow of sex hormones (see Hormones)—estrogens in girls, androgens in boys—and are controlled by the pituitary gland at the base of the brain. Differences in the times and rates of growth and sexual maturity are caused by a combination of inherited tendencies (see Genetics), nutrition, and the environment. Along with increasing sexual maturity comes a growing interest in the opposite sex. Children

47

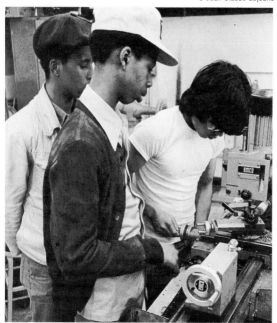

© Jean-Claude Lejeune

Adolescent boys in their high school metal shop class may find it to be one place where they will begin to consider future work possibilities.

frequently are embarrassed and self-conscious if their development timetable is different from those of their friends, but by the end of their adolescence most young people are equally grown and developed.

Emotional Changes

Much of the confusion felt by adolescents is caused by moving into an adult world in which relationships and responsibilities are quite different from those known as a child. The way in which an adolescent handles these changes depends on many things. Family attitudes and the way one's own group feels about issues, such as money and sex, largely determine what is and is not acceptable behavior. During the mid-20th century rapid changes in social attitudes have put teenagers at odds with the older generation in many instances.

A common area of disagreement with the family is how much freedom and responsibility the adolescent should have. Parents often feel that an adolescent is not mature enough to have the freedom he or she insists on taking. Many adolescents resent being treated like children and often respond to discipline with anger and sometimes with defiant behavior. Although the concerns of both the young person and the parents are more or less the same, each has a different way of thinking about them. This difference, and a seeming lack of understanding, is what is often referred to as "the generation gap."

Adolescents usually prefer the company and interests of their own friends to those of their family. Activities, such as music and sports, with friends are far more enjoyable than those with their family most

of the time. While most parents understand this, it is difficult for them to be shut out of the lives of those whom they still think of as their children. This lack of balance works itself out over the years, and new relationships between the generations develop.

That it is difficult for many young people to deal with the confusion of these years is seen in the increased use of alcohol, marijuana, or other consciousness-changing substances. Seeming to offer a way to escape for a few hours, the use of drugs can create more problems than it solves. A major cause of death among teenagers is automobile accidents that are largely the result of driving while intoxicated. (For other consequences of heavy drinking, see Alcoholism.) The use of drugs other than alcohol may also have damaging effects on the body and cause additional emotional problems. Family and social problems resulting from the use of drugs can be serious. All drugs used for social purposes have a potential to cause physical and emotional dependence.

Attitudes

An adolescent has a great deal to think about. This is the time of seeing other people in an objective way, of weighing oneself against others. Popularity in the social group, accomplishments or failures in school, how one looks compared to others of the same age— all these can cause anxiety. There is social and family pressure to plan for further education and to decide on the work area that one will enter, and the adolescent is seldom clear about what he or she wants to do. What some adolescents would most like to do— "hang out" and entertain themselves with friends— is not always acceptable to their parents. As one reaches the last years of high school, however, the adult view of planning and working for the future gradually becomes more sensible to the adolescent.

Sexuality is another area that can be confusing to the adolescent. Many young people are unsure of their attractiveness and worry about how to manage their strong feelings of sexuality. The wide differences in development between boys and girls often mean classrooms roughly divided between well developed young women and less mature boys. Concerns about birth control and venereal disease (see Birth Control; Venereal Disease) may be a problem for some adolescents.

Many adolescents become somewhat disillusioned about adult institutions such as religion, politics, the school system, and family relationships. What they have been taught to regard as honest and good is seen to be far less straightforward than they had thought. Gradually, as the adolescent matures, the value systems and the weaknesses of all people are put into a more workable, useful perspective.

BIBLIOGRAPHY FOR ADOLESCENCE

Calderone, M. S. and Johnson, E. W. The Family Book About Sexuality (Harper, 1981).
Ginott, H. G. Between Parent and Teen-ager (Avon, 1971).
LeShan, Eda. You and Your Feelings (Macmillan, 1975).
Thornburg, H. D. You and Your Adolescent (H.E.L.P., 1977).

ADONIS. According to Greek and Phoenician mythology, the handsomest of the gods was a youth named Adonis. His name came from the Semitic word *adonay,* meaning "my lord, my master."

Adonis was born of a tree, into which his mother had transformed herself. His relationship to a tree established the belief that his spirit lived in vegetative matter—particularly in the seed of corn. The annual Phoenician festival of Adonia commemorated Adonis as a god of fertility and plenty.

The goddess Aphrodite first saw Adonis at his birth. She was so taken by his great beauty that she hid him away in a coffer, or treasure chest. She told this secret to Persephone, another goddess. Unknown to Aphrodite, Persephone opened up the coffer. When she beheld Adonis she was also struck by his beauty. She kidnapped him and refused to give him up. Aphrodite appealed to the god Zeus, who decreed that Adonis must spend half of each year on earth with Aphrodite and the other half in the underworld with Persephone.

Aphrodite tried vainly to dissuade Adonis from his passion for hunting dangerous game. One day he was killed by a wild boar he had wounded with his spear. As Aphrodite knelt over him, anemones sprang from the ground where her tears had fallen.

ADOPTION. The act of establishing a person as parent to one who is not in fact or in law that person's child is called adoption. This procedure can be formal through the legal system of a state, or it can be informal as when a relative of the natural parents permanently takes over the care and responsibility of a child. In a strict sense, however, adoption is done through petitioning a court or government agency for permanent custody of a child or, rarely, of an older person. When the custody is granted, the adopted child is legally the child of the adoptive parents. Today, it is also not uncommon for single people to apply to adopt a child.

Although the adoption procedure concentrates on its legal aspects, much emotional energy is involved in such a family change. However, most adopters will acknowledge that as difficult as it was to go through the legal process and cope with its infringements, it was worth it to gain the protections the law affords. Adoption is so widely recognized that it can be considered an almost worldwide institution. Most countries have laws and practices that promote child welfare with an emphasis on the best interests of the child to be adopted. This contrasts with earlier civilizations in which the interests of the adopter were paramount, usually relating to the continuance of the male line. In the United States individual states enact laws and make regulations, but they are generally guided by the Adoption Assistance Child Welfare Act, passed by the United States Congress in 1980.

Process

There are many reasons for wishing to adopt a child. The most common is a couple's inability to have a child of their own because of infertility. If it is known that either partner is, or both partners are, unable to conceive a baby, and one or more is wanted, the couple may go to a government or private agency to make a request to adopt a child. This is usually a long process. Many questions must be answered, including inquiries into the health of the couple, their ability to support and educate a child, the soundness of their marriage, and the amount of available living space. Also important in planning for the best child–adult combination for making a family unit are the physical characteristics of the parents, such as height and weight, and racial, ethnic, and religious backgrounds. Once approval has been given to adoptive parents, their names are placed on a waiting list for a child who will most closely match the desired characteristics.

Newborn or Older Child?

Most people want a newborn infant whom they can raise from the first weeks of life. This is considered an ideal adoption, allowing the early bond between child and parents to form as in a natural family. Frequently, however, it can take an extended period, often many years, to find an available infant. Those who do not wish to wait can adopt an older child. As there is less call for older children, many wait for adoption while living in foster homes or state institutions. Adolescent mothers, many unmarried, often decide initially to keep their babies. The care and support of an infant, though, demands much time and expense, and, after several years, many young mothers find that they cannot care properly for their children. They may then turn to adoption so that the children can be raised in a more suitable way. This provides a large number of children between two and four who are available for adoption. In such an adoption it is often difficult for the child and parents to relate to one another as a family; but after the early months of getting to know and care for one another family bonding usually occurs.

What, in the United States in the latter half of the 20th century, is sometimes referred to as the "sexual revolution" has changed many elements of society, adoption among them. When birth control devices became widely available in the 1960's, the number of unplanned pregnancies fell sharply (*see* Birth Control). The legalization of abortion has also reduced the number of births (*see* Abortion). Both of these events have greatly reduced the number of babies who need parents.

There are, on the other hand, many older children of minority or mixed racial backgrounds and children suffering from physical or mental disabilities who are available for adoption. Many never are adopted and remain wards of the state until they are old enough to be on their own. The problems of adopting older children who know or remember their natural parents and who have experiences, attachments, and problems from the past often make couples reluctant to undertake such adoptions.

Relatives and Foster Parents

In the United States most adoptions occur when family members adopt children of a relative. Because of death or the inability of the natural parents to care for a child, an aunt, cousin, grandparent, or other relation undertakes the care and responsibility for such a child. This is often done without a formal legal process. Many children are adopted by their foster parents, people who care for children until permanent homes are found for them. Individual states pay small amounts for foster services, but most foster parents perform this function out of care and concern for children who need homes.

Special Problems

There are special problems in adoption. It is generally thought best to tell a child who was adopted as an infant that he or she had another set of parents—the natural, or biological, parents. This raises questions of identity for the adopted child, who naturally is curious about the "real" parents. This information is often revealed when a child is near adolescence—a time of figuring out "who am I?" The search for an answer to this question may take on a wider meaning for those who are adopted.

In the United States each state has slightly different laws, and most protect the identity of the natural parents. Changes late in the 20th century have made it possible for people who were adopted to get information about their biological parents—their ages, ethnic backgrounds, and health history—but in only a few states can the actual names and addresses of these parents be revealed. Groups of adopted adults have formed to discuss the legal, and sometimes emotional, problems related to adoption. In the spirit of "the right to know," these groups, and some individuals, have petitioned and sued governments and agencies for information about their histories.

ADRENAL GLANDS *see* HORMONES.

ADRIATIC SEA. Italy is separated from Yugoslavia and Albania by a baylike arm of the Mediterranean—the Adriatic Sea. It was named for Adria, which was a flourishing port during Roman times. About 500 miles (800 kilo-meters) long, the Adriatic has an average width of about 100 miles (160 kilometers). Its maximum depth is 4,100 feet (1,250 meters).

The Adriatic extends from its northerly head, the Gulf of Venice, southeastward to the Strait of Otranto, which leads to the Ionian Sea. The Po and the Adige rivers empty into the Adriatic at its head. Its western, or Italian, coast is low and straight. The eastern, or Yugoslav-Albanian, coast is rocky and mountainous, with numerous inlets and offshore is-

lands. In general, the Adriatic seabed consists of a yellowish mud and sand mixture, which contains fragments of shells, fossil mollusks, and corals. Two main winds prevail in the area of the sea—the bora, a strong northeasterly wind that blows from the near-by mountains, and a southeasterly wind called the sirocco, which is calmer. The tides of the Adriatic, which follow a complicated pattern, have been studied intensively, mainly by Italian and Yugoslav scientific institutes.

Temperatures in the surface layers of the sea are 75° to 77° F (25° C) during August. The minimum readings, some 50° F (10° C), are usually reached during January and February. In the northern Adriatic, river mouth temperatures are even lower because the waters are cooled by melting ice and snow.

The principal Italian ports on the Adriatic are Bari, Brindisi, Venice, and the free port of Trieste (*see* Trieste). The main Yugoslav ports are Rijeka, Split, Dubrovnik, and Kotor. Durrës and Vlorë are the chief Albanian ports. The fishing catch includes lobsters, sardines, and tuna.

ADULT EDUCATION. Voluntary learning undertaken in organized courses by mature men and women is called adult education. Adult students come to this learning from all walks of life. Such education is offered, among other broad reasons, to enable people to enlarge and interpret their experience as adults. The specific reasons for undertaking such learning are many: Adults may want to study something missed in earlier schooling, acquire new skills or job training, find out about new technological developments, seek better self-understanding, or develop new talents and skills. This kind of education may be pursued with guidance on an individual basis through the use of libraries, correspondence courses, or broadcast media. It may also be acquired collectively in schools and colleges, study groups, seminars, workshops, clubs, and professional associations.

Background

The ideal of education as a lifelong process was put forward centuries ago by the Greek philosophers Plato and Aristotle. They envisioned that an adult would devote himself throughout his life to what they called the "pursuits of leisure," the endeavor to gain for himself ever greater understanding of himself, society, and the world. This was one of the chief aims of the many philosophical schools in the ancient world of Greece and Rome.

The beginnings of modern adult education for large numbers of people occurred in the 18th and 19th centuries with the rise of the Industrial Revolution. Great economic and social changes were taking place: people were moving from rural areas to cities; new types of work were being instituted in an expanding factory system; more people were being allowed to vote in elections. These, and other factors, produced a need for further education—and in some cases, re-education—of adult populations.

A group of adults learns to expand educational skills in order to function effectively in society. In addition to their instructional responsibilities, many teachers provide personal counseling and job placement assistance.

U.S. Department of Education

The earliest programs of organized adult education arose in Great Britain in the 1790's, with the establishment of an adult school at Nottingham and a mechanics' institute at Glasgow. Mechanics' institutes taught artisans the applications of science to industry. Other adult schools, founded largely by religious groups, had as their main goal improving adult literacy. These, and more adult schools that appeared in the next 50 years, were all dependent on voluntary effort and voluntary financing. There were as yet no government-sponsored efforts to educate adults. In fact, widespread, government-supported education even of the young did not become generally accepted until the 19th century.

The founding in Great Britain of the Sheffield People's College in 1842 and the London Working Men's College in 1854 grew out of an awareness of the need for education of the adult poor. A movement called Christian Socialism was behind this attempt to bring literacy to the lower classes. It was in these colleges that the distinction between technical, or useful, education and liberal, or humane, education was first made. Technical education aimed at improving work skills, while education in the humanities sought to enrich the lives of students with courses in literature, arts and sciences, and history.

In 1873 a nondegree institution for adult men and women was started as an extension at Cambridge University in England. One of the most valuable contributions of this institution and others like it was the new opportunities they gave to women, who had previously been excluded from most educational programs.

The earliest adult education institution in the United States, called the Junto, was founded by Benjamin Franklin and some friends in Philadelphia in 1727. It was a club for the discussion of scientific matters and questions on morals and political philosophy. Within a few years, the Junto's collection of books was transformed into the Library Company of Philadelphia, the first public subscription library in the United States. The Junto itself formed the basis for the founding of the American Philosophical Society in 1769.

In 1826 the first large-scale attempt at popular adult education was started by a man named Josiah Holbrook. He was interested in bringing educational opportunities to people in rural areas. He published an article, 'Associations of Adults for Mutual Education', in 1826, outlining a program for establishing voluntary associations in small towns and villages throughout the United States. These associations served as meeting places for adults interested in self-improvement. In that year he founded the first such association at Millbury, Mass., calling it a "lyceum" after the school of the Greek philosopher Aristotle in ancient Athens. The idea caught on rapidly in the Eastern and Middle Western states, and within eight years there were about 3,000 lyceums organized into an American Lyceum Association with headquarters in New York City. The local lyceums were more than adult meeting places for discussion groups. The association sent out lecturers on a regular annual circuit. Many prominent Americans served as lecturers, but the most popular of them all was the writer Ralph Waldo Emerson (see Emerson).

An organization similar to the lyceum was started at Lake Chautauqua in New York state in 1874. Founded for the training of Sunday school teachers, the early Chautauqua education was entirely religious in nature. But as the annual summer gathering increased in popularity, the program became more varied and the summer classes were supplemented by home reading courses and correspondence courses.

The success of the Chautauqua programs led to the founding of many "chautauquas" throughout the United States. By 1900 there were more than 400 such local assemblies. Lecturers, musicians, and per-

A group of adult students attends a course in which they are learning a second language.

formers traveled from one local chautauqua to another each year. Touring "chautauqua companies" were seen by as many as 40 million Americans annually in the 1920's. In the next decade the chautauquas declined in popularity, owing to the emergence of radio and the movies as entertainment media.

During the 19th century millions of immigrants came to the United States. These people aspired to become American citizens and to learn the English language. To assist them, night schools, using day school facilities, were set up in most major cities and in other locations where the foreign-born were numerous. The first of these evening schools was organized in New York City in 1833. There are still many adult schools of this type in the United States. Often associated with community colleges, they teach English and other basic skills.

One of the most noteworthy and successful experiments in adult education was pioneered in Denmark in the late 19th century and spread to the other Scandinavian countries. Called "folk high schools," they were founded under the urging of Nikolai F. S. Grundtvig, a Danish educator, theologian, historian, and poet. The folk schools are residential schools for young adults with some work experience. Grundtvig's original intention was to instill in young adults of every class a thorough knowledge of the Danish language, history, and Biblical literature. In the 20th century the curriculum has become much more varied. Although the folk schools were originally independent local institutions, they are now frequently supported by community boards of education. The folk high school concept has been exported with some modifications to countries as diverse as Canada, India, Kenya, and The Netherlands.

Adult Education Today

Adult education assumes many different forms throughout the world, depending on a nation's history, economic development, and political system. In the United States educational opportunities for adults are many and varied. Adults may pursue courses in remedial education, job retraining, and self-improvement. They may also follow complete college courses leading to a degree. In many careers, advanced education is a means to promotion and higher salaries. Advances in modern technology frequently require further job training for both office and factory work.

One uniquely American development in adult education is the agricultural extension service. Started in 1914 under the auspices of the United States Department of Agriculture, the extension service conducts programs on farming, home economics, and public affairs in every county in the United States.

In Great Britain a new kind of institution, the Open University, was founded in 1970. It is located at Milton Keynes in Buckinghamshire and provides part-time education for adults. To reach a wide audience, it uses radio and television programs as well as local study and lecture courses. The Open University attempts to do nationally what many other adult education institutions do locally.

In the Soviet Union and other Eastern European countries adult education is part of a comprehensive system embracing the whole population. There are "palaces of culture"—nonresident institutions offering instruction in practical crafts, fine arts, music and drama, foreign languages, and social problems, as well as remedial courses. Similar nonresident educational centers exist in Germany, Austria, Finland, Italy, The Netherlands, Switzerland, and Japan.

One of the most original adult education institutions was started in Yugoslavia after World War II. Called "workers' universities," they were established because of the government's decision to turn over control of the factories to the workers. Their basic aim is to train workers in management and commerce, but they have broadened their curriculums to include courses in the arts and sciences, psychology, and politics.

Illiteracy has been one of the greatest challenges facing underdeveloped nations. Many countries have devoted substantial amounts of their resources to public schooling for children and to overcoming adult illiteracy. To assist in this endeavor, the United Nations Experimental World Literacy Program has, since 1965, carried out adult instruction courses in several countries, including Algeria, Ecuador, Ethiopia, India, Iran, Madagascar, Mali, the Sudan, and Tanzania. This program teaches reading in conjunction with basic skills related to daily life or employment. The teaching of reading alone has not proved very successful, because those who have learned frequently lapse back into illiteracy unless some practical uses can be found for their reading ability.

An unusual experiment in adult education has been carried out since the 1970's in underdeveloped countries by the Fujitsu Company, Japan's largest manufacturer of computers. The company has sent teams into many areas of the Far East, teaching people to use computers. Apart from the basic goal of raising adult educational levels, the company has a more ambitious aim: improving economic progress without the need for industrialization.

The rapid pace of technological change has had a significant impact in the industrialized nations. There is a recognized need for continued learning in most forms of employment. Segments of the adult population in many countries find it necessary to undergo retraining programs at work or to learn entirely new jobs. Adult education programs are springing up constantly to meet these and other needs.

Encouragement in this trend is being given by professional adult education associations. Such organizations exist in Australia, Canada, Denmark, Great Britain, New Zealand, Norway, Sweden, Switzerland, and the United States. Their activities are supported by the United Nations Educational, Scientific, and Cultural Organization (UNESCO) and by such regional bodies as the European Bureau of Adult Education and the Asian-South Pacific Association for Adult Education. The existence of the organizations suggests a growing awareness of the need for adult education throughout the world.

ADVENTISTS. The Old and New Testaments of the Bible both foretell the advent (coming) of a Savior, or Messiah. When he appears, as an agent of God, the wicked will be punished and a new Heaven and Earth created. This expectation of an imminent coming of the Messiah, along with the end of the present world, is called Adventism. In a sense, all Jews and Christians are Adventists. But they disagree on whether Jesus Christ was the Messiah that was promised in the Old Testament.

Christians expect a second appearance of Jesus on Earth some time in the future. The precise nature of this expectation varies among the many Christian denominations. Some hardly emphasize it at all, while others make it one of their chief doctrines and devise elaborate scenarios concerning the end of the world. In very troubled periods of the world's history, Christians have frequently expected a sudden return of Christ to inaugurate his personal kingdom. Among the churches, besides Adventists, that have attached special significance to doctrines of the Second Coming are Fundamentalists, Pentacostals, and Jehovah's Witnesses.

The churches specifically named Adventist began in the United States during the 1840's. William Miller, founder of the movement, predicted that the Second Coming would take place on March 21, 1844. When Christ did not appear, the predicted date was put off until Oct. 22, 1844. Even though this prophecy failed, his followers, known as Millerites, insisted that choosing a date had started a long process of preparing the world for the Second Coming. In 1863 the Millerites formally organized the denomination known as Seventh-day Adventists.

This, the largest of the Adventist groups, has a worldwide membership of more than 1½ million. The name Seventh-day Adventists was adopted because members of the group celebrate the Sabbath, the day of rest and worship, on Saturday. They base this observance on a literal interpretation of Gen. ii, 3: "So God blessed the seventh day [Saturday] and hallowed it, because on it God rested from all his work which he had done in creation."

Seventh-day Adventists believe that the human body is the temple of God's spirit and should be kept pure. Hence they follow strict dietary laws, eating no meat and avoiding narcotics and stimulants such as coffee and tea.

Members of the church give one tenth of their incomes to support a worldwide program of missions, hospitals, education, and publishing. The General Conference, the governing body based in Washington D.C., also sends missionaries from door to door with religious literature.

Seventh-day Adventists have suffered ridicule and discrimination for their beliefs and practices. It is not easy, for example, to keep Saturday as a holy day when most employers give Sunday off. For years they were also scorned for their dietary regulations, but an increase in health consciousness has led many other people to reexamine their own dietary views.

The work of William Miller resulted in the founding of other Adventist groups, all much smaller than the Seventh-day Adventists. These include: Evangelical Adventists (1845), the Advent Christian Church (1860), the Life and Advent Union (1862), the Church of God (1866), and the Church of God General Conference (1888). The Life and Advent Union merged with the Advent Christian Church in 1964. These churches differ among each other and from the Seventh-day Adventists on a number of issues, including the issue of whether Saturday or Sunday is the proper day for worship. But the doctrine concerning the Second Coming is central for all groups.

Ken Short

An advertising art director prepares the pictures, art, and typography that make up a product's printed advertisement that will appear in magazines.

ADVERTISING. Advertising is a form of selling. For thousands of years there have been individuals who have tried to persuade others to buy the food they have produced or the goods they have made or the services they can perform. But the mass production of goods resulting from the Industrial Revolution in the 19th century made person-to-person selling less efficient than previously for most products. The mass distribution of goods that followed the development of rail and highway systems made person-to-person selling too slow and expensive. At the same time, however, a growth in mass communication occurred—first newspapers and magazines, then radio and television—that made mass selling possible. Advertising, then, is merely selling—or salesmanship—functioning in the paid space or time of various mass communication media.

The objective of any advertisement is to convince people that it is in their best interests to take an action the advertiser is recommending. The action may be to purchase a product, go to a showroom to try the product, use a service, vote for a political candidate, make a contribution, or even to join the

This article was contributed by John E. O'Toole, Chairman of the Board, Foote, Cone & Belding Communications, Inc., and author of 'The Trouble with Advertising' (Chelsea House, 1981).

Army. Like any personal salesperson, the advertisement tries to persuade. The decision is the prospect's.

Advertising as a business developed first and most rapidly in the United States, the country that uses it to the greatest extent. In 1980 advertising expenditures in the United States exceeded 55 billion dollars, or about 2 percent of the gross national product. Canada spends about 1.2 percent of its gross national product on advertising, Brazil 1.1 percent, Japan .88 percent and West Germany .87 percent.

Almost every company in the United States that manufactures a product, that provides a service, or that sells products or services through retail outlets uses advertising. Those that use it most are companies that must create a demand for several products or services among many people residing in a large area. In 1980 Sears, Roebuck & Company, the largest advertiser in the United States, spent more than 700 million dollars in national and local communications media. Procter & Gamble spent 650 million dollars, primarily in national media. General Foods Corporation spent 410 million dollars, predominantly in national media. The 28th largest United States advertiser in 1980 was the United States government, promoting such projects as recruitment for the military services and encouraging use of the United States Postal Service.

While advertising brings the economies of mass selling to the manufacturer, it produces benefits for the consumer as well. Some of those economies are passed along to the purchaser so that the cost of a product sold primarily through advertising is usually far less than one sold through personal salespeople. Advertising brings people immediate news about products that have just come on the market. Finally, advertising pays for the programs on commercial television and radio and for about two thirds of the cost of publishing magazines and newspapers.

Development

An advertisement, or a campaign of advertisements, is planned in much the same way a successful salesperson plans the approach to be used on a personal call. The first stage is working out the strategy. This requires a thorough analysis of all available market research, personal discussions—or focus groups—with typical prospective buyers of the product, and a knowledge of all competitive products and their advertising. Based on the understanding and insights derived from this information, advertising professionals write a strategy that defines the prospects who constitute the target market to whom they must direct the message and what must be communicated in order to persuade the prospects to take the action that is desired.

With this strategy as a guide, copywriters and art directors begin to create the advertisements. At this second stage they try to come up with an idea that involves the prospect, pertains to his life or problems, and is memorable. The idea can take the form of an unexpected set of words (for example, "The U.S. Army wants to join *you*.") or a graphic symbol (Smokey the Bear or the Jolly Green Giant). It also can be a combination of words and graphics, and even music. An advertising idea works best when it is a totally unexpected yet thoroughly relevant fulfillment of the strategy.

The third stage is the execution of the idea. This means turning the idea into some form of communication that a prospect can see or hear. For print advertising, execution involves writing text, taking photographs or commissioning drawings, arranging elements on the page (layout), setting type, making photoengravings, and so on. For broadcast advertising, it may mean writing dialogue and composing music, hiring actors and recording voices, filming in a studio or on location.

Throughout all three of these stages, research plays an active role. Market research provides the information on which the strategy is based. Copy research may test the relative strength of several ideas on small groups of consumers or larger national samples. Focus groups may uncover communications problems in various headlines, photographs, actors, or musical compositions along the way. Research remains active after the advertisement has been executed. Often a finished print ad or broadcast commercial is tested before it appears in print or on the air, and it is not unusual to track the effect of advertising in the marketplace during the course of a campaign.

A rough proof (below) and finished proof (bottom) of an advertisement for Wedgwood bone china prepared for the print medium show the changes in the development of the idea to the final stages of execution.

Prepared by J. Walter Thompson U.S.A., Inc. © 1982 Wedgwood plc.

J. Walter Thompson U.S.A., Inc.

An employee of an advertising agency works at a regional media-planning computer terminal doing research for a client's television advertising campaign.

Despite all the developmental thinking and planning and despite all the copy research, no one can predict how effective an ad or campaign will be. Much remains unknown about how advertising works. Most experts agree, however, that an ad that involves its prospect in a personal way, that offers a benefit important to that prospect's life, and that does this simply and memorably will be successful.

The Communication Media

At the same time advertising is being developed, other specialists are at work determining where that advertising should be placed in order to accomplish the advertiser's objectives most effectively and most economically. The result is the media plan. This states which communication media should be used to reach as many prospects as possible. It also specifies how much of the available money should go into each medium, thereby determining how many times a prospect will be reached. These two factors are known as reach and frequency. The various media choices are evaluated in terms of how many dollars it will take to reach 1,000 prospects—the cost per thousand. They are also evaluated in terms of the nature of each as carriers of advertising.

Posters. What are now called out-of-home media are the earliest form of advertising known. Poster advertising reached a high state of development in Europe before the turn of the 20th century, employing the talents of artists such as Henri de Toulouse-Lautrec, and remains a more important medium there than in other parts of the world. There are posters of all sizes (the larger ones are called billboards, or in Britain hoardings) along streets and highways, on the sides of buildings, on the outside of buses, and on the inside of commuter trains and subways. Because the prospect has little time to devote to a poster, usually only a glance, the information communicated is brief. For this reason posters are usually used as a reminder medium, supplementing a major exposure of an idea in another medium. Posters are usually rented by an advertiser on a local basis, but a number of local "showings" can be put together to achieve national coverage.

Newspapers. Because they attract so much local advertising, newspapers are the most popular medium in the United States and in most other parts of the world. Newspapers offer an advertiser coverage of a specific geographical area. This can be important to national advertisers as well as local ones. For example, newspapers added to a national television or magazine campaign can tell prospects the names and addresses of stores where the product can be bought locally. Newspapers also offer advertisers speed. A newspaper ad can be set in type and appear within a day after it is delivered to the newspaper office.

Lithograph posters by Ludwig Hohlwein, 'Hermann Scherrer. Breechesmaker Sporting-Tailor', 1911 (far left), and (left) by Henri de Toulouse-Lautrec, 'Divan Japonais', 1892, are examples of early European advertisements.

Courtesy of the Museum of Modern Art, New York (far left) gift of Peter Muller-Munk, (left) Abby Aldrich Rockefeller Purchase Fund

What you see...is what you get.

A billboard poster advertising Sunkist oranges is based on visual appeal, and says so.

Speed is important in announcing special sales or relating advertising messages to events in the news.

Magazines. For the advertiser interested in reaching prospects with specific interests or life-styles, magazines provide the ideal medium. For instance, if a fishing rod is being sold, the advertiser knows that the readers of *Sports Illustrated* come to that publication with a keen interest in sports. There are also magazines devoted exclusively to fishing. If the advertiser wants to appeal to both men and women with an interest in current events (to advertise a book club, perhaps), they can be reached by means of *Time* or *Newsweek*. Furthermore, those magazines will allow an advertiser to run an ad in only those copies going to a particular region of the country.

Most magazines offer full color to advertisers as opposed to the more limited color available in newspapers. This kind of color is called four-color printing because it is achieved by using four separate engraved plates (*see* Color, section "Techniques for Reproducing Color"). Full color is especially desirable for food and fashion advertising because the color of these products is part of their appeal.

Radio. In those countries in which it can be used for advertising, radio offers the advertiser a geographically defined audience and, at the same time, a choice among certain kinds of audiences. The latter is important if these kinds of audiences can be related to the definition of the prospect. For example, in the United States one or more radio stations in each market broadcasts music designed to attract a young audience; another appeals to the musical tastes of an older generation; still another attracts listeners interested in classical music and notices of cultural events in the community. Like newspapers, radio affords the advertiser speed in getting a message to prospects.

Television. This newest of media carries more national advertising than any other medium in the United States. The same is true in some smaller countries such as Spain and Portugal, where it is the only medium reaching a general national audience. In many countries, Sweden and Denmark, for example,

the state-owned television accepts no advertising. In many other countries the amount of commercial time is so limited that few advertisers can employ it. This is the case in France, Germany, and Italy.

The chief reason for the popularity of United States television among national advertisers is that it reaches a vast number of people at the same time. While it can cost well over 100,000 dollars, a 30-second commercial on network television can be seen

A magazine advertisement that has stood the test of time was used originally in 1958 and has appeared repeatedly ever since that year.

© McGraw-Hill Magazines

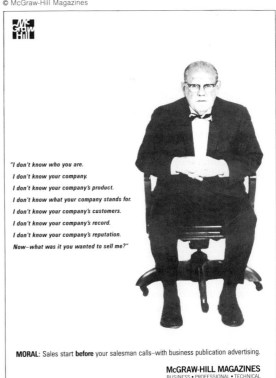

"I don't know who you are.
I don't know your company.
I don't know your company's product.
I don't know what your company stands for.
I don't know your company's customers.
I don't know your company's record.
I don't know your company's reputation.
Now—what was it you wanted to sell me?"

MORAL: Sales start **before** your salesman calls—with business publication advertising.

McGRAW-HILL MAGAZINES
BUSINESS • PROFESSIONAL • TECHNICAL

© BBC Hulton Picture Library

A 19th-century example of a business sign that uses a representation of its name serves the Goat Tavern in London, England. The sign was photographed about 1940.

and heard by as many as 25 million viewers. For a manufacturer who has succeeded in placing a product in stores across the country and must make prospects aware of the product and convince them of its benefits immediately, there is nothing as efficient as television advertising.

Because it employs motion as well as words, graphics, sound, and music, television is a valuable medium for products that lend themselves to demonstration. No other medium is as effective in showing how quickly an automobile can accelerate, how easily a typewriter ribbon can be replaced, or how well a brand of wristwatch will stand up under abuse and continue to run. Similarly, it is an ideal medium for conveying a mood or an emotional benefit for products such as long-distance telephone calls.

Media Comparison. The differences in the nature of these media effect how the public feels about advertising in them. Newspaper ads are generally welcomed by readers. In polls many say that the advertisements are a reason for buying newspapers. Advertisements are usually well received in magazines, too. They are placed in a particular publication because the advertiser feels the product and the reader have something in common. In any case the reader of either a newspaper or magazine can ignore any ad that does not hold interest after a quick glance.

Broadcast advertisements, however, intrude themselves on the listener or viewer with little or no warning. On television—where the audience is less defined in terms of where the people live, how they live, or what they are interested in—messages intended for one kind of viewer are likely to intrude on another. For example, a man is just as likely as a woman to see a commercial for lipstick or pantyhose. This kind of

intrusion has resulted in annoyance with television advertising being expressed in public polls.

History

Advertising originated in the signs that merchants once put over their doors to inform the public, with symbols or pictures, exactly what was for sale inside. For example, the barber's sign was a red and white striped pole. Posters and handbills began appearing in England after the invention in 1440 of movable type in Germany. The first newspapers appeared in England in the 17th century and in the New World at the beginning of the 18th. Advertising soon became part of these newspapers as it became part of the magazines that followed in the early 19th century.

Advertising agencies began to emerge in the United States in the 1840's. They were actually space brokers, selling space in newspapers and magazines for a commission. By 1900 the major agencies of the day—J. Walter Thompson, N. W. Ayer, and Lord & Thomas—were providing copy to fill that space. The copy consisted primarily of outlandish claims and advertiser identification. In fact, the generally accepted definition of advertising was "keeping your name before the public."

A 19th-century advertisement reflects the elaborate taste of the period. Its appeal is through suggestion.

Library of Congress

Modern advertising began in the Chicago agency Lord & Thomas (now Foote, Cone & Belding) in 1904. It was there that Albert Lasker, known as "the father of modern advertising," and a copywriter named John E. Kennedy coined the definition "salesmanship in print." For the first time the idea of persuasion and the comparison to the role of an individual salesperson was brought to advertising. This led to further concepts such as the consumer benefit, putting forth not simply a feature of the product but the benefit it would bring to the prospect when used. This led in turn to reason-why advertising, in which a logical argument showed the prospect why it was in his or her individual interest to use the product. Then followed market research as it became apparent that an understanding of the prospect was at least as important as an understanding of the product.

This redefinition of advertising, along with the introduction of radio in the United States in the 1920's, gave the industry a surge that carried it through the Great Depression and the years of World War II. Immediately following the war, television stations in the United States began broadcasting in major cities, and coast-to-coast television began in the early 1950's. This was the start of the big advertising boom in which advertising expenditures increased tenfold between 1950 and 1980.

After World War II a number of large United States companies began to renew the markets they had lost overseas or began to enter them for the first time. These companies often urged their advertising agencies to open offices abroad and introduce the techniques, particularly in television advertising, that were resulting in sales success at home. Thus did the McCann-Erickson agency follow Coca-Cola in its worldwide expansion; J. Walter Thompson followed Ford and Kodak; Young & Rubicam, General Foods and some other clients. Even agencies without multinational clients began opening offices in foreign marketing capitals or began acquiring local agencies there and Americanizing them. As a result, the advertising theory, techniques, and even vocabulary that dominate every major world market originated in the United States, although national adaptations are strong and growing. So, too, United States agencies and their affiliates dominate most world markets. One exception is France. Another is Japan, whose Dentsu agency is the largest in the world, exceeding the worldwide volume of the largest United States agency by a considerable margin.

Other Varieties

As advertising has grown, it has also become more complex. In addition to the kind of advertising directed to consumers for products and services through the media already described, some other varieties have developed. The most important are:

Direct Response. In this form the advertisement is the only salesperson. Direct mail/direct response employs a brochure mailed to the prospect with a coupon for ordering. Media/direct response uses a news-paper or magazine ad to deliver the coupon. The prospect fills in the coupon, sends it in with a check, and the product is sent by mail.

Yellow Pages. This is the advertising that appears only in classified telephone directories. Its purpose is to direct prospects who have learned about a product through media advertising to the dealer or representative who can provide it.

Business-to-Business. This is advertising from one manufacturer to another in publications read primarily by people in a specific industry. It usually sells a product used in manufacturing another product; or it might be a message from the manufacturer to the independent dealer who sells the product.

Recruitment. This is advertising from a company that needs certain skills or talents. Its purpose is to attract individuals with those skills to the advertiser's work force.

Health Care. This specialized field uses medical journals and direct mail to bring news of new drugs and other medical products to physicians and hospital administrators. The advertisers are major manufacturers of prescription and over-the-counter drugs.

Regulation

Because of the power and pervasiveness of advertising in so many countries, there are official restrictions imposed everywhere. As mentioned, television advertising is not allowed in many countries, and radio advertising is prohibited in some. In almost every country there is a restriction of some sort on the advertising of alcoholic beverages. This can take the form of an outright ban, a restriction to certain media, or actually a direction as to what may and may not be said or shown in an ad. In the United States, for example, alcoholic beverage advertising,

A billboard advertisement in the Peoples Republic of China represents the spread of American advertisers and advertisements.
© 1979 Harry Redl—Black Star

The Bettmann Archive, Inc.

A United States Army recruiting poster, first used in World War I, is one of the best known of all ads. The figure of Uncle Sam is by James Montgomery Flagg.

except for wine and beer, is restricted to print and out-of-home media.

In the United States there are federal laws concerning advertising that are enforced by the Federal Trade Commission. There is also self-regulation. Most newspapers and magazines enforce their own standards in accepting advertisements. Television networks check every submitted commercial for accuracy and good taste. For many years those television stations belonging to the National Association of Broadcasters (NAB) sent any proposed commercial directed to children, for personal products, or for foods in which fat or cholesterol is mentioned to the NAB Code Review Board for clearance. The code, however, was suspended in 1982. The National Advertising Review Board, sponsored by several advertising associations and the Council of Better Business Bureaus, deals with any advertiser it finds guilty of using false or misleading claims.

None of this restriction, law, or self-regulation applies to political advertising as it is practiced in the United States. This is one reason why there is such controversy over the practice of candidates for public office purchasing television spots to influence voters. Another is the contention that television campaigns, being both expensive and powerful, help to give the office to the wealthiest candidate.

Careers

Careers in advertising fall generally into three categories: advertising agencies, advertiser companies, and advertising media.

Agencies. People in an advertising agency work in one of four departments, and each requires a somewhat different set of skills and educational background. In account management the people who represent the agency to the client organize the service of the agency to serve the client. Account managers often have degrees in business and usually have a broad range of interests.

The creative department actually conceives and produces the advertisements. The copywriters generally have a liberal arts education and a strong interest in verbal communication. A copywriter is usually teamed with an art director who has had some formal training in art and design.

The research department does a great deal of statistical work and analysis. Since much of this has to do with the responses of people to communications, a background in the social sciences is valuable.

The media department is also statistically oriented, though media jobs involve a good deal of negotiating in the course of buying vast amounts of space and time. Media specialists are, to a certain extent, purchasing agents.

Advertisers. The involvement with advertising in an advertiser company is less direct and total than it is in an advertising agency. While there may be a marketing services department that coordinates media schedules of many brands of products, advertising involvement is primarily a function of brand managers. These people deal with all aspects of the marketing of a brand, including advertising. They are the providers of information to the agency and the approvers of the agency's work. Most brand managers have degrees in business.

Media. The people in media companies who are most directly involved with advertising are those who sell the space or time to the advertiser through the agency. They are called representatives and come from varied educational backgrounds as well as from other areas of selling.

TOP TEN ADVERTISING AGENCIES IN THE WORLD

(According to Billings in the Early 1980's)

Dentsu Advertising Ltd., Tokyo
Young & Rubicam Inc., New York City
J. Walter Thompson Co., New York City
Ogilvy & Mather, New York City
McCann-Erickson, Inc., New York City
Ted Bates Worldwide, Inc., New York City
BBDO International, Inc., New York City
Leo Burnett Company, Inc., Chicago
SSC & B Inc. Advertising, New York City
Foote, Cone & Belding, Chicago

AEGEAN CIVILIZATION

MINOAN-MYCENAEAN CIVILIZATION
+ IMPORTANT CENTERS ABOUT 1400 B.C.

AEGEAN CIVILIZATION. The earliest civilization in Europe appeared on the coasts and islands of the Aegean Sea. Here, while Western Europe was still in the Stone Age, the Minoan-Mycenaean peoples achieved a highly organized Bronze Age culture.

Two different civilizations flourished in this region some 2,000 years before the Christian Era. One is known as *Minoan*, because its center at Cnossus on the island of Crete was the legendary home of King Minos, son of Zeus and Europa. The other is called *Mycenaean*, after Mycenae in Greece (the city of King Agamemnon, the Achaean leader in the Trojan War).

The Mycenaeans, or Achaeans, had invaded the Greek mainland between 1900 B.C. and 1600 B.C. The center of their culture was Mycenae. The city flourished from about 1500 to 1100 B.C. Before 1400 B.C. the Mycenaeans conquered the Minoans, and about 1200 B.C. they sacked Troy (*see* Trojan War).

Mycenae and Other Achaean Cities

In 1876 Heinrich Schliemann began excavating Mycenae (*see* Schliemann). Alan J. B. Wace contin-

ued the work in the 20th century. Still visible today is the acropolis, with its broken stone walls and Lion Gate. Within the walls Schliemann uncovered the graves of bodies covered with gold masks, breastplates, armbands, and girdles. In the graves of the women were golden diadems, golden laurel leaves, and exquisite ornaments shaped like animals, flowers, butterflies, and cuttlefish.

Schliemann thought he had found the burial place of Agamemnon and his followers. Later study proved the bodies belonged to a period 400 years earlier than the Trojan War. Rulers of another dynasty were buried outside the walls in strange beehive tombs.

Ewing Galloway

Metropolitan Museum of Art
Here are a porch of the palace of Cnossus and a snake goddess.

Other great cities of the same period were Pylos, the legendary home of King Nestor, and Tiryns. It is not known to what extent Mycenae controlled other centers of the Achaean civilization. Trade extended to Sicily, Egypt, Palestine, Troy, Cyprus, and Macedonia. Mycenaeans settled on Cyprus and at Miletus on the coast of Asia Minor.

Scholars once believed that the Mycenaeans were illiterate. The evidences of culture in their massive walled cities, their fine goldwork, pottery, and vases were attributed to the influence of the Minoans, who conquered the mainland about 1600 B.C.

Deciphering the Mycenaean Writings

In 1952 great light was thrown on the Mycenaean civilization by the deciphering of an ancient writing on clay tablets, known as Linear Script B. Michael Ventris, a young English architect, accomplished the task on which scholars had labored for 50 years These tablets were among some 2,000 uncovered at Cnossus on Crete by Sir Arthur Evans, beginning in 1900. With them were tablets in an older writing, which Evans called Linear Script A, and some still older hieroglyphics. Linear Scripts A and B are in a kind of writing which uses symbols for syllables. In 1939 about 600 more tablets in Linear Script B were found at Pylos, on the Greek mainland, and in 1952 and 1953 some were discovered at Mycenae.

Ventris found that Linear Script B is an *archaic Greek dialect*. It is the oldest Indo-European system of writing yet discovered. The language is at a stage 700 years older than the earliest classical Greek.

A huge gate pierces the wall around the acropolis of Mycenae. Above the lintel are two lions, their forepaws on an altar.

The tablets appeared at Cnossus because the Mycenaeans had conquered the Minoans.

The tablets are only inventories of palace storerooms and arsenals. They reveal a great deal about the life of the Mycenaeans, however. They engaged in agriculture, industry, commerce, and war. At the head of the society was a king. Under him was a "leader of the people," perhaps an army commander. There were landowning barons, tenants, servants and slaves, priests and priestesses. There were many trades and professions. The Mycenaeans worshiped Zeus, Hera, Poseidon, Ares, Artemis, and Athena.

The Minoan Civilization

The language of Linear Script A has not yet been identified, and it is uncertain where the Minoans originated. They lived on Crete from about 2500 B.C. to 1400 B.C., when they were conquered by Mycenaeans from the Greek mainland. By 1600 B.C. they were a world power. Prosperity depended upon seafaring and trade, especially with the East and with Egypt. Minoan influence spread also to the Greek mainland.

Evans' excavations at Cnossus revealed a great palace which covered six acres. There were no surrounding walls at Cnossus, as in the Mycenaean cities. The palace and the city had been protected by a powerful navy.

Evans found storerooms with huge oil jars still in place, elaborate bathrooms, ventilation and drainage systems, and waste disposal chutes. The pottery was as fine as porcelain. Paintings on walls and pottery showed the "modern" dress of the women, with puffed sleeves and flounced skirts.

Myth of the Labyrinth

The Minoans worshiped a mother goddess, whose symbol was the double-bladed ax, called a *labrys*. The name of the symbol and the maze of rooms in the palace recall the story of the labyrinth. According to Greek mythology, Daedalus built a labyrinth for Minos to house the man-eating Minotaur, half man and half bull (*see* Theseus). Painted on the palace walls are pictures of acrobats vaulting over the backs of bulls. This sport may have given rise to the myth. (For picture of one of the frescoes, *see* Design.) After the Greeks conquered the Minoans such stories became a part of their mythology.

End of Minoan-Mycenaean Civilizations

About 1100 B.C. Greece was overrun by an invasion of barbaric tribes from the north. The Dorians and later the Ionians occupied the areas where the Minoan-Mycenaean cultures had flourished. Greece was not to be as rich and powerful again until the golden age of Pericles, in the 5th century B.C. (*See also* Archaeology.)

AEGEAN SEA. The sparkling blue Aegean Sea lies between the peninsula of Greece on the west and Turkey on the east. Named after Aegeus, a legendary Athenian king, the Aegean Sea was the cradle of two of the great early civilizations, Crete and Greece.

An arm of the Mediterranean Sea, the Aegean contains numerous islands known as the Grecian archipelago (group of islands). It is connected to the Black Sea through the straits of the Dardanelles, the Sea of Marmara, and the Bosporus strait. The southern boundary of the sea is the island of Crete. Its shoreline is quite irregular, broken with bays, harbors, and other inlets. Because of the need for frequent docking, such inlets made it easier for early seamen to make extensive voyages.

The total area of the Aegean is about 83,000 square miles (214,000 square kilometers). It is about 380 miles (610 kilometers) long and 185 miles (300 kilometers) wide. Its maximum depth, which occurs near Crete, is 11,627 feet (3,544 meters), although its average depth is 1,188 feet (362 meters).

There is little marine life in the Aegean because of its low nutrient content. However, many fishes, mainly from the Black Sea, enter the Aegean for breeding purposes because the water is warm.

Other than its fishes the sea provides few resources. Research has revealed the possibility of oil deposits beneath the seabed, plus mineral and chemical deposits on the seafloor, which is composed mainly of limestone. (*See also* Aegean Civilization.)

AENEAS. In mythology Aeneas was regarded as a Roman god. Homer's 'Iliad' compares him with the legendary Hector. He is the hero of Vergil's 'Aeneid' but was revered by the Romans long before the 'Aeneid' was written. They called him *Jupiter indiges*—"the founder of the race."

Aeneas was not of Roman origin. Anchises, his father, was a member of the Trojan royal house. His mother was the goddess of love, Aphrodite. Anchises was sworn never to reveal his marriage to Aphrodite. When Aeneas was born, however, Anchises boasted to his companions. In punishment, he was blinded.

When Troy was conquered in the Trojan War, Aeneas led his warriors out of the burning city, carrying his blind father on his shoulders. Aeneas and his companions then roamed the Mediterranean area for seven years in search of a new homeland. His ships were wrecked off the African coast, near Carthage. Dido, the Carthaginian queen, fell deeply in love with Aeneas and begged him to stay. When he left, Dido killed herself in grief.

Aeneas and his companions settled briefly in Thrace, Crete, and Sicily, before coming to Latium, on the banks of the Tiber. King Latinus made them welcome. Aeneas aided the ruler in his struggles against the Rutuli. Later, Aeneas married Lavinia, daughter of Latinus. He inherited the kingdom after Latinus died, reigning happily and successfully over his united Trojans and Latins. He was killed in a battle with the Etruscans.

AERIAL SPORTS. The dream of flight is perhaps as old as humanity. Most modern flight is for commercial or military purposes, but the pioneers of aviation wanted to fly just for the thrill of it. Today, a growing number of people throughout the world enjoy that thrill in a variety of aerial sports. These sports may use powered planes, lighter-than-air balloons, gliders, parachutes, or hang gliders. Organized aerial sports are governed by the Federation Aéronautique Internationale (FAI), founded in Paris in 1905.

Power-Plane Sports

Power-plane sports include all sports that use a self-propelled airplane. They began after the Wright brothers made the first successful flight in a heavier-than-air machine in 1903. There are five major power-plane sports: racing, aerobatics, and activities involving homebuilts, antiques, or rotorcraft.

Racing. The first international racing meet was held in Reims, France, in 1909. About 28 of the 38 entrants crashed. Nevertheless, air races became extremely popular from then until World War II. The Bennett races, Thompson Trophy race, and similar events helped pilots, mechanics, and designers improve their airplanes. In 1939 a propeller-plane speed

A hang glider soars over Dead Horse Point State Park in Moab, Utah, in the western United States. The hang-glider pilot's view is a beautiful panorama of the naturally sculptured canyons of the Colorado River.

Leroy F. Grannis

record of 496.22 miles (798.59 kilometers) per hour, which stood for 30 years, was set by a German Messerschmitt.

After World War II, when powerful wartime fighter planes dominated air racing, the sport became too expensive for fliers to compete without commercial or military backing. The growing expense, plus the number of fatal crashes, led to a lapse in air racing from 1949 until 1964. Meanwhile, pilots turned to smaller, less powerful planes, such as sport biplanes, midget, single-wing aircraft, and modified World War II fighter planes called "unlimiteds." The sport also attracted many women. Today, the Powder Puff Derby, held in the United States, is the leading women's transcontinental air race.

Aerobatics. This sport, also known as stunt flying, calls for pilots to perform difficult turns, loops, and spins. It has become widely popular since 1964.

Homebuilts. In the early 1900's, almost all aircraft were homebuilts, or made by their fliers. These planes caused many fatal crashes. In 1924, the United States government established strict rules for aircraft construction. Other governments set similar regulations, and the sport of making and flying homebuilts almost ended. It revived after the rules were relaxed in the United States in 1947.

Antiques. Planes at least 30 years old qualify as antiques. Pilots modify these aircraft largely by putting in new engines.

Rotorcraft. These have wings that work like large propellers mounted on the top. The wings whirl around on a central axis to give the planes their upward lift, and enable them to fly very slowly. For sport rotorcraft flying, many pilots use autogiros, the forerunners of helicopters (*see* Helicopter).

Ballooning

After the first successful manned balloon flight in 1783, ballooning grew more and more popular until World War I. Then public attention turned toward heavier-than-air aviation. Sport ballooning made a comeback in the 1960's, when aviators developed new lightweight materials and an inexpensive propane gas burner to heat the air in the balloon.

Balloon contests began as rallies in which the entrants tried to outdo one another in tests of distance, time aloft, and landing accuracy. Outstanding figures during the early years of the sport included John Wise of the United States, who flew 1,200 miles (1,930 kilometers) in 20 hours in 1859. In 1963, two other Americans, Paul E. Yost and Donald Piccard, became the first hot-air balloonists to soar across the English Channel.

Many balloon contests include a "hare and hounds" race, in which balloonists follow an official and try to land as close to him or her as possible. In the cross-country event balloonists compete to see who can fly the farthest in a certain period of time. (*See also* Balloon and Airship.)

Soaring

Soaring, or gliding, uses a motorless single-wing aircraft called a glider or sailplane. This lightweight craft soars on the upward motion of air to gain or maintain height. Skillful pilots seek thermals, or updrafts of warm air, to prolong flights over great distances and to reach high altitudes. Gliders reach speeds of more than 100 miles (160 kilometers) per hour and fly more than 500 miles (800 kilometers).

Crude gliders made of wood and fabric were flown in the mid-19th century. The sport advanced greatly during the 1890's when Otto Lilienthal, a German designer, made more than 2,000 glider flights. The Wright brothers aided glider development in the early 1900's. By 1926, flights of 30 miles (48 kilometers) or more were common. Distance records for glider flights exceeded 500 miles by 1951. Modern gliders can be flown more than 600 miles (960 kilometers) and higher than 46,000 feet (14,000 meters).

Gliders are made of fiberglass and aluminum. Some have a small motor that the pilot uses mostly to take off without being towed by a powered plane. A pilot

Nine sport parachutists perform a free-fall hookup while five others look on at approximately 4,500 feet (1,373 meters) above the city of Elsinore, Calif.

Carl Boenish

Flight International

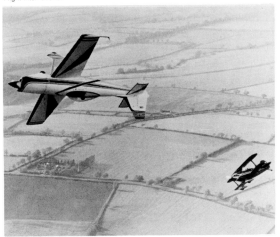

Aerobatic planes perform during the 1970 world meet at Hullavington, Wiltshire, in southern England. A world aerobatics meet is held every two years.

may also start the engine for brief periods to regain lost altitude if a thermal cannot be found.

Glider competitions feature several "tasks," or events, that stress basic principles. These include speed, altitude, distance, and accuracy in returning to the starting point. World championships take place every other year, and United States national championships are held annually. John Robinson of the United States was the first pilot to fly more than 300 miles (500 kilometers) in a glider. He won the United States title three times. Pelagia Majewski of Poland won the first women's international championship, which took place in Poland in 1973.

Sport Parachuting

Parachuting for sport has grown tremendously since 1960, when fewer than 1,000 organized parachute jumpers competed. By 1980, the number had increased to more than 250,000 men and women in 28 countries. Sport jumping consists of various types of competitions. In style jumping, entrants are judged by the speed and style of their stunts. In accuracy jumping, contestants receive scores based on how close they land to a target on the ground. Team events involve two or more persons who jump together. They may pass batons, form patterns, or perform various other stunts while descending.

Sport parachuting began in 1914 with the first free-fall, a jump made with a delayed opening of the parachute. The sport did not become popular until the 1950's, when some French enthusiasts began jumping for fun. They experimented with free-falls and designed their parachutes to make them easier to steer. The United States Parachuting Association was established in 1957 to promote jumping as a safe sport.

Jumpers wear both a main parachute and a safety reserve parachute, plus helmet, goggles, gloves, and boots. They leap from an airplane at a height of about 2,000 to 6,600 feet (600 to 2,000 meters). Jumpers descend in free-fall for a few seconds or for

more than a minute, depending on their original altitude. They open the parachute when about 2,000 feet above the ground to allow enough time for it to spread out properly.

The first world sport parachuting championship was held in Yugoslavia in 1951. They are now held every two years. (*See also* Parachute.)

Hang Gliding

A hang glider consists of a piece of fabric, called a wing, attached to a frame. A person who goes hang gliding, or "sky surfing," is said to be as close to being a bird as is possible for a human.

Otto Lilienthal of Germany experimented with hang gliders as well as regular gliders, but few others showed much interest in them until 1951. That year, Francis Rogallo, a United States space scientist, and his wife, Gertrude, patented what they called a flexible kite. This new kind of kite had no sticks, and its frame was flexible, rather than rigid. The flexible kite developed into the first modern hang glider later in the 1950's. Today, one of the most popular and easily flown models is called the Rogallo wing.

Modern hang gliders include airfoils, which have a rigid frame and are larger, heavier, and harder to fly than the flexible types. They need a ground crew for launching. The semirigid hang gliders have a collapsible frame and no tail. The wings of most hang gliders are made of Dacron, which can withstand great stress. Aluminum tubing is used to brace the rigid and semirigid models. The pilot hangs beneath the wing in a harness and grips a horizontal control bar.

A hang-glider pilot can take off by running down-hill. Skilled fliers may take off from a cliff, but this method is both dangerous and difficult. In the air, the pilot moves his or her body and the control bar to change the center of gravity of the glider. This movement causes the glider to turn or to go up or down. Like regular glider pilots, the hang-glider pilot uses thermals to help gain altitude and maintain it.

Competition in hang gliding grew rapidly during the 1970's. Most events test the pilots' form and skill in distance runs, target landings, banked turns, and full-circle turns. (*See also* Aviation.)

A high-performance fiberglass sailplane flies over majestic Mt. Rainier in the state of Washington.

Linn Emrich

AEROSOL. A liquid or solid that is finely dispersed in air and is in a stable state is an aerosol. A cloud is a natural aerosol of water droplets in air. Smoke, which contains solid particles of carbon and ash, combined with fog and certain other chemicals is the harmful aerosol called smog (*see* Fog; Smoke).

Manufactured aerosols—pressurized products—include insecticides, disinfectants and sanitizers, detergents and cleaning compounds, waxes, automotive products, and coatings, such as paints and hair sprays. Edible aerosol products include whipped cream and processed cheese spreads.

How Aerosol Products Work

In manufactured aerosols the product to be dispensed from a container is held under pressure by a gas, called a propellant. When a valve is released, the gas drives out the product as spray or foam.

In some commercial aerosols the gas is stored under pressure in the can. It fills the space above the product when the can is sealed and expands as the product is used. Pressure is continuously lost as the product is consumed. This type of aerosol is used to deliver a coarse spray as is desirable for laundry prespotters, surface insecticides, and engine starters.

For uniform pressures the product is mixed with the propellant, which may be a liquid that evaporates rapidly into the space left as the product is used. The same effect is obtained if a suitable gas under enough pressure is dissolved in the product. The gas must evaporate to keep up the pressure.

The type of propellant employed depends on the end use of the product. Common propellants for food products—which must be flavorless and nontoxic—include carbon dioxide, nitrogen, and nitrous oxide. The most common propellant for non-food aerosols is the hydrocarbon type, which is usually a blend of propane, isobutane, and n-butane. Members of the chlorofluorocarbon (CFC) family of synthetic chemicals have also been used widely. The CFC's, also called fluorocarbons, are seldom used today in several countries because they may harm the environment.

Environmental Effects of Aerosols

Ozone, a form of oxygen, occurs naturally in the Earth's upper atmosphere where it forms a layer that prevents some ultraviolet solar radiation from striking the Earth. If this atmospheric ozone were to become less dense, more ultraviolet rays would reach the Earth, possibly damaging crops and perhaps leading to increased incidence of human skin cancer.

During the 1970's some scientists concluded that ozone concentrations were slowly lessening. They said that CFC's from aerosols and other sources are rising to the upper atmosphere and being decomposed there by ultraviolet light. This action frees a chlorine atom that reacts with the ozone to form new compounds. Theoretically, atmospheric ozone is diminished by this process.

These findings received wide publicity, and in 1978 the United States government banned CFC aerosols in most products. Two years later the United States announced its intention first to halt the growth of CFC production in all products and then to curtail production sharply. The aerosol industry protested these actions, declaring that the ozone depletion theory is questionable. They also maintain that action by the United States without international cooperation punishes United States industry and solves no problems. By the end of 1981 only Canada, Sweden, and Norway had joined the United States in banning CFC aerosols. A cutback in fluorocarbon propellant use has been implemented by Europe's Common Market countries.

Smog can damage many substances including plant and animal life. A cloud of chemically laden smog stings the eyes and makes breathing difficult. If smogs occur over regions where much coal is burned and industries discharge gaseous wastes, the harmful gases usually include sulfur dioxide and oxides of nitrogen. Automobile exhausts contribute incompletely burned portions of fuel.

Harmful substances sometimes travel great distances. Sulfur dioxide, for example, may combine with atmospheric water to form sulfuric acid. Winds may then blow acid-laden clouds many miles before they release their moisture as polluting acid rain (*see* Acid Rain).

The worst smogs occur where strong sunshine is abundant and winds are light. In such circumstances atmospheric inversions often hold a mass of air stationary over a region. (During an inversion heavy air lies over lighter air and pins it down.) The sunshine turns some of the automobile exhaust fumes into ozone. The increased ozone in the stagnant air causes most of the damage. The harmful effects of smogs have been a major factor in the enactment of antipollution laws. (*See also* Pollution, Environmental.)

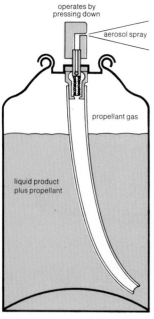

operates by pressing down

aerosol spray

propellant gas

liquid product plus propellant

An aerosol spray container works when the top is pressed. This opens a valve that allows the product, propelled by gas under pressure, to escape. Because such cans are under pressure, they should not be placed near a flame or be punctured.

From 'Kirk-Othmer Encyclopedia of Chemical Technology', vol. 1 (© 1963); by permission of John Wiley & Sons, Inc.

AEROSPACE INDUSTRY

AEROSPACE INDUSTRY. The Earth's atmosphere is usually referred to as "the air" (*see* Air; Atmosphere). "Aircrew," "aircraft," and "air force" are some of the names of persons, machines, and organizations concerned with manned air travel.

Man-made vehicles have gone beyond the air, entering interplanetary regions outside the Earth's atmosphere. Since 1961, people have been traveling alone or in crews in vehicles through outer space. Therefore, a whole new terminology, or system of names, has been devised to describe the technology and science of all space beyond the Earth's surface.

Aerospace is such a word. It describes all the regions beyond the Earth's surface. It includes the atmosphere and the vast expanse of outer space.

The research, design, and production of airplanes, missiles, and spacecraft constitute the aerospace industry. Until shortly after World War II it was called the aircraft or aviation industry. Increasing production of missiles and spacecraft by the same manufacturers that formerly made only aircraft necessitated the name change (*see* Guided Missiles; Space Travel). In 1959 the Aircraft Industries Association was renamed the Aerospace Industries Association to reflect the transition in its members' products.

It is a relatively young industry, less than a century old. Its birthplace was the tiny bicycle shop of Orville and Wilbur Wright in Dayton, Ohio, where they built the first successful airplane (*see* Wright Brothers). Today an aerospace manufacturing plant resembles a small city. Its offices, warehouses, factories, and other buildings stretch for blocks.

How Air and Space Vehicles Are Built

Vehicles that travel through the air or through space have the same basic structure—an airframe,

Fact Finder for Aerospace Articles

The subject of aerospace is a broad one. Additional information will be found in the many articles listed here.

Air Force	Jet Propulsion
Airline	Military Education
Airplane	Navy
Airport	Parachute
Aviation	Rocket
Balloon and Airship	Sailplane
Glider	Space Travel
Guided Missiles	Wind Tunnel
Helicopter	

See additional references in the Fact-Index. For bibliography, *see* Space Travel.

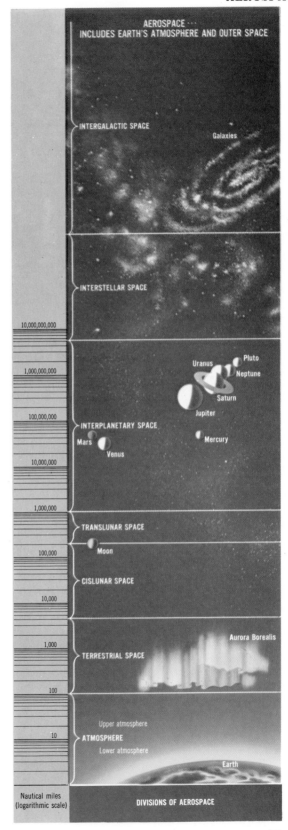

AEROSPACE ··· INCLUDES EARTH'S ATMOSPHERE AND OUTER SPACE

INTERGALACTIC SPACE

Galaxies

INTERSTELLAR SPACE

10,000,000,000

1,000,000,000

Uranus — Pluto — Neptune — Saturn — Jupiter

100,000,000

INTERPLANETARY SPACE — Mars — Venus — Mercury

10,000,000

1,000,000

TRANSLUNAR SPACE

100,000 — Moon

CISLUNAR SPACE

10,000

Aurora Borealis

1,000

TERRESTRIAL SPACE

100

Upper atmosphere

10 — ATMOSPHERE

Lower atmosphere — Earth

Nautical miles (logarithmic scale)

DIVISIONS OF AEROSPACE

A Boeing 747 jet airliner nears completion in one of the company's manufacturing and assembly buildings. Boeing has long been a leader in the United States aerospace industry.

engine, and supporting equipment (*see* Airplane). A jet airplane has many thousands of parts. It therefore takes a long time—at least four or five years—to initiate, develop, and produce an aerospace vehicle. This is called lead time.

The important preliminary steps before manufacturing itself begins are research and development, including engineering and testing (*see* section on Research and Development). Military or business leaders first specify the characteristics of the vehicle they want built. In a military plane fast takeoff, supersonic speed, armament, and bomb load are important. In an airliner the number of passengers and cargo weight are considered. Manufacturers of aerospace vehicles often develop their own design ideas.

The engineering department may have a thousand specialists. They prepare drawings that show the configuration, or general outlines, of the vehicle. Scale models are made for testing in a wind tunnel (*see* Wind Tunnel). Next a mock-up, or full-sized replica, is built. Accuracy of calculations is checked with electronic computers, slide rules, and graphs.

Draftsmen then draw blueprints. A medium-sized jet plane may require up to 18,000 blueprints. An experimental model, or prototype, is constructed. Test pilots prove its airworthiness in actual flight.

The production of the vehicle takes careful planning. Plant layout experts make a miniature scale model of the plant to solve production problems. Contracts are let to subcontractors who will supply the parts. Workers must be trained.

Machines, tools, fixtures, and jigs are ordered. Fixtures are devices for holding parts during machining or assembly. A jig is a device for guiding a tool, such as a drill. Huge hydraulic presses, two stories high and exerting 3,000 tons of pressure, are used to form as many as 24 parts from a sheet of metal at one time. The metal parts are anodized to give them a tough, thin film that prevents corrosion and bonds paint. They are heat-treated to make them stronger and sprayed with paint to protect them.

When production begins, the factory is a noisy and busy place. People work with riveting guns, mechanical hammers, saws, and many other tools. Overhead cranes carry materials. Tractors, trailers, and lift trucks move supplies.

In different shops and departments in the plant, parts are built into sections called subassemblies. Routers constantly check on supplies. Hundreds of inspectors examine parts and assemblies.

The aerospace manufacturing industry has borrowed the assembly-line method from the automobile makers. As the vehicle moves down the line, assemblers, riveters, and welders fit sections to it—the nose, fuselage, wings, tail, engines, and so on—until the craft is completed. It is then test-flown.

HISTORY OF THE AEROSPACE INDUSTRY IN THE UNITED STATES

About a year after their first successful flight the Wright brothers began negotiations with the United States government to build an airplane. The United States Army signed a contract for a Wright plane in 1908. Glenn H. Curtiss became a competitor of the Wrights and later one of the leading aircraft manufacturers in the United States.

By 1914 there were 16 aircraft manufacturers in the United States. In the next two years they had produced fewer than 1,000 airplanes. During World War I American pilots flew Allied planes. Few American-built planes were used in combat, although the

This article was critically reviewed by Robert van der Linden, Assistant Curator, Department of Aeronautics, National Air and Space Museum, Smithsonian Institution.

United States eventually produced 14,000 planes and flying boats. The greatest American contribution was the 12-cylinder 400-horsepower Liberty engine. After the war the aircraft industry decreased substantially. Surplus war planes glutted the market.

After Charles A. Lindbergh's transatlantic flight in 1927 interest in aviation boomed (*see* Lindbergh). By 1929 the industry had greatly expanded, but production dropped during the depression of the 1930's.

The development of economical multiengine planes, such as the Boeing 247 and Douglas DC-2 and DC-3, stimulated the growth of airlines and aircraft production. Military aircraft orders also increased in the period before World War II as nations rearmed.

Wartime Production

When Germany attacked France, President Franklin D. Roosevelt called on the industry to produce a staggering 50,000 planes a year during World War II. In its whole history it had made less than 45,000. In 1944, however, its production was almost double this goal. During the entire war it made some 300,000 military aircraft. In 1943 the industry had 1,345,600 employees. The manufacture of aircraft had become one of the nation's leading industries.

After the war the aviation industry curtailed production drastically. By 1949 output had dropped to 6,100. When the Korean War broke out in 1950 the industry again increased production. More than 19,000 military aircraft were built during that war.

In the 1950's significant developments included the conversion of commercial airlines from propeller and piston-engine aircraft to jet planes (*see* Jet Propulsion; Airplane; Rocket). The greatest growth in aviation was in smaller planes used for private and business flying (*see* Aviation). Helicopter production also increased. The aviation industry became the aerospace industry as the United States and the Soviet Union competed in production of intercontinental su-

Lockheed-Georgia Co.

Computers aid engineers and mathematicians in designing modern aircraft. Thousands of specialists are required to plan and build the complex vehicles.

personic missiles and Earth-girdling satellites. From 1964 to 1973, when the United States was actively involved in the Vietnam conflict, almost 30,000 military aircraft—including helicopters—were built.

The Aerospace Industry Today

In the United States major producers of aircraft, aircraft engines, missiles, and space vehicles number more than a dozen. Some concentrate principally upon military equipment, others upon civilian products. Most, however, either manufacture for both markets or are prepared to do so. As vehicles become increasingly complex, companies often work in partnership on major projects. They also depend upon specialized suppliers for many items. Tens of thousands of smaller firms make parts for the primary

One of the world's largest buildings, Boeing's 747 assembly plant in Everett, Wash., was expanded to accommodate production of the 767. After the jetliners emerge from one of the giant doors along the front of the main building, they are towed across a highway overpass to a preflight area (lower left).

Boeing Co.

Ablation. The melting, erosion, evaporation, or vaporization of nose cone materials of vehicles entering a planetary atmosphere at high speeds.

Aerodynamics. The science that studies the motion of air and other gases and the forces that act on bodies moving through them.

Aeronautics. The science or art of operating both lighter-than-air and heavier-than-air craft.

Aerospace. The earth's atmosphere and the space above it, in which fly aircraft, missiles, and spacecraft.

Afterburner. An auxiliary combustion chamber at rear of a jet engine into which additional fuel is injected and burned, utilizing unburned oxygen in the exhaust gases to increase thrust.

Aileron. A movable control surface, usually on trailing edge of wing, used to control rolling of airplane.

Airfoil. A surface designed to obtain a reaction from air, such as a wing for lift, fin for stability, elevator for control, and propeller blade for thrust.

Airspeed. Speed of an aircraft relative to the air in contrast to *ground speed*, or its speed relative to the ground.

Airway. A designated air route equipped with navigational aids.

Angle of attack. The angle formed by the chord of an airfoil and the line of air flow, or relative wind.

Angle of incidence. Angle made by the chord of an airfoil and the longitudinal axis of the aircraft; that is, the angle at which the airfoil is attached to the airplane.

Area rule. A method of aircraft design for minimizing drag. The cross-sectional area of transonic aircraft is distributed to resemble that of an ideal body of minimum drag by lengthening the nose, adding a tail blister, or indenting the fuselage in a *Coke-bottle* shape.

Aspect ratio of airfoil wing. Ratio of span of a wing to its mean chord.

Attitude. The position of an aircraft or spacecraft as determined by the relationship of its axes to some reference line, plane, or system of reference axes.

Automatic direction finder (ADF). A radio compass that automatically indicates the direction of the station to which it is tuned.

Automatic pilot, or autopilot. A device that maintains an aircraft in straight and level flight on a set course.

Aviation. The art or practice of designing, developing, manufacturing, or operating heavier-than-air craft.

Axis. A line passing through an airplane about which it may revolve. An airplane has three mutually perpendicular axes, each passing through the center of gravity—*longitudinal* from nose to tail, measuring roll;

lateral, from wing tip to wing tip, measuring pitch; and *vertical*, from back to belly, measuring yaw.

Bail out. To make a parachute jump.

Bank. To incline an airplane laterally.

Beacon. A device that guides aircraft with light, radio, or radar beams.

Beam. A stream of radio or radar impulses or light rays used for aircraft guidance.

Blackout. Temporary loss of vision, sometimes followed by unconsciousness, in making a fast turn or pulling out of a dive when centrifugal force decreases blood pressure in the head, resulting in insufficient oxygen. A *redout* results at the top of a dive when blood rushes to the head.

Blind flying. Flight with the use of instruments when the pilot cannot see out because of darkness or weather.

Boundary layer. A thin layer of air next to an airfoil, distinct from the main air flow, with flow characteristics resulting from friction. Its flow may be *laminar* (smooth) or *turbulent* (eddying).

Braking ellipses. A series of orbital approaches to the atmosphere of the earth or other planet to slow a spacecraft before landing.

Ceiling. 1. Maximum altitude an aircraft can attain. 2. Upper limit of flying visibility because of clouds.

Chord. The dimension between the leading and trailing edges of an airfoil section.

Clearance. Authorization for a flight to depart from an airfield or to fly a specified route.

Collective pitch control. The control in a helicopter for changing the pitch of all the main rotor blades simultaneously to regulate lift.

Condensation trail, or vapor trail. A visible trail of water droplets or ice crystals formed in the wake of high-altitude aircraft by disturbing supercooled air and by ejecting water vapor of the exhaust into cold air.

Control stick, or stick. A lever which controls movements of a plane by operating elevators and ailerons. Some aircraft have a *wheel* on a *control column* instead of a stick.

Convertiplane. An aircraft designed to fly vertically (like a helicopter) and horizontally (like a fixed-wing plane).

Crabbing. To point an aircraft partly into the wind to offset drift.

Crosswind landing gear. A landing gear with wheels that turn from side to side enabling the airplane to land in a crabbed attitude.

Cruising speed. Speed at which a plane flies best under given conditions.

Cyclic pitch control. Helicopter control for changing angle of each rotor blade during the cycle of rotation to regulate horizontal flight.

Dead reckoning. Calculation of position using earlier known position, elapsed time, speed, heading, and wind.

Deicer. Device for removing ice from wings, propeller, or control surfaces.

Dihedral. Upward (positive) or downward (negative) inclination of a wing or stabilizer from the horizontal.

Drag. Resistance to the passage of an airplane through the air.

Ejection seat. A seat designed to be catapulted with its occupant from high-speed aircraft in an emergency.

Elevator. A control surface hinged to a horizontal stabilizer for rotating an aircraft about its lateral axis.

Empennage, or tail assembly. Horizontal and vertical stabilizers and control surfaces at rear of an aircraft.

Feather. 1. To turn a propeller blade edgewise into the airflow to minimize resistance. 2. To change blade angle or a rotor blade or rotating wing.

Flap. A movable control surface at rear of wing for increasing lift or drag in takeoff or landing.

Flight plan. A detailed statement about a proposed flight submitted to Air Traffic Control prior to takeoff, including point of departure and destination, flight route, altitude, and airspeed.

Free fall. The drop of a parachutist before opening his parachute.

Fuselage. The main body of an airplane.

G-force. A force exerted by gravity or by reaction to acceleration or deceleration when direction is changed. Measured in g's, or multiples of the force of gravity.

Glide path. The line of flight of an aircraft in controlled descent.

Ground controlled approach (GCA). An instrument landing system, used during poor visibility, in which a ground operator observes a plane's position and direction on a radarscope and directs the pilot by radio.

Ground loop. A violent turn made while moving on the ground.

Gull wing. A wing which slants upward from its roots and then flattens out or angles upward. An *inverted gull wing* slants downward and then straightens out or slants upward.

Heat barrier. *See in this table* Thermal barrier.

Helicopter. An aircraft capable of both vertical and horizontal flight, which derives both lift and thrust from rotating wings power-driven about a vertical axis.

High-wing monoplane. An airplane whose wing is mounted at, near, or above the top of the fuselage. A *parasol monoplane* has its wing mounted above the fuselage on struts.

Hypoxia. Oxygen deficiency in the blood in high-altitude flight, impairing physical faculties.

Icing. Atmospheric moisture freezing on the surfaces of an aircraft.

Instrument flight rules (IFR). Traffic and procedure rules governing flight under instrument conditions.

Instrument flying. Navigating and controlling an aircraft solely by the use of instruments.

Instrument Landing System (ILS). Radio system for guiding aircraft in landing during poor visibility. Directional radio transmitters indicate direction of runway and angle of glide path, and radio marker beacons establish position along approach path.

Jet. *See in this table* Turbofan; Turbojet.

Jet stream. 1. Narrow band of high-speed wind in upper troposphere or in stratosphere moving west to east. 2. Stream of combustion products expelled from a reaction engine.

Lift. Aerodynamic force which acts on an airfoil perpendicular to the relative wind and is usually exerted upward, opposing force of gravity.

Loop. Maneuver in which an airplane makes a circular path in the vertical plane, with its lateral axis horizontal.

Low-wing monoplane. An airplane whose wing is mounted at or near the bottom of the fuselage.

Mach number. A number expressing the ratio of the speed of a moving body or of air to the speed of sound, with Mach 1.0 equal to the speed of sound.

Mid-wing monoplane. An airplane whose wing is mounted halfway between the top and bottom of the fuselage.

Mush. To settle or to gain little or no altitude while flying with the airplane's nose held high.

Nacelle. A housing on an aircraft for engines, personnel, or equipment.

Nose cone. The shield that fits over, or is, the nose of an aerospace vehicle; constructed to resist the high temperatures generated by friction with air particles.

Omnidirectional range or omnirange. A radio navigation system that gives bearings in all directions from a transmitter.

Pilotage. Navigation by visual reference to check points and by comparing landmarks with symbols on a chart.

Pilot chute. A small parachute which pulls out main parachute from pack.

Pitch. The up-and-down, or vertical, movement of an aircraft about its lateral axis.

Pitot-static tube. A device, consisting of a pitot tube and a static tube, that measures impact and static pressures. The pressure difference registers airspeed in an air-speed indicator. The static pressure may operate an altimeter or similar instruments.

Pressurize. To maintain normal pressure in a cabin at high altitudes.

Radius of action, or radius. The distance an airplane can fly and return to its starting point.

Range. Maximum distance an aircraft can fly from takeoff until its fuel supply is exhausted.

Reaction engine. An engine, such as a jet or rocket type, which derives thrust by its reaction to a substance ejected rearward.

Reciprocating engine. An engine which develops thrust by back-and-forth motion of pistons in cylinders to rotate a crankshaft.

Reduction gear. A gear assembly used to run a propeller or a rotor at a slower rate than the engine.

Relative wind. Flow of air with reference to an object passing through it.

Rendezvous. The meeting in flight of two or more aerospace vehicles at a planned time and place; also, the point in aerospace where the meeting occurs.

Rev, or rev up. To revolve or to increase the revolutions per minute of an engine.

Reversible-pitch propeller. A propeller whose blade angle can be changed to give reverse thrust for braking the airplane in landing.

Rocket. An engine which derives thrust from expulsion of hot gases and carries an oxidizer, making it independent of atmosphere for combustion.

Roger. 1. A code word meaning "message received and understood." 2. An expression of agreement meaning "O. K." or "all right."

Roll. Rotation of an airplane about its longitudinal axis.

Run, or run up. To increase engine speed while the aircraft is standing still to check or to warm up the engine.

Sideslip. 1. To slide sideways and downward along the lateral axis with wings sharply banked. 2. In a turn, a sidewise movement toward the inside of a turn. A *skid* is a slide sideways away from the center of the turn.

Solo. Flying alone.

Sonic. Pertaining to speed of sound.

Sonic barrier, or sound barrier. Large increase in drag when approaching the speed of sound.

Space platform or station. A large habitable satellite for scientific and military uses.

Span. The dimension of an airfoil from tip to tip.

Spar. The principal longitudinal member in a wing or other airfoil.

Spin. A maneuver, controlled or uncontrolled, in which an airplane dives and spirals at the same time.

Stability. Ability of an aircraft to return to level flight.

Stabilizer. An airfoil which keeps an aircraft steady in flight; includes horizontal member of the tail assembly.

Stall. A condition which occurs when an airplane flies at insufficient airspeed and with the nose too high, creating an excessive angle of attack on the wings and resulting in a loss of lift.

Strut. A rigid member that bears compression loads, such as between longerons in a fuselage or in a landing gear.

Subsonic. Less than speed of sound.

Supercharger. A pump or compressor for forcing air into a reciprocating engine for high-altitude flights.

Supersonic. Greater than speed of sound.

Sweepback. The backward slant of a wing or other airfoil.

Tab. A small airfoil hinged to a control surface and used to move the larger surface or to trim or balance the plane. May be a *balancing tab, servo tab,* or *trim tab.*

Taxi. To move an airplane over ground or water under its own power.

Thermal barrier, or heat barrier. Zone of speed at which friction heat generated by passage of an object through air endangers its operation.

Three-point landing. A landing in which the tail skid or tail or nose wheel of an airplane and its two main wheels touch ground at the same instant.

Torque. A force which produces twisting, such as rolling of an airplane in reaction to the rotating propeller or turning of a helicopter fuselage because of the revolving rotor.

Transonic. The transitional speed between subsonic and supersonic.

Turbofan. A jet engine of the bypass, or ducted-fan, type in which part of the air taken in at the front by a compressor or fan bypasses the combustion chamber to give extra thrust; one type has a fan at the rear.

Turbojet. A jet engine with a turbine-driven compressor that takes in and compresses air for combustion of fuel, producing hot exhaust gases that rotate the turbine and create a jet steam for thrust.

Turboprop, or prop jet. A jet engine whose exhaust gases drive a turbine-connected propeller and also produce thrust.

Visual flight rules (VFR). Rules for minimum altitudes and limits of visibility to govern contact flight by visual reference to the ground.

Warm-up. Running an engine to heat it to operating temperature.

Wind sock. A cloth cone pivoted on a pole to show wind direction.

Wind tee. A pivoted T-shaped device that indicates wind direction.

Wing loading. Gross weight of loaded airplane divided by the wing area.

Yaw. Movement about vertical axis.

Zoom. A brief, steep climb.

BIRTHPLACE OF THE AEROSPACE INDUSTRY

Interior and exterior views show the bicycle shop where the Wright brothers made parts for the first airplane. Henry Ford moved the shop to his historic Greenfield Village in Michigan.

producers. Overall, the aerospace industry employs more than a million persons.

The leading manufacturers of airframes for aircraft, missiles, and space vehicles include Boeing, Fairchild Republic, General Dynamics, Grumman, Hughes, Ling-Temco-Vought, Lockheed, Martin Marietta, McDonnell Douglas, North American Aircraft, and Northrop. Among the producers of private aircraft are Beech, Cessna, and Piper. Engine makers include Avco Lycoming, General Electric, and Pratt and Whitney. Helicopter manufacturers include Bell, Boeing, Hiller, Hughes, Kaman, and Sikorsky.

The federal government is the major customer for missiles, space vehicles, aircraft, and their components. Annual government purchases of these vehicles and parts total some 23 billion dollars, about 54 percent of the United States aerospace products and services sold. In 1968 the aerospace industry produced a record high of about 19,000 aircraft—15,000 civil and 4,000 military.

Private Industry in the Satellite Program

In 1962, after the launching of the privately developed Telstar communications satellite, Congress passed the Communications Satellite Act. This authorized the formation of a private corporation, the first time such a step had been taken by the government. On Feb. 1, 1963, the Communications Satellite Corporation (COMSAT) was chartered.

On April 6, 1965, COMSAT launched Early Bird, the world's first commercial communications satellite. The satellite relayed telephone messages and television and other transmissions between North America and Europe. The Early Bird program is an

international venture. It is supported by many nations, each of which has its own ground station. More than 100 countries cooperate in a global system of communications satellites.

Other Production Techniques

Aerospace industry companies have done research in manufacturing methods as well as in design. Several of these companies have explored the use of explosive forming to shape hard missile metals. These require even more power to mold them than the tremendous force of hydraulic presses. The release of a great amount of electrical energy in a few millionths of a second underwater produces an explosion that is similar to lightning. This "spark" creates a shock wave that travels rapidly through the water, pushing the metal into a mold.

Another development is the honeycomb panel for wings and fuselages. The skins of both aircraft and missiles need to be more durable to withstand stress at higher speeds, but strong metals are heavy. Designers join cells of thin aluminum or stainless steel to resemble a honeycomb. Thin layers of metal are stretched across the open ends of the cells and bonded to them by heat to form a honeycomb sandwich. It is lighter than a solid piece of metal of the same thickness but is very strong. The brazing technique devised for honeycomb panels is widely used. It eliminates drilling, punching, rolling, and welding.

Automation, or the use of electronic and mechanical devices to control machine operations, also has had a major effect on the industry (see Automation). Parts can be cut, drilled, or punched more precisely and quickly in this way than by a human operator.

A jetliner has fuel tanks located in the wings. This Qantas 747B is being refueled for an overseas flight from Australia.

Qantas

Aerospace Fuels

Aircraft that fly within the Earth's atmosphere and spaceships that travel in outer space require fuels to power them. The reciprocating, or piston-type, aircraft engine uses gasoline (*see* Airplane, section on Power Plants; Gasoline). This petroleum substance produces heat by burning. The heat energy is converted into pressure energy which produces mechanical power to turn a propeller.

Jet engines use kerosene or a gasoline and kerosene mixture (*see* Jet Propulsion). They also change heat to pressure energy but use expanding gases directly.

Rocket engines also propel aircraft or spacecraft by using the jet thrust (*see* Rocket). They burn a wide range of fuels. Under development are nuclear and ion power plants (*see* Space Travel; *see also* section on Research and Development).

Aviation Gasoline

Until World War II aviation gasoline underwent little change (*see* Petroleum). The octane rating, however, was increased from about 87 to 100. The octane number is the antiknock value of a fuel. Knocking indicates that combustion in the cylinder is too rapid. The higher the octane number the greater is the fuel's ability to reduce engine knock. Octane numbers range from 0 to 100. Tetraethyl lead is added to give the proper octane number. The larger aircraft require fuels of higher than 100 octane. The performance number scale was devised to rate such fuels.

Midair refueling increases the range of military aircraft. An Air Force HC-130P tanker (below left) refuels an HH-3E rescue helicopter as it flies on duty over Vietnam. A B-52 bomber (below right) takes on fuel from a KC-135 tanker.

Lockheed-Georgia Co.

Boeing Co.

73

Grades of Fuel

Aircraft engines, like those of automobiles, require different grades of fuel. The aviation gasoline now used is graded 81/87, 91/98, 100/130, and, for the later planes, such as the Boeing Stratocruiser, 115/145.

Aircraft engine developments created the dual number fuel rating. The first number is the "lean mixture rating." It indicates how the fuel resists knocking with the engine adjusted for economy while cruising. The second number is the "rich mixture rating." It designates antiknock quality with the engine at maximum power during take-off and climb.

Jets Burn Kerosene

The first jet engines used a special kerosene. Since the early jets were military aircraft and the petroleum industry was set up to produce gasoline, a compromise fuel had to be developed. This jet fuel, which was a combination of gasoline and kerosene, was called JP-4. The majority of jet airliners burn highly refined kerosene.

Rocket and Spaceship Fuels

Rocket engines carry their own supply of oxygen in the form of chemical oxidizers, which enable them to burn materials not usually considered aircraft fuels. These range from liquid hydrogen and liquid oxygen, or kerosene and liquid oxygen, to exotic hydrazine-based fuels used in combination with liquid oxygen or acid oxidizers.

Liquid fuels generally produce more energy and power than the solid fuels used in present-day rocket engines. Solid fuels being considered for use include uranium for nuclear engines and cesium for ion engines. The nuclear reactor may be used to furnish heat for a jet engine; or the products of the nuclear reaction may serve as the propellant.

Fuels with Greater Heat Content

Chemists are attempting to develop fuels that have greater heat content. The planes that utilize such fuels could carry lighter fuel loads, as well as more passengers, and the craft would also be able to fly longer without refueling.

A large automobile may get 10 to 15 miles per gallon of gasoline, whereas a Douglas DC-7 flying at a speed of 300 miles per hour will get only about a half mile per gallon and a jet transport will get only about a quarter mile per gallon. Jet airliners are equipped

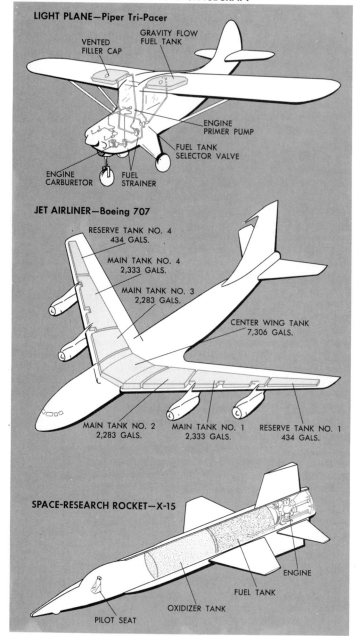

FUEL SYSTEMS OF AIRCRAFT AND SPACECRAFT

LIGHT PLANE—Piper Tri-Pacer

VENTED FILLER CAP
GRAVITY FLOW FUEL TANK
ENGINE PRIMER PUMP
FUEL TANK SELECTOR VALVE
ENGINE CARBURETOR
FUEL STRAINER

JET AIRLINER—Boeing 707

RESERVE TANK NO. 4 434 GALS.
MAIN TANK NO. 4 2,333 GALS.
MAIN TANK NO. 3 2,283 GALS.
CENTER WING TANK 7,306 GALS.
MAIN TANK NO. 2 2,283 GALS.
MAIN TANK NO. 1 2,333 GALS.
RESERVE TANK NO. 1 434 GALS.

SPACE-RESEARCH ROCKET—X-15

ENGINE
FUEL TANK
OXIDIZER TANK
PILOT SEAT

to carry up to 23,000 gallons, or 138,000 pounds, of fuel. Jet engine fuel consumption is measured in pounds per hour, which is indicated on the plane's instrument panel.

Fueling Systems

Aircraft are refueled from tank trucks or hydrant systems. The hydrant systems, which are faster, pump the fuel from airport storage tanks directly to the aircraft through underground pipes. These systems are capable of fueling a plane at the rate of 600 gallons per minute.

Research and Development

Flight by humans resulted from the study and experiments of patient and curious dreamers. When, in 1961, a person finally was able to fly in outer space, it came about because of research and development. This is the systematic search for scientific principles as well as their application in a practical way.

Various types of vehicles fly in aerospace. Aircraft are machines designed to operate through the atmosphere of the Earth (*see* Airplane). Spacecraft are devices, unmanned or manned, for flight in outer space (*see* Guided Missiles; Space Travel). Space-air vehicles operate both within and above the atmosphere (*see* Atmosphere).

Steps in Research and Development

Research is of two types, basic and applied (*see* Science). Basic research attempts to discover fundamental principles. Applied research tries to find uses for these principles. When research has shown that it is feasible to construct an aerospace vehicle, development begins.

Development goes through three main stages—engineering, production, and testing. In the engineering stage the vehicle is designed and blueprints are made. Frequently a mock-up is built. This is a nonflying model, sometimes constructed in full size. Then the engineers develop a prototype. This is the master model that serves as the pattern for production.

Manufacturing begins with the production stage. Before the assembly lines turn out the vehicle in quantity, it goes through the testing stage. Tests show whether the craft will perform as planned. The steps from research through development are not clearly separated but go on at the same time.

Fields of Research

Aerospace research concerns itself with many fields of investigation. They involve the aeronautical or space vehicle, its performance, and its pilot. Research on a vehicle includes aerodynamics, propulsion systems, structures, and materials. While in flight, its communication and navigation systems and operating and meteorological problems are investigated. Pilot research involves human reactions to flight.

Aerodynamics is concerned with the forces acting on a vehicle in motion in the air (*see* Airplane, section on Aerodynamics). It attempts to discover the most efficient shape for flight. Designers increase speed by streamlining the craft so that it offers the least resistance, or drag, to air. A streamlined shape is particularly important in supersonic flight. When an airplane flies near, at, or beyond the speed of sound, it creates shock waves. The air piles up because it cannot move aside quickly enough to make space for the airplane. Shock waves resist motion through them and therefore cause drag.

NASA

A shuttle orbiter is lowered into a test stand at the Marshall Space Flight Center for further assembly and testing.

Propulsion, Structure, and Materials

Propulsion research has played a key role in man's growing ability to move through and beyond the atmosphere (*see* Airplane, section on Power Plants). Reciprocating engines have progressed from the 12-horsepower engine of the Wright brothers to the 3,500-horsepower propeller-driven airliners that were developed by the late 1950's. Jet engines are now capable of more than 50,000 pounds of thrust at 600 miles an hour (*see* Jet Propulsion).

Structural research has resulted in new techniques for forming the frame and skin of aircraft. Thinner wings for higher speed meant that rib and skin construction had to be replaced by panels machined from heavy slabs of solid metal alloys. Swept-back wings like those of the B-52 are flexible yet strong.

On each square foot of wing surface a fighter plane may support 110 pounds of pressure on takeoff and 70 pounds in landing. Designers allow a margin of strength well beyond what may be needed in flight.

The search for new materials goes hand in hand with structural research. The aluminum alloys used in World War II airplanes proved excellent for subsonic flying. Supersonic flight, however, subjects a plane to much higher temperatures, and stronger

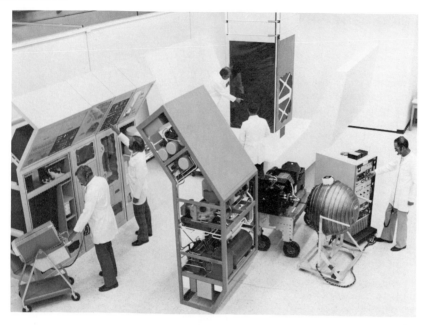

During a simulation of tasks to be performed on a space shuttle mission, scientists check out equipment that will be used for biological and chemical experiments.

metals are needed. Today stainless steel, molybdenum, and titanium are most commonly used. The X-15 research rocket plane was built with a nickel alloy, Inconel-X, which can withstand temperatures of 1,000° F (540° C). In addition, new airplanes are being constructed of strong, lightweight composites—for example, graphite and boron.

Operation Problems and Pilot Research

The advent of jet aircraft has created a demand for communication and navigation facilities geared to flights at higher speeds. Communication with satellites has developed to a high stage. For example, in 1960 Pioneer 5 sent information 5 million miles to Earth, and its transmitters were designed to send a signal 50 million miles. Increasingly sophisticated equipment was acquired for the growing number of deep-space probes that were launched by many nations during the 1970's and 1980's.

Advances in the speed of aircraft bring new operating problems for research to solve. Higher cruising speeds mean higher landing speeds; therefore pilot control of high-performance aircraft during landings must be improved. Many airliners carry instruments to measure airspeed and altitude during flight from takeoff to landing. These records promote safety in day-to-day operations.

In meteorology much research remains to be done (see Aviation, section on Meteorology). High-speed aircraft fly quickly through a wide range of weather conditions of which the pilot must be kept informed.

A great step forward in meteorological research was the launching in 1960 of the first weather observation satellite, Tiros 1, by the National Aeronautics and Space Administration (NASA). As it orbited, it photographed the clouds covering Earth. Meteorologists study such photographs for a more complete picture of global weather. The first Synchronous Meteorological Satellite was launched in 1974.

Advanced aeronautical and space vehicles require an understanding of human reactions to high gravity conditions, weightlessness, disorientation, confinement, and other unfamiliar experiences (see section on Aerospace Medicine).

Early Research

Throughout the history of people's attempts to fly, they not only experimented with flying machines but also developed the scientific foundations of flight (see Airplane, section on History). As early as the 4th century B.C., Aristotle studied hydrodynamics, from which the science of aerodynamics springs. Hydrodynamics deals with fluids in motion. Later contributors to this science included Leonardo da Vinci, Galileo, Sir Isaac Newton, Johann and Daniel Bernoulli, Leonhard Euler, and Jean le Rond d'Alembert.

In the 19th century interest in science and aeronautics grew. Investigators of fluid flow included Augustin Louis Cauchy, Sir G. G. Stokes, Hermann von Helmholtz, and Gustav Robert Kirchhoff.

Sir George Cayley was one of the first experimenters to see the problem of flight clearly. In 1809 he stated that the solution to flight would be "to make a surface support a given weight by the application of power to the resistance of air." He suggested the use of a propeller and an "explosion" engine. Cayley experimented with gliders and models. Francis H. Wenham built the first wind tunnel in 1871.

In 1883 Sir Osborne Reynolds determined that fluid flow is either laminar (smooth) or turbulent. He expressed the type of flow as a ratio between the velocity, density, and length of a fluid stream and the viscosity of the fluid. Today this fraction is called the Reynolds number. It is important in relating wind-tunnel research with scale models to the actual flights of full-sized vehicles.

Ernst Mach was the first to do laboratory research in the motion of fluids at supersonic speeds. In 1887 he photographed shock waves at the nose of a projectile in flight. Later he experimented with a model in a supersonic jet of air. His work is recognized in the term Mach number, which designates flight speeds in relation to the speed of sound. The principle of lift and drag was developed in 1894 by F. W. Lanchester.

Samuel P. Langley spent many years studying air resistance before he built powered models (see Langley). His experiments ended in his ill-fated attempts at full-scale flight in 1903.

The Wright brothers familiarized themselves with the earlier experiments and theories on flight. Dissatisfied with the scientific data, they built a wind tunnel. Their tests of airfoil shapes contributed to their successful flights.

A vast organization of scientific and technological specialists has since emerged to study the flight of aircraft and spacecraft. Research is usually undertaken by teams due to its complexity. Much research is government sponsored because of its high cost and military requirements.

Research Institutions

Aerospace research in the United States is carried on by governmental agencies and private institutions. The major research organization is the National Aeronautics and Space Administration (NASA). Congress created NASA as an independent civilian agency in 1958. It succeeded the National Advisory Committee for Aeronautics, which had been established in 1915. Among NASA research centers are:

Ames Research Center: gas dynamics; automatic stabilization, guidance, and control of space vehicles; biomedical and biophysical research.

George C. Marshall Space Flight Center: launch-vehicle systems; spacecraft structures and materials.

Goddard Space Flight Center: emphasis on Earth, sun, and astronomy aspects of space-science program; tracking and data-gathering functions.

Hugh L. Dryden Research Center: flight-evaluation tests of research aircraft such as the X-15.

Jet Propulsion Laboratory: emphasis on deep-space exploration, including moon and interplanetary flights; Earth and ocean dynamics.

John F. Kennedy Space Center: principal launch site for manned and unmanned spacecraft.

Langley Research Center: aerodynamics of reentry vehicles; spacecraft structures and materials.

Lewis Research Center: propulsion and power-plant research on technology for space vehicles, including nuclear rockets.

Lyndon B. Johnson Space Center: responsibility for spacecraft for Projects Mercury, Gemini, Apollo.

National Space Technology Laboratories: tests of space shuttle engines; environmental research.

Wallops Flight Center: launching smaller Earth satellites; firing sounding rockets.

SOME PRINCIPAL UNITED STATES GOVERNMENT RESEARCH AND DEVELOPMENT CENTERS

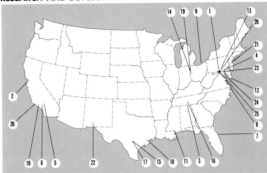

Federal Aviation Administration
1. FAA headquarters, Washington, D. C.

National Aeronautics and Space Administration
2. Ames Research Center, Moffett Field, Calif.
3. George C. Marshall Space Flight Center, Huntsville, Ala.
4. Goddard Space Flight Center, Greenbelt, Md.
5. Hugh L. Dryden Research Center, Edwards, Calif.
6. Jet Propulsion Laboratory, California Institute of Technology, Pasadena, Calif.
7. John F. Kennedy Space Center, Cape Canaveral, Fla.
8. Langley Research Center, Langley Field, Va.
9. Lewis Research Center, Cleveland, Ohio
10. Lyndon B. Johnson Space Center, Houston, Tex.
11. National Space Technology Laboratories, Bay St. Louis, Miss.
12. Wallops Flight Center, Wallops Island, Va.

National Bureau of Standards
13. NBS headquarters, Washington, D. C.

United States Air Force
14. Aeronautical Systems Division, Wright-Patterson AFB, Ohio
15. Aerospace Medical Division, Brooks AFB, Tex.
16. Arnold Engineering Development Center, Arnold AFS, Tenn.
17. School of Aerospace Medicine, Brooks AFB, Tex.
18. Space and Missile Systems Organization, Los Angeles AFS, Calif.
19. Wright Aeronautical Laboratories, Wright-Patterson AFB, Ohio

United States Army
20. Army Ballistics Research Laboratory, Aberdeen, Md.
21. Electronic Technology and Devices Laboratory, Fort Monmouth, N. J.
22. White Sands Missile Range, Las Cruces, N. M.

United States Department of Defense
23. Defense Advanced Research Projects Agency, Washington, D. C.

United States Navy
24. Naval Air Test Center, Naval Air Station, Patuxent River, Md.
25. Naval Research Laboratory, Washington, D. C.
26. Pacific Missile Test Center, Point Mugu, Calif.

The Department of Defense and its three military services—the Air Force, Navy, and Army—also engage in aerospace research. The Defense Advanced Research Projects Agency, an organization within the Defense Department, is responsible for all proj-

NASA

Some experimental aircraft are air-launched. Here an X-15 drops away from its B-52 "mother" plane.

The YF-12A is used by the Air Force and by NASA in high-performance tests.

A new airfoil shape that could substantially lower jetliner operating costs is tested on this modified Navy F-8.

Manned lifting bodies, such as this X-24, have been tested as the forerunners of space-shuttle craft.

Aircraft that can take off and land vertically have received a great deal of study in the United States and abroad.

ects that relate to space research. Other governmental agencies engaged in aerospace research are the Federal Aviation Administration, National Oceanic and Atmospheric Administration, and National Bureau of Standards.

Private research organizations include educational institutions, industrial groups, and laboratories and foundations. Among these are the Battelle Memorial Institute, IIT (Illinois Institute of Technology) Research Institute, Stanford Research Institute, Rand Corporation, and Brookings Institution.

Most of the major European countries, including the Soviet Union, have some aerospace research activity under government, industrial, or university sponsorship. Many belong to the European Space Agency, a counterpart of NASA. In the Far East, Japan has a growing interest in research. The United Nations has been making an effort to coordinate aerospace work throughout the world.

Tools for Research

Many specialized facilities and instruments have been developed for aerospace research. The chief tool in the first half of the 20th century was the wind tunnel (see Wind Tunnel). New facilities that reach beyond the speed limitations of the wind tunnel have been invented. The wind tunnel, however, is far from being outmoded. No matter how far space vehicles travel they must slow down for landing. The flying qualities of spacecraft over their entire range of speed must continually be investigated.

The evolution of power plants from piston engines through jets and to rockets and other space propulsion systems has called for new research techniques. Test cells, strong enough to withstand high temperatures and thrust, have been devised for jet and rocket engines. Fuel and lubricant research requires chemical and mechanical laboratory equipment. Lubricants are tested for atomic radiation reaction to learn whether they will suit the special requirements of various types of spacecraft.

Structural research laboratories use large machines for twisting or crushing a part under study. Quartz-lamp heaters generate the high temperatures typical of those endured in high-speed flights. Re-

National Aviation Education Council   North American Rockwell Corp.

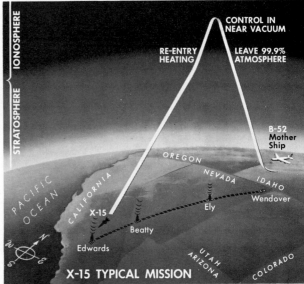

search on material examines new metals, plastics, and cermets (ceramic-metal combinations) that will retain their strength under extreme temperatures.

Flight testing is a useful research technique because measurements can be made under actual flight conditions. It is the earliest aeronautical research method. For many years experimental aircraft have been so thoroughly instrumented that they are flying laboratories. Frequently the test pilots of these vehicles are aeronautical engineers.

Other important facilities are aeromedical laboratories, including those of the military and NASA. These laboratories monitor and explore the effects of aerospace flight on pilots.

Many instruments have been devised to measure the results of experiments. In wind tunnel work an optical device called a schlieren system makes visible

Friendship 7, a Project Mercury space capsule, carried astronaut John H. Glenn, Jr., into orbit on Feb. 20, 1962.

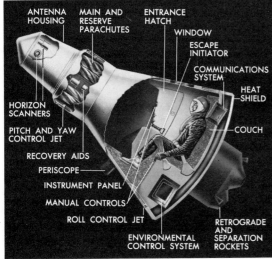

North American Rockwell Corp.

U.S. Air Force

In 1962, for the first time, the North American X-15 flew into outer space, nearly 60 miles above the earth. The rocket plane was carried into the air by a B-52 and then launched.

the shock-wave pattern at supersonic speeds. High-intensity electric sparks produce shock-wave pictures in one ten-millionth of a second for studying models launched from guns at 16,000 miles per hour. A wide range of mechanical instruments measures forces on models in wind tunnels. Electronic devices are used for small quantities and short periods of time.

Pinched-in Fuselages and Blunt Noses

In recent decades new principles of design have appeared. Richard T. Whitcomb, then with the National Advisory Committee for Aeronautics (NACA), discovered the area rule in 1951. It reduced by 25 percent the drag on a plane approaching the speed of sound. The combined cross-sectional area of the wing and fuselage should be no greater than that of an ideal body of minimum drag. Aircraft designers apply the rule by pinching in the fuselage where the wings of the craft are attached.

H. Julian Allen, also of NACA, proposed the blunt nose-cone shape in 1952 as a way to protect a missile from friction as it reenters the atmosphere. A slim, sharp-nosed shape would burn like a needle point held in a flame. He found that a blunt shape creates high drag and a heavy shock wave that dissipates heat. Another type of nose cone is made of material that

79

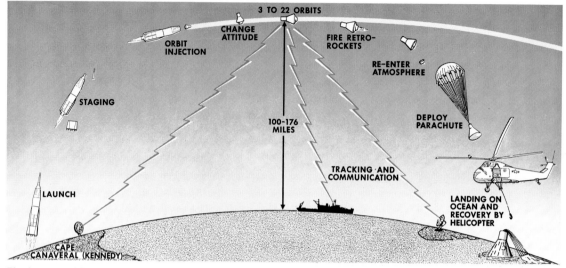

The first United States manned orbital flight, made by John H. Glenn, Jr., in 1962, had been preceded by two manned suborbital flights in 1961. The last of the three Project Mercury flights was made by Leroy Gordon Cooper, Jr., who completed 22 orbits in 1963.

can be ablated, or vaporized, during reentry. This cuts down on drag. The ablating nose cone is longer and more pointed than the blunt type.

New applications of the boundary-layer-control principle were made in the 1950's. The idea that a film of slow-moving air clings to a wing dates back to the discoveries of Reynolds, the British physicist. In experimental planes the boundary layer has been mechanically removed, leaving air of higher velocity to flow and provide more lift.

In the early 1960's a new design to reduce air-friction drag, called Laminar Flow Control (LFC), was successfully tested. The airflow is drawn into slots in the wing surfaces and is expelled through nacelles at the rear. The Northrop X-21A used this design.

Aircraft of Advanced Design

Experiments are continually being conducted with unusual aerospace vehicles. Ground-effect machines hover above the earth or water on an air cushion created by the downdraft of fans. Such vehicles include the Bell SK-1 Hydroskimmer and the English-built SR-N3 Hovercraft.

Many experimental VTOL (vertical takeoff and landing) and STOL (short takeoff and landing) aircraft have been designed and built. The Ryan XV-5B used fans in its wings to gain vertical lift. The Bell X-22A and Curtiss-Wright X-19 used tiltable propellers. The Ling-Temco-Vought XC-142A employed a movable "tilt wing" that pointed the propellers upward or forward. The Piasecki VZ-8P AirGeep, a "flying jeep," used ducted fans for vertical flight.

Advanced power plants are also under continuous development. The ramjet engine is capable of much greater speeds than the turbojet engine. It is used in the United States Air Force's supersonic interceptor Bomarc missile. Rocket engines that develop high thrust have been used in the Bell X-1, the first air-

plane to fly faster than sound, and in the North American X-15 research airplane. A more advanced version, the X-15A-2, was also rocket-powered.

In 1964 the Lockheed YF-12A and SR-71 were unveiled. These planes reached speeds of more than 2,000 miles an hour (over Mach 3) and altitudes above 70,000 feet. Two versatile jet fighters were unveiled in 1972. The McDonnell Douglas F-15 has unprecedented maneuverability, mainly because of its lightweight twin engines and revolutionary wing design. Northrop's F-5E Tiger II is a tactical fighter capable of supersonic flight.

Satellites and Men in Space

The Air Force, Navy, and NASA have launched many artificial satellites in research programs. The satellites developed by the Environmental Science Services Administration, for example, relayed pictures of clouds to the Earth as an aid in weather forecasting. (*See also* Weather.)

The first man to orbit the Earth was the Soviet Union's Maj. Yuri Gagarin, in 1961. John H. Glenn, Jr., made the first United States manned orbital flight, in 1962. Three manned Project Mercury flights followed. Ten orbital flights of two-man Project Gemini spacecraft were made in 1965–66. Manned flights of three-man Project Apollo "moonships" began in 1968. Apollo astronauts made the first lunar landing in 1969. The final United States mission to the moon—Apollo 17—ended with recovery in the Pacific Ocean on Dec. 19, 1972. In May 1973 the manned Skylab program was launched. In July 1975, in a joint United States–Soviet Union space mission, Apollo and Soyuz crews visited each other during a two-day linkup some 140 miles above the Earth. During 1981–82 the space shuttle Columbia made four test flights in preparation for commercial operations, which began in November 1982.

Aerospace Medicine

Although the human body is not structured for flight, men and women have been able to achieve their dreams of being airborne. Their flights in aircraft and in spacecraft subject their bodies to unusual physical, mental, and emotional strains. The branch of medical science concerned with the effects of flight upon human beings both within and beyond the atmosphere is called aerospace medicine. A medical officer who specializes in this field is a flight surgeon.

The health of persons who fly within the atmosphere is the concern of aviation medicine. Among the hazards studied in this field are altitude, speed, fatigue, noise and vibration, airsickness, and toxic substances.

The health of people who fly beyond the atmosphere of the Earth is the concern of space medicine. It involves the study of such problems as weightlessness, radiation, isolation, and the provision for food, water, and air in a sealed space capsule.

Pressure and Temperature Hazards of Flight

The dangers of high-altitude flight include hypoxia and decompression sickness. The extremely low temperatures encountered also create problems.

Hypoxia is a lack of enough oxygen to maintain normal body processes. Mild hypoxia causes a mistaken feeling of well-being coupled with confusion and poor coordination and judgment. Severe hypoxia leads to unconsciousness and death. Hypoxia results from the decrease in air pressure at higher altitudes. As the pressure drops, the air becomes thinner and there is less oxygen present. Oxygen masks can protect fliers from hypoxia up to about 43,000 feet. Above that altitude a pressure suit must be worn or the cabin must be pressurized to permit satisfactory breathing and adequate oxygen intake.

An airman making a rapid climb into the thinner air above 25,000 feet may also be subject to decompression sickness, or aeroembolism. This is similar to the "bends" experienced by deep-sea divers who surface too quickly. The fast reduction of atmospheric pressure causes formation of gas bubbles, largely nitrogen, in the body tissues and fluids. This produces aching joints, itching, coughing and choking, blurred vision, paralysis, and, in severe cases, unconsciousness and death. A pressurized cabin prevents decompression sickness.

A sudden loss of pressure at high altitudes produces explosive decompression. If a broken window or skin puncture allows the cabin pressure to fall, the occupants may experience hypoxia and decompression sickness. Pilots of pressurized aircraft wear oxygen masks as a precaution, and passengers have emergency masks readily available.

Another high-altitude flight hazard is temperature extremes, which may reach −80° F or lower. Electrically heated suits for the crew and heated cabins protect against the cold. High-speed flights or reentry of a space capsule into the atmosphere produces intense heat. This requires special clothing, refrigeration, insulation, and heat-dispersing devices.

Acceleration and Other Hazards

If an aircraft flies at a constant speed, its occupants feel no bodily effects. If, however, the rate of speed or the direction of flight is changed suddenly, there may be human stresses.

An increase in velocity, or rate of speed, is called acceleration. Negative acceleration, or decreasing speed, is called deceleration. Acceleration forces react on the body in three directions—head to foot, chest to back, and side to side. Acceleration produces a pull

The United States has developed medical equipment to simulate problems that astronauts encounter during long space missions. Through suction, this machine places stress on a pilot's heart and blood vessels.

NASA

The KC-135 aircraft flies in parabolic patterns to create a weightless environment for testing astronauts' reactions to the various stresses that are created by space flight and for developing their space tools and working procedures.

like gravity. It is measured in g (gravity) units. One g is equal to the pull of gravity in a body at rest on the Earth's surface.

Human tolerance to acceleration varies with the direction and duration of the force. In a tight turn or pullout from a steep dive, a blackout may occur. This temporary loss of vision and eventual unconsciousness are caused by blood rushing from the head. To combat this a pilot may wear a G-suit, which exerts pressure on the abdomen and legs to prevent the pooling of blood in the lower body. During an outside loop a redout may occur. This reddening of vision and possible loss of consciousness result from the blood rushing to the head. An airman can withstand a force of several hundred g's for a fraction of a second if it builds up gradually. Lap belts, harnesses, helmets, and a supported body position help fliers tolerate acceleration stresses.

Emergency escape from high-speed aircraft requires an ejection seat. Beyond the speed of sound the airman must be enclosed in a capsule if he is to survive wind blast and deceleration. An explosive charge propels the seat or capsule and pilot clear of the tail.

Fatigue is a problem on long flights. Noise and vibration add to fatigue. Vibration may cause physical disturbances. Noise may impair hearing sensitivity. Cabin insulation, earplugs, helmets, and radio headsets protect aircrews from excessive noise.

Turbulent air may cause airsickness, nausea, and discomfort. Toxic compounds such as carbon monoxide from engines or fumes from fire extinguishers must be kept from the cabin. Fuels must be handled with care. The oxygen supply should be pure.

Hazards of Flight in Space

Space travelers encounter weightlessness. They float in the capsule, free of the Earth's gravity at zero-g. In the closed cabin they must process carbon dioxide and other human wastes chemically or by photosynthesis into oxygen, water, and food. Astronauts must be trained to guard against the mental confusion that comes with isolation and confinement. They must also be protected against radiation.

Research Devices and Organizations

Research tools for aerospace medical problems are highly specialized. Low-pressure chambers duplicate the rarified atmosphere at high altitudes. Human centrifuges produce acceleration forces. Rocket-powered sleds and centrifuges test high acceleration and deceleration effects. Vertical accelerators simulate vibration stress. Closed cabins duplicate isolation conditions. Radios send data to ground stations from measuring devices attached to animals and human beings in flight. The astronauts of Project Mercury underwent long training before the first American space flight was made in 1961 (see Space Travel).

In the United States aerospace medicine is practiced by military and civilian branches of the federal government, educational institutions, research institutes, airlines, and aircraft manufacturers.

The Air Force maintains the School of Aerospace Medicine and the Aerospace Medical Research Laboratory. The Navy has the School of Naval Aviation Medicine, Aviation Medical Acceleration Laboratories, and Equipment and Material Laboratories.

A NASA test engineer, wearing an Apollo pressure suit, climbs out of a simulated moon crater. He is strapped in a device that produces the effect of lunar, or one sixth Earth, gravity on his body and uses a Jacob's staff as an aid for walking.

NASA

Careers in Aerospace

All occupations dealing with the manufacture and operation of aircraft and spacecraft may be classified as careers in the aerospace industry. More than one million men and women work on civilian aerospace jobs. Thousands of servicemen and women are in military aerospace work.

About three fourths of the civilians are in the aircraft and parts manufacturing industry. The remainder are airmen. These include pilots and nonpilots, such as mechanics and air traffic control operators.

Occupations in aviation are found both in the air and on the ground, and virtually every job is open to both men and women. The major fields are aircraft and missile manufacturing, air transportation, federal government aviation, and general aviation. Examples of aerospace careers are described on the pages that follow.

The aerospace industry offers careers for more than a million men and women of varied skills. Job opportunities range from aircraft mechanics (left) to reservations agents (right).

Eastern Airlines

American Airlines

83

Aircraft and Missile Manufacturing Occupations

These occupations are concerned with the manufacture of airframes, engines, electronic systems, and accessories for aircraft and missiles. Scientists, engineers, mathematicians, and technicians work on research, design, and testing. Mechanics make the parts and assemble them.

Aerodynamics Engineer. Studies aircraft and missile flight performances with models in wind tunnel.

Assembler. Puts together parts of aircraft and missiles.

Chemist. Develops or tests aircraft and rocket fuels and materials such as plastics and ceramics.

Design Engineer. Plans shape, size, and structure of aircraft and missile airframes.

Design Layout Draftsman. Makes designs to engineers' specifications.

Electronics Engineer. Designs sensing and control devices.

Equipment Engineer. Designs heating, pressurizing, hydraulic, and oxygen-equipment systems.

Flight Line Mechanic. Prepares airplane for test flight after final assembly.

Inspector. Checks materials from suppliers and finished parts.

Jig and Fixture Builder. Makes jigs to hold work or to guide tools in production or assembly.

Mathematician. Develops formulas for engineering design problems; records wind tunnel data; analyzes flight test results.

Metallurgist. Develops or tests metals and alloys used for parts.

Mock-Up Builder. Makes full-size aircraft and spacecraft models for solving engineering problems.

Model Builder. Makes scale models for wind tunnel testing.

Physicist. Works on scientific problems for aircraft and missiles, such as overcoming heat barrier.

Power Plant Engineer. Designs piston, jet, turboprop, ram-jet, or rocket engines and their parts.

Sheet-Metal Fabricator. Cuts and shapes aircraft and missile parts from sheet metal.

Structures Engineer. Checks strength of materials with vibration and stress and strain tests.

Technical Illustrator. Makes drawings for operation handbooks.

Test Pilot. Flies aircraft to test flight performance.

Tool- and Diemaker. Makes tools and dies for machine parts.

Tool Designer. Designs tools for making aircraft or missile parts.

Weight Engineer. Studies weight and center of gravity of aircraft and missiles under different loads.

AERODYNAMICS ENGINEER

ASSEMBLER

MATHEMATICIAN

MODEL BUILDER

AIR CARGO AGENT

Air Transportation Occupations

These occupations involve the transportation of passengers, mail, and freight by scheduled and nonscheduled airlines, charter aircraft, and air-cargo carriers. About 80 per cent of these are ground jobs.

Air Cargo Agent. Supervises cargo terminal; records airfreight and arranges for delivery.

Aircraft Instrument Technician. Installs, repairs, and tests aircraft instruments.

Aircraft Maintenance Inspector. Checks aircraft parts and the work of mechanics and technicians.

Aircraft Mechanic. Services aircraft airframes and engines.

Aircraft Radio Technician. Installs and repairs radio equipment.

Airline Station Manager. Is in charge of ground and flight operations for his airline at his station.

Check Pilot. Observes pilot's efficiency on check flights; trains new pilots in company regulations.

Copilot. Assists pilot in operation of flight controls; watches instruments and weather; keeps log.

Flight Dispatcher. Plans flight with pilot; authorizes take-offs or cancels flights; advises pilots in air on weather or route changes.

Flight Engineer. Is responsible for in-flight operation of engines and aircraft systems.

Flight Simulator Instructor. Trains pilots and checks their skills, using a flight simulator.

Ground Radio Operator. Operates airline station radio equipment.

Meteorologist. Makes weather reports to pilot and dispatcher.

Navigator. Plots course; reports position; estimates arrival time.

INSTRUMENT TECHNICIAN

MAINTENANCE INSPECTOR

RADIO TECHNICIAN

FLIGHT ENGINEER

PILOT

Operations Agent. Oversees loading and unloading; checks distribution of aircraft load and fuel.

Pilot. Is in command of plane; is responsible for safety of passengers and cargo; makes flight plan and preflight check of aircraft; operates controls; supervises crew.

Propeller Specialist. Repairs and checks propellers and governors.

Ramp Serviceman. Handles cargo and baggage; refuels aircraft.

Reservations Clerk. Makes flight reservations for airline passengers.

Stewardess or Steward. Checks passengers' names and destinations; enforces safety rules; serves food; oversees riders' comfort.

Teletype Operator. Runs airline's teletype equipment.

Ticket Agent. Sells tickets; weighs and tags baggage; answers questions on schedules and fares.

Traffic Representative. Promotes airline travel; calls on customers; arranges charter flights.

Aviation Occupations in the Federal Government

The federal government offers hundreds of occupations in aviation. Most of them are in the armed forces. The others are civilian occupations with government agencies. Most of the civilian jobs are concerned with air safety or with aerospace research and development.

Military Aviation

Many aviation occupations in the armed forces are similar to those in air transportation. All the armed services require pilots, mechanics, meteorologists, radio operators, etc. Many careers are open to women. Some aviation occupations not found in civilian life are:

Air-Borne Weather Operator. Operates weather instruments aboard weather reconnaissance plane.

Aviation Boatswain's Mate. Handles aircraft aboard carriers and at naval air stations.

Aviation Machinist's Mate. Participates in rescue work aboard Coast Guard helicopters.

Bomber Navigator. Keeps plane on course; locates target; drops bombs; directs return course.

Fighter Pilot. Operates jet plane to intercept enemy craft or missiles.

Flight Nurse. Attends sick or injured military personnel in flight.

Guided Missile Mechanic. Installs, maintains, tests, and repairs guided missile control systems.

Parachute Rigger. Packs personnel, cargo, and aircraft parachutes.

Paramedic. Parachutes to give medical aid; rescues injured or lost persons in rough country.

Rocket Specialist. Installs, inspects, and repairs liquid propellant rockets.

Federal Aviation Administration

This agency employs thousands of workers who direct air traffic, maintain navigational aids, check pilot compliance with safety rules, or certify worthiness of aircraft.

Air Traffic Controller. Mans airport control tower, air route traffic control center, and communications station.

Airways Engineer. Plans electronic navigational aids, such as radar, instrument landing systems, and airport approach lighting.

Airways Flight Inspector. Pilots aircraft to check navigational aids, such as radio beacons and ground-controlled approach systems.

Electromechanic. Maintains teletype equipment, landing lights, beacons, and stand-by generators.

Electronics Inspector. Examines airline's compliance with safety rules for electronic equipment; checks competency of electronics repairmen; inspects electronic equipment of general aviation craft.

Electronics Installation Technician. Installs air navigational aids, such as radar, approach lighting, and communications equipment.

Electronics Maintenance Technician. Maintains navigational aids and communications equipment, such as radar and radio beacons.

Engineering Flight Test Inspector. Checks worthiness of new aircraft for certification purposes.

Maintenance Inspector. Checks airline maintenance practices, training methods, spare-parts stock; inspects aircraft engines, systems, instruments; checks compliance with safety rules in general aviation.

Manufacturing Inspector. Examines aircraft parts, engines, systems, and instruments as produced.

Operations Inspector. Oversees airline flight operations; tests general aviation pilots and instructors.

Planning Engineer. Plans airport construction and improvements.

Program Officer. Estimates costs of construction or improvements at airports.

Civil Aeronautics Board

Occupations with the Civil Aeronautics Board, which is gradually being abolished, have dealt with approval of flight schedules and establishment of fares. They also involve the determination of rates to be paid by the Postal Service for hauling airmail.

Economist. Studies airline operating costs, revenues, and profits when airlines request changes in fares and services.

Statistician. Gathers statistics for decisions on airline fares and services.

National Aeronautics and Space Administration

Occupations with NASA are concerned with the research and development of advanced aircraft or with the design and testing of space vehicles for nonmilitary use. NASA employs thousands of scientists, engineers, and technicians.

Aeronautical Research Scientist. Carries on aircraft design research in chemistry, electronics, physics, metallurgy, and other areas.

Space Research Scientist. Conducts research on space travel problems, such as satellite guidance, propulsion, launching, and tracking.

RAMP SERVICEMAN

STEWARDESS

General Aviation Occupations

These occupations have to do with the flight of aircraft other than military or airline. All sizes of aircraft are included, from the light plane used for sport or for farming to the four-engine executive transport. In each case the airplane is a tool that helps do the job better.

Aerial Fire Fighter. Observes forest fires from air; directs fire fighters on ground by radio; dumps water or chemicals on fires.

Aerial Prospector. Uses air-borne electronic instruments to locate and map mineral deposit areas.

Aerial Sight-Seeing Guide. Conducts sight-seeing tours in aircraft.

Agricultural Pilot. Sprays, dusts, fertilizes, or seeds crops and orchards.

Air Taxi Operator. Provides air taxi service for the public.

Executive Pilot. Flies aircraft owned by business firms.

Flying Instructor. Teaches student pilots how to fly.

Helicopter Pilot. Carries loads to otherwise inaccessible areas.

Pipeline Patrol Pilot. Inspects oil pipelines from low-flying plane.

Skywriter. Pilots skywriting aircraft; releases chemicals.

TICKET AGENT

Related Occupations

These occupations are closely connected with aviation. They contribute necessary or desirable services to all areas of aviation.

Air Cargo Forwarder. Delivers airfreight to and from airlines

Aircraft Conversion Specialist. Makes major changes on used aircraft; installs new interiors and other improvements; converts transports to executive or cargo planes.

Aircraft Designer. Designs interiors of aircraft.

Aircraft Salesman. Demonstrates light planes to customers; sells aircraft parts and accessories.

Airport Operator. Manages airport services; administers airport regulations.

Aviation Educationist. Assists schools, teachers, and youth groups to increase knowledge of aviation.

Aviation Writer. Reports on new developments in aviation and space exploration for newspapers, magazines, and books.

Flight Safety Research Specialist. Studies air accidents; promotes safety by recommending improved procedures and design.

State Aeronautics Director. Promotes aviation within his state; administers state regulations; aids communities in building airports.

RESEARCH SCIENTIST

AIR TRAFFIC CONTROLLER

AESCHYLUS (525–456 B.C.). The first great tragic dramatist of Greece was Aeschylus. His plays focused on the conflicting concerns of political leaders for their people and for themselves.

Little is known of Aeschylus' youth. He was probably born and grew up in Eleusis, northwest of Athens. He was recorded as having entered the Dionysia, Athens' major dramatic competition, shortly after its reorganization in 501 or 500 B.C. He won his first success in the theater in 484 B.C. at the age of 41.

Aeschylus is said to have introduced into Greek drama the second actor. This not only was an exciting break from the traditional single performer and chorus but also allowed for a variety of plots and dialogue. Aeschylus reduced the size and the role of the chorus. He used some unusual scenic effects as well as exotic and often terrifying masks and costumes. He probably acted in most of his own plays, which was the usual practice among dramatists of his time.

This sculpture of Aeschylus is a Roman copy of a Greek original. It dates from the second half of the 4th century B.C.

Ny Carlsberg Glyptothek, Copenhagen

Aeschylus died at the age of 69 in Gela, Sicily. After his death the Athenians took the unprecedented step of decreeing that his plays could be revived for festival competitions. He was awarded the title "Father of Tragedy."

Out of more than 80 known titles, 52 of his plays won first prizes. Only seven of the tragedies survive: the trilogy 'Oresteia', which includes 'Agamemnon', 'Choephoroi', and 'Eumenides'; 'The Suppliants'; 'The Persians'; 'Seven Against Thebes'; and 'Prometheus'. (*See also* Drama.)

AESCULAPIUS. The Greek god of medicine, Asclepius—in Latin, Aesculapius—appears in art holding a staff with a serpent coiled around it. The serpent, which was sacred to him, symbolized renewal of youth because it casts off its skin.

Aesculapius was the son of Apollo and Coronis. The centaur Chiron brought him up and taught him the art of healing. His daughter Hygeia personified health, and his daughter Panacea, healing. Two of his sons appear in Homer's 'Iliad' as physicians in the Greek army. Their supposed descendants, called Asclepiadae, formed a large order of priest-physicians. The sacred secrets of medicine belonged only to them and were passed on from father to son.

The serpent was sacred to Aesculapius, god of medicine, because it was supposed to have healing powers. The god's clublike staff, with a serpent coiled round it, is a symbol of medicine. In this classical sculpture he is attended by his daughter Hygeia.

Alinari—E.P.A., Inc.

The Asclepiadae practiced their art in magnificent temples of health, called Asclepieia. The temples were actually sanatoriums equipped with gymnasiums, baths, and even theaters. The patient was first put to sleep. His dream, interpreted by the priests, was supposed to furnish directions for treatment. All cures were recorded as miracles. In the course of time the priests probably accumulated considerable medical knowledge and skill.

AESOP (died 564? B.C.). What little is known of Aesop, the legendary Greek teller of fables, is recounted by such ancient Greek authors as Herodotus, Aristotle, Aristophanes, and Plutarch. Even from the mentions of him in this literature it is difficult to separate fact from fiction and to get a true picture of his life.

It seems generally agreed that Aesop was a native of Thrace, lived during the first half of the 6th century B.C., and spent part of his life as a slave on the island of Samos. The story in Plutarch's 'Lives' that Aesop was a highly esteemed writer of fables living at the court of King Croesus of Lydia is probably untrue. That he was a writer of fables at all is unlikely, although he certainly gained a wide reputation in the ancient world as a teller of such stories.

Fables, or metaphorical animal stories, were often told to illustrate a point or teach a moral lesson, much as they are still told. Such was Aesop's reputation that most of the fables in ancient times were ascribed to him. They include such well-known stories as 'The Shepherd Boy and the Wolf', 'The Fox and the Grapes', and 'The Hare and the Tortoise'.

Modern editions of Aesop's fables are based on various ancient collections made by different authors from the 4th century B.C. to the 2d century A.D. Two of these collections are the anonymous 'Augustana' and the compilation made by Babrius, a Greek writer of the 2d century A.D. (*See also* Fables.)

The Kunar River, flanked by mountains, winds through Afghanistan near the Pakistan border. Irrigation is practiced in the valley, which contains many villages. Major crops in this region are wheat and corn (maize).

John F. Shroder, Jr.

AFGHANISTAN. The mountainous country of Afghanistan lies in south central Asia. It shares borders with the Soviet Union, Iran, and Pakistan, and a highland panhandle on the northeast, the Wakhan

Corridor, connects it with China. The southernmost part of Afghanistan is separated from the nearest sea, the Arabian Sea, by 300 miles (483 kilometers) of Pakistani territory.

Afghanistan has been known as a crossroad between East and West. Isolated and landlocked, it clung to traditional ways of life. By the mid-1900's the Afghans began to accept the ideas, methods, and machines of modern industrial societies.

Afghanistan is about 252,000 square miles (652,000 square kilometers) in area. In the early 1980's the country's population was estimated at about 16 million. Kabul, the capital and largest city, had about 900,000 inhabitants.

The Land and Climate

Mountains cover about four fifths of Afghanistan. From the Pamir Mountains in the northeast, the giant Hindu Kush range stretches west across the country. The range is highest in the Wakhan Corridor, where Nowshak Peak rises up to 24,557 feet (7,485 meters) above sea level. Narrow river valleys and broad plains spread from the central highlands to barren desert country in the west.

Afghanistan's rivers are fed by melting snow and glaciers in the mountains. Northern streams flow toward the Amu Darya, which forms part of the country's border with the Soviet Union (*see* Amu

Darya). The Amu Darya is Afghanistan's largest river; but the Helmand in the southwest is longer. The Kabul River provides water for the fertile valleys and basins around Kabul and Jalalabad.

Facts About Afghanistan

Official Name: Democratic Republic of Afghanistan.

Capital: Kabul.

Area: 251,733 square miles (652,090 square kilometers).

Population (1981 estimate): 15,960,000; 63 persons per square mile (24 persons per square kilometer); 13 percent urban, 87 percent rural.

Major Languages: Pashto and Dari (Persian).

Major Religion: Islam (official).

Literacy: 24 percent of the people attend school or have completed at least one grade.

Mountain Ranges: Hindu Kush, Pamirs.

Highest Peak: Nowshak, 24,557 feet (7,485 meters).

Largest Lakes: Ab e Istadeh ye Moqor, Sari Qul, Band e Kajaki.

Major Rivers: Amu Darya, Helmand.

Form of Government: People's Republic.

Chief of State and Head of Government: President of the Revolutionary Council.

Legislature: Revolutionary Council and Central Committee of the People's Democratic Party of Afghanistan.

Voting Qualifications: All citizens 18 years of age.

Political Divisions: 26 provinces.

Major Cities (1979 census): Kabul (913,164), Qandahar (178,409), Herat (140,323), Mazar e Sharif (103,372).

Chief Manufactured and Mined Products: Cement, cotton fabrics, fertilizer, hard coal, natural gas, rayon fabrics, woolen fabrics.

Chief Agricultural Products: *Crops*—barley, corn (maize), fruits, rice, vegetables, wheat. *Livestock*—cattle, donkeys, goats, poultry, sheep.

Flag: *Colors*—red and yellow (*see* Flags).

Monetary Unit: 1 afghani = 100 puli.

In winter and spring most of Afghanistan's meager rain and snow falls. Temperatures drop below 0° F (−18° C) in the windswept uplands. The lowlands have milder winters. But the summer sun may raise desert temperatures to 115° F (46° C) or higher. Frontal winds sweeping in from the west may bring huge sand storms or dust storms. The desert regions receive less than 4 inches (100 millimeters) of rain a year; the high mountains receive more than 40 inches (1,000 millimeters) of precipitation, most of which falls as snow.

Plant and Animal Life

Like its climate, Afghanistan's plant life is diverse. In the southern deserts, few trees grow. Spring rains may bring flowering grasses and herbs. Farther north, plant life becomes richer; at higher altitudes it may be almost luxuriant. Plants, shrubs, and herbs include the camel thorn, the locoweed, the spiny restharrow, mimosa, and the common wormwood. In addition to stands of conifers, trees include wild walnut, oak, alder, hazel, wild peach, and others. North of the Hindu Kush are pistachio trees, which yield nuts for export.

Afghanistan has more than a hundred mammal species, some of which are nearing extinction. They include the leopard, snow leopard, goitered gazelle, markhor goat, and Bactrian deer. Other wild animals that survive in the country's subtropical Temperate Zone include wolves, foxes, hyenas, jackals, and mongooses. Grazing animals include ibex, wild goats, and sheep. Wild boar, hedgehogs, shrews, hares, mouse hares, bats, and various rodents also occur. More than 380 bird species have been identified in Afghanistan; 200 of them breed there. Birds are widely hunted, and some species are becoming rare. Few Siberian cranes, for example, survive. Snakes, lizards, skinks, salamanders, and frogs are also common to the country. There are many varieties of freshwater fish in the rivers, streams, and lakes.

Desertification, in which human intervention causes good land to turn into desert, is far advanced in Afghanistan (see Desert). Because many Afghans are poor, they collect dung, uproot shrubs, and cut trees for fuel. Domestic animals overgraze the ranges. Improper irrigation adds salt to fields. Ancient records and archaeology show that once-rich areas have become stretches of rock and sand.

The People

Afghanistan's people reflect their country's location astride historic migration and invasion routes. Most Afghans belong to the Pashtoon (Pathan), Tadzhik, Hazara, Turkmen, and Aimak ethnic groups. Constituting about 50 percent of the population, the Pashtoons claim to be related to the Hebrews. The Turkish-descended Uzbeks and Turkmens farm the plains north of the Hindu Kush. The Tadzhiks, who live near Iran, are of Persian descent. The Hazaras, a Mongol people who remained after the invasion of Genghis Khan, live in the central highlands.

Islam, the official religion, pervades all aspects of Afghan life (see Islam). Religious codes provide standards of conduct and means of settling legal disputes. About 99 percent of the population is Muslim, and of them about 80 percent belong to the Sunni sect. Most of the Hazaras are Shiites. The country also has small numbers of Hindus, Sikhs, Jews, and Parsis (Zoroastrians).

The official languages of Afghanistan are Pashto and Dari, which are spoken by 80 percent of the people. Pashto, or Pushtu, is the native tongue of the Pathans; Dari is a Persian dialect. Turkmen and Uzbek are spoken widely in the north. In the isolated eastern mountain valleys, the smaller Kafir, or Nuristani, tribes speak a variety of languages.

About 13 percent of Afghanistan's people live in cities. The remainder are farmers or nomads. Living mainly in small villages, farmers cultivate land irrigated by rivers. In the highlands, seminomadic farmers may move their herds to upland pastures, remaining all summer and returning to their villages in the fall. Nomadic groups, mainly Pashtoons, move repeatedly, taking their families, belongings, and animals with them.

Kabul forms the focal point of Afghanistan's artistic and cultural life. The city has theaters, concert halls, and libraries. Other cities offer historic, cultural, and artistic attractions to a lesser extent. A revival of the arts took place in the 1960's, bringing renewed interest in traditional and Western-style painting, the development of a dramatic theater, and a revival of older singing and dancing forms.

The Economy

About two thirds of Afghanistan's people are farmers or herdsmen, but only about 12 percent of the land is cultivated. The remainder is either too rugged or too dry for farming. The country has extensive natural gas, coal, and iron deposits. About 4 percent of the total land area is irrigated. Farmers use terrace, tunnel, and well methods to irrigate their land.

In the early 1980's about 77 percent of Afghanistan's land area was being used for grazing. Afghanistan has vast herds of sheep, goats, cattle, horses, donkeys, and camels—as many as 30 million head. Of these, sheep number about 23 million and goats, 3 million. The sheep provide wool and skins for clothing and flesh for meat.

The farmers live in the fertile valleys or on the plain, wherever water is available for irrigation. Wheat, corn (maize), rice, and barley are the most important crops. Industrial crops include cotton, sugar beets, and sugarcane. Oilseed, nuts, and fruits, particularly grapes, are also important, and large quantities of vegetables, especially potatoes, are grown. Agriculture contributes more than half of the gross domestic product.

Aided by loans and grants from the World Bank and other sources, Afghanistan's government has tried since World War II to improve economic conditions. The Helmand Valley project, undertaken with

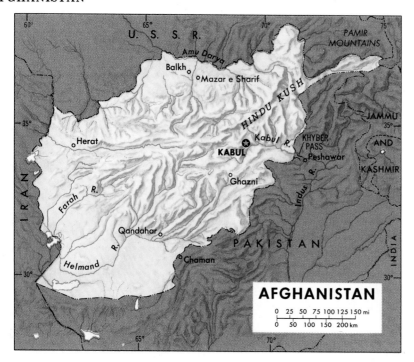

AFGHANISTAN

```
0  25  50  75 100 125 150 mi
0    50   100   150   200 km
```

aid from the United States, was designed to supply water for 1,000 square miles (2,600 square kilometers) of desert. With aid from the Soviet Union, the Afghan government built the Nangarhar Canal near Jalalabad in the south.

Afghanistan has little industry. By estimate, only about 20,000 persons make up the industrial labor force; most of them are employed in the cotton-textile industry. Others work in the cement, sugar, vegetable oil, woolen and artificial silk textile, and fruit-processing industries. Handworkers in cottage industries produce woven, embroidered, metal, pottery, and wooden goods and utensils. Cottage industries account for some 8 percent of the gross domestic product while manufacturing industries account for only about 4 percent. The yearly income per person in Afghanistan was about $153 in the early 1980's.

Fruits and nuts account for about one third of the country's exports. Natural gas, cotton, carpets, and karakul skins are also exported. Leading imports include textiles, machinery, vehicles, and petroleum.

Transportation and Communication

In the early 1980's Afghanistan had no railways. But the country has more than 7,000 miles (11,265 kilometers) of roads and highways. The most important roads connect Kabul with Shir Kahn, on the Soviet border in the north, and with Peshawar in Pakistan in the east. Paved roads also link Kabul with Qandahar (the country's second largest city), Herat, and Mazar e Sharif.

Other forms of transportation range from the very primitive to the very advanced. Camels and donkeys serve as draft animals in many parts of the country.

Jet-age airports, however, have been built in Kabul, Qandahar, Shindand, and Baghram, near Kabul. About 30 other airports of varying quality are located in more remote parts of the country.

Government-operated telephone, telegraph, and postal facilities form the heart of the communications system. The facilities serve only the principal cities and some towns, however. Radio and television programs are broadcast from Kabul, and plans have been developed to expand both types of programming in a greater variety of languages.

Education and Health

Afghanistan's 1964 constitution provided that education would be free and compulsory at all levels. Regardless, relatively few children attended school, and literacy was near only 16 percent in the early 1980's. Some 30 percent of the country's children now attend the more than 3,700 schools. Before the Soviet invasion of 1979 the country had more than 300 general secondary schools and 27 vocational secondary schools; some of these were destroyed, however, in fighting that followed the invasion of the country. Kabul University has an enrollment of about 8,800 students. To earn their degrees, some Afghan students go abroad, now mostly to Communist countries.

Afghanistan's public health services have long been handicapped by a lack of doctors, hospitals, and sanitary facilities. Neglect of the rules of health and hygiene has also been a problem. Diseases such as malaria, smallpox, and cholera had been eliminated in the early 1980's, but the country had fewer than 60 hospitals and only 1,500 doctors. Thirty-eight percent of all newborn children do not survive beyond their first birthday; this is one of the world's highest infant mortality rates.

Government

On July 17, 1973, a military coup overturned the two-century-old Afghan kingdom and established a republic. From 1964 to 1973 the country had been run as a true constitutional monarchy, with royalty barred from high public office. Members of the lower house of parliament and most members of the upper house were elected.

The 1964 constitution provided that parliament would pass laws, ratify treaties, and perform other functions of government. A prime minister appointed by the king, or shah, directed the government. He was assisted by a 14-man cabinet. This constitution was abolished in 1973. Another constitution was abolished in 1978, after which a Revolutionary Council ruled by decree.

History

The remains of buried cities indicate that settled peoples lived in Afghanistan more than 5,000 years ago. The land was invaded repeatedly by nomads and conquering armies. Historic figures who passed through Afghanistan included Darius I of Persia, Alexander the Great, the Muslim invaders, Genghis Khan, Timur (Tamerlane), and Baber (see Darius I; Alexander the Great; Baber). Through Afghanistan's mountain passes, China's trade flowed west and south on the ancient silk route.

The modern Afghan kingdom dates from 1747 when Ahmad Shah freed the country from Persian domination. To preserve their independence, the Afghans shut their country off from the outside world.

In the 19th century Afghanistan was caught in the rivalries of great empires. Russia, on the north, threatened Britain's domination of India, to the east. Britain waged two bloody wars from 1839 to 1842 and 1878 to 1880 to gain control over Afghanistan (see Afghan Wars). Defeated in the first war but victorious in the second, Britain bought Afghanistan's cooperation by paying a large annual subsidy to 'Abdor Rahman Khan and supporting his rule.

When Amanollah Khan ascended the Afghan throne in 1919, he declared war on Britain. Britain's third Afghan war ended in the same year with neither side winning a clear-cut victory; but Afghanistan gained its independence. Amanollah turned to internal reform, especially women's rights, and tried to modernize the country. The mullahs, religious teachers and leaders, incited a revolt against him, and he abdicated in 1929. Mohammad Zahir Shah became king in 1933. After World War II Mohammad renewed efforts to modernize the country.

The Westernization policy begun by Amanollah made important advances. Under the 1964 constitution, women voted and ran for office for the first time in 1965. The separation of the state's executive, legislative, and judicial powers was completed when a supreme court was established in 1967. Except for border problems with Pakistan, the country remained largely neutral in foreign affairs.

In 1973 the country was taken over by a military regime, which was in turn overthrown in 1978 by another coup. A Revolutionary Council with leanings toward the Soviet Union was then established. A treaty of friendship was signed with that country in December 1978. The new government was oppressive and highly offensive to the Islamic majority. Civil war broke out. In December 1979, as the military regime weakened, the Soviet Union claimed Western interference, invaded the country, and joined government forces in their battles with Muslim rebels. The council president, Hafizuallah Amin, was killed in the invasion, and the Soviets installed Babrak Karmal to replace him. Scores of Soviet advisers were sent into Afghanistan to aid the government. Opposition to them and to Karmal spread rapidly. Urban demonstrations and violence increased, and resistance escalated in all regions. In April 1982 Afghan diplomat Abdul Rahman Pazhwak, former president of the United Nations General Assembly, called for establishment of an Afghan government in exile. Afghan guerrillas continue to battle Soviet invasion forces.

AFGHAN WARS. During the 19th century there were two wars between the rulers of Afghanistan and British forces in India. The origin of both wars lay in the weakness of the Afghan state. The nation had become independent of foreign rule in the middle of the 18th century, but there were still many internal divisions as local chieftains attempted to establish their own power against the central government. The British, who were consolidating their hold on India, wanted a strong Afghanistan between Persia on the west and Russia to the north.

The first Afghan War (1839–42) started when the ruler of Afghanistan, Dost Mohammad, refused to make an alliance with the British. The British invaded the country and restored a former king, Shah Shoja, to the throne. Local uprisings throughout the country eventually drove the British out, and Dost Mohammad returned as ruler in 1843.

The second Afghan War (1878–80) was prompted by the refusal of Afghanistan's ruler, Shir 'Ali Khan, to accept a British mission in the capital at Kabul, when he had already accepted a Russian mission. The British armies again invaded. Shir 'Ali fled, leaving his son, Ya'qub Khan, as regent. He made peace on British terms in May 1879, but the murder of the British envoy in Kabul a few months later caused a renewal of hostilities. The British occupied Kabul, and Ya'qub Khan was forced to abdicate.

In July 1880 the British recognized 'Abdor Rahman Khan, grandson of Dost Mohammad, as ruler at Kabul. The British then helped 'Abdor Rahman fend off an attempt by the brother of Ya'qub Khan to take over the government. British forces evacuated Afghanistan in 1880, and 'Abdor Rahman was able to establish peace and a strong central government.

Kay Lawson—Rapho/Photo Researchers

People of northern Cameroon work in the ruggedly beautiful land typical of the dry interior of north-central Africa.

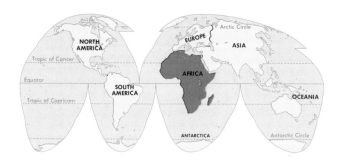

AFRICA

AFRICA. There are more than 50 independent countries in Africa and on the islands off its coasts. Together, they make up more than one third of the membership of the United Nations.

After World War II, the African people gained their independence from European countries that had controlled most of the continent since the 19th century. France and the United Kingdom had the largest colonial empires, although Spain, Portugal, Belgium, Germany, and Italy also had African possessions. By the early 1980's, South Africa and Namibia (South West Africa) were the only remaining countries that were under the control of white minority governments.

Today, the African countries have and are developing political and economic relations with nations

---

Preview

The article Africa is divided into the following sections:

For a brief review of essential information about Africa, see AFRICA FACT SUMMARY.

throughout the world. In the 1970's, for example, Nigeria became the largest African trading partner of the United States and its second most important supplier of oil. Many of the world's essential minerals, including copper, gold, and uranium, are mined in Africa. The continent's extensive river system represents one of the world's major potential sources of hydroelectric power.

Long before the colonial period, there were great African kingdoms whose rulers presided over magnificent courts. Their merchants traded in gold, salt, and other goods with faraway countries, often traveling vast distances over caravan routes across the plains and deserts. The art, language, and, especially, the music of the Western world have been affected by African culture. Jazz has its roots in Central and West African rhythms. Many modern European artists, such as Picasso, have drawn inspiration from African sculpture and design.

THE NATURAL ENVIRONMENT

The Land

The continent of Africa lies astride the equator, extending beyond 35° N. latitude and reaching almost 35° S., or about as far north as Washington, D.C., and about as far south as Uruguay. It is the second largest landmass in the world, after Eurasia, and its area is more than three times that of the United States. Its population in 1980 was estimated at 448 million, increasing at a rate of 2.9 percent a year and doubling every 24 years. The average population density is only 38.4 per square mile (14.8 per square kilometer), but this is misleading because much of the land is almost uninhabitable desert or rain forest. Roughly one third of Africa's total land area is devoted to agriculture, but in nearly half the countries less than 10 percent of the land is cultivated.

Physiographic regions of Africa

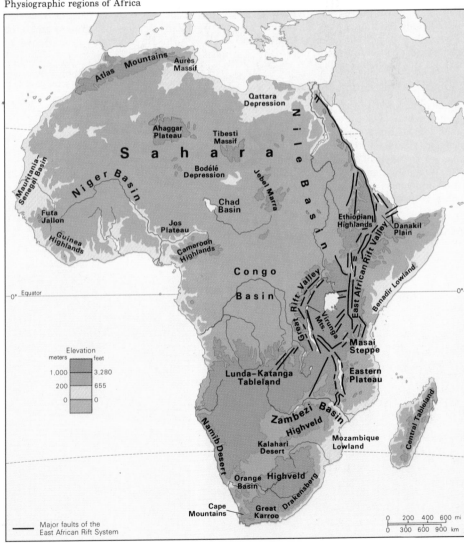

Elevation

meters	feet
1,000	3,280
200	655
0	0

0   200   400   600 mi
0 300   600   900 km

——— Major faults of the
East African Rift System

Geologically, Africa is the oldest of the continents. It formed the core of the ancient landmass of Gondwanaland, from which the Southern Hemisphere continents are said to have drifted. Because of its age, Africa has undergone erosion for hundreds of millions of years. Most of the mountains have been worn away, and today much of the area is a rolling plateau ranging between 500 and 4,500 feet (150 and 1,400 meters) above sea level. While Africa has no massive mountain ranges like the Rocky Mountains or the Himalayas, it does have the Atlas Mountains in the northwest, the Ahaggar and Tibesti ranges in the Sahara, and the East African highlands stretching from Ethiopia to Tanzania. The highest mountain in Africa, snow-capped Mt. Kilimanjaro at 19,340 feet (5,895 meters) high, is in the Eastern Highlands.

Running the length of the highlands is the great Rift Valley. This deep, narrow break in the Earth's surface has a number of branches in which long, narrow lakes such as Tanganyika, Nyasa, and Rudolf are located. The valley is nearly 3,500 miles (5,600 kilometers) long and varies in width between 20 and 60 miles (30 and 100 kilometers). Of several islands off the coast of Africa, Madagascar is the largest. Others include the Cape Verde Islands, the Comoros, Mauritius, and the Seychelles.

Climate and Vegetation

The climate and vegetation reflect the position of the continent astride the equator. A sequence of ecological zones extends north and south of the equator: the equatorial forest, the savanna grasslands, the desert, and the area of mild, Mediterranean-type climate. Where highlands occur within these zones, conditions are cooler and wetter. The rainfall of these zones is associated with the movement of air masses,

caused by the seasonal warming and cooling of different parts of the Earth as it rotates around the sun. In the Northern Hemisphere, or north of the equator, rain falls from April to September. In the Southern Hemisphere, it rains from October to March. The exceptions are the equatorial regions, which have year-round rainfall; the extreme north and south of the continent, which have only winter rainfall (Mediterranean climate); and parts of West and East Africa, where the climate is affected by the seasonal monsoon winds. The heaviest rainfall occurs in the equatorial regions. The savanna areas receive moderate rainfall. In the deserts rainfall is uncommon, but when it does occur it usually comes in the form of heavy downpours. In the savanna and desert areas rain falls mainly in the summer months; winters are almost completely dry.

Because of the differences in rainfall between one part of the continent and another, the vegetation is also widely varied. In the areas around the equator, where it rains the year around, are dense rain forests that may contain as many as 3,000 different tree and plant species per square mile. The forest usually forms three layers: a ground cover of shrubs and ferns

Torrents of water plunge over steep embankments into a lush rain forest in Zimbabwe, a country of southern Africa.

Carl Frank—Photo Researchers

Egyptian sail boats ply the Nile River, an important trade route and source of irrigation in arid northeast Africa.

Carl Frank—Photo Researchers

between 6 and 10 feet (2 and 3 meters) high; a woody layer of trees and climbers reaching about 60 feet (18 meters); and a canopy of broad-leaved evergreen trees growing as high as 150 feet (46 meters).

Between the equatorial rain forests and the great deserts to the north and south are the savanna areas. These are open grasslands scattered with trees such as acacias and baobabs. Farmers and herders live in the savanna. In the eastern and southern regions of Africa, certain savanna areas contain large numbers of wild animals.

A serious problem for the people of the savanna is that the vegetation is being used up, leaving the land bare. The population in these areas has grown rapidly since the 1950's, creating a rising demand for pasture and for wood to be used as fuel and for construction. There is concern among conservationists that the removal of vegetation may cause the savanna to become more desert-like.

Another problem is that the summer rains are unpredictable in amount, duration, and distribution. Occasionally the monsoons fail and drought results. Between 1970 and 1974 a drought occurred over much of the African savanna. It was particularly severe in West Africa, where it is estimated that 250,000 people and 6 million head of livestock died.

Beyond the savanna, where the annual rainfall is less than 16 inches (40 centimeters), are dry deserts. These include the Sahara, the Namib, and the Kalahari. The deserts cannot support large populations. In the Sahara there are a few nomadic herders, such as the Tuareg and the Gabbra. A number of countries extract minerals, notably oil in Algeria and Libya.

While the rain forest, savanna, and deserts cover most of the continent, there are smaller areas of mountain and Mediterranean environments. The mountain environments are found in such highland areas as the Atlas Mountains and the Ethiopian Highlands. The Mediterranean climatic zones are restricted to two narrow bands, one in Morocco, Algeria, and Tunisia and one in South Africa.

Animal Life

Africa is the home of some of the largest and most varied wildlife populations in the world, from the rare mountain gorillas in the highlands of Rwanda and Zaire to the lemurs of Madagascar. In the savanna regions are vast populations of zebras, wildebeest, and antelopes and their predators—the lions, cheetahs, and leopards—as well as hyenas, jackals, rhinoceros, hippopotamus, and elephants.

The wildlife of Africa has been greatly reduced in the past 50 years, partly as a result of hunting and poaching and partly because large areas of their nat-

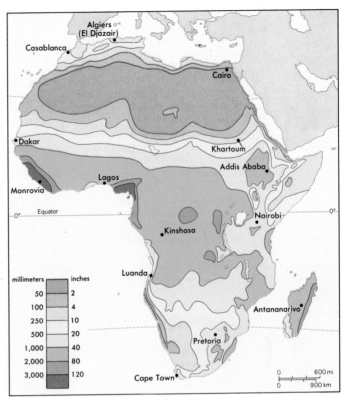

Average annual precipitation for Africa

ural habitats have been taken over for farming. Today some species are threatened with extinction. To protect wildlife, several countries have set aside land for the exclusive use of wild animals. These areas, called national parks, have tourist facilities that permit visitors to watch the animals in a natural setting. Among the countries that have established such parks are Upper Volta, Cameroon, Kenya, Tanzania, Zimbabwe, and South Africa. Besides providing greater protection for the animals and promoting tourism, the parks make it possible for scientists to study animal behavior in the wild.

While scientists, tourists, and animal lovers praise the national parks, the creation of these areas has led to conflict with people who would like to use the land for other purposes. The population of Africa is growing rapidly, and where there is a shortage of land for herders and farmers, the parks are seen as depriving people of land. The conflict is a difficult one, and it appears that it could continue for decades.

One place where this problem is particularly serious is Kenya. There the government deals with the conflict by paying money earned from tourism to people who live next to the parks as compensation for the loss of land. It also spends money on projects that

This article was prepared by the African Studies Center/Michigan State University under the direction of Dr. David Wiley and Marylee Crofts Wiley.

will directly benefit these people. The Kenyan government hopes that if people see and share in the economic benefits of the parks, they will be more willing to accept their presence.

Although many people associate Africa with big game, the most important animals are the cattle, poultry, goats, and pigs that are raised for food. There are far more domestic farm animals in Africa than there are wild ones.

Insects are another important form of African animal life. This importance may be negative or positive. One common ant in southern Africa builds high anthills. The clay mud from these anthills is very good for making bricks for houses and farm buildings. Most insects, however, are not helpful. The *Anopheles* mosquito is a carrier of malaria and other diseases. The tsetse fly, which transmits sleeping sickness, has made large tracts of land in East and Central Africa uninhabitable for people or cattle. Rodents are also a problem. They eat grain and can carry diseases, such as cholera. Even the beautiful birds of Africa can be destructive to grain crops.

PEOPLES AND CULTURES

The People

The people and cultures of Africa are as diverse as its geography, and they cannot be described in general terms. North of the Sahara the inhabitants are a mixture of Arab stock with indigenous peoples such as the Berbers. Egypt, Libya, and the Maghreb (Arabic for "west," comprising Tunisia, Algeria, and Morocco) have strong cultural and ethnic ties with the Arabic Middle East. In many ways they are more a part of the Middle Eastern and Mediterranean worlds than the world of Africa south of the Sahara.

Vegetation zones of Africa

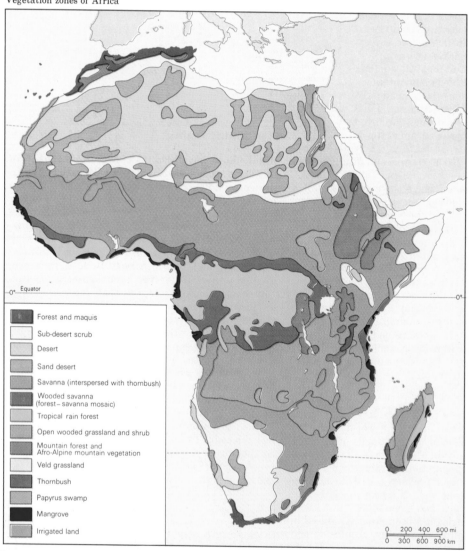

Forest and maquis

Sub-desert scrub

Desert

Sand desert

Savanna (interspersed with thornbush)

Wooded savanna
(forest–savanna mosaic)

Tropical rain forest

Open wooded grassland and shrub

Mountain forest and
Afro-Alpine mountain vegetation

Veld grassland

Thornbush

Papyrus swamp

Mangrove

Irrigated land

Equator

0   200   400   600 mi
0   300   600   900 km

Arabic influence is also strong in East Africa, where intermarriage of Arabs with the local Bantu produced the distinctive Swahili culture, and in western and central Africa just south of the Sahara. Hamito-Semitic peoples are found in the Horn of Africa (Ethiopia and Somalia), as well as in Egypt, while the extreme southwestern part of the continent is the home of certain Khoisan peoples—the Bushmen and Hottentots. Most of the rest of the continent is dominated by black peoples of various ethnic groups. Anthropologists have identified almost 3,000 different ethnic groups or peoples in Africa, speaking approximately a thousand different languages. (*See also* African Languages.)

During the colonial period, many Europeans went to Africa to live, temporarily or permanently. Most gravitated to the possessions of their respective countries. Many people from Lebanon, Syria, India, and Palestine also immigrated to Africa. Some went to work for the colonial governments and then became involved in business and trade. Asians are still found in a number of African countries, often earning their living as shopkeepers and traders.

For the most part, Europeans who planned to settle in Africa went to the southern parts of the continent. The Dutch arrived in South Africa as early as the mid-17th century, settling first in the Cape and then moving north, where they fought a series of wars with the Africans. Later, the British also settled in South Africa, principally in Natal, as well as in Northern and Southern Rhodesia (now Zambia and Zimbabwe) and in the Eastern Highlands. The Germans went to South West Africa (Namibia) and the Portuguese to Angola and Mozambique.

The presence of these white settler populations, which usually controlled the local government and economy, complicated the arrangements made at independence. In most parts of Africa, however, people of different races have learned to live together peacefully. Most African nations have official policies of equal rights under the law regardless of race, color, or creed. Even Zimbabwe, where the whites fought a bitter rearguard action for 15 years, became independent in 1980 under black leadership with an official multiracial policy. Most white settlers in Kenya and Zambia have been accepted by the native peoples of those two countries.

The major exception is South Africa. Whites make up less than one fifth of the South African population. If the so-called Bantu homelands are included, the percentage is even smaller. (These homelands have been granted "independence" by South Africa but are not recognized by any other country.) Nevertheless, the whites continue to maintain control over the African and Asian people in the country. Racial segregation is an official government policy, and blacks and whites who protest against it may be arrested and imprisoned. Securing racial equality in South Africa is a major aim of all other African countries. Another is independence for Namibia, which is controlled by South Africa.

Traditional Societies. Usually foreigners in Africa have referred to African people who spoke the same language as members of the same "tribe." However, the family is the most important social unit in Africa, and non-Africans tend to overemphasize the importance of the "tribe." Indeed, the use of the term tribe is now regarded as inappropriate and unfortunate. Rather, African people should be referred to as belonging to different societies.

Six major types of societies developed in Africa before colonial rule in the 19th century. They were: hunting and gathering societies; cattle-herding societies; forest dwellers; fishermen; grain-raising societies; and city, or urban, societies.

The hunting and gathering societies were those whose livelihood was based on hunting wild game. When game was scarce, they relied on roots, herbs, and berries. Few of these societies still exist, although the Khoisan of the Kalahari Desert are an example.

Cattle-herding societies still live on the savanna, in areas where there are no cattle-killing tsetse flies. These groups have developed around the herding and trading of beef cattle. Cattle herders include, among others, the Fulani of northern Nigeria, the Masai of Kenya, and the Zulu of South Africa. They have a division of labor: men herd and hunt, while women garden and build houses. Such societies require a great deal of land for grazing cattle because there is little grass on the plain. Thus the population, sometimes nomadic, is scattered over wide areas.

The tropical forest societies related to nature in a different way. Because the land was relatively more fertile, large populations could be supported in these

Extensive desert and savanna regions are found in Africa. The Kalahari Desert (left) is in southern Africa. Baobab trees (right) grow in the savanna region of Senegal in western Africa.

(Below) Gerald Cubitt; (below right) Scholz—Shostal

(Top left) Anthony Merieca from Root Resources—EB Inc.;
(top right) © Animals Animals; (left) Tierbilder Okapia,
Frankfurt am Main; (above) Leonard Lee Rue III

Wildlife in Africa is especially rich and varied on the savanna. There the elephant, the giraffe, and the zebra roam along with many other types of large game animals typically identified with the continent. The tree-climbing lemur (far left), on the other hand, is an animal of the forest. African wildlife has been diminishing because of poaching and the expansion of human population.

areas. Most often, people lived in scattered villages. This scattering prevented overuse of the land. With axes and hoes, these people cut away at the dense brush, piled and burned it, and used the ashes for fertilizer (slash-and burn agriculture). Their crops included cassava (a large tuber that tastes like potatoes), sweet potatoes, bananas, plantains (hard, green "bananas" that must be cooked), and some cereal grains. The villagers were bound to one another in tightly knit groups whose members depended on each other. Together they cleared the dense forest and in times of trouble they assisted one another.

On the coasts and along the rivers, the societies of fishermen found good sources of protein for their diet. Their life centered around fishing, usually with nets. They traded the fishes for animal skins and other necessities produced by the people of the interior forests. Some members of the village were specialists in boat building or net making, but all the work required cooperation. The high quality of these people's diet was a major factor in their producing large and dense populations.

The granary societies developed on the open plateau and in areas infested with tsetse flies. These people used the slash-and-burn technique to clear land in order to grow millet, sorghum, cassava, rice, and corn. Unlike the cattle herders who moved from place to place, they had more settled life-styles that required order and stability. Stable systems of land use guaranteed each family adequate land for growing grain and other crops.

Before European colonization large urban societies had flourished for centuries in West Africa along the edge of the forest-savanna areas. Successful cattle herding and grain agriculture created agricultural surpluses that supported these societies. As the cities grew wealthy, trade became possible, and long trade routes developed southward into the Congo region (now largely Zaire) and northeastward across the Sahara to the Arab societies of the Mediterranean. Leather, ivory, gold, animal skins, feathers, timber, metal artwork, and other trade goods were sold. Bureaucracies were established to control taxes, trade, and land. Great urban centers developed in the kingdoms of Ghana, Mali, and Songhai. The influence of these urban trading societies can still be seen in Kano and Zaria in Nigeria, Ouagadougou in Upper Volta, and Timbuktu in Mali, as well as in the lakeside and port cities that are located in Central and East Africa.

Contemporary Societies. Today, these different types of societies have become mixed in regions, cities, and even rural areas. Intermarriage among different groups has made it difficult to identify people according to these categories. Herding societies now have gardens, and grain-growing people keep milk and beef cattle or goats and pigs. Some hunting and gathering peoples have become soldiers, traders, or farm workers.

Once the people living in the same geographic area tended to have work and life-styles in common, but now there are many differences. People's work and standards of living vary not according to where they live but according to the opportunities they have had to go to school and to find better jobs. As these changes occur, the people learn to identify with many different groups. Thus, Africans, like other peoples, have many loyalties: to their family, neighborhood, school, social class, state, and nation. People in the large cities share a life-style and culture similar to those of urban people in other parts of the world.

Although over 70 percent of the people of Africa still live in rural areas, African cities and towns are growing more rapidly than those of any other continent. More than in any other continent, people in Africa are moving to urban areas. From 1950 to 1980, as much as 15 to 20 percent of some rural populations moved to cities and towns. In Zambia, for example, nearly 50 percent of the population now lives in urban areas and mining towns. This is still much lower than in the United States, where nearly 90 percent of the people live in cities and towns. However, urbanization in Africa continues to grow.

The establishment of independent national governments in Africa after the end of colonial rule led to

Persons	
per sq km	per sq mi
0	0
1	2.6
10	25
50	130
100	260
400	1,035

Population density of Africa

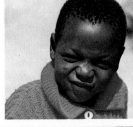

African peoples reflect a variety of physical types and cultures. (Right) a Zambian boy; (center) a woman of Madagascar; (far right) a Muslim man in Kenya; (below) a Soninke girl in Mali.

(Right and far right) Michael Bratton, MSU; (center) Kitty Thuermer, African Studies Center, MSU; (below) Harriet Gaines, Floral Park, NY

the growth of cities, as well as regional and district administrative towns. New towns have arisen and old cities have expanded near mines, industries, ports, and markets. Even though the urban areas in any given African country generally contain less than one fourth of the population, they are exceedingly important. They include the centers of government, colleges and universities, and the headquarters of businesses and industry.

Religions

Three major forms of religion exist in Africa: Christianity, Islam, and African traditional religions. The African traditional religions vary from society to society, but most share certain common beliefs and practices. For example, most Africans who follow traditional religions believe in a supreme creator god or spirit. Other "lesser gods" or spirits work and speak through the ancestors of the community. Most traditional religions include prayers for good health and plentiful harvests, and most practice rituals of celebration through dance and song that involve the entire community. The belief in a supreme being and in spirits that reveal themselves through ancestors is somewhat similar to the Roman Catholic belief in one god and many saints.

Christianity first came to Africa, according to tradition, when the holy family of Jesus, Mary, and Joseph fled to Egypt from Bethlehem. Later, Christianity spread across North Africa through the work of early missionaries such as St. Augustine of Hippo, an African. The six-million-member Coptic Church in Egypt and the Ethiopian Church are the direct heirs of that long Christian history. In sub-Saharan Africa, Christianity was introduced by Roman Catholic and Protestant missionaries from Europe and North America. Portuguese Catholic missionaries arrived

Women of Dabola, Guinea, buy their food at an open marketplace. African urban population is growing steadily.

Paul Conklin—Pix

as early as the late 15th century, at about the same time that Columbus sailed to North America. However, most missionaries came after 1880.

Today, it is estimated that more than 25 percent of Africa is Christian. Christian churches are growing rapidly in the nations south of the Sahara and especially in southern Africa. Indeed, some statisticians think that by the year A.D. 2000 there will be more Christians in the Southern Hemisphere than in the Northern Hemisphere, which is the traditional stronghold of Christianity.

Islam, a monotheistic religion related to the Jewish and Christian traditions, originated in Arabia in the 7th century A.D. when Muhammad proclaimed himself as the prophet of Allah, the one god. After the death of Muhammad in A.D. 632, it swept across North Africa in the wake of conquering Arab armies. Like Christianity, Islam is making many African converts. Today, Muslims, the followers of Islam, number about 146 million in all of Africa and probably constitute more than 25 percent of the population. The largest Muslim populations are found in Egypt, Nigeria, Algeria, Sudan, and Morocco, but there are Muslims as far south as Malawi, Zambia, and Mozambique. Most African Muslims belong to the Sunni branch of Islam.

Art and Literature

African art is as diverse as the cultures and languages of the continent. The artistic styles of the countries of North Africa have been strongly influenced by Islamic art and are, in large measure, part of the Middle Eastern tradition. South of the Sahara there exists a rich diversity of artistic forms that Westerners have begun to appreciate only recently.

One artistic activity common to all African cultures consists of crafts or cottage industries, where specialists make objects needed by other members of the society. In the case of textiles, these specialists include spinners, weavers, dyers of cloth, tailors, and seamstresses. Others work in leather, wood, clay, or metal. Another branch of art consists of wood and metal sculpture used in religious and cultural ceremonies. Craftsmen and craftswomen are called upon to fashion objects to be worn as part of a costume at a New Year festival, a dance in hope of the first rains, or a harvest ceremony where the guardian spirits are thanked for providing food. Many of these objects have found their way into art exhibitions and museums in Europe and North America, where they have influenced Western arts and crafts.

Another branch of the arts can be called court art. This consists of objects made at the courts of the kingdoms that dominated many parts of Africa before colonial rule. The artists were full-time professionals maintained at the court, where they fashioned clay, wood, and metal sculptures in honor of the king, the queen mother, and various officials. Often they produced naturalistic or realistic art as they tried to capture the expression of a person. The bronze and terra-cotta sculptures of Ife and Benin, two very old

A street of downtown Nairobi, Kenya, is jammed with automobile and foot traffic during a business day. Nairobi is a major city of East Africa. Although crowded in some parts, the city includes a 45-square-mile game preserve within its limits.

Georg Gerster—Rapho/Photo Researchers

cities in Nigeria, are the best-known objects in this category. Power and authority were expressed through other arts, as well. Kente cloth, for example, was only made for the political leaders of the Ashanti state (now southern Ghana). This brightly colored cloth included threads laced with gold.

Not all African societies have a tradition in all arts, but every community has its own music, which is intertwined with everyday life. Traditional music and dance form an important part of the festivals, rites, and religious celebrations of the community. Work songs accompany such activities as hoeing and threshing, often with a leader singing different phrases and the others singing the refrain, in the manner of a Western sea chantey. Spontaneous music making takes place during recreation. Although Westerners tend to associate African music with drums, a wide variety of stringed instruments, wind instruments, and vibrating instruments such as xylophones, rattles, and clappers are used. In recent years African musicians, especially in urban areas, have tended to adopt Western harmonies and instruments. On the other hand, through the music brought to America by African slaves, elements of traditional African music have entered the mainstream of the music of the West.

Africa also has a strong literary tradition. For centuries specialists in the kingdoms composed chronicles and epics, some in Arabic, the Ge'ez language of Ethiopia, or other languages with a long written tradition. Others were transmitted orally from one generation to another. The epic of Sundiata, who founded the kingdom of Mali in West Africa in the 13th century, is one of the best examples of this "oral literature." Since the 19th century, many Africans have been writing poetry, novels, and a variety of nonfiction works in European languages. Chinua Achebe of Nigeria and Ngugi wa Thiong'o of Kenya are two of Africa's most brilliant contemporary authors. (*See also* African Literature.)

Contemporary art takes many other forms. One is cinema, a field in which the Senegalese filmmaker Ousmane Sembene is especially noteworthy. Building on a long tradition of dance dramas and dramatic presentations, several African playwrights have done outstanding work. Painters, weavers of tapestry, photographers, and a variety of musicians and dancers are at work all over the continent, often without workshops, good materials, or much recognition from the larger society. Many have achieved a new synthesis of older traditions and contemporary styles.

Education and Health

A majority of the African population cannot read or write, but African governments are well aware that an educated population is a necessary prerequisite for economic development. Literacy drives are given a high priority in many countries, and national budgets usually allot more money to education than to military expenditures. The people, too, realize that education is a first step to better jobs and higher social status. Schools and colleges across the continent are crowded with students. Thousands of Africans also are enrolled in European, Asian, and North American colleges and universities. Most African governments support these overseas students.

Even though literacy is still at a low level by Western standards, modern communications media such as television and, especially, radio have spread information about the rest of the world. Through them, Africans have learned about Europe, Japan, and North America where the standards of living for most people are higher. They hear about people whose lives are made easier through good health care, efficient transportation systems, well-equipped schools, and time-saving conveniences in their homes. Some scholars describe the resulting attitude as a "revolution of rising expectations"—the demand of increasing numbers of Africans for a quality of life that North Americans and Europeans enjoy.

Africa has the highest death rate of any continent, reflecting the poor level of health care, sanitation, and, more basically, protein and caloric deficiencies in many African countries. The United Nations estimates the death rates in some very poor African nations at more than 18 deaths per 1,000 population,

101

compared with approximately 11 for the world as a whole and 7 to 12 for most Western countries. An even more dramatic figure is the infant mortality rate, or number of deaths of infants under one year of age per 1,000 live births. The United Nations estimates this at around 50 for many less developed African nations, compared with approximately 10 to 15 in the West. Expectation of life at birth in these countries ranges between about 40 and 50 years of age; in the United States it is over 70. Even so, the population of Africa is growing rapidly because of extremely high birthrates and the introduction of modern medical treatment techniques.

Because much of Africa is near the equator, large areas suffer from fatal or debilitating tropical diseases such as malaria, sleeping sickness, schistosomiasis, and river blindness, or onchoceriasis. Many of these diseases are caused by parasites that are extremely difficult to eradicate. Malaria, for example, is caused by a protozoan that is transmitted to humans by the bite of the female *Anopheles* mosquito. Despite a long and expensive World Health Organization campaign to exterminate the mosquito carrier, the disease has not been eliminated; in some areas it appears to be staging a comeback.

The blood fluke that causes schistosomiasis, a painful and debilitating disease that afflicts millions in the tropics, spends part of its life cycle in certain species of freshwater snail. Ironically, the snails and the disease have been introduced into previously free areas—including parts of Egypt and Ghana—by irrigation projects that were meant to better the lot of the people. Conquering these diseases requires vast sums of money and immense efforts in medical research and education in better hygiene.

Another cause of poor health in Africa is malnutrition. Large parts of the continent, especially marginal areas such as the region just south of the Sahara, are subject to crop failures resulting from droughts, locust plagues, and other natural disasters. Wars and revolutions have driven refugees into countries where the people have difficulty feeding themselves, much less the newcomers. Even in those areas where the diet provides enough calories, it may consist largely of starchy foods such as cassava. As a result the people do not consume enough protein to insure good health.

As with education, the African governments recognize these problems, and national budgets typically reflect high expenditures on health care. In addition to training doctors and nurses and building hospitals and clinics, some governments are experimenting with the use of paramedical helpers who can provide everyday health care and teach the people improved methods of sanitation and hygiene. Traditional medicines, utilizing native plants and herbs, are being examined for possible useful properties. Unfortunately, resources for health care are frequently inadequate.

Clergy of the Legion of Mary (left) hold a prayer meeting at Nairobi, Kenya. The Qarawiyin mosque and Islamic University (below) was founded in Fez, Morocco, in A.D. 859. The Christian and Islamic faiths have spread throughout much of Africa.

(Left) Marion Kaplan; (below) Adeline Haaga—Focal Point

African artists' work includes sculpture and cottage crafts. In the ancient Nigerian city of Benin sculptors created Bronze images (right) before colonization. Colorful basketry (far right) was woven by Ethiopian craftsmen. In Ghana some young Ashanti girls and pregnant women carry *Akuamma*, a wood doll that represents the ideal of beauty. They believe it will help insure the birth of beautiful babies.

(Right) Museum für Völkerkunde, Berlin; (far right) Maude Wahlman; (bottom right) Frank Willett

THE ECONOMY

Because most African nations have inherited economic problems from the colonial period and because the prices for African products on world markets have been low, governments there are finding it very difficult to fulfill the hopes and demands of their people. Living standards have improved since independence, but they are still below expectations.

At the time of independence, many African countries relied on a single crop or mineral to export for sale in other countries, a pattern that had been encouraged by the colonial powers. This was their only source of national income, and as a result they were highly exposed to the fluctuations of international prices for their products. Since independence, African governments have tried to diversify their exports so their income does not depend on just one item. They also have begun to sell their goods to more countries to avoid being dependent on only one foreign buyer.

Senegal is an example of a country that has been relatively successful in changing its export pattern. At the time of independence, peanut products made up 83 percent of Senegal's exports and France bought more than three quarters of Senegal's produce. By 1975, peanuts had been reduced to 39 percent of exports and France's portion of the market was less than half the total. Not all countries have done as well, and trade in a single product remains a problem for certain countries, among them Zambia (copper), The Gambia (peanuts), and Mauritius (sugar).

Agriculture

Even though Africa is wealthy in minerals and other raw materials, agriculture continues to be the economic base of life for most people. Since independence, African farmers have greatly increased the cultivation of cash crops, such as cocoa, coffee, tea,

and bananas, for export. However, small-scale or subsistence farming to meet the daily needs of the family continues to be the most common rural life-style. Sixty percent of Africa's farmlands and nearly three fourths of the working population are involved in subsistence agriculture.

The biggest problem facing Africa today is the failure of agricultural production to keep pace with the very rapid increase in population. In the 1970's food production per person declined in most African countries. Even in Nigeria, Africa's most populous and resource-rich nation, the population is growing at a rate of nearly 3 percent per year while agricultural output has grown at less than 2 percent per year.

If Africa is to overcome the food crisis, African governments must give more attention to the rural areas. Some governments have recognized this and have put special emphasis on agriculture, generally with positive results; Senegal, Ivory Coast, Tanzania, and Malawi are examples. On the other hand, until recently Nigeria spent only one percent of the

103

The John F. Kennedy Library on the Addis Ababa University campus in Ethiopia is symbolic of the growing emphasis on education in Africa. Although the majority of people in most African countries cannot read and write, strong efforts are being made across the continent to raise the literacy rate.

Jim & Sandi McCann

government budget on agriculture. African governments also require cooperation from the rest of the global community to help keep down the costs of farm equipment, fertilizers, and imported oil, all needed to improve food production.

In the forest areas of Africa, subsistence farming is carried out under a form of land use known as shifting agriculture. A farmer clears a plot in the forest, grows crops such as bananas and yams until the soil fertility declines, then abandons the area to let the soil recover (lie fallow), and moves on to a new plot. Where population growth is rapid, the land often is not left fallow long enough to allow the soil to regain its fertility.

Over the years large areas of forest have been cleared by this process. Land has also been cleared for plantation crops, such as rubber in Liberia, cocoa in Ghana, and palm oil in Ivory Coast.

Farmers can cultivate crops in the wetter parts of the savanna. They grow grains such as millet, sorghum, and corn (maize), often in the same field as other crops such as beans, cassava, and sweet potatoes. Many also produce crops for sale, such as cotton, peanuts, and soybeans. These crops must be grown during the short rainy season, but in some

areas along rivers it has been possible to build irrigation projects that allow farmers to grow crops over a longer period of time.

Herders also live in the savanna, moving their herds of camels, cattle, sheep, and goats from place to place to find water and pasture. During the dry season they go to the hills, swamps, and river valleys that have water and grasses all year. When the rains arrive, they spread out over the savanna, grazing their herds on the grasses and shrubs that grow during the wet season.

Forestry and Fishing

Lumbering is an important activity in the forest areas. Countries such as Gabon, Ghana, Liberia, and Ivory Coast have lumbering industries that exploit such valuable tree species as mahogany. Together with agriculture and mining, lumbering has contributed to the deforestation that is becoming a serious problem in some areas. Removal of the vegetation cover increases soil erosion, ultimately reducing agricultural productivity.

The long coastline and large number of rivers and lakes provide Africa with ample fish resources. Fishes are caught by spear and net from dugout canoes,

Sisal grows on a Tanzanian farm rimmed by mountains. Agriculture is the economic basis of most African countries, but some, like Tanzania, are diversifying their economies.

Shirley Gause

Cattle led by Fulani herdsmen raise dust before huge pyramids of sacked peanuts at Kano, Nigeria. This style of stacking protects the peanuts from insect damage. Once a local subsistence crop, peanuts are now a major export for Nigeria as well as other African countries.

Marc & Evelyne Bernheim—Rapho/ Photo Researchers

from motorboats, and in some countries such as Senegal and Morocco by fleets of trawlers. Fish farming is being developed in low-lying areas of the savanna where water can be retained for the entire year (*see* Fish Culture).

Among African nations, South Africa, Nigeria, Tanzania, Namibia, Senegal, Morocco, Ghana, and Uganda account for the greatest catches, but even larger amounts are caught by highly mechanized fleets from Japan, the Soviet Union, and the United States which operate in African waters. Fishing agreements, such as those between Kenya and Japan and Ghana and the Soviet Union regulate this exploitation of Africa's fishing grounds. To help protect African waters, proposals have been made to extend territorial waters from 12 to 200 miles (19 to 320 kilometers) offshore and to strengthen national naval forces to control illegal fishing.

Mining

Africa has tremendous mineral wealth. Many different minerals are found in large deposits of high quality. The continent produces 70 percent of the world's diamonds (Zaire, South Africa, Botswana, Namibia, Ghana, Angola), 55 percent of its gold (South Africa, Ghana, Zimbabwe, Zaire), and at least 25 percent of its chromite for hardening steel (South Africa, Zimbabwe), phosphate for fertilizer (Morocco, Tunisia, South Africa), beryllium for hardening copper or nickel (Rwanda, Zimbabwe, Mozambique), and copper (Zambia, Zaire, South Africa). It is also an important producer of oil (Nigeria, Libya, Algeria, Egypt), uranium (South Africa, Namibia, Niger, Gabon), tin (Zaire, South Africa, Nigeria), and iron ore (South Africa, Liberia, Mauritania, Algeria). Cobalt is mined in Zaire, Zambia, and Morocco and bauxite in Guinea, Sierra Leone, and Ghana. Almost all of the mining and petroleum operations are managed by foreigners, although African governments are committed to increasing their share of ownership.

Manufacturing

At independence, most African countries had little industry. Under colonial rule, African raw materials were exported to Europe to be manufactured into finished goods, some of which were exported back to Africa and sold at very high prices. To change this pattern, many African leaders have encouraged industrial expansion in their countries so that they will not need to depend on imported textiles, automobile tires, canned goods, and other manufactured products. But economic independence is often more difficult to achieve than political independence. Despite successes in industrial expansion, manufacturing still accounts for only a small fraction of the total economic activity in most countries. Generally, manufacturing is concentrated in the areas of textiles, building materials, and the processing of fish, fruits, and other agricultural crops. Most of these industries are owned by foreign companies. However, some African private businesses and governments have become partners with foreign businesses in building new enterprises.

Africanization

As in the case of mining, African governments are committed to becoming more involved in "Africanizing" their countries' businesses and industry. One thing that Africanization does is place African people in leadership positions in these enterprises. Thus, for example, Zambian businessmen and women would make decisions affecting other Zambians, rather than leaving those decisions to foreigners who may not even consider Zambia their home. The East African countries of Kenya and Tanzania have taken the lead in limiting the role and power of foreigners in their economies. The effects of this drive on African living standards have been mixed. Africanization in some countries, such as Kenya and Nigeria, has made a few people very rich while the others remain poor. In other countries, such as Angola and Tanzania, most people are better off than before, but the total increase in economic development has been small.

The sharp increases in the world price of oil that began in the 1970's have created serious problems for oil-importing African countries that are seeking to expand their industrial base. However, Africa possesses a great potential source of energy in its many rivers, and as oil prices rise, African nations are actively exploiting hydroelectric power. Some rivers, like the Nile, Congo, and Niger, are very long and are navigable over much of the interior but not at the coast. While this limits their use as transport links to the coast, they have the potential to produce 23 percent of the world's hydroelectric power. At present only about 2 percent is used. Among the largest hydroelectric dams are the Kariba Dam on the Zambezi River between Zambia and Zimbabwe, the Aswan High Dam on the Nile in Egypt, the Akosombo Dam on the Volta River in Ghana, and Cabora Bassa Dam on the Zambezi in Mozambique.

Transportation and Communications

Africa had extensive transportation networks long before the colonial period. Camel caravans crossed the Sahara carrying goods between Africa and Europe. In eastern and southern Africa traders brought goods to the coast, where they were exchanged for products brought by Arab traders from as far away as China. Boats carried trade goods on the major rivers like the Nile and the Niger.

The colonial period brought major changes in the transportation systems of the continent, in terms of both technology and the pattern of routes. Since 1900 railways have been built and roads improved to allow motor transport. Steamboats are found on rivers and lakes, and aircraft fly from the major cities of Africa to Europe, Asia, and the Americas.

These modern modes of transport required large investments. They were justified by the colonial powers as a means to exploit the mineral and agricultural resources of Africa. Since independence, few changes have been made in the transportation systems created during the colonial period.

The transportation systems within most African countries tend to be treelike, with a major rail line or road fed by a few branches. These routes were built to connect mines and plantations with the coast, so minerals and crops could be exported to the colonial country. Only a few countries have integrated systems designed for people rather than goods.

The countries that do not have direct access to the sea require road and rail links to a port if they are to engage in trade. Some landlocked countries do have good transportation systems. These are the countries whose mineral or agricultural resources were valuable enough to make a heavy investment in transport facilities worthwhile for the colonial powers. Countries without such resources were neglected, however. Many of these countries are among the poorest in the world, and their lack of transportation facilities and landlocked positions contribute to their poverty.

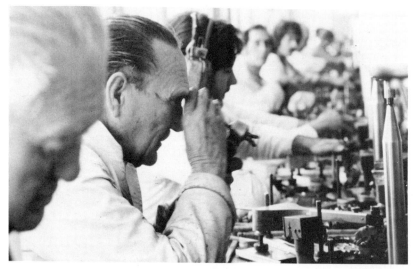

Diamond cutters in Johannesburg, South Africa, process the precious stones that come from the rich mines of that country. Most of the world's diamonds come from African nations, including Zaire, Botswana, Namibia, Ghana, and Angola, as well as South Africa.

One of Nigeria's major petroleum operations is offshore in the Atlantic Ocean near Port Harcourt. Oil discoveries in Nigeria and other countries, such as Libya, Algeria, and Egypt, have been an important factor in the growth of African export trade.

Harriet Gaines, Floral Park, NY

Brightly colored fabrics are displayed in an open-air market in Sikasso, Mali. The country is famous for its textiles.

Another consequence of the colonial transportation pattern is that communications among African countries are not well developed. The highest priority was given to linking areas that produced export goods with the port in each country. Furthermore, the colonial powers themselves were often at odds with one another, and they had no interest in improving communications between their own colonies and those of rival powers.

This is changing to some extent. New railroads have been built, such as the Tanzam Railway between Tanzania and Zambia, and others are proposed between Cameroon and Chad and between Benin and Niger. Transcontinental highways from Cairo to the Cape of Good Hope and from Kenya to Nigeria are under construction. Communications among African nations are being steadily improved, even though the systems of most of the countries are still oriented toward Europe.

Improved transportation and communications are important if Africa is to achieve a measure of unity and integration in its economic, social, and political development. Regional economic associations among African countries exist, and their continued success depends to a large degree on better communications.

INTERNATIONAL RELATIONS

Contemporary Africa is marked by a great variety of political and economic systems. There are, however, certain common themes that most African countries share. Many of these arise from the fact that almost all of the African countries attained independence from European colonial rule only recently. The arrival of the Europeans in Africa, and the political and economic ideas they brought with them, deeply affected the way of life of the local inhabitants and greatly influenced the thinking of important segments of the African population. The colonial legacy has created serious problems for the independent African governments.

The Colonial Legacy

Perhaps the most important legacy of colonialism is the division of Africa into more than 50 states

whose boundaries were set without regard for where the people lived or how they organized their own political divisions. The present boundaries often divide single African ethnic communities among two or more nation-states. For example, although most of the Somali people live in Somalia, there are significant minorities in Kenya and Ethiopia, many of whom would like to become citizens of Somalia. This has led to tension, and on occasion to border warfare, among Kenyan, Ethiopian, and Somali governments. Similarly, the Bakongo people of central Africa were colonized by three different European powers—Belgium, Portugal, and France—and now live in three different independent African nations—Zaire, Angola, and the Congo.

A second important legacy of colonialism was its effect on the economic life of the African people. All the colonial systems disrupted existing economic patterns, although the extent of the disruption varied from area to area. The change from food-crop to cash-crop production is an example. Colonialism also linked Africa economically to the European colonial powers. The benefits of these new patterns usually went to the European countries rather than to the African colonies. This history of economic exploitation has played an important role in shaping the way independent African governments have attempted to develop their own economies. Some countries, such as Ivory Coast, have built on the export-oriented economic base created by colonial rule. Others, such as Tanzania, have attempted to redirect their economies away from the production of exports and toward producing crops and goods needed by the Tanzanian people. President Julius Nyerere of Tanzania described this approach as "Self-Reliance."

The third important legacy of colonialism was the introduction of ideas of European racial and cultural superiority. The colonial powers attempted to convince Africans that effective participation in the modern world required them to discard their own identities and cultures and become more like Europeans. Schools in colonial Africa taught African children about European history and European literature, while neglecting the history and cultural heritage of Africa itself.

The experience of colonialism in Africa, as in the 13 American Colonies, also generated a powerful desire among the colonized to be free. This feeling was strengthened after thousands of African soldiers fought for France and Britain in World Wars I and II. They returned home with a renewed spirit of freedom and desire to build independent countries that would take their proper place among the global community of nations. While the colonial authorities first resisted these notions, by the late 1950's they had become too strong to be denied.

Government

European Political Systems. At independence, the new African nations inherited European forms of government. Most former British colonies had a parliamentary system that included a legislature and competing political parties. The head of government was a prime minister chosen by the legislature rather than directly by the people, and the prime minister and his Cabinet of ministers could be dismissed by the legislature. Former French colonies generally inherited governments that were modeled on the French presidential system. These countries also had political parties competing for legislative office, but the president was elected directly by the people, as is the case in France.

By and large, these European-style political systems have not lasted. In the decades after 1960, when most of Africa became independent, African countries have moved away from the forms of government left by the Europeans, and their political systems have become more diverse.

One noteworthy feature of the African political scene has been the importance of individual political leaders, "fathers" of their countries, like Kwame Nkrumah of Ghana, Nyerere of Tanzania, and Jomo Kenyatta of Kenya. As the African countries gained independence, their leaders felt that they themselves could become symbols that would bring together the various regions and peoples and create a sense of nationhood and loyalty. They proposed strong leadership to achieve national unity and to begin the difficult tasks of economic and social development.

In order to be successful, however, the new national leaders had to recognize the continuing strength of the traditional African political systems. The authority of the traditional leaders, especially over the rural population, had not been destroyed by colonial rule. Some of the new leaders, like Nyerere and President Félix Houphouët-Boigny of Ivory Coast, worked with them successfully. President Nkrumah of Ghana and President Milton Obote of Uganda, on the other hand, failed to take them into account. Their governments lost support and were overthrown.

One-Party States. Another important general feature of African political life has been the emergence of states with only one political party. At the time of independence, most African governments had competitive party systems, but the parties usually did not function as they do in Europe and the United States. African political parties were often based on regional or ethnic loyalties, and this led to conflict and instability rather than to compromise and stability. In response, many African countries attempted to create broad-based, single-party political systems in order to build a strong basis for national unity and development. Some single-party states became authoritarian with no political choice, but others—notably Tanzania, Mozambique, Kenya, and Zambia—encouraged political competition and choice within the single-party framework.

Eventually, some countries became disillusioned with single-party systems and military governments and began experimenting with a return to competitive party politics. These included Senegal, Sierra Leone, Nigeria, and Uganda.

Military Governments. In most African countries, political power has become more centralized at the top, and the influence of representative legislatures has decreased. However, as nonmilitary or civilian leaders centralized their authority and attempted to build single-party states, their governments often became more fragile. These leaders sought help from the military. In many cases, the military became so discouraged with civilian government that they took over political power directly. In a one-year period during the mid-1960's, military coups that overthrew civilian governments were especially evident. They occurred in eight African countries, including the most populous nation, Nigeria.

In Africa today, about half of the countries either have military governments or have been ruled recently by the army. There are many reasons why African military leaders lost confidence in civilian governments and why military intervention has been accepted by the people. Some civilian governments have not managed economic development well, and in many cases political corruption has been widespread, causing unrest and rebellion.

In general, however, the governments that have come to power in military takeovers or "coups" have not proved any better at the tasks of governing than the civilian governments they replaced. Military regimes also are usually reluctant to step down from power, although there have been several exceptions. Most notably, Nigeria returned to civilian rule within a democratic political framework after nearly 15 years of military government.

One important cause of political instability in Africa is the inability of governments to meet the rapidly growing demands for more schools, roads, hospitals, and other expensive services that were denied by the colonial powers. The people thought that political freedom would bring quick changes in their standard of living. When such hopes are not fulfilled, these people lose faith in their government.

Regional and Continental Organizations

Many Africans have long dreamed of unifying their continent into a giant "United States of Africa." After World War II, along with the rise of nationalism in colonial territories, there emerged a continent-wide Pan-African movement. While the dream of a United States of Africa remains distant, African governments have participated in several international and regional organizations designed to promote African cooperation and unity.

The most important of these organizations is the Organization of African Unity (OAU), founded in 1963. The goals of the OAU are to promote unity and solidarity among African states; coordinate efforts to improve living standards; defend the territorial integrity and independence of African states; eradicate all forms of colonialism; and promote international cooperation in keeping with the United Nations Charter. The OAU has played an important role in the struggle to end colonialism and racial domination in southern Africa and has been generally successful in settling disputes between African nations.

African governments also have established regional organizations for economic and political cooperation. In recent years these organizations have achieved some success in strengthening the economic and political positions of their members. The two most important regional organizations in Africa today are the Economic Community of West African States (ECOWAS) and the Southern African Development Coordination Conference (SADCC).

ECOWAS is comprised of 16 West African nations that are trying to expand trade and economic cooperation among the member countries and to promote self-reliance. Currently, only 10 percent of West African trade is within the region. The ECOWAS countries encompass a vast area with almost 150 million people and a wide range of agricultural, mineral, and petroleum resources. Their chances of developing trade within the region are good.

SADCC is comprised of nine independent African-ruled countries in southern Africa. SADCC has two major goals: to expand and coordinate the economic and transportation ties among member countries and to decrease the power and influence of white-ruled South Africa within the region. Both ECOWAS and SADCC have sought and received support from non-African nations, including the United States, to assist them in their efforts at regional economic and political development.

HISTORY

It has been generally agreed that the first human beings evolved on the African continent more than one million years ago. Archaeological excavations at various sites in eastern and southern Africa have produced evidence for this theory. If this is correct, all human history began with a series of migrations from Africa to other world regions.

Settled agriculture and iron working are two important developments in human history. The first known instance of settled agriculture was in the Middle East around 7000 B.C., although Africans in various regions also were experimenting with wild plants at about the same time. These Africans adapted Middle Eastern agricultural techniques to the African context and produced local food crops. Iron working also has a long history on the African continent. Archaeologists have found iron objects in Nigeria that were constructed by the people of Nok more than two thousand years ago. Agricultural tools made of iron helped African societies bring more land into cultivation and, at the same time, expand the process of agricultural experimentation.

Agricultural production in Africa has been dominated by people organized into small groups or societies. The Africans in these small societies usually identified themselves as the descendants of an important ancestor, often the leader of a migration. These societies treated everyone equally, although special respect was shown to elders who were considered wise

Jacques Jangoux—Peter Arnold Inc.

The Akosombo Dam on the Volta River in Ghana generates a surplus of power, which is exported to Togo and Benin.

and experienced leaders of the community. Elders were assisted by others in governing the community; together they discussed the common problems of the people and sought solutions that would bring the most good to the greatest number. The purpose of their decisions was to help the community remain peaceful and prosperous. Under this system everyone in the community shared in the wealth as well as the hardships of their common life.

Most people in these societies were engaged in agricultural production. After the harvest season, people had time to produce useful household objects, such as kitchen utensils, and to practice other arts and crafts. Societies that had a particularly skillful group of ironsmiths or other specialized craftsmen traded their products to societies that specialized in other products. Such local systems of trade and specialization developed in several regions. If an area had a particularly valuable resource, such as fertile land or rich iron deposits, a small chiefdom or state often emerged to control that resource.

Kingdoms and Empires

The African continent had many kingdoms and empires during its early history. Ancient Egypt, one of the first centralized states in human history, developed in the lower Nile River valley nearly five thousand years ago. Although this Egyptian state eventually dissolved, state control over fertile agricultural regions was a pattern that reappeared elsewhere in Egypt, northern Africa, and Ethiopia. At various times, the northern African states were controlled by outside powers. For example, the Romans conquered part of North Africa, and its fertile lands became the granary of the Roman Empire. In the 2d to 5th centuries A.D., an Ethiopian state called Axum developed, based on the rich agricultural resources of that region, and exercised control over the trade routes on

109

the Red Sea and the Gulf of Aden. Other regions of Africa did not have such extensive international trading systems until much later.

Muslims and the Growth of Trade

Beginning in the 7th century A.D., the Arabs, inspired by the newly founded religion of Islam, conquered a vast territory, including much of North Africa. These Arabs established an Islamic state structure called the Caliphate to control the conquered areas. The Caliphate lasted in name until the 13th century, though it had actually divided into smaller states much earlier. In many cases the leaders of non-Arab Muslim groups took control of territories within the domain of the Caliphate. For example, the Almoravids, a nomadic people from the western Sahara, conquered several North African provinces during the 11th century.

Merchants from the Muslim world soon became aware of the economic potential of the African continent. North African merchants, for example, began to trade regularly with areas of West Africa during the 9th century. This system of trade was based primarily on the exchange of North African salt for West African gold. West Africa soon became the most important source of gold for North Africa, the Middle East, and Europe. Through their trade contacts with North Africa, the West African merchants were introduced to Islam and became the first West African converts to that religion. Political leaders of West African states that benefited from this trade also became converts to Islam, though they continued to respect the ideas and cultural practices of those groups of non-Muslim peoples who still lived within their states.

In East Africa merchants from Arabia established cities along the coast during the 12th century. These cities were part of a trading system that reached as far away as China and Indonesia. The Arab merchants were primarily interested in gold, which was mined in what is now Zimbabwe. A large state emerged there that controlled the flow of gold to the coast. Massive stone ruins now known as the Great Zimbabwe are the remnants of a structure built by one of the dynasties of that state, which reached its greatest glory in the 15th century. The Arab merchants traded with East Africans all along the coast, and some settled there. This cross-cultural interaction resulted in the creation of a new language, Swahili, which combines a Bantu language foundation with an extensive Arabic vocabulary.

Slavery and the Slave Trade

The capture, sale, and use of slaves on the African continent had a long history. The ancient Egyptians enslaved people; slavery was an important form of labor in the Roman Empire and in the Muslim states. Africans from south of the Sahara were exported to North Africa and to the Middle East beginning with the arrival of Muslim traders in these regions. Thus, the Europeans who came later continued a well-established tradition of selling human beings as slaves to work for others.

Europeans first appeared along the African coast during the late 15th century, when improvements in the technology of ocean travel made long voyages possible. The Portuguese dominated European activity on the African coasts during the 16th century. In West Africa, the Dutch, French, and British established outposts and forts to compete with the Portuguese and eventually forced them out.

African slaves were imported into Spain's New World possessions in the early 16th century, as well as into the Portuguese possession of Brazil and, somewhat later, into the British colonies of North America. However, it was not until the development of sugar, cotton, and tobacco plantations in the Americas that the Atlantic slave trade reached huge proportions, exceeding any such earlier trade. The British became the major traders in slaves, although the French, Dutch, and others also took part.

African societies that had not participated in the slave trade prior to the European presence began to do so. Small African states that lay near the coast served as suppliers to the Europeans and grew into sizable empires because of their new wealth and power. Ashanti and Oyo in West Africa are examples. They supplied European merchants with slaves that they obtained through warfare with neighboring states. These states did not merely trade slaves to Europeans; Oyo, for example, used slaves at its capital to staff its expanding bureaucracy and on plantations to produce the surplus food needed to support it. The Oyo state fell in the early 19th century, partly because it had been disrupted by a slave revolt.

In 1807 the British government declared the slave trade illegal and ordered British merchants to cease trading in slaves. States like Ashanti that had traded directly with the British were forced to find new ways to support themselves, and Ashanti began to export kola nuts to its northern neighbors. Other Africans continued to trade with Europeans who did not accept Britain's decree. The British navy patrolled the West African coast during the first half of the 19th century to enforce the abolition, but slave dealers moved their operations southward; even some slaves from East Africa were sent to the Americas. In many areas slavery was not abolished effectively until the Europeans established their colonial presence late in the 19th century. Until then, Europeans could not stop internal African slavery because they did not have any power or influence beyond the coast.

The Christian Church in Africa

Christianity has had a long history in Africa. There were Christians throughout North Africa and Ethiopia during the first centuries of the Christian era. The expansion of Islam slowed the growth of Christianity in North Africa, but Ethiopia remained predominantly Christian with a strong kingdom supported by the Ethiopian Church.

European Christian missionaries began coming to

Africa in the late 19th century. They concentrated on West, Central, and southern Africa—areas that had not been part of the ancient Christian world. Several African political leaders encouraged missionary activity because the missionaries taught Africans new skills that were becoming important as contact with Europe increased. Unfortunately, in several areas, missionaries supported colonial policies that benefited Europeans rather than Africans. Even today in South Africa there are white Christians who use religion to justify their belief that African people are inferior to whites.

The Colonial Period

In the mid-19th century, the European colonial presence was confined to Dutch and British settlers in South Africa and to British and French military personnel in North Africa. The discovery of diamonds in South Africa and the opening of the Suez Canal, both in 1869, focused European attention on the continent's economic and strategic importance. A scramble among European powers to claim African territories soon followed.

In some areas Europeans used military force to conquer territory. In others, European and African leaders came to an understanding about mutual control over territory. These agreements were essential to the Europeans because they could not have controlled all their colonial territory otherwise. They needed the consent of African political leaders who saw an advantage for themselves in associating with the European powers. However, other African people continued to resist European control throughout the colonial period.

Britain, France, Portugal, and Belgium controlled the most territory in Africa. Germany also had several African territories, though it lost them after World War I. Although styles of rule varied, in general the colonial powers made little effort to develop their colonies, except as sources of raw materials and markets for their manufactured goods. Africans were, by and large, excluded from participation in the decisions that vitally affected their lives. European settlers established themselves in parts of Africa where the land was fertile and the climate relatively temperate, often pushing Africans off the best land with the help of colonial administrators.

Independence

Decolonization has been one of the most striking developments of the mid-20th century. The colonial empires that once seemed so stable have dissolved as the European powers, weakened by World War II, proved unable to resist the rising tide of nationalism. However, the process has been a lengthy one, often marked by bloodshed.

Two countries in Africa never were colonies. The first of these is the ancient country of Ethiopia. The second is Liberia, founded in West Africa in the early 18th century as a home for freed American slaves. The first colonial area on the continent to gain independence was Egypt in 1947. The first in sub-Saharan Africa were Ghana (formerly Gold Coast), from the British, in 1957, and Guinea, from the French, in 1958. Most of the remaining French colonies became independent in 1960 and most of the British colonies shortly thereafter. The transfer of power in most British and French territories was to educated Africans who had served the colonial government. Usually these Africans had been educated in mission schools and then in European universities.

In general, independence proceeded most easily in countries where Europeans had worked mostly as colonial administrators or businessmen and had not established permanent homes. In countries where large numbers of Europeans had settled and lived for generations, it proved more painful. The Algerians forced the French to recognize independence in 1962 only after a long and costly war, and the Portuguese colonies in Africa finally gained independence in the mid-1970's after 15 years of guerrilla warfare and a revolution in the home country. In 1965 the white minority in Rhodesia unilaterally declared independence from Britain rather than share power with the Africans. Many years of negotiation and warfare elapsed before they agreed to the establishment of the multiracial nation of Zimbabwe in 1980. South Africa, the last stronghold of white supremacy in Africa, is an independent country. Its government and economy are tightly controlled by the white minority. South Africa also maintains control of Namibia, although its mandate over that territory has been revoked by the United Nations. (*See also* the various main articles on African countries and geographic features.)

BIBLIOGRAPHY FOR AFRICA

Books for Children

Achebe, Chinua and Iroaganachi, John. How the Leopard Got His Claws (Joseph Okpaku Pub., 1973).

Appiah, Peggy. Ananse the Spider: Tales from an Ashanti Village (Pantheon, 1966).

Bernheim, Marc and Evelyne. In Africa (Atheneum, 1973).

Clayton, Robert. Central and East Africa (John Day, 1971).

Gilroy, Tom. In Bikole: Eight Modern Stories of Life in a West African Village (Knopf, 1978).

Kotzwinkle, William. The Leopard's Tooth (Houghton, 1976).

Ojigbo, A. O., ed. Young and Black in Africa (Random, 1971).

Books for Young Adults and Teachers

Abrahams, Peter. Tell Freedom (Macmillan, 1970).

Addison, John. Traditional Africa (Greenhaven, 1980).

Bohannan, Paul and Curtin, Philip. Africa and Africans, rev. ed. (Natural History, 1971).

Davidson, Basil and others. African Kingdoms (Time-Life, 1971).

Fage, John. History of Africa (Little, Brown & Co., 1978).

Hughes, Langston. Poems from Black Africa (Indiana Univ. Press, 1963).

Maquet, Jacques. Civilizations of Black Africa (Oxford Univ. Press, 1972).

Murphy, E. J. Understanding Africa (Crowell, 1978).

Schmidt, N. J. Children's Books on Africa and Their Authors: an Annotated Bibliography. (Africana, 1975). A supplement was published in 1979.

Sembene, Ousmane. The Money Order with White Genesis (Heinemann, 1972).

Willett, Frank. African Art (Praeger, 1971).

Political Units of Africa

Political Unit	Status	Area (sq mi)	Area (sq km)	Population (1980 est.)	Capital
Algeria	Republic	919,595	2,381,741	18,594,000	Algiers
Angola	People's Republic	481,351	1,246,700	7,078,000	Luanda
Benin	Republic	43,475	112,600	3,567,000	Porto Novo
Bophuthatswana	Republic*	15,610	40,430	1,268,000	Mmabatho
Botswana	Republic	224,600	581,700	819,000	Gaborone
British Indian Ocean Territory	Colony (United Kingdom)	23	60	2,000	(no capital)
Burundi	Republic	10,747	27,834	4,512,000	Bujumbura
Cameroon	Republic	179,558	465,054	8,444,000	Yaoundé
Cape Verde	Republic	1,557	4,033	296,000	Praia
Central African Republic	Republic	240,324	622,436	2,362,000	Bangui
Chad	Republic	495,755	1,284,000	4,524,000	N'Djamena
Ciskei	Republic*	3,200	8,300	720,000	Bisho
Comoros	Republic	692	1,792	347,000	Moroni
Congo	People's Republic	132,047	342,000	1,537,000	Brazzaville
Djibouti	Republic	8,900	23,200	315,000	Djibouti
Egypt	Republic	385,201	997,667	41,955,000	Cairo
Equatorial Guinea	Republic	10,831	28,051	363,000	Malabo
Ethiopia	Socialist State	472,400	1,223,600	31,065,000	Addis Ababa
Gabon	Republic	103,347	267,667	1,356,000	Libreville
Gambia, The	Republic	4,127	10,690	601,000	Banjul
Ghana	Republic	92,098	238,533	11,542,000	Accra
Guinea	Republic	94,926	245,857	5,014,000	Conakry
Guinea-Bissau	Republic	13,948	36,125	792,000	Bissau
Ivory Coast	Republic	124,504	322,463	8,245,000	Abidjan
Kenya	Republic	224,081	580,367	16,402,000	Nairobi
Lesotho	Constitutional Monarchy	11,716	30,352	1,339,000	Maseru
Liberia	Republic	37,757	97,790	1,873,000	Monrovia
Libya	Republic	675,000	1,749,000	3,250,000	Tripoli
Madagascar	Republic	226,658	587,041	8,714,000	Antananarivo
Malawi	Republic	45,747	118,484	5,968,000	Lilongwe
Mali	Republic	478,841	1,240,192	6,646,000	Bamako
Mauritania	Republic	398,000	1,030,700	1,634,000	Nouakchott
Mauritius	Parliamentary State	788	2,040	959,000	Port Louis
Mayotte	Dependency (France)	146	378	50,000	Dzaoudzi
Morocco	Constitutional Monarchy	177,117	458,730	20,242,000	Rabat
Mozambique	People's Republic	308,642	799,380	12,375,000	Maputo
Namibia (South West Africa)	Status undetermined	318,251	824,268	989,000	Windhoek
Niger	Republic	459,100	1,189,000	5,305,000	Niamey
Nigeria	Republic	356,700	923,800	77,082,000	Lagos
Réunion	Overseas Department (France)	970	2,512	491,000	Saint-Denis
Rwanda	Republic	10,169	26,338	5,130,000	Kigali
St. Helena	Colony (United Kingdom)	159	412	5,000	Jamestown
São Tomé and Príncipe	Republic	372	964	85,000	São Tomé
Senegal	Republic	75,955	196,722	5,661,000	Dakar
Seychelles	Republic	171	444	63,000	Victoria
Sierra Leone	Republic	27,699	71,740	3,474,000	Freetown
Somalia	Republic	246,300	638,000	3,645,000	Mogadishu
South Africa	Republic	435,868	1,125,459	25,083,000	Pretoria
Sudan	Republic	966,757	2,503,890	1,621,000	Khartoum
Swaziland	Monarchy	6,704	17,364	547,000	Mbabane
Tanzania	Republic	364,886	945,050	18,618,000	Dar es Salaam
Togo	Republic	21,925	56,785	2,505,000	Lomé
Transkei	Republic*	15,831	41,002	2,263,000	Umtata
Tunisia	Republic	52,664	154,530	6,367,000	Tunis
Uganda	Republic	93,104	241,139	12,600,000	Kampala
Upper Volta	Republic	105,900	274,200	235,000	Ouagadougou
Venda	Republic*	2,448	7,184	358,000	Thohoyandou
Western Sahara	Status undetermined	103,000	266,769	135,000	El Aaiún
Zaire	Republic	905,365	2,344,885	28,291,000	Kinshasa
Zambia	Republic	290,586	752,614	5,680,000	Lusaka
Zimbabwe	Republic	150,873	390,759	7,360,000	Harare

*Recognized only by South Africa.

Africa Fact Summary

NATURAL FEATURES

Area: 11,667,000 square miles (30,218,000 square kilometers).

Mountain Ranges: Ahaggar, Atlas, Cameroon Highlands, Drakensberg, Ethiopian Highlands, Kenya Highland, Tibesti.

Highest Peaks: Kilimanjaro (19,340 feet, 5,895 meters); Kenya (17,058 feet, 5,199 meters).

Largest Lakes: Victoria (26,418 square miles, 68,422 square kilometers); Tanganyika (12,700 square miles, 32,893 square kilometers); Nyasa (11,430 square miles, 29,604 square kilometers).

Major Rivers: Congo, Limpopo, Niger, Nile, Orange, Senegal, Zambezi.

Climate: Regions—hot desert, semi-arid, tropical wet and dry, equatorial (tropical wet), mediterranean, humid sub-tropical marine, warm temperate upland, and mountain.

Total annual precipitation and average annual temperature at selected stations:

Station	Precipitation		Temperature	
	in	*mm*	*°F*	*°C*
Agadir	9	226	66	19
Cairo	1	22	72	22
Nairobi	36	926	64	18
Yaoundé	60	1,547	75	24

THE LAND

Lowest point Qattara Depression 436 ft (133 m) below sea level

Greatest width 4,580 mi (7,370 km)

Highest point Mt. Kilimanjaro 19,340 ft (5,895 m)

Greatest length 4,850 mi (7,800 km)

Coastline 18,950 mi (30,500 km)

Extremes in temperature and precipitation:

Dalul, Ethiopia, with the highest annual average temperature, 94.0° F (34.4° C). Ifrane, Morocco, with the lowest annual average temperature, 51.4° F (10.8° C). Debundscha, Cameroon, with the highest annual average precipitation, 404.6 in (10,277 mm). Wadi Halfa, Sudan, with the lowest annual average precipitation, 0.1 in (2.5 mm).

Major Deserts: Sahara (3,500,000 square miles, 9,100,000 square kilometers); Kalahari (275,000 square miles, 712,000 square kilometers); Namib (40,000 square miles, 104,000 square kilometers).

THE CONTINENTS COMPARED

Region	Area		Population	GNP per Capita (U.S. $)	Literacy %	Life Expectancy	
	sq mi	*sq km*				*Male*	*Female*
World	57,976,000*†	150,157,000†	4,368,000,000*†	2,430	65.8	56.1	59.0
Africa	11,667,000	30,218,000	448,000,000	700	26.3	47.2	50.3
Asia	17,236,000‡	44,642,000‡	2,607,000,000‡	310§	53.2	57.2	59.4
Europe	4,056,000	10,505,000	680,000,000	6,760‖	96.4	68.9	75.0
North America	9,355,000	24,230,000	369,000,000	10,500¶	87.3	69.2	77.0
Oceania	3,283,000	8,503,000	23,000,000	7,000	—	63.7	67.8
South America	6,878,000	17,814,000	242,000,000	1,730	87.3	61.1	65.8

*Details do not add to total given because of rounding.
†Includes 5,500,000 sq mi (14,245,000 sq km) of area for Antarctica not listed separately.
‡Area and population figures include Asian portion of the Soviet Union.
§Excludes Japan, which had a GNP per capita of U.S. $8,730, and Middle East, which had a GNP per capita of U.S. $4,310; also
  excludes Afghanistan, Iran, Kampuchea, North Korea, Lebanon, Mongolia, and Vietnam.
‖Excludes Soviet Union, which had a GNP per capita of U.S. $4,040.
¶Excludes Central America, which had a GNP per capita of U.S. $1,620.

Africa Fact Summary

PEOPLE

Population (1980 estimate): 448,000,000.

Density: 38.4 persons per square mile (14.8 persons per square kilometer).

Vital Statistics (per 1,000 population): Birth rate, 46.0; death rate, 17.1; annual growth rate, 2.9 percent.

Main Language Groups: Arabic (103,855,000); Hausa (18,450,000); Yoruba (15,780,000); Fulani (13,915,000); Igbo (13,340,000); Amharic (11,200,000); Galla (10,620,000); Malagasy (8,200,000); Rundi (6,630,000); Kongo (6,170,000); Afrikaans (2,725,000).

Principal Religions: Traditional beliefs (largest group); Islam (145,715,000); Christian (130,917,000); Hindu (1,380,000).

Literacy: 26.3 percent.

POPULATION TRENDS

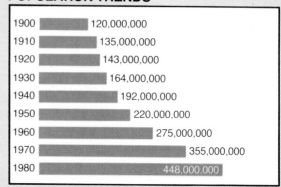

1900	120,000,000
1910	135,000,000
1920	143,000,000
1930	164,000,000
1940	192,000,000
1950	220,000,000
1960	275,000,000
1970	355,000,000
1980	448,000,000

Largest Cities: Cairo, Egypt (5,399,000); Alexandria, Egypt (2,462,000); Kinshasa, Zaire (2,242,000); Casablanca, Morocco (2,220,000); Algiers, Algeria (1,998,000); Johannesburg, South Africa (1,536,000); Lagos, Nigeria (1,450,000).

ECONOMY

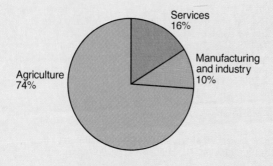

EMPLOYMENT*
(percentage of labor force)

Services 16%
Manufacturing and industry 10%
Agriculture 74%

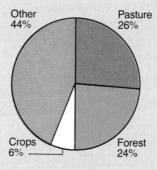

LAND USE

Other 44%
Pasture 26%
Crops 6%
Forest 24%

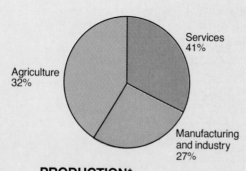

PRODUCTION*
(percentage of gross domestic product)
*Excludes North Africa

Services 41%
Agriculture 32%
Manufacturing and industry 27%

Agricultural Products: *Crops*—bananas and plantains, beans, cashews, cassava, citrus fruits, cocoa, coffee, corn (maize), cotton, dates, manioc, millet, olives, palm nuts and oil, peanuts (groundnuts), pulses, rice, sorghum, soybeans, sugarcane, sweet potatoes and yams, tea. *Livestock*—camels, cattle, goats, pigs, poultry, sheep.

Manufactured Products: Cement and building materials, chemicals and petrochemicals, processed food, pulp and paper, refined petroleum, textiles, wood products.

Mined Products: Bauxite, beryllium, chromite, coal, cobalt, copper, crude petroleum, diamonds, gold, iron ore, manganese, natural gas, phosphates, platinum, tin, uranium.

Total Foreign Trade: $189,800,000,000; imports, 49.4 percent; exports, 50.6 percent.

AFRICA

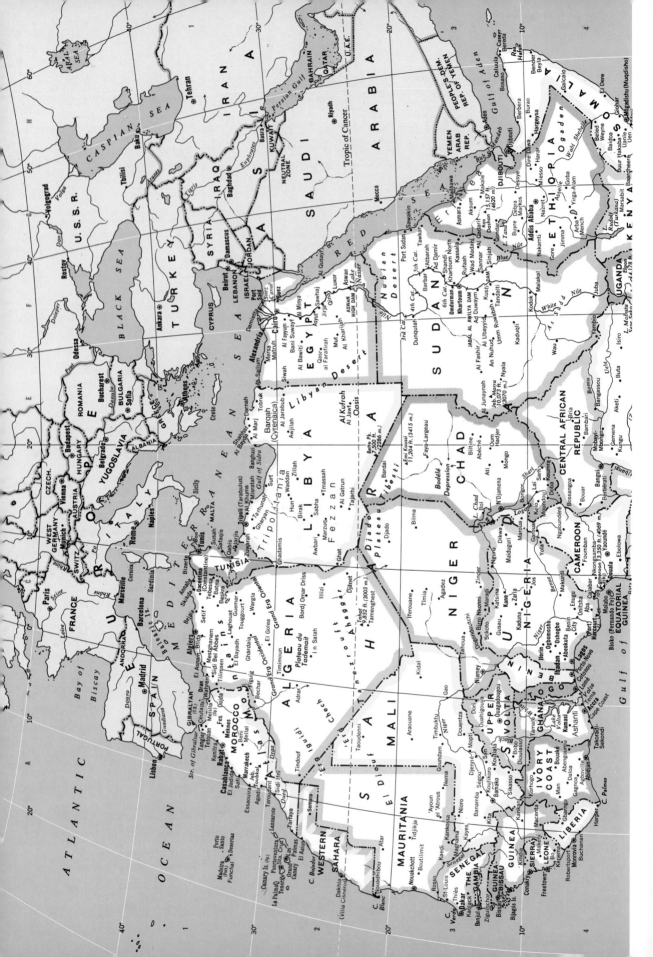

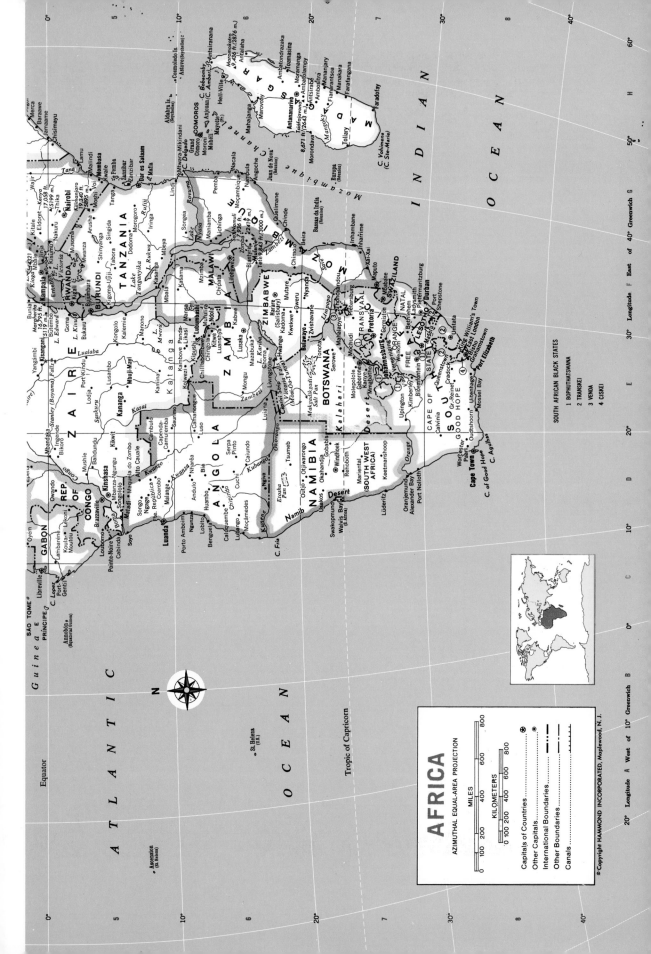

AFRICA

AZIMUTHAL EQUAL-AREA PROJECTION

MILES
0 100 200 400 600 800

KILOMETERS
0 100 200 400 600 800

Capitals of Countries .... ⊛
Other Capitals .... ⊛
International Boundaries ....
Other Boundaries ....
Canals ....

®Copyright HAMMOND INCORPORATED, Maplewood, N.J.

SOUTH AFRICAN BLACK STATES

1 BOPHUTHATSWANA

2 TRANSKEI

3 VENDA

4 CISKEI

AFRICAN LANGUAGES.

AFRICAN LANGUAGES. The 700 to 1,000 languages spoken in Africa today can be grouped into four families, or groups of languages thought to have common origins—Afro-Asiatic, Niger-Congo-Kordofanian, Nilo-Saharan, and Khoisan (*see* map). The large number of African languages does not include dialects, which are regional varieties of a language that can be understood by speakers who use other regional varieties.

The language diversity of Africa is considerable as compared with Europe, where there are two language families—Finno-Ugric and Indo-European. In Europe, excluding the Soviet Union, just ten languages are spoken by 80 percent of the people. In Africa, by contrast, the 20 most widespread languages are spoken by considerably less than half of the people. This means that multilingualism, or the ability to use more than one language, is a fact of life in almost every community in Africa. One exception to this is North Africa, where Arabic is used to the general exclusion of other languages. In parts of Africa—for example, the upper Niger River area and the highlands of southern Ethiopia—dozens of languages are spoken within an area of a few hundred square miles. People there may understand several languages, especially if they travel in their work or if they meet people from other areas.

Probably most Africans know at least two languages well, and many know a third, often a European language. This multilingualism provides cultural diversity, a richness of expression, and broad-mindedness because one group can understand the customs of another group as well as their language. The costs of such multilingualism are in the difficulty of accomplishing nationwide tasks such as public education and mass communication. When dozens of languages are spoken widely in a single country—as in Zaire, Nigeria, and Angola—it is impossible to produce newspapers, radio broadcasts, and school textbooks in all of them.

Lingua Francas

Africans solve these problems by adopting certain languages for purposes of wider communication, so-called lingua francas. Hausa is becoming widespread in north-central Africa, Yoruba in west-central Africa, and Swahili in East Africa. Amharic is known throughout Ethiopia, and Lingala is spoken widely in Zaire and in large parts of central Africa. English functions as the lingua franca in some African countries that were once British colonies; likewise, French may be the lingua franca in former French colonies. A typical African child may be required to learn a second African language in order to participate in primary school and then a European language upon entering high school.

Especially in the rapidly growing urban centers—such as Lagos, Nigeria, and Nairobi, Kenya—certain languages become a basic choice for use in the frequent casual encounters of city life; for example, Yoruba is used in Lagos and Swahili in Nairobi, even

LANGUAGE FAMILIES AND LANGUAGES OF AFRICA

NIGER-CONGO-KORDOFANIAN
Bantu: Ganda, Kikuyu, Kongo, Ruanda, Rundi, Shona, Sotho, Swahili, Tswana, Zulu
Non-Bantu: Fulani, Igbo, Mandingo, Mende, Mossi, Twi, Wolof, Yoruba

NILO-SAHARAN
Kanuri, Massai, Nubian, Nuer, and others

AFRO-ASIATIC
Amharic, Arabic, Hausa, Oromo (Galla), Somali, Tamazight, and others

KHOISAN
!Kung (N. Bushman), Xam (S. Bushman), Hottentot, and others

MALAYO-POLYNESIAN
Malagasy

INDO-EUROPEAN
Afrikaans, English, and others

The language families and languages shown are not the only ones in a particular area and are not confined to that area.

though they are second languages for many. In such circumstances languages play an important role in group identification and cohesion.

Most of the languages of Europe were established there by 1000 B.C. The history of African languages is even older. African language families include languages which are so different from one another that they must have been spoken for many centuries before Indo-European languages were known in western Europe. The older a language family, the greater the differences among its individual languages.

Features

There are no linguistic features by which all or even most African languages can be characterized. The widespread Bantu languages—spoken in central, eastern, and southern Africa—have special prefixes for identifying types of nouns, and the Afro-Asiatic languages of North and northeastern Africa have prefixes on verbs that identify the subject of the verb. Many African languages are tonal—that is, they employ voice pitch to distinguish meanings of words. The Khoisan languages of southwestern Africa—for example, Hottentot and !Kung—have what is perhaps the only language feature found exclusively in Africa: consonants known as clicks (which, however, are no more odd in comparison with other languages than the unusual American English *r* sound).

Some African languages have ancient written literatures—for example, Amharic of Ethiopia, Meroitic of the Sudan, and the Berber languages of North Africa. Modern printed literature—including daily newspapers, poetry, and novels—is immense for such urban African languages as Swahili, Hausa, Wolof, and Zulu. Indeed the English, Latin-based writing system is descended from that invented 5,000 years ago for the ancient African language, Egyptian. Over the years African languages have contributed a number of words to English—for example, oasis, banjo, and tote, and probably even coffee. The hundreds of languages spoken in the more than 50 nations of Africa represent the breadth and wealth of cultural diversity in that immense continent.

Even when African tribal ways change, the oral tradition survives in its performances and in the memories that they create. Here a Ghanaian cocoa farmer recounts for his children stories from the past of the Ashanti people.

© Ian Berry—Magnum

AFRICAN LITERATURE.

AFRICAN LITERATURE. Black Africa, south of the Sahara, has two distinct kinds of literature. Traditional poetry and folklore, which was oral, date back to the early days of various tribal cultures. Written literature first emerged in the 18th century, but most has been produced in the 20th century.

African literature has been influenced by two great colonizing movements—that of Islamic Arabs in the 7th century and that of Christian Europeans in the 19th. Although the number of books written in African languages is growing, many African writers find a larger audience for works written in Portuguese, and English.

Some of the most important themes in African literature chart the effects of European colonization. The earlier published works by converted Christians express religious zeal and acceptance of Western values. Acceptance gives way to disillusionment and a sense of loss in the European-educated writers who followed. Cut off from their traditions, yet not accepted in the Western world, they write about their experiences of culture conflict. Many also reinstate the African oral traditions in their work.

ORAL TRADITION

The oldest African myths, stories, and poems have been told for hundreds of years. Sometimes a storyteller or singer memorizes a tribe's poems and songs for recitation during festivals. African children grow up hearing stories that they later tell to their own children. All these tales are part of an oral tradition that is ritually passed on. Since the 1930's, oral performances have been preserved in books.

An oral work may be simple or complex. Many spells or incantations are very short. Among the Nyanga people in Zaire, a performance of the Mwindo story about a magician king takes 12 days.

Myths

The different peoples in Africa each have their own myths about the creation of the world. In many of these stories, one all-powerful god creates the world, then leaves a group of lesser gods to oversee it. According to nearly all African mythologies, a god first

agreed to give man eternal life, but his message was perverted through the stupidity or malice of the messenger. Several hundred variants of the perverted message myth are known south of the Sahara.

The most elaborate deities are probably those of the Yoruba of Nigeria and the Fon of Benin. They are often seen as being legendary kings, founders of cities, supernatural spirits, and controllers of the elements—all at the same time.

Poetry

Some oral poems are composed on the spot to praise a chief, mourn the dead, or make fun of an unfriendly town. Others are recited to get favors from the gods or to cure a disease. Such ritual incantations must be recited, word for word, the same way every time, for their presumed magic to work.

Religious poems must also be recited exactly, because they contain all of a tribe's wisdom and history. Priests among the Yoruba study for years to memorize a part of the 'Ifa' oracle, a massive poem used to give advice on how to behave toward the gods.

Poems of praise list the powers and accomplishments of a god or a chief in a series of praise names. For example, a poem to the violent Yoruba god Ogun refers to him by names like "the forest god," "master of iron," "chief of robbers," and "mad dog." Dirges are songs that praise the dead and express the sorrow of those left behind.

Folktales, Proverbs, and Riddles

For an evening's entertainment, a group of family or friends may sit around telling folktales. The hero is often a clever trickster—usually named Tortoise, Hare, or Spider—who outsmarts the other animal characters. Some stories are called dilemma tales because the ending is left up to the listeners, who must decide on the fairest solution to a problem.

Proverbs, an important part of conversation all over Africa, contain advice on behavior or observations on human nature. Many are entertaining because they express ideas in a surprising way. Instead of saying, "Be careful," a Ewe mother might tell her child, "The housefly does not play a sticky drum."

When a Kikuyu says, "The staring frogs do not prevent cattle from drinking," he means, "Don't worry about other people's opinions."

Riddles usually take the form of a statement, not a question. So, in the riddle "People run away from her when she is pregnant, but they rejoice when she has delivered," the question "What is it?" is understood. (The answer is "A gun.") Often the riddle is intended to display the questioner's imagination rather than to test the cleverness of the audience.

WRITTEN TRADITION

Poems or stories cannot be recorded unless there is a written language, and authors need readers who can understand them. For centuries, African languages had no written alphabet. The Swahili and Hausa languages, which have the oldest written traditions, were both subjected to the presence and influence of Muslim Arabs in Africa. Early African writers used Arabic script and followed Arabic models, gradually developing their own forms and themes.

Written literature exists in only 49 of the approximately 700 to 1,000 African languages. Most of this literature has been produced in South Africa and other former English colonies; writing in African languages was discouraged in the French and Portuguese colonies. Even where it has been encouraged, African-language works may reach only a small audience. Although a cultural group may speak the same basic language, there are variations of wording, spelling, and pronunciation in different settlements.

Swahili Literature

The Swahili of Tanzania were the first Africans to put the sounds of their language in writing. Since the 14th century, Arab traders had settled in East African cities, spreading the Islamic religion (*see* Islam). When people began to write in Swahili, they used the Arabic alphabet because they had none of their own. The oldest piece of Swahili literature (1728) is a long religious poem praising Muhammad, the founder of the Islamic faith. In Swahili epic poems, Islamic heroes fight against human and supernatural enemies.

Since the 19th century, many nonreligious poems have been written in a form called *shairi* that developed out of poetry contests. One poet makes up two lines and another must finish the stanza by making up two lines with the same rhyme and rhythm.

The first Swahili novella, 'Uhuru wa Watumwa' (Freedom for the Slaves, 1934) was written by James Mbotela. Muhammed Said Abdulla of Kenya published the first Swahili detective novel in 1960. Shaaban Robert of Tanzania was acclaimed for his Swahili poems, essays, and satires.

Hausa Literature

The Islamic Arabs who conquered and converted northern Africa in the 7th century had a great influence on the Hausa literature of Nigeria. The first poems in Hausa were written by Islamic scholars. In the early 19th century, they used the Arabic alphabet to write religious poems called *ajami*. Poets like Nagwamatse wrote about the conflict between European culture and the Islamic ways.

By the 20th century, Hausa was written in the Roman alphabet instead of in Arabic script. This change did not affect the political and religious subjects of the poetry. There are also Hausa novels.

Yoruba Literature

Despite the difficulties of finding publishers and readership, some authors have had success with African-language works. A Yoruba novelist, Chief D. O. Fagunwa, was one of Nigeria's most popular writers; his fantasy, 'Igbo Olodumare' (The Forest of the Lord, 1947), has been reprinted 16 times. In his series of adventure novels, the heroes meet with magicians, gods, demons, and other creatures drawn from Yoruba oral tradition. These tales are written in a colorful, vivid style. For example, Fagunwa described Death's eyes as "big as a food bowl, round like moons and red like fire. . . ."

Yoruba plays range from the social and political satires of Hubert Ogunde, who formed Nigeria's first theatrical company in the 1940's, to the tragedies of Duro Lapido. Many of Ogunde's plays are based on Biblical stories; his satires incorporate elements of music hall and slapstick. Lapido's trilogy about the kingdom of Oyo (1964) has the structure of classical Greek tragedy; however, the Nigerian playwright draws his characters from African history and uses traditional Yoruba poetry and music.

Other African-Language Literature

Most African languages had no written tradition until the arrival of Christian missionaries from Europe in the second half of the 19th century. The missionaries converted African languages into written form and also began teaching European languages and literatures. Missionaries translated the Bible, hymns, and religious books, such as John Bunyan's 'Pilgrim's Progress', into various languages. In many of the languages, these books were the first written materials. As with Islamic-based literature, the Christian texts became models for African writers. For example, the first writings in the Ewe language were Christian hymns.

One of the first works inspired by Christian teachings was 'Moeti oa Bochabela' (Traveller of the East, 1934), by Thomas Mokopu Mofolo of Lesotho. Originally published by a mission printing press in 1906, Mofolo's novel about a man's joyful conversion to Christianity was written in the Sotho language. In his third Sotho novel, 'Chaka' (1925), he criticizes the pagan ways of a bloodthirsty Zulu king. Because the book includes descriptions of war and witchcraft, subjects that the missionaries did not approve, its publication was delayed for 17 years.

Gradually, African-language writers tried to blend African and Christian traditions. The Rwandan priest Abbé Kagame modeled his religious poem, 'The Song of the Mother of Creation' (1949–51), on

AFRICAN LITERATURE

oral praise poems. Literary content developed from religious writings to popular fiction, though often stories contained a moral lesson.

South Africa's S. E. K. Mqhayi, a Xhosa poet, novelist, and translator, was known as "the poet of the whole nation." His work recalls African traditions and expresses the tensions between European and African ways of life. The Xhosa poet James J. R. Jolobe and the Zulu poet-novelist B. W. Vilakazi praised the wholeness of tribal life and protested economic exploitation of their people. Called the "father of modern Zulu poetry," Vilakazi adapted traditional blank verse forms to a contemporary style.

Writers working in other African languages included: in Ewe, poets Kofi Awoonor and Kolu Hoh of Ghana; in Bemba, novelist Stephen Andrea Mpashi of Zambia; in Runyoro-Rutooro, novelist Timothy Bazzarabusa of Uganda; in Luganda, poet Y. B. Lubambula of Uganda; and in Shona, novelists Solomon Mutswairo and Patrick Chakaipa of Zimbabwe. (*See also* African Languages.)

French-Language Works

The French colonial governments tried to assimilate the native peoples by replacing their African culture with French culture. The brightest African students continued their education in France, which they slowly realized could not replace their African homelands. In Paris during the 1930's a group of African and West Indian writers began to write—in French—about their feelings of loss and anger. They tried to reclaim their bond with African traditions and celebrated their blackness. A West Indian poet, Aimé Césaire of Martinique, first used the word *negritude* to describe this movement.

An exponent of the negritude movement was Léopold Sédar Senghor, a poet who became the first president of Senegal in 1960. In his poetry the color black is not a symbol of death but of magical life.

Another Senegalese negritude poet, David Diop, scorned the Africans who tried to become part of the colonial system in his book of poems, 'Coups de Pilon' (Pounding, 1956). 'Leurres et lueurs' (Lures and Lights, 1960), by the Senegalese poet and story writer Birago Diop, reflects a movement away from the "lures" of imitating French poetry toward the "light" of following African forms and themes.

Two of the best Francophone poets, Jean Joseph Rabearivelo of Madagascar and Tchicaya U Tam'si of the Congo, wrote poetry that is personal rather than political. Rabearivelo, who wrote before the surge of negritude poetry, created a dream world where familiar things seem strange and beautiful. Tchicaya U Tam'si, who published his poetry in Paris after 1955, wrote about his sense of rootlessness. His surrealist poems explore his personal agonies in the dense texture of which mythological, Christian, historical, and sexual imagery is juxtaposed.

Negritude themes also appear in Francophone novels. In the 1950's, two novelists from Cameroon, Ferdinand Oyono and Mongo Beti (pseudonym of

Wole Soyinka   Tchicaya U Tam'si

Alexandre Biyidi), exploded the French colonial myth that educated Africans were simply black Frenchmen. Oyono's 'Une Vie de boy' (Houseboy, 1956) ridicules an innocent youth, full of admiration for Europeans, who is exploited as a house servant. In Beti's radical novels, particularly 'Le Pauvre Christ de Bomba' (Poor Christ of Bomba, 1956), even well-meaning attempts to impose European education create harm. At the end of 'Mission Terminée' (Mission to Kala, 1957), the hero symbolizes the African tragedy in a man "left to his own devices in a world which does not belong to him, which he has not made and does not understand."

One of the noted pre-independence Francophone authors, Camara Laye of Guinea, wrote an idyllic description of his own village childhood in 'L'Enfant Noir' (The Dark Child, 1954). After Guinea became a republic in 1958, the president, who distrusted intellectuals, placed Laye under house arrest. In 1965 he became a political refugee in Senegal; a year later he published 'Dramouss' (Dream of Africa), a bitter attack on Guinea's repressive government.

African drama in French began in the 1930's with school plays written by students at École William Ponty in Senegal. The first play by Bernard Dadié, of the Ivory Coast, was staged there in 1936. Dadié, a noted poet and novelist, also published three renditions of works in the oral tradition.

Portuguese-Language Works

The first African poet to write in Portuguese was Caetano da Costa Alegre of São Tomé. In the 1880's while a medical student in Portugal, he described his loneliness and isolation in white society. Two prominent political poets were Agostinha Neto, who was active in the Angolan liberation movement, and Mário de Andrade.

Although Valente Malangatana and Jose Craveirinha of Mozambique were not as militant and nationalistic as the Angolan poets, both were concerned with the problems of racial discrimination. In his short stories, Luis Honwana of Mozambique described the hard living conditions of black laborers in a realistic style. Like Neto, Craveirinha, and Malangatana, he suffered harassment and imprisonment by Portuguese authorities for his writings.

Kofi Awoonor   Ngugi Wa Thiong'o

English-Language Works

The first African writers who produced works in English were freed slaves writing in England and America in the 18th century. A body of Anglophone (written in English) literature did not really emerge until the 20th century. The Anglophone pioneer poets of the 1940's were not much influenced by the earlier negritude poetry. Their models were Christian hymns and English Victorian poetry. Many of their poems are statements of racial and national pride, but a good number also give homage to European and Christian values. R. E. G. Armattoe, who was born in Ghana, expressed both his love for Africa and his disappointment in its leaders.

Like many West African poets of the 1950's who wrote in French or Portuguese, those who wrote in English were concerned with social issues. Among the wide variety of styles they used, imitation of the forms and rhythms of oral poetry was common. The poetry of Gabriel Okara of Nigeria shows the influence of Ijaw oral poetry. Ewe dirges and war poems were models for the Ghanaian poet Awoonor, who used these traditional forms to show how hard it is to recapture the past. The complex, polished poetry of Christopher Okigbo of Nigeria shows his knowledge of Igbo oral tradition, the Bible, and Indian, French, English, and American poetry. Okot p'Bitek of Uganda wrote long dramatic monologues.

The apartheid imposed by the South African government has been a pressing concern for that country's black poets (see Apartheid). Many writers, like poet Dennis Brutus, have had to leave South Africa for their own safety. His 'A Simple Lust' (1973) describes living in fear under a brutal political system; however, the poems are also concerned with spiritual survival. Raymond Mazisu Kunine recreated praise songs and dirges in 'Zulu Songs' (1970).

In 1911 the Ghanaian political leader Joseph Ephraim Casely-Hayford published 'Ethiopa Unbound', the first African novel in English. By the 1940's there was a growing audience in western Africa for short popular fiction, called Onitsha novels after the market in Nigeria where they were sold.

With publication of 'The Palm-Wine Drinkard' (1952), Amos Tutuola was the first Nigerian writer to gain international recognition. Tutuola gave English a new flow and rhythm. His plots blend invented creatures with those from Yoruba folklore. For example, one of the ghosts in 'My Life in the Bush of Ghosts' (1954) has television sets in her fingertips.

In the 1950's descriptions of tribal life were common in West African novels. Nigerian Chinua Achebe's famous 'Things Fall Apart' (1958), tells much about the family life and religious rituals of the Igbo. Achebe's novels often focus on a hero torn between old and new ways (see Achebe).

As the colonies in Africa achieved independence in the mid-20th century, many African authors turned to writing about social and political problems in the new nations. In 'The Beautyful Ones Are Not Yet Born' (1968), for example, Ayi Kwei Armah criticized the corruption, greed, and arrogance of the black officials who replaced Europeans in his native Ghana.

Leonard Kibera of Kenya published a collection of short stories about the Mau Mau uprising and a novel, 'Voices in the Dark' (1970), about post-independence Kenya. 'Village in Uhuru' (1969), by Gabriel Ruhumbika of Tanzania, describes the disturbance and confusion of independence. 'Weep Not Child' (1964), by Ngugi Wa Thiong'o (formerly called James Ngugi) of Kenya, shows how one family is torn apart by the Mau Mau rebellion.

Three important South African novelists were Peter Abrahams, Alex La Guma, and Ezekiel Mphalele. Abrahams was one of the earliest African novelists to write in English about the problems of black South Africans. While imprisoned for opposing apartheid in the 1960's, La Guma produced three novels. Mphalele wrote two autobiographical novels—'Down Second Avenue' (1959), about growing up in the slums of South Africa, and 'The Wanderers' (1971), about the loneliness of political exile.

H. I. E. Dhlomo of South Africa wrote the first Anglophone play, 'The Girl Who Killed to Save' (1935). Nigerian James Ene Henshaw's first volume of plays, 'This is Our Chance' (1956), merited ten printings by 1970. In the popular title play, a tribal chief realizes that some of his people's traditions are outmoded.

Other important Anglophone playwrights were the Nigerians J. P. Clark and Wole Soyinka. Clark's 'Ozidi' (1966), follows an Ijaw myth about a child who revenges his father's death and rescues his tribe from the Smallpox King; the mythical power struggle was used in 'Ozidi' to comment on modern political coups.

Africa's most famous playwright, Soyinka is also considered its most versatile. He has written farces, such as 'The Lion and the Jewel' (1959); dramas, such as 'The Strong Breed' (1963); and political satires, such as 'Madmen and Specialists' (1971). His works successfully merge Western plot structure with Yoruba characters and themes; traditional European forms with African mime, dance, and music; symbolism with irony. For Soyinka, who rejected the philosophy of negritude, the proper function of the artist is to record the values and experiences of his society and to provide a perspective on his era.

123

AGAMEMNON. Most of what is known of the ancient Greek hero Agamemnon is narrated in the Homeric legend of the 'Iliad' and in the dramas of Aeschylus. The son of Atreus, who was the king of Mycenae in Greece, Agamemnon was probably a historical personage, a king who ruled either at Mycenae or at nearby Argos during the Trojan War. From the mythic tales of the ancient Greeks, however, it is impossible to separate fact from legend.

The stories relate that Agamemnon was the brother of Menelaus, king of Sparta, whose wife, Helen, was carried off to Troy by Paris, a prince of that city in Asia Minor. This event led Agamemnon to muster the military might of the Greek city-states in a war of revenge. After the long war and the eventual destruction of Troy, he sailed home to his wife, Clytemnestra, and his family. Upon arriving, he was murdered either by his wife or by her lover, Aegisthus.

To avenge this treachery, Agamemnon's son, Orestes, killed both Clytemnestra and Aegisthus. The story of this revenge and its outcome is told in three plays by Aeschylus—'Agamemnon', 'Choephoroi', and 'Eumenides'. It is also the basis of the plot in the 'Electra' of Sophocles and the 'Electra' of Euripides. All three of these playwrights lived in the 5th century B.C. The 20th-century American playwright Eugene O'Neill wrote an adaptation of the Agamemnon legend entitled 'Mourning Becomes Electra'.

AGASSIZ, Louis (1807–1873). The interests of the celebrated Swiss-American naturalist Louis Agassiz ranged from fishes to glaciers. He was the greatest authority of his day on zoology and geology. He was also an outstanding teacher.

Jean Louis Rodolphe Agassiz was born May 28, 1807, in the Swiss village of Môtiers, near Lake Neuchâtel. His father was a pastor. As a boy Louis loved all animals, including insects.

Agassiz studied medicine at the universities of Zurich, Heidelberg, and Munich. His greatest enthusiasm, however, was for zoology. He welcomed an invitation to edit a work on Brazilian fishes in 1829. This was followed by an extended investigation of European fishes. He studied not only living specimens but also fossil fishes. This led to an interest in geology. His research during a summer spent in a hut on the edge of a glacier helped establish the theory that at different times the greater part of Europe and other northern continents was covered by vast sheets of ice (*see* Ice Age).

Agassiz became professor of natural history at Neuchâtel in 1832. He remained there until 1846, when he came to America to deliver a series of lectures in Boston. In 1848 he accepted the chair of natural history at Harvard University and lived in America until the end of his life.

Agassiz wrote extensively, delivered popular lectures on scientific subjects, and engaged in expeditions in various parts of the United States and Brazil. He was the first director of the Museum of Comparative Zoology at Harvard, often called the Agassiz

Louis Agassiz

Museum. When urged to turn his great scientific knowledge to financial profit, he impatiently replied that he "had no time to make money."

A few months before his death Agassiz established a summer school of science on the island of Penikese in Buzzards Bay, off the southeast coast of Massachusetts. This was the first school for studying science directly from specimens and in close contact with nature. Agassiz died at Cambridge in 1873. On his grave were placed a boulder that came from the glacier near the spot where his hut once stood and pine trees sent from his old home in Switzerland.

His son Alexander (1835–1910) was also a distinguished naturalist and writer. From 1874 to 1897 he was chief curator of the Museum of Comparative Zoology, which his father had founded.

Louis Agassiz's most important American publications are 'Methods of Study in Natural History'; 'Geological Sketches'; 'The Structure of Animal Life'; 'A Journey in Brazil' (with his wife, Elizabeth Agassiz); and 'Contributions to the Natural History of the United States' (only four volumes of the ten planned were completed).

AGAVE. The most familiar species of the agave is the American aloe, commonly known as the century plant through a mistaken idea that it blooms only after reaching 100 years of age. Actually the time of blooming depends upon the plant's vigor and the conditions under which it grows. In warm countries flowers appear in a few years. In colder climates it requires from 40 to 60 years. After blooming one time, the plant dies.

Agaves grow in the arid regions of the Southwestern United States, Mexico, and Central America. The more than 300 species are cultivated for ornamental purposes. In their native Mexico they are among the most useful of plants. Three species are grown for the fibers sisal, henequen, and cantala, or manila maguey. Of these, sisal is the most valuable (*see* Sisal).

Jim Annan—Photo Trends

The American agave is called a century plant.

Pulque, a common drink, is the fermented sap of the maguey species. Mescal and tequila are distilled beverages made from the sap. The juice of the leaves lathers in water and is used in washing.

The century plant has thick, fleshy leaves, edged and tipped with sharp spines. They grow in a tight rosette, each leaf 5 to 6 feet (1.5 to 1.8 meters) long. The stem is short and thick. At the time of flowering the stem springs up 25 to 40 feet (7.5 to 12 meters). It is many-branched and bears clusters of greenish-yellow flowers. The flower has a 6-parted, funnel-shaped perianth, 3 stamens, and a 3-lobed stigma. When the plant has flowered the leaves die, but suckers are frequently produced from the base of the stem to become new plants.

The agave is a genus of the amaryllis family, Amaryllidaceae. The scientific name of the century plant is *Agave americana*.

AGINCOURT, Battle of. The third great English victory over the French in the Hundred Years' War was won Oct. 25, 1415, near the village of Agincourt in northern France. The young king Henry V had recently succeeded to the insecure Lancastrian throne of England. On the advice of his father, Henry IV, he resolved, in the words of Shakespeare, "to busy giddy minds with foreign quarrels" by reviving England's claim to the French throne.

Henry's forces landed in Normandy and captured the port of Harfleur. En route to the port of Calais (then held by England), their way was blocked by a great French army. The French knights, four times as numerous as the English foot soldiers, foolishly dismounted. They advanced in their heavy armor through the deep mud of newly plowed fields. Each of the three times they came on, in a narrow defile between two woods, they were forced back by clouds of arrows released by skilled English archers. More than 5,000 Frenchmen were killed, including many princes and nobles. The English lost only 113 men.

This decisive battle, along with Crécy and Poitiers, proved the superiority of the longbow over the crossbow. It hastened the end of the heavily armored knight, the military basis of feudalism. (*See also* Hundred Years' War; Henry, Kings of England.)

AGING. Medical advances in the 20th century have produced for the first time in human history national populations with more than 10 percent over the age of 65. In the United States this has been referred to as "the graying of America" and has awakened interest in the consequences of aging and the care of the elderly. Geriatrics is the branch of medicine that deals with the medical problems and care of the elderly. Gerontology is the more broadly based scientific discipline that deals with all the aspects of aging—social, biological, psychological, and so on.

Characteristics

It is an everyday observation that animals are born, grow, and mature—then begin to lose some of their capabilities, and finally die. This loss of capabilities is progressive, irreversible, and universal for all members of a species and is called aging. In humans it shows in many ways, some very visible: decline in height, shrinkage of muscle, thinning and graying of hair, and wrinkling of skin. Internally, and even more significantly, there is the progressive loss of cells in the brain, kidneys, and other vital organs. This cell loss has been ascribed to, among other things, errors in DNA replication, resulting in stoppage of a vital process (*see* Genetics, section "Genes and the Genetic Code"). Whatever the reason, important tissues—ranging from the muscles to the brain—shrink and become less competent with age. Many of these changes are reflected in functional declines. Not only do nerve cells at levels from the brain to the spinal cord diminish, but also those that remain conduct impulses at a slower rate so that the reaction time of the older animal is slowed. Memory often shows a decline, especially for recent events.

Another widespread decline is in the loss of cells involved in the hearing process. The loss is most marked for high pitches and may require the assistance of a battery-operated hearing aid. More subtle are such declines as those in the processes involved

Eight-year-old Fransie Geringer of South Africa, left, and nine-year-old Mickey Hays of the United States—are victims of the premature aging disease, progeria.

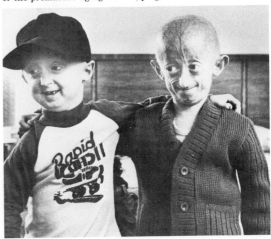
Eddie Adams—Gamma/Liaison

with being immune to disease, which result in a lessened ability of the older organism to cope with infection. Thus infections due to the pneumococcus organism (a bacterium that causes pneumonia) are more common at the extremes of age—in the infant whose immune processes are not fully mature and in the elderly whose formerly high levels of resistance have diminished. Indeed pneumonia is perhaps the most common cause of death.

Mixed with true aging processes are disease processes that may be so common as to be mistaken for aging. For instance, the buildup of deposits of fatty materials in arteries (atherosclerosis, or hardening of the arteries) tends to be progressive with aging; everything else being equal, the narrowing of arteries results in such serious illnesses as stroke (in arteries to the brain) or heart attack (in arteries to the heart), occurring with increasing frequency as an individual ages. However, many persons escape significant atherosclerosis, and some undernourished populations as a group have very little incidence of the disease. It is now recognized that atherosclerosis is the result of many factors, not only genetic but also environmental—high blood pressure, high saturated-fat diets, and smoking, the effects of which become more obvious with the passage of time. It is therefore an age-related, but not a universal aging, process and thus gives hope for control.

Life Span

Everyday observation indicates that the onset of aging and the length of life span are quite different in each species. The dog becomes old after a dozen years, developing graying, visual problems, and stiffness. The pet rodent grows old and dies in two or three years, the horse at 15 to 20 years. The time of the onset of aging is thus specific in each species and appears to be built into the organizational plan. Until more is known about the unfolding of this plan and its ability to be modified, it appears unlikely that major prolongation of life or postponement of the onset of aging can be controlled.

A strange and rare human disease illustrates what can happen when the organizational plan goes awry. The disease is called progeria, and though it does not actually reproduce the pattern of aging, an accelerated aging process does typically occur. The infant with progeria appears normal at birth but within a few years begins to look odd, developing a relatively large head and beaked nose. The skin becomes thin, hair is lost, accelerated atherosclerosis develops, and heart attacks become common by the age of ten or so. The life span is often no longer than 15 years.

At the cell level, one expression of an organizational plan is the discovery that cells removed from an organism and allowed to grow in tissue culture will

The life spans of four species of animals (top) are compared with cells removed from each species (bottom) and allowed to grow in tissue cultures. The graph shows the number of divisions, or population doublings, that each cell may undergo before death.

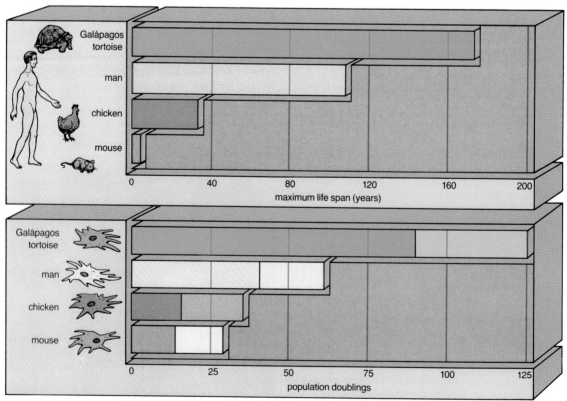

undergo a limited number of divisions and then die. In the human the number of such cell divisions is around 50, in the chicken about 25, in the mouse 14 to 28. In the long-lived Galápagos tortoise, with a life span of about 175 years, explanted cells will undergo 90 to 125 doublings. (In progeria, by comparison, the number of doublings is about ten.) Furthermore, if the normal explanted human cells that have attained, say, 40 doublings are put into a deep freeze for a period of years, then thawed and put back into culture, the cells "remember." They go through only another ten or so multiplications and then cease. This is referred to as the Hayflick phenomenon after the American biologist who first described it. It seems to point to factors within the cell of a species that predetermine its capacity to multiply, the final exhaustion of this capacity, and the relation to life span.

Variability

Not only the fixing but also the biological variability of aging must be recognized. Perhaps around 90 to 100 years is the typical limit for the human fixed life span, but only a few hardy persons attain this age. Generally such long-lived persons seem to show a later onset of aging signs and a slower progression in the rate of aging than is normal. There is a genetic factor to this in that long life does seem to run in families. The changes caused by aging at the level of vital organs, especially the brain, are also quite variable. Some individuals of 50 show obvious slowing of mental processes; others at 70 are still quite sharp.

Disuse may be a significant factor in the impairment of memory and thinking just as it is in muscle weakness associated with aging. Disuse from an inactive physical life-style has been shown to accelerate the loss of bone, which results in the fractures so common in old age. Exercise slows this process and may even increase the bone mass. The increased susceptibility of the aged to pneumonia and influenza may be improved by vaccines. Progress in the medical area indicates that some of the declines produced by aging can be retarded. This ability to be modified indicates that though the aging process is inevitable, it need not be regarded with complete passiveness.

Modification

Since aging and life span are broadly determined by the genetic plan of a species, attention has been directed to the possibilities of their modification by altering the environment. The German-born biologist Jacques Loeb showed early in the 20th century that the life span of the fruit fly was halved by every ten-degree rise in temperature. This led to impractical speculations about prolonging the human life span by experimenting with various degrees of cooling the body. Fairly severe restriction of caloric intake in the laboratory rat can more than double its life span, chiefly by prolonging the period of immaturity. This is known as the McKay effect, and caloric restriction is so far the only factor shown to have a major effect on aging and the life span. Unfortunate-ly, food restriction has less effect on species other than the rodent, although experiments indicate the possibility of some life-span prolongation in other animals. It has not been shown that undernourished human populations live longer, but vitamin deficiency, disease, and poor medical care found in such groups complicate the analysis.

In geriatric medicine the hope is to eliminate the disease processes that prevent human beings from living to the end of their natural life span. The elimination of such diseases as cancer and those of the cardiovascular (circulatory) system would add several years to the average life span. The avoidance of cigarette smoking alone can add more than four years.

Effects on Society

Social and economic aspects of aging are troublesome and an increasing burden on society. For example, there are more than a million Americans who are institutionalized in such facilities as nursing homes. Many of them have multiple impairments such as stroke with its resulting paralysis, crippling arthritis, and cancer. About half suffer from an advanced degree of brain impairment known as senile dementia. They may be so confused as not to recognize members of their own families and may wander much of the time or, conversely, sleep much of the time. The cost of maintaining them is a major element in the total medical bill of the elderly. The overlap of disabling disease and aging processes has given aging many negative connotations; but, in the United States, only 5 percent of the population past age 65 are in institutions, and most are in reasonably good health.

AGNELLI, Giovanni (1866–1945). The dynamic founder of the Italian Fiat automobile company, Giovanni Agnelli, was born on Aug. 13, 1866, in Villar Perosa, in the Piedmont region of northwestern Italy. He was educated at the Classical and Military Academy and graduated in engineering with honors.

With a group of industrialists, Agnelli founded his now well-known company in 1899. Named Fabbrica Italiana Automobili Torino (Fiat), it was the first automobile factory in Italy. Agnelli was chairman and managing director. By 1903 four Fiat factories were producing 1,300 cars a year.

In 1906 Agnelli founded the Officine di Villar Perosa company, which manufactured ball and roller bearings. Agnelli is considered largely responsible for the growth of this industry in Italy. In 1907 he was named a Knight of Labor. One year later he built the first Fiat airplane engine, making him again a pioneer, this time in the aeronautical industry.

In 1923 he was made a senator by the Italian dictator, Benito Mussolini. Agnelli was a promoter of war industries before and during World War II. He and his family were involved in the mining, smelting, cement, radio, and newspaper industries. Agnelli died in Turin, Italy, on Dec. 16, 1945.

AGRIBUSINESS see AGRICULTURE.

Wheat is harvested with modern equipment in the Palouse Hills of southeastern Washington. Wheat farming is a major agricultural business in the western part of the United States.

AGRICULTURE. As soon as humans began to form permanent settlements and gave up wandering in search of food, agriculture was born. The Latin roots of the word agriculture mean "cultivation of the fields." From the beginning, agriculture has included raising both crops and livestock. At first, this new way of providing food and other raw materials developed slowly. But, because it made life much easier for many people, it became the preferred way of supplying a basic human need. The people who worked at agriculture came to be called farmers.

Society was different before there were farmers. Nearly everybody devoted much time to gathering plants for food or to hunting or fishing. When food was abundant, there were feasts; when it was not, there was famine. Gradually people discovered the advantages of caring for animals in flocks and herds. They learned to grow plants for food, medicine, clothing, and shelter in areas set aside for that purpose.

As the food supply became more reliable and raw materials became more abundant, some people were free to do other things besides farming and hunting.

Many of them chose to live in towns and cities, using their talents in various ways, including becoming expert in different trades. They made a variety of goods, which they could trade with the farmers for food. This began the division of labor into the rural farming community and the urban industrial complex, a fundamental partnership that still exists throughout the world.

Other people used their new leisure to observe, to think, to experiment. With the passage of centuries, such activity led to the bases of science, religion, government, and the arts, the foundation of modern civilization. (*See also* Civilization; Family.)

A CHANGING INDUSTRY

Farming used to be primarily a family enterprise and to a large extent still is in most countries. In the more developed areas, however, more efficient large-scale operations are overtaking the smaller family farms. These large farms usually specialize in one crop or one type of crop and often are run by giant parent corporations. Such farms are part of the current trend toward more controlled and cost-effective agriculture, called agribusiness.

The goal in agriculture has almost always been increased production and decreased labor. In the early 1900's the American farm, for example, was run by the muscles of men and draft animals. Today machines of great size and complexity, some computerized, accomplish in hours what took many of those men and animals days to complete.

There are still family farms similar to those of an earlier era even in the most industrialized nations, but they are becoming fewer every year. There are also small-scale agricultural systems in many emerging nations of the world. But the trend almost everywhere is toward larger farms that are mechanized and utilize the latest scientific agricultural methods to provide products more efficiently.

Production: Too Much and Too Little

There is a great range in agricultural production around the world. Some countries, using high technology and advanced methods, produce more through agriculture than they need or can use, while others—underdeveloped and poorer—never produce enough to sustain their populations.

The farming systems that maintained ancient civilizations in Asia Minor or in the Mayan kingdom in the New World are incapable of supporting populations in those areas today. In underdeveloped Africa, farming techniques are improving but are not even as advanced as those of ancient Babylon or the Incas.

Nations with more advanced agriculture often attempt to help such areas improve farm productivity. This aid is often invaluable, but sometimes questionable for the long term. Agricultural systems are intimately connected to places and peoples. Propelling such areas into modern agricultural cropping techniques may be a shock to the local culture. Advanced technologies may not be advisable under the climatic and soil conditions of the area. The native method is often a marvel of ingenuity developed over many generations through intimate contact with a unique

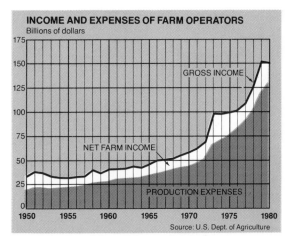

INCOME AND EXPENSES OF FARM OPERATORS
Billions of dollars

GROSS INCOME

NET FARM INCOME

PRODUCTION EXPENSES

Source: U.S. Dept. of Agriculture

Figures for United States farm operators only

situation. There may be no bumper crops, but the wonder is that there is any crop at all.

Many countries in the Western Hemisphere consistently produce more food than they use. The surpluses are stored in granaries and warehouses for later use or sale to other countries. Storing the surpluses costs money because giant bins and huge buildings must be built and maintained. Techniques for reducing spoilage and loss to insects and rodents add to the cost.

As farmers continue to seek the greatest possible yield for the most reasonable cost, advanced agriculture is becoming as elaborate and as complicated as other modern industries. In the United States and in other wealthy nations where population is not yet a burden, the cost of labor is relatively high and is the limiting factor in production. Thus there has been more and more mechanization and automation.

Feeding the World

In general, the world is no better fed today than decades ago. The world's population is growing at an alarming rate, and agriculture has just barely kept up with it. Despite overproduction in some nations, perhaps one out of six persons throughout the world is undernourished. Some studies show that as much as half of the world's population may be suffering from malnutrition or starvation.

Distribution of agricultural surpluses to areas of deficiency seems an ideal solution. But it is far more difficult than it seems. The surpluses currently produced by agriculturally advanced countries are often given to school lunch programs, to families on public assistance, and to welfare institutions within the nations themselves. Food and fiber crops are sold abroad for foreign currencies to improve the producing country's balance of trade.

Even if the food could be easily distributed to other nations, the costs for transporting it run high. Some nations may complain that others ruin their markets by giving a commodity away or selling it at cut-rate prices. These problems, too, must be carefully weighed against the benefits to poorer countries.

Cotton is picked rapidly and efficiently by large machines in the fields of Mississippi.

Mississippi Department of Agriculture and Commerce

129

Plowing and sowing took place in ancient Egypt as in a painting from a tomb at Thebes.

Andre Held

Government's Role

Because agriculture is so important to a nation's well-being, governments have always been concerned with it. For example, the United States and Canada have long produced surpluses that complicate their economies. Surpluses tend to lower prices to farmers and seriously endanger the agriculture industry. Governments have instituted systems of price supports to maintain a fair price when surpluses cause prices to drop. The system in the United States is a good example. A government program supports the prices paid to farmers for grains, soybeans, cotton-seed and other oilseeds, peanuts, cotton, tobacco, butter, cheese, dried milk, wool, mohair, and honey.

Support prices are based on parity, which is the ratio between the prices farmers receive for their crops and the prices they must pay for things they need. The government selected the period from 1910 to 1914 as a time when farm prices were in a fair ratio with farming costs. This is the base period now used to determine parity prices.

The idea is to assure farmers that what they get for a bushel of wheat will buy the same amount of, say, seed as it did in the years of the base period. If prices drop too far below this ideal the government can help in a number of ways. For example, it may buy much of a surplus at parity prices. Governments have instituted a wide variety of other controls for prices and, also, for farm output, mainly at the request of the farmers themselves. Farm prices tend to fluctuate more than other prices do, and the incomes of farmers fluctuate along with farm prices.

Various measures for maintaining farm prices and incomes include tariff or import levies, import quotas, export subsidies, direct payment to farmers, and limitations on production. All of these measures are useful and are used to some extent by most developed countries. An important example of such a program is the soil-bank plan, which aimed at limiting production while improving farmland. The soil-bank plan was passed by the United States Congress in 1956. It allowed a farmer to withdraw land from production for three-, five-, or ten-year periods and receive rental payments from the government for doing so. The

farmer planted such land with grass, trees, or other vegetation that would help prevent erosion and aid fertility. New soil-bank rentals ended in 1960.

The European Economic Community (EEC) established a common agricultural policy (CAP) for its member nations, called the Common Market countries. The aim is to create free trade for individual commodities within the community. When production of a commodity exceeds EEC consumption, the EEC may buy the excess for storage, pay to have it reprocessed, or export it to countries outside the Common Market. In this way the EEC can maintain its members' farm prices at levels equal to or even higher than those in such market-competitive nations as the United States and Canada.

DEVELOPMENT OF FARMING

Agriculture is the basis of civilization. It began about 10,000 years ago, somewhere in the Middle East. Perhaps primitive attempts at agriculture were underway even earlier in Southeast Asia. Both of these areas were rich in animals that were suitable for domestication and in varieties of plants, and both have mild climates.

Agricultural Landmarks

Grazing animals were likely domesticated before plants were tended. Among the earliest animals domesticated were the elk in Scandinavia, the gazelle in the Middle East, and the dog in western North America. Sheep, cattle, and pigs came later.

The first crops probably included grains such as wheat, oats, rye, barley, and millet; and legumes such as peas, lentils, vetch, chick-peas, and horsebeans. Grapes, olives, dates, apples, pears, cherries, and figs were among early domesticated fruits.

Mesopotamia, called the cradle of civilization, influenced all of antiquity, especially Syria and Egypt and perhaps India and China. Its ancient cultures—Sumerian, Babylonian, Assyrian, and Chaldean—developed an increasingly complex and rich agricultural system that freed many people from farming. As a result, the first cities arose in Mesopotamia.

Ancient farming is clearly recorded in Egypt, where it flourished along the Nile. Egyptian farmers developed drainage and irrigation techniques through construction of a system of dikes and canals. During this time farming tools were developed and refined, foremost among them being the hoe.

Greek influence upon agriculture was the establishment of the science of botany. Roman agricultural practices are well recorded. The earliest writing, about 200 B.C., on farming is Cato's 'De agricultura', an essay on the practical aspects of crop and livestock management. Up to 200 B.C. Roman agriculture consisted of farms of one to four acres, intensively managed. Larger farms owned by absentee landowners were developed later, with slaves used to run them. Despite social upheavals in the Roman Empire, its agricultural technology—although inferior to that of the Egyptians—was not equaled in Europe until the Renaissance. The Romans discovered and carefully noted relatively sophisticated techniques such as grafting and budding, crop rotation, and the use of fertilizers. They also originated an early type of greenhouse. (*See also* Ancient Civilizations.)

With the decline of the Roman Empire in the 3d century A.D., the Middle East and the Far East became the centers of technological advance, especially between A.D. 500 and 1500. Crop growing was based on extensive production in large fields and intensive production in small gardens. There were common pastures for the cattle or other domestic animals.

The usual method of crop farming was a fallow system, in which one third of the land was not planted each year, to restore soil fertility. Fields were partitioned into strips that were rotated among the tenant farmers. Strip farming gave way ultimately to an enclosed system, with individual farmers responsible for their own lands. Crop rotation and improved plowing techniques evolved.

By the end of the Middle Ages, most of the tillable land of Europe was cleared, drained, and in cultivation. At that time the transition from medieval to modern agricultural practices began. This transition

M. Petruzska/F.A.O.

Jute is harvested in Nepal by field workers, who cut the stalks by hand.

is called the agricultural revolution. New foods entered European farming. During the 16th century the potato and maize (corn), imported from the New World, and rice, introduced earlier from Asia, came under cultivation in Europe.

The classification of agriculture into agronomy, horticulture, and forestry has been traced to medieval times. Agronomy came to refer to the growing of grains and forage plants, or field crops. Horticulture developed from small garden plots that provided

TOTAL POPULATION AND POPULATION ENGAGED IN AGRICULTURE, WORLD AND REGIONS: 1937, 1980

	1937			1980		
	Total Population (000,000)	Population Engaged in Agriculture (000,000)	Percentage of Total Engaged in Agriculture	Total Population (000,000)	Population Engaged in Agriculture (000,000)	Percentage of Total Engaged in Agriculture
Europe	372	133	36	484	71	15
U.S.S.R.	190	108	57	266	44	16
North and Central America*	178	56	31	370	53	14
North America	140	32	23	246	6	2
Central America	38	24	63	124	47	38
South America	84	52	62	245	79	32
Asia†	691	504	73	1,601	915	57
Africa	168	128	76	470	298	63
Oceania	11	3	26	23	5	21
World†	1,694	985	58	3,458	1,465	42
China	447	40	76	957	572	60
World total	2,141	1,325	62	4,415	2,037	46

*Combined figures; figures for individual regions given below. †Excluding China.
Source: UN Food and Agriculture Organization, *Production Yearbook*.

fruits and herbs as well as ornamental plants for the medieval manor. Forestry developed from the wild lands that produced timber for the landowner and supported game animals hunted by the nobles.

As feudalism ended, technology was developing and agricultural methods, tools, and products were improving. New industries arose, creating markets for some crops such as sugarcane, hemp, flax, vegetable oils, and dyes. The growing of grapes for wine became a key industry. New farming systems of enclosed fields, crop rotation, and feeding animals in stalls became more efficient with time. Mechanization was beginning for agriculture. Plows, seed sowers, threshers, and harvesters were introduced and became increasingly complex.

KINDS OF MODERN FARMS

Today, about one half of the world's people are farmers. Most of them struggle along as subsistence farmers. This means that they raise plants and animals to provide for their families, usually having little or nothing left over to sell or trade for other goods. Subsistence farming is common in crowded, poorer, underdeveloped countries and in depressed areas even in advanced countries. In this type of farming, a farm may be less than an acre in size and the land of poor quality. The family that works such a farm usually coaxes it to provide enough to live on only through intensive hand labor.

In more developed, less crowded countries, such as the United States, Australia, and Canada, a single farm may reach as far as the eye can see in any direction, and may be run by a large corporation that uses only the latest machines and technology. Such commercial farms are the big agricultural producers in developed nations. They are operated much like other industries. Many are family run, but the family functions as management for the parent corporation.

The amount of farmland owned by those who farm is smaller than most people realize. Many farms are rented, and often sharecropping, in which income from the crop is shared, is arranged to pay the land's owner. In countries such as Israel and the Soviet Union, there are communal farms owned by the state.

Diversified, general farming, in which many crops and different kinds of animals are raised, is the traditional farming in Western countries with temperate climates. These farms are often composed of land claimed from forest and prairie.

A specialized farm is a commercial farm that produces a major crop or a few major crops that account for half or more of the farm's gross sales. These are crops best suited to the land and climate and to the skill and financial ability of the farmer.

Farms on flat to rolling lands are usually used for row crops or grains. Rocky, irregular lands are usually used as pasture, left wooded, or used for tree farms.

Dryland farming, practiced on prairies and other places where rainfall is light (less than 20 inches, or 50 centimeters), is common in many parts of North America and Europe. Soils are generally deep and rich, but yields vary because rainfall is not only light, but also uneven from year to year. Crops planted in such areas include winter wheat and grain sorghum.

Tropical farming, practiced where the climate is predominantly warm and wet, is common throughout

Erosion is controlled with a cover of grasses and weeds in an orange grove in the Eagle Valley at Riverside, Calif. The cover is mowed to keep it from becoming overgrown.

Soil Conservation Service/USDA

Thomas Höpker—Stern/Black Star

Terraced rice paddies are common in the northern part of the island of Sumatra in Indonesia.

Latin America, Africa, India, Australia, and Southeast Asia. The amount of land suitable for tropical farming is limited and requires careful management to be productive and sustaining. The soil is leached of nutrients rapidly by the heavy rainfalls typical of the tropics. Tropical crops include coconut, palm oil, rice, sugarcane, pineapple, sisal, cocoa, tea, coffee, jute, rubber, pepper, banana, and breadfruit.

FARMING METHODS AROUND THE WORLD

In underdeveloped countries more than 70 percent of the people live by farming. In wealthy industrialized countries less than 10 percent are so engaged.

Farming in the Economy

Most of the farmers throughout the world live in underdeveloped countries and practice subsistence farming. They raise just enough plants and tend just enough animals for their own needs and have little, if anything, to trade for other goods. This type of farming hinders a nation's development. More productive agriculture has played a major part in the growth of developed countries. Typically, a country's development depends upon its ability to produce a surplus of food to maintain a nonfarming labor force in its urban areas. Put another way, the economic develop-

ment of a nation requires a growing nonfarm labor force, and so the diminishing farm community must produce more food with fewer hands. Many countries find it difficult to reach this goal.

Agricultural systems have developed in response to tradition, geographic area, type of crop, and level of technology. They are also shaped by many factors not obviously related to them. Farming in North America, for example, developed out of traditional farming in the Old World. Corn was soon seen to be a valuable crop and became the dominant grain raised. Tobacco, cotton, and rice, which require many hands to tend, stimulated slavery.

The United States was originally an agricultural nation. In 1800, 90 percent of the working population was engaged in farming. By the 1980's, only about 5 percent worked on farms, but each worker produced enough for more than 20 people. In contrast, in India and other poorer countries a typical farm worker produced enough only for about four persons.

Shifting Agriculture

While technology is advancing in many parts of the world, some primitive cultures in sparsely populated tropical areas still practice a shifting system of agriculture. This system is a type of slash-and-burn agriculture, in which land is cleared of plant life, which is burned to add some nutrients to the soil. This is followed by planting. When the land is exhausted, it is abandoned and new clearings are slashed and burned. This process is wasteful of native vegetation and is abusive to the land. The milpa of tropical America and the ladang system of the Orient are examples of such farming practices.

Plantation Agriculture

A plantation is a large area of land that is usually privately or government owned and employs resident labor to cultivate a single commercial crop. Plantation agriculture is generally found in tropical and subtropical regions. This type of agriculture has achieved new degrees of efficiency in Central and South America and some other areas where such crops as cacao, sugarcane, coconut, banana, pineapple, breadfruit, and other tropical plants are raised under efficient agricultural methods.

Typically plantations develop as settlements grow and slash-and-burn farming exhausts the land. Villagers then turn to tending groves of coconut, breadfruit, banana, citrus, and avocado trees that can thrive permanently under tropical and subtropical soil and climate conditions. The rubber plantations of Sumatra and Malaya, cacao plantations of Africa and Central America, and the sugar and coffee plantations throughout the tropics are probably the best methods of using the land under existing conditions.

Forests have only recently became regarded as croplands to be managed for continuous production, like plantations, with specialized techniques and machines for planting, harvesting, and replanting. (*See also* Forests and Forestry.)

Orcharding

Orcharding is a more intensive method of fruit and nut tree cropping than plantation agriculture. In other words, it demands more skill and effort to be done successfully. The first orchards came into being in the Temperate Zones of Europe, Asia, and North America. Crops such as apples, pears, plums, apricots, and cherries are grown in orchards.

In the United States, many orchards are found concentrated in the coastal Northwest and the Great Lakes regions. There are extensive pear orchards in the Rhone Valley of Europe, and apple and pear or-

Methods of harvest vary dramatically in different parts of the world. Potatoes are harvested (below) by machinery in Michigan. In Bangladesh (bottom) the radish crop is harvested and processed by hand.

chards in Northern Italy. Southern Australia, South Africa, and Southern Argentina are also areas of fruit orcharding. China has about 12 million acres (4.9 million hectares) of orchards, yielding in excess of 5 million tons (4.5 million metric tons) of fruit each year.

In the United States and Europe, apple, citrus, pear, peach, plum, apricot, cherry, pecan, and walnut are the principal orchard-grown crops. Although grapes are sometimes grown in orchards, along with some other fruit, they are more usually grown in vineyards. (*See also* Fruitgrowing).

Floodplain Farming

Farming in the tropics often includes floodplain cropping with periodic irrigation. A river's floodplain is the area on either side of the river over which it deposits soil when it floods. Farming is practiced along the floodplains of rivers such as the Nile in Egypt and large waterways in the Orient, where paddies are formed by terracing. Floodplain farming is most successfully used in Southeast Asia.

Burning-grazing

In many parts of the world grasses cover the land to the horizon. Livestock grazing is ideal in these areas, which include the prairies of the Western United States, the pampas of South America, tropical savannas of Africa, and steppes of Asia. Periodic, controlled burning is practiced in such areas to keep woody brush from gaining a foothold and to stimulate continuing grass growth.

Desert Farming

Some of the richest plant areas are along stream borders in desert valleys. Desert land apparently lacks only water to be productive. Now, irrigation projects transport water for many miles to produce large crops in places like the interior desert valleys of California, Arizona, Colorado, and Texas in the United States. The deserts of the Middle East are in the beginning phases of large-scale agricultural production in such places as Egypt and Israel. A host of innovative irrigation techniques, such as drip irrigation, have originated in these areas.

Diversified General Farming

The farming traditional to Western cultures in temperate regions is diversified general farming. In this type of farming, a variety of crops is grown, including most of the Temperate Zone crops, and especially corn, small grains, and soybeans. In the south, tobacco, beans, peanuts, corn, small grains, hay and forage crops, and fruit trees are grown. Diversified general farming produces great self-sufficiency for the farmer, even more so if some livestock are also raised, as is often the case.

Prairie Farming

Much prairie land is used for the burning-grazing agriculture described earlier. Large acreages are usually devoted to a single crop or only a few. The prairie

(Top) Soil Conservation Service/USDA
(bottom) Kay Chernush—World Bank

wheat fields of Canada and the cornfields of the United States are examples. Each year, with rare exceptions, this land yields larger and larger harvests because of more productive crop strains and improved farming techniques.

TWENTIETH-CENTURY TRENDS

Agriculture has developed more rapidly in the 20th century than in all previous history. Up to the 1950's, industrial countries such as the United States, England, Germany, and Japan were the major centers of agricultural innovation and progress. Since that time, the newly developing nations in Latin America, Africa, and Asia have begun impressive large-scale efforts to improve their agriculture.

Mechanization

The full influence of mechanization began shortly after 1850, when a variety of machines came rapidly into use. The introduction of these machines frequently created rebellions by workers who were fearful that the machines would rob them of their work. Patrick Bell, in Scotland, and Cyrus McCormick, in the United States, produced threshing machines. Ingenious improvements were made in plows to compensate for different soil types. Steam power came into use in the 1860's on large farms. Hay rakes, hay-loaders, and various special harvesting machines were produced. Milking machines appeared. The internal-combustion engine—run by gasoline—became the chief power source for the farm.

In time, the number of certain farm machines that came into use skyrocketed and changed the nature of farming. Between 1940 and 1960, for example, 12 million horses and mules gave way to 5 million tractors. Tractors offer many features that are attractive to farmers. There are, for example, numerous attachments: cultivators that can penetrate the soil to varying depths, rotary hoes that chop weeds; spray devices that can spray pesticides in bands 100 feet (30 meters) across, and many others.

A piece of equipment has now been invented or adapted for virtually every laborious hand or animal operation on the farm. In the United States, for example, cotton, tobacco, hay, and grain are planted, treated for pests and diseases, fertilized, cultivated, and harvested by machine. Large devices shake fruit and nuts from trees, grind and blend feeds, and dry grain and hay. Equipment is now available to put just the right amount of fertilizer in just the right place, to spray an exact row width with herbicides, and to count out, space, and plant just the right number of seeds for a row.

Mechanization is not used in agriculture in many parts of Latin America, Africa, and heavily populated areas of the Orient, where human and animal labor is usually far less expensive than are machines. Agricultural innovation is accepted fastest where agriculture is already profitable and progressive. Some mechanization has reached the level of plantation agriculture in parts of the tropics, but even today

Ray Witlin—World Bank

An agricultural extension worker gives instruction in the use of a metal plow to a farmer in the West African Republic of Upper Volta.

much of that land is laboriously worked by people leading draft animals pulling primitive plows.

The problems of mechanizing some areas are not only cultural in nature. For example, tropical soils and crops differ markedly from those in temperate areas that the machines are designed for; so adaptations have to be made. But the greatest obstacle to mechanization is the fear in underdeveloped countries that the workers who are displaced by machines would not find work elsewhere. Introducing mechanization into such areas requires careful planning.

Tillage Systems

Deep tilling, in which the soil is plowed deeply, is being superseded in many areas by shallow plowing or no plowing at all. This is one of several techniques that are effective in controlling soil erosion. In the fallow system, which dates back to ancient times, land is plowed and tilled but not planted to a crop. This is to rest and rejuvenate the land. The disadvantage is that such fallow land is more vulnerable to wind and water erosion than is planted land. Plowing along the contours of the land is called contour tillage. This and building terraces on sloping land help to conserve moisture by preventing excessive water runoff on moderately sloping land.

Minimum tillage appears to be gaining acceptance in many areas of the world. With minimum tillage,

135

Insect damage is a major problem to agriculture throughout the world. An invasion of locusts in Morocco is sprayed by an airplane (left). The grain on an ear of corn (right) failed to develop because rootworm beetles disrupted pollination by eating the corn silk.

soil is disturbed as little as possible. In fact, in some areas zero tillage, or no tillage at all, is a growing practice. Weeds can be killed chemically and left as a soil-improving mulch. Crops are planted in untilled land by special machines. Yields of potatoes, parsnips, carrots, gooseberries, broad beans, and brussels sprouts are close to, and sometimes slightly better than, yields under traditional cultivation practices, which consume more time and energy. Corn and soybeans under zero tillage often yield more than under standard cultivation.

Intensive Cropping

Another trend is toward growing more plants in any given space. Increased fertilization and irrigation are often required to do this. But the dense growth usually reduces soil erosion and chokes out weeds, making weeding unnecessary. Cotton, sorghum, sugar beets, soybeans, and corn are effectively grown in such dense plantings.

Field Processing

In some areas field processing of crops is becoming a standard practice. The farmers use machines that process crops as they are harvested. Corn is shelled, or removed from the cob, as it is picked. Hay is baled and tossed onto a wagon, ready to be stored or sold. The idea behind machine processing in the field is to avoid unnecessary handling and storage of unprocessed crops.

Crop and Livestock Improvement

Crop improvement is continuous. Professional plant breeders are constantly working, through genetics, on the improvement of plants to meet changing needs and standards. For example, with the introduction of mechanical pickers for tomatoes, a tomato resistant to bruising by the machine was needed. Such a variety was created by plant breeders.

Better, higher-yielding crop varieties have played an important part in the increase in crop production per acre in the United States and some other nations. Varieties of rice, cotton, vegetable-oil crops, and sugar crops have changed almost completely since 1950. By the late 1960's most crop acreage in the United States was producing varieties unknown in earlier decades. Best known of the improved crops are the many varieties of hybrid corn that are planted on more than 97 percent of the total corn acreage in the United States. Government experimental laboratories and commercial seed companies shared in the research and development of the high-yield plant varieties that provide such superior characteristics as resistance to cold, drought, diseases, and pests.

Improvements in livestock, such as more efficient use of feed, has added greatly to farm output. Such improvements are the result of breeding and improved husbandry and veterinary techniques. Special-purpose stock has been developed through selective breeding. It includes cattle that are able to thrive in subtropical regions, hogs that yield lean bacon instead of lard, and small and broad-breasted turkeys. Between 1970 and 1980 average milk production per cow, worldwide, increased about 40 percent. (*See also* Cattle; Hog; Poultry; Turkey.)

Artificial insemination has become a major factor in cattle improvement. In this technique the sperm of genetically superior bulls is used to inseminate thousands of cows. In this way a herd can be upgraded significantly in a single generation.

Some people feel that the tendency of agriculture to produce plants and animals that conform to the needs of mechanization and increased production has resulted in less desirable farm products. They say that the new varieties of plants and specially bred animals yield less tasty, and sometimes less nutritious, vegetables, fruit, meat, and dairy products.

Pesticides and Growth Regulators

Better control of plant and animal diseases and pests has aided the increase in agricultural output. Inorganic chemical pesticides were generally used before 1945. Organic chemicals developed later include chlorinated hydrocarbons, such as toxaphene and benzene hexachloride. They also include organic phosphates, such as malathion and parathion.

The use of airplanes in spraying made the work more efficient. A plane can spray 1,000 acres (405 hectares) in a matter of minutes. Research in insecticides must go on continuously, since insects tend to develop immunity to sprays. Each new chemical is tested to be sure that no harmful residue will poison treated food plants. The natural enemies of some pests have also been used. The combined use of chemicals and natural enemies is called integrated pest management and is considered by many to be the most desirable control technique. Improvement in storage methods, especially for cereals and hay, has also cut losses from molds, insects, and rodents.

Insects, mites, and ticks that attack domestic animals cause them enough distress and disease to cost stock raisers millions of dollars annually. Control methods worked out to free the animals from several types of pests have resulted, for example, in desirable weight gains and increased milk production. Antibiotics are given to animals in feed and as medicine. By checking and preventing disease, the antibiotics promote growth, weight, and efficient use of feed. (*See also* Insects; Scale Insects.)

The use of chemicals to kill weeds has saved much labor and has led to crop increases. The application of chemicals began on a large scale after the discovery in 1944 that 2,4-D (2,4-dichlorophenoxyacetic acid) kills broad-leaved weeds, but not grasses. This kind of selective action is ideal if some plants (the crop) are to be saved, while others (the weeds) are killed. Since that time more than 100 weed killers have been developed. They may be applied by special machines before or after the crop plant emerges. (*See also* Weeds.)

Research has shown ways to regulate or control the growth of plants by means of chemicals. Such regulators may be used to increase the size of fruits. Hormones can retard the falling of fruit, thus extending the harvest period.

Fertilizers and Lime

Agricultural experts credit greater and more scientific use of fertilizers and lime with a major share of the increase in farm production since 1940. Liming of acid soils in humid areas is a general practice in advanced agricultural countries. The lime reduces the acidity of the soils, making them more productive when planted with most crops.

Modern farmers dig soil samples from their fields and send them to soil laboratories operated by the government or private companies. After testing the samples, the technicians recommend a fertilizer mixture, in terms of pounds per acre, of nitrogen, phosphorus, and potassium—the chief elements used by plants. Modern fertilizers may also contain small amounts of minor elements, called micronutrients or trace elements. Many machines have been developed for applying fertilizers to various crops.

To return organic matter to the soil, thus keeping it in good physical condition as well as providing fertilizer, farmers plow under available manure and cornstalks, alfalfa, clover, and other "green manure" plants. Residue from the processing of plants and animals is used as organic fertilizer. Waste from fish canneries and meat-packing plants is also widely used. (*See also* Fertilizers.)

Fertilizer and Pesticide Improvement

Farm manure is the major source of organic matter and plant nutrients in many parts of the world. Manure is refuse from stables and barnyards, including both animal excrement and bedding materials such as straw, wood chips, and the like.

Research in plant nutrition, begun in the 18th century, is reaching new heights in the 20th century. The beneficial effects of organic matter and chemicals in the growth of crops have been long known. But only recently have sophisticated systems of chemical release and application been generated rapidly. The goal now is to determine precisely how much nutrient to add and when it is best to add it.

Materials with higher percentages of nutrients are used increasingly. Although there is continued use of standard chemical sources of nitrogen—the most needed and most expensive nutrient—such as anhydrous ammonia, ammonium nitrate, and urea; cheaper and better ways of providing nitrogen are being developed. Concentrated liquid fertilizers are becoming more useful, as is customized mixing of fertilizers based on soil and plant analysis.

Larger and more precise fertilizing machines are being developed. Biodegradable tapes, with seed, fertilizer, and pesticide incorporated, have found acceptance in gardening. They may find some application in commercial agriculture in the future.

The pesticide industry continues to produce standard control products while actively engaging in the search for more effective and safer ones. Herbicides are of increasing importance, especially under zero tillage systems of farming. Fungicides and other protectants against disease are expensive and may not be as advantageous in the long run as the breeding of disease-resistant strains of crops.

The future of chemical pesticides—including insecticides, fungicides, and herbicides—is being reconsidered on several levels: by the manufacturers, the sellers, and the buyers. The concern for environmental quality demands that greater care be given to development and use of these valuable yet potentially hazardous substances. Integrated control—the use of biological agents along with chemicals when necessary—is perceived as more and more desirable.

Fish-farming and Other Aquaculture

Fish-farming involves raising small immature fishes as livestock, under the best conditions possible. The Chinese have raised carp for several thousands of years, and the Japanese and others have raised certain other species of fishes with varying degrees of success. Now some researchers claim that the time is near when the problem of feeding a growing world population could be solved by farming the edges of the sea, raising not only fishes, but also lobsters, shrimps, and other shellfishes under optimum conditions. Commercial culture of lobsters, shrimps, and clams is in its infancy, but continues to develop. Under ideal conditions, such as those found in parts of Spain, mussels and other edible bivalves are raised and harvested in great numbers.

Commercial farming of algae as human or farm-animal food has yet to begin. However, seaweed and other algae are collected for food and other uses in several parts of the world. (*See also* Aquaculture.)

Hydroponics, or soilless culture of plants in liquids, is used on a small scale in greenhouses for production of off-season vegetables. Large-scale production would be economical only for certain kinds of farming, under special conditions, perhaps on some of the coral islands of the Pacific.

Young members of a production brigade in Jiangsu province of China are proud of the harvest of silver carp at their aquaculture farm.

F. Mattioli/F.A.O.

Soil and Water Management

Farmers have become more expert in soil and water management in the past half century. The science of agronomy includes land management. The huge yields today are partly due to intelligent use of the land. Farmers use areas with the least fertile soil, poor drainage, steep slopes, or other disadvantages as pasture and woods rather than for crops. They work and plant their land in ways that hold the rainfall and prevent or check erosion. The farmers of a district may join in soil conservation projects with federal aid. (*See also* Conservation.)

Irrigation has long played an important part in the agriculture of many countries. Individual farmers and groups of farmers may get water for their fields from streams and wells. Others may get water from large government irrigation systems. These systems dam the snow-fed mountain rivers of the area and send their water through canals to the fields. About two thirds of the increase in irrigated acreage in the United States after 1949 was in the West. (*See also* Irrigation and Reclamation.)

Until recently farmers in moister areas relied entirely upon rainfall for moisture. Since World War II many farmers in such areas have turned to irrigation to compensate for periods of poor rainfall during the growing season. This has insured more dependable crops and high yields even in times of drought. More than 400 million acres (162 million hectares) were being irrigated worldwide in the 1970's.

Livestock Production

As the need for grain as human food grows, the practice of feeding it to cattle and other livestock is increasingly questioned. New sources of livestock feed seem likely to emerge. Some research has focused on and appears to be headed toward increasing the yield of animal products just on the food that can be provided by rangeland and permanent pastures. Large-scale fertilization of this kind of land could, therefore, become justified in the future.

Genetic improvement through controlled breeding of dairy cows, better nutrition, and improved management have resulted in unparalleled gains in milk production in the past 40 years. Improvement is expected to continue. Research on climate control and increasing the number of multiple births is expected to result in improved production of beef cattle and pigs. Efficiency of poultry production, already high, could reach even higher levels through techniques that now seem fantastic. For example, the potential efficiency limit for a laying hen is one egg each day for a year from three pounds of feed per dozen eggs. The average hen, however, lays about 230 eggs per year from four pounds of feed per dozen eggs. Much energy goes into producing the shell around an egg. Research may result in hens' laying eggs without shells, thereby increasing the total number that are laid. The question then becomes one of packaging and acceptance by the public.

USDA

Soil erosion is reduced by intercropping near Fresno, Ohio. Intercrops are typically small grains or sod such as alfalfa or clover grown between rows of a field crop.

The limits in most livestock productivity are still not within sight. Much remains to be done, but supplements in feed to fatten animals and keep them healthy may have reached its limit. There is growing concern over the appearance of such additives in the human food derived from treated animals.

Agricultural Research

As competition for land increases and agricultural productivity peaks, agricultural research enters the area of bioengineering, through which plants can be redesigned by genetic manipulation. This offers the hope for crops that can take nitrogen out of the air, lessening the need for nitrogen fertilizer. Disease resistance increasingly will be built into crops. Plants will be able to grow on arid land or in salt marshes. Almost any desired genetic change is possible. What to modify is the question, not how to modify.

Agribusiness

In agriculturally progressive areas, such as Japan, the United States, Canada, and many parts of Europe, agriculture has become big business. The farmer is more and more a manager, running a business, which may be part of a huge corporation, based soundly on chemistry, biology, engineering, and economics. The goal is the same as for any businessman: to maximize profits. The agribusiness manager must be alert to government programs and regulations, must be aware of the newest varieties and growing techniques, and must be knowledgeable about pesticide hazards and hundreds of other details. Every segment of the operation is examined. The most select crop variety suited to soil conditions is chosen; special fertilizer is blended for maximum growth and yield. Chemical weed control is practiced. Irrigation may be used. Pesticides are applied at the best times.

All of these have been done by farmers in the past, but now many of these activities are computerized.

AGRICULTURAL MANAGEMENT

Farming has become a highly complex and competitive business. Today's farmer must be a careful businessman as well as a trained agriculturist. There is now the need to understand and use economics, marketing, and several other business-related fields in addition to having a knowledge of agronomy, animal husbandry, breeding techniques, and other fields traditionally related to agriculture.

Capital Outlay

The young person who selects farming as a career makes a large investment on entering it. Often there are years of expensive schooling. Then if the decision is to start one's own farm, there is the problem that the machines and equipment for scientific farming are expensive. The up-to-date farmer also must spend a great deal of money on such items as fertilizer, seed and livestock, special feeds, insect sprays, tractor fuel, and special buildings, such as milking parlors and poultry houses.

The price per acre of farm real estate (including land and buildings and other improvements) continues to rise. Net income, however, has changed little. A part of the rise in real estate has been caused by inflation. The demand for land for nonfarm uses also has boosted the average price.

Few farmers pay cash for their land. It may be months before money comes in from crops or animals. Like the city dweller buying a home, the average farmer must borrow. The farmer may also borrow to purchase seed, fertilizer, stock feed, and other supplies. The farm renter also needs money for the portion of machinery or livestock he or she must supply. Government and private agencies assist the farmers in securing this needed credit.

Records and Accounts

The modern farm family finds that it is necessary to keep numerous records. This task often falls to members of the farmer's family. The farmer needs data provided by the records for income tax returns and as a basis for making business decisions. Careful accounting is required to show whether the input— into a crop or into the farm as a whole—is warranted by the value of the output.

A dairy farmer may weigh and record the yield of every cow at each milking in order to find and then keep only the most productive animals. The poultry farmer may tally the number of eggs each hen lays and then cull the poor layers. The grain farmer must know the cost of seed, fertilizer, weed spray, labor, machinery depreciation, and other production items to calculate profit or loss on a crop.

After a careful study of investment, costs, and output, a farmer may make major changes in operations. The grain farmer, for example, may decide to rent more land to get greater use from machines. If yield is high and the price is low, the farmer may buy beef cattle to feed on the grain and hope to make a better profit on the beef. The farmer may decide to plant soybeans or another crop instead of grain the next year. A series of poor yearly results may reveal that the output of a small farm is not paying a fair wage for the labor. The farmer may then decide to take other work and run the farm only part time.

Modern Marketing

Marketing has changed as much over the years as other aspects of farming. A century ago much of the farmer's output was sold and consumed at the nearest marketing town. The farmer might also deliver barrels of potatoes and apples directly to nearby homes. Grain was usually sold to a nearby mill, a steer or hog to the local slaughterhouse, and eggs and butter might be sold to a local store.

In some parts of the world farmers still carry their small surplus to a town market where they trade or sell it to their neighbors. In the United States, roadside vegetable stands and farmers' markets are the chief remnants of such direct trade between farmer and consumer. In general the modern farmer's output reaches the market through the hands of many businesses that buy, store, transport, process, package, and deliver it before it is sold to the consumer.

This system is necessary because people use few commodities in the form in which they come from the farm. People want cuts of meat or hamburger—not a steer; bread—not wheat; a dress or a coat—not cotton or wool. A farm's product may be used thousands of miles away, completely changed in form. More than a million commercial firms are engaged in agricultural marketing and processing. (*See also* Trade; Food Processing; Meat Industry; Food Buying.)

The people who handle farm produce en route to the consumer must be paid. In the United States, more than 60 cents of every dollar people spend for farm commodities goes to the people who buy, handle, sell, package, and advertise it. This leaves about 40 cents for those who raise the produce.

To avoid dealing with commercial buyers and processors, farm groups often organize cooperatives for the processing and selling of their produce. The extra profits are shared among the cooperative members. Farm cooperatives may also buy such items as fertilizer, seed, and gasoline in large, money-saving quantities, then sell them to members, passing along the savings. (*See also* Cooperative Societies.)

Understanding the Market

To sell produce most advantageously, the farmer needs to understand the market for particular commodities. He or she must keep in touch with price trends to determine the most favorable time to sell. Various services in different countries issue reports on the production and prices of crops and livestock. They also forecast future output and furnish market news to newspapers and radio broadcasters. Boards of trade, or commodity exchanges, issue reports of prices for current sales and futures on grains, cotton, soybeans, and other commodities

The farmer can increase profits by producing commodities that meet high standards. The Agricultural Marketing Service in the United States has played an important role in setting standards and grades for agricultural products. The service also inspects many foods for wholesomeness.

GOVERNMENTS AND ORGANIZATIONS

Since World War II modern farming methods have been spread by national and international organizations. Governments have continued their traditional role of overseeing and influencing agriculture. Numerous countries have set up development programs and five-year plans to improve agriculture, marketing, and processing. Many nations have been especially eager to improve their economies at least partly through improving their agriculture. Irrigation systems have been built by many countries, notably India, Pakistan, Israel, and Egypt. To improve their agriculture, some of these countries have borrowed money from the World Bank and wealthy countries such as the United States.

The Food and Agriculture Organization (FAO) and the World Health Organization of the United

Eggs inoculated with HVT vaccine produce protected chicks. Agricultural production has increased through research.

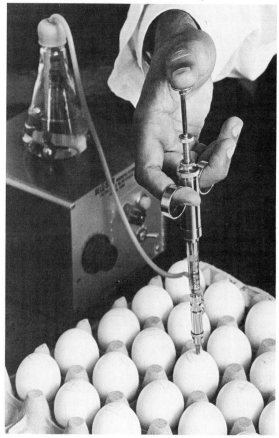

Nations are working to extend new farming methods and to fight diseases and pests. Groups that are active in improving agriculture in specific regions of the world include the Commonwealth of Nations, the Colombo Plan nations, and the Organization of American States. Agencies of the Organization of American States maintain numerous technical institutions. Prominent among these are the Inter-American Institute of Agricultural Sciences in Costa Rica and the Pan American Foot and Mouth Disease Center in Brazil.

The United States economic and technical-aid programs are supervised by the State Department's Agency for International Development (AID). Agricultural experts work with farmers of other lands and show how modern methods may be applied to help solve their problems. They introduce improved seed and better implements and devices to take the place of traditional seed and equipment. Philanthropic organizations such as the Ford Foundation and the Rockefeller Foundation are also active in giving technical assistance abroad. (*See also* in Fact-Index international agencies mentioned.)

Farming in Communist Countries

Communist governments have worked to increase the supply of food and fiber in their countries. They have set up large cooperative and state farms, which use the labor and land of former private owners. In many cases they have met resistance. Also, crop results often have not come up to the expectations of leaders. The Soviet Union's output of grain per acre, for example, is one third less than that of Western Europe, where intensive farming is carried on. Seeking to improve production, the Soviet government made several changes. For instance, they ended the system whereby collective farms had to sell grain to the state at low prices.

Communist China set up a commune system. Peasant families give up their property and are housed in dormitories. Then they work in the fields or on state projects under government-appointed supervisors. (*See also* Russia; China, People's Republic of.) China is also experimenting with Western methods.

Cooperative International Research

Progress in cooperative research is slow. Billions of dollars have been offered in agricultural aid through the AID, funded by the United States. Other billions are channeled through the FAO.

Grants from private foundations and various nations help to fund regional and international agricultural research centers in the tropics and subtropics. The centers provide educational opportunities as well as research services. At least half of the board members of these centers are distinguished authorities from the nations served.

The World Food Conference, sponsored by the United Nations, was held in Rome, Italy, in November 1974. Important resolutions dealing with the food crisis were passed, but progress remains unsteady.

United States Department of Agriculture

The activities of the United States Department of Agriculture are an outstanding example of how a government can aid and influence a nation's agriculture. Within the United States Department of Agriculture are numerous divisions, generally called bureaus, services, or administrations. Their activities and responsibilities are discussed in the article United States Government, section "Department of Agriculture." Most divisions assist in problems with farm methods. Several divisions, however, have programs to aid the farmers financially. Each of the 50 states also has an agricultural department. Federal and state departments work in cooperation with each other and with local committees, farmers' organizations, and individual farm families.

Research in Agriculture. The United States Department of Agriculture is best known for its research, which is often associated with colleges and universities, thus providing added educational opportunities to students at these institutions. Just a few of the areas of research are crops, farm and land management, livestock, human nutrition, home economics, and utilization of agricultural products. Extensive staffs of scientists carry on this work at the large Beltsville, Md., research center and in laboratories and field stations throughout the United States and in several foreign countries. State agricultural experiment stations work on local problems and join with other state stations in regional research.

Discoveries of scientists at these facilities have played a major role in the growth of farm output. Stock-breeding experiments have produced animals that provide more meat, milk, and other products than did previous varieties. The scientists have tailored crops to fit the needs and demands of consumers, processors, and machine cultivation. They have searched for disease-resistant seed that will thrive in United States soils and climates. They have discovered pesticides, medicines, and other cures for diseases of plants and animals. At Utilization Research and Development Laboratories, they have discovered new industrial uses for farm produce.

Publications and Extension Work. Federal and state agricultural departments reveal the results of their research to farmers through broad programs of publishing and the extension service. All offer free or inexpensive bulletins on thousands of practical farm topics. The extension service is a cooperative undertaking of federal and state departments. Each agricultural county in the nation is served by extension workers. They are as a rule the county agent, usually a man, and the home demonstration agent, usually a woman. They work directly with farm families in meetings and in farm or home consultations and demonstrations. The latest scientific knowledge is thus quickly made available. State extension staffs usually include experts in soils, livestock, landscaping, youth organizations, community improvement, wildlife conservation, and other topics of rural interest.

F. Mattioli/F.A.O.

Grain is harvested on a slope in the Irbid area of Jordan. In the background is land that has been contoured to combat soil erosion.

Aid in Conservation and Marketing. Farmers get assistance in land and water management from the Soil Conservation Service and the Agricultural Stabilization and Conservation Service. The United States Forest Service helps in the management of woodlands. Aid in marketing farm crops is supplied by the Agricultural Marketing Service and the Foreign Agricultural Service. The Farmer Cooperative Service assists marketing cooperatives. The Commodity Exchange Authority supervises the commodity markets, or boards of trade.

Aid in Economic Problems. Programs that help farmers solve financial problems were introduced in 1929 and the 1930's during the Great Depression. They have been continued and revised over the years, as mounting crop surpluses threatened a slump in prices that would impoverish the farmers and the businesses that were dependent upon them.

Laws creating programs to provide various types of aid are passed by Congress. The administration of the program is in the hands of the secretary of agriculture. For more detail, *see* earlier subheads "A Changing Industry" and "Government's Role."

The Commodity Credit Corporation (CCC) is the Department of Agriculture agency that handles commodity price agreements with the farmer. To get the support price, the farmer must usually agree to plant only a certain number of acres with a certain crop. This does not necessarily reduce output, as modern techniques permit more to be raised per acre.

The CCC offers to buy supported crops or to lend the farmer money at support prices. The farmer who pledges a crop for a loan will pay the loan when it comes due if the market price produces a profit on the crop. If the market price is lower than the support price, the CCC takes full rights to the commodity.

The federal government also helps the farmer obtain low-cost credit. The Farmers Home Administration lends money to farmers to buy, improve, and operate farms in cases where credit is not available from other lenders. The Farm Credit Administration supervises a nationwide system of cooperative lending associations. The Rural Electrification Administration makes loans to companies and cooperatives to take electric power and telephone service to rural districts. The Federal Crop Insurance Corporation insures crops against loss from natural hazards.

AGRICULTURAL EDUCATION

At the turn of the 18th century a movement arose in central Europe to train farmers in special academies. The earliest were founded in Hungary in 1796 and in Germany in 1818. In these schools farmers were taught the experiences of other farmers.

Formal Studies

By about 1840 a scientific approach to farming had begun. The old training centers were eventually replaced by schools that taught this approach in all European countries and in the United States.

There were four parts to the European system:

1. Compulsory agricultural school training from age 15 to 18

2. Voluntary attendance at day schools (usually one day per week) to train farm managers

3. Attendance at schools of engineering for a period of about three years

4. College training for four or five years at special institutions of higher learning

This system, with some variation, is still the basic one used to train farmers in much of Europe.

In some countries schools work in conjunction with farms to provide agricultural training. Agricultural colleges operate in almost all countries, and many manage experimental farms where students receive practical training. In most nations agricultural research and training are promoted by both government and private industry. International bodies such as the Food and Agriculture Organization, the World Health Organization, and the International Rice Research Institute, which was established at the University of the Philippines by the Ford and Rockefeller foundations in 1962, have made great contributions to agricultural technology since World War II, especially in the developing nations. Most agricultural students study the following:

1. Soil science as it relates to farm production

2. Plant production, including breeding, weed control, fertilization, plant diseases, and pest control

3. Animal production, including breeding, nutrition, and care (usually not animal disease, which is a separate study)

4. Economics and management science, including agricultural policy, business, and marketing

5. Agricultural engineering, including construction and hydraulics

In addition, several other studies, including land reclamation, conservation techniques, processing technology, meteorology, agricultural law, and agricultural history, are required in various countries.

Agricultural Education in the United States

In the United States young people may study agriculture in high school and in college. Under the Smith-Hughes Act of 1917, the federal government grants funds to high schools for teaching vocational agriculture. High school students usually learn by doing. Their courses are coordinated with farming programs supervised by their teachers. Students carry on long-term productive projects, such as raising livestock as a business venture. They grade, process, and market their produce. They also undertake improvement projects to increase the value and efficiency of the farm. Examples include building a poultry house or repairing farm machinery using skills learned in shop class. In addition they are taught supplementary farm practices. For example, they learn to keep records and figure profits and losses.

High school vocational agriculture departments also offer evening classes to young farmers and adult farmers. These classes help keep those who are already farming up-to-date on new agricultural information, methods, skills, and practices.

In each state at least one college or university offers professional agricultural training. These institutions resulted from the Morrill Act of 1862 in which Congress provided public land grants to state colleges that would teach agriculture and mechanical arts. Later legislation provided more federal aid.

The state experiment stations are connected with the agricultural colleges. They carry on research in laboratories and on experimental farms.

Farm Organizations

Farm boys and girls learn some farming methods and may develop as rural leaders through their young people's clubs. Students in vocational agriculture courses are eligible to join the Future Farmers of America and similar organizations elsewhere. The 4-H Clubs, sponsored by the United States Department of Agriculture and state agricultural colleges, carry on extensive programs in farming and homemaking. The Juvenile Grange, sponsored by the National Grange, is another such group.

Adult farmers have independent dues-supported organizations for advancing their welfare, including providing specialist speakers, idea exchange, and other educational functions. The three principal groups in the United States are the National Grange, organized in 1867; the American Farm Bureau Federation, begun in 1919; and the Farmers' Union, set up as a national organization in 1906.

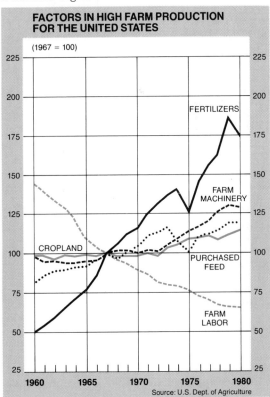

FACTORS IN HIGH FARM PRODUCTION FOR THE UNITED STATES

(1967 = 100)

FERTILIZERS

FARM MACHINERY

CROPLAND

PURCHASED FEED

FARM LABOR

Source: U.S. Dept. of Agriculture

Careers in Agriculture

Worldwide, most graduates of agricultural colleges become farmers. In agriculturally advanced countries there are also many related occupations in which they may use their training and knowledge. Government departments of agriculture are the largest employers of professional agriculturists. They hire specialists for research, inspection, and other jobs in their programs. Teaching and agricultural assistance work, such as the extension services in the United States, offer a wide range of jobs.

Businesses that cater to the farmer or that utilize farm products need agricultural graduates for research, production, marketing, and servicing activities. Agricultural publishing also requires people with a knowledge of modern farming to write and to edit farm publications. Graduates in agriculture may also find work in radio, television, motion pictures, and advertising.

BIBLIOGRAPHY FOR AGRICULTURE

Books for Children

Dunlop, Stewart and MacDonald, Donald. Farming and the Countryside (Heinemann, 1976).
Gemming, Elizabeth and Klaus. Born in a Barn: Farm Animals and Their Young (Coward, 1974).
Gurney, Gene and Clare. Agriculture Careers (Watts, 1978).
Hellman, Hal. Feeding the World of the Future (Evans, 1972).
Higham, Charles. The Earliest Farmer and the First Cities (Lerner Publications, 1977).
Reynolds, P. J. Farming in the Iron Age (Cambridge Univ. Press, 1976).
Shuttlesworth, D. E. and G. J. Farms for Today and Tomorrow: the Wonders of Food Production (Doubleday, 1979).

Books for Young Adults and Teachers

Cannon, G. G. Great Men of Modern Agriculture (Macmillan, 1963).
Edlin, H. L. Trees and Man (Columbia Univ. Press, 1976).
Farm Quarterly (Periodical). A journal that highlights new techniques and modern practices (F & W Pub. Co.).
Fite, G. C. American Farmers: the New Minority (Indiana Univ. Press, 1981).
Fite, G. C. The Farmers' Frontier, 1865–1900 (Univ. of N.M. Press, 1977).
Harwood, R. R. Small Farm Development (Westview, 1979).
Kohls, R. L. and Uhl, J. N. Marketing of Agricultural Products, 5th ed. (Macmillan, 1980).
Leonard, J. N. and others. The First Farmers (Time-Life, 1973).
Sloane, Eric. The Seasons of America Past (Funk, 1958).
Smith, H. P. and Wilkes, L. H. Farm Machinery and Equipment, 6th ed. (McGraw, 1976).
Snodgrass, M. M. and Wallace, L. T. Agriculture, Economics, and Resource Management, 2d ed. (Prentice, 1980).
Von Hagen, V. W. The Ancient Sun Kingdoms of the Americas (Beekman, 1977).
Wolfe, Louis. Aquaculture: Farming in Water (Putnam, 1972).

AGUINALDO, Emilio (1869–1964). The first president of the Philippines was the revolutionary general and hero Emilio Aguinaldo.

Aguinaldo was born on March 22, 1869, in Cavite, one of eight children born to Trinidad Famy y Valero and Carlos Aguinaldo, the town's mayor. He attended college in Manila. Instead of graduating, he returned home to help support his family.

In 1895 Aguinaldo joined the Katipunan, a secret society that opposed the Spanish government of the Philippines. After fighting broke out in 1896, he rose to become a general of the revolutionary army and president of a revolutionary government declared in 1897. Rivalry erupted between Aguinaldo and Andres Bonifacio, the Katipunan leader. Aguinaldo had Bonifacio charged with treason and executed.

In December 1897 Aguinaldo went into exile in Hong Kong as part of a peace agreement with the Spanish, but he returned home when the Spanish-American War began in 1898. Aguinaldo became president of a Philippine republic declared in 1899 to oppose United States rule in the Philippines. He fought United States forces until his capture in 1901. Aguinaldo then retired and worked on behalf of veterans of the revolution. In 1935 he was defeated by Manuel Quezon for the presidency.

Aguinaldo had married Hilaria del Rosario in 1896. They had six children before her death in 1921. In 1930 he married Maria Agoncillo, who died in 1963. His own death was in Quezon City on Feb. 6, 1964. (*See also* Philippines, section on history.)

AHMADABAD, India. The largest city in the Gujarat state of west-central India, Ahmadabad is located on the Sabarmati River, north of Bombay. The city lies in a major cotton-growing region, and approximately one half of its population depends on the cotton textile industry.

Ahmadabad was founded in 1411 by a Muslim ruler, Ahmad Shah I, the first independent sultan of Gujarat. For the next 100 years Ahmadabad grew larger and wealthier. It then experienced various declines under different rulers until the British annexed Gujarat in 1818. The city's first cotton mills were opened in 1859–61. Ahmadabad grew to become the largest inland industrial center in India and the seventh most populous city. It became the state's temporary administrative headquarters in 1960 and remained so until 1970 when Gandhinagar was named the capital. Ahmadabad is also the place where Mahatma Gandhi, the 20th-century leader of nonviolent Indian nationalism, established his famous Sabarmati *asrama* ("retreat").

One of Ahmadabad's most interesting features is the sharp contrast between the remains of magnificent ancient temples and the modern designs of mills and factories. The area surrounding Lake Kankariya, a popular and attractive site, contains promenades, a hill garden, and a museum designed by the famous Swiss architect Le Corbusier. The city is the home of Gujarat University, founded in 1949, and of the Lalbhai Dalpatbhai Institute for Indological Research, which undertakes studies relating to India and its people.

Roads from the city lead to Bombay and central India, the Kathiawar Peninsula, and north to the Rajasthan border. Ahmadabad is a major junction on India's Western Railway. (*See also* India.) Population (1981 census), 2,123,831.

AIR

NITROGEN		78%
OXYGEN		21%
ARGON		.93%
CARBON DIOXIDE AND OTHERS		.07%

The Gases That Make Up Air

In addition to nitrogen, oxygen, argon, and carbon dioxide, the composition of air includes traces of hydrogen, neon, krypton, helium, ozone, and xenon.

AIR. In countless tasks, from running blast furnaces to blowing up tires, people use air. Airplanes and kites need it to fly. The sound of thunder or a clap of hands requires air to be heard. Birds, fish, dogs, and man would die without it. Trees, flowers, and grass also need air to live.

Human beings are in contact with air every second that they live. It is all around, and it extends upward for many miles as the earth's atmosphere (see Atmosphere). Sometimes, on a windy day, people feel it brushing against their skin. They can hear it move when the wind howls or a tire blows out. Most of the time, however, people are completely unaware of the air, because it has no color, taste, or odor. They even think of a container of air as being empty.

What Is Air?

This invisible substance called air is really a mixture of several gases. Each gas is present in the form of separate, tiny particles called *molecules*. The molecules are much too small to be seen even with

HEATED AIR EXPANDS

Heat causes air in the bottle to expand. As the air requires more room, it flows into the balloon and inflates it.

the most powerful microscope. They make up for their small size, however, by being present in tremendous numbers. Scientists estimate that one cubic inch of ordinary air contains about 300 billion billion of them. They are so tiny, however, that there is plenty of space between them.

Under ordinary conditions, each molecule has energy enough to shoot through space at a speed of about 1,000 miles an hour. Very few molecules, however, travel far in a straight line at this speed. One reason is that the earth's force of gravity holds most of them within a few miles of the ground in spite of their speed. In this space they fly about, colliding with each other at a tremendous rate. In usual situations near the ground, each molecule collides with other molecules about 5 billion times a second.

Different Elements That Make Up Air

The molecules of two different elements, nitrogen and oxygen, make up about 99 per cent of the air. The rest includes small amounts of argon and carbon dioxide. (Other gases such as hydrogen, neon, krypton, helium, ozone, and xenon are present in traces.)

Oxygen is the life-giving element in the air. It helps plants make food and helps animals use these substances as though they were fuel. The heat given off by this process supplies energy, just as the burning of gasoline keeps an engine running. Oxygen supports fire and other chemical changes in matter. It also causes metals to rust. (*See also* Oxygen.)

Certain compounds of nitrogen help build tissue in living things. Nitrogen also serves to dilute the oxygen in the air. Plants, men, and animals are used to the diluted mixture and would soon "burn out" if they lived in pure oxygen. Indeed, the living world would soon burn up, for in pure oxygen every spark or flash of lightning would start raging fires which could never be controlled. (*See also* Nitrogen.)

Carbon dioxide is formed by the union of oxygen and carbon. Every fire produces it, as do the bodies of men and animals. They give it off in every breath they expel. Plants use the carbon in it for making food and give back the oxygen to the air. Thus they continually renew the supply of oxygen. (*See also* Carbon; Plants.)

Most air contains water vapor. The amount varies greatly from time to time and place to place. Air also contains dust, pollen, spores, bacteria, and other bits of solid and liquid matter.

145

The Properties of Air

Air can be compressed almost without limit. All the air in a space as big as a house can be squeezed into a small tank. On the other hand, air can expand almost indefinitely. If all the air were taken from inside a house and then one cubic foot of air were supplied, it would expand throughout the building.

This *elastic* quality comes from the nature of air as a mass of flying molecules. It can be compressed because there is plenty of space between the molecules. Pressure simply squeezes them closer together. A mass of air also will expand to fill any space which has fewer molecules. The colliding molecules merely spread out.

Although the molecules in air are unbelievably tiny, they still have weight; and there are many of them. Therefore any given mass of air has weight. At sea level and at standard pressure and temperature (29.921 inches of mercury and 59° F.) a cubic foot of air weighs about .0765 pounds. This is a little more than one ounce.

A vacuum is a space from which all matter, including air, has been removed. The concept of a complete, or "perfect," vacuum (zero internal pressure) is useful for many theoretical purposes. In practice, however, there is no equipment that can remove all the air from an airtight container. A confined space with almost all air removed from it is described as a "high vacuum" and is equal to a very *low* pressure. High vacuum techniques and compressed-air equipment have many uses in industrial plants and laboratories. (*See also* Vacuum; Pneumatic Appliances.)

Compressed Air

Air compressors serve numerous purposes in the home and in industry. A simple type is the hand pump used to inflate bicycle tires. To show that air

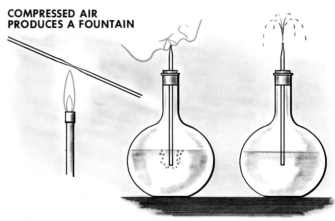

COMPRESSED AIR PRODUCES A FOUNTAIN

A glass tube is drawn into a nozzle. Air is blown through the nozzle into a stoppered bottle containing water. The compressed air produces a fountain.

has weight, let the air out of a basketball until it is quite soft. Weigh it on sensitive scales. Now pump it hard and weigh it again. It will be heavier by the weight of the extra air pumped into it. Similarly, every bit of extra air inside an automobile tire (the air that shows a pressure above zero on a tire gauge) adds to the weight of the tire.

In the toy air gun, bullets are fired with compressed air instead of gunpowder. A lever attached to the piston forces the air into a chamber, usually in the stock, and compresses it. When the trigger is pulled, a valve opens and the compressed air enters the barrel, forcing the bullet out.

Compressed air is used in manufacturing plants for a wide variety of purposes. It is used for paint spraying, for laundry and dry-cleaning equipment, and for heating-control units. Compressed air provides the power to drive many small tools, including grinders, drills, wrenches, and hoists. Stone blocks are engraved by blasts of compressed air. Bottling plants use it to operate their filling machines. Foundries depend upon it as power for hoisting operations and for cleaning molds, core boxes, and tools. Railroads

FLAME TAKES OXYGEN FROM THE AIR

A tube covered with a piece of rubber is placed over a flame and into putty. The hot air makes the rubber bulge. When the air cools, the loss of oxygen used by the flame causes a partial vacuum. Outside pressure pushes the rubber downward.

CARBON DIOXIDE PUTS OUT FIRE

A candle, baking soda, and water are placed in a glass. Vinegar is added, forming carbon dioxide, which smothers the flame.

use compressed air for many tasks. It operates pneumatic switches and serves to retard and charge air brakes. When air is compressed and also reduced to a temperature of about −312° F. it becomes a liquid with odd properties (see Liquid Air).

Air Pollution

Although air supports animal and plant life, it can also help produce effects that harm all living things. In a single year in the United States millions of tons of rubbish and wastes are poured into the air. When air is carrying such foreign particles it is said to be *polluted*.

Pollution arises from many sources. The burning of gasoline in automobiles causes harmful gases and combustion products. From cement and metal factories come millions of particles that are carried off in the air. Chemical plants produce gaseous by-products that are toxic when the concentration is high enough. Smoke from trash fires and garbage incinerators increases pollution. As the United States has

become more and more industrialized, air pollution has generally increased and new health hazards have developed. Officials at many levels of government have the responsibility of enforcing laws to limit air pollution for the protection of the people.

A Demonstration of Atmospheric Pressure

Many interesting experiments with air can be performed with materials that are available in almost any home. For example, place a sheet of paper over the top of a glass filled with water. Hold the paper firmly in place and turn the glass upside down. Now the water will remain in the glass even if the paper is not held. This is because the paper prevents air from entering the glass. If the water ran out, it would create a vacuum. This demonstrates that pressure of air against the paper is greater than the weight of the water.

More Demonstrations of Air Pressure

To show the increase of air pressure under certain conditions, tie a rubber balloon onto the neck of an empty pop bottle. Place the bottle in a pan of warm water and set the pan on a hot burner. This heats the water, the bottle, and the air inside the bottle. As the air is heated, it expands and fills the balloon.

An experiment can be performed to show the power of air pressure. Boil a cup of water in an open can. The heated vapor expands and some flows out. Carefully put on the cover, making the can airtight. Next place the can into a sink and drench it with cold water. This causes the vapor to contract and create a vacuum inside the container. The air pressure on the outside will then crumple the can.

Compressed Air Produces a Fountain

Still another experiment demonstrates the effects of compressed air. Hold a glass tube over a gas flame until the glass softens. Then draw it thin

AIR PRESSURE CRUMPLES CAN

A cup of water is boiled in an open can. Heated vapor expands and some escapes. Then the container is sealed. Cold water is poured onto it. The heated vapor contracts, creating a vacuum inside the can. Air pressure on the outside crumples it.

FIRE NEEDS AIR SUPPLY

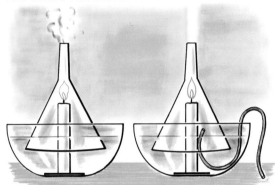

A candle flame under a glass funnel in a bowl of water smothers. A rubber tube is needed to supply air for combustion.

PRESSURE MAKES TEST TUBE SINK

A test tube is filled with water until it barely floats upside down in a container of water. For fine adjustment, air is blown in with a medicine dropper. Rubber is tied over the container's mouth. Pressure on the rubber causes the tube to sink.

and break it off to leave a small nozzle. Next fit the tube into a stopper, which is used to plug a bottle that is partially filled with water. The nozzle end points up, and the other end extends into the water.

Blowing through the nozzle into the bottle compresses the air. When blowing stops, the compressed air forces water out, making a fountain. The action is prolonged because of the tube's fine tip.

A Strange Diver

A diving experiment was devised by the French scientist René Descartes in the 17th century. To perform this experiment, pour water into a test tube until it will barely float. Place it upside down in a tall container of water and tie a piece of rubber over the mouth of the container.

Pressure on the rubber will compress the air in the container and in the test tube. This forces some water into the tube and makes it sink until the pressure is released. The air in the test tube displaces just enough water to balance the tube's weight. Archimedes discovered the principle some 2,000 years ago. (*See also* Archimedes; Liquid.)

Air Contains Oxygen

Oxygen in the air supports combustion. To demonstrate this, tie a piece of rubber over one end of a glass tube open on both ends. Next, insert a small candle into a piece of putty. Then light the candle, place the open end of the tube over the candle, and push the tube into the putty.

As the flame consumes oxygen, it heats up the other gases in the air and the rubber bulges outward. When the gases cool, there is a partial vacuum in the tube because of the loss of oxygen. Pressure from the outside air then forces the rubber into the tube.

Carbon Dioxide Suffocates Flame

Carbon dioxide extinguishes fire. To prove this, stand a candle upright inside a glass. Pour a little water mixed with baking soda into the glass. Light the candle. Next pour vinegar into the baking soda and water mixture. This forms carbon dioxide. When carbon dioxide fills the glass, the flame suffocates from lack of oxygen. This principle is used in some fire extinguishers.

To show how fire needs a steady supply of air, stand a candle in a bowl of water. Light the candle and lower a glass funnel over it down into the water. Soon the flame smokes and goes out from lack of oxygen. Now relight the candle and lead an empty tube from outside the bowl into the funnel near the flame. This will keep the flame burning by supplying air (and oxygen) for combustion.

The Egg Trick

A final experiment can be performed with an egg and a milk bottle. Light a long strip of wax paper or newspaper and drop it into the empty bottle. When the paper has burned, place a hard-boiled egg (with the shell removed) small end down on the mouth of the bottle. In a few seconds the egg will start moving down into the neck. Soon it will pop into the bottle.

The egg moves into the bottle because the burning paper heated the air inside the bottle, driving some of it out. When the flame died, the air cooled and contracted. Since the egg was now sealing the bottle, air pressure forced it down the neck.

AIR CONDITIONING. One reason human beings can thrive in all kinds of climates is that they can control the qualities of the air in the enclosed spaces in which they live. Air conditioning is the use of mechanical systems to achieve that control in such places as homes, offices, theaters, institutions, factories, airplanes, and automobiles. The most familiar type of air conditioning is summertime cooling. Although important, this is but one of several aspects of air conditioning. Other applications include the control of the humidity (or air moisture), cleanliness, circulation of the air, and heating.

EFFECTS ON PEOPLE AND PRODUCTS

Tests have determined that people generally feel and function best under certain temperature, humidity, and air velocity conditions. Temperatures can range from 71° F (21.5° C) with 70 percent relative humidity to 83.5° F (28° C) with 30 percent relative humidity. Relative humidity is the amount of moisture in the air at a specific temperature compared with the amount it could hold at that temperature. Agreeable air velocities range from 15 to 35 feet (4.5 to 10.5 meters) per minute. It is also desirable that an air conditioner for people remove dust, pollen, smoke, and odors from the air.

In many industrial environments, air conditioning is essential. Most print shops, for example, require constant humidity in order to control paper shrinkage and to ensure uniform operation in processes such as collotype and offset lithography. Libraries, especially ones with rare books, require air control to preserve the physical quality of their collections. Bakeries and the tobacco and cotton industries require high humidities for their products, and perishables such as fruits must be stored in cool, dry rooms. Some electronic components, drugs, and chemicals must be manufactured where the air is as free as possible of dust and other particles. Air conditioning is vital in hospitals, especially in operating rooms.

HOW AIR CONDITIONERS WORK

There are many kinds of air conditioners, but their functions are essentially the same. Nearly all air conditioners cool and clean the air while they ventilate the space. Some air conditioners humidify, dehumidify, and heat as well.

Cooling

Air conditioners customarily cool by blowing the air through a coil of tubing that contains a cold fluid. The fluid, usually a special chemical, is most often cooled by the process of refrigeration. This process makes use of the relationship between the volume of a substance and its capacity for holding heat. For example, if a quantity of gas at a given temperature is suddenly compressed, its temperature momentarily rises. If the gas is then suddenly expanded, the temperature will momentarily fall.

Refrigeration air conditioners compress their fluids with a mechanical compressor system. The most common compressor is the reciprocating type. It employs a piston in a cylinder.

These compressor-type air conditioners circulate a refrigerant fluid in a closed tube system, compressing it, exhausting the heat the compression creates, and expanding the fluid. Warm interior air is circulated over the coil that contains the refrigerant, which becomes a cool vapor as it expands. The cool vapor removes heat from the air and the cooled air is re-

Most air conditioners work according to the same principles of refrigeration. Warm interior air circulated through the air conditioner passes over evaporator coils that contain a refrigerant. The refrigerant has been cooled by a process of compression and expansion. Heat is transferred from the air to the refrigerant and a blower forces the cooled air back into the room. The warmed refrigerant then circulates through a condenser and its heat is removed and exhausted to the outside air.

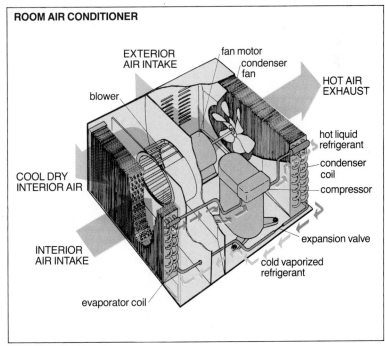

ROOM AIR CONDITIONER

EXTERIOR AIR INTAKE

fan motor

condenser fan

HOT AIR EXHAUST

blower

hot liquid refrigerant

condenser coil

compressor

COOL DRY INTERIOR AIR

INTERIOR AIR INTAKE

expansion valve

cold vaporized refrigerant

evaporator coil

turned to the interior. The refrigerant is compressed and its heat exhausted to the exterior again.

Many refrigeration units employ fluids that alternate between liquid and gaseous forms when compressed and expanded. The change from gas to liquid can involve large degrees of compression and expansion, and equally large amounts of heating and cooling. A condenser transfers the heat from refrigerant to the outdoor air. The more efficiently this is done, the more efficient the air conditioner.

There are several types of condensers. Air-cooled condensers, which are generally used in small air conditioners, transfer heat to the outdoors through a coil of finned tubing. In water-cooled condensers, water flows through tubing within a refrigerant chamber to pick up and convey heat outdoors. The water may be cooled in a device that resembles an automobile radiator or it may be cooled by evaporation. In evaporative cooling, water is pumped to a high, narrow outdoor structure called a cooling tower. These towers are frequently seen atop large factories and office buildings. The water is released from the top of the tower in a fine spray. Air blown through the spray causes some evaporation. The water is cooled in the process, and fresh water is added to the tower to replace the small amount lost by evaporation.

Cleaning

The air is usually cleaned by passing it through a filter in the duct that carries it into the air conditioner. Three main types of air filter are used today: impingement, dry, and electronic. Impingement filters, the most common type, consist of fiberglass or stranded metal formed into a sheet and coated with a thick, sticky substance such as oil or liquid adhesive. Relatively large particles in the intake air stream impinge upon, or strike, a fiber of the filter and stick to it. Such filters are commonly enclosed in a cardboard frame and changed at regular intervals. Large air-conditioning systems often use large impingement filters held on rollers, as is film in a camera, and moved across the air stream in stages. Some impingement filters can be cleaned or even clean themselves.

Dry filters work like a kitchen strainer, capturing impurities while clean intake air passes through. Any dirt particle that cannot fit between two filter fibers is trapped. A dry filter is made of small cellulose, synthetic, or bonded glass fibers packed closely together and shaped like a sheet or blanket. Dry filters are commonly arranged in the form of accordion pleats, folds, or pockets. They are held on light frameworks and discarded when filled with dirt.

Electronic filters work by ionization or polarization. The ionization filter employs high-voltage charged wires or screens to ionize, or impose an electrical charge on, all particles. The particles next pass between metal plates that are coated with oil or liquid adhesive and are either grounded or charged oppositely from the particles. The particles are drawn to the plates and stick to them. From time to time, the plates are washed clean and recoated.

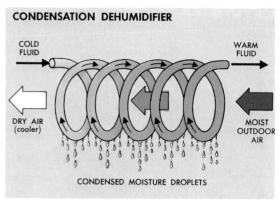

CONDENSATION DEHUMIDIFIER

Moist air is cooled as it passes through the coil, causing it to release some of its moisture through condensation.

Polarization filters are similar, but need not be washed and recoated. The charged particles stick on oppositely charged plates, like iron filings on an electromagnet. The filter is cleaned by momentarily turning off the electricity and rapping the plates. The particles fall off and are discarded.

Air washers are also used to clean the air. Air is passed through sprays of water to trap particles and wash them away. The air is not only cleaned but also cooled and made more humid. Air washers are used in industry when high humidity is desirable.

Ventilating

Most air conditioners can draw fresh air in and exhaust stale air out. Most also permit or create air movement within the conditioned space. Air motion alone can have a slight cooling effect on the body. But the motion has to be too fast for comfort to achieve significant cooling.

Most air conditioners use both fresh and recirculated air. Air circulation, or movement, may be natural, caused by the tendency of warm air to rise, or it may be forced by a fan. Natural circulation is sometimes used in heating systems, but cooling systems generally employ forced circulation.

Air-conditioning fans other than those in small, window units are usually arranged in ducts, which are essentially long tubes. Typically rectangular in shape and made from galvanized steel, the ducts may be attached to the ceilings, walls, or floors of the conditioned space. Ducts often contain metal vanes that direct the air flow to increase system efficiency. Room air inlets and outlets are customarily rectangular in shape and fitted with a metal grill which often has dampers that open and close to control flow.

Centrifugal fans, or blowers, are the type of fan most commonly used. The familiar three-bladed propeller-type fan is often noisy and is inefficient. Centrifugals have a rotating cylinder (called an impeller) mounted inside a scroll-type housing, which somewhat resembles a snail's shell in shape. These fans have scoop-like blades that collect air and throw it against the inside of the housing to create the desired air stream for efficient cooling.

Humidifying

Moisture is added to the air by injecting steam directly, by spraying water into the air stream, or by evaporating water from electrically heated pans. Air is often humidified after being heated. Warm air is able to hold more moisture than cool air.

Dehumidifying

Because it is warmer, summer air often contains more moisture than winter air. The more moisture there is in the air, the more slowly perspiration evaporates. Since perspiration evaporation is an important mechanism for cooling the human body, high humidity increases discomfort during warm weather.

When warm, moist air passes over an air conditioner's cooling coil, its temperature can fall to a point where it can no longer hold all the moisture it contains. The moisture then condenses on the coil as droplets which may be drained away. This process, called condensation dehumidification, is the one most often used in air conditioning.

Adsorbent dehumidification employs a bed of silica gel, the common metal silica in a finely divided state. The gel adsorbs, or picks up on its surface, moisture from air that is passed through it. As it removes the water vapor in the air stream, the silica-gel bed generates heat, which is removed by cooling water. Once the bed is saturated, it can be taken out, heated to drive off the adsorbed water, and then reused.

Heating

Air conditioners heat by blowing air through coils that contain hot water or steam or over devices that create heat by passing electricity through resistant metal wires and plates.

Many air-conditioning systems, particularly those in large buildings, recover and reuse waste heat in winter. Sources of such heat include refrigeration compressors, lights and machines, and even the bodies of the building's human occupants. Sharply rising energy costs have made waste heat recovery economically attractive, leading to a rapid development and widespread adoption of the technology.

To recover waste heat, the warm air exhausted from a room by an air conditioner is passed through a heat exchanger. This device transfers the heat from the air to a fluid such as water. The heated fluid is then used within the building's basic heating system. Only cool air leaves the structure. Every unit of waste heat that is recovered and reused saves a unit that would otherwise be created with fuel.

The technology makes possible dramatic reductions in energy use. Some newer buildings in cold-winter areas have such efficient waste heat recovery systems that they need no boiler at all.

TYPES OF AIR CONDITIONERS

There are several ways to classify air conditioners. Most people tend to group them by size and complexity. For example, the familiar boxy device, commonly referred to as a room or window air conditioner, is also called a self-contained air conditioner. This is because all of its working parts are in a single unit. Many homes and other buildings have central air conditioners. These have their controls in one area, machinery in another, and ducting throughout the structure. Systems in hospitals, factories, or other large buildings may perform several functions at once in widely separated areas. These large air conditioners, often controlled by computers, are properly called environmental control systems.

Another way to classify air conditioners is according to the details of how they work. Common air-conditioner types classified in this way include refrigeration compressor (described earlier), heat pumps, steam-jet, and air-cycle.

Heat Pumps

All refrigeration systems are essentially pumps that transfer heat from one place to another. The process of cooling is reversible; that is, a refrigeration system can transfer heat into an enclosure. This is easier to understand by considering the heat that comes out of the back of a refrigerator. In fact, some air-conditioning systems used for summer cooling can be used for heating in winter. These and other types of heat pumps take the heat that is already in the air and boost its temperature. This is done, for example, in waste heat recovery systems, where the recovered heat is not intense. A heat pump is used to amplify heat, raising the temperature to a useful level.

Central air-conditioning machinery is separate from the areas it serves. Most such units can both cool and heat. For heating, the furnace portion is used.

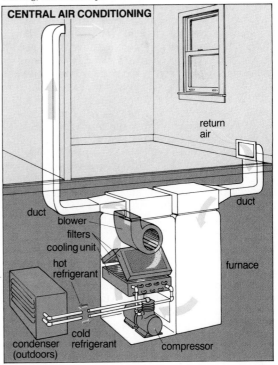

CENTRAL AIR CONDITIONING

return air

duct

duct

blower

filters

cooling unit

hot refrigerant

furnace

condenser (outdoors)

cold refrigerant

compressor

Steam-jet

Coolers of this type employ water as a refrigerant, vaporizing it at low temperatures in a partial vacuum that is induced by a strong jet of superheated steam. The process is similar to compressor refrigeration except that low pressures are used to expand a liquid refrigerant into a vapor.

Steam-jet coolers fit well into systems that use a boiler to provide heat. The same boiler may be used to produce steam both for heating and for cooling, and the same piping may transmit both hot and cold fluids. Coolers of this kind are used only in systems with large capacities.

Air-cycle

Commonly employed to cool high-speed aircraft such as jets, this system uses a forward-facing tube in which air is compressed by the motion of the aircraft. The operation resembles that of an ordinary compressor cooler, except that the refrigerant, which is air, does not liquefy. In this case, air is cooled by air.

HISTORY

Mechanical air conditioning did not come into existence until refrigeration machines were invented at the end of the 19th century. As scientists learned more about the properties of fluids, the physics of air movement, and human comfort conditions, their findings were used to improve air conditioning.

At first, air-conditioning systems were designed with initial cost as a major consideration. Operating costs were virtually ignored because electrical energy was cheap. Rapid energy price increases during the 1970's, however, caused a shift in emphasis toward energy-efficient operation. Special units that conserve energy became available for the home. Many owners of large structures modified or replaced existing systems to cut energy use. The focus of the industry on increasing efficiency continued into the 1980's.

Efficient Home Units

The amount of cooling produced by a home air conditioner compared with the electricity it consumes is its energy efficiency ratio (EER). The higher the EER, the more efficient the air conditioner is. Air conditioners with an EER of 7.5 or higher are the most efficient and best to buy. They cost more initially but cost less to operate and are thus money savers in the long run.

High efficiency also results from careful sizing of the home system. An oversized unit will consume more energy than is needed to condition the space and also may not lower humidity sufficiently. If the unit is too small, however, it will not get the cooling job done and may dry the air out too much. The size air conditioner required for a given job is best determined by calculating a cooling load—that is, the amount of cooling that the machine will have to put out to condition the space. Cooling load depends upon the size and shape of the space; the number and

size of windows and their orientation toward the sun; the areas of walls, ceilings, and floors and the extent to which they are insulated; local climatic conditions; the wattage of electrical equipment present; and the number of people who normally occupy the space. Standardized forms are available from some air conditioning manufacturers, public utilities, and consumer groups for calculating cooling load.

Larger Systems

Rising energy costs increase operating costs drastically for many older air-conditioning systems in large buildings, causing owners to seek help. In some cases, existing equipment must be replaced completely with more efficient new systems. Most of the time, however, the old system can be reengineered, with some new components replacing older ones.

Often engineers achieve large energy savings by reviewing operations, making adjustments so that the system operates according to original design, and setting up a program of careful maintenance. A single dirty filter or slipping fan belt does not in itself waste much energy. But many such problems in a large system add up to large efficiency losses.

Engineers also make changes to reduce the resistance to air flow in ducts, grills, and piping. Lowered resistance results in less energy needed to drive the fan or pump, and sometimes a lower horsepower fan can be used.

"Turning down" the entire system is another way to save energy. Without seriously affecting occupant comfort, the engineer can reduce the extent to which the air is heated or cooled.

Each type of large-building system presents engineers with its own unique set of problems. For example, the single-duct–single-zone system—which is probably the most common—supplies air at a constant temperature to one complete zone, or area, of a building or to the entire structure all at once. Because it is not easy to control zones, this system wastes energy by heating or cooling unoccupied rooms.

The terminal reheat system allows for better zone control. It has a heating coil in each branch duct to zones of similar loads. Terminal reheat wastes energy in the cooling season, however, because all air in the system must be cooled to the lowest temperature demanded in the structure and then reheated in zones where the coolest air is not needed. Energy is thus used twice, first to cool the air, then to reheat it. Two improved systems—multi-zone and dual duct—have better zoning capabilities but still waste energy.

In variable air volume (VAV) systems, a central unit supplies cooled or heated air at constant, controllable temperatures to VAV boxes for each zone. These boxes vary the quantity rather than the temperature of the air. This mode of operation is energy efficient because no air is heated or cooled beyond need. In structures where zoned air conditioning is required, engineers selecting systems often choose VAV for its energy efficiency without even considering other systems. (*See also* Heating and Ventilating.)

A pair of F-106 interceptor jets thunder past Mt. Ranier in Washington on their way back to their home base near Tacoma. They are part of the North American Air Defense Command at McChord Air Force Base.

AIR FORCE. This is an age of air power, and the military strength of a nation depends in great part upon the effectiveness of its air force. All of the major countries of the world maintain air forces as part of their defense systems. Air power also reaches into outer space, where satellites control modern weapons and communications systems.

The contemporary air force relies on computer and radar technology to control fleets of fighters, bombers, transports, and reconnaissance (spy) craft. Modern airplanes can carry missiles and bombs, as well as machine guns. Tanker planes can refuel fighters and bombers in the air to lengthen flight time.

ORGANIZATION AND TRAINING

Most of the world's air forces organize their resources in similar ways. Air forces either are dependent units of an army, navy, or unified defense system or are autonomous service branches.

Air force members hold military ranks similar to those of other services. Commissioned officers are usually headed by generals, as in France, or by marshals, as in Great Britain. These are followed by some mix of commodores, colonels, group captains, lieuten-

ant colonels, commanders, wing and squadron leaders, lieutenants, and pilot officers. Enlisted men and women generally include warrant officers, sergeants, corporals, privates, and aircraftsmen.

In many nations the smallest units of planes and personnel are called flights. These traditionally consist of three or four aircraft. Larger organizational units include squadrons, wings, divisions, and commands. The major combat commands of the United States Air Force, for example, are each organized into at least two divisions. They, in turn, contain wings of 28 to 75 planes. Wings are further divided into squadrons composed of several flights of aircraft.

Air force commands usually perform one of five military functions: strategic, tactical, air defense, logistical, and training. Often the duties of a command change in response to new national and international needs and improved weapons.

Strategic commands involve attack and bombing missions. They rely on the use of heavy bombers as well as strategic missile systems. These systems include intercontinental ballistic missiles, which are equipped with nuclear warheads and are launched from underground silos, and air-to-surface attack

153

missiles, which are launched from aircraft onto enemy defenses. In some countries, such as the United States and the Soviet Union, the strategic command also uses space satellites for surveillance and for reconnaissance.

Tactical commands are responsible for fighting enemy aircraft and for providing air support to ground troops. These commands rely on fighter and fighter-bomber aircraft for their operations. Tactical planes are often armed with guns, rockets, nuclear bombs, and guided missiles.

Air defense commands protect the airspace of a nation and provide reconnaissance systems to monitor enemy attacks. Equipment for air defense ranges from single reconnaissance planes to surveillance satellites and complex airborne warning and control systems (AWACS). AWACS planes, first flown by the Soviet Union and the United States in 1968, are high-speed jets outfitted with radar sensors, computers, and antennae to monitor a large combat area. Larger nations also use semi-automated ground environment systems, composed of computer and radar equipment, to scan for enemy radar signals and possible missile attacks.

Logistical commands direct the movement of troops and supplies. They primarily use large transport planes and helicopters for their duties. They also procure and maintain equipment. Training commands recruit men and women and use special training aircraft and weapons systems to prepare air force members for actual combat conditions.

Air force personnel can train for a variety of military careers, including those of pilot, technician, specialist, and instructor. New recruits go through basic training before specializing in a field of work. Future officers can attend special college and university programs, such as the Air Force Reserve Officer Training Corps (AFROTC) courses in the United States, or they can enroll in national service academies. In France, the air officer trainee studies at the École de l'Air (School of the Air) at Salon-de-Provence. In Great Britain, air force officer candidates train at the Royal Air Force College at Cranwell. United States Air Force cadets enroll at the United States Air Force Academy in Colorado Springs, Colo.

Training prepares air force members for actual warfare conditions. Pilots learn their trade in special trainer airplanes that simulate realistic combat flight conditions. This method of military pilot training was first devised by Maj. Robert Smith-Barry of the British Royal Flying Corps. During World War I, when most air force trainees learned how to pilot by flying obsolete planes, Smith-Barry adapted the Avro 504J fighter craft with dual controls for both student and instructor. This paved the way for more efficient flying experience before combat.

During World War I pilots went into action with about 20 hours of flying time in training. By the late 1960's, they needed some 400 hours and 18 months of training, reflecting the increased complexity of aircraft operation and maintenance.

HISTORY OF AIR POWER

Air power has been used for military purposes since the late 18th century. Although the Chinese may have used huge kites some 2,000 years ago to lift men into the skies for military reconnaissance, the first practical aircraft was the hot-air balloon invented by the brothers Joseph-Michel and Jacques-Étienne Montgolfier of France in 1783. This balloon was capable of rising to 6,000 feet (1,830 meters) and carried baskets to hold crews. This and other balloons were controlled by reheating air, releasing hydrogen gas, or eliminating ballast (weight). In 1793 the French government formed what may have been the world's first air force when it set up a corps of Aérostiers (Aeronauts) for the purpose of military observation from tethered balloons.

Balloons were first used as offensive weapons in 1849 when the Austrians unsuccessfully attempted to bombard Venice with bombs connected to time fuzes. Hot-air balloons proved most useful as reconnaissance craft. This was demonstrated by their employment by both sides in the American Civil War (1861–65), by the British in Africa during the Boer War (1899–1902), and by the Russians in Japan (1904–5) during the Russo-Japanese War.

In 1852 air power took a new direction with the first successful demonstration of the dirigible (steerable) balloon airship. Designed by the Frenchman Henri Giffard, the first dirigible was a nonrigid cylindrical-shaped airship composed of a gasbag, 144 feet (44 meters) long, propelled by a steam engine. This dirigible was the prototype of increasingly sophisticated craft, which promised more navigational control than that offered by wind-borne balloons.

True military aviation began with the perfection of the navigable airship and the airplane. In 1897 the Austrian David Schwartz designed the world's first rigid airship. It had an aluminum framework and was covered with aluminum sheeting. Although this craft was wrecked on a test flight, the rigid airship was subsequently improved by Count Ferdinand von Zeppelin of Germany. In 1900 Zeppelin built a huge cigar-shaped, metal-framed ship covered by a smooth cotton cloth, which he named the LZ-1. This ship, 420 feet (128 meters) long and driven by two 16-horsepower engines, was the forerunner of the more powerful Zeppelin craft used with some success by the Germans in World War I. (*See also* Balloon and Airship.)

In 1903 the American brothers Wilbur and Orville Wright took the first controlled and sustained flight in a heavier-than-air craft, an airplane capable of flying at 30 miles (48 kilometers) per hour. Airplane experimentation soon flourished in other countries. Early models were distinguished by the number of wing levels. Monoplanes were designed with a single set of wings; biplanes had two sets of wings; and triplanes had three.

Among the other early airplane pioneers was Louis Blériot of France. In 1907 Blériot made a flight of over a quarter of a mile (400 meters), and in 1909 he

U.S. Air Force

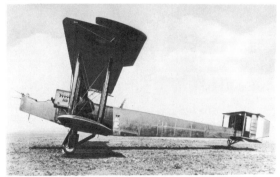

Handley Page HP-400

Smithsonian Institution, Washington, D.C.

Gotha G-III

Smithsonian Institution, Washington, D.C.

Morane-Saulnier monoplane

RAF Museum, London

British reconnaissance-fighter from World War I

demonstrated his type XI airplane with the first flight across the English Channel, a distance of about 25 miles (40 kilometers).

The Wright brothers had foreseen that the airplane would be a most useful machine for military reconnaissance. This prediction was first fulfilled on Oct. 23, 1911, during the Italo-Turkish War, when an Italian pilot made a one-hour reconnaissance flight over North Africa in a Blériot XI monoplane. Nine days later the Italians demonstrated another, deadlier use of the airplane, when they tossed heavy hand-grenade bombs from a plane flying over Libya. In 1912 the use of aircraft for psychological warfare was first demonstrated, when propaganda leaflets were showered over Libya from Italian planes.

Bombing techniques subsequently improved. Dummy bombs were dropped on a sea target in 1910 by Glenn Curtiss of the United States, and soon thereafter bomb carriers and bombsights were developed. The first bomb carrier consisted of a small rack, placed behind the observer's cockpit, in which small bombs were retained by a pin. The pin was removed over the target by pulling a string.

Soon airplanes were armed with other weapons. By 1910 work had begun on the installation of machine guns. In 1913 Col. Isaac Newton Lewis of the United States went to Belgium to manufacture his Lewis gun, which was a low-recoil weapon that was to come into widespread use in fighter planes that flew during World War I.

By 1911 deteriorating international relations led many countries to build up military capacity, including air fleets. In this period the first air forces were organized. They were established as subordinate divisions within existing armies.

World War I

At the outbreak of World War I, Germany led the world in air power with 260 airplanes and a fleet of 14 Zeppelins. Other allies of Germany, including Italy, also had newly formed air arms. The British had about 100 aircraft at this time; the French, backed by the world's leading aviation industry, had 156. Some 100,000 aircraft flew in the war, primarily in support of ground and sea troops.

During the war, rapid advances were made in both air power strategy and technology. In 1914 the airplanes mobilized for war were flimsy, kitelike structures powered by engines of uncertain power. At best, they could climb 2,000 to 3,000 feet (600 to 900 meters) and fly at speeds of 60 to 70 miles (95 to 110 kilometers) per hour. At worst, they could barely get off the ground. Only four years later, single-seat airplane fighters with 150- to 200-horsepower engines were outfitted with machine guns to do battle at 15,000 feet (4,600 meters) in the air.

The aircraft that were developed during World War I were of three main types, each with its own specific purpose. These airplanes were reconnaissance craft, fighter planes, and bombers.

The use of aircraft for reconnaissance was probably the most important contribution of air power to the war effort. In the first weeks of hostilities, French aircraft spotted the movements of the German First Army, and this led to the battle of the Marne. The Germans, in turn, successfully used Zeppelin airships to monitor their opponents'—the Allies'—shipping movements. By 1917 these craft could stay in the air for more than 95 hours at a time.

The British revived interest in nonrigid airships with their design of the blimp (from "British" Class B Airship and "limp," that is, nonrigid). Hundreds of blimps were built during the war for antisubmarine convoy and coastal patrol work.

Reconnaissance techniques were greatly improved during World War I. Photography was added to visual observation by the British in 1914, when pictures were taken of German troop positions during the first battle of the Aisne. Radio came into use at this time as a means of passing messages between reconnaissance aircraft and ground personnel.

At the start of the war, reconnaissance craft were usually unarmed, except for the rifles and pistols carried by fliers. Soon the realization that these craft were vulnerable to attack led to the widespread adoption of the fighter plane—an aircraft designed to attack enemy reconnaissance and bombing aircraft.

Fighter planes were pioneered by Britain, which in 1913 had developed the Vickers *Destroyer*, a fighting biplane. In 1915 the French adapted the interrupter to a Morane-Saulnier monoplane. This gun synchronizer allowed machine gun bullets to pass between the blades of a spinning propeller.

When a French fighter plane was shot down by the Germans in 1915, the Dutch designer Anthony Fokker used the captured French craft as a model for his Fokker Eindecker, a single-seat fighter that was to give the German Luftwaffe (air force) temporary air superiority on the Western Front. From October 1915 until May 1916, Fokker Eindeckers blasted the French and British from the skies, a mastery that was ended only when the Allied forces improved their own fighter craft in 1916. In that year the British developed D.H.2 and F.E.2b "pusher" fighters. These airplanes were fitted with one or more nose-fixed guns that fired forward, and the pilot could aim his aircraft as a firing weapon.

The aerial warfare made possible by these fighting airplanes led to individual combat in dogfights, one-on-one battles between pilots who used machine guns against enemy fliers. The war produced hundreds of flying aces, pilots who were credited with shooting down five or more enemy aircraft. Among the most famous were Capt. Edward ("Eddie") Rickenbacker of the United States, Baron Manfred von Richthofen of Germany, René Fonck of France, and Edward Mannock of Great Britain. These pilots also introduced the strategy of flying planes in a "circus" formation, or an air armada. The flying circus led to enormous air battles involving more than 100 fighter planes at a time.

A related development was the building of aircraft carriers to launch fighter planes from platforms built over battleship gun turrets. Some aircraft carriers were merely barges that were towed behind high-speed destroyers.

A third type of aircraft developed during the war was the bomber. After 1915 both sides used bombers to attack enemy targets, such as railway stations and weapons storehouses. These targets were deep behind enemy lines and out of the range of conventional ground troops.

The Germans used their Zeppelin aircraft as strategic bombers during the war, launching raids against London and other European cities. But Zeppelins proved to be too vulnerable, and by 1916 the Germans were building bomber airplanes.

The German Gotha biplanes of 1916 had a wingspan of nearly 90 feet (27 meters) and two engines of 260 horsepower each. The Gothas could carry a 2,000-pound (900-kilogram) bombload and fly 300 miles (480 kilometers) without refueling. Even larger was the Siemens-Schückert R-VIII, a bomber with a wingspread of more than 150 feet (45 meters) and powered by six 300-horsepower engines.

The Russians, British, and French also developed bomber airplanes. In 1915 Igor Sikorsky of Russia designed the first successful four-engined airplane. The British contributed the twin-engined Handley Page, the first heavy bomber used by British and American forces. The Voisin bomber of France was also in service in World War I. Known as the "chicken coop" because of its profusion of struts and wires, the Voisin type L had an 80-horsepower engine and could carry 130 pounds (58 kilograms) of bombs to be hand dropped overboard by the flier.

While large numbers of aircraft were used in World War I, they exercised little direct influence on the outcome of the conflict. The importance of air power in this war was rather in the development of increasingly sophisticated types of aircraft and of new strategic policies, which would be significant for military use in the later wars of the 20th century. (*See also* World War I.)

The Interwar Years

During the years between World Wars I and II, national air forces emerged around the world. There were also a number of tremendous advances in aircraft technology and strategy.

Immediately after World War I progress was slow. This was because there was a surplus of airplanes during peacetime, and governments were reluctant to spend money on the development of new military aircraft. Moreover, the Treaty of Versailles forbade the Germans to arm for military purposes, and what had been one of the world's most powerful air forces was disbanded.

Two important strategic concepts were shaped in this period. The first was the doctrine of strategic bombing. The Italian brigadier general Giulio Douhet argued in 'The Command of the Air', an influen-

The American B-17 (top left), the Soviet Union's Ilyushin IL-2 Shturmovik (above left), and the German Junkers JU-87 dive bomber (above right) are bombers that saw service in World War II.

tial essay that was first published in 1921, that future wars would be won by huge formations of bomber planes striking deep into enemy territory against industrial targets and civilian population centers. This would, Douhet stated, disrupt production and destroy national morale. The need for this kind of air power meant that nations should concentrate their military resources to build up powerful independent air forces with which to defeat their enemies without the aid of land or sea power.

This idea of the independent air force was the second important air power concept of the interwar era. Supporters included the British general Hugh Montague Trenchard and the American general William (Billy) Mitchell. Mitchell claimed that the airplane was the most important instrument of war and that the failure of United States military leaders to expand the air force amounted to no less than "criminal negligence." Mitchell's outspoken views led to his court-martial in 1925. But his vision of the future of air power proved to be correct (*see* Mitchell).

Other countries began to form independent air forces. In Britain the Royal Air Force was firmly established as an independent power by 1923, when the government began an air defense program. The

Italians established their Regia Aeronautica in 1923. The French followed in 1928 with an air ministry and later with the creation of the Armée de l'Air. In 1935 Versailles Treaty restrictions against German rearmament ended, and Adolf Hitler established the Luftwaffe as an independent military service. In the United States, the Soviet Union, and Japan, air arms remained under the control of previously established military branches.

Perhaps the most important technical improvement in this era was the development of jet propulsion. In 1930 Frank Whittle of Great Britain patented the first jet engine. On Aug. 27, 1939, the first flight of a jet-powered aircraft was made by a Heinkel He-178 airplane in Germany. Few people realized the significance of the event.

Great Britain's Hawker Hurricane fighter bomber (right). Japan's Mitsubishi A6M, or "Zero" (below).

Rocket research also began in the interwar years. Both the Germans and the Soviets were experimenting with rocket-powered aircraft by 1930, and, in the United States, Robert Goddard was researching liquid-fueled rockets in New Mexico.

The military airplane was completely transformed between the world wars. Wood construction gave way to metal. Typical of the new fighter craft was the British Supermarine Spitfire, first flown in 1936. Its metal structure and a new type of machine armament on the wings to eliminate the need for bulky interrupter gear made it an advanced craft for its time.

In 1931 the Boeing Airplane Company of the United States built the B-9 bomber. Also of all-metal design, it was a great improvement over all previous bombers. In 1932 the Martin B-10 added enclosed cockpits and an internal weapons bay for further structural improvement.

In 1935 the Boeing B-17 was flight-tested. This was the prototype for the Flying Fortress, the bombardment mainstay of World War II. By the late 1930's bombers and fighter planes were equipped with bulletproof windshields, armor plating, gun turrets, and radar attachments.

As airplane technology advanced in these ways, the airship received a blow from which it never recovered. In May 1937 the German passenger dirigible *Hindenburg* exploded at the Lakehurst (N.J.) Naval Air Station, killing 35 people. With its destruction, the era of the great dirigible balloons passed.

During the 1930's air power was increasingly a factor in wars throughout the world. The British used air power in colonial conflicts in Iraq, Aden, and India; and the Italians used a tactical air force against Ethiopia in 1935. In the Spanish Civil War (1936–39), the air forces of Italy and Germany supported Gen. Francisco Franco with the bombing of cities, including Barcelona, Madrid, and Guernica. Japan mounted an air attack against China in a 1931 dispute over the control of Manchuria. By the time the Germans used air power in their invasions of Czechoslovakia and Poland in 1938 and 1939, it was evident that air power had come into its own.

World War II

Air power was a decisive factor in the outcome of World War II. An early German lead in air power was overcome by Allied advances in both radar technology and the use of strategic weapons (*see* Radar).

At the start of the war in September 1939 the German Luftwaffe was the best equipped air force in the world, with some 500,000 air force personnel and about 5,000 aircraft. In contrast, the British Royal Air Force (RAF) was composed of some 100,000 men and some 2,000 aircraft.

Strategic bombing became an early part of the war effort. The Germans successfully used intensive bombing raids to assault Norway, The Netherlands, Belgium, and France. Luftwaffe bombers destroyed Allied cities and transportation networks and flew in support of advancing German ground troops.

U.S. Air Force

A formation of Republic F-84 Thunderjets of the 20th Fighter Wing returns to Shaw Air Force Base in South Carolina.

In the Battle of Britain in the summer of 1940, British RAF forces of about 600 aircraft, mostly Hawker Hurricanes and Supermarine Spitfires, faced over 2,700 Luftwaffe planes, including the powerful Junkers JU-87 Stuka dive-bomber. But this imbalance was overcome by pioneering developments in British radar, which allowed the RAF to manage its aircraft efficiently by using an early-warning system. As a result, the RAF was largely responsible for preventing a German invasion of England.

The German air raids on London in 1940 and 1941 further demonstrated the potential of strategic bombing. For over a month in the fall of 1940, German bombers dropped nearly 14,000 tons (12,700 metric tons) of high explosives and more than 12,000 incendiary canisters on the city. These attacks subsided as Germany became engaged on other fronts, particularly with the Soviet Union.

At the same time, Allied forces were developing improved aircraft able to match those of the Luftwaffe. The Americans produced the Boeing B-17 Flying Fortress day bomber and the four-engine B-24 Liberator. By 1942 the British had added the Bristol Beaufighter long-range fighter and the Avro Lancaster, a four-engined heavy bomber.

By 1943 the Allied bombing offensive led to the round-the-clock bombing of Germany, shifting the balance of air power away from the Luftwaffe. The United States bombed German cities by day, and the RAF continued the assault at night. By 1945 this bombing strategy had caused some 600,000 casualties and inflicted great damage on German cities, including Dresden, Hamburg, Essen, and Berlin. On March 11, 1945, 1,079 United States Eighth Air Force planes released 4,738 tons (4,298 metric tons) of explosives on Essen. This was the greatest weight of bombs dropped on a single target in Europe.

On the Pacific Front the Japanese displayed an awesome use of airmanship with the surprise attack on the American fleet at Pearl Harbor, Hawaii, on Dec. 7, 1941. They crippled 8 battleships, 10 warships, and 349 aircraft, and killed or wounded 3,581 troops. By 1944 the Allies had countered with systematic bombing raids over Japan. These raids utilized the Boeing B-29 Superfortress, a long-range bomber operating from bases in China and later from islands in the central Pacific.

In 1945 United States Maj. Gen. Curtis E. LeMay of the 20th Bomber Command ordered his Superforts to attack Japanese industrial centers with firebombs. Seventeen strikes totaling 6,960 flights dropped 41,600 tons (37,700 metric tons) of incendiaries and set afire 102 square miles (264 square kilometers) of Tokyo, Nagoya, Kobe, Osaka, and Yokohama.

In 1944 and 1945 the Japanese tried a new tactic. Kamikaze (Divine Wind) pilots, believing in the Shinto philosophy of honorable death in battle, committed suicide by diving bomb-laden Mitsubishi A6M planes into sea targets. These kamikaze attacks sank 34 ships and damaged 288 others.

Air power was decisive in battles on other fronts, including the Mediterranean, where British air forces supported Gen. Bernard Montgomery's march to Tripoli. Allied air forces also contributed to the German collapse in North Africa in 1943.

In the Soviet Union inferior equipment and training allowed German air supremacy on the Eastern Front until 1944. By then the Soviet air force was able to dominate in clashes with the Luftwaffe. In the spring of 1945 the Soviet air force devastated Berlin with more than 7,500 bombers.

While bombers were used extensively in World War II, other aircraft also had a great impact. Planes used for tactical support contributed to the Allied landing at Normandy on June 6, 1944, when United States forces flew more than 8,000 sorties in support of the operation. By that time Allied forces had won air superiority over most of Europe.

Fighter planes, used to battle enemy fighters and attack enemy bombers, increased in speed during the war. Among the first small high-speed strike aircraft was the heavily armored Soviet Ilyushin IL-2 Shturmovik. In 1943 and 1944 American P-47 and P-51 fighters, equipped with external fuel tanks, flew long-range cover for heavy bombers. These fighters were in great part responsible for gaining Allied air superiority over Europe. Jet and rocket-powered planes in use by 1944 boosted fighter speeds from about 350 miles (565 kilometers) per hour to 600 miles (965 kilometers) per hour. The first jet fighter, the Gloster Meteor, was put into operation by the RAF in 1944. The Germans soon followed with the Messerschmitt ME-262 twin jet fighter.

In 1944 the Germans used V-1 flying bombs and, later, V-2 rockets carrying high explosives to threaten British cities. These bombs caused considerable damage for a short period but were developed too late to play a major role in the war. Allied forces bombed the launching sites in northern Europe and overran them soon after the Allied invasion of Europe in June 1944. These early rockets were prototypes for the guided missiles of the postwar era.

Reconnaissance developments included the use of streamlined high-speed fighter planes that sped low over enemy targets to take photographs and then escaped homeward at maximum speed. High-altitude craft took photographs on motion-picture film that was later processed into mosaic large-scale maps, foreshadowing developments in aerial mapmaking.

Air transport advances during the war included the use of airborne parachute troops dropped by plane into combat areas. The German air force first tried this technique during the battle of Crete in May 1941, using the Junkers JU-52 transport plane and troop-carrying gliders.

World War II ended in 1945. The war in Europe came to an end in May, when the German forces surrendered to the Allies. The war in the Pacific ended in August with the bombing of two Japanese cities. On August 6 a B-29, the *Enola Gay,* dropped an atomic bomb on Hiroshima, and three days later another B-29 dropped an atomic bomb on Nagasaki. The next day the Japanese surrendered to the United States forces.

The Korean War

The conflict over the control of Korea, fought from 1950 to 1953, was between the Democratic People's Republic of Korea (North Korea), supported by the Soviet Union and China, and the Republic of Korea (South Korea), supported by United Nations (UN) forces dominated by the United States. Both sides suppressed the use of all-out air power strategies in an effort to avoid a world war (*see* Korean War).

Air power in Korea was used only against precise targets in a limited area of conflict. Bombers at-

The Boeing B-52H missile bomber, first built in 1961, was the last of Boeing's Stratofortress series.

Boeing Aerospace Co.

Britain's Sea Harrier fighter-reconnaissance plane (above left). Sweden's Saab SF-37 supersonic STOL photo-reconnaissance aircraft (above). American Phantom F-4 multirole fighter (left).

(Above left) Aircraft Group/British Aerospace; (above) I. Thuresson-Saab-Scania; (left) McDonnell Aircraft Corp.

tacked bridges, roads, and industrial centers, while planes such as the B-26 flew in support of ground armies. The UN forces limited the air power capacity of the North Koreans by destroying their air bases as they neared completion.

The first jet fighter battles were fought in this war, as Republic F-84 Thunderjets, Lockheed P-80C Shooting Stars, and North American F-86 Sabres faced Mikoyan MiG-15's in the skies over Korea. The first heavy jet bomber, the Boeing B-47 Stratofortress, was in use by 1951.

Another important development in Korea was the use of the helicopter in warfare. Helicopters were used to transport men, supplies, and guns to otherwise inaccessible places. They were also used to fire rockets and other missiles. They could evacuate casualties quickly, resulting in a reduction of the death rate to the lowest figure in modern military history.

The Indochinese War

United States military involvement in Indochina began in 1961, when American troops entered Vietnam as advisers in a conflict between the South Vietnamese government and Communist rebels. By 1965 United States military forces were heavily engaged in attacks on the Viet Cong and North Vietnamese targets (*see* Vietnam Conflict).

The use of air power in this war, as in Korea, was primarily for tactical support. Air Force pilots used fighter and bomber planes to destroy enemy supplies, support ground troops, and deliver both supplies and personnel. American pilots also dropped defoliants—chemical substances that destroy plant life—over the countryside. They hoped in this way to deny the cover of trees to guerrilla fighters. Unmanned drone planes were used to penetrate bombed areas at high speeds and photograph earlier strikes.

The high cost and complex operation requirements of jet planes made the use of less powerful aircraft more expedient. In Vietnam the A-4 Skyhawk, with a maximum speed of 685 miles (1,102 kilometers) per hour, proved most effective for tactical support.

The Boeing B-52 jet bomber was also used in this conflict. First used in 1955, the B-52 was a huge jet airplane with a range greater than 12,000 miles (19,300 kilometers), a wingspan of 185 feet (56 meters), and speeds up to 630 miles (1,015 kilometers) per hour. Among the weapons it carried were precision guided munitions (PGMs), including the "smart bomb"—an explosive directed to its target by the use of a laser beam.

Air power advances were made in the development of short-takeoff-and-landing (STOL) craft, which reduced the need for long concrete runways, and in counterinsurgency aircraft (COIN), designed to operate from rough terrain. Helicopters were used in an air patrol system that also employed transport planes. The air patrol system brought mobility to ground troops by transporting men, guns, ammunition, and supplies to remote locations. In October 1965 the relief of an outpost was accomplished by the arrival of a whole division in helicopters.

The main use of strategic bombing occurred in December 1971 and in April 1972. United States Air Force (USAF) Strategic Air Command pilots blanketed Hanoi and Haiphong in North Vietnam with bombs dropped from B-52's in an intensive series of raids. As in Korea, the lesson in Indochina was that conventional bombing and fighter strategies would not by themselves win a guerrilla war.

Middle Eastern Wars

Several conflicts in the Middle East between Israel and its Arab neighbors have been shaped by the use

U.S. Air Force

of air power. The Suez crisis of 1956 began when British, French, and Israeli forces dominated Egyptian airspace by using fighter and bomber aircraft as a tactical support force for advancing ground troops. Within two days the Egyptian air force was destroyed, and a cease-fire was subsequently accepted.

In 1967 the Six-Day War between Egypt and Israel was won by the superior air strategy of Israel. Both Egypt and Israel had equal air forces, although Egypt could call upon the military resources of other Arab nations. But in three hours, on June 5, 1967, the Israeli air force completed a preemptive strike against Egyptian airfields and destroyed nearly 300 aircraft. This attack, along with raids on the airfields of Syria, Jordan, and Iraq, led to Israel's eventual victory, which was achieved without a strike on enemy cities. The Israelis lost about 50 aircraft compared to 452 aircraft of Egypt and its allies.

At the start of the Yom Kippur War of October 1973, a surprise strike by Arab forces killed more than 2,500 Israelis and destroyed a fifth of their air fleet. While Israel countered with the use of paratroopers, ground tank forces, and conventional air power to end the war, the Egyptian use of missiles reduced the effectiveness of Israeli air efforts. (*See also* Egypt; Israel.)

Air Power in the Missile Age

One of the most important developments after World War II was the achievement of supersonic flight. On Oct. 14, 1947, Maj. Charles Yeager of the USAF became the first person to fly faster than the speed of sound. He made his historic flight in a Bell X-1 rocket-powered airplane. The Soviets also broke the sound barrier in 1947, using the MiG-15 fighter. By the time of the Korean War, fighters could fly at supersonic speeds of Mach 2, or twice the speed of sound. By 1959 planes such as the Mirage III and the Lockheed F-104 could fly as fast as 1,650 miles (2,655 kilometers) per hour. Perhaps the greatest of the supersonic fighter planes has been the McDonnell Douglas F-4 Phantom, which can fly at Mach 2.27 (1,584 miles, or 2,549 kilometers, per hour) with a range greater than 2,600 miles (4,180 kilometers).

Although missiles have to some degree made the heavy bomber obsolete, both the Soviet Union and the United States retain long-range supersonic bomb-

Aircraft Group/British Aerospace

American B-1 bomber in flight (top). European swing-wing Tornado multi-role aircraft (above).

ers equipped with automatic navigation and electronic countermeasure (ECM) systems. These automated systems arose because supersonic speeds in aircraft made the human navigation and control of the planes extremely difficult. Aircraft control was made easier with the development of avionics, the use of electronic aids in aviation.

Avionics relies on the use of miniature electronic components and computer and radar technology to automate navigation and weapons systems. For example, avionic-equipped jets can be flown on preset courses, while radar searches for and "locks onto" enemy aircraft. After firing at the most favorable moment, the electronic fighter can break away to return to base. The devices used for this kind of detection, pursuit, and destruction of enemy aircraft also are used for ECM devices, which attempt to disable enemy countermeasures and jam radar.

The external design of aircraft has changed as flying speeds have increased. Swept-back wings and delta plane forms replaced the straight or tapered wings of World War II. By the late 1960's, variable-geometry arrangements—to allow wing flexibility—were under development.

Long-range capabilities of postwar aircraft were further extended with the growth of aerial refueling. In 1949 the Boeing B-50 *Lucky Lady II* flew nonstop around the world in 94 hours, proving the feasibility of aerial refueling for long-range missions. In another demonstration of in-flight refueling, two Republic F-84-E Thunderjet fighters flew across the Atlantic in 1950 in just over ten hours, completing the first nonstop, transoceanic jet flight.

Missile development began in earnest in the early 1950's, when both the Soviets and the Americans in-

Israel's KFIR C2
ground attack fighter
and missiles

Israel Aircraft Industries Ltd.

troduced their first missiles. Since then these two nations have continued to seek equality in military strength by balancing and counterbalancing various types of offensive and defensive missile forces.

In air defense, where missiles have an irreplaceable role, fighter-interceptor aircraft also play a part. Airborne for long periods, they can meet attacking aircraft or missiles far from the target. In strategic warfare, bombers and missiles complement one another.

The manned bomber is flexible. It can be recalled or directed to switch targets. Its crew can take radar-map pictures of the area it has destroyed and use them to plan subsequent missions. Jet bombers can carry far heavier and more varied loads of explosives than can earlier types of bombers. The manned plane is essential in search and rescue, transport, evacuation of wounded troops, antisubmarine patrol, and other missions where the human factor is decisive.

In the 1970's both the Soviet Union and the United States developed high-performance, complex airplanes for manned flight. The Soviet MiG-25 Foxbat attack and fighter plane can fly up to Mach 3 in short bursts and is capable of firing the air-to-air Acrid missile. The United States has developed the Mc-Donnell Douglas F-15 Eagle, an effective long-range flier that carries Sparrow and Sidewinder missiles.

Among other specialized manned planes designed in the postwar era have been the short-takeoff-and-landing (STOL) and vertical-takeoff-and-landing (VTOL) crafts. The wars in Korea and Indochina proved the need for planes able to take off and land in remote jungles, forested areas, and on ships. The STOL and VTOL craft provided some independence from long permanent runways. Typical of these craft is the Swedish Saab SF-37 Viggen; another example is the British Hawker-Siddeley Sea Harrier, which uses a single turbofan (a jet that uses air for fuel combustion) for both takeoff and propulsion.

The high production cost of specialized aircraft has led to the growing use by many smaller nations of the multirole combat aircraft (MRCA). The MRCA is an airplane that can be adapted to a variety of func-

tions—bomber, fighter, and reconnaissance. An example is the European-made Panavia Tornado, commissioned by Britain, West Germany, and Italy, and made operational in 1976. The Tornado carries up to 18,000 pounds (8,200 kilograms) of bombs, missiles, and a mix of laser, radar, and electronic aids.

The MRCA may become more widely used in the next decades by nations looking for cost-effectiveness in their military spending. So will other low-cost strike aircraft. These have been developed from such trainers as the Cessna A-37 and are relatively inexpensive, small, and highly maneuverable. (*See also* Airplane; Aviation.)

Air Forces in Outer Space

The nations of the world have been reaching into outer space since the development of jet and rocket propulsion in the late 1940's. In 1956 the United States Air Force launched the Bell X-2, a rocket-powered research craft, to an altitude of nearly 24 miles (39 kilometers). On Oct. 4, 1957, the Space Age began in earnest as the Soviet Union used an intercontinental ballistic missile to launch the 184-pound (83-kilogram) Sputnik satellite into orbit.

The actual and potential military uses of outer space are many. Arsenals of the future may include weapons-carrying satellites. By the early 1980's, in both the Soviet Union and the United States, satellites that could use laser beams and particle beams to destroy ground-based targets and spacecraft were under study. Orbital bombardment weapons have also been under study. The Soviets have researched the SS-9 Scarp, a satellite armed with a nuclear warhead, which would remain in orbit until needed.

The ability of space vehicles to gather intelligence has grown. Some reconnaissance satellites furnish detailed pictures of military installations, either by television or by photographic film returned to Earth in reentry capsules. Others eavesdrop on electronic conversations. Reconnaissance satellites carrying infrared sensors can also detect missile launchings or heat-producing craft.

Israel Aircraft Industries Ltd.

Israel's Scout Mini-RPV, a reconnaissance-surveillance drone, is an unmanned, remotely piloted craft.

The Soviet Union first launched a military observation satellite, the Kosmos 112, in 1969, to provide coverage of Norway, Alaska, and Greenland. Vela satellites now orbit some 70,000 miles (113,000 kilometers) from the Earth to monitor nuclear explosions in space. Manned spacecraft may eventually be more effective in reconnaissance duties.

TWENTIETH-CENTURY AIR FORCES

Few nations had air forces prior to World War I. By 1980 more than 120 nations had established air forces. These ranged from the powerful military organizations of the United States, the Soviet Union, and the People's Republic of China—each with hundreds of thousands of members and thousands of aircraft—to such tiny groups as the air force of the People's Republic of Benin, which had 100 men operating five aircraft.

There are two methods of staffing an air force. In some countries, such as the United States, Canada, and Japan, the air force relies on volunteers who enlist for a specific number of years. In other nations, such as the Soviet Union and Israel, young people are drafted into military service to supplement air force strength. In terms of size, strength, advanced technology, and combat readiness, the two leading air forces of the late 20th century are those of the Soviet Union and the United States.

SOVIET UNION

Soviet military aviation began in 1969, with the establishment of the Commission on the Use of Aeronautics for Military Purposes. Currently the Union of Soviet Socialist Republics divides its air force into five commands. These are Long-range Aviation, a strategic nuclear force oriented to operations against Western Europe and China; Frontal Aviation, a tactical force; Air Defense; Air Transport; and Naval Aviation. Each command consists of divisions of three or more regiments, which, in turn, contain three squadrons of 12 aircraft each.

The estimated 475,000 members of the Soviet air force are supplemented by some 950,000 reserves and 550,000 members of the national air defense. The Soviets maintain at least 500 air bases, including 100 in the Arctic and subarctic regions. Their air forces are

deployed in the Soviet Union and in the German Democratic Republic (East Germany), Hungary, Poland, and Czechoslovakia. The Soviets are the mainstay of the Warsaw Treaty Organization (WTO), an Eastern bloc defense alliance, and they supply most of its direction and equipment.

Soviet aircraft include MiG fighters and interceptors, Tupolev Tu-26 bombers, Bison refuelers, and Sukhoi Su-7b Fitter-A ground attack aircraft. In addition, they control a wide-ranging missile system that includes more than 12,000 surface-to-air missiles and 1,500 intercontinental ballistic missiles. In the 1980's airborne warning and control systems, missile-equipped interceptors, and military satellites were under intensive development.

THE UNITED STATES AIR FORCE

The Air Force has been a separate branch of the United States armed services only since 1947. Before that time it was part of the Army. The first air arm was established in 1907 as the Aeronautical Division of the Army Signal Corps. The First Aero Squadron was organized in 1914. It served with the Mexican Border Expedition in 1916, the first United States military air unit to see action.

The three components of the United States Department of Defense are the departments of the Air Force, the Army, and the Navy. The Department of the Air Force is headed by a civilian secretary, who is appointed by the president of the United States.

The Air Force's military staff is headed by the

Britain's Airborne Early Warning Nimrod operates beyond the range of ground-based radar.

Aircraft Group/British Aerospace

chief of staff who is also appointed by the president. Together with the chiefs of staff of the Army and the Navy, he is a member of the Joint Chiefs of Staff, who serve as the principal military advisers to the president and to the secretary of defense.

Major Commands

Eleven major commands are responsible for specific areas of the Air Force's mission. They may be grouped into combat, overseas, training, and support commands, according to their primary functions. The basic combat organizations are the Strategic Air Command and the Tactical Air Command.

The Strategic Air Command (SAC), a specified command of the Joint Chiefs of Staff, includes a strike force of long-range combat aircraft and of intercontinental ballistic missiles. The forces of SAC support the government's international policy of deterrence. In the event of attack on the United States or its allies, however, SAC planes and missiles could inflict heavy damage on the enemy.

In 1979 SAC also began to assume responsibility for space surveillance and warning of missile attack, which had been functions of the former Aerospace Defense Command (ADCOM). As a part of these duties SAC took control of the Distant Early Warning (DEW) line and of the Ballistic Missile Early Warning System (BMEWS). These radar networks, located in extreme northern areas of North America, can detect unidentified aircraft and missiles.

The Tactical Air Command (TAC) is a mobile strike force. Its principal duties include support of ground troops, strikes against the enemy, and disruption of enemy transportation, communications, and supply networks. TAC supplies the Air Force components to two unified military commands—the Atlantic Command, at Norfolk, Va., and the Readiness Command, at MacDill Air Force Base (AFB), near Tampa, Fla.

Beginning in 1979 TAC also began to assume some of the former ADCOM responsibilities, including the management of interceptor units and of ground-based radar and air-traffic-control centers. The Air Force component of the North American Aerospace Defense Command, a network maintained jointly by the United States and Canada, came under the temporary control of TAC.

TAC's headquarters are at Langley AFB, Norfolk, Va. TAC is made up of two numbered air forces—the Ninth, at Shaw AFB, near Sumter, S.C., and the Twelfth, at Bergstrom AFB, near Austin, Tex. Units of the two are stationed at more than 15 air bases.

Other Major Commands

There are nine other major Air Force commands. The three overseas commands are:

United States Air Forces in Europe (USAFE), with headquarters at Ramstein Air Base, West Germany. USAFE is responsible for Air Force operations in the unified European Command. Its forces include SAC's Seventh Air Division.

Pacific Air Forces (PACAF), Hickam AFB, Oahu, Hawaii. PACAF is responsible for Air Force operations in the unified Pacific Command. Its forces include SAC's 3d Air Division, at Anderson AFB, near Agana, Guam.

Alaskan Air Command (AAC), Elmendorf AFB, at Anchorage, Alaska. Strategically located, AAC is an important part of the electronic defense system that has been established to warn of air attack.

The five support commands are:

Air Force Communications Command (AFCC), Scott AFB, near Belleville, Ill. AFCC provides communications, flight facilities, and air-traffic-control services for the Air Force and for other government and civil agencies, including those of some foreign countries. In 1979 AFCC began to assume the communications responsibilities of the former ADCOM.

Air Force Logistics Command (AFLC), Wright-Patterson AFB, near Dayton, Ohio. AFLC procures, stores, distributes, and provides maintenance for supplies for the Air Force.

Air Force Systems Command (AFSC), Andrews AFB, Md., near Washington, D.C. AFSC promotes the advancement of aerospace technology and its adaptation to new weapons systems for the Air Force.

Military Airlift Command (MAC), Scott AFB, near Belleville, Ill. Also a Joint Chiefs of Staff specified command, MAC provides air transportation for personnel and cargo for all branches of the armed services of the United States. MAC also provides weather, rescue, and audiovisual services for the Air Force.

Electronic Security Command (ESC), Kelly AFB, near San Antonio, Tex. ESC monitors Air Force communications facilities and conducts intelligence work and electronic warfare analysis for the government.

The training command is:

Air Training Command (ATC), Randolph AFB, also near San Antonio, Tex. ATC is responsible for the recruitment and training of airmen and officers and for the education of officers. Its educational programs include the Air University, headquartered at Maxwell AFB, near Montgomery, Ala.

Separate Air Force Agencies

Separate operating agencies include the Accounting and Finance Center, the Audit Agency, the Commissary Service, the Engineering and Services Center, the Inspection and Safety Center, the Intelligence Service, the Legal Services Center, the Manpower and Personnel Center, the Medical Service Center, the Office of Security Police, the Office of Special Investigation, the Service Information and News Center, and the Test and Evaluation Center.

BIBLIOGRAPHY FOR AIR FORCE

Encyclopedia of Air Warfare (Crowell, 1975).
Hickey, S. M. Out of the Sky: a History of Airborne Warfare (Scribner, 1979).
Jablonski, Edward. Air War (Doubleday, 1979).
Macksey, Kenneth and others. History of Air Warfare (Sterling, 1980).
Wheeler, Barry. Air Forces of the World (Scribner, 1980).

TWA Ambassador
Boeing 747 jetliner in the service of Trans World Airlines

AIRLINE. The newest form of mass travel in the world's transportation network, airlines are organizations of people, airplanes, equipment, and buildings for transporting passengers, freight, and mail by air between specified points. The airliner is as significant economically and socially as the train, bus, truck, or ship. In many industrialized countries, intercity air passenger traffic has been growing at a far greater rate than that of either railroads or bus lines. International air travel is so extensive that it is possible to reach almost any major city in less than a day on one of the more than 350 airlines operating throughout the world. The United States has the largest air transportation system. It includes more than 60 commercial airlines, which carry more than half of the world's air passengers and cargo.

Routes

Airliners travel along designated airways, or routes, in controlled airspace. The routes, which are numbered like highways on the ground, are set by radio beams sent out by navigation stations along the routes. Air traffic controllers are responsible for directing traffic on these routes. They follow international guidelines to ensure that aircraft on a specific route are separated by at least ten minutes and/or a safe vertical distance.

Most flights are routed with the aid of computers. The computer is provided with data about the freight, baggage, fuel, number of passengers, and weather. It then prints out several possible routes and designates one as the most desirable, taking into account distance, time, and cost. Long-distance flights often follow the great circle route, which is the shortest distance on the Earth's surface between two points. All routes begin and end at air traffic "hubs." The term hub is used to designate cities and areas that require aviation services.

Classification

Airlines are classified by their routes and by their schedules. The two major classifications are domestic and international. Domestic airlines provide services within a country. International airlines operate both within a nation and between two or more nations. The International Civil Aviation Organization (ICAO) also distinguishes between scheduled and nonscheduled operators. Nonscheduled airlines offer either domestic or international air transportation services, but they do not maintain definite departure or arrival times.

Many individual countries have established various classes of air carriers. These categories often include local service airlines, trunk airlines that service large hubs, international airlines, all-cargo lines, and charter services.

Passenger Services

By far the largest source of revenue for airlines in the second half of the 20th century has been transporting passengers. Competing airlines offer attractive fares and various services to entice travelers to fly on their individual planes. Special discounts—including family plans, student or youth fares, round trip excursion rates, night flights, and other promotional schemes—can lower the cost of air travel. In general, the more flexible arrangements cost more. These include plans that allow the passenger the choice of buying an open-date ticket or making a firm reservation, stopovers at intermediate airports, or even failing to show up with no penalty.

Traditionally, first-class service has been more luxurious than coach and other services, with fewer and wider seats, more elaborate meals, and, generally, more flight personnel attending passengers. Coach service is less expensive, with cabins of a larger seat-

SOME MAJOR INTERNATIONAL AIRLINES*

 AEROFLOT: Owned by the government of the U.S.S.R. Began operations in 1956. Passenger-miles (kilometers): 100.0 (161.0).

 AIR CANADA: Government owned. Organized in 1937. Passenger-miles (kilometers): 14.4 (23.1).

 AIR FRANCE: Government owned. Organized in 1933. Passenger-miles (kilometers): 16.2 (26.1).

 ALITALIA: Privately owned, regulated by Italian government. Organized in 1946. Passenger-miles (kilometers): 7.7 (12.5).

 AMERICAN AIRLINES, INC., (AA): Privately owned U.S. company. Organized in 1934. Passenger-miles (kilometers): 28.0 (45.0).

 BRITISH AIRWAYS: Government owned. Organized in 1974. Passenger-miles (kilometers): 24.6 (39.6).

 CONTINENTAL AIRLINES: Privately owned U.S. company. Organized in 1934; adopted present name in 1937. Passenger-miles (kilometers): 7.9 (12.7).

 DELTA AIR LINES, INC.: Privately owned U.S. company. Organized in 1924; adopted present name in 1928. Passenger-miles (kilometers): 24.2 (39.0).

 EASTERN AIR LINES, INC.: Privately owned U.S. company. Organized under present name in 1929. Passenger-miles (kilometers): 27.5 (44.3).

 IBERIA: Owned by Spanish government. Organized in 1927. Passenger-miles (kilometers): 9.4 (15.0).

 JAPAN AIR LINES CO., LTD. (JAL): Government directed. Organized in 1951. Passenger-miles (kilometers): 18.9 (30.4).

 KLM—ROYAL DUTCH AIRLINES: Partly government owned. Organized in 1919. Passenger-miles (kilometers): 9.1 (14.6).

 LUFTHANSA GERMAN AIRLINES: Privately owned. Organized in 1926. Passenger-miles (kilometers): 13.3 (21.4).

 NORTHWEST ORIENT AIRLINES, INC.: Privately owned U.S. company. Organized in 1926. Passenger-miles (kilometers): 14.3 (22.9).

 PAN AMERICAN WORLD AIRWAYS, INC. (PAN AM): Privately owned U.S. company. Organized in 1927. Passenger-miles (kilometers): 28.9 (46.5).

 QANTAS AIRWAYS LTD.: Owned by the government of Australia. Organized in 1920. Passenger-miles (kilometers): 9.4 (15.1).

 **SAS—SCANDINAVIAN AIRLINES:** Owned partly by the governments of Norway, Sweden, and Denmark. Organized in 1946. Passenger-miles (kilometers): 6.8 (10.9).

 SWISSAIR: Privately owned. Organized in 1931. Passenger-miles (kilometers): 7.0 (11.2).

 TRANS WORLD AIRLINES, INC. (TWA): Privately owned U.S. company. Organized in 1925. Passenger-miles (kilometers): 27.2 (43.8).

 UNITED AIRLINES, INC.: Privately owned U.S. company. Organized in 1931. Passenger-miles (kilometers): 36.6 (58.9).

*Passenger-miles (kilometers) in billions.

ing capacity and thus more crowded conditions, and, usually, less-attentive service. Depending on the type of fare and the length of trip, passenger services often include music, magazines, and in-flight movies.

Lower-cost charter service is usually available for organized groups at lower rates than those provided by scheduled passenger flights. Charter flights, which have contributed significantly to the growth of world tourism since the 1960's, are an outgrowth of the post-World War II expansion of small airlines. These airlines acquired long-haul jets by the mid-1960's and developed group charters—agreements by which an aircraft's capacity was leased to a club or organization for the use of its members.

Cargo Services

Because scheduled flights are frequently under-booked, airlines rely on the carrying of cargo to be sure of making a profit. Air cargo is the load carried by airliners in addition to passengers and their baggage. All aircraft used by airlines have space available for carrying freight and mail. Some airlines fly special convertible versions of standard jet airliners. The convertible airliners can be outfitted rather quickly to carry cargo only, passengers only, or both cargo and passengers.

All-cargo airlines and all-cargo aircraft offering specialized facilities and services exist throughout the world; nearly 200 such companies were operating in the 1980's. All-cargo aircraft have special features geared to facilitate efficient loading, storage, and delivery. For example, the Boeing 747-200 F can carry a load of 200,000 pounds (91,000 kilograms) almost 5,000 miles (8,000 kilometers) without stopping to refuel. This aircraft has a hinged nose that facilitates the loading of cargo.

Cargo and luggage usually are carried in compartments in the lower part of the fuselage—the main body of the airplane that accommodates the crew and passengers. Cargo is generally assembled on large pallets (metal sheets that usually measure ten by seven feet [two to three meters]) that are loaded into the fuselage from the ground through doors and hatches and secured by stout netting to prevent movement during flight.

Airport cargo terminals are often similar to post-office sorting offices. They are automated with a minimum of human supervision and organized to process freight by computer. These facilities are capable of storing materials that require special treatment; they provide cages for animals, lead-lined rooms for radioactive chemicals, and vaults for valuables. The bulk of airfreight shipments includes engineering goods, chemical and pharmaceutical products, textiles, paper products, livestock, and commercial samples of all kinds.

Air cargo services are especially valuable in areas where surface transportation is difficult such as the frozen wastes of northern Canada and the Soviet Union and the mountainous areas of South America. This means of transport is also used in torrid areas

Qantas

In an airline's operational hub, its flight control center, the airline's fleet of planes is tracked 24 hours a day.

such as Africa and the Middle East, where heat causes spoilage of perishable goods unless transported speedily or in refrigerated vehicles.

Although the price per ton-mile (the carrying of one ton of cargo for one mile) is higher than that of other forms of transportation, users of air cargo services believe that the reliability, frequency, security, and speed of delivery make it worth the price.

Mail Services

Airmail service, including parcels, is available at relatively low cost throughout the world. Regular airmail and air parcel post are considered priority mail. Nonpriority mail is first-class postal matter carried by air on a space-available basis.

Scheduled air transportation in much of the world began with the carrying of the mails. The first recorded airmail delivery occurred in 1910, when the United States flier Glenn Curtiss flew a plane he designed for 142½ miles (229.3 kilometers) in 2 hours and 50 minutes. Airmail service was begun experimentally in 1911 between Windsor and London, England, to celebrate the coronation of King George V. Over a period of three weeks, Gustave Hamel carried 25,000 letters and 90,000 postcards, all of which were stamped in honor of the occasion. Also in 1911 the first airmail in Italy was carried between Bologna and Venice and between Venice and Rimini.

In 1918 the United States Post Office opened the first regularly scheduled airmail service between Washington, D.C., and New York City, using army pilots. Airmail service between New York and Chicago began in 1919 and was extended to San Francisco the following year. The first regular airmail parcel service was inaugurated in 1921 between London and Paris, and transatlantic airmail service began in 1939 from New York via Bermuda and Portugal to Marseilles, France, and soon was extended across the Pacific Ocean to Singapore and Hong Kong.

The Soviet airline, Aeroflot, also relied on mail and other freight services in its early days. Such deliveries constituted 85 percent of its transport volume prior to 1939.

Safety

The safety record of airlines has improved dramatically over the years. In retrospect, it is a wonder that people risked traveling by air in the early days.

In the United States, for instance, by 1929 airlines' fatality rate was approximately 1,500 times higher than that of railroads and 900 times above that of bus lines. In 1980, however, of 2,966,000,000 miles (4,773,000,000 kilometers) flown by all United States certificated route air carriers, there were but 13 deaths, a fatality rate of only .0044 per million passenger miles. The safest year in United States aviation was 1981, when no fatal crashes were recorded among major airlines.

Regulation and Deregulation

A high degree of international and national organization and cooperation has always been required for efficient and safe air transportation. Problems of international traffic rights and freedom of passage and questions of air safety, health, and commercial competition began to arise in the decade after World War I, but these did not receive full attention until the development of air transportation after World War II. Regulations apply to aspects of air travel as varied as the routes that an airline is permitted to fly, passengers' legroom, fares, training standards, and noise levels around airports.

In most industrialized Western nations, the regulatory agencies are separate from the airlines. In the Soviet Union, on the other hand, the state airline, Aeroflot, also functions as its own regulatory agency. Other airlines that are owned or operated by their governments include Air Canada, Air France, British European Airways, Lufthansa German Airlines, Qantas Airways (Australia), Royal Dutch Airlines (KLM), and Scandinavian Airlines System (SAS; owned partly by the governments of Norway, Sweden, and Denmark). Government-directed airlines include Alitalia and Japan Air Lines.

Air safety standards are generally set by the civil aviation board of the country in which an aircraft is registered. The Federal Aviation Administration (FAA) in the United States and the Civil Aviation Authority (CAA) in the United Kingdom are two such boards. In addition to these organizations, consumer groups such as the Aviation Consumer Action Project in the United States and the International Airline Passengers' Association protect passenger rights. Professional associations of air personnel, such as the International Federation of Airline Pilots' Association (IFAPA), work for the adoption of particular safety measures.

Two relatively recent concerns of both consumer and professional groups have been air traffic congestion and airplane noise around airports. To control these effects of air transportation, extensive research has been undertaken to suggest ways to assess and minimize these potential hazards.

Specific approaches to airline regulation vary from country to country. Some of the most stringent legislation has been enacted in the United States.

United States. In the United States the major legislation governing air transportation is the Federal Aviation Act of 1958. This act created the Federal Aviation Agency (FAA), renamed the Federal Aviation Administration in 1966. Among the powers and duties of the agency are the development of aviation, regulations for the use of airspace, design of aircraft, training and certifying of air personnel, and construction of airports. Although the FAA began as an agency that reported directly to the president, its operations are now overseen by the Department of Transportation.

Early legislation in the United States was concerned with airmail as was air legislation throughout much of the world. The United States government also established an agency to regulate civil aviation. The Civil Aeronautics Board (CAB) was directed to grant airlines permission to fly specific routes and to charge certain fares.

Later legislation—the Airline Deregulation Act of 1978—reversed earlier policy. An intention of this legislation was to free the airlines from certain restrictions in order to encourage, through competition, an increased fare flexibility. This act provides for the phasing out of the CAB and the transferring of some of its functions to other agencies such as the departments of Transportation and Justice. Two stipulations of the Airline Deregulation Act include the expiration of the CAB's power to assign specific routes to airlines and the cessation of its authority over the setting of domestic fares.

International Agreements. By 1970 a large body of international regulations, focusing largely on air traffic rights and on international airline procedures recommended by the United Nations' International Civil Aviation Organization (ICAO), were established. These regulations are intended to guide the operation of worldwide air services.

The earliest international agreements were concerned with the rights of a nation to fly over another nation's airspace. The Paris Convention of 1919 granted exclusive national sovereignty over airspace above each nation that signed the agreement. The first official agreement involving the United States is found in the Air Commerce Act of 1926, providing for the navigation of foreign aircraft over United States territory if the same rights are provided for United States aircraft over foreign territory. The Havana Convention of 1928, signed by the Dominican Republic, Guatemala, Mexico, Nicaragua, Panama, and eventually the United States, also stated specific conditions for the passage of foreign aircraft over the airspaces of the ratifying nations.

The International Civil Aviation Organization (ICAO), proposed by the Chicago Convention of

Food is prepared (above) at the flight catering center. Meals are served (above right) in the economy class section. Passengers collect their luggage (right) at the baggage carousel.

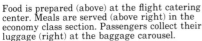

Qantas

1944, came into being in 1947. An agency of the United Nations, it had about 150 member countries in the early 1980's. This agency is concerned with establishing international standards for technical and operational matters such as takeoff and landing noise. The Chicago Convention also established degrees of "freedoms of the air," which are incorporated into official agreements. These freedoms include the privileges of flying over a country without landing and of making a technical landing to refuel or for repairs.

A conference of airlines, the International Air Transport Association (IATA), is sanctioned to determine rates, subject to the approval of the involved countries. The IATA has also updated and revised the 1929 Warsaw Convention's regulations concerning such matters as an airline's liability for loss of or damage to passengers' luggage and compensation for injury or death. Although not all are still in effect, these agreements have set the stage for most contemporary international airline policies.

History

Commercial air transportation is a relatively recent development. The first significant air service of any kind was the dirigible line organized in Germany by Count Ferdinand von Zeppelin in 1910. A dirigible differs from a balloon in that it is steerable under power at the control of its pilot. The *Graf Zeppelin* and the *Hindenburg* were developed for transatlantic flights from Frankfurt am Main, Germany, to Lakehurst, N.J., and to South America as well. This dirigible service came to an end with the destruction by fire of the *Hindenburg* in 1937, temporarily terminating all interest in transatlantic air services.

The first regularly scheduled air passenger flight took place on Jan. 1, 1914, when a Benoist flying boat—a seaplane with a hull adapted for floating—traveled 22 miles (35 kilometers) from Tampa to St. Petersburg, Fla. This service offered two flights a day for four months. The first scheduled international airline service originating in the United States began in 1920 on a flight between Florida and Cuba.

World War I halted the development of civil air transportation as military concerns took precedence, but public interest in aviation increased in the 1920's, fostered by events such as the Paris Air Show in France and the Hendon Air Show of the Royal Air Force in England. Some countries, including the Soviet Union, officially sponsored air clubs.

Successful air transportation systems were developed on both sides of the Atlantic during the 1920's. By 1921 there were at least 10 services operating flights between major European cities. By 1924 the European air transport system was well on its way, operating in 17 countries. In the United States 14 routes were established by 1926. Passenger interest lagged, however, until Charles Lindbergh's solo flight across the Atlantic Ocean on May 20–21, 1927.

Efforts were first made in the 1920's to produce aircraft that were—in addition to being economical, safe, and reliable—attractive to passengers. The earliest passenger planes were converted World War I bombers. These were soon replaced in the United States by planes designed by early manufacturers such as William Boeing, Claude L. Ryan, and Donald Douglas. A Ford trimotor, called the *Tin Goose*, carried up to 15 passengers and was used by all major United States airlines in the 1930's.

British aircraft of the early 1920's included the De Havilland 18, the Handley Page W.8B, and the Blackburn Kangaroo. The French had the Bréguet 14T and the Potez 9; German aircraft of the period included the Fokker F.2 and the Junkers F.13.

Air transportation continued to develop in the 1930's. Japan established a strong network of mail services, and air transportation was inaugurated in Australia, South America, and Africa as well. By 1930 there were 43 scheduled airlines in the United States that depended chiefly on airmail for revenue. Revolving beacons, radio communication, and more accurate weather service improved airway facilities and safety records. Aircraft developed during this period included the Douglas DC-2 and DC-3. The DC-2, a machine that could fly from coast to coast in a little more than 13 hours, was introduced by Douglas in 1934. A year later the DC-3 offered carrying space for 21 passengers, a speed of 180 miles (290 kilometers) per hour, and considerably advanced safety and comfort features. This aircraft was flown from New York City to Los Angeles, with three or four stops, in about 18 flying hours.

Extensive overseas flights began in earnest in the mid-1930's. In 1936 Pan American Airways (since 1950, Pan American World Airways) inaugurated transpacific service—San Francisco to Hawaii and the Philippines—with *China Clipper* flying boats. Transatlantic service began in 1939. A route between England and the Far East was operated by British Imperial Airways in 1937. Limitations of aircraft range and capability and navigational and landing aids restricted the development of this venture. Australia was accessible through an eight-day service offered by both British Imperial Airways and the Royal Dutch Airlines (KLM). In Europe the colonial empires of Great Britain and France and the ambitious governments of Germany and Italy encouraged the development of long-distance overseas flights. The Soviet Union also developed long-distance airlines to link its own distant regions with Moscow. By the outbreak of World War II, a worldwide network of air services existed.

United States airlines established routes during World War II in support of military operations and soon became the dominant world airline power. By the end of the war, the scheduled routes with the largest passenger volume within the United States were the New York City to San Francisco and Los Angeles, and the New York to Chicago routes. The postwar availability of large numbers of former military transport aircraft (particularly the Douglas DC-3 and DC-4), along with a rising demand for air transportation, furthered the expansion of United States airline activity. During this period some 20 local service airlines were established, mainly operating DC-3's, to develop feeder services that connected with the major points on the trunk airline routes.

The British European Airways (BEA), formed in 1946, was soon established as the leading airline in Europe. Its expansion was aided by the use of the Vickers Viking, an airplane significantly faster than the DC-3. Other European airlines at this time included British Overseas Airways Corporation (BOAC; formerly British Imperial Airways), Britain's principal long-haul airline; Air France; and Scandinavian Airlines System (SAS).

Until World War II most aircraft were propeller driven and powered by internal-combustion engines. A major technological breakthrough occurred with the introduction of the turbine engine. The first successful flight of a turbojet aircraft took place in 1939. The first commercial service was not offered, however, until 1952 on BOAC's London to Johannesburg, South Africa, route, using a 36-seat De Havilland Comet. Britain used Viscount turboprop models in 1953 on the London–Cyprus route, and the first large turboprop aircraft, the Bristol Britannia, was operating by 1957. By 1960 United States airlines had Boeing 707, Convair 880, Douglas DC-8 turbojet, and Lockheed Electra turboprop aircraft in service.

Jet engines proved to be well suited to high-speed aircraft and were rapidly put into use. The airlines achieved even greater passenger and cargo capacity as they switched to jet aircraft. Transatlantic jet service began in 1958, when BOAC and then Pan American provided London to New York City service. By the 1960's international jet air travel was firmly established worldwide.

A trend in the 1950's and 1960's toward increased size was continued in the 1970's with the introduction of the "jumbo" jets, an innovation that resulted in chronic congestion at many major airports. In 1970 the Boeing 747 was introduced into service. This first of the wide-bodied jets could seat as many as 500 tourist-class passengers. Its first competitors, the Lockheed 1011 and McDonnell Douglas DC-10, could each seat up to 400 passengers.

Increased size was only one goal of aircraft design; speed was also an increasingly important consideration. During the 1960's three supersonic transport (SST) planes were developed: the British–French Concorde, the Soviet Tu-144, and a United States airliner planned by Boeing, which was discontinued in 1971 when federal government funds were cut off for economic and environmental reasons. The basic

WORLD AIR CARGO TRANSPORT

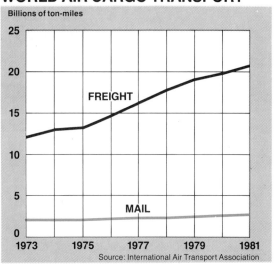

Billions of ton-miles

FREIGHT

MAIL

1973   1975   1977   1979   1981

Source: International Air Transport Association

Photos. courtesy (above) Air France; (below) Pan American; (bottom left) Aeroport de Paris; (bottom right) Qantas

An employee uses a computer (top left) to check airfreight. Freight is loaded onto an all-cargo plane (above) through its nose. Luggage is loaded onto a passenger plane (below). Special cargo is prepared for shipment (right).

HOW SPEED OF AIRLINERS HAS INCREASED

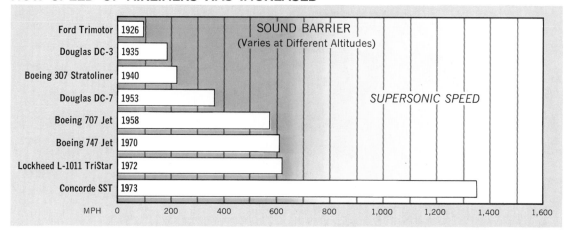

objections were the high investment cost, the noise, and the potential pollution of the stratosphere.

The Soviet Tu-144, which reaches a speed of 1,550 miles (2,494 kilometers) per hour, was first tested in 1968 and was the first SST to complete a flight. Tu-144 passenger flights were inaugurated in 1977. The 1,354-miles- (2,179-kilometers-) per-hour Concorde began undergoing tests in 1969 and was first used for commercial flights in 1976 on routes from Europe to South America and Asia.

Airline Personnel

Requirements for airline personnel vary according to the company and the position. Many of the jobs require training programs after employment as well as before. Specialized certificates of competence are necessary for many airline employees, including pilots, mechanics, ground instructors, control tower operators, flight engineers, and flight instructors. Pilots, for example, are often required to possess a college education or a satisfactory equivalent and to log a specified number of flying hours. Requirements for flight attendants vary according to the individual airline, but these employees also must meet certain educational requirements in addition to standards for age, weight, and appearance.

Airline personnel may be certified in more than one field. Flight engineers—crew members who are responsible for mechanical operations—are generally promoted from the airline maintenance force or from personnel who have a pilot's experience. Navigators—those who determine position, course, and distance traveled—are often copilots who are trained in navigation skills.

Finances

Governments subsidized airlines for many years to promote strong national defenses and national economies. Air transportation stimulates trade and industry and provides essential services such as mail delivery. As the airlines became capable of developing profitable services on their own, the subsidies in some countries lessened considerably. In the early 1980's in the United States, for example, less than one percent of airline revenues was from subsidies, compared with 28 percent in 1938. Many airlines remained owned or operated by their national governments. The largest source of revenue for an airline is passenger transportation (about 80 percent), followed by airfreight and, finally, mail.

An airline's principal expenses include labor, fuel, passenger meals, maintenance, landing fees, advertising, traffic commissions, and capital with which to buy aircraft and other property. Even a small aircraft is expensive, costing millions of dollars. Each time an airliner takes off and lands, the airline is charged according to factors such as weight, number of passengers, and time of day.

Throughout most of their history, airlines have made a profit (helped by subsidies in some instances). This trend was reversed in the late 1970's and early 1980's. Although the airlines suffered losses during earlier periods (for example, during the transition from piston aircraft to jets in the early 1960's and after the petroleum price increases in 1973), they were unprepared for the effect that an inflation-ridden world economy would have on their finances. For a variety of reasons, including the sharpest decline of passenger boardings in 50 years of scheduled air transportation, high interest rates, and a drastic increase in the price of fuel, airlines throughout the world suffered a financial reversal in 1980 of more than a billion dollars. Several airlines subsequently declared bankruptcy.

In response many airlines reduced the number of scheduled flights and offered special promotional fares. Some of their services are geared toward business travelers—those who are not deterred by large increases in the price of airline tickets. It seems likely in the long run, however, that the demand for air travel will increase as industries continue to expand and technology increases the speed and the comfort of aircraft. (*See also* Aerospace Industry; Airplane; Airport; Aviation.)

McDonnell Douglas Corporation

AIRPLANE

AIRPLANE. When the Wright brothers mastered the secret of flight, they did not try to imitate the flying of birds but built a machine for flying. That is exactly what an airplane is, a flying machine.

An airplane is heavier than air and yet it flies. It does this by propelling itself through the air and by supporting itself on wings so shaped that the air flowing over them gives them lift.

Used in a broad sense, the term airplane includes piston-engine and jet-driven aircraft, gliders, helicopters, and winged guided missiles (*see* Glider; Helicopter; Guided Missiles).

In a narrower sense, airplane means any power-driven aircraft with a fixed wing. This is the usual meaning of the word. The British use the form aeroplane. The word plane is short for airplane.

Airplane and Aircraft Distinguished

Airplane and aircraft are widely used to mean the same thing, though aircraft is a broader term. It includes both lighter-than-air and heavier-than-air craft. The lighter-than-air group includes balloons, blimps, and dirigibles, which get lift from gases lighter than air (*see* Balloon and Airship). Heavier-than-air craft include airplanes, helicopters, Autogiros, ornithopters, and convertiplanes.

The helicopter uses power-driven rotating wings for both lift and thrust. The Autogiro is another

This article was critically reviewed by Robert van der Linden, Assistant Curator, Department of Aeronautics, National Air and Space Museum, Smithsonian Institution.

LANDPLANE—Champion Challenger

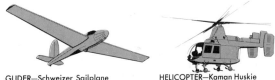

SEAPLANE—Cessna 172   FLYING BOAT—Martin Marlin

TYPES OF AIRPLANES

AMPHIBIAN—Colonial Skimmer IV

GLIDER—Schweizer Sailplane   HELICOPTER—Kaman Huskie

Airplanes are built in many shapes and sizes to do many things. They are designed to take off and land on land or water or both.

Fact Finder for Airplane Articles

The subject of the airplane is a broad one. Readers will find exactly what they want to know about it in the many articles listed here.

Aerospace	Helicopter
Air Force	Jet Propulsion
Airline	Navy
Airport	Parachute
Aviation	Rockets
Balloon and Airship	Sailplane
Glider	Space Travel
Guided Missiles	Wind Tunnel

See also additional references in the Fact-Index.

AIRPLANES MAY BE CLASSIFIED IN MANY WAYS

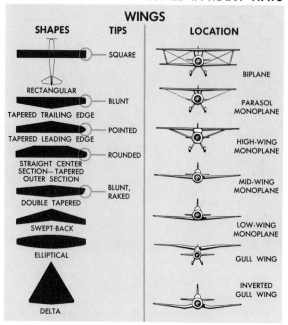

WINGS

SHAPES **TIPS** **LOCATION**

- SQUARE
- RECTANGULAR
- BLUNT
- TAPERED TRAILING EDGE
- POINTED
- TAPERED LEADING EDGE
- ROUNDED
- STRAIGHT CENTER SECTION—TAPERED OUTER SECTION
- BLUNT, RAKED
- DOUBLE TAPERED
- SWEPT-BACK
- ELLIPTICAL
- DELTA

BIPLANE

PARASOL MONOPLANE

HIGH-WING MONOPLANE

MID-WING MONOPLANE

LOW-WING MONOPLANE

GULL WING

INVERTED GULL WING

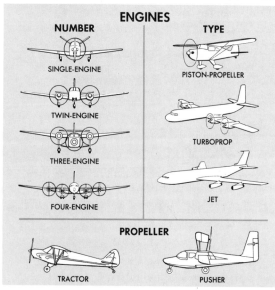

ENGINES

NUMBER **TYPE**

- SINGLE-ENGINE
- TWIN-ENGINE
- THREE-ENGINE
- FOUR-ENGINE

PISTON-PROPELLER

TURBOPROP

JET

PROPELLER

TRACTOR   PUSHER

The **airframe** includes the fuselage, wings, tail assembly, landing gear, and engine mount. The fuselage is the body of the airplane.

The wings are the airfoils that provide lift. Ailerons are hinged portions of the wing that control rolling of the airplane. Flaps are also hinged sections, usually at the rear of a wing. They increase lift or drag, making possible shorter takeoffs and slower landings. Spoilers are sections that move up from the top or bottom of the wing to increase drag and decrease lift. Slots are narrow, spanwise passages along the leading edge of a wing to improve airflow at high angles of attack.

The tail assembly, or empennage, consists of the horizontal and vertical stabilizers and their control surfaces. The fixed horizontal stabilizer keeps the plane from pitching. Hinged to it is the elevator. When it is moved up or down it raises or lowers the nose of the plane. The fixed vertical stabilizer, or fin, keeps the tail from whipping from side to side. The rudder is hinged to it. When the rudder is swung to the left or right it turns the plane.

The landing gear is an apparatus for supporting the airplane while on land, water, or snow and when taking off or landing. The engine mount is a metal frame for attaching an engine to the airplane. (*See also* section on Airframe.)

The **power plant** consists of an engine, propeller (if any), accessories such as carburetors and fuel pumps, and fuel and oil tanks and lines (*see* Aerospace, section on Fuels). The engine is a machine that powers, or propels, the aircraft. (*See also* section on Power Plants.)

The **instruments** are devices for helping the pilot fly the airplane, for navigating, for checking engine performance, and for indicating the operation of equipment, such as deicing systems. (*See also* section on Flight Controls and Instruments.)

The **furnishings** include such equipment as seats, safety belts, fire extinguishers, and cupboards.

The **accessories** are devices that facilitate the use of some piece of equipment. They may be aircraft accessories, such as lighting systems, or engine accessories, such as superchargers.

Kinds of Airplanes

Airplanes are of three broad types, depending upon whether they take off on land, on water, or on both. A landplane has a landing gear for support while at rest or in motion on the ground and during takeoff and landing. The landing gear may be wheels, skids, endless tracks, or skis. A seaplane has floats shaped like small airtight boats for landing gear. A flying boat has a hull or boatlike fuselage. An amphibian can take off and land on either land or water. It has wheels for use on the ground and a hull or floats for use on the water.

Airplanes may be classified by the number, location, and shape of the wings or by the type, number, and position of the engines. Another designation is by landing gear—fixed or retractable.

rotary-wing craft, but its blades revolve without power for lift and it uses a conventional propeller for forward motion.

The ornithopter, not yet flown successfully, is designed with wings that flap. The convertiplane can be adjusted to fly as a conventional airplane or as a helicopter or an Autogiro. It is also called a VTOL (vertical takeoff and landing). A related aircraft is the STOL (short takeoff and landing).

Parts of the Airplane

An airplane usually consists of an airframe, power plant, instruments, furnishings, and accessories.

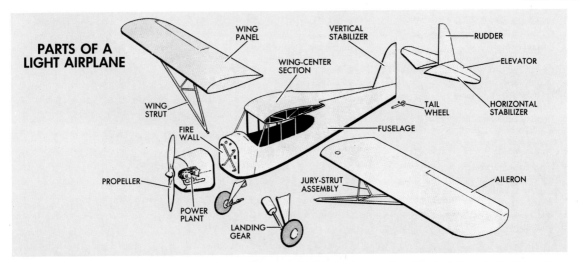

PARTS OF A LIGHT AIRPLANE

The first flying machine was a biplane. Almost universal today is the monoplane, whose single wing creates less drag. Triplanes and other multiplane aircraft have been built.

Monoplanes are high-wing when the wing is attached high on the fuselage; low-wing when it is fastened below the fuselage; and mid-wing when it is mounted through the fuselage. A parasol monoplane has the wing carried on struts above the fuselage.

The tips of a dihedral wing are higher than the wing roots; those of an anhedral wing are lower. A gull wing slants upward and then straightens out so that it resembles the wing of a gull. An inverted gull wing slants downward and then either flattens out or slopes upward. A flying wing is an airplane without a tail and with its fuselage incorporated into the wing. Wings are designed in many different shapes, such as rectangular, tapered, and elliptical. A swept-back wing has a backward slant; some aircraft are built with forward sweep. A delta wing looks like an isosceles triangle. Wing tips also vary and may be square, rounded, or pointed.

Power Plants, or Engines

Two types of power plants are the most widely used in aircraft today. They are the reciprocating engine and the jet engine. The reciprocating, or piston-driven, internal combustion engine is similar to the automobile engine (see Internal Combustion Engine). The jet, or reaction, engine may be of three principal types. The turbojet, or pure jet, does not have a propeller. The turbofan is a turbojet with a large fan supplementing the total thrust. In the turboprop, or prop jet, a turbine drives a propeller.

Most combat military aircraft and airline transports use jet engines. Most of the business-operated planes, trainers, and personally owned aircraft are powered by reciprocating engines.

Engines may be classified as single-engine, twin-engine, three-engine, and so on. They may also be grouped by location of the propeller. In the more common tractor type it is at the front of the engine and pulls the airplane through the air. In the pusher type it is at the rear and pushes the plane.

Civil and Military Aircraft

As airplanes have been required to do more things they have become more specialized in design (see Aviation). The bush pilot needs an airplane that can take off and land in a small space. The air force pilot requires a swift airplane. The airline pilot flies an airplane that can carry heavy loads long distances.

This specialization has produced two broad classes, military and civil. Military aircraft include bombers, fighters, and other planes of a country's air force, army, and navy. Civil aircraft are those used in general aviation or flown by the air carriers.

General aviation aircraft consist of all civil types except air carriers. They range from single-engine, one- and two-place planes flown by sportsmen to large multiengine, multiplace transports used by business corporations. The air carriers, or airlines, use many kinds of aircraft, depending upon the service required (see Airline). The planes may be short-, medium-, or long-range aircraft for intercity, transcontinental, or intercontinental flights.

Military aircraft include many specialized planes (see Air Force). There are long-range heavy bombers and low-altitude supersonic swing-wing bombers. Fighters are of two classes, fighter-interceptor and fighter-bomber or tactical fighter; the fast-climbing interceptor meets the enemy quickly to destroy it. The fighter-bomber can both fight and drop bombs.

Transports carry passengers, troops, and supplies. Tankers have large tanks to refuel other aircraft in flight; fuel is transferred by booms, which extend from the tanker to openings in the receiving aircraft.

Trainers are used to teach aircrews. They are of two types—pilot trainers and observer trainers for instructing navigators, bombardiers, engineers, and radio and gunnery specialists. Other types of military aircraft include reconnaissance, search and rescue, helicopter, observation, utility, research (or experimental), antisubmarine, carrier, and seaplanes.

PARTS OF A PASSENGER JET AIRPLANE

1. Weather Radar Scanner
2. Forward Retracting Wheels
3. Passenger Stairs That Telescope Under Floor
4. Center Section Fuel Cells (under floor)
5. Main Retracting Landing Gear
6. Leading Edge Slats and Anti-Icers
7. Low-Speed Outboard Aileron
8. Aileron Control Tab
9. Flight Speed Brakes
10. High-Speed Inboard Aileron
11. Ground Speed Brakes
12. Turbofan Engines (sides and center)
13. Dual Rudder Segments
14. Horizontal Stabilizer
15. Elevator
16. Elevator Control Tab
17. Passenger Seating
18. High Lift Trailing Edge Flaps
19. Galley
20. Control Cabin

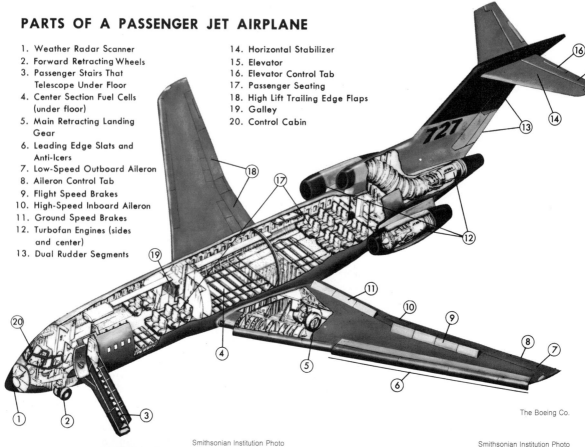

The Boeing Co.

Cessna 172

Beech Baron

Gates Learjet 50

Douglas DC-7C

The Boeing Co.

Boeing 767

Smithsonian Institution Photo

McDonnell Douglas DC-10

Boeing 747

Smithsonian Institution Photo

Concorde

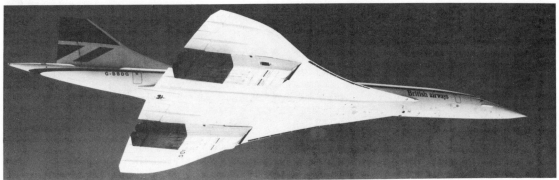

Smithsonian Institution Photo

The Boeing Co.

The Boeing Co.

E-3A Sentry warning and control aircraft

Boeing KC-135 Stratotanker

U.S. Air Force Photo

F-15 Fighter-bomber

Beech C-12

McDonnell Douglas F-18A Hornet

Smithsonian Institution Photo

Smithsonian Institution Photo

Lockheed S-3A Viking

ARAVA/STOL

Smithsonian Institution Photo

Israel Aircraft Industries Ltd.

FORCES WHICH ACT UPON AN AIRPLANE IN FLIGHT

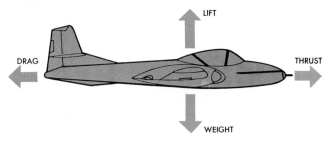

Aerodynamics

AIRPLANE MOVES ALONG 3 AXES

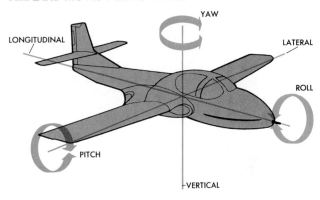

How is an airplane able to fly? The answer is explained by the science called aerodynamics. This is the study of air in motion and the forces that act on solid surfaces moving through the air. The name aerodynamics is a combination of the Greek terms *aer*, meaning "air," and *dynamis*, meaning "power." It is the reaction of the air on the specially shaped wing, or airfoil, that lifts an airplane off the ground and supports it aloft.

Four Forces of Flight

Lift is one of the four forces that act on an airplane. The others are weight (or gravity), drag, and thrust. Lift is an upward force that offsets the airplane's weight. Drag is air resistance to forward motion. Thrust produced by the power plant counteracts drag.

Scientific principles developed by Sir Isaac Newton and Daniel Bernoulli explain what makes lift possible. Newton's third law of motion states that for every action there must be an opposite and equal reaction. Therefore, since a wing is an inclined plane similar to a kite, it deflects the air downward and the air in turn deflects the wing upward. Impact pressure of the air striking the wing's under-surface produces about 30 percent of the lift of a wing.

Bernoulli's law, called the Bernoulli effect, states that an increase in the velocity of air reduces the static pressure. The Venturi tube of a carburetor illustrates this law. It is wide at each end but narrows in the middle. As moving air passes through the throat it speeds up and its static pressure decreases. The low static air pressure in the nozzle leading from the throat draws fuel into the tube from a bowl that is under normal atmospheric pressure.

A wing in cross section is shaped like a side of a Venturi tube. Moving air has farther to go over its curved, or cambered, upper surface than over its flatter lower surface. The air moves more rapidly over the top than it does over the bottom and thus exerts

CENTER OF GRAVITY

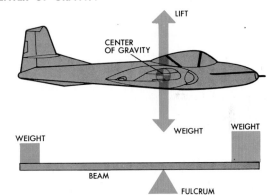

Airplane is like a beam on a fulcrum.
Lift force must be at or near center
of gravity for plane to be level in flight.

less downward pressure. This pressure differential between the top and the bottom of the wing produces about 70 percent of its lift.

Factors Affecting Lift

The lift of a wing may be increased by the angle of attack, airfoil shape, outline shape, airspeed, wing size, and air density. The angle of attack is the angle formed by the airfoil chord and relative wind. The chord is the line joining the leading and trailing edges. Relative wind is the flow of air in relation to the wing. It is parallel to and opposite the flight path.

179

AIR PRESSURE KEEPS AIRPLANE ALOFT

A simple experiment to demonstrate lift of a wing

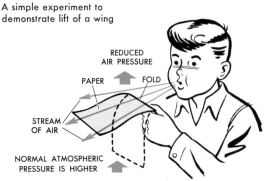

Blowing over upper surface of paper makes it rise, not fall. Blowing increases speed of air and lowers pressure. Normal higher atmospheric pressure beneath paper pushes it up. This illustrates Bernoulli's law.

VENTURI TUBE BASED ON BERNOULLI'S LAW

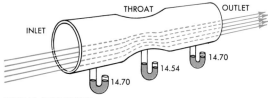

NORMAL ATMOSPHERIC PRESSURE 14.70 LBS. PER SQUARE INCH

WING WAS DEVELOPED FROM VENTURI TUBE

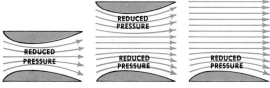

Narrowing of Venturi tube speeds air flow

Same action in larger tube as long as there is any restriction to flow

Same action over half of Venturi tube which is like a section of a wing

HOW AIR PRESSURE GIVES LIFT TO A WING

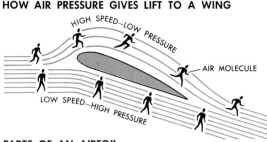

PARTS OF AN AIRFOIL

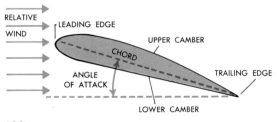

The motion may be that of air flowing past the wing or of the wing moving through the air.

The greater the angle of attack the more the lift. If a pilot wishes to climb he pulls up the nose of the plane and thereby increases the angle of attack. If he points the nose too high, however, the angle of attack will be too great and the plane will stall. At too high an angle the air no longer flows smoothly over the wing but burbles and slows down, decreasing lift. The angle of attack differs from the angle of incidence, which is formed by the chord of the wing and the longitudinal axis of the airplane.

Larger wings have more lift, as do wings with greater camber, or curvature. A long narrow wing has more lift than a short wide one because less of a swirl, or vortex, develops at the smaller tip to produce drag. The ratio between length, or span, and average chord width is aspect ratio. Wings with high aspect ratio are more efficient.

The faster the airplane flies the greater is the lift. At higher speeds the air travels faster around the wing, decreasing the pressure on the top surface and increasing the impact pressure on the lower surface. Finally, the density of the air itself affects lift (see Atmosphere). The density varies with altitude, temperature, and humidity.

High-lift devices, such as flaps and slots, reduce landing speed. A flap is a control surface hinged at the trailing edge of each wing. When lowered it increases the curved surface of the wing for more lift. It also acts as an air brake by increasing drag. A slot is a long narrow opening between the leading edge of a wing and an auxiliary airfoil. It permits air to flow smoothly over the wing and increases lift.

Forms of Drag

Since drag makes an engine work harder to provide thrust to overcome it, engineers have streamlined aircraft. The total drag is the sum of an airplane's profile, induced, and parasite drag.

Profile drag is caused by the shape of the airfoil and by skin friction. The clinging of air to the outer surface of the airplane is called skin friction. Air is fluid and therefore has viscosity, or stickiness. Aircraft surfaces are made smooth in order to reduce skin friction.

The thin layer of air next to the airplane skin is called the boundary layer. Its velocity is slower than that of the main airstream because of skin friction. Airflow in the boundary layer may be laminar or turbulent. In laminar flow the air moves in sheets, or layers, which slide smoothly over each other. In turbulent flow the layers mix and cause drag.

Systems that control the boundary layer reduce drag. These include porous surfaces, slots, and other devices that are designed for blowing or sucking the air over the wings (see Aerospace, section on Research and Development).

Induced drag is due to lift. It is caused by the sheet of high-speed air rushing across the wing's curved upper surface. As this sheet of air leaves the trailing edge of the wing, it has a slight downward direction so that it interrupts the smooth flow of lower-speed air under the wing. This causes drag. Parasite drag is resistance from parts of the airplane other than the lifting surfaces.

Thrust is the force that drives an airplane forward and opposes drag. A propeller or a jet or rocket engine develops thrust (*see* section on Power Plants; Jet Propulsion; Rockets).

Weight is the force of gravity acting on the airplane and its contents. The point where the total weight of the airplane is concentrated is the center of gravity. The loading of an airplane must be planned with care so that it will be in balance. The lift force must act on or very near the center of gravity if the airplane is to be level in flight.

Aircraft Stability and Control

Aeronautical engineers design stability and controllability into aircraft. An airplane is stable if it flies a straight and level course with no attention to the controls by the pilot. If a gust of wind disturbs a stable plane whose controls are held at neutral it rights itself.

An airplane rotates around three axes—the lateral, vertical, and longitudinal. All three pass through the center of gravity and are perpendicular to each other. The airplane pitches, or raises or lowers its nose, along its lateral axis, which extends from one wing tip to the other. It yaws, or turns right or left, about its vertical axis, which runs from the top to the bottom of the fuselage. It rolls, or dips its wings up or down, along its longitudinal axis, which extends from the nose to the tail.

The tail assembly and the wings provide stability along the axes. The fixed horizontal stabilizer prevents pitching. The fixed vertical stabilizer stops yawing. The wings counteract rolling and sideslipping. Dihedral, in which the wings' tips are higher than the roots, contributes to stability. If one wing drops, it has more lift than the raised wing and the plane rights itself. Sweepback, or backward slant of the wings, produces stability in almost the same manner. It also corrects yawing by creating more drag farther ahead on the wing than on the aft portion.

An airplane has controllability if it can be flown effectively and easily. The controls include the control stick or wheel, rudder pedals, and throttle (*see* section on Flight Controls and Instruments). The control surfaces include ailerons, elevators, rudders, flaps, and trim tabs.

High-Speed Flight

During World War II fighter planes with piston engines approached the speed of sound (*see* Sound). After the war jet aircraft flew faster than sound. High-speed flight has created problems for engineers.

The basic problem is the compressibility of air. At subsonic speeds (less than the speed of sound) the wing creates pressure waves that move in front of it at the speed of sound to "warn" air particles in its

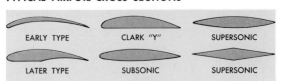

TYPICAL AIRFOIL CROSS SECTIONS

EARLY TYPE   CLARK "Y"   SUPERSONIC

LATER TYPE   SUBSONIC   SUPERSONIC

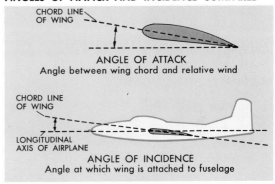

LIFT VARIES WITH ANGLE OF ATTACK

LOW ANGLE OF ATTACK

AIR PRESSURE   AIR FLOW

RELATIVE WIND

8°

HIGH ANGLE OF ATTACK

AIR PRESSURE   AIR FLOW

RELATIVE WIND

BURBLING

16°

Arrows pointing toward wing mean pressure is greater than that of atmosphere. Arrows pointing away from wing mean pressure is less than atmospheric. Lengths of arrows show intensity of pressure.

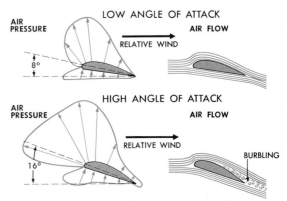

ANGLES OF ATTACK AND INCIDENCE COMPARED

CHORD LINE OF WING

ANGLE OF ATTACK
Angle between wing chord and relative wind

CHORD LINE OF WING

LONGITUDINAL AXIS OF AIRPLANE

ANGLE OF INCIDENCE
Angle at which wing is attached to fuselage

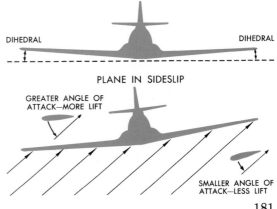

HOW DIHEDRAL RIGHTS AIRPLANE

LEVEL FLIGHT

DIHEDRAL   DIHEDRAL

PLANE IN SIDESLIP

GREATER ANGLE OF ATTACK—MORE LIFT

SMALLER ANGLE OF ATTACK—LESS LIFT

BREAKING THE SOUND BARRIER

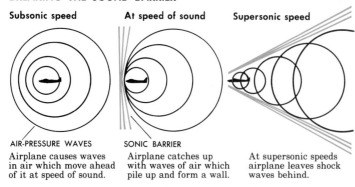

Subsonic speed

At speed of sound

Supersonic speed

AIR-PRESSURE WAVES

Airplane causes waves in air which move ahead of it at speed of sound.

SONIC BARRIER

Airplane catches up with waves of air which pile up and form a wall.

At supersonic speeds airplane leaves shock waves behind.

CHANGE IN SHAPE MAKES SUCCESS OUT OF FAILURE

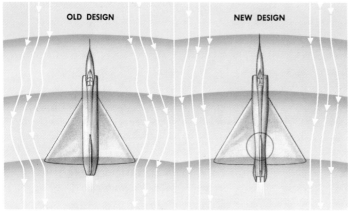

OLD DESIGN

NEW DESIGN

The Convair F-102 (left) failed to fly faster than sound. The redesigned pinched waist F-102A (right) applies the area rule and flies at supersonic speed.

BOUNDARY-LAYER CONTROL

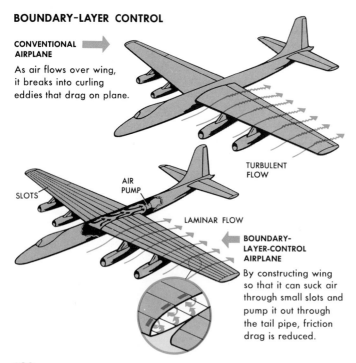

CONVENTIONAL AIRPLANE

As air flows over wing, it breaks into curling eddies that drag on plane.

TURBULENT FLOW

AIR PUMP

SLOTS

LAMINAR FLOW

BOUNDARY-LAYER-CONTROL AIRPLANE

By constructing wing so that it can suck air through small slots and pump it out through the tail pipe, friction drag is reduced.

182

path of its coming. The alerted particles change their direction and follow the shape of the wing.

At transonic speeds, in which different parts of an airplane may be near, at, or beyond the speed of sound, the pressure waves cannot warn air particles ahead that the airplane is coming because it is moving as fast as they are. The air piles up into a shock wave. The wings and control surfaces vibrate and buzz; controls become uncertain; and the airplane is buffeted. Swept-back and triangular delta wings and boundary-layer control reduce drag.

A shock wave causes a thunderlike sonic boom as it spreads away from the plane. Sometimes persons on the ground can hear the boom. The shock wave may even break windows.

Supersonic speeds are faster than the speed of sound. They are measured by a Mach number instead of miles per hour. It is named for Austrian scientist Ernst Mach and expresses the ratio of the speed of an airplane to that of sound. At sea level the speed of sound is 760 mph, but the speed varies with air temperature and density. At the much colder altitude of 35,000 feet it is only 660 mph. At Mach 1 an airplane is flying at the speed of sound. At Mach 2 it is flying at twice the speed of sound. Hypersonic speed is Mach 5 or greater.

After an airplane penetrates the sonic, or sound, barrier, its flight is smooth because it is moving faster than the pressure waves it produces. They fall behind and cause no shock waves. Airplanes capable of supersonic flight have short, thin wings with knifelike leading edges. Engineers use the area rule principle to minimize drag. At the point where the wings are attached they give the fuselage a so-called wasp-waist, or Coke-bottle, shape.

At extremely high speeds airplanes encounter the thermal barrier. The friction of the air heats the airplane's skin to very high temperatures. At Mach 3 the boundary-layer temperature is above 600° F. Only such materials as toughened glass, titanium alloys, and stainless steel retain their strength at such temperatures. The plane may be cooled by internal refrigeration systems; transpiration cooling, which forces a coolant through holes in the skin; and ablation coatings on the plane's surface, which absorb heat by vaporizing.

Airplane Airframe

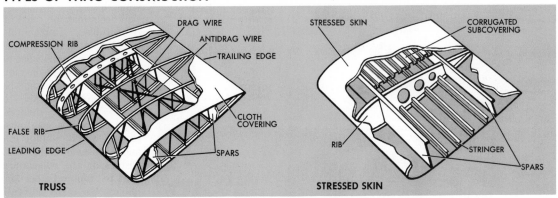

The airframe of an airplane is the basic plane without the power plant and other parts that are regularly replaced (*see* section on Power Plants). The major parts of the airframe are the fuselage, wings, tail assembly, engine mounts, and landing gear.

The Fuselage, or Body

The fuselage is the body of the airplane. The name comes from the French word *fuselé*, meaning "spindle-shaped." There are two main types of fuselage construction—truss and stressed skin.

The truss type is used in light planes. It consists of a framework of steel tubes that are welded, riveted, or bolted together in a series of trusses, or triangles. The tubes running the length of the fuselage are longerons. Connecting them are bracing membranes called struts. Formers and stringers are added to give the fuselage a streamlined shape.

Over the framework is a skin, or covering, of fabric, sheet aluminum or magnesium, or molded plastic or fiberglass. Fabric covering is painted with dope to shrink and waterproof it.

In the stressed-skin type of fuselage the skin bears all or part of the stresses acting on the airplane. The skin is usually sheet aluminum. There are two variations—monocoque and semimonocoque.

In the monocoque fuselage the skin is essentially a thin-walled tube that bears all the stresses. Monocoque is a French word meaning "single shell." More common is the semimonocoque. Its skin is reinforced by longerons. Rings, frames, and bulkheads shape and strengthen the skin.

The truss fuselage is built up with triangles. The monocoque is shaped like a tube; the semimonocoque has reinforcements.

The Wings

There are three types of wing structure—cantilever, semicantilever, and externally braced. The cantilever wing is made very strong and carries all stresses within itself. It is internally braced and not externally supported by struts or wires to the fuselage or landing gear. The semicantilever wing requires some external bracing. It can be made lighter. The externally braced wing is supported entirely by struts or wires. It can be made light in weight, but the external

TYPES OF WING CONSTRUCTION

The truss wing utilizes the principle of the triangle. It is a framework of spars, ribs, and braces.
In the stressed-skin wing the metal covering bears all or part of the bending and twisting stresses.

SOME TAIL ASSEMBLY DESIGNS

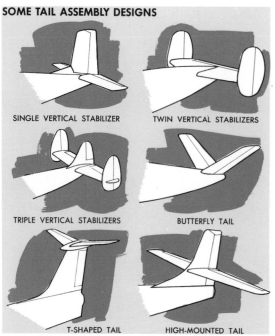

SINGLE VERTICAL STABILIZER

TWIN VERTICAL STABILIZERS

TRIPLE VERTICAL STABILIZERS

BUTTERFLY TAIL

T-SHAPED TAIL

HIGH-MOUNTED TAIL

There are many variations in the arrangement of the tail surfaces of an airplane. Some common types are shown here.

braces increase air drag. It is used for light planes.

Two types of construction are used for wings—truss and stressed skin. In the first type, truss design and external bracing to the fuselage withstand stresses. In the second type, the wing itself carries all or part of the stresses.

Both truss and stressed-skin wings consist of a

The Piper Cub (top) has a fixed landing gear. The landing gear on the McDonnell Douglas Phantom (bottom) is retractable.

Photos, (top) Piper Aircraft Corp.; (bottom) McDonnell Douglas Corp.

framework of spars and ribs. Long spars extend the length of the wing and bear most of the load. Fastened to the spars are curved ribs, which give the wing its shape. Over the ribs is a covering, or skin. Sometimes corrugated metal sheets or long stringers are placed under the skin for added strength.

The wing parts may be made of wood, but lightweight aluminum is more common. The skin may be doped fabric, plastic-bonded plywood, aluminum or magnesium alloy, stainless steel, or titanium.

The Tail Assembly, or Empennage

At the rear of the fuselage is the tail assembly, or empennage. The name empennage is derived from the French word *empenner*, meaning "to feather the arrow." Like feathers on an arrow, the empennage stabilizes the aircraft. The tail surfaces, like the wings, are made of spars, ribs, strings, and skin.

Engine Mounts

An engine mount is a framework of metal for attaching an engine to an airplane. It is often considered a part of the fuselage. Rubber pads cushion the vibration between the engine and the fuselage. Behind the engine is a fire wall for fire protection. The hollow pod-shaped structure in which an engine is mounted is called the nacelle. Detachable sections covering a power plant are engine cowlings.

The Landing Gear

The undercarriage on which an airplane rests while taking off or landing is the landing gear. It may consist of wheels or skids for land, skis for snow or ice, and floats, or pontoons, for water.

Landplanes have conventional, tricycle, or tandem landing gear. A conventional gear includes two main

HOW OLEO STRUT WORKS

The oleo strut absorbs the shock of landing. Oil and air help cushion the impact.

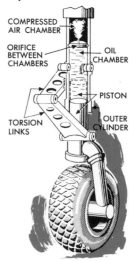

COMPRESSED AIR CHAMBER

ORIFICE BETWEEN CHAMBERS

OIL CHAMBER

PISTON

TORSION LINKS

OUTER CYLINDER

wheels and a tail wheel. A tricycle gear consists of two main wheels and a nose wheel. A tandem, or bicycle, gear has two main wheels or sets of wheels, one behind the other. Outrigger wheels support the wing tips.

Wheels may be fixed or retractable. Retractable wheels fold up into the fuselage, wings, or nacelles to reduce air drag. To cushion the impact of landing, the wheels are attached to shock-absorbing devices. Most airplanes use oleo struts, which employ oil and air to cushion the blow. Brakes on the wheels are used to stop and steer airplanes. On many aircraft the tail or nose wheel may be steered.

General Electric

General Electric CF6-6 high-bypass turbofan engines power
several versions of the McDonnell Douglas DC-10.

Power Plants

The power plant of an airplane corresponds with
the muscles of a bird. The muscles of a bird give it the
power to flap its wings and fly. Similarly, an engine
propels an airplane forward so that its fixed wings develop lift as they move through the air (*see* section on
Aerodynamics).

Years before the first powered flight, the Wright
brothers and others had flown in gliders (*see* section
on History). Perhaps the greatest achievement of Orville and Wilbur Wright was the building of an engine for their historic airplane (*see* Wright Brothers).

The Wright brothers built a 4-cylinder gasoline
engine that produced 12 horsepower and weighed 180
pounds. In contrast is the Pratt and Whitney R-4360
Wasp Major, ranked as one of the world's most pow-

The Wright brothers could not find a suitable engine to
power their airplane, so they built one themselves.

Smithsonian Institution

erful reciprocating engines. The Pratt and Whitney
has 28 cylinders in four banks, delivers 3,500 horsepower, and has 11,000 parts.

AIRPLANE ENGINES

The power plant of an airplane consists of its engine or engines, plus its propeller or propellers (if it
has any), accessories, and fuel and oil tanks and lines.
Its engine is a machine that converts energy, usually
in the form of heat, into work. Accessories include
carburetors, fuel and oil pumps, and other elements
not actually a part of the engine.

The internal combustion engine powers most aircraft today (*see* Internal Combustion Engine). The
combustion of fuel inside a chamber produces gas
pressure that gives the engine power. Two types of
internal combustion engines in wide use are the reciprocating, or piston, engine and the reaction engine.
The automobile has a reciprocating engine, and a
skyrocket has a reaction engine. The two general
classes of reaction engines are the jet, or air-breath-
ing, and the rocket, or non-air-breathing, engines.

A number of other types of propulsion systems for
aircraft and spacecraft are in the experimental stage
(*see* Aerospace, section on Research and Development; Space Travel). These include nuclear jet and
rocket, ionic, photon, solar, and antigravitational
propulsion.

Horsepower and Thrust

The power of aircraft engines is rated in different
ways. That of reciprocating engines is given in horsepower. One horsepower is specified as a unit of power
equal to the force necessary to raise 33,000 pounds
one foot in one minute.

185

AIRPLANE POWER PLANTS

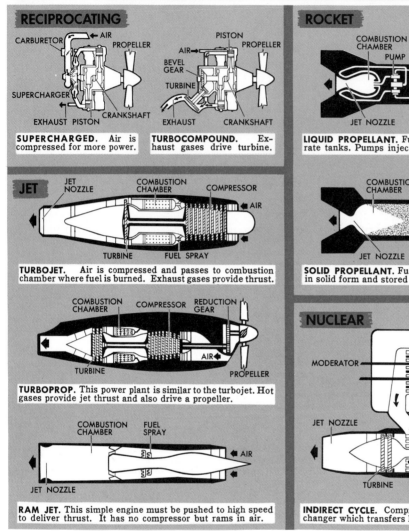

RECIPROCATING

SUPERCHARGED. Air is compressed for more power.

TURBOCOMPOUND. Exhaust gases drive turbine.

JET

TURBOJET. Air is compressed and passes to combustion chamber where fuel is burned. Exhaust gases provide thrust.

TURBOPROP. This power plant is similar to the turbojet. Hot gases provide jet thrust and also drive a propeller.

RAM JET. This simple engine must be pushed to high speed to deliver thrust. It has no compressor but rams in air.

ROCKET

LIQUID PROPELLANT. Fuel and oxidizer are liquids in separate tanks. Pumps inject them into combustion chamber.

SOLID PROPELLANT. Fuel and oxidizer are mixed together in solid form and stored in the combustion chamber itself.

NUCLEAR

INDIRECT CYCLE. Compressor forces air through an exchanger which transfers heat from the reactor to the air.

Turbojet, turbofan, pulse-jet, ramjet, and rocket engines are rated by the pounds of thrust they produce. One pound of thrust equals one horsepower at 375 miles an hour. The turboprop engine uses almost all the gas turbine's thrust to turn a propeller, and its power is stated as equivalent-shaft horsepower.

Reciprocating Engines

The reciprocating engine is the type most widely used in aircraft. It gets its name from the back-and-forth movement of a piston in a cylinder (*see* Motors and Engines; Automobile). When a fuel-air mixture is ignited, it burns. The expanding gases push the piston downward in order to rotate a crankshaft and turn a propeller.

Reciprocating engines may be radial, in-line, or opposed, depending upon the arrangement of their cylinders. In the radial engine the cylinders are distributed around the crankshaft like spokes on a wheel.

The cylinders may be in a single row, in twin rows, or in multiple rows. The in-line engine has one or more rows of cylinders, each behind the other. The rows may be arranged in a "V," "X," or "W" pattern. The opposed engine has two rows of cylinders placed across from each other horizontally, one on either side of the crankshaft.

Piston engines may be air-cooled or liquid-cooled. Today most of them are cooled by air blowing over fins on the cylinders. In the automobilelike liquid-cooled system a liquid circulates around the cylinders and through a radiator to carry away heat.

Airplanes that fly in the thin air of high altitudes may be equipped with a supercharger. This is a compressor that pumps extra air into the engine for added power. Most superchargers are of the centrifugal type, with an impeller, or bevel gear, which is driven by the crankshaft. In the turbosupercharger an exhaust-driven turbine rotates the impeller. The compound, or turbocompound, engine also uses exhaust gases for more power by driving a turbine geared to the crankshaft.

Reaction Engines

A reaction engine gets its thrust from gases blasting rearward like a blowtorch. It moves forward, or reacts, in accordance with Sir Isaac Newton's third law of motion. This law states that to every action there is an equal and opposite reaction.

An example of this principle is the holiday firework rocket. When a skyrocket is fired, expanding gases escape from it to hurl it high into the sky. It is not the gases rushing out of the skyrocket and pushing against the outside air that drive it ahead. Rather it is the gases inside the skyrocket pressing against the inside front wall that thrust it forward.

Reaction engines are classified according to whether or not they carry their own oxygen for fuel combustion. The jet engine obtains oxygen from the atmosphere. The rocket engine, however, does not depend upon atmospheric oxygen and can go into outer space.

Jet Engines

Jet engines are of three types—the gas turbine, pulse-jet, and ramjet (see Jet Propulsion). The gas turbine has a turbine-driven compressor that compresses air for combustion. The pulse-jet and ramjet compress air by other means.

The two main types of gas-turbine engines are the turbojet and turboprop. In the turbojet the gases resulting from combustion not only rotate the turbine to drive the compressor but also create the thrust-producing jet. In the turboprop, or propjet, the turbine drives both the compressor and a propeller. It creates thrust from its jet but produces most of it from its propeller. An afterburner added to a turbojet increases its thrust. It is an auxiliary combustion chamber, attached to the tail pipe, in which additional fuel is burned to utilize unused oxygen in the exhaust gases from the turbine.

Another turbojet with increased thrust is the turbofan engine. It gets more power by handling more air. It is also called the ducted-fan, aft-fan, or bypass engine. One version has a propellerlike fan enclosed in a duct at the front of the engine. It gulps in air in great quantities and passes some of it around the combustion chamber to add an independent thrust to the exhaust gases in the jet stream. In another type the fan takes in air behind the combustion chamber.

The British bypass engine has a low-pressure compressor in front of a high-pressure compressor. Part of the airflow goes to the high-pressure compressor. The balance bypasses it and mixes with the exhaust.

The pulse-jet is an intermittent-firing jet, while the ramjet is a continuous-firing type. Both must be boosted to high speed by some other kind of propulsion to start combustion.

Shutters in the front end of the pulse-jet open and close to take in air intermittently. This produces power in a series of rapid explosions. It is not as efficient as the turbojet or ramjet. The noisy pulse-jet engine powered the German V-1 buzz bomb during World War II.

The ramjet is the simplest jet engine because it has no moving parts. It is an open-end smoke pipe that rams air in as the engine moves forward and burns fuel continuously to produce forward thrust. It is used for missiles and experimental aircraft.

Rocket Engines

The rocket engine powered the German V-2 missile during World War II (see Guided Missiles; Rockets). There are two types—liquid propellant and solid propellant. Hybrid-propellant rocket engines under development use a solid fuel and a liquid oxidizer or the reverse. Rocket engines are used in missiles and research planes such as the North American X-15A-2.

Electric Engines

Electric engines can be used to propel spaceships on deep-space missions. These engines produce low thrust for long periods. There are three basic types, each differing in the method used to accelerate the propellant. The arc-jet, or electrothermal, engine utilizes an electric arc discharge to heat a propellant gas. The gas expands through a nozzle, producing thrust. The ion, or electrostatic, engine employs cesium ions accelerated by an electrostatic field to create thrust. The plasma, or magnetohydrodynamic (MHD), engine uses an ionized gas accelerated by an electromagnetic field to produce thrust.

ELECTRIC PROPULSION ENGINES

ION ENGINE (CONTACT TYPE)

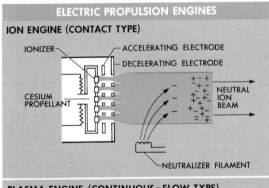

PLASMA ENGINE (CONTINUOUS - FLOW TYPE)

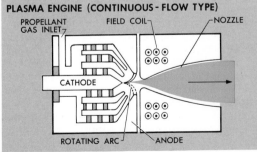

In the ion engine the positive cesium ions are first accelerated, then decelerated to adjust their velocities, and finally neutralized by electrons to prevent the buildup of an electric charge on the spacecraft. The plasma engine uses an ionized propellant gas such as argon or nitrogen.

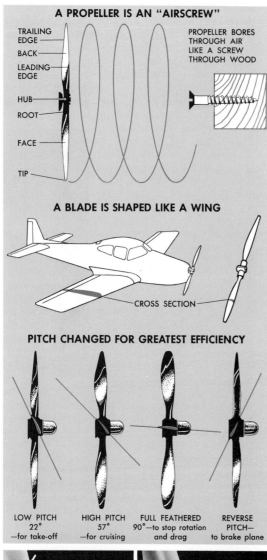

A PROPELLER IS AN "AIRSCREW"

TRAILING EDGE
BACK
LEADING EDGE
HUB
ROOT
FACE
TIP

PROPELLER BORES THROUGH AIR LIKE A SCREW THROUGH WOOD

A BLADE IS SHAPED LIKE A WING

CROSS SECTION

PITCH CHANGED FOR GREATEST EFFICIENCY

LOW PITCH 22° —for take-off

HIGH PITCH 57° —for cruising

FULL FEATHERED 90°—to stop rotation and drag

REVERSE PITCH— to brake plane

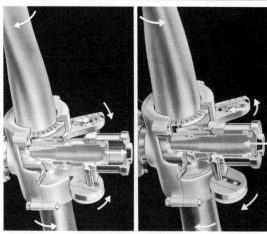

When the hubcap of a controllable-pitch propeller is moved forward, the blades turn at low pitch (left). For high pitch (right), the cap is pulled back.

AIRPLANE PROPELLERS

In the jet age more and more aircraft have propellerless turbojet engines. Many airplanes, however, are still being powered by piston or turboprop engines that turn propellers (*see* Jet Propulsion).

A propeller is a device so shaped that when it is rotated it produces a force, or thrust, which pulls or pushes an airplane through the air. It is called a prop for short. It may have two, three, four, or more arms, or blades. They are fastened to a hub that is attached to the crankshaft.

A propeller blade is actually a small wing. In cross section it is an airfoil (*see* section on Aerodynamics). When it rotates, its curved front surface creates a low-pressure area in front of it just as the top of a wing does. Its flatter rear surface creates a high-pressure area and pushes air rearward. A forward lift or thrust results that causes the propeller to move forward, pulling the airplane with it.

Most aircraft have tractor propellers. They are mounted at the front of the engine ahead of the wing and pull the airplane through the air. A few aircraft have pusher propellers. They are at the rear of an engine behind the wing and push the plane. Counterrotating propellers have two sets of blades, one behind the other, revolving in opposite directions.

Light planes often have laminated wood propellers. Aluminum or magnesium alloy props are machined from forgings. Steel props may be solid or hollow.

Variable Pitch

The British call a propeller an airscrew, because a propeller bites into the air as a screw bores into wood. It is twisted to provide a small blade angle at its tip, where greater speed is needed, and a large blade angle at its root, where less speed is required. The angle, or pitch, determines the distance the blade moves forward in one revolution. A blade at high pitch takes a bigger bite of air than at low pitch. A plane with a prop at high pitch is like an automobile in high gear. It moves forward a great distance with each turn of the prop. High pitch is best for cruising; low pitch, for taking off or climbing.

Many small aircraft use a one-piece fixed-pitch propeller whose angle cannot be changed. The blades of the adjustable-pitch propeller are clamped in the hub and their angle can be altered on the ground. The pilot can change the blade angle of a controllable-pitch propeller while in flight. He operates the controls mechanically, hydraulically, or electrically. A variation is the constant-speed propeller. A governor automatically adjusts the pitch of this type of propeller to the engine's speed.

If engine failure occurs, a propeller will windmill, or continue to rotate, and cause drag. Props on multiengine planes can be feathered, or turned edgewise to the air, in order to stop rotation. Reversible-pitch propellers can be adjusted to change the direction of the thrust. This slows down the plane in flight or when it is landing.

Flight Controls and Instruments

Beech Aircraft Corporation

Primary flight controls on an airplane are the wheel, rudder pedals, and throttle. Some aircraft have a verticle control stick instead of a wheel.

To regulate the movement and position, or attitude, of an airplane a pilot uses a number of different flight controls. They consist of a system of levers, pedals, throttles, cables, pulleys, instruments, and other equipment.

FLIGHT CONTROLS

Flight controls include a control stick between the pilot's knees or a control wheel, a pair of rudder pedals, and a throttle. The pilot pulls the stick backward to raise the aircraft's nose and pushes the stick forward to lower the nose. He moves the stick sideways to bank the plane. He turns the nose right or left with the foot pedals. He controls engine power by using the throttle.

The Control Stick and Wheel

The control stick is connected by cables to the elevator, which is hinged to the horizontal stabilizer. Pushing the stick forward tilts the elevator down. This changes the angle of attack of the stabilizer; that is, the angle at which the stabilizer strikes the airflow. It now has more lift so that the tail is raised and the nose is lowered (*see* section on Aerodynamics). Pulling the stick backward lowers the tail and raises the nose.

The control stick is also connected to cables that run into each wing to the ailerons. These are small hinged surfaces on the trailing edge of the wings near the tips. When the control stick is pushed to the right, the aileron on the right wing is raised and the aileron on the left wing is lowered. This reduces the airflow over the right aileron and decreases its lift, which lowers the right wing. At the same time the lowered aileron on the left wing increases its lift. This banks the airplane to the right. In a similar manner the aircraft is banked to the left.

Instead of a vertical control stick on the floor, some airplanes have a wheel extending out from the instrument panel. Turning the wheel to the right or left has the same effect as moving the stick in the same direction. Moving the wheel backward or forward raises or lowers the airplane's nose.

The Rudder

The two foot pedals are connected by cables to the rudder, which is hinged to the vertical stabilizer on the tail. If the left pedal is pushed forward, the rudder turns to the left and a sideways force to the right is created on the tail. The airplane's nose then moves to the left.

Some airplanes have a single rudder bar instead of separate pedals. The pilot's feet rest on the bar, which is pivoted in the center.

Secondary Controls

Modern airplanes have secondary high-lift devices and control surfaces. Among these are flaps, slots and slats, and trim tabs.

Flaps are hinged control surfaces on the trailing edge of the wing. The pilot lowers them a little in takeoff to get lift with a small increase in drag. In landing he lowers them much more for a proportionately greater increase in drag, thus permitting a steeper approach. He controls them with a wheel or crank in the cockpit.

The slot is a narrow air gap on the leading edge of a wing. Air passes through the slot and flows smoothly over the wing to prevent stalls. Slots may be fixed or movable, operating automatically. A movable slot operated by small motors under the pilot's control is called a slat.

189

HOW ELEVATORS CAUSE AIRPLANE TO CLIMB AND DIVE

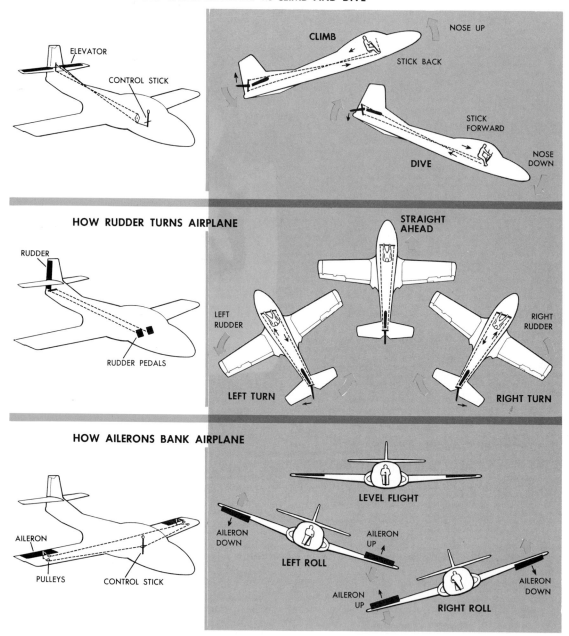

Trim tabs are small control surfaces on the rudder, elevators, and ailerons. They balance the airplane by adjusting for small shifts in weight as fuel is used up or passengers move about. Usually they are operated by small wheels next to the pilot.

Basic Flight Techniques

The flight maneuvers that the pilot masters first are takeoff, landing, turns, stalls, climbing, gliding, dives, and sideslips. Spins are usually not taught until the pilot has become proficient in the basic maneuvers, because modern training planes are considered spinproof. Aerobatics such as loops, rolls, and Immelmann turns are learned later.

The Takeoff

Takeoff is preceded by a walk-around inspection of the airplane by the pilot. After the engine is started he taxis to the runway. Takeoffs are made into the wind rather than downwind or crosswind. The added speed of the air over the wings gives greater lift and permits a shorter takeoff run.

The pilot stops the airplane near the end of the runway and opens the throttle wide to check the engine performance. When he sees no aircraft nearby he taxis out on the runway. The throttle is pushed forward until maximum power is obtained.

If the airplane has a conventional landing gear with a tail wheel, there is a tendency for the tail to rise. The pilot aids this by pushing the stick forward slightly. When the tail has come up so that the wings are parallel to the runway the pilot centers the stick again. In this attitude the airplane will fly itself off the ground. If the airplane has a tricycle landing gear with a nose wheel, its normal position is suited for quick acceleration.

Once the airplane has lifted off the runway the pilot tries to climb quickly to a safe altitude and to fly out of the airport's traffic pattern. Under normal circumstances the aircraft is leveled off and engine power is reduced from maximum to cruising setting as soon as an altitude of 400 feet is reached. To enter the traffic pattern a level 90-degree left turn is made. If the pilot wants to leave the pattern, he then turns away at a 45-degree angle to the right. If he wants to go around the airport and land again he is required to climb to 600 feet.

The Climb, Glide, and Dive

To climb the pilot pulls back on the stick to put the wings at a higher angle of attack for more lift. This raises the nose of the plane. At the same time he opens the throttle.

In a glide the pilot reduces or cuts his throttle. Earth's gravity provides the power for descent. As speed is reduced a decrease in lift results. The nose of the airplane is lowered but it still remains above the glide path.

To dive the pilot pushes the stick forward. This lessens the angle of attack and noses the plane down. Unlike the glide, in the dive the nose is lower than the horizon. The descent, made with or without engine power, is rapid.

Turns

A turn is made by using both the rudder and ailerons at the same time. If the rudder alone is used the airplane will skid, or slide sideways, just as an automobile does on an icy street. If the ailerons alone are used the airplane will sideslip, or slip sideways and downward. A pilot sometimes purposely sideslips to lose altitude quickly.

Stalls

When an airplane does not have enough lift to keep it airborne, it stalls. A stall may occur when the pilot pulls back on the stick, raising the nose and increasing the angle of attack of the wing to too great a degree for the speed at which the plane is flying. The aircraft continues to lose speed and the controls feel sloppy. Air burbles over the top of the wing and causes the airplane to shudder. When the stall occurs, the nose drops suddenly and the aircraft loses altitude rapidly even though the pilot has the stick pulled back.

The pilot recovers from the stall by pushing the stick forward to lower the nose and build up airspeed. When the controls become effective again, he pulls the stick back and resumes level flight.

If during the stall the pilot pushes the rudder full right or left, the airplane will spin. In a spin the airplane dives and spirals at the same time.

Landing

Landings must be made according to government regulations. If the airport is a large one with a traffic control tower, the aircraft should receive a radio or blinker-light signal for clearance to land, except in an emergency. The pilot should fly over a small airport at about 1,500 feet to determine wind direction and which runway is in use. Landings are made into the wind to lower the plane's ground speed.

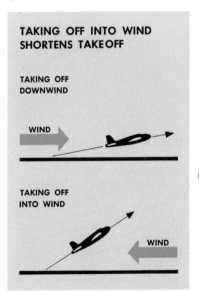

TAKING OFF INTO WIND SHORTENS TAKEOFF

TAKING OFF DOWNWIND

WIND

TAKING OFF INTO WIND

WIND

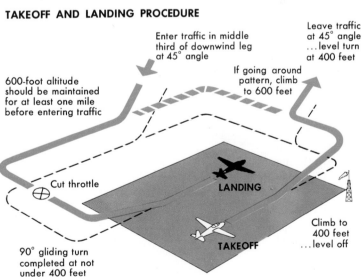

TAKEOFF AND LANDING PROCEDURE

Enter traffic in middle third of downwind leg at 45° angle

Leave traffic at 45° angle ...level turn at 400 feet

600-foot altitude should be maintained for at least one mile before entering traffic

If going around pattern, climb to 600 feet

Cut throttle

LANDING

90° gliding turn completed at not under 400 feet

TAKEOFF

Climb to 400 feet ...level off

HOW AN AIRPLANE STALLS AND RECOVERS

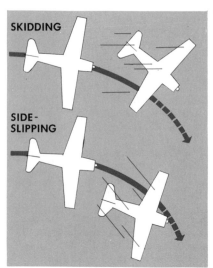

ANGLE OF ATTACK
5°

1.
5°
2.
20°
3.
+ STALL
20°
4.
5. 10°
10° 5°
6. 7.

1. Normal flight

2. Throttle closed
...nose drops

3. Back pressure on elevator
increases angle of attack
...plane stalls

4. Plane descends

5. Back pressure
released...nose drops

6. Plane regains speed
and lift

7. Throttle opened...
normal flight resumed

SKIDDING

SIDE-
SLIPPING

In preparing to land, the pilot flies at least one mile beyond the airport and descends to 600 feet. He approaches the downwind leg of the traffic pattern at a 45-degree angle. At the end of the runway he makes a 90-degree left turn into the base leg. Then he cuts back his throttle and makes another 90-degree gliding turn to the left into the final approach.

If it looks as though the airplane will touch ground short of the runway, the pilot must avoid the danger of trying to stretch his glide. The normal reaction is to pull the nose of the airplane up. This will cut down the airspeed and possibly cause a stall. The proper procedure is to nose the airplane down so that it will pick up speed. Even though it will lose altitude it will have sufficient forward speed to remain under control for a safe landing.

Landings are essentially abbreviated stalls made just above the runway so that the airplane's lift is reduced to slightly less than its weight. The plane then settles gently to the ground. The pilot must accurately control the speed and angle of attack as he skims over the runway. When the wheels are only a few feet above the ground, the pilot pulls his stick all the way back. The airplane settles to the runway.

A perfect landing for an airplane with a tail wheel is for all three wheels to touch the ground at once in a three-point landing. Usually the two main wheels are touched down first to avoid damaging the tail. The two main wheels should always touch first in landing an aircraft with tricycle landing gear.

If a pilot begins the final stage of landing (called flare-out) too high in the air, he will stall the airplane. The aircraft then drops down with great force in a pancake landing. It will bounce if the pilot begins his flare-out too late or lands too fast.

After all the wheels are on the ground a great deal of forward momentum remains. The pilot must use the brakes to steer and stop the airplane.

FLAPS INCREASE LIFT

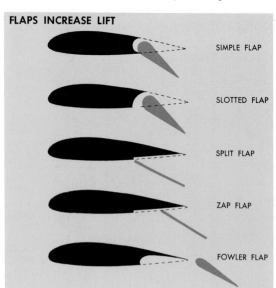

SIMPLE FLAP

SLOTTED FLAP

SPLIT FLAP

ZAP FLAP

FOWLER FLAP

SLOTS REDUCE TURBULENCE

SLOT

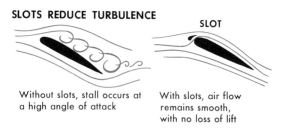

Without slots, stall occurs at a high angle of attack

With slots, air flow remains smooth, with no loss of lift

FLAPS PERMIT SMALLER LANDING SPACE

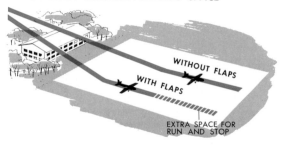

WITHOUT FLAPS

WITH FLAPS

EXTRA SPACE FOR
RUN AND STOP

AIRPLANE INSTRUMENTS

The instrument panel of an airliner or a bomber presents a seemingly confusing cluster of dials, switches, and levers. The pilot does not have to watch all of these hundreds of instruments at one time, however. In addition, they are conveniently grouped, according to their special use.

The early aviators flew "by the seat of their pants," relying on their senses to tell them the position, or attitude, of their plane. Flying by instinct, however, was unreliable because the pilot could easily become confused. He might, for example, confuse the pull of centrifugal force with that of the Earth's gravity. Airplane instruments prevent such mistakes. They also permit "blind," or instrument, flying when the ground or horizon is obscured by fog, rain, clouds, snow, or darkness.

Airplane instruments are mechanical, electrical, and electronic devices that tell the pilot about the plane and its performance. Flight instruments indicate speed, altitude, and direction. Navigation instruments give directional bearings. Engine instruments show how the power plant is functioning. Equipment instruments tell how the mechanical and electrical systems are operating.

Boeing Co.

In the cockpit of the Boeing 707 jet airliner, the captain sits at the left, the copilot at the right, and the flight engineer in the right foreground.

Aircraft instruments are conveniently grouped. In this Beechcraft *Bonanza*, for example, primary flight instruments (left) are in front of the pilot's seat; engine instruments in the center; and radios for communication and navigation at the pilot's far right.

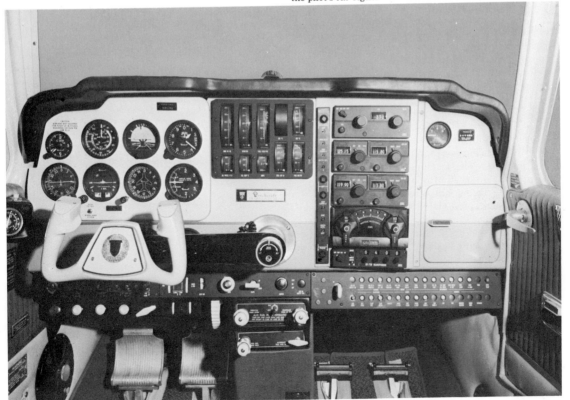

By courtesy of Beech Aircraft Corp.

Flight Instruments

The only flight instruments a light plane actually needs are an airspeed indicator, an altimeter, and a turn-and-bank indicator. A compass and a clock will suffice for navigation. A tachometer, oil-pressure and oil-temperature gauges, and a fuel gauge are the necessary engine instruments. Most planes, however, require many more instruments.

The airspeed indicator tells the pilot the speed of air flowing past the airplane. If there is no wind, the airspeed and the ground speed are the same. A tail wind increases the ground speed. For example, if an airplane has an airspeed of 100 mph with a 25 mph tail wind, the ground speed is 125 mph. On the other hand, a head wind decreases the ground speed.

The airspeed indicator operates by air pressure transmitted from the Pitot-static tube. Actually this is two tubes in one. The Pitot tube has an open end that protrudes from the wing, nose, or vertical stabilizer. It measures the impact of the airstream. The static tube is closed in front, but small holes in its sides supply it with still air. It measures the atmospheric pressure. The airspeed indicator is a hollow diaphragm connected to the Pitot tube. Its case is joined to the static tube. The Pitot pressure forces the diaphragm to expand or contract with the increase or decrease in speed. The difference between Pitot and static pressures is registered by levers and gears leading to a pointer.

The airspeed is indicated on the dial in statute miles or nautical miles (knots) per hour. The instrument registers true airspeed only in still air at normal atmospheric pressure (*see* Atmosphere). At different altitudes and temperatures the atmospheric pressure varies. The indicated airspeed (IAS) must be corrected to true airspeed (TAS) by adding 2 percent to the IAS for every 1,000 feet that the plane climbs above sea level.

Jet aircraft have a special airspeed indicator, the machmeter. It measures the airspeed in relation to the speed of sound and gives the maximum safe speed. High performance aircraft also use the accelerometer, or G-meter. It shows how great a load is being imposed on the plane's structure in high-speed dives and turns.

The altimeter indicates the altitude above sea level or the ground in feet. The barometric altimeter is an aneroid barometer (*see* Barometer). It measures variations in air pressure with changes in altitude. A metal diaphragm is housed in a case connected to the static tube. The diaphragm expands and contracts as air pressure in the case changes. Levers and gears connect the diaphragm to a pointer.

The altimeter reads zero at the average sea-level pressure of 29.92 inches. At different geographical locations the barometric pressure varies according to the elevation and weather conditions. The pilot en route radios for the local sea-level barometric reading and adjusts his altimeter to this setting with a knob. When landing he asks the controller for the airport barometric pressure and adjusts his altimeter to show the height above the runway.

The absolute altimeter, or terrain-clearance indicator, gives the height of the plane above the earth. It measures the time lapse between the transmission of a radio signal to the ground and its return.

The rate-of-climb, or vertical-speed, indicator shows the rate of ascent or descent in thousands of feet per minute. It consists of a metal diaphragm connected to the Pitot-static tube. Its case is vented to the static line through a small hole, the "calibrated leak." As the plane changes altitude, the pressure change in the case lags behind that in the diaphragm. This pressure difference moves the diaphragm, which is mechanically linked to a pointer.

The turn-and-bank indicator is two instruments in one. The turn indicator tells the direction and rate of the plane's turn. The dial needle, vertical when the plane is in straight flight, shows turns in degrees per second. A gyroscope operates the needle (*see* Gyroscope). The bank indicator shows slipping or skidding in a turn. A ball is sealed in a curved, liquid-filled

The air-speed indicator measures the difference between Pitot, or impact, and static, or still, air pressures as transmitted from the Pitot-static tube.

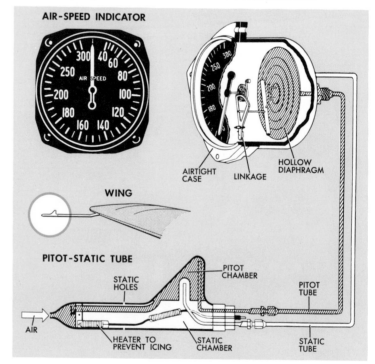

AIR-SPEED INDICATOR

AIR SPEED

AIRTIGHT CASE   LINKAGE   HOLLOW DIAPHRAGM

WING

PITOT-STATIC TUBE

STATIC HOLES

PITOT CHAMBER

AIR

PITOT TUBE

HEATER TO PREVENT ICING

STATIC CHAMBER

STATIC TUBE

FLIGHT INSTRUMENTS HELP THE PILOT FLY

ALTIMETER

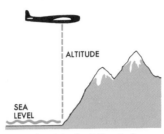

ALTITUDE

SEA LEVEL

The pressure altimeter indicates the altitude of the airplane in feet. It uses an aneroid barometer to measure air pressure.

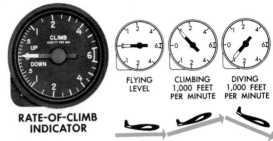

RATE-OF-CLIMB INDICATOR

FLYING LEVEL   CLIMBING 1,000 FEET PER MINUTE   DIVING 1,000 FEET PER MINUTE

Differences in air pressure operate this instrument to indicate the plane's rate of climb or descent in feet per minute.

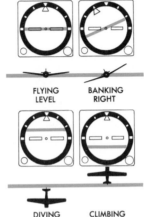

ATTITUDE GYRO

FLYING LEVEL   BANKING RIGHT

DIVING   CLIMBING

This gyro-operated instrument provides an artificial horizon to show the attitude of the airplane in relation to the Earth.

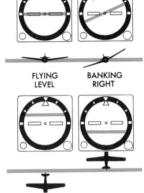

TURN-AND-BANK INDICATOR

This flight instrument indicates the direction rate of turn of an airplane and also shows its skidding or slipping in a turn.

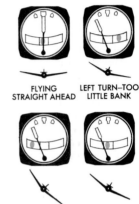

FLYING STRAIGHT AHEAD   LEFT TURN—TOO LITTLE BANK

LEFT TURN—TOO MUCH BANK   LEFT TURN—CORRECT BANK

glass tube. If a turn is executed properly, the ball remains in the center. If the plane skids, centrifugal force drives the ball to the high side. If the plane slips, gravity pulls the ball to the low side.

The gyro horizon, or artificial horizon, helps the pilot keep the wings of the aircraft level and the nose fixed in relation to the horizon. On the dial are a miniature airplane and a horizon bar. In climbs or dives the index airplane appears above or below the bar. When the pilot banks, the index airplane banks. A suction-driven gyroscope operates the instrument. The attitude gyro performs the same function as the artificial horizon, but its gyroscope is electrically operated. Instead of an index airplane and horizon bar

The magnetic compass is a directional instrument that indicates the heading on which the airplane is flying.

it has a horizontal pattern. It can be used even in acrobatic maneuvers when the plane is upside down.

Navigation Instruments

There are many types of navigation aids. The magnetic compass shows the heading of the airplane (*see* Compass, Magnetic). Magnetic interference may make the compass inaccurate. A correction card allows for these errors. The compass card swings when the airplane turns or flies in rough weather, making it difficult to read.

The directional gyro holds its compass card steady with a gyroscope. It does not seek north but must be set with a knob to agree with the magnetic compass. It must be reset every 15 minutes. The gyrocompass needs no resetting. It combines the functions of the magnetic compass and the directional gyro.

Radio and radar are valuable air navigation tools (*see* Radio; Radar). Air-to-ground communications include low to ultrahigh frequency range radio signals. The radio compass, or automatic direction finder, is a receiving set with a directional antenna that indicates the heading to a transmitter. One of the pilot's most effective course-guidance aids is the very-high-frequency omnidirectional range (VOR) receiver. Instrument landing system (ILS) equipment guides aircraft in landing.

An instrument that relieves strain on long flights is the automatic pilot, or Gyropilot. It keeps the plane on course without the pilot's help. Gyroscopes control the plane's elevators, ailerons, and rudder.

Engine Instruments

A large plane has so many engine instruments that they are mounted on a separate panel under the supervision of a flight engineer. These devices indicate when the engine is warmed up, delivering full power in takeoffs, or operating at maximum efficiency.

The tachometer measures the revolutions per minute (rpm) of the engine shaft. Thermometers check the oil, carburetor, and cylinder-head temperatures. One type is a Bourdon tube, a curved, flexible metal device. The liquid inside it expands when it is heated, causing the tube to straighten. The motion drives a pointer. Some thermometers use a thermocouple of two dissimilar metals that generate electricity when heated.

The oil-pressure gauge and fuel-pressure gauge show the pressures at which lubricants are forced into the bearings and fuel is delivered to the engine. A manifold-pressure gauge registers the power the engine is developing by indicating pressure in the intake manifold.

The engine analyzer detects ignition and vibration disorders in an engine. The flight engineer scans the screen of a cathode-ray tube for deviations from normal. The synchroscope is an indicator on multiengine aircraft that is used to maintain the same rpm on each engine and thereby prevent vibration.

Jet Engine Instruments

Jet aircraft require fewer instruments than aircraft equipped with piston engines (see section on Power Plants; Jet Propulsion). The engine-pressure-ratio indicator (EPR) registers jet thrust by measuring the ratio between the engine compressor inlet pressure and the exhaust pressures.

Tachometers measure compressor speed of rotation in percentage of maximum revolutions per minute. The exhaust-gas temperature (EGT) instrument monitors overheating of the engine. The fuel flowmeter indicates the rate at which fuel is being used by an engine. Each tank has a fuel gauge.

Equipment Instruments

The mechanical, hydraulic, and electrical systems of modern aircraft require instruments to show if they are operating properly. Loadmeters mea-

sure the generators' output. The landing-gear-position indicator tells whether the gear is retracted. Gauges measure air pressure in the cabins and in hydraulic systems for the flaps and brakes. Instruments show the position of the landing flaps, engine cowlings, and other parts not visible from the cockpit. Lights warn of fire and indicate autopilot cutout.

United Airlines

The flight, or systems, engineer in the foreground has a separate panel with instruments for monitoring the aircraft's performance in flight.

INSTRUMENTS THAT INDICATE ENGINE PERFORMANCE

TACHOMETER
This electric tachometer shows the rotation speed of a jet rotor.

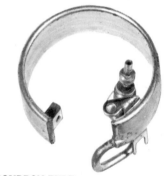

BOURDON TUBE
Fluid or gas in the hollow tube reacts to measure oil and other pressures.

FUEL FLOWMETER
This instrument indicates the rate of fuel flow to the engine.

OIL-PRESSURE GAUGE
The dial shows the pressure at which oil is being forced into the bearings.

American Airlines

Airplane
Pilot and Crew

Many airplanes can be operated by one person—a pilot. On airliners, military bombers, transports, and other large and complex aircraft the pilot is assisted by a crew.

Private Pilots

In the United States a civilian pilot must have a certificate issued by the Federal Aviation Administration (FAA). This may be a Student, Private, Commercial, or Flight Instructor Certificate. Ratings on the certificate indicate the ability to fly under instrument flight rules or in single- or multiengine aircraft, helicopters, gliders, landplanes, or seaplanes.

A private pilot flies for recreation or business. He must pass a physical examination and both a written and a practical examination in flying. He must also have 20 hours of solo flying. Flight schools or airport operators offer flying instruction.

Airplane Flight Crews

A flight crew operates an airliner (*see* Airline). Smaller planes have a captain and a copilot in the cockpit, or flight deck, and a flight attendant in the cabin. Larger airliners also have a flight engineer, a navigator, and up to 16 flight attendants. Many major airlines have hired women as pilots and engineers.

The captain, or first pilot, flies the airliner and is responsible for the safety of passengers and cargo. The captain is in command and his decision is law at all times. The position is comparable to that of the captain of a ship at sea.

Airlines require the age of a male pilot candidate (captain or copilot) to be from 20–23 to 27–30. He must be between 5 feet 7 inches and 6 feet 4 inches tall. Some airlines narrow this to between 5 feet 8 inches and 6 feet. Weight must be normal for height. Most airlines insist on 20/20 vision, uncorrected.

College graduates are preferred, but at least two years of college or the equivalent in experience is required. Pilots must have 400 to 1,000 hours of flying and FAA ratings for flying transports.

Pilots obtain training at private flying schools or while in military service. Airlines give them intensive training before assigning them to flight duty. The copilot, or first officer, assists the captain. After he serves some time as copilot he may become a captain.

Before each flight, commercial airline pilots consult weather reports in order to select the safest, smoothest route.

Both men and women are employed as flight attendants on airplanes. Here the chief steward and a hostess are serving a meal on an international flight.

Qantas Airways

American Airlines

In a simulated 747 cockpit, pilots receive the training they need for resolving actual problems in flight.

The number of certified civilian pilots in the United States more than doubled between 1960 and 1980.

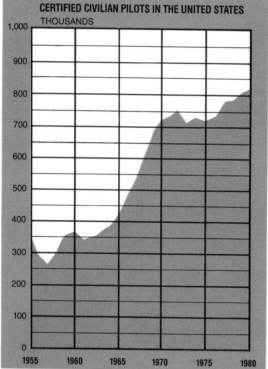

CERTIFIED CIVILIAN PILOTS IN THE UNITED STATES
THOUSANDS

TOTAL NUMBER OF PILOTS
Each symbol represents 50,000 pilots.

Private	Student and Other	Commercial	Airline
357,479	216,581	183,442	69,569

Total 827,071

Source: Aerospace Industries Association of America, Inc.

Pilots advance according to seniority. Pilots and co-pilots earn more on international runs than on domestic flights.

The flight engineer is responsible for mechanical performance of the airliner in flight. Applicants must be from 20–23 to 35 years old. Height and weight requirements are the same as for pilots. Most airlines insist on 20/50 vision, correctable to 20/20. A flight engineer must have a high school education and an FAA license. One airline requires 600 hours of solo flying; another, four years of aircraft mechanic experience.

A navigator is carried on some international flights, especially those over water. He determines the aircraft's position at any time (*see* Aviation, section on Navigation).

Flight attendants cater to passenger comfort and needs. Most of them are women stewardesses, or hostesses, although there are men stewards. A purser may be in charge of the cabin crew. Before takeoff a stewardess helps passengers put away wraps and luggage and instructs them in the use of safety belts and oxygen masks. In flight she serves food and supplies such things as magazines, mints, gum, and pillows.

Most airlines require that female flight attendants be at least 20 years of age. Preferred height is generally between 5 feet 2 inches and 5 feet 9 inches; weight, between 100 and 140 pounds. Minimum uncorrected vision is usually 20/50 in each eye, but some airlines allow stewardesses to wear contact lenses or plain eyeglasses in flight. Good posture and a pleasing personality and voice are important.

On some airlines stewardesses must have two years of college or be registered nurses. Others require one year of college plus one year of business training. Stewardesses on international airlines must speak foreign languages. Airlines provide special schools for stewardesses. Some courses take six weeks. Like pilots and flight engineers, flight attendants earn more on international routes.

Flight crews fly no more than 85 hours a month on domestic routes and 255 hours in a calendar quarter on international flights. Flight deck personnel must pass a physical examination every six months and demonstrate proficiency in flight to airline and FAA check pilots. The airlines pay expenses of flight crews while away from the base station. They are allowed free or reduced-rate air travel.

Military Aircrews

The size of a military aircrew varies with the type of plane and mission (*see* Air Force). In a fighter the pilot acts as navigator, gunner, and bombardier. The B-52 bomber has six crewmen, and the FB-111 has two. A multiengine plane must have at least a pilot and a copilot. Usually there is a flight engineer. On long flights there may be a navigator and a radio operator. Military pilots and flight engineers need not obtain FAA licenses but must meet rigid health and proficiency standards. Women may actively serve as military pilots and crew members.

Airplane History

Man's desire to rule the skies has been the driving force behind one of his greatest adventures. In prehistoric times birds and dragonlike flying reptiles sailed through the air. When man appeared on Earth, he watched and envied the birds flying in the sky.

Early man also wondered about the smoke climbing from his campfires and about the "falling stars" streaking through the sky. These mysteries of nature—the bird, the smoke, and the meteor—symbolize the three principal types of vehicles that today fly in the aerospace within and above the Earth's atmosphere (*see* Aerospace Industry). Heavier-than-air craft and lighter-than-air craft fly in the atmosphere, while spacecraft hurtle through space.

Flights in Myth and Fantasy

Stories of the flight of men, animals, and gods abound in the myths, art, and religions of ancient civilizations. As far back as 3500 B.C. the Babylonians engraved the adventure of Etana, a shepherd who flew on the back of an eagle, on semiprecious stones.

The legendary Chinese prince Ki Kung-shi flew a flying chariot; and the Persian king Kai Ka'us, a flying throne. Khonsu was a winged Egyptian god; and Assur, the chief Assyrian god, had an eagle's wings. In Arabic folklore a magic carpet glided over Baghdad. In a Greek myth Bellerophon rode Pegasus, the flying horse. In Roman mythology Mercury

North American Rockwell Corp.

Within a half century aviation progressed from the 60-mile-an-hour, 80-horsepower pusher-type biplane to the 670-mile-an-hour, 9,000-horsepower F-86 Sabre jet.

was the winged messenger of the gods. A famous Greek legend of flight is that of Daedalus and his son Icarus. One day Icarus soared too close to the sun, which melted his wings made of feathers and wax. (*See also* Mythology.)

First Man-Made Objects in the Sky

Long before men learned how to fly they sent objects soaring through the air. The arrow dates from

FLIGHT IN FANTASY

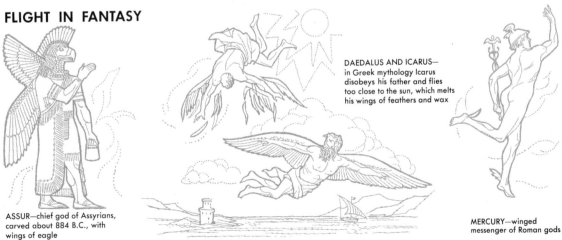

DAEDALUS AND ICARUS— in Greek mythology Icarus disobeys his father and flies too close to the sun, which melts his wings of feathers and wax

ASSUR—chief god of Assyrians, carved about 884 B.C., with wings of eagle

MERCURY—winged messenger of Roman gods

DREAMERS OF FLIGHT—DESIGNERS OF MODELS

Leonardo da Vinci, the great Italian genius, designed this bat-like orthopter, with flapping wings, about 1490.

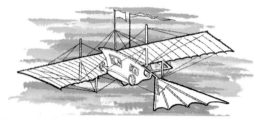

William S. Henson of England patented his "aerial steam carriage" in 1842. It was to provide world-wide airline service.

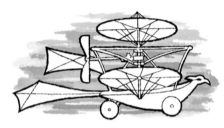

Sir George Cayley designed this "aerial carriage" in England in 1843. It was a combination of an airplane and a helicopter.

John Stringfellow, an English lace machinery manufacturer, flew this model, powered by a tiny steam engine, in 1848.

Alphonse Pénaud of France built his *Planaphore*, powered by a rubber band, in 1871. It resembled today's pusher-stick models.

the Stone Age. The ancient Chinese flew kites (*see* Kites). The early inhabitants of Australia invented the boomerang, the blades of which they carved in the shape of an airfoil (*see* Boomerang).

As early as the Middle Ages men of scientific mind prophesied human flight. About 1250 Roger Bacon, an English friar, suggested the *orthopter*, a machine that flaps its wings like a bird (*see* Bacon, Roger). He also conceived the balloon, proposing "a hollow globe filled with ethereal air or liquid fire."

Some 250 years later the great Italian artist and scientist Leonardo da Vinci studied the flight of birds (*see* Vinci). About 1490 he drew sketches for flying machines, also of the orthopter type. Da Vinci made drawings of a propeller and a helicopter and described the principle of the parachute.

Man Flies in the Balloon

An Italian monk, Francesco de Lana, in 1670 proposed a vacuum balloon. Four spheres, from which air had been exhausted, were to support a car equipped with oars and a sail. He overlooked atmospheric pressure, however, which would have crushed the spheres.

Not until a hundred years later was the first balloon flown successfully in public. In 1783 J. Étienne and Joseph M. Montgolfier inflated a big paper balloon with hot air. It rose 6,000 feet (*see* Balloon). That same year the Montgolfier brothers sent up Jean Pilâtre de Rozier in one of their balloons in the first human ascent.

Balloonists sought a way of steering their craft instead of merely floating with the wind. They proposed oars, man-powered propellers, and even harnessed eagles. In 1852 Henri Giffard, a Frenchman, flew a dirigible powered by a steam engine and propeller.

Interest Grows in Heavier-Than-Air Craft

Not satisfied with the limitations of the balloon in controlling flight direction, Sir George Cayley of England turned to the study of heavier-than-air craft. He advanced the basic principle of the airplane and is called the "father of British aeronautics." Beginning in 1810 he built model gliders. In 1843 he proposed the "aerial carriage," which combined the principle of the airplane and the helicopter.

In 1842 William S. Henson, a British inventor, had patented an "aerial steam carriage," the *Ariel*. He and John Stringfellow, a lace machinery manufacturer, organized the Aerial Transit Company, a world-wide airline service, but a model of Henson's airplane failed to fly. Stringfellow continued to experiment and in 1848 flew a steam-powered model.

Alphonse Pénaud of France made models powered by rubber bands. His models of the airplane, orthopter, and helicopter were successful. His *Planaphore* model of 1871 was a single-stick pusher monoplane that looks like the models built today.

Heavier-Than-Air Flight with the Glider

During the second half of the 19th century less attention was given to the idea of flapping the wings

PIONEER GLIDERS

Otto Lilienthal of Germany made more than 2,000 glides until killed in 1896.

An American engineer, Octave Chanute, built this biplane glider in 1898.

In 1905 John J. Montgomery of California launched his glider from a balloon.

of airplanes by means of the arm and leg muscles of the pilot. Instead, gliders were built with wings braced by struts and wires (*see* Glider). They had no engines but relied on gravity and wind for force.

In France Jean Marie le Bris built the *Artificial Albatross*, a birdlike glider, in 1857. Louis Pierre Mouillard, also a Frenchman, in 1881 wrote a book on gliding, which applied bird flight to aviation.

In Germany Otto and Gustav Lilienthal contributed greatly to aeronautics. They made glider flights from an artificial hill. Otto made more than 2,000 glides before he was killed in a flight in 1896. Percy Sinclair Pilcher introduced the Lilienthal glider to Great Britain. He too was killed, while flying his fourth monoplane, the *Hawk*, in 1899.

In Australia Lawrence Hargrave experimented with models, including an orthopter powered by compressed air. In 1893 he invented the box kite, upon which early European airplane designers based their biplanes.

EARLY ATTEMPTS AT POWERED FLIGHT

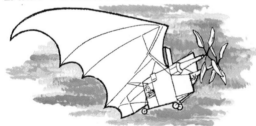

Clement F. Ader of France claimed to have flown his batlike *Avion*, powered by steam engines and twin propellers, in 1897.

In the United States John Joseph Montgomery of California built gliders. His most spectacular demonstration was made in 1905, when his glider was cut loose from a balloon several thousand feet in the air.

Another American, the civil engineer Octave Chanute, influenced the achievement of powered flight by his writings and experiments. From his work with bridges, he developed the truss construction of the biplane. Numerous flights were made with his gliders. Movable control surfaces added to their stability.

Experiments with Powered Flight

At the turn of the century four men came close to actual flight in a power-driven, manned flying machine. They were Ader in France, Phillips and Maxim in England, and Langley in the United States.

Clement F. Ader built batlike monoplanes powered by steam engines. He claimed he flew his *Eole* in 1890 and his *Avion* in 1897. There was some question, however, whether they hopped rather than flew.

Horatio Phillips in 1893 constructed a strange steam-powered multiplane with 50 narrow wings that resembled a Venetian blind. Tethered and without a pilot, it rose a few feet off the ground.

Sir Hiram Maxim, an American-born inventor who lived in England, constructed another curious machine, in 1893. It was a $3\frac{1}{2}$-ton multiplane monster powered by a steam engine. In a test flight on a circular track, it rose, ripped up a guard rail, and then crashed.

Meanwhile in the United States Samuel P. Langley, an American scientist and secretary of the Smithsonian Institution, attempted to solve the problem of

Sir Hiram Maxim built this steam-powered giant in England in 1893. It rose from its railroad track and crashed.

Samuel P. Langley twice catapulted his large aerodrome from a houseboat on the Potomac River in 1903. Both attempts failed.

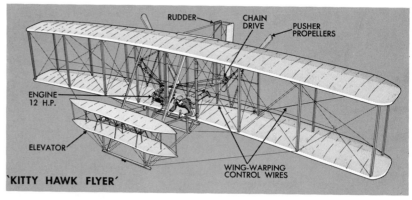

'KITTY HAWK FLYER'

This historic photograph shows Orville Wright making the first powered flight by man in a heavier-than-air craft, Dec. 17, 1903, near Kitty Hawk, N.C. His brother, Wilbur, runs alongside.

flight with large powered models after years of scientific research (see Langley). He called his models *aerodromes*, meaning "air runners." In 1896 his *Aerodrome No. 5*, powered by a steam engine, flew for a minute and a half and covered more than a half mile.

In 1898 while at war with Spain the United States government granted Langley $50,000 to build a man-carrying aerodrome for aerial observation. In 1903 a gasoline-engined model flew successfully. Charles M. Manly, Langley's assistant, developed a radial engine that produced 52.4 horsepower. Manly was aboard the aerodrome in two attempted flights in 1903. It

was catapulted from the roof of a houseboat on the Potomac but plunged into the river both times.

Wright Brothers Conquer the Air

Just nine days after Langley's second test, two Americans, Orville and Wilbur Wright, made the world's first successful man-carrying, engine-powered, heavier-than-air flight (see Wright Brothers).

The brothers had read about Lilienthal's gliders and studied the writings of Mouillard, Chanute, Langley, and other pioneers. In their bicycle shop in Dayton, Ohio, they built gliders and a wind tunnel. In their 1902 glider they solved the problem of lateral control with vertical rudders and wing tips that could be warped or twisted up and down. The Wrights added power to their next machine. They built a four-cylinder, 12-horsepower gasoline engine and propellers. The craft weighed 750 pounds, with the pilot. Its wing span was 40 feet, 4 inches.

In the fall of 1903 the Wright brothers shipped their airplane to Kitty Hawk, on the coast of North Carolina. Here they had tested their gliders previously because of the hills and steady winds. On Dec. 17, 1903, Orville made the first flight, which lasted 12 seconds and covered 120 feet.

The Wrights improved their machine so that by 1905 they could fly more than 24 miles in 38 minutes. In

GREAT PIONEER FLIGHTS

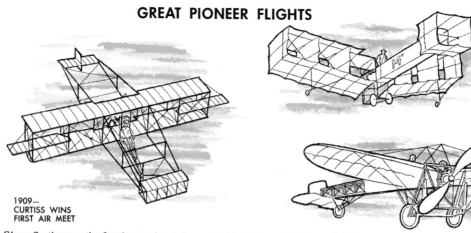

1909—
CURTISS WINS
FIRST AIR MEET

1906—
SANTOS-DUMONT
MAKES FIRST
FLIGHT IN EUROPE

1909—
BLÉRIOT FLIES
ENGLISH CHANNEL

Glenn Curtiss won the first international air meet in his *Golden Flyer* (left), 1909. Alberto Santos-Dumont made the first flight in Europe in his *14 Bis* (upper right), 1906. Louis Blériot flew the English Channel in his *Blériot XI* (lower right), 1909.

1908 Wilbur went to France and flew a Wright machine before the royalty of Europe. That same year Orville demonstrated one of the Wright planes at Fort Myer, Va., before government officials. During one of his flights, Orville took up a passenger, Lieut. Thomas E. Selfridge of the United States Army Signal Corps. Trouble developed and the plane crashed, killing Selfridge. He was the first person to be killed in an airplane crash. In 1909 the trials were successful and the War Department purchased the improved machine. Thus the United States became the first nation to own a military airplane.

Pioneer Daredevils

From 1900 to 1910 many pioneer airmen in many nations flew airplanes. Cash prizes for record flights and air meets stimulated the development of aviation. Fliers were particularly active in France. Alberto Santos-Dumont made the first officially observed airplane flight in Europe in his *14 Bis* in 1906. Henri Farman won a prize in 1908 for flying a kilometer course in a Voisin. In 1909 Louis Blériot flew across the English Channel in his *Blériot XI* and Hubert Latham almost succeeded twice in crossing the channel in an Antoinette monoplane.

Also in 1909 the first international air meet was held, at Reims, France. An American, Glenn H. Curtiss, flew his *Golden Flyer* a record 47.8 miles an hour. In 1910 he won the *New York World* prize of $10,000 for flying from Albany to New York City.

Curtiss had joined the Aerial Experiment Association, organized by Alexander Graham Bell in 1907, and he later became a leading aircraft manufacturer. When he used the aileron for lateral control, the Wright brothers claimed this was based on their wing-warping system and sued him for infringement of their patent. Their claim was sustained by the court.

A remarkable feat was the first transcontinental flight, by Calbraith Perry Rodgers in 1911. He flew a Wright brothers type EX airplane from Long Island, N. Y., to Long Beach, Calif., in 49 days.

The Airplane Becomes a Weapon of War

World War I accelerated the expansion of aviation (*see* World War I). Airplanes were first used for observation and later for aerial duels, bombing, and other purposes. Roland Garros, a French pilot, fired a machine gun through a whirling propeller by attaching steel deflectors on the blades to protect them. Anthony Fokker, a Dutch airplane designer, improved this idea by synchronizing the engine and machine gun.

Aircraft improved in structure and power plants as more military uses were found for them. Famous fighters included the Fokker and Albatros of Germany; the Nieuport and Spad of France; and the Sopwith Camel, Sopwith Snipe, Bristol F2B, and SE-5 of Great Britain. Outstanding bombers were the German Junkers, the British Vickers, and the Italian Capronis.

American fliers flew planes purchased from the Allies. The only United States-built craft used in combat were DH-4's. They were based on the British

NOTABLE LONG-DISTANCE FLIGHTS

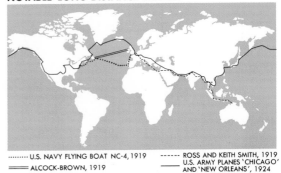

.... U.S. NAVY FLYING BOAT NC-4, 1919   ------ ROSS AND KEITH SMITH, 1919
═══ ALCOCK-BROWN, 1919   U.S. ARMY PLANES 'CHICAGO'
                                 AND 'NEW ORLEANS', 1924

This United States Navy flying boat, the NC-4, made the first transatlantic flight, in 1919 from New York to England.

Captain John Alcock and Lieut. A. W. Brown made the first nonstop Atlantic crossing, in 1919 in this Vickers-Vimy.

Captains Ross and Keith Smith and two crewmen made a flight from England to Australia in a Vickers-Vimy in 1919.

United States Army airmen made the first round-the-world flight, in 1924 in two Douglas planes. This one is the *Chicago*.

LINDBERGH'S FLIGHT

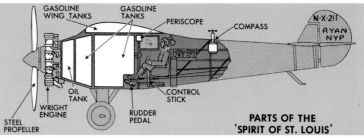

GASOLINE WING TANKS — GASOLINE TANKS — PERISCOPE — COMPASS — N-X-211 RYAN NYP — OIL TANK — CONTROL STICK — WRIGHT ENGINE — RUDDER PEDAL — STEEL PROPELLER

PARTS OF THE 'SPIRIT OF ST. LOUIS'

De Havilland-4 but had American-designed Liberty engines. The United States also produced several thousand Curtiss Jennies for training planes.

During the war continuously scheduled public service airmail began in the United States. In 1918 Army pilots flew regular airmail between Washington, D. C., and New York City by way of Philadelphia.

After the war, pilots found little use for their skills.

Charles A. Lindbergh made the first nonstop solo flight across the Atlantic, in 1927. "Lindy" flew his Ryan monoplane, the *Spirit of St. Louis*, from New York City to Paris in 33½ hours.

Many of them bought surplus warplanes and became barnstormers. They offered rides in their craft or did stunt flying at county fairs and carnivals. These courageous and often foolhardy fliers promoted interest in aviation in the United States.

Across the Atlantic and Around the World

Flights over oceans, continents, and poles were made after World War I. In 1919 three huge United States Navy flying boats attempted the first Atlantic crossing. Only one, the NC-4, succeeded. It flew from Rockaway, N. Y., via Newfoundland, the Azores, and Lisbon, Portugal, to Plymouth, England.

A few weeks later Capt. John Alcock and Lieut. Arthur Whitten Brown made the first nonstop Atlantic flight. They flew a Vickers-Vimy from Newfoundland to Ireland. Later in the year Capts. Ross and Keith Smith and two crewmen flew a Vickers-Vimy from England to Australia. The next year the United States Army Air Service flew four DH-4–B's from New York City to Nome, Alaska, and back.

In 1923 Lieuts. John Macready and Oakley Kelly flew nonstop coast-to-coast from New York City to San Diego, Calif., in a Fokker T-2. The following year the first round-the-world flight was made. United States Army airmen took off in four Douglas World Cruisers from Seattle, Wash., but only two completed the trip, in 15 days, 3 hours, and 7 minutes flying time.

In 1926 Lieut. Comdr. Richard E. Byrd of the United States Navy and Floyd Bennett flew over the

Clarence D. Chamberlain and his passenger, Charles Levine, flew nonstop from New York to Germany in this Bellanca in 1927.

Commander Richard E. Byrd and a crew of three flew in the Fokker trimotor *America* from New York to France in 1927.

204

North Pole in a Fokker trimotor (*see* Byrd). In 1929 Byrd flew over the South Pole in a Ford trimotor.

The Lone Eagle Defies the Atlantic

The Atlantic Ocean continued to fascinate the airmen. In 1919 Raymond Orteig of France had offered $25,000 for the first nonstop flight between New York City and Paris. Several French and American fliers made unsuccessful and often tragic attempts.

Finally, in 1927, Charles A. Lindbergh succeeded in his Ryan monoplane, the *Spirit of St. Louis* (*see* Lindbergh). His brave solo flight of 33½ hours not only conquered the Atlantic but also made the nation and the world more air-minded.

Two weeks after Lindbergh's feat, Clarence Chamberlain and Charles Levine flew nonstop from New York to Germany in a Bellanca monoplane. A month later Byrd and a crew of three also crossed the Atlantic, in a Fokker trimotor.

With the Atlantic conquered, fliers turned to the Pacific. In 1927 Lieuts. Lester J. Maitland and Albert F. Hegenberger of the United States Army flew from Oakland, Calif., to Honolulu, Hawaii.

The next year Capts. Charles Kingsford Smith and Charles Ulm of Australia and two Americans flew from Oakland, Calif., via Hawaii and the Fiji Islands, to Brisbane, Australia, in the *Southern Cross*. In 1929 Lieut. James Doolittle made the first "blind" flight in history, using instruments to guide him.

General Italo Balbo led a mass flight of Savoia-Marchettis from Rome, Italy, across the South Atlantic to Rio de Janeiro, Brazil, in 1931. Also in that year Wiley Post and Harold Gatty flew around the world in a Lockheed monoplane, the *Winnie Mae*, in 8 days, 15 hours, and 51 minutes. Two years later Post made a solo flight around the world in the same plane.

Women became interested in aviation in increasing numbers. Amelia Earhart flew the Atlantic as the first woman passenger in 1928 in the Fokker *Friendship*. She became the first woman to solo the ocean, in 1932 in a Lockheed Vega. She and her navigator, Fred Noonan, disappeared over the Pacific in 1937.

Commercial aviation also developed in the 1920's and 1930's (*see* Airlines). The Kelly bill of 1925 turned over the airmail routes to private carriers. This encouraged the growth of airlines. More efficient aircraft were produced, including the all-metal Ford trimotor, Douglas DC-3, Sikorsky flying boat, Martin Clipper, and Boeing Stratoliner.

In the 1930's the airplane again became an instrument of destruction. Military craft were used in battles in Manchuria, Ethiopia, Spain, China, and Finland. These conflicts tested the design and tactics of warplanes for their roles in World War II.

Air Power Decisive in World War II

World War II demonstrated the vital importance of air power in modern total war (*see* World War II). Hitler's Junkers JU-87 Stuka dive bombers spearheaded his blitzkrieg of France. When the *Luftwaffe*, Germany's air force, attacked Great Britain, the

OVER THE TOP AND AROUND THE WORLD

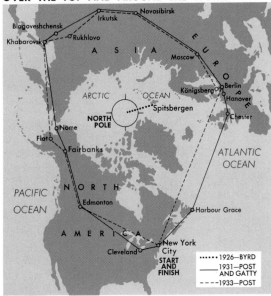

Richard E. Byrd and Floyd Bennett flew this Fokker trimotor, the *Josephine Ford*, over the North Pole in 1926.

Wiley Post and Harold Gatty flew around the world in the *Winnie Mae* in 1931. Post circled the globe solo in 1933.

Hawker Hurricanes and Supermarine Spitfires of the Royal Air Force fought it to a standstill.

The *Luftwaffe*'s planes included the Messerschmitt Me-109, Focke-Wulf FW 190, and Messerschmitt Me-262, all fighters, and the Dornier bombers. Other planes of the RAF were the fighters Hawker Tempest and Westland Whirlwind, the bombers Avro Lancaster, Short Stirling, Halifax, and Bristol Blenheim MK-1, and the fighter-bomber De Havilland Mosquito.

After the Japanese bombers attacked Pearl Harbor, the United States entered the war. Its aircraft production skyrocketed until in 1944 its output was almost 100,000 planes for the year.

Among the American fighters were the North American P-51 Mustang, Lockheed P-38 Lightning, Grum-

1903 'KITTY HAWK FLYER'   1919 NC-4 FLYING BOAT   1924 'CHICAGO'   1926 'JOSEPHINE FORD'

FAMOUS FLIGHTS IN HISTORY

1903 Dec. 17—Orville and Wilbur Wright make first successful flight, at Kitty Hawk, N.C.; 120 feet in 12 seconds.

1906 Oct. 23—Alberto Santos-Dumont makes first officially observed flight in Europe, nearly 200 feet in 6 seconds, in France.

1909 July 25—Louis Blériot of France in *Blériot XI*, which he designed, makes first crossing of English Channel by airplane, 25 miles in 37 minutes.

1909 Aug. 22–29—Glenn H. Curtiss in *Golden Flyer* wins first James Gordon Bennett international airplane race and other events in first International Flying Meet, Reims, France.

1910 May 28—Glenn H. Curtiss flies *Hudson Flyer* in record flight, 135.4 miles, from Albany to New York City, in 2 hours, 32 minutes.

1910 Nov. 14—Eugene Ely takes off from deck of U.S. cruiser *Birmingham* at Hampton Roads, Va., in first flight from deck of a ship.

1911 Sept. 17–Dec. 10—Calbraith P. Rodgers in Wright EX *Vin Fiz* makes first transcontinental flight, 4,231 miles, from Sheepshead Bay, Long Island, N.Y., to Long Beach, Calif., in 84 days and 70 hops; flying time—82 hours, 14 minutes.

1911 Sept. 23—Earle L. Ovington in Blériot monoplane flies first officially sanctioned airmail in U.S., from Hempstead to Mineola, Long Island, N.Y.

1913 May 13—Igor Sikorsky, Russian engineer, flies *Grand*, first four-engine airplane.

1914 Jan. 1—Anthony Jannus in Benoist flying boat begins world's first scheduled airline service with heavier-than-air craft, from Tampa to St. Petersburg, Fla.

1918 May 15—U.S. Army pilots in Curtiss JN4-H Jennies begin first continuous scheduled public-service airmail in U.S. between New York City and Washington, D.C., via Philadelphia.

Transoceanic Flights

1919 May 8–31—U.S. Navy flying boat NC-4 makes first transatlantic flight, 4,526 miles, from Rockaway, N.Y., to Plymouth, England, via Newfoundland, Azores, Lisbon, Portugal, and other intermediate stops, in 53 hours, 58 minutes.

1919 June 14–15—Capt. John Alcock and Lieut. A. W. Brown of Britain in Vickers-Vimy bomber make first nonstop transatlantic flight, 1,960 miles, from Newfoundland to Ireland, in 16 hours, 12 minutes.

1919 Nov. 12–Dec. 10—Capts. Ross and Keith Smith and two crewmen in Vickers-Vimy fly from Hounslow, England, to Darwin, Australia, 11,130 miles, in 27 days, 20 hours; flying time—124 hours.

1920 July 15–Oct. 20—U.S. Army Air Service pilots in four De Havilland DH-4-B biplanes make New York–Alaska flight and back, 9,329 miles, in 112 flying hours.

1923 May 2–3—Lieuts. John A. Macready and Oakley G. Kelly fly Fokker T-2 monoplane in first nonstop transcontinental flight, 2,516 miles, from New York City to San Diego, Calif., in 26 hours, 50 minutes, 3 seconds.

1924 April 6–Sept. 28—Two U.S. Army Douglas World Cruisers *Chicago* and *New Orleans* make first round-the-world flight, 26,345 miles, from Seattle, Wash., in 175 days; flying time—363 hours, 7 minutes.

1926 May 8–9—Lieut. Comdr. Richard E. Byrd and Floyd Bennett fly Fokker trimotor nonstop from Spitsbergen to North Pole and back, 1,545 miles, in 15½ hours.

1926 Dec. 21–May 2, 1927—U.S. Army Air Service pilots starting with five Loening OA-1 amphibians fly Pan American goodwill flight, over 22,000 miles, from U.S. to Central and South America and back.

1927 May 20–21—Charles A. Lindbergh flies Ryan monoplane, *Spirit of St. Louis*, in first nonstop solo transatlantic flight, 3,600 miles, from New York City to Paris, in 33½ hours.

1927 June 4–5—Clarence D. Chamberlain and Charles Levine in Bellanca monoplane make first nonstop New York–Germany flight, 3,911 miles, in 43 hours, 49 minutes, 33 seconds.

1927 June 28–29—U.S. Army Air Corps pilots fly Fokker C-2 trimotor across Pacific, 2,407 miles, from Oakland, Calif., to Honolulu, Hawaii, in 25 hours, 50 minutes.

1927 July 14–15—Emory Bronte and Ernest L. Smith are first civilians to make U.S.–Hawaii flight, 2,340 miles, in 25½ hours.

1928 April 12–13—Günther von Huenefeld and Capt. Hermann Koehl of Germany and Comdr. James Fitzmaurice of Ireland fly Junkers monoplane *Bremen* in first nonstop westbound flight over North Atlantic, 2,070 miles, from Ireland to Labrador, in 36½ hours.

1928 May 31–June 10—Capts. Charles Kingsford Smith and Charles T. P. Ulm of Australia and Harry W. Lyon, Jr., and James W. Warner of U.S. in Fokker trimotor *Southern Cross* make U.S.–Australia flight, more than 8,000 miles, in 83 hours, 19 minutes.

1928 June 17–18—Amelia Earhart in Fokker trimotor *Friendship* is first woman to fly Atlantic as a passenger.

1929 Jan. 1–7—Maj. Carl Spaatz and crew in Fokker C-2 trimotor set refueling endurance record of 150 hours, 40 minutes, 51 seconds, over Los Angeles, Calif.

1929 Sept. 24—Lieut. James H. Doolittle makes first demonstration of "blind" flight, at Mitchel Field, N.Y.

man F6F Hellcat, and Chance-Vought F4U Corsair (*see* Air Force; Navy). The Boeing B-17 Flying Fortress and the Consolidated B-24 Liberator were used in mass bombings in Europe. The North American B-25 Mitchell attacked Japanese ships. The Martin B-26 Marauder was used in support of ground troops. The Boeing B-29 Superfortresses dropped atomic bombs on Japan.

Famous Japanese fighters were the Mitsubishi A6M Zero, or "Zeke," and the Nakajima Ki 43 "Oscar." Soviet fighter planes included the Lavochkin La-5 and the Yakovlev Yak-3 and Yak-9.

During World War II the era of jet-propelled airplanes began. In 1939 the Germans flew the world's first successful turbojet airplane, the Heinkel He 178. Germany and Great Britain were the only nations to have operational jet fighters.

After the war the United States, Britain, and the Soviet Union made rapid progress in jet and rocket power (*see* Rockets). In 1947 the rocket plane Bell X-1 became the first aircraft to fly faster than the speed of sound. In the war in Korea American F-86 Sabre jets outflew the Soviet MiG-15 jets. During the 1960's and 1970's Mach 2 jets, such as the McDonnell Douglas F-4 Phantom II and the MiG-21, were used in fighting in Vietnam and the Middle East.

The jet engine also showed its superiority for commercial transports. In 1952 Great Britain began the

1927 'SPIRIT OF ST. LOUIS' **1931** 'WINNIE MAE' **1947** BELL X-1 **1959** NORTH AMERICAN X-15

1929 **Nov. 28–29**—Comdr. Richard E. Byrd, Bernt Balchen, Harold June, and Capt. Ashley McKinley in Ford trimotor monoplane *Floyd Bennett* make first flight over South Pole, 1,600 miles, from Little America over pole and back, in 18 hours, 59 minutes.

1931 **June 23–July 1**—Wiley Post as pilot and Harold Gatty as navigator fly Lockheed monoplane *Winnie Mae* in round-the-world flight, 15,477 miles, from Long Island, N.Y., in 14 stops, in 8 days, 15 hours, 51 minutes; flying time—107 hours, 2 minutes.

1931 **Oct. 4–5**—Clyde Pangborn and Hugh Herndon, Jr., fly Bellanca monoplane *Miss Veedol* in first nonstop transpacific flight, 4,860 miles, from Tokyo, Japan, to Wenatchee, Wash., in 41 hours, 13 minutes.

1932 **May 20–21**—Amelia Earhart in Lockheed Vega monoplane makes first transatlantic solo flight by a woman, 2,026 miles, from Harbour Grace, Nfld., to Londonderry, Ireland, in 15 hours, 18 minutes.

1933 **July 1–15**—Gen. Italo Balbo of Italy leads 24 Savoia-Marchetti seaplanes in mass transatlantic flight, 6,100 miles, from Orbetello, Italy, to Chicago, Ill., in 47 hours, 52 minutes.

1933 **July 15–22**—Wiley Post flies Lockheed Vega monoplane *Winnie Mae* in first round-the-world solo flight, 15,596 miles in 11 stops, in 7 days, 8 hours, 49 minutes; flying time—115 hours, 36 minutes.

1935 **Jan. 11–12**—Amelia Earhart makes first solo flight by a woman, from Hawaii to California.

1935 **Nov. 22–29**—Capt. Edwin C. Musick in Martin China Clipper flies first regular transpacific airmail, between San Francisco and Hawaii and Manila.

1937 **Jan. 19**—Howard Hughes sets transcontinental speed record, 2,453 miles, from Burbank, Calif., to Newark, N.J., in 7 hours, 28 minutes, 25 seconds.

1938 **July 10–14**—Howard Hughes and crew fly Lockheed "14" around the world, 14,971 miles, from Long Island, in 3 days, 19 hours, 8 minutes.

The Jet Era Begins

1939 **Aug. 27**—Germans fly Heinkel He-178, world's first turbojet airplane, at Rostock, Germany.

1942 **Oct. 1**—Robert M. Stanley flies first U.S. jet plane, Bell XP-59 Airacomet, at Muroc, Calif.

1946 **Sept. 29–Oct. 1**—Comdr. Thomas D. Davis and crew of three other U.S. Navy fliers in Lockheed P2V Neptune *Truculent Turtle* flies nonstop from Perth, Australia, to Columbus, Ohio, 11,235.6 miles in 55¼ hours.

1947 **Aug. 7–10**—William P. Odom in Douglas A-26 flies solo around the world, 19,645 miles, in 3 days, 1 hour, 5 minutes, 11 seconds.

1947 **Oct. 14**—Maj. Charles E. Yeager of USAF flies Bell X-1, first plane to fly faster than sound.

1949 **Feb. 26–March 2**—Capt. James Gallagher and crew of 13 fly USAF Boeing B-50 bomber *Lucky Lady II* in first nonstop round-the-world flight, 23,452 miles (4 in-flight refuelings), in 3 days, 22 hours, 1 minute.

1950 **Sept. 22**—Two USAF Republic F-84-E's fly first nonstop jet transatlantic flights (3 in-flight refuelings).

1952 **May 2**—British Overseas Airways Corporation with De Havilland Comets begins first turbojet airline service, between London and Johannesburg, South Africa.

1957 **Jan. 16–18**—Three B-52 Stratofortresses make first nonstop jet round-the-world flight, 24,325 miles (3 in-flight refuelings), in 45 hours, 20 minutes.

1958 **Oct. 26**—Pan American World Airways begins first regular jet service between New York City and Paris, using American-built Boeing 707 jet transports.

1959 **Jan. 25**—American Airlines, using Boeing 707's begins transcontinental jet service between Los Angeles and New York City; 4 hours, 3 minutes, 53.8 seconds.

1962 **July 17**—North American rocket research plane X-15 penetrates outer space.

1964 **March 19–April 17**—Jerrie Mock makes first round-the-world solo flight by a woman; flies a single-engine Cessna 22,858.8 miles, in 21 stops.

1974 **Sept. 1**—Transatlantic speed record of 1 hour, 54 minutes, 56 seconds set by USAF Lockheed SR-71.

1976 **Jan. 21**—Regular supersonic transport service begins with Concorde flights from Britain to Bahrain and from France to Brazil.

1977 **Oct. 28–30**—Pan American Boeing 747 sets speed record for circling globe over both poles on 26,383-mile passenger flight from San Francisco; elapsed time, including 3 on-ground refuelings: 54 hours, 7 minutes, 12 seconds.

Alternative Aircraft

1979 **June 12**—Bryan Allen, who helped develop first successful human-powered aircraft with Paul MacCready in 1977, pedals chain-driven *Gossamer Albatross* across English Channel.

1980 **Aug. 7**—Janice Brown pilots Paul MacCready's *Gossamer Penguin*, first solar-powered aircraft without battery-stored energy, in 15-minute test flight in California.

1981 **July 7**—MacCready's *Solar Challenger* is first solar-powered aircraft to cross English Channel.

world's first jet airline service, with De Havilland Comets between London and Johannesburg, South Africa. By 1960 United States airlines had in service the American-built turbojets Boeing 707, Convair 880, and Douglas DC-8 and the turboprop Lockheed Electra. The first jumbo jet, the Boeing 747, began flying in 1970. Other so-called wide bodies are the Lockheed L-1011 Tristar, the McDonnell Douglas DC-10, and the Airbus A-1300. In the late 1960's the United States, Great Britain and France, and the Soviet Union worked to develop supersonic transport planes (SST's). The first SST to fly was the Soviet TU-144, tested in 1968. The British-French Concorde began commercial flights in 1976.

From Buzz Bombs to Earth Satellites

After World War II research was also conducted on many unusual types of aircraft. The helicopter was not a new machine, but it was brought to a high degree of efficiency (*see* Helicopter). Developments that grew out of war research included missiles and man-made satellites. These devices marked the transition from craft that fly in the Earth's atmosphere to craft that journey in outer space.

During World War II the Germans not only led in jet propulsion but also in rocketry. Among their weapons were the jet-propelled V-1, or buzz bomb, and the rocket-propelled V-2.

207

After the war the United States and the Soviet Union also built missiles and experimented with satellites using rocket power. The Soviets were the first to launch a man-made satellite, in 1957.

In 1961 the United States and the Soviet Union began sending men into outer space and back. The North American rocket research plane X-15 penetrated the lower reaches of outer space in 1962. Man thus passed through the Air Age and entered the Space Age. (*See also* Space Travel; Guided Missiles.)

BIBLIOGRAPHY FOR AIRPLANE

Books for Children

Anastasio, Dina. Who Puts the Plane in the Air? (Random, 1977).

Elting, Mary. Aircraft at Work (Harvey House, 1964).

Hoare, Robert. The Story of Aircraft and Travel by Air (Dufour, 1966).

Peet, Creighton. Man in Flight: How the Airlines Operate (Macrae, 1972).

Place, M. T. New York to Nome: the First International Cross-Country Flight (Macmillan, 1972).

Rosenblum, Richard. Wings: the Early Years of Aviation (Scholastic, 1980).

Scribner, Kimball. Your Future in Aviation Careers in the Air (Rosen, 1979).

Scribner, Kimball. Your Future in Aviation Careers on the Ground (Rosen, 1979).

Wilson, Mike and Scagell, Robin. Jet Journey (Viking, 1978).

Books for Young Adults and Teachers

Benkert, J. W. Introduction to Aviation Science (Prentice, 1971).

Bowen, Ezra. Knights of the Air (Time-Life, 1980).

Cole, Martin. Their Eyes on the Skies (Aviation, 1979).

Douty, E. M. The Brave Balloonists (Garrard, 1969).

Fay, John. The Helicopter: History, Piloting, and How It Flies, 3rd rev. ed. (David and Charles, 1977).

Gann, E. K. Fate Is the Hunter (Simon & Schuster, 1961).

Jablonski, Edward. Man with Wings: a Pictorial History of Aviation (Doubleday, 1980).

Jane's All the World's Aircraft (Watts, annual).

Lindbergh, C. A. Spirit of St. Louis (Scribner, 1953).

McKee, Alexander. Great Mysteries of Aviation (Stein & Day, 1981).

O'Neil, Paul. Barnstormers and Speed Kings (Time-Life, 1981).

Rausa, Rosario. The Blue Angels (Aviation, 1979).

Read, P. P. Alive: the Story of the Andes Survivors (Harper, 1974).

Smith, Elinor. Aviatrix (Harcourt, 1981).

Smith, R. K. First Across! The U.S. Navy's Transatlantic Flight of 1919 (Naval Institute, 1973).

Solberg, Carl. Conquest of the Skies: a History of Commercial Aviation in America (Little, 1979).

Who's Who in Aviation. (Pergamon, 1974).

Wykes, Alan, ed. Air Atlantic (David White, 1968).

NOTABLE FIGURES IN AIRPLANE HISTORY

Some prominent persons are not included below because they are covered in the main text of this article or in other articles in Compton's Encyclopedia (*see* Fact-Index).

ALCOCK, John (1892–1919). Born Manchester, England. As World War I pilot, was captured by Turks after bombing Constantinople. Made first nonstop transatlantic flight on June 14 and 15, 1919, from Newfoundland to Ireland. With Lieut. Arthur Whitten Brown as navigator, flight took 16 hours, 12 minutes in Vickers-Vimy biplane. Both men, knighted for feat, shared *London Daily Mail* prize of £10,000. Alcock died from injuries sustained in plane crash en route to Paris.

ARNOLD, Hap (1886–1950). Born Gladwyne, Pa. As commanding general of United States air forces during World War II, Henry Harley Arnold pioneered in military education. After West Point graduation (1907), served in infantry. Trained to fly by Orville Wright in 1911. Advocated creation of independent air force and supported development of four-engine bomber airplanes. During his command the air force grew from 25,000 men with 4,000 planes to 2.5 million men with 75,000 planes. Retired in 1946. Ranked 5-star general in 1949.

BENNETT, Floyd (1890–1928). Born near Warrensburg, N.Y. Selected by Adm. Richard Byrd, he participated in MacMillan expedition to Greenland in 1925. Piloted Byrd in first successful flight over polar region on May 8 and 9, 1926. Awarded Congressional Medal of Honor. Conducted 8,000-mile flight around the United States to demonstrate feasibility of commercial airline routes. Developed pneumonia in flight to aid German-Irish transatlantic fliers and was stranded near Quebec, where he died. Floyd Bennett Field named for him.

BLÉRIOT, Louis (1872–1936). Born Cambrai, France. An engineer and pilot, Blériot made first over-the-ocean flight in heavier-than-air craft, from Calais to Dover, in 1909. Designed and built first successful mid-wing monoplane. Contracted by French army to produce military planes during World War I.

DOOLITTLE, Jimmy (born 1896). Born Alameda, Calif. During two separate periods of military service, James Doolittle was first pilot to cross the North American continent in less than 24 hours (1922) and leader of first United States air attack on Tokyo (1942). In 1920s and 1930s, made several record-breaking flights, winning a number of trophies. Chairman of National Advisory Committee for Aeronautics (1956–58).

FOKKER, Anthony (1890–1939). Born in Java. Dutch airplane designer and manufacturer of World War I fighter planes and long-range transport airplanes. Designed synchronizer that enabled machine guns to fire through propeller of an airplane. German air force built thousands of Fokker pursuit biplanes and triplanes during World War II. Fokker designs used in first nonstop coast-to-coast United States flight (1923), in Admiral Byrd's North Pole flight (1926), and in early transatlantic and transpacific flight.

LINK, Edwin (1904–81). Born Huntington, Ind. Inventor of flight simulators for airline-pilot training, blind-flying instruments, ground-based airplane guidance systems, small submarines for undersea exploration, and underwater dwellings. Learned to fly as hobby in 1920s. Left high school to work in father's piano and organ factory. Simulator, first used in amusement parks, became standard equipment at every United States and Allied air-training school.

POST, Wiley (1899–1935). Born near Grand Plain, Tex. Became first solo flier to circle the Earth (1933). Began career as stunt parachutist, moving on as the private pilot of wealthy oilman. First circled the globe in 1931, with navigator Harold Gatty. Designed early version of pressure suit while experimenting with high-altitude flights. With the famous American comedian Will Rogers aboard as a passenger, Post died in plane crash in Alaska in 1935.

RICHTHOFEN, Baron von (1892–1918). Born Breslau, Germany. Leading World War I flying ace, Manfred Richthofen was credited with shooting down 80 Allied planes. As squadron leader of combat group called "Richthofen's Flying Circus," was famous as "Red Baron," after the color of his plane. Fatally shot down in aerial combat over France.

RICKENBACKER, Eddie (1890–1973). Born Columbus, Ohio. Automobile racing driver, airline executive, and World War I flying hero, Edward Vernon Rickenbacker was leading American combat pilot of World War I. He shot down 26 enemy planes before Armistice. Had entered Army as chauffeur. Purchased Eastern Airlines (1938). In World War II, on a United States mission was stranded on raft in Pacific Ocean for 23 days (1942). Died in Zurich, Switzerland.

Orly International Airport, near Paris, is among the world's busiest air stations.

AIRPORT. Airplanes must have airports just as ships require docks and trains need railroad stations. An airport provides a place for planes to take off and land. It also includes areas for aircraft to be loaded, unloaded, fueled, repaired, and stored.

Airports vary in size. The large ones used by the airlines are called air carrier airports, and the smaller facilities that serve private planes are known as general aviation airports. Airports used by the United States Air Force, Army, Navy, Marines, and Coast Guard are called air bases, airfields, or air stations.

A heliport is an airport for helicopters. Some heliports are on the roofs of buildings. A helicopter landing pad may be no larger than a baseball diamond. A seaplane base is an airport for planes that can take off and land on water. It may be on a river or a lake, or in coastal waters.

Visiting an Airport

A visit to a large airport can be an exciting experience. The roar of engines usually can be heard even

This article was contributed by James T. Murphy, Assistant Vice President, and Gary Church, Air Traffic Control Specialist, both of the Air Transportation Association, Washington, D.C.

before reaching an airport, and giant airliners and small private planes can be seen taking off and landing. People who drive to an airport may park in a large parking lot or in a building many stories high that holds thousands of cars.

An airport has three main types of facilities. One is for passengers, one for airplanes on the ground, and one for planes that are taking off or landing.

The facilities for passengers help make the change between ground and air transportation as efficient as possible. They include roads; bus, taxi, limousine, and subway facilities; and the terminal building.

Among the facilities for airplanes on the ground are loading bridges connected to the terminal building, maintenance shops, cargo terminals, in-flight food kitchens, and a fueling system. Some United States airports have areas for Air National Guard, Air Force, or Navy Reserve units, including hangars for military planes. Aerospace factories and warehouses are sometimes on airport grounds.

Facilities that serve airplanes during takeoff and landing include runways, taxiways, parking ramps, and the air traffic control tower. Traffic controllers in the tower regulate air traffic at and near the airport. Many kinds of special devices assist planes in taking off and landing, among them instrument landing systems, radar, and approach lights.

United Airlines

Qantas

Flight schedules are electronically posted on a large overhead board in easy view of air travelers at Chicago-O'Hare International Airport (left). A ticket agent (right) at Kingsford Smith International Airport in Sydney, Australia, checks reservations on a computer screen.

The Terminal Building

The busiest and perhaps the most interesting airport building is the terminal building. People buy airline tickets and make flight reservations at ticket counters there. Flight information boards, which can be television screens or electronic signs, display information about arriving and departing flights.

The airline employees behind the ticket counters are called passenger service agents. In addition to selling tickets and making reservations, they take passengers' baggage and give them claim checks. The baggage moves on a conveyor belt from the ticket counter to the baggage makeup room. There, the luggage for each flight is sorted and placed in containers or on carts to be loaded on the proper airplane.

Modern airport terminals resemble shopping malls. They have restaurants, cocktail lounges, snack bars, ice-cream parlors, gift shops, newsstands, barbershops, game rooms, bookstores, banks, flower shops, candy stores, flight-insurance booths or machines, boutiques, and even hotels.

The terminal building also includes each airline's operations area, where the flight crews make their

In the terminal building each airline has an operations area where pilots prepare their final flight plans. Weather reports and all other details of the flight are checked out prior to takeoff.

American Airlines

flight plans. The crew examines weather reports and determines the fastest and safest route for each flight. Dispatchers determine the weight of the plane's fuel, baggage, and cargo, including mail.

Planning and coordination are important to assure the on-time arrival and departure of a plane. Workers clean the cabin, put food from the in-flight kitchen on the plane, pump drinking water aboard, and load baggage and cargo. Fuel is pumped into tanks in the plane's wings. The flight crew checks the tires, control surfaces, and other vital areas of the plane. An airline usually takes about 45 minutes to unload a plane and then load and service it for its next flight. The period required to complete this operation is called turnaround time.

The Airfield

The airfield is the area of an airport where planes take off and land. Many runways are more than two miles (three kilometers) long, and most measure about 150 feet (46 meters) wide. Planes move to and from the runways on taxiways, most of which are about 75 feet (23 meters) wide. Taxiways connect the runways to the ramps, the areas where planes are loaded, unloaded, and serviced.

On the airfield are large hangars where skilled mechanics check and repair the planes and their engines. A hangar has special shops for the repair of sensitive navigational or communications equipment. Spare parts for aircraft and engines are stocked in hangars so that defective parts can be replaced quickly. Other buildings on the airfield house heating and power plants, rescue vehicles and ambulances in case of a plane crash or fire, snow-removal plows and trucks, and various other equipment.

Airplane fuel is stored in huge tanks above or be-

Airline mechanics inspect the jet engine of a huge Boeing 747 airplane. Enormous airfield hangars house airplanes and are equipped with spare parts for quick repairs. Within the hangar are special shops for the repair of sensitive flight instruments.

SAS

low the ground. It is either pumped into trucks for delivery to the planes or moved through underground pipes to hydrants from which it is loaded aboard the aircraft.

Marking Airports for Safety

Airfields have various kinds of markings to help make flying safe. The Federal Aviation Administration (FAA) sets the standards for marking the airfields in the United States. The FAA works with the International Civil Aviation Organization (ICAO), an agency of the United Nations, so that these standards match those at airports in other countries. Representatives of member nations meet regularly to establish worldwide standards and procedures for airfields, airplane navigation, and air traffic control. As a result, airfields in the United States have the same markings as those in France, the Soviet Union,

Canada, Brazil, and Japan. This system helps maintain a high level of safety in airline operations.

Runways have numbers painted at each end to correspond with compass directions. For example, a runway that points north and south has the number 36 (for compass direction 360 degrees or north) at its south end and the number 18 (for 180 degrees or south) at the north end. Airplanes land and take off into the wind, and so if the wind is from the north the control tower will tell the pilot to land on runway 36. The plane will approach the airfield from the south so that it can land into the wind.

A threshold marker, consisting of eight large stripes, is painted at each end of a runway. Six smaller stripes indicate the proper place to land on the runway. A broken stripe down the center of the pavement indicates a runway, and a continuous center stripe marks a taxiway. A runway may also have side

Eastern Airlines

stripes along its borders. A holding line marker on a taxiway warns a pilot not to go beyond that point until cleared by an air traffic controller. Obstructions, such as smokestacks, water tanks, and television towers more than 150 feet (46 meters) high and within three miles (five kilometers) of an airport, are painted with alternate bands of orange and white. These structures also must have a bright red light on top that pilots can see in the dark.

A heliport is marked by a large Maltese cross, or an *H* enclosed in a segmented triangle. The symbol is painted at the center of the landing pad.

Airport Lighting Systems

Lighting at an airport is essential for night flying or during periods of poor daytime visibility. The rotating beacon on top of the control tower or on the roof of the terminal or a hangar helps the pilot locate the airport. It flashes two beams—one of which is white and the other green.

Lights outline the runways. They are white, except for those within the final 2,000 feet (600 meters) at the end of each runway, where they are yellow. Runways also have center-line lights running their full length and touchdown lights at each end of their landing area. High- or medium-intensity approach lights on the ends of posts extend 1,000 feet (300 meters) from each end of a runway to help pilots properly line up their planes for landing. Green threshold lights mark the ends of the runway.

Blue taxiway lights outline the taxiways, and floodlights illuminate the ramps. Red obstruction lights warn of hazards. Lighted wind direction indicators may be in the form of cones, tees, or cloth-covered devices called tetrahedrons.

A heliport may have a flashing or rotating beacon to identify it. It also has boundary lights that outline

An aircraft fueler pumps jet fuel into an airplane being prepared for takeoff. The fuel is stored in large tanks that may be either above or below the surface of the airfield.

the landing pad, plus floodlights and a lighted wind direction indicator.

Taking Off on a Flight

Departing passengers go to the gate for their flight shown on the flight information board. On the way to the gate, they must go through a security checkpoint as a safeguard against hijacking. Armed hijackers have taken over many planes in an effort to extort

In the United States, Federal Aviation Administration rules govern airport markings. Runway and taxiway markings help pilots to take off and land safely. The segmented circle marker locates and identifies an airport and indicates landing strip direction and traffic pattern. The hangar marker gives the name and location of the airport.

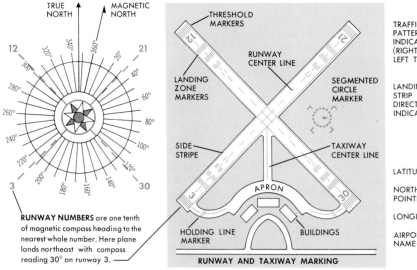

RUNWAY AND TAXIWAY MARKING

RUNWAY NUMBERS are one tenth of magnetic compass heading to the nearest whole number. Here plane lands northeast with compass reading 30° on runway 3.

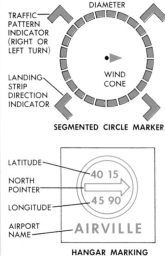

SEGMENTED CIRCLE MARKER

HANGAR MARKING

money or other things in exchange for the safety of the passengers and crews. Since 1973 the FAA has required every passenger to be screened prior to boarding an airliner. The passenger walks through a metal detector, which makes sure he or she is not carrying a weapon or explosives. At the same time, the passenger's hand-carried luggage goes through a special X-ray machine to be checked for dangerous items. This preboarding security check has practically eliminated the hijacking threat in the United States. Similar procedures have been adopted at major airports all over the world.

At the flight gate, a passenger service agent checks the passengers' tickets and asks them whether they would prefer seats next to a window or on an aisle, and in a smoking or nonsmoking section. The agent gives each person a boarding pass, which includes the date and flight number and the traveler's destination and seat assignment. About 15 minutes before departure time, a loudspeaker announcement asks the pas-sengers to board the aircraft. They show their boarding passes to a flight attendant at the door of the plane and then go to their seats.

When the plane is ready for takeoff, the pilot starts the engines and a tractor pushes the aircraft to an area on the ramp where it can start to taxi. After the tractor has been disconnected, the pilot moves the plane down a taxiway to the runway designated by an air traffic controller. The plane stops at the end of the runway and waits there until the pilot receives a radio call from an air traffic controller giving permission to take off.

The pilot sets the plane's wing flaps at the proper angle to help it rise from the ground. The aircraft turns onto the runway, and the pilot pushes the throttles forward as the engine generates power and the plane gains speed. When it reaches takeoff speed, the plane rises from the runway and the pilot retracts the landing gear and starts to climb to the assigned altitude. The flight has begun.

Approach lights and runway lights guide pilots to safe landings at Washington National Airport, Washington, D.C. Airport lighting is essential to night flying and during days of low visibility.

By courtesy of Federal Aviation Administration

Departing passengers go through a security check before entering the boarding area. An alarm sounds if any heavy metal objects—possible weapons—are carried through a detector. Often baggage goes through a separate device that X-rays it for any possible dangerous materials.

Bill Osmun—Air Transport Association

The Development of Air Traffic Control

Soon after the Wright brothers' first powered airplane flight in 1903, a growing number of pilots realized that some type of aviation rules would be necessary for their safety. The first attempt at air traffic control came when some pilots began to use maritime rules of right-of-way to avoid collisions.

In 1910, 19 European nations attempted to reach agreement on uniform rules of the air. They finally succeeded in 1919, when the International Commission for Aerial Navigation was established and the General Rules for Air Traffic Control were created.

The early rules for air traffic control were based on "see and be seen." If a pilot saw another plane, he simply maneuvered his aircraft to avoid a collision. The standardized rules told both pilots what to do in various situations, and these procedures worked well in daylight and good weather.

Pilots also needed daylight and fair weather to navigate. Until 1921 pilots navigated by recognizing rivers, roads, and other natural landmarks. The first night flight occurred that year, with bonfires used to mark the route for navigation. In 1924 the United States Post Office Department established the first air route marked by lighted beacons.

At the flight gate passengers file past airline service agents on their way to boarding. Each passenger must display a boarding pass that is issued at the gate before being allowed on the plane. The pass indicates the passenger's seat assignment and other flight details.

Bill Osmun—Air Transport Association

Aviation began to grow rapidly after World War I, particularly, in the United States. The United States Congress passed the Air Commerce Act in 1926, instructing the Department of Commerce to develop air traffic rules for the navigation, protection, and identification of aircraft. These rules included policies regarding safe flying altitudes and the prevention of collisions between vessels and aircraft. As a result of the Air Commerce Act, the Federal Airways System was established in 1927, establishing the use of radio signals for navigation. Pilots no longer needed to see natural landmarks, bonfires, or lighted beacons to navigate their planes. But even with radio signals to guide them, pilots could not safely fly into clouds or bad weather. A better system of navigation was still needed.

Pilots who could not see outside their airplanes often suffered from vertigo, or dizziness. Without

Air traffic controllers (right), who direct flight movements at the airfield, are crucial to flight and airport safety. At most large airports controllers operate from a tall traffic control tower (below), which stands above the other airport buildings and provides an unobstructed view of the airfield and surrounding skies.

Photos, (right) Goodyear Aerospace Corporation; (below) American Airlines

FEDERAL AVIATION AGENCY **FLIGHT PLAN**				FORM APPROVED BUDGET BUREAU NO. 04-R072.1		

1. TYPE OF FLIGHT PLAN	2. AIRCRAFT IDENTIFICATION	3. AIRCRAFT TYPE	4. ESTIMATED TRUE AIR SPEED (Knots)	5. DEPARTURE TIME	
☐ FVFR ☐ VFR ☒ IFR ☐ DVFR	N6864S	Fastflight	180	PROPOSED (Z) 1730	ACTUAL (Z)

6. INITIAL CRUISING ALTITUDE	7. POINT OF DEPARTURE	8. ROUTE OF FLIGHT
5000	Will Rogers OKC	V14S Shawnee Intersection, V15W OKM, V15 DAL, V15 ADM, V163 OKC

9. DESTINATION (Airport & City)	10. ALTITUDE CHANGES EN ROUTE		11. ESTIMATED TIME EN ROUTE		12. FUEL ON BOARD	
Will Rogers OKC	6000 OKM/ADM 5000 ADM/DAL 6000 DAL/OKC		HOURS 2	MINUTES 30	HOURS 4	MINUTES 55

13. ALTERNATE AIRPORT	14. REMARKS
SPS	----

15. NAME OF PILOT	16. ADDRESS OF PILOT OR AIRCRAFT HOME BASE	17. NO. OF PERSONS ABOARD
J. Smith	----	2

18. COLOR OF AIRCRAFT	19. FLIGHT WATCH STATIONS (FAA use)
-----	----

FAA Form 398 (6-62)
USE PREVIOUS EDITIONS.   **CLOSE FLIGHT PLAN UPON ARRIVAL**   SEE REVERSE

A flight plan to be filed with air traffic control allows close monitoring of the flight. It is mandatory to file flight plans that follow Instrument Flight Rules (IFR). It is recommended for those following Visual Flight Rules (VFR).

seeing the horizon, pilots did not know if they were climbing, diving, or turning. Sometimes they flew upside down out of a cloud while thinking they were flying straight and level. The invention of flight instruments in the early 1930's enabled pilots to know if they were flying straight and level. In 1933 the United States government established standards and rules for instrument flying and required airline pilots to demonstrate their skills while looking only at the instruments in the plane. These rules, which have been designated Instrument Flight Rules, were added to the see-and-be-seen rules, which are now known as Visual Flight Rules.

Between 1930 and 1932 two-way radios were installed in almost all airline planes. At some airports, these radios enabled pilots to talk to their company representatives. In 1934 American Airlines' radio operators in Chicago started a system of advising their pilots of weather and the presence of other company planes within 100 miles (160 kilometers) of Chicago. Other airlines soon began to cooperate in sending such advisory messages in Chicago and then in Newark, N.J. The airlines using Chicago and Newark agreed in 1935 to establish airway traffic control centers in Chicago, Newark, and Cleveland, Ohio. All three centers were operating by June 1936 under an airline plan to control airline airplanes within 50 miles (80 kilometers) of these airports. In 1936 the United States government took over the operation of the centers. By 1935 in addition to these facilities, 20 United States airports had control towers owned by city governments. The towers provided air traffic and local weather information to pilots during takeoffs and landings.

The Very High Frequency Omnidirectional Range (VOR) is a widely used system of electronic navigation. The omnirange station sends out an infinite number of radio signals, or radials, like wheel spokes. The pilot uses a VOR receiver and other cockpit instruments to stay on course.

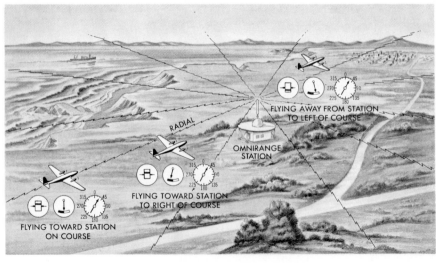

FLYING AWAY FROM STATION TO LEFT OF COURSE

RADIAL

OMNIRANGE STATION

FLYING TOWARD STATION TO RIGHT OF COURSE

FLYING TOWARD STATION ON COURSE

INSTRUMENTS IN AIRPLANE

Frequency Selector for tuning omnirange station desired

Omnibearing Selector and "To-From" Indicator for selecting magnetic bearing and for indicating whether bearing is to or from station

Course Line Deviation Indicator for indicating whether plane is on course

Federal Aviation Administration

In an air-route traffic control center computers help keep track of aircraft that are flying heavily traveled airways. For safety, airplanes in flight are kept well separated.

The Civil Aeronautics Act, passed by the United States Congress in 1938, established the Civil Aeronautics Authority (CAA), which developed a regulatory code known as Civil Air Regulations. These regulations set air traffic rules that, for the first time, required pilots to follow instructions issued by an airway traffic control center.

By 1942, 23 airway traffic control centers were serving airways throughout the United States. Because of the labor shortages during World War II, the CAA assumed responsibility for the operation of control towers as well as the control centers. By 1946 the CAA was operating 113 control towers and 24 centers employing about 1,800 air traffic controllers.

In 1946, the Radio Technical Commission for Aeronautics developed a traffic control system for commercial, military, and private planes. The International Civil Aviation Organization (ICAO) was formed in 1947 and put the air traffic control rules into effect in international airspace.

Incoming aircraft must sometimes be stacked when bad weather slows landings. Stacking requires pilots to go into a holding pattern that circles radio marker beacons. Each plane is assigned a level in a stack. If a primary stack is filled, planes are assigned to a secondary stack. When the lowest plane lands, the other planes descend one level.

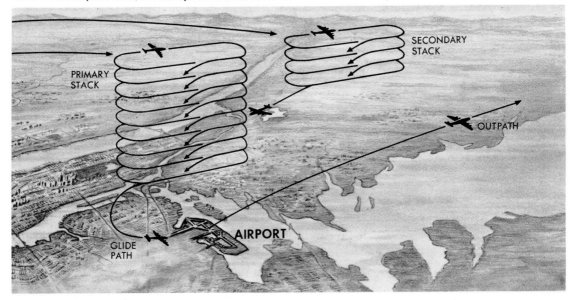

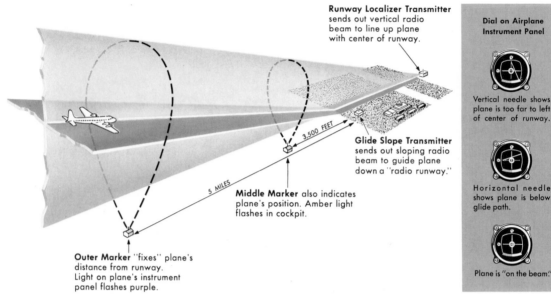

Runway Localizer Transmitter sends out vertical radio beam to line up plane with center of runway.

Glide Slope Transmitter sends out sloping radio beam to guide plane down a "radio runway."

Middle Marker also indicates plane's position. Amber light flashes in cockpit.

3,500 FEET

5 MILES

Outer Marker "fixes" plane's distance from runway. Light on plane's instrument panel flashes purple.

Dial on Airplane Instrument Panel

Vertical needle shows plane is too far to left of center of runway.

Horizontal needle shows plane is below glide path.

Plane is "on the beam."

Instrument Landing System (ILS) is used to land planes in bad weather. One transmitter sends out a vertical radio beam to line up the plane on the runway and another sends out a sloping beam to guide it down. Vertical and horizontal needles on a dial tell the pilot if the plane is on course. The distance of the plane from the runway is sent by two other transmitters, which cause cockpit lights to flash when the plane passes over them.

Direct communication between pilots and air traffic controllers by two-way radio came into use in the early 1950's. During this period, radar enabled controllers to "see" the location of aircraft far from an airport (*see* Radar). The United States Congress established the Airways Modernization Board (AMB) in 1957 to improve air traffic control.

Commercial aviation entered the jet age in 1958, and many changes were needed to modernize air traffic control because of the size, speed, and altitudes at which jet planes operated. That year, Congress passed the Federal Aviation Act of 1958, which established the Federal Aviation Agency to promote air commerce and regulate air safety. In 1967 this agency became the Federal Aviation Administration (FAA), under the Department of Transportation.

Air Traffic Control Today

Air traffic controllers throughout the world provide information and instructions to pilots according to the rules of the air. These rules are the same in all countries, and air traffic controllers everywhere use the same procedures. Most of these rules are established by the International Civil Aviation Organization (ICAO). The ICAO made English the international language of air traffic control. Controllers use these rules to prevent collisions between aircraft and to maintain an orderly flow of air traffic.

There are two sets of flight rules. During the daytime and in fair weather, pilots can use Visual Flight Rules, or VFR, watching for landmarks and other planes. At night, in bad weather, and in congested airspace, they follow Instrument Flight Rules, or IFR. In the United States, airline pilots are required

by the federal government to operate aircraft by Instrument Flight Rules only.

Pilots flying by IFR must obey all instructions issued by an air traffic controller. They must receive permission from a controller to take off and land and must have approval for the route and altitude they plan to fly. Air traffic controllers keep planes flying by IFR away from one another by instructing pilots when to take off and land and when to change altitude or direction.

Pilots using VFR must only receive permission from a controller to take off and land at airports that have an air traffic control tower. They are responsible for keeping their planes away from other aircraft. However, even if pilots flying by VFR do not talk to an air traffic controller, they must obey certain rules of the air. For example, they must fly only in good weather and avoid flying into areas where they are restricted. They must also fly at certain altitudes, depending upon their flight direction. If the airplane has navigation instruments, a VFR pilot can use the same electronic navigation systems as are available to the IFR pilot.

Electronic Navigation

IFR flight must be conducted without being able to see landmarks for navigation, and so electronic navigation is required. The most widely used aviation navigation system is called Very High Frequency Omnidirectional Range, or VOR. A VOR transmitter in a station on the ground sends radio signals that are received by a VOR receiver in a plane. The radio signals are transmitted in all directions, but they are identified for each of the 360 degrees radiating from the transmitter. By tuning in the radio frequency of a VOR, pilots are able to determine their direction from the VOR station. In addition, most VOR's are equipped with distance-measuring equipment, or DME. If an aircraft has the proper navigational equipment, the pilot is able to determine not only the direction of a ground station but also the plane's distance from the station up to 199 nautical miles (369 kilometers). If a VOR has DME, it is known as a VORTAC.

In the United States, more than 900 VORTAC stations make up a system of electronic highways called Victor Airways or Jet Routes, depending on their height. The electronic airways between these VOR's are control areas. Victor Airways begin at 1,200 feet (366 meters) above the ground and extend to 17,999 feet (5,486 meters) above sea level. Most of these routes are 8 nautical miles (15 kilometers) wide between VOR's spaced every 80 nautical miles (148 kilometers). Jet Routes are airways from 18,000 feet (5,486 meters) through 45,000 feet (13,716 meters) above sea level. The Positive Control Area also begins at 18,000 feet. Only IFR flights are permitted in this area between 18,000 feet and 60,000 feet (18,288 meters) above sea level. VOR's for high altitude jet routes are spaced as much as 260 nautical miles (482 kilometers) apart.

When planes get within 10 miles (16 kilometers) of an airport, they need a more accurate electronic navigation system than a VOR to guide them to the end of a runway. This system is called an Instrument Landing System, or ILS. It includes a localizer, which gives pilots directions to fly right or left, and a glide slope, which tells how fast to descend in order to arrive at just the right altitude for a perfect landing.

Air traffic controllers use radar to help guide airplanes that are flying within 35 miles (56 kilometers) of the airport. Radio signals from the radar antenna bounce off the metal aircraft or trigger an electronic box, called a transponder, in the plane to send a signal to the radar receiver. These signals are displayed on the air traffic controller's radarscope so he or she can see the location of the airplane.

How Airports Are Built

When engineers build airports, they first draw up a master plan. They take surveys that show the present volume of air traffic in the area and also forecast what it will be in the future. In addition, the engineers study the types of airplanes that will use the airport. Their master plan develops the airport by stages and allows for future expansion.

The planners determine how the new airport will fit into the system of airports and airways in the area. In the United States they must fit it into the National Airport System Plan prepared by the FAA.

An airport should be close to the center of population that it serves. It also should be planned so that residents of nearby areas are protected as much as possible from airplane noise.

There must be no flight obstructions at the airport itself, in the approach and departure zones, or in the vicinity of the airport. Clearance over highways and railroad tracks in the approach and departure zones should be adequate. The location of the airport must not interfere with the traffic at other nearby airports.

The direction of prevailing winds is important because planes take off and land into the wind. To study wind data, engineers construct a wind rose, a diagram shaped like a wheel. Its spokes indicate the direction and relative strength of the wind.

The amount and type of traffic served by an airport determine its size. The FAA classifies airports into four general categories. *General Aviation Airports* handle small private planes weighing less than 12,500 pounds (5,670 kilograms) and engaged in nonscheduled flying activities. *Reliever Airports* are specially designated general aviation airports that provide re-

An air traffic controller uses radar to monitor aircraft movements. Each dot on the radar screen represents an airplane, and it is the controller's responsibility to be sure that the dots are kept a safe distance apart.

Wide World

lief for congested major airports. *Air Carrier Airports-Commuter* are designed for scheduled operations conducted by commuter-type planes. *Air Carrier Airports-Certificated Service* serve airlines that operate large transport-type aircraft.

The lengths of runways are determined by a formula that consists of the thrust of jet engines, the degree of the flap-takeoff setting, and the elevation of the airport. At higher elevations, where the atmosphere is increasingly less dense, a plane needs more takeoff time to get the necessary lift to become airborne. Runways must be strong enough to bear the great pressure exerted by aircraft.

Leading Airports of the World

Most of the busiest airports are near capital cities and large population centers. The chief air traffic hub of the United States is the New York City metropolitan area. Three airports serve this area: John F. Kennedy International and LaGuardia in New York City and Newark International in New Jersey. Chicago's O'Hare International handles more flights annually than any other airport in the world.

Other major United States airports include Los Angeles International, Hartsfield Atlanta International, San Francisco International, Miami International, Dallas-Fort Worth, Washington (D.C.) National, Logan International in Boston, Stapleton International in Denver, Detroit Metropolitan, and Philadelphia International. Honolulu International is a major transoceanic airport. Canada has the world's largest airport—Mirabel, which serves the Montreal area. Toronto International ranks among the busiest Canadian airports. One of Latin America's busiest airports is Mexico City International.

Major international airports in Europe include Heathrow in London, England; Orly and Charles de Gaulle in Paris, France; Tegel in West Berlin, and Rhein-Main Airport in Frankfurt, West Germany; Fiumicino in Rome, Italy; Kastrup in Copenhagen, Denmark; Sheremetyedo in Moscow, the Soviet Union; and Palma de Majorca off the east coast of Spain. Japan's Haneda, near Tokyo, and Osaka International airports are among the busiest in Asia.

The History of United States Airports

In the early days of aviation in the United States, pilots often used a cow pasture as a "flying field" and a barn as a hangar. After World War I, the Army Air Service encouraged cities to build airports. The federal government spent about 393 million dollars between 1932 and 1942 to aid airport development. In the Federal Airport Act of 1946, the United States Congress directed the Civil Aeronautics Authority (now, in part, the Federal Aviation Administration) to prepare a National Airport Plan. This act authorized expenditures of up to 500 million dollars over a period of seven years. In 1955 a new law provided federal aid for another four years. The program was extended in 1959 and 1961, and it was renewed in 1964 for another three years.

The Airport and Airway Development Act, passed in 1970 and renewed in 1975, provides federal funds, raised principally through taxes on airline passenger tickets, for airport and airway development. The program allocated 4.4 billion dollars to build and improve airports. This was followed by the 1982 Airport and Airway Improvement Act, which allocates almost 5 billion dollars over a five-year period.

By 1982 the United States had more than 15,000 civil and civil-military airports, seaplane bases, and heliports. The nation's military airport facilities numbered about 300. (*See also* Aerospace; Airline; Airplane; Aviation.)

AIRSHIP *See* BALLOON AND AIRSHIP.

AIR TRAFFIC CONTROL *See* AIRPORT.

AJAX. Among the Greek warriors who besieged Troy, Ajax the Great ranked second only to Achilles in strength and courage. He was the son of Telamon and was half-brother of Teucer. Homer in the 'Iliad' describes him as being gigantic in stature.

At the death of Achilles, Ajax as the bravest of the Greeks claimed Achilles' armor. The prize, however, went to Odysseus (Ulysses) as the wisest. So enraged was Ajax that he went insane and killed himself. His story is told by the Greek playwright Sophocles in the tragedy 'Ajax'.

Another Greek hero of the same name was the "Lesser" Ajax, son of Oileus, king of Locris. He was small of stature but brave and skilled in throwing the spear. Only Achilles could run more swiftly. Like the Telamonian Ajax, he was the enemy of Odysseus. Boastful and arrogant, he defied even the gods. As punishment for his rash behavior he was wrecked and drowned on a return voyage from Troy.

AKBAR (1542–1605). The Mughal (or Mogul) dynasty ruled India for about 200 years, from 1530 to the middle of the 18th century. The Mughals were a Muslim (Islamic) power governing a basically Hindu country, but the greatest of their emperors, Akbar, managed to enlist the cooperation of Hindu leaders in conquering and governing virtually the whole of the Indian subcontinent.

Akbar was born in the province of Sind (now in Pakistan) on Oct. 15, 1542. He was a descendant of the great Mongol conquerors, Genghis Khan and Timur Leng (Tamerlane). Akbar's father, Humayun, had a very weak hold on his throne and was, in fact, driven from it for a period of more than ten years. He returned to power in 1555, only to die a year later. It was left to the young Akbar to consolidate the power of the monarchy and extend Mughal rule over India from his base in Punjab. This he did in a series of campaigns from 1561 to 1601.

Akbar's reign was noted for good government and a flourishing cultural life. He reformed the army, the civil service, and the collection of taxes. Foremost among his accomplishments was the centralization of all authority in the person of the emperor. This enabled him to find the best persons available for careers in public service. It also helped prevent abuses of power by local administrators and tax collectors.

Inequalities of wealth and poverty persisted in India despite Akbar's efforts to achieve good government. The emperor urged those who had great wealth to use it to become patrons of the arts. Although he was himself illiterate, his intelligent and inquiring mind led him to establish an elaborate court in which culture and the exchange of learned opinions were welcomed and could flourish. Akbar promoted tolerance in religion and invited Muslims, Christians, and Hindus to debate their ideas before him.

By the time Akbar died in 1605, his kingdom included most of the Indian subcontinent, Baluchistan, and Afghanistan. Such was the excellence of his administrative reforms that vestiges of them persist in the provincial governments of 20th-century India and Pakistan.

AKIBA BEN JOSEPH (40?–135). The destruction of Jerusalem by the Romans in A.D. 70 eliminated most of the competing sects and parties of ancient Judaism. The loss of the Temple as the focal point of worship had the effect of transferring the leadership of Judaism from the priests at Jerusalem to the rabbis, or scholars, in other parts of Palestine. It was the rabbinic Judaism that emerged from the disastrous war against the Roman Empire strong enough to provide guidance and cohesion to the Jews dispersed throughout the empire. One of the founders of rabbinic Judaism was Akiba ben Joseph, a scholar whose teaching helped shape the development of Jewish religious thought for centuries.

The facts concerning Akiba's life are somewhat sketchy. After he was put to death by the Romans in 135, many legends grew up about him. From these it is not always easy to disentangle fact from fiction.

Tradition has it that Akiba was born in Palestine about A.D. 40 and spent the first 40 years of his life as an uneducated farmer or shepherd. Only then did he turn his attention to the study of religion. Strongly supported by his wife, Rachel, he is said to have spent 12 years in the academy at Jabneh (or Jamnia) in Palestine learning the Law, or Torah, which makes up the first five books of the Old Testament.

Following his return home, Akiba opened his own academy in the town of Bene Baraq, near present-day Tel Aviv. From this school came many of the great teachers of 2d-century Judaism.

Akiba believed that every word and letter of the Old Testament had a special meaning. On the basis of this literalism, he devised principles of legal interpretation that pertained to virtually all aspects of an individual's life. He is said to have been the first rabbi to organize into a codified system all the legal and ethical standards of previous scholars. This codification is called the Mishna, the first standardization of Jewish law outside the Bible. Yet for all his emphasis on law, Akiba is considered to have been an outstanding humanitarian who was more concerned with justice than with punishment.

It is probable that late in his life Akiba was involved in the rebellion against the Roman emperor Hadrian. The rebellion was led by Simeon bar Kokhba in Palestine from 132 to 135. Akiba may even have been hailed as a Messiah, or Savior, by the Jews. The Romans imprisoned him at Caesarea in 132 and executed him in 135.

AKRON, Ohio. The city of Akron is known as the rubber capital of the world. Although the principal rubber product is tires, several factories make a great variety of other rubber articles, varying from rubber bands to logging balloons that are 142 feet (43 meters) long.  Other manufactures include toys, heating and air conditioning equipment, automobile bodies and parts, salt, clay products, paper and boxboard, wrought iron and steel products, children's books, and dairy products.

Akron is located on the Cuyahoga River, 35 miles (56 kilometers) southeast of Cleveland. In 1807 Capt. Joseph Hart formed the settlement of Middlebury, which is now East Akron. In 1825 Gen. Simon Perkins laid out a new town on the site of the present city. Because it was among the highest points in Ohio, it was named Akron, from the Greek *akros*, meaning "high."

The town was served by the Ohio and Erie Canal after the section between Akron and Lake Erie opened in 1827 and by the Pennsylvania and Ohio Canal after its completion in 1840. The water and transportation that were supplied to Akron by these canals led to its development as an industrial center. The north–south railroad that was completed in 1852 and the abundant water supply prompted Benjamin F. Goodrich to move his little rubber factory from Melrose, N.Y., to Akron in 1871. Thus began the industry which made the city famous. In the 1890's the first "horseless carriages" brought a demand for rubber tires. Akron prospered and grew as the demand for automobile tires increased.

Akron is an important truck terminal and distribution point between the Eastern Seaboard and the Midwestern United States. The city is the manufacturing center for lighter-than-air craft in the United States. At its municipal airport is the huge Goodyear Aerospace Air Dock, which is for blimps.

Akron is the home of the annual All-American Soap Box Derby for boys and girls who drive homemade gravity-propelled cars. The city's cultural centers include the Akron Art Institute and the Stan Hywet Hall, with antiques dating from the 16th century. The University of Akron, founded in 1913, has an Institute of Rubber Research. The city has a mayor-council form of government. (*See also* Ohio.) Population (1980 census), 236,820.

Beautiful gardens abound in and around Mobile, a major seaport and Alabama's second largest city. Here, flanked by azaleas, the Ile-aux-Oies River winds through Bellingrath Gardens.

Alabama Bureau of Publicity and Information

ALABAMA

ALABAMA. Few states have made as much progress during the 1900's as has Alabama. Before this century the economy of the entire state was based on cotton. Today Alabama farms produce a variety of crops and livestock products. Manufacturing is worth more than 8 billion dollars a year, and Birmingham has become the iron and steel capital of the South.

Most of Alabama's progress can be traced to three factors. The first was the discovery and use of the coal, iron ore, and limestone in the Birmingham area. These resources made possible the development of the city's steel industry. The second was the coming of the boll weevil, which, by destroying cotton crops, forced farmers to turn to other crops and to the raising of hogs and cattle. The third was the development of hydroelectric power.

The name Alabama is from Choctaw Indian words meaning "to clear (or reap) vegetation." The nickname Yellowhammer State originated during the Civil War, when Alabama troops stuck yellowhammer feathers in their caps. The yellowhammer, a member of the finch family, is Alabama's state bird.

Population (1980): 3,890,061 — rank, 22d state. Urban, 60.0%; rural, 40.0%. Persons per square mile, 76.6 (persons per square kilometer, 29.6) — rank, 26th state.

Extent: Area, 51,705 square miles (133,915 square kilometers), including 938 square miles (2,429 square kilometers) of water surface (28th state in size).

Elevation: Highest, Cheaha Mountain, 2,407 feet (734 meters) near Talladega; lowest, sea level; average, 500 feet (152 meters).

Geographic Center: 12 miles (19 kilometers) southwest of Clanton.

Temperature: Extremes — lowest, −27° F (−33° C) at New Market, Jan. 30, 1966; highest, 112° F (44° C) at Centerville, Sept. 5, 1925. Averages at Birmingham — January, 46.0° F (7.8° C); July, 80.2° F (26.8° C); annual, 62.9° F (17.2° C). Averages at Mobile — January, 52.5° F (11.4° C); July, 81.3° F (27.4° C); annual, 67.4° F (19.7° C).

Precipitation: At Birmingham — annual average, 51.86 inches (1,317 millimeters). At Mobile — annual average, 62.23 inches (1,581 millimeters).

Land Use: Crops, 18%; pasture, 6%; forest, 66%; other, 10%.

For statistical information about Agriculture, Education, Employment, Finance, Government, Manufacturing, Mining, Population Trends, and Vital Statistics, see ALABAMA FACT SUMMARY.

A Survey of Alabama

The Yellowhammer State lies in the central part of the Deep South. It is bordered on the north by Tennessee and on the west by Mississippi. On the south a panhandle extends along the Gulf of Mexico for 53 miles. The remainder of the southern boundary is shared with Florida. To the east is Georgia, separated in part from Alabama by the Chattahoochee River.

Alabama's greatest length, north to south, is 336 miles. Its greatest width, east to west, is 208 miles.

A State of Five Natural Regions

Almost all the northern part of Alabama lies in four distinct highland regions. Three of these regions form the southern end of the Appalachian Mountains system (*see* Appalachian Highlands). The remainder of the state lies in the coastal plain of the Gulf of Mexico. The boundary between the highlands and the plain is marked by the curving *fall line* of the rivers. The fall line enters the state on the east at Phenix City, passes west to Wetumpka, turns northwest to Tuscaloosa, and then runs north and west to the Tennessee River valley in Colbert County.

The Interior Low Plateaus form a rolling upland in the northwestern corner of the state on both sides of the Tennessee River. This region extends northward into Tennessee, where it is called the Highland Rim. The surface rises 200 to 300 feet above the Gulf Coastal Plain to the southwest.

The Appalachian Plateau, also called the Cumberland Plateau, juts into Alabama from the northeast as far south as Tuscaloosa County. Its highest point is the northern end of Lookout Mountain in De Kalb County, about 2,000 feet above sea level. From here the plateau slopes down to about 1,600 feet in the west and 500 feet in the south.

The Valley and Ridge region lies east of the Appalachian Plateau. It reaches south into Tuscaloosa, Bibb,

and Chilton counties. This region is a series of long narrow valleys lying between sharp mountain ridges. The city of Birmingham lies in Jones Valley northwest of Red Mountain. Another important lowland is the valley of the Coosa River.

The Piedmont Plateau is a triangular wedge, 500 to 1,000 feet in elevation, in the east-central part of the state. It is subdivided into the Opelika Plateau to the east and the Ashland Plateau in the west. In the Ashland Plateau is Cheaha Mountain (2,407 feet), the highest point in the state.

The Gulf Coastal Plain is the largest natural region in the state. Its highest part (about 600 feet) is the Central Pine Belt, which borders the Appalachian uplands. From here the surface slopes down to sea level along the coast. Near the center of Alabama a gently rolling prairie, the Black Belt, runs from Sumter County on the west to Russell County on the east. This section, named for its fertile black soil, is 25 to 50 miles wide. South of the Black Belt are the Southern Red Hills, named for their red, sandy clay soil. Pine flats and marshes fringe the coast.

The chief river of northern Alabama is the Tennessee, which bends northward to flow back into Tennessee. The other rivers of the state flow generally south. The Tombigbee and its principal branch, the Black Warrior, drain into the Mobile River, then into Mobile Bay. Also entering the bay is the Alabama, formed by the union of the Coosa and the Tallapoosa near Montgomery. The chief river in the east is the Chattahoochee, along the Georgia border.

Weather and Climate

Most of Alabama has a mild climate, with short, moderate winters and long, warm summers. At Birmingham, in the north-central part of the state, the average annual temperature is about 64° F.; at Mobile, in the southwest, it is about 68° F. De Kalb County, in the north, is the coldest part of the state, with

The largest city in Alabama is Birmingham, one of the nation's great producers of iron and steel. The city's skyline is seen here from Vulcan Park atop Red Mountain. The statue of Vulcan was cast from iron ore produced in Birmingham.

Metropolitan Development Board, Birmingham, Alabama

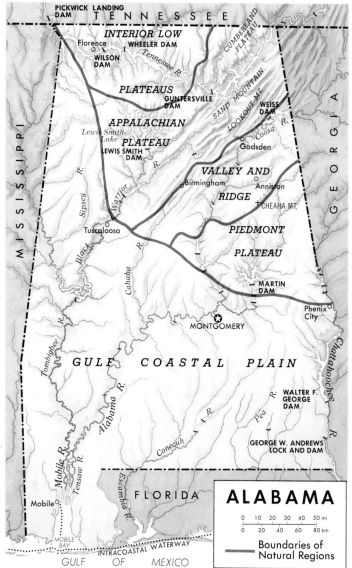

This map shows the five natural regions and the surface features of Alabama. The use that can be made of the land is related to the physical features of each region.

is one of the leading lumber-producing states. The chief commercial trees are pines; other important woods are oak, gum, and yellow poplar.

Valuable industrial resources include rich deposits of coal, iron ore, limestone, bauxite, and white marble, and streams for hydroelectric power. Navigable waterways reach far inland. Mobile Bay has a huge sheltered harbor. Tourism is important, particularly in the historic cities of Mobile and Montgomery.

Alabama's long dependence upon cotton led to erosion and depletion of soil nutrients. Farms have been rebuilt by the use of fertilizer, crop rotation, and other conservation methods. Another important conservation program has been the building of dams to prevent flooding. Hydroelectric generators have been installed in many of the dams. A valuable source of waterpower is at Muscle Shoals, near Florence, where the Tennessee River drops 134 feet in 37 miles. The Tennessee Valley Authority built Wheeler and Guntersville dams. Other projects in the state include Martin Dam, on the Tallapoosa River, and Lewis Smith Dam, on the Sipsey Fork. Brown's Ferry, near Decatur, and Farley, near Dothan, are two nuclear power complexes completed during the 1970's. The newer Bellefonte complex is located near Scottsboro. Most of the natural resources in the state are administered by the Department of Conservation and Natural Resources, the State Forestry Commission, and the Geological Survey.

The People of Alabama

Early inhabitants of the Alabama region were the Mound Builders. The first white settlers found the area occupied by four of the Five Civilized Tribes of Indians—Chickasaw, Choctaw, Cherokee, and Creek (the Seminole lived in Florida). The Alabama, or Alibamu, were part of the Creek Confederacy.

The Chickasaw were the most peaceful tribe, the Creek the most warlike. Beginning in 1805 all the tribes but the Creek began ceding their land to the United States. The Creek resisted white settlement until their power was crushed in 1814 by Gen. Andrew Jackson in the battle of Horseshoe Bend on the Tallapoosa River. By 1839 all the major bands of Indians had moved west of the Mississippi River.

Alabama was settled chiefly by people from Georgia, the Carolinas, and other Eastern states. It has attracted few immigrants from abroad. Today one percent of its people are foreign born. About one fourth of the people are blacks. They are largely con-

an average annual temperature about 8 Fahrenheit degrees less than that of the Mobile region. The southwest is the wettest part of Alabama. It receives an average of more than 65 inches of precipitation a year. Some areas in the center of the state receive the least precipitation—about 50 inches a year.

The growing season is long throughout the state. It ranges from about 200 days a year in the northwest and northeast to about 300 days along Mobile Bay.

Natural Resources and Conservation

Alabama's rich natural resources for agriculture include a long growing season, plenty of rainfall, and a variety of soils. The land produces much timber, with almost two thirds of the state forested. Alabama

Ewing Galloway

Much of Alabama's cotton is shipped from the government-owned State Docks and Terminals built along the Mobile River.

centrated in central Alabama. From 1970 to 1980 the state's black population has increased. It ranks thirteenth nationally and seventh among the Southern states in black population.

Manufacturing and Cities

Before World War II the value of manufacturing in Alabama was less than a quarter of a billion dollars a year. By 1947 it had more than tripled. By the late 1970's the value of manufacturing had reached almost 8½ billion dollars a year, having increased by almost 3½ billion dollars in the five-year period from 1972 to 1977. Manufacturing income is almost six times that from farming and mining combined.

Today there are in Alabama more than 5,000 manufacturing establishments employing approximately 350,000 workers. The growth and diversification of industry in Alabama between 1947 and 1977 has been reflected in a dispersion of workers among more industry groups. In 1947, three traditional industries—textiles, primary metals, and lumbering—accounted for 62 percent of manufacturing employment. In 1977, the six most valuable industries—primary metals, paper, chemicals, fabricated metal, textiles, and rubber and plastics—accounted for only 45 percent of manufacturing employment.

The most important of these industries is primary metals, centered in the Birmingham district, which contains most of the resources necessary for the manufacture of iron, steel, and aluminum. The abundant supply of these metals has been responsible for Alabama's development of its metal fabrication industry. Textile mills have developed because of the hydroelectric power plants on the Tennessee River and on streams in the Piedmont Plateau. The ready availability of fabrics fostered the development of an extensive wearing-apparel industry. Other industries are also important, including food processing, machinery, and electronics. The state's forests provide raw materials for the manufacture of lumber and wood, furniture, and paper and paper products.

The state's chief industrial center and largest city is Birmingham, in north-central Alabama. It is a highway and railroad hub and also has a water outlet to the Gulf of Mexico (*see* Birmingham). Mobile, the second largest city, is a port on Mobile Bay and a ship-repair center (*see* Mobile). The state capital is Montgomery, the fourth largest city and the chief trade center of the Black Belt (*see* Montgomery).

Gadsden, Anniston, and Bessemer are large steelmaking cities in the northern half of the state. Tuscaloosa is a lumbering and agricultural center on the Black Warrior River. Huntsville, in north-central Alabama, is the third largest city. It is the home of the United States Army's Redstone Arsenal, which includes the George C. Marshall Space Flight Center, and the Alabama Space and Rocket Center.

Agriculture, Mining, and Fishing

Farms occupy about 12 million acres in Alabama. In recent years they have grown fewer in number and larger in size. In the mid-1950's Alabama farms numbered nearly 116,000. By 1980 they numbered some 58,000, with an average acreage of about 219. Only about 8 percent are operated by tenants; in 1950 more than 41 percent were tenant operated.

Alabama farmers have increasingly turned from growing crops to raising livestock and poultry. In a typical year sales of livestock and livestock products account for about two thirds of farm receipts. Most important are poultry, including eggs, and cattle, swine, and dairy products. The poultry industry is concentrated in the northern counties. Beef cattle are raised largely in the central Black Belt. The leading hog-producing counties are in the southeast.

Automation, which has been the key to increased livestock and poultry production, has also influenced crop production. In general, crops requiring large numbers of workers have given way to crops that can be planted, cultivated, and harvested largely by ma-

At Enterprise a statue honors the boll weevil for helping change the cotton-based economy.

chine. Cotton, though still an important cash crop, is no longer king in Alabama. In the late 1970's cotton acreage was less than soybeans or corn (maize).

The principal corn- and soybean-producing counties are in the southern part of the state and in the Tennessee Valley of the north. Peanuts are the principal cash crop in southeastern Alabama. Alabama is among the leading states in pecan production.

The state's most valuable mineral resource is coal. Most of the coal lies in fields in the north-central part of Alabama. The largest is the Warrior field near Birmingham, which covers about 3,000 square miles. Petroleum, found in the coastal regions, is the second-ranking mineral resource and natural gas, the third. By 1980 Alabama had leased about 28,000 acres offshore for oil and gas production. In that same year, production of petroleum was 22 million barrels while natural gas was 106 billion cubic feet. Stone, especially marble, is also a valuable product of the Piedmont Plateau. Red Mountain, adjoining Birmingham,

Wheeler Dam on the Tennessee River supplies hydroelectric power for northern Alabama's industries.

bears a huge seam of hematite (iron ore), which is the basis of the state's steel industry.

Most of Alabama's fish catch comes from the Gulf of Mexico and from coastal rivers. Among the most valuable catches are shrimp, red snapper, oysters, mullet, and menhaden.

Transportation by Land and Water

The first wagon road into Alabama was the Natchez Trace, across the Tennessee River near Muscle Shoals (*see* Road and Street). The Federal Road, called the Three Notch Road from markings chopped on trees, opened in 1805 and ran from the site of Phenix City to the Alabama River. Branches extended to Natchez, Miss., and to Fort Stoddert. Alabama's modern road system began in 1911 with the formation of the State Highway Department. There are about 87,000 miles of state and county roads.

River-barge traffic is heavy on the Tennessee and on the Black Warrior-Tombigbee-Mobile system. Mobile has a fine harbor, which includes the Alabama State Docks, a major ocean terminal. A 36-mile channel leads to the Intracoastal Waterway.

One of the first railroads in the South connected Tuscumbia with the Tennessee River at Muscle Shoals in 1832. This two-mile line was extended to Decatur three years later. Today the state is served by some 20 major and secondary railroad lines. Air transportation is also well developed.

Recreation in Alabama

Tourists provide the basis of a multimillion-dollar industry in the Yellowhammer State. Mobile has two of the leading attractions in the nation—a Mardi Gras festival and the Azalea Trail. The Dogwood Trail and the annual Festival of Arts and state fair attract many visitors to Birmingham. The Blessing of the Shrimp Fleet at Bayou La Batre and the Deep Sea Fishing Rodeo at Dauphin Island south of Mobile Bay are popular. The Natchez Trace Parkway, Horseshoe Bend National Military Park, and Russell Cave National Monument are administered as national park areas (*see* National Parks).

Education in Alabama

For many years education in Alabama was limited to tutors and private academies. It was not until 1854 that the legislature was able to provide an effective public school system. The Civil War halted educational activities and forced an extensive program of rebuilding schools and colleges.

In 1907, high schools were established in every county except those which already had normal or agricultural schools. Today each county has at least two high schools.

State-supported schools include the University of Alabama, at University, with branch campuses in Birmingham and Huntsville; Auburn University, at Auburn, with a branch at Montgomery; Jacksonville State University, at Jacksonville; the University of South Alabama, at Mobile; the University of North

Fire consumed the Capitol building in Montgomery just two years after that city had become the seat of government, destroying many valuable records.

Alabama, at Florence; University of Montevallo, at Montevallo; and Alabama Agricultural and Mechanical University, at Normal. There are also state universities at Troy, Montgomery, and Livingston.

Other large schools are Samford University, at Birmingham; Spring Hill College, at Mobile; and Huntingdon College, at Montgomery. Tuskegee Institute was opened by Booker T. Washington in 1881 (*see* Washington, Booker T.).

Government and Politics

While Alabama was a territory, its capital was at St. Stephens. Huntsville was the first state capital, followed by Cahaba, Tuscaloosa, and, since 1847, Montgomery. The state is governed under its sixth constitution, adopted in 1901.

The chief executive officer is the governor, elected every four years. The state legislature consists of a Senate and a House of Representatives. Heading the judiciary is the Supreme Court. All judges and justices are elected for six-year terms.

Alabama traditionally has been a politically conservative state in both local and national politics. Since 1876 it has voted for the Democratic candidate for president in all except six elections. The Republican candidate won in 1964, 1972, and 1980, and third-party candidates won in 1948, 1960, and 1968.

HISTORY OF ALABAMA

Alabama's southern boundary along the 31st parallel of north latitude was fixed while Florida was still a possession of Spain. It was determined by a treaty signed in 1795. The Perdido River boundary with Spanish Florida was established in 1813. By the time Alabama was ready to become a state, its other boundaries had been set by the admission into the Union of neighboring states to the east, north, and west—Georgia (one of the original states), Tennessee (1796), and Mississippi (1817). The following sections tell the development of Alabama into a modern state.

Exploration and Settlement

In 1540 the Spanish adventurer Hernando de Soto became the first European to explore what is now Alabama (*see* De Soto). A permanent settlement was not made until 1702, when the French built Fort Louis de la Mobile on the Mobile River. The governor was Jean Baptiste le Moyne, sieur de Bienville (*see* Bienville). In 1719 slave ships brought the first blacks to clear the land for rice and indigo.

France ceded the region to Great Britain in 1763 (*see* French and Indian War). Many British traders and colonists moved in at this time. In 1783 Great Britain surrendered all Alabama except the Mobile area to the United States. In 1813 the Creeks destroyed Fort Mims, near the junction of the Alabama and Tombigbee rivers. The next year Gen. Andrew Jackson defeated them at Horseshoe Bend. In 1817 Alabama was made a territory, and two years later it was admitted to the Union as the 22d state.

The Civil War Period

The first half of the 1800's was a period of extensive cotton planting. Production was encouraged by Abraham Mordecai, who built Alabama's first cotton gin in 1802 at Coosada Bluff near Montgomery. The Black Belt and other rich cotton-growing areas had large plantations with beautiful homes.

Wealthy planters who held many slaves dominated the state. One of their chief spokesmen was William

227

L. Yancey, the fiery editor of the *Wetumpka Argus*. Alabama seceded from the Union on Jan. 11, 1861. Montgomery became the first capital of the Confederacy. It was here that Jefferson Davis was inaugurated as president of the Confederacy. (*See also* Confederate States of America.)

Early in the Civil War Union forces occupied the Tennessee Valley. In August 1864 Adm. David G. Farragut destroyed the Confederate fleet in Mobile Bay. By April 1865 the whole state was occupied by Federal forces. One of the most famous of Alabama's leaders in the war was Adm. Raphael Semmes, commander of the sea raider *Alabama* (*see* 'Alabama' Claims). Other outstanding Confederate leaders from the state were John Morgan, John Pelham, and Joseph Wheeler. (*See also* Civil War, American.)

After the Civil War, Alabama was placed under military rule. The state was readmitted to the Union in 1868 when the Republicans were in control, but by 1875 the Democrats were again in power (*see* Reconstruction Period).

The Modern State

There have been marked industrial changes in Alabama in the 20th century. Many cotton mills have moved there, providing more jobs. Steel-manufacturing towns in the state send their products all over the world. Hydroelectric power has contributed to the development of manufacturing, and dams have helped to protect farmlands from flooding and soil erosion. Development of petroleum and natural gas reserves has enhanced the economic importance of the state's mineral resources.

During this time many Alabamians made outstanding contributions to the nation. George Washington Carver pioneered in scientific agriculture (*see* Carver). The Panama Canal could not have been built without the work of William C. Gorgas (*see* Gorgas). Robert J. Van de Graaff invented the high-voltage generator (*see* X Rays). From 1970 to 1980 the population of Alabama increased by nearly 445,707 persons, a gain of about 13 percent.

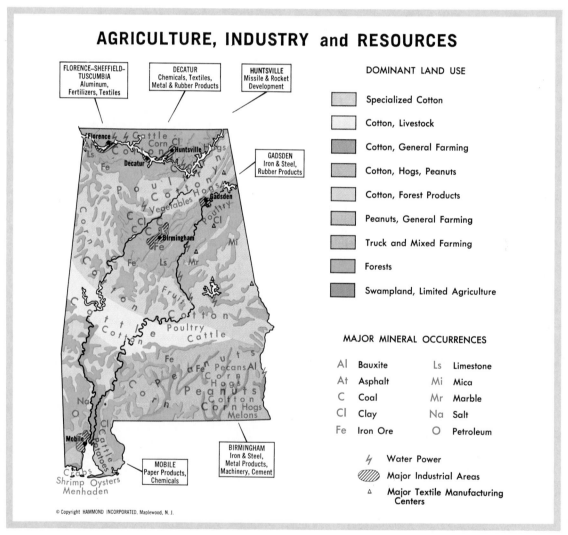

Notable Events in Alabama History

1540—De Soto crosses Alabama; battles Indians at Mauvila, near Choctaw Bluff.

1629—Charles I makes Carolina grant; includes Alabama area.

1699—Pierre le Moyne, sieur d'Iberville, founds colony near Biloxi, Miss. Alabama, as part of Louisiana, is governed from there.

1702—Jean Baptiste le Moyne, sieur de Bienville, builds Fort Louis de la Mobile on Mobile River above Mobile; moves capital from Biloxi to fort.

1711—Fort Louis moved to present site of Mobile; name changed to Fort Condé la Mobile in 1720.

1719—First shipload of slaves arrives at Dauphin Island.

1763—Alabama included in area ceded by France to Great Britain in Treaty of Paris.

1780—Bernardo de Galvez, governor of Spanish Louisiana, captures Mobile from English.

1783—Great Britain cedes Alabama north of 31st parallel to U. S.; Florida, including Mobile, to Spain.

1798—Mississippi Territory created; includes Alabama.

1802—**First cotton gin built, in Montgomery County.**

1803—U. S. claims Mobile as part of Louisiana Purchase.

1805—Chickasaw, Cherokee, and Choctaw cede part of land claims in Alabama region to U. S.

1813—U. S. Gen. James Wilkinson seizes Mobile from Spaniards. Creek Indians massacre colonists at Fort Mims. Creek defeated by Gen. Andrew Jackson at battle of Horseshoe Bend in 1814; site dedicated as national military park in 1964.

1817—Congress creates Alabama Territory; capital, St. Stephens; governor, William W. Bibb.

1819—Alabama becomes 22d state, December 14; capital, Huntsville; governor, Bibb.

1820—Capital moved to Cahaba. University of Alabama chartered; opened near Tuscaloosa in 1831.

1826—State capital moved to Tuscaloosa.

1832—State's first cotton mill built in Madison County.

1846—Legislature votes to move state capital to Montgomery; holds first session there in 1847.

1851—Present State Capitol completed.

1861—**Alabama secedes from Union; Confederate government formed at Montgomery; Jefferson Davis inaugurated Confederate president there.**

1862—Federal forces invade Alabama; capture Huntsville, Decatur, and Tuscumbia.

1864—**Adm. David Farragut's Union fleet wins battle of Mobile Bay; Mobile captured in 1865.**

1868—Alabama readmitted to the Union.

1871—Birmingham founded as railroad junction point.

1880—Blast furnace built at Birmingham.

1881—Booker T. Washington founds Tuskegee Institute.

1901—Present state constitution adopted.

1933—**Wilson Dam at Muscle Shoals, completed in 1924, becomes first unit in Tennessee Valley Authority.**

1949—Redstone rocket center established at Huntsville.

1962—Alabama's state legislature is first to be reapportioned by federal court order.

1965—Drive for Negro voter registration dramatized by "Freedom March," from Selma to Montgomery.

1966—Tennessee Valley Authority awards contract for its first nuclear power plant, near Decatur.

1970—First blacks elected to state legislature since Reconstruction period.

1972—Jones Bluff Lock and Dam officially opened, making possible barge traffic on the Alabama River as far north as Montgomery.

1974—Tornadoes and hurricanes in northern part of state kill 81 persons.

1802

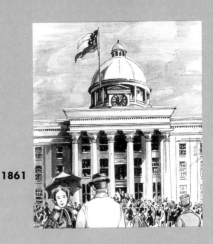

1861

1864

1933

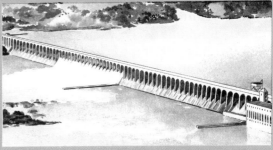

229

STATE FLOWER:
Camellia

STATE TREE:
Longleaf Pine

STATE BIRD:
Yellowhammer

STATE SEAL: State map shows
chief rivers.

Alabama Profile

FLAG: *See* Flags of the United States.
MOTTO: Audemus Jura Nostra
   Defendere (We Dare Defend
   Our Rights).
SONG: 'Alabama'—words, Julia S.
   Tutwiler; music, Edna G. Gussen.

For a hundred years, King Cotton ruled in Alabama. Cotton is still a major crop, but the state's diversified agriculture of today, flourishing in a mild climate with adequate rainfall, produces crops ranging from corn to peanuts, from soybeans to watermelons. Cattle, hogs, and chickens are also important farm products of Alabama.

Even more dramatic than its agricultural growth has been Alabama's industrial emergence. The state is situated in the Deep South, commonly considered an agricultural region. Yet its income from manufacturing is twice the combined total obtained from farming, mining, forestry, and fishing. Rich resources of iron ore, coal, and limestone have helped make Alabama a major steel-producing state. Great dams on its rivers provide flood control and hydroelectric power—much of which is consumed by a thriving textile industry. Alabama has the world's largest known deposits of white marble and contains vast areas of pine and hardwood forest. It also has one of the best water-transportation systems in the South. The city of Mobile, linked by Mobile Bay with the Gulf of Mexico, is an important seaport.

Despite all its newly tapped industrial wealth, Alabama is still confronted with problems rooted in the pre-Civil War era. It is working to reclaim hundreds of square miles of land that too many years of one-crop farming left eroded and infertile and to replant vast stretches of cutover forest. The state is also trying to strengthen its educational system and to resolve long-standing problems in human relations. Alabama's Negro citizens are intensifying their efforts to secure the equalities guaranteed by the federal Constitution, and men of goodwill—both whites and Negroes—are working to achieve a climate of mutual understanding and respect.

Floodlit against a night sky, Alabama's State Capitol stands in Montgomery. The Capitol's center section and dome were completed in 1851. It was the first Capitol of the Confederacy and the scene in 1861 of Jefferson Davis' inauguration as president of the Confederate States of America.

Near the center of the University of Alabama's Tuscaloosa campus stands its main library, completed in 1940. The university, which opened in 1831, has branches at Birmingham and Huntsville as well as numerous other facilities.

Many of the rockets and space vehicles for United States space exploration programs are designed and built at the George C. Marshall Space Flight Center at Huntsville. Nearby is the United States Army's Redstone Arsenal.

Alabama picture profile

Images of the grace and elegance of a bygone era are evoked by the many fine plantation homes that Alabama maintains as tourist attractions. Above are exterior and interior views of Gaineswood, an antebellum mansion set in a spacious lawn near Demopolis.

Billets of steel emerge from a continuous casting machine at Birmingham, the largest city in Alabama. Near the city lie rich deposits of iron ore, coal, and limestone. Making iron and steel products is Alabama's major industry.

Now a state park, historic Fort Morgan overlooks the mouth of Mobile Bay. Troops of seven flags have manned the star-shaped fort. It was built in the 1700's and was a key strongpoint in the War of 1812 and the Civil War.

A parade in Mobile is a highlight of the annual Mardi Gras celebration, one of Alabama's colorful festivals. Mobile was the site of the first such carnival parade to be held in the New World.

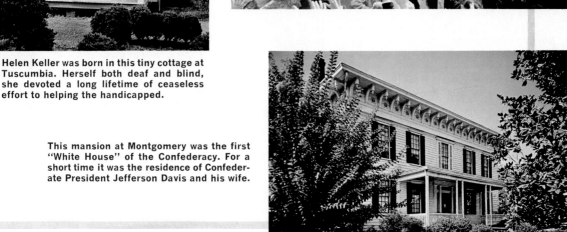

Helen Keller was born in this tiny cottage at Tuscumbia. Herself both deaf and blind, she devoted a long lifetime of ceaseless effort to helping the handicapped.

This mansion at Montgomery was the first "White House" of the Confederacy. For a short time it was the residence of Confederate President Jefferson Davis and his wife.

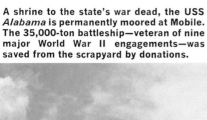

A shrine to the state's war dead, the USS *Alabama* is permanently moored at Mobile. The 35,000-ton battleship—veteran of nine major World War II engagements—was saved from the scrapyard by donations.

ALABAMA FACT SUMMARY

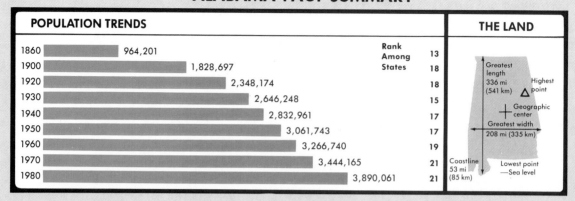

POPULATION TRENDS

Year	Population	Rank Among States
1860	964,201	13
1900	1,828,697	18
1920	2,348,174	18
1930	2,646,248	15
1940	2,832,961	17
1950	3,061,743	17
1960	3,266,740	19
1970	3,444,165	21
1980	3,890,061	21

THE LAND

Greatest length 336 mi (541 km)
Highest point
Geographic center
Greatest width 208 mi (335 km)
Coastline 53 mi (85 km)
Lowest point —Sea level

LARGEST CITIES (1980 census)

Birmingham (284,413): leading iron and steel center of South; industrial city; railroad shops; iron state of Vulcan (*see* Birmingham, Ala.).

Mobile (200,452): seaport on Mobile Bay; state docks; industrial center; shipyards; 37-mile (60-kilometer) Azalea Trail (*see* Mobile, Ala.).

Montgomery (178,157): state capital; manufacturing center; Victorian furniture reproductions; dairying and livestock market; first White House of Confederacy (*see* Montgomery, Ala.).

Huntsville (142,513): missile and space research center; textiles, other manufactures; first state capital (1819–1820); Redstone Arsenal nearby.

Tuscaloosa (75,143): trade center; University of Alabama; Old Tavern (1826); Gorgas home.

Dothan (48,750): lumber and wood products; hosiery, clothing; meat processing; National Peanut Festival.

Gadsden (47,565): industrial city; steel and fabricated metal products; Noccalula Falls.

Decatur (42,002): on Tennessee River; chemical fibers, tire fabrics, metal products.

Prichard (39,541): industrial suburb of Mobile.

Florence (37,029): aluminum, fertilizer, and textile manufacturing; livestock; Wilson Dam nearby.

VITAL STATISTICS 1980 (per 1,000 population)

Birthrate:	16.6
Death Rate:	9.4
Marriage Rate:	13.0
Divorce Rate:	7.1

GOVERNMENT

Capital: Montgomery (voted, 1846; first session of state legislature, 1847).

Statehood: became 22d state in the Union on Dec. 14, 1819.

Constitution: adopted 1901; amendment may be passed by three-fifths vote of Legislature; ratified by majority voting on it in a popular election.

Representation in U.S. Congress: Senate—2. House of Representatives—7. Electoral votes—9.

Legislature: Senators—35; term, 4 years. Representatives—105; term, 4 years.

Executive Officers: governor—term, 4 years; may succeed self once. Other officials—lieutenant governor, secretary of state.

Judiciary: all justices and judges elected for 6-year terms. Supreme Court—9 justices; Court of Civil Appeals—3 judges; Court of Criminal Appeals—5 judges; Circuit Courts—112 judges.

County: 67 counties; governed by boards of commissioners; members elected for 4-year terms.

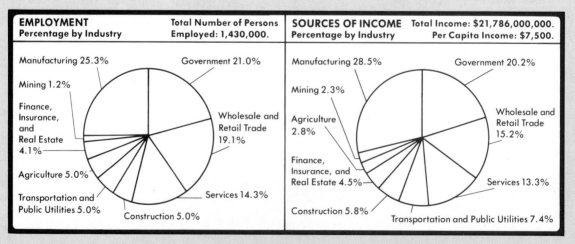

EMPLOYMENT Percentage by Industry — Total Number of Persons Employed: 1,430,000.

- Manufacturing 25.3%
- Government 21.0%
- Mining 1.2%
- Finance, Insurance, and Real Estate 4.1%
- Wholesale and Retail Trade 19.1%
- Agriculture 5.0%
- Transportation and Public Utilities 5.0%
- Construction 5.0%
- Services 14.3%

SOURCES OF INCOME Percentage by Industry — Total Income: $21,786,000,000. Per Capita Income: $7,500.

- Manufacturing 28.5%
- Government 20.2%
- Mining 2.3%
- Agriculture 2.8%
- Wholesale and Retail Trade 15.2%
- Finance, Insurance, and Real Estate 4.5%
- Services 13.3%
- Construction 5.8%
- Transportation and Public Utilities 7.4%

MAJOR PRODUCTS

Agricultural: soybeans, peanuts, cotton and cottonseed, corn (maize), poultry, dairy and beef cattle.

Manufactured: iron and steel, paper, chemicals, dairy products.

Mined: coal, crude petroleum, natural gas, cement, limestone, marble, asphalt, mica, bauxite.

EDUCATION AND CULTURE

Universities and Colleges: Auburn University, Auburn; Jacksonville State University, Jacksonville; Troy State University, Troy; Tuskegee Institute, Tuskegee; University of Alabama, University (Tuscaloosa).

Libraries: Air University Library, Maxwell Air Force Base; Alabama Public Library Service; Birmingham Public and Jefferson County Free Library; Choctanhatchee Regional Library System; Public Library of Anniston and Calhoun County.

Notable Museums: Alabama Department of Archives and History, Montgomery; Anniston Museum of Natural History; Birmingham Museum of Art; George Washington Carver Museum, Tuskegee Institute; University of Alabama Museum of Natural History.

PLACES OF INTEREST

Alabama Space and Rocket Center: at Huntsville; museum of rocketry and space travel.

Ave Maria Grotto: at St. Bernard College in St. Bernard; miniature reproduction of the Holy Land.

Bellingrath Gardens: near Mobile along Azalea Trail; azaleas, camellias, and other flowers; moss-hung live oaks.

Cathedral Caverns: near Grant; large stalagmite forest; frozen waterfall.

Dauphin Island: at entrance to Mobile Bay; French settlement (1669); Fort Gaines.

Demopolis: in Marengo County; Gaineswood, Bluff Hall, and other beautiful plantation mansions.

DeSoto Caverns: near Childersburg; oldest recorded U.S. caverns.

Horseshoe Bend National Military Park: near Dadeville; Andrew Jackson defeated Creek Indians near here on March 27, 1814, during the War of 1812.

Ivy Green: at Tuscumbia; birthplace and home of Helen Keller, noted deaf and blind author-lecturer.

Jasmine Hill Garden: in Mobile; Greek sculpture, ruins, and art objects.

Magnolia Grove: at Greensboro; home of Adm. Richmond P. Hobson, hero of Spanish-American War.

Magnolia Springs: in Baldwin County; fishing resort with only all-water mail route in Alabama.

Mentone: in DeKalb County; resort on top of Lookout Mountain; scenic drives.

Monument to the Boll Weevil: erected by the grateful farmers of Enterprise; damage done to cotton by this insect forced them to diversify their crops.

Mound State Monument: near Moundville; prehistoric Indian city of 34 mounds; museum.

Pope's Tavern: in Florence; during Civil War served as both hospital and tavern.

Russell Cave National Monument: near Bridgeport; oldest known home of primitive man in southeastern U.S.

Sequoyah Caverns: in Valley Head; crystal-clear reflecting pools of water; stalagmites.

State Parks: total of 21, including Chattahoochee, DeSoto, Gulf, Joe Wheeler, Little River, Oak Mountain, Cheaha.

The Dismals: near Phil Campbell; rock walls rise 100 feet (30 meters) above bottom of ravine; wild flowers.

Tuskegee: in Macon County; old homes; Tuskegee Institute.

TVA Dams: Wilson, at Muscle Shoals, Wheeler, near Rogersville, and Guntersville, near Guntersville; fishing, boating, and other recreation on lakes formed by dams (see Tennessee Valley Authority).

USS Alabama: in Mobile Bay; battleship bought by the people of Alabama; established as a state shrine.

Vestavia Temple and Gardens: near Birmingham; replica of a Roman temple.

BIBLIOGRAPHY FOR ALABAMA

Akens, H. M. and Brown, V. P. Alabama Mounds to Missiles (Strode, 1966).

Bailey, B. F. Picture Book of Alabama, rev. ed. (Whitman, 1966).

Brown, V. P. and Akens, H. M. Alabama Heritage (Strode, 1967).

Carmer, C. L. Stars Fell on Alabama (Hill, 1961) o.p.

Carpenter, Allan. Enchantment of Alabama (Childrens, 1968) o.p.

Hamilton, V. V. Alabama: a Bicentennial History (Norton, 1977).

Lee, Mildred. The Rock and the Willow (Archway, n.d.).

Stribling, T. S. The Forge (Scholarly, 1971).

Swindler, W. F. and Trover, E. L., eds. Chronology & Documentary Handbook of the State of Alabama (Oceana, 1972).

Writers' Program. Alabama: a Guide to the Deep South (Somerset, 1941).

All Fact Summary data are based on current government reports.

ALABAMA

236

ALABAMA

MILES

0   20   40   60

KILOMETERS

0   20   40   60

State Capitals ✪
County Seats ✪
Major Limited
Access Hwys. ―――

© Copyright HAMMOND INCORPORATED, Maplewood, N.J.

'ALABAMA' CLAIMS. In spite of warnings by the American minister to England, Charles Francis Adams, the British-built steam cruiser *Alabama* was allowed to put to sea on July 29, 1862. Adams said the *Alabama* was intended as a warship for the Confederate government during the American Civil War. He was right; for two years the *Alabama* destroyed Northern merchantmen, until it was finally sunk by the cruiser *Kearsarge* on June 19, 1864.

After long discussions the British government agreed to submit to arbitration the claims of the United States for damages arising out of the *Alabama* case. Five arbitrators met at Geneva, Switzerland, in December 1871. They decided that Britain had not exercised "due diligence" to prevent the ship's departure and awarded $15,500,000 damages. This ended the dispute, which had threatened the friendly relations between the two countries. It was also a victory for the principle of the peaceable settlement of international disputes by arbitration (*see* Arbitration).

ALABASTER. Two different mineral substances are called alabaster. The alabaster used by the ancient Greeks and Romans was actually marble, a granular aggregate of crystals of calcium carbonate (*see* Marble). Modern alabaster is a compact form of granular gypsum.

Alabaster is white, pink, or yellow. It often has darker streaks, or bands, of color. The best quality is pure white and translucent. It is so soft that it can be scratched with a fingernail. This softness makes it good for carving. It is used for statues, vases, and other ornaments. Florence, Italy, is the center of its production. It is also found in England and France. Nova Scotia and New York have small deposits.

ALAMO. An old mission-fort, the Alamo, in San Antonio, has been called the "cradle of Texas liberty." Its gallant defense and the horrible massacre of the more than 180 men who fought there inspired the cry, "Remember the Alamo!" Texas soldiers shouted this at the battle of San Jacinto, which brought independence to Texas. (*See also* Texas.)

The Alamo was originally the Mission San Antonio de Valero, founded in 1718 (*see* San Antonio). It ceased to function as a church institution in 1793. At the time of its famous siege the mission chapel was a roofless ruin, but a high rock wall about three feet (one meter) thick enclosed an area around the chapel large enough to accommodate 1,000 men. Within that enclosure the battle of the Alamo was fought.

In 1835, during the battle for Texas independence from Mexico, San Antonio had been captured by the Texans. Only 144 soldiers, most of them volunteers, were left to guard the city. They were under the command of Lieut. Col. W. B. Travis. On Feb. 22, 1836, a Mexican force of almost 5,000 troops under Santa Anna arrived at San Antonio. Travis and Col. James Bowie, for whom the bowie knife was named, believed that the Alamo must be held to prevent Santa Anna's march into the interior. On February 23 they and their forces went into the fort, with about 30 refugees, and prepared to withstand attack by the Mexicans. Santa Anna hoisted a flag of no quarter and demanded unconditional surrender. This was answered by a cannon shot from the fort. The Mexican bombardment began. Meanwhile, on February 22, the frontiersman David Crockett and some of his Tennessee riflemen had arrived to help in the defense. On March 1, 32 more volunteers were brought from Gonzales by James Butler Bonham.

The siege lasted 12 days. On the morning of March 6 several thousand Mexicans stormed the fort. As they attacked, a Mexican trumpeter sounded the *deguello*—the no-quarter bugle call of Spain—as a signal to the soldiers to butcher all in the fort. Every Alamo defender died fighting, and their bodies were burned at Santa Anna's order. The only survivors were 16 women and children. About 1,600 Mexicans were killed. The Alamo is preserved as a state park. Located in front of the old fort is a monument to the heroes who died there.

The Alamo, a famous fort which Texas heroes defended with their lives, is today owned by Texas and maintained by the Daughters of the Republic of Texas.

San Antonio Chamber of Commerce

Mount McKinley, the highest peak in North America, is the crowning glory of Denali National Park. The park is located in the central part of the Alaska Range.

ALASKA

ALASKA. The Stars and Stripes have flown over Alaska since 1867. In that year Russia sold this vast land to the United States for $7,200,000. In 1912 Alaska was incorporated as a territory. This was the first step toward statehood.

In 1958 the United States Congress approved Alaska's admission to the Union as the 49th state. The news was flashed to the entire territory. The people celebrated with parades and parties. Alaska officially became a state Jan. 3, 1959, when President Dwight D. Eisenhower signed the statehood papers.

Alaska was the first new state to be added since 1912, when New Mexico and Arizona achieved statehood. Its admission required the adding of one more star to the 48 in the United States flag.

Alaska Means "Great Land"

The name Alaska comes from an Aleut word meaning "mainland" or "great land." The state is so large that it increased the area of the United States by a fifth. Texas, long the largest state, had to give up first place to Alaska, more than twice its size.

California lost the distinction of having the highest peak, Mount Whitney. Alaska's Mount McKinley is almost 6,000 feet higher—the tallest mountain in North America (*see* McKinley, Mount).

Population (1980): 400,481—rank, 50th state. Urban, 64.5%; rural, 35.5%. Persons per square mile, 0.7 (persons per square kilometer, 0.3)—rank, 50th state.

Extent: Area, 591,004 square miles (1,530,693 square kilometers), including 20,171 square miles (52,243 square kilometers) of water surface (1st state in size).

Elevation: Highest, Mount McKinley, 20,320 feet (6,194 meters), highest point in North America; lowest, sea level; average, 1,900 feet (580 meters).

Geographic Center: About 95 miles (153 kilometers) south of Tanana.

Temperature: Extremes—lowest −80° F (−62° C), Prospect Creek, 1971; highest 100° F (38° C), Fort Yukon, 1915. Averages at Barrow—January, −15.6° F (−26.4° C); July, 39.6° F (4.2° C); annual, 9.8° F (−12.3° C). Averages at Fairbanks—January, −10.9° F (−23.8° C); July, 60.4° F (15.8° C); annual, 25.6° F (−3.6° C). Averages at Juneau—January, 29.0° F (−1.7° C); July, 56.7° F (13.7° C); annual, 42.7° F (5.9° C).

Precipitation (annual average): At Barrow—4.47 inches (113.54 millimeters). At Fairbanks—11.01 inches (279.65 millimeters). At Juneau—90.71 inches (2,304.03 millimeters).

Land Use: Crops and pasture, 0.4%; forest, 32.5%; other, 67.1%

For statistical information about Agriculture, Education, Employment, Finance, Government, Manufacturing, Mining, Population Trends, and Vital Statistics, see ALASKA FACT SUMMARY.

239

The new state also took first place for scenic beauty. Mount McKinley is only one of its many towering snowcapped peaks. Glaciers cover hundreds of square miles. About one third of the entire area is forested. Big-game animals are abundant. Thousands of tourists visit Alaska every summer to hunt or fish or simply to enjoy its spectacular beauty.

In natural resources the immense state also takes high rank. However, it is still a frontier country, waiting to be developed. When the 1980 census was taken, Alaska had fewer people than any of the other states in the Union.

Alaska is of great importance to the defense of the United States. Army, Air Force, and Navy units are stationed there, and billions of dollars have been spent for Alaska defense installations. Radar warning stations situated around Alaska's perimeter are designed to prevent surprise attacks on North America from across the polar regions.

Size and Location

Alaska occupies a huge peninsula, from which hang two long extensions. To the southwest stretch the Alaska Peninsula and the Aleutian Islands chain. To the southeast is a 500-mile-long strip bordering on British Columbia. On its eastern side the Alaskan mainland is adjacent to Canada's Yukon Territory. Alaska's total area is about 586,412 square miles, including 19,980 square miles of lakes and rivers. Its coastline, 6,640 miles in length, is longer than the coastline of all the other states combined—including Hawaii.

Northward, Alaska extends the United States to Point Barrow on the Arctic Ocean. About one third of Alaska is within the Arctic Circle. Westward, the Aleutian Islands chain stretches across the Pacific Ocean into the Eastern Hemisphere. Attu, Alaska's westernmost island, is located at 173° east longitude. This is directly north of New Zealand. The distance from Attu, in the Aleutians, to Ketchikan, in the Panhandle, is greater than the distance from San Francisco, Calif., to New York City.

The tip of Seward Peninsula, on the Alaskan mainland, is a little over 50 miles across the Bering Strait from the Russian mainland. Through the Bering Strait runs the international date line. On one side is Little Diomede Island, a part of the United States. On the other side, less than 3 miles away, is Big Diomede Island, a part of Russia.

Natural Regions and Their Climates

From north to south, the four main natural regions of Alaska are: (1) the Arctic Slope; (2) the Rocky Mountain System; (3) the Interior Plateau, basin of the great Yukon River; and (4) the Pacific Mountain System. The fourth region includes three very different sections: south-central Alaska; the Panhandle; and the Alaska Peninsula and Aleutian Islands chain.

This map shows the four major natural regions and the surface features of Alaska. The use that can be made of the land is related to the physical features of each region.

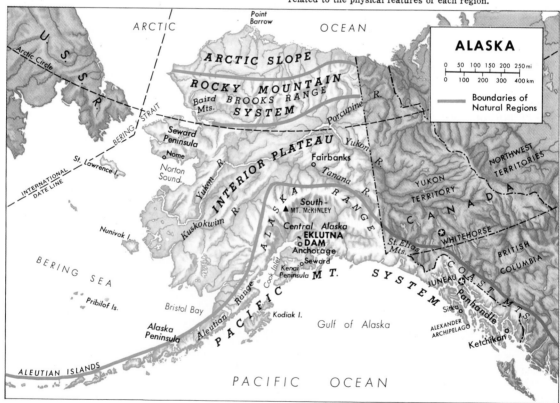

Alaska Visitors Association

Alaska Pictorial Service

In March 1964 a violent earthquake struck southern Alaska. Much of the downtown area of Anchorage, the state's largest city, was demolished. As can be seen from the photograph at the right, the damaged area was subsequently rebuilt.

The Arctic Slope covers about a sixth of Alaska. The climate is the true Arctic type, with light snow and little rain. The soil is tundra (*see* Soil). Continuous sunshine in summer brings up mosses and bright flowers, although the soil thaws only to a depth of one or two feet. At Point Barrow the sun remains above the horizon for 82 consecutive days.

The Rocky Mountain System separates the Arctic Slope from the Interior Plateau. The backbone of the system is the Brooks Range, 600 miles long, a wilderness of ice and snow. Some peaks rise above 8,000 feet. Only the southern foothills are forested. All of the Brooks Range is inside the Arctic Circle.

The Interior Plateau is a vast rolling upland, larger than Texas. Westward across it flows the great Yukon River with its tributaries and the shorter Kuskokwim (*see* Yukon River). On the Bering Sea these rivers have built up huge deltas. There are millions of acres of sub-Arctic forest interspersed with marshes, lakes, and ponds.

The climate in this region is the extreme continental type, with a wide range from summer to winter. Annual precipitation (rain and snow) is 8 to 15 inches. Summers are short, but daylight lasts up to 20 hours, and the temperature has risen as high as 100° F. During the summer the topsoil thaws, but the frozen subsoil causes water to remain on the surface.

The Pacific Mountain System curves around the entire south coast. The climate is the cool wet marine type, tempered by warm ocean currents and warm winds from the Asian mainland. Descriptions of the three sections of this region follow.

Southeastern Alaska—The Panhandle

Geographically, the Panhandle is the coastal section of northern British Columbia. The mainland strip is about 30 miles wide. The Coast Mountains rise sharply almost from the water's edge. Off the coast an outer range of mountains forms the islands of the Alexander Archipelago. The most beautiful approach to Alaska is by boat through the famous Inside Passage between these islands and the shore. The lower mountain slopes are covered with forests. The tops are capped with ice. Glaciers flowing down their sides have deepened the river valleys, forming mountain-walled fjords like those in Norway. Alaskans call these passageways "canals."

The Panhandle is one of the wettest regions in North America. Most of the rain falls from November to March. The heavy rainfall gives rise to great glaciers and to many streams, where Pacific salmon spawn. The largest forest growth of the state is the Tongass National Forest in the Panhandle.

Few peaks in the Coast Mountains are higher than 10,000 feet. To the north, where the coastline turns westward, rise the lofty St. Elias Mountains. Here vast glaciers fill the valleys. Malaspina Glacier, the largest, pours down from Mount St. Elias (18,008 ft.). The beautiful Muir Glacier, in Glacier Bay National Monument, also flows out of the St. Elias Mountains.

South-Central Alaska

South-central Alaska extends from the Panhandle to Cook Inlet. The spectacular Alaska Range, 150 miles wide, sweeps inland in a 400-mile arc, separating the coastal region from the Interior Plateau. The crown of this range is Mount McKinley. Many mountains in this region reach elevations of more than 15,000 feet.

Along the coast, west of the St. Elias Mountains, rise the Chugach Mountains. The Chugach National Forest covers their southern slopes. This range blends with the Kenai Mountains, backbone of the Kenai Peninsula, and is continued in the low mountains of Kodiak Island.

The Kenai Peninsula and Kodiak Island, like the Panhandle, have a mild climate and ample rainfall. The mainland climate is colder but drier, and valleys sheltered by mountain walls are suitable for farming. Just west of these is the Aleutian Range, which runs about 500 miles, the entire length of the Alaska Peninsula. (*See also* Aleutian Islands.)

Big Game and Other Wildlife

Alaska offers sportsmen the finest hunting and fishing in the United States. Among the many types of brown bears found in Alaska is the famous Kodiak bear, the largest of all carnivorous land mammals, weighing up to 1,700 pounds. Other species are the closely related grizzly bear, the black bear, and the polar bear. Other wildlife includes reindeer, moose, elk, bison, Sitka black-tailed deer, the Dall mountain sheep, and the Alaska mountain goat.

Millions of waterfowl summer on Alaska's rocky islands. Birds of prey include bald and golden eagles, owls, hawks, and falcons. The ptarmigan (white grouse), seen in flocks of several hundred, is Alaska's state bird. Fur seals breed on the Pribilof Islands (*see* Seal). Sea otter, now carefully protected, are increasing in numbers.

People and Population

Alaska is so thinly populated that there are about 1½ square miles for each person. Since World War II, however, the population has been growing rapidly. In 1940 it was 72,524; by 1980 the population had risen to 400,481.

There are about 64,000 Eskimos, Indians, and Aleuts, the three major groups of native Alaskans. About 16,000 Alaskans are foreign born. Of the total foreign stock, the largest groups historically had their origins in Canada, Germany, Norway, Asian nations, Great Britain, and Sweden.

Eskimos are the most numerous of the native Alaskans. They live along the coast of the Arctic Ocean and Bering Sea and in the great deltas formed by the Yukon and Kuskokwim rivers. They are good fishermen and fur trappers, and some earn their livelihoods from the hides and meat of large herds of reindeer. Many Eskimos live nontraditional lives. Some live in cities and work in construction and mining. Others have continued to maintain the traditional customs. (*See also* Eskimos.)

Indians rank second in number among native Alaskans. About half of them are Tlingit, living on islands and coasts of the Panhandle. Most of them have their own fishing boats. Others work in canneries during the summer and trap and hunt in the fall and winter. Some still carry on the craft traditions of their people.

The Haida and Tsimshian Indians came to the Panhandle from British Columbia. The Haida are related to the Tlingit and are noted for fine argillite carvings and delicate articles made of wood, bone, and shell. Most of the Tsimshian live in the model village of Metlakatla, which is run partly on a cooperative basis. They own their own fishing boats and operate a salmon cannery and a sawmill.

The Athapaskan Indians live in thinly scattered villages in the interior and in south-central Alaska. Most of them are hunters and trappers.

Aleuts are closely related to the Eskimos but have their own language and customs. Able seamen and fishermen, they live on the foggy Aleutian and Pribilof islands, the Alaska Peninsula, and Kodiak Island.

Alaska's Four Major Cities

About two thirds of the Alaskans live in towns and cities. The larger towns are as modern as those in the other states but are widely separated and surrounded by sparsely populated areas. Some can be reached only by ship, riverboat, or airplane.

Anchorage is by far the largest city and also the fastest growing. It is situated in south-central Alaska at the head of Cook Inlet on a bluff overlooking Knik Arm. As Alaska's chief center for air transportation and as headquarters for the northern defense, Anchorage has grown rapidly since 1946. Its population in 1970 was 48,081. In 1980 it was 174,431, a ten-year gain of about 260 percent. In 1964 much of Anchorage's downtown section was demolished by an earthquake that struck the southern part of the state. (*See also* Anchorage.)

Fairbanks is Alaska's second largest city. It is situated on the broad Interior Plateau on the Tanana River, the chief tributary of the Yukon. Its major importance is as the transportation hub for the remote hamlets on the plateau and in the Arctic region. It is the terminus of the Alaska Railroad, the Alaska Highway, the George Parks Highway, and the Steese Highway. (*See also* Fairbanks.)

Juneau, the capital, is near the northern end of the Panhandle. Its chief industries, apart from government, are tourism and fishing. (*See also* Juneau.)

Ketchikan, at the southern end of the Panhandle, is the first port of call in Alaska for northbound ships. It has the largest pulp mill in the state and is also the chief salmon-canning center.

Alaska Is Rich in Fish and Furs

Salmon is one of Alaska's leading products, although the catch has been declining because of over-fishing. Sockeye and pink salmon rank first in number, but dog, silver, and king salmon are also taken (*see* Salmon). About 90 percent of the catch is processed in about 80 canneries. The rest is sold fresh, frozen, or cured. Other commercial catches are shellfish (crabs, shrimps, and clams), halibut, and herring.

The most valuable furs come from the Pribilof Islands fur seal herd, which is managed by the federal government. The Alaska statehood bill provided that the state should receive from the federal government 70 percent of the profits from sales of both sealskin and sea otter skin. (*See also* Seal; Otter.)

Mink is the most valuable fur taken by trappers. Also important are beaver, marten, lynx, land otter, and muskrat. Fur farming in Alaska, mostly mink and fox, is also an important industry.

Mining and Mineral Resources

Alaska is known to have large reserves of gold, nickel, tin, lead, zinc, copper, and molybdenum. However, because of transportation difficulties, the development of its mineral resources has been slow. The minerals that reach outside markets are chiefly those of high value and low volume, such as gold, platinum, chrome, mercury, and silver. The chief minerals are petroleum, sand and gravel, coal, gold, and natural gas, which make up more than half of Alaska's mineral production. Deposits of subbituminous coal are widespread, but mining has been limited to two areas close to the Alaska Railroad.

Important petroleum operations began with the discovery of oil on the Kenai Peninsula in 1957. Even larger petroleum deposits were discovered in the northern Prudhoe Bay area in 1968. An 800-mile pipeline from the area to the all-year port of Valdez, in the south, was completed in 1977. The construction of the pipeline and the increase in oil production created significant growth of Alaska's economy and population.

Forests and Forest Products

Alaska's forests are capable of supplying a sustained production of several billion board feet of timber annually. In the interior are extensive stands of spruce, Alaska birch, cottonwood, willow, alder, aspen, and larch. These forests occupy about 32 percent of the land of Alaska. They have been little worked because of transportation difficulties. The usable forests are along the south coast and in the Panhandle, where deep inlets make the timber readily accessible. Here the principal trees are western hemlock and Sitka spruce, intermixed with some western red cedar and Alaska cedar.

Most of the commercial timber is purchased from Tongass National Forest, which covers more than half of southeastern Alaska, and Chugach National Forest, on the south coast. Logs are manufactured into pulp at a plant at Ketchikan and into lumber at a number of sawmills. A second large pulp mill, which supplies great quantities of cellulose to paper and rayon manufacturers in Japan, is located near Sitka.

Farming in Alaska

Alaska imports from the other states about 90 percent of its food. Very little of its vast area is suitable for farming. Good land is usually covered with trees and is difficult and expensive to clear. Farm machinery and fertilizer are expensive too, because they must be imported. The growing season (the time between killing frosts) is short, but plants grow rapidly because of the long summer daylight.

Farmland is being steadily added but totals only about 2 million acres. The best farmlands are in the Matanuska Valley, 50 miles northeast of Anchorage; in the Tanana River valley, near Fairbanks; in the lowlands of the Kenai Peninsula; and in the limited flatland of the Panhandle. The Matanuska district is by far the largest and the most prosperous.

The most profitable crops are perishable products. Garden vegetables, milk, and eggs command a good price in Alaska markets because of their freshness. Long hours of daylight produce potatoes, carrots, and cabbages of enormous size. Potatoes are a standard crop. Almost all kinds of berries can be raised. Dairying is one of the principal farm activities. Oats and legumes take the place of corn for silage and are also used for hay.

Hydroelectric Resources

Alaska's waterpower resources are known to be enormous. They have not yet been fully surveyed, but more than 200 possible sites have been located that could be used for providing electric energy. Most of them are in the Panhandle. Only small projects have so far been developed. Snettisham, near Juneau, and Eklutna, near Anchorage, are the largest.

Recreation—For Tourists and Alaskans

Thousands of tourists visit Alaska every summer. Most come by plane or ship, but a growing number

Western Electric Co.

Huge antennas like this relay telephone and telegraph messages. The checkerboard pattern (red and white) is a warning to fliers.

243

Steve and Dolores McCutcheon

Eskimo children predominate in this modern classroom. Their school is at Point Hope, which juts into the Arctic Ocean.

travel by car or bus over the scenic Alaska Highway (*see* Alaska Highway). This highway is linked with Alaska's main tourist attraction, Mount McKinley National Park, in the spectacular Alaska Range. Within the vast park is Muldrow Glacier, more than 50 miles long, fed by snow from Mount McKinley and other peaks. The park is also one of the great wildlife sanctuaries of the nation. Hunting is not allowed here, but fishing and camping are permitted.

Glacier Bay National Monument, 100 miles northwest of Juneau, is famous for its vast ice fields and fjordlike bays. Totem poles are the principal attractions of Sitka National Historical Park, in the Panhandle. Katmai National Monument, on the Alaska Peninsula, is noted for its volcanoes. (*See also* National Parks, United States.)

Communication and Transportation

Regular telephone communication is now available between Alaska and the other states. Submarine telephone cables from Port Angeles, Wash., to Skagway, at the northern end of the Panhandle, were completed in 1957. An overland system links Skagway to central Alaska. Radiotelephone makes it possible to place calls to many remote towns and villages.

About four families out of five have television. Network programs on tape or film are flown in and shown by Alaska stations.

South-central Alaska is linked with the interior by the Alaska Railroad and by a network of paved roads that connect with the Alaska Highway. The only town in the Panhandle that has access by motor road to the Alaska Highway is Haines, at the northern end of the Panhandle. The Haines Highway runs through Canada.

The backbone of transportation is the airplane. Established routes connect all cities and towns, and many small villages receive mail and freight by airplane only. In addition to scheduled flights, there

are the daring "bush pilots" who own their own planes and will fly anywhere anytime.

State and Local Government

In preparation for statehood, an Alaska convention drafted a constitution, which was ratified by the voters in 1956. It was praised as a model constitution and approved by Congress in the statehood bill.

The voting age is 18. The governor has great power. He appoints the heads of all important departments and the judges. The constitution provides for 22 election districts, based on population. The governor is required to reapportion the districts after each United States census. The people may propose and enact laws by initiative and approve or reject acts of the legislature by referendum. Elected officials are subject to recall by the voters.

Local government is vested in boroughs and cities. A borough is governed by an assembly and a city by a council. The city is represented on the borough assembly by one or more of its council members. The area of a borough is not based solely on population but on common interests, such as its industries.

Conservation of Natural Resources

The United States owned 99 percent of the land in the Territory of Alaska. The statehood act provided for deeding to the state, within 25 years, up to 102,500,000 acres—more than a quarter of Alaska's total area. Alaska may select the lands to take over. The state also gained permission to select from lands within the great national forests up to 400,000 acres. Lands taken over by the state may be sold to individuals or corporations for farms, homesites, or factory sites. Ownership does not include mineral rights. The state reserves the authority to lease such rights. Producing oil wells must pay royalties to the state.

AIR DISTANCES FROM FAIRBANKS
Alaska's strategic location makes it important to the United States both for defensive and offensive operations.

The statehood act also provides that fisheries and wildlife resources should continue to be managed by the federal government until the secretary of the interior decides that Alaska has made adequate provision for the conservation of these resources.

The Alaska constitution provides that all replenishable resources belonging to the state—fish, wildlife, forests, and grasslands—shall be utilized on the "sustained yield" principle.

In 1971 Congress passed the Alaska Native Claims Settlement Act, which awarded natives nearly one billion dollars and 40 million acres of land. Corporations were established to manage the terms of the settlement.

Public Schools and Universities

Alaska's constitution provides that public schools shall be open to all the children of the state. Schools maintained by the Bureau of Indian Affairs for Indians, Aleuts, and Eskimos are gradually being transferred to the state's public school system.

The University of Alaska, a land-grant college, was opened in 1922 at College, near Fairbanks. In addition, there are senior campuses at Anchorage and Juneau. The university also maintains community colleges at Anchorage, Auke Bay (Juneau-Douglas branch), Bethel, Kenai, Ketchikan, Kodiak, Palmer, and Sitka. Other institutions in the state are Inupiat University of the Arctic, at Barrow, and Sheldon Jackson College, at Sitka.

A Bulwark of American Defense

The shortest routes between many of the world's great centers lie across the Arctic region. Many North American defense installations are therefore concentrated in the Far North. Anchorage is the headquarters for the defense of the area. The statehood act provides that in an emergency about 260,500 square miles of state land in northern and western Alaska, including the entire Aleutian Islands chain, will be withdrawn from the state and placed under federal control.

At Anchorage the federal government constructed Elmendorf Air Force Base, one of the world's largest airfields, and Fort Richardson, the Army's headquarters. Near Fairbanks are Eielson Air Force Base and Fort Wainwright, an Army installation. The Arctic Indoctrination Center at Big Delta, near Fairbanks, provides instruction in winter ground operations and tests equipment for Arctic use.

DEW (Distant Early Warning) radar sites were set up in the Arctic wastes to alert the Air Force against attack. The federal government also installed the "White Alice" long-distance radiophone and telegraph communications network.

HISTORY OF ALASKA

Alaska was once a Russian possession. Russia sold it to the United States in 1867 by a treaty negotiated by Secretary of State William H. Seward during the Administration of President Andrew Johnson. The

Wide World

Alaskans celebrated their statehood on June 30, 1958. These youngsters climbed on a fire wagon to join the parade.

following sections trace the growth and development of Alaska from the period of exploration to statehood.

Discovery and Russian Occupation

In 1725 Peter the Great, czar of Russia, ordered Capt. Vitus Bering, a Dane in the service of the Russian navy, to explore the land east of Siberia. On his second trip, in 1741, Bering visited the Alaskan mainland and established Russia's claim to the region. He died on the return voyage, but part of his crew made their way back to Russia (see Bering Sea). Their tales of wealth in furs sent trappers and traders to the new lands.

Russian fur traders set up their first outpost on Kodiak Island in 1784. The natives were cheated, abused, and massacred. Fur-bearing animals of sea and land were wantonly slaughtered. The sea otter was almost exterminated. Some of the abuses were reduced when, in 1799, the czar chartered the Russian-American Company. The director for 19 years was Alexander Baranov, who ruled Russian America like an emperor. In 1804 Baranov moved the capital of the company from Kodiak to a new settlement at Sitka, which the Russians called New Archangel, and made it the most brilliant "court" in America. Alaska's many Russian churches with their onion-shaped domes date from this period.

"Seward's Folly"—The Alaska Purchase

Russia tried to sell its American possession to the United States as early as 1855. United States and British competition had made the Russian-American Company unprofitable, and Russian involvement in the Crimean War left the Alaskan colony vulnerable (see Crimean War). The sale was finally made in 1867 at the insistence of Seward. The price paid was $7,200,000. Charles Sumner supported the measure in the Senate and suggested that the new possession should be named Alaska. The date of the actual transfer of ownership was October 18, Alaska Day.

The American people called Alaska "Seward's folly" and "Seward's icebox." The Army, the Treasury Department, and the Navy in turn took charge. No civil government was provided until in 1884 Alaska became a "district" governed by the laws of the state of Oregon.

The discovery of gold in the Klondike region of Canada in 1896 brought armies of prospectors because the most accessible route was through southeastern Alaska (*see* Klondike; Alaska Boundary Dispute). Before the Klondike strike subsided, a fresh rush began at Nome, on the Seward Peninsula. Again, in 1902, there was a scramble to stake claims in the Fairbanks region. It was a violent, colorful era.

Under Territorial Government

The Organic Act of 1912, signed by President William Howard Taft on August 24, made Alaska an incorporated territory. In 1942, during World War II, Japanese forces occupied and fortified Kiska and Attu islands in the Aleutian chain. In the summer of 1943 United States forces, aided by Canadian troops, recaptured the islands. To ensure Alaska's safety, the United States rushed construction of the Alaska Highway (*see* Alaska Highway). At the same time a huge military construction program was begun. This was continued after the war, bringing about a boom in Alaska's economy and a rapid increase in population.

Steps to Statehood

For more than 40 years the people of Alaska fought for statehood. Finally they had a constitution drafted by a convention of 55 delegates in a meeting held at the University of Alaska, Nov. 8, 1955, to Feb. 6, 1956. In April the voters ratified it, 17,447 to 7,180. At the same time they approved the Tennessee Plan, by which they elected in October two "senators" and one "representative" to plead their cause in the federal Congress.

On June 30, 1958, the United States Senate voted 64 to 20 its approval of the statehood bill passed by the House of Representatives. President Eisenhower signed the statehood proclamation on Jan. 3, 1959 (*see* Statehood), and Alaska became officially the 49th state.

Earthquake!

On March 27, 1964, the most intense earthquake ever recorded on North America struck southern Alaska. More than 100 lives were lost, and damage reached an estimated 500 million dollars. Much of Anchorage's business district was leveled; some of its suburbs, especially Turnagain, suffered heavy damage. Kodiak, Chenega, Seward, Valdez, and surrounding areas were also hard hit. (*See also* United States, section "Alaska"; and individual entries in the Fact-Index on Alaska persons, places, products, and events.)

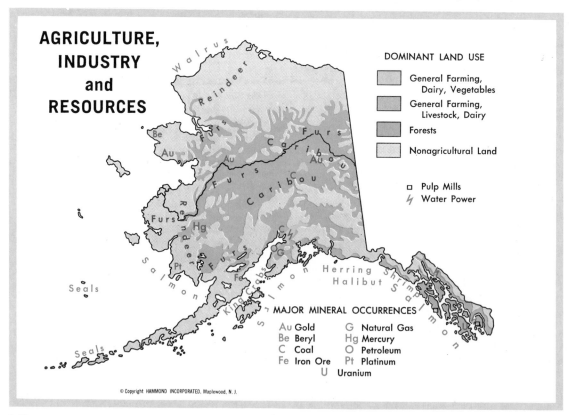

AGRICULTURE, INDUSTRY and RESOURCES

DOMINANT LAND USE

General Farming, Dairy, Vegetables

General Farming, Livestock, Dairy

Forests

Nonagricultural Land

□ Pulp Mills

⚡ Water Power

MAJOR MINERAL OCCURRENCES

Au Gold   G Natural Gas
Be Beryl   Hg Mercury
C Coal   O Petroleum
Fe Iron Ore   Pt Platinum
U Uranium

© Copyright HAMMOND INCORPORATED, Maplewood, N. J.

Notable Events in Alaska History

1728—Vitus Bering proves Asia and North America are separate. His lieutenant, Aleksei Chirikov, sights Prince of Wales Island, and Bering, St. Elias Mountains, in 1741.

1774-92—Spanish expeditions explore southeast coast.

1778—British Capt. James Cook surveys Alaskan coast.

1784—Russians make first settlement at Three Saints Bay on Kodiak Island; moved to present site of Kodiak in 1792.

1791—Capt. George Vancouver, British navigator, charts southeast corner of Alaska.

1799—Russian-American Company chartered by Russia for trade; director, Alexander Baranov. Sitka founded; becomes company capital in 1804.

1823—Father Ivan Veniaminov, Russian missionary, begins work among the Aleuts.

1824-25—Limit of Russian colony set at 54° 40′ in negotiations with U. S. and Great Britain.

1867—Secretary of State William H. Seward purchases Alaska from Russia for U. S. for $7,200,000.

1878—First commercial Salmon cannery built at Klawock.

1884—District of Alaska created; capital, Sitka; governor, John H. Kinkead.

1891—Rev. Sheldon Jackson, Presbyterian missionary, introduces reindeer into Alaska to aid Eskimos.

1896—Gold discovered in Klondike Basin of Canadian Yukon; at Nome, in 1899; at Fairbanks in 1902.

1900—White Pass and Yukon Route completed, Skagway to Whitehorse, Y. T. Alaska's civil government reformed by U. S. Congress; capital moved to Juneau; government offices transferred in 1906.

1903—Boundary between Panhandle and Canada settled.

1906—Alaska allowed an elected delegate to Congress.

1911—U. S. joins international agreement to regulate seal hunting on Pribilof and other islands.

1912—Territory of Alaska created; capital, Juneau. Katmai volcano erupts.

1916—First statehood bill introduced in Congress.

1917—Mount McKinley National Park established. University of Alaska founded at College.

1920—Four U. S. Army planes make round trip between New York and Nome.

1923—Naval Petroleum Reserve No. 4 established. Alaska Railroad completed, Seward to Fairbanks.

1924—Lieut. Carl Ben Eielson flies first airmail.

1931—Federal Building, territorial capitol, completed at Juneau; designated State Capitol in 1959.

1935—Families from Middle West resettle in agricultural community in Matanuska Valley.

1942—Japan attacks Dutch Harbor; occupies Attu and Kiska.

1942-43—U. S. constructs Alaska Highway; turns over Canadian section to Canada in 1946.

1943—U. S. recaptures Aleutians from Japan.

1946—Alaskans approve statehood in referendum.

1954—First pulp mill in Alaska completed at Ketchikan.

1955—Eklutna power project operates near Palmer; military fuel pipeline opened, Haines to Fairbanks.

1956—Alaskans adopt state constitution.

1957—Oil discovered on Kenai Peninsula; first oil refinery opens in 1963.

1959—Alaska becomes 49th state, January 3.

1964—Alaska devastated by earthquake.

1967—Record floods damage Fairbanks and Nenana.

1976—Voters choose site near Willow, 35 miles north of Anchorage, for new state capital.

1977—Petroleum pipeline 800 miles long from Prudhoe Bay to Valdez completed.

1728

1799

1878

1942-43

STATE FLOWER:
Forget-me-not

STATE TREE:
Sitka Spruce

STATE BIRD:
Willow Ptarmigan

STATE SEAL: Revised territorial seal adopted in constitution; shows natural features and industries.

Alaska Profile

FLAG: *See* **Flags of the United States.**
MOTTO: None official.
SONG: 'Alaska's Flag'—words, Marie Drake; music, Elinor Dusenbury.

Alaska is the last United States frontier. The largest of the states in size, this vast, raw, and rugged land is the smallest in population. Twice as big as Texas, it thrusts a chain of volcanic islands more than a thousand miles into the Bering Sea. It juts northward far into the Arctic Circle, and to the south its Panhandle extends about 500 miles between the Pacific Ocean and the Canadian Rockies. Alaska is a land of spectacular contrasts—smoking volcanoes and frozen tundra, hot springs and ice floes, creeping glaciers and virgin forests.

Nearly everything about this 49th state is big. Its Mount McKinley is higher than any other peak in North America. Its Yukon River is one of the longest navigable waterways in the world. Big animals still thrive here—Kodiak, grizzly, and polar bears; moose, caribou, musk-oxen, wolves; otter, walrus, seals.

After its purchase by the United States from Russia in 1867, Alaska remained a remote and lonely fur-trading territory until, late in the 19th century, gold was discovered. The chaotic, primitive life of the gold-rush era is gone. Present-day Alaskans are engaged in a variety of pursuits, including lumbering, commercial fishing and trapping, cattle raising and truck farming, and oil production.

Alaska's Eskimos find it hard to adjust to modern conditions; extinction threatens some wildlife species; and the cost of living is high, since many foods and manufactured goods must be imported. Alaska's unused water resources may provide a solution to the last of these problems. New dams are being planned to generate the power required to attract new industries. In the years ahead, Alaska will have to devise ways of conserving its natural and human resources while utilizing them to meet the needs of an advancing economy.

Columns of Alaskan marble dominate the entrance of Alaska's State Capitol, in Juneau. Completed in 1931 to house federal offices, the building became the Capitol when Alaska attained statehood in 1959. It is the meeting place of the state legislature and houses the governor's offices.

Juneau, the capital since 1900, lies on the Gastineau Channel in southeastern Alaska. It was settled in 1881 by gold miners and named for Joe Juneau, who made Alaska's first major gold discovery here in 1880. Its industrial plants include salmon canneries.

Opened in 1922 as a land-grant college, the University of Alaska achieved its present status in 1935. Its central campus is in College, five miles from Fairbanks. With branches in other cities, the university provides public higher education for the entire state.

The fishing fleet of Kodiak Island brings in an annual catch of halibut, salmon, and shellfish worth millions of dollars. On Kodiak Island are fish canneries, livestock ranches, dairy farms, and a Coast Guard base. The island is also the home of the Kodiak bear.

Alaska picture profile

An offshore oil rig at Cook Inlet, near Anchorage, is evidence of Alaska's developing petroleum industry. Oil was discovered in Alaska in 1853 and was produced commercially from 1902 to 1933. Since the 1950's oil has become one of Alaska's most important products.

Eskimos in native dress entertain a crowd. Alaska's 28,000 Eskimos comprise its largest native group. There are also more than 16,000 Indians and over 6,000 Aleuts.

Mendenhall Glacier, north of Juneau, is 12 miles long and 1½ miles wide. A recreation area maintained here by the United States Forest Service has trails and campsites.

In the Matanuska Valley, northeast of Anchorage, two thirds of Alaska's farm produce is grown. Other farming areas are the Tanana River valley and the lowlands of the Kenai Peninsula and the Panhandle.

Fairbanks, Alaska's second largest city, is a gold mining, farming, and transportation center. It is the northern terminus of the Alaska Highway and the Alaska Railroad.

Craters, lakes, and the Alaska brown bear are features of Katmai National Monument, one of Alaska's four national park areas. The others are the Glacier Bay and Sitka National monuments and Mount McKinley National Park.

The old Russian Orthodox church at Kenai was built in the early 19th century, when Russian traders dominated Alaska. Russia established Alaska's first white settlement in 1784 on Kodiak Island.

Through the Inside Passage between Prince Rupert, B. C., and Skagway, a modern ferryboat carries motorists and other travelers along the Alaska Marine Highway. Another ferry route lies between the Kenai Peninsula and Kodiak Island.

ALASKA FACT SUMMARY

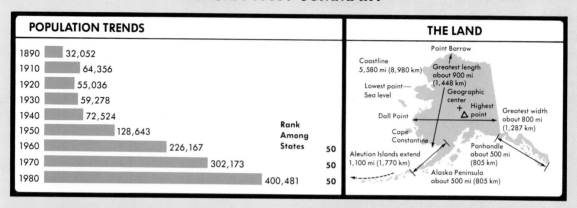

POPULATION TRENDS

Year	Population
1890	32,052
1910	64,356
1920	55,036
1930	59,278
1940	72,524
1950	128,643
1960	226,167
1970	302,173
1980	400,481

Rank Among States 50

THE LAND

Point Barrow

Coastline 5,580 mi (8,980 km)

Greatest length about 900 mi (1,448 km)

Lowest point— Sea level

Geographic center

Highest point

Dall Point

Greatest width about 800 mi (1,287 km)

Cape Constantine

Panhandle about 500 mi (805 km)

Aleutian Islands extend 1,100 mi (1,770 km)

Alaska Peninsula about 500 mi (805 km)

LARGEST CITIES (1980 census)

Anchorage (174,431): trade and transportation center at head of Cook Inlet; Alaska Railroad headquarters; International Airport; called "Air Crossroads of World"; Fort Richardson, Elmendorf Air Force Base nearby (*see* Anchorage).

Fairbanks (22,645): on Chena Slough, branch of Tanana River; gold-mining, farming, and transportation center; Eielson Air Force Base and Fort Wainwright nearby; northern terminus of Alaska Highway and Alaska Railroad (*see* Fairbanks).

Juneau (19,528): capital of Alaska on Gastineau Channel at foot of Mounts Juneau and Roberts; ice-free sea and fishing port; salmon canneries; Alaska Historical Library and Alaska State Museum (*see* Juneau).

Sitka (7,803): historic town on Baranof Island; Russian blockhouse; Sitka National Cemetery; Pioneers' Home; Sheldon Jackson College; Mount Edgecumbe on nearby Kruzof Island.

Ketchikan (7,198): trade center on Revillagigedo Island; port on Inside Passage; called "Salmon-Packing Capital of World"; saw and pulp mills; Indian totem poles and community house nearby.

VITAL STATISTICS 1980 (per 1,000 population)

Birthrate:	23.0
Death Rate:	12.3
Marriage Rate:	13.0
Divorce Rate:	8.4

GOVERNMENT

Capital: Juneau (designated, 1900).

Statehood: Became 49th state in the Union on Jan. 3, 1959.

Constitution: Adopted 1956; amendment may be passed by two-thirds majority of each house; ratified by majority voting on it in an election.

Representation in U.S. Congress: Senate—2. House of Representatives—1. Electoral votes—3.

Legislature: Senators—20; term, 4 years. Representatives—40; term, 2 years.

Executive Officers: Governor—term, 4 years; may serve two successive terms; then eligible after one term has intervened. Other officials—lieutenant governor, elected; term, 4 years.

Judiciary: Governor appoints justices of the Supreme Court, the Court of Appeals, the Superior Court, and the District Court, who are subject to periodic voter approval or rejection. The presiding judge in each of the four Superior Court districts appoints District Magistrates.

County: No counties; state divided into 11 organized boroughs and 1 "unorganized borough." Elected assemblies govern organized boroughs; the State Legislature is responsible for unorganized areas of the state.

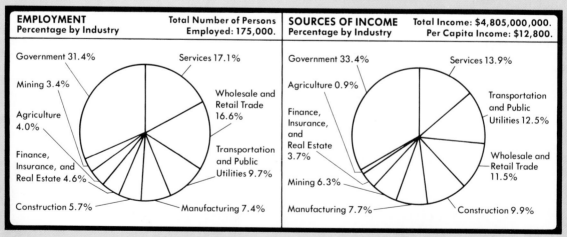

EMPLOYMENT
Percentage by Industry

Total Number of Persons Employed: 175,000.

- Government 31.4%
- Services 17.1%
- Mining 3.4%
- Wholesale and Retail Trade 16.6%
- Agriculture 4.0%
- Finance, Insurance, and Real Estate 4.6%
- Transportation and Public Utilities 9.7%
- Construction 5.7%
- Manufacturing 7.4%

SOURCES OF INCOME
Percentage by Industry

Total Income: $4,805,000,000. Per Capita Income: $12,800.

- Government 33.4%
- Services 13.9%
- Agriculture 0.9%
- Transportation and Public Utilities 12.5%
- Finance, Insurance, and Real Estate 3.7%
- Wholesale and Retail Trade 11.5%
- Mining 6.3%
- Manufacturing 7.7%
- Construction 9.9%

MAJOR PRODUCTS

Agricultural: Hay, vegetables, nursery and greenhouse products, cattle.

Manufactured: Processed fish and seafood (fresh, frozen, canned, and cured), printing and publishing.

Mined: Crude petroleum, natural gas, sand and gravel, stone, mercury.

EDUCATION AND CULTURE

Universities and Colleges: The University of Alaska statewide system of higher education has urban centers at Fairbanks, Anchorage, and Auke Lake (Juneau) and community colleges at Anchorage, Bethel, Fairbanks, Kenai-Soldatna, Ketchikan, Kodiak, Kotzebue, Nome, Palmer, Sitka, and Valdez.

Libraries: Alaska State Library aids in developing public libraries; Anchorage Municipal Libraries; University of Alaska, Fairbanks.

Notable Museums: Alaska State Museum, Juneau; Sheldon Jackson Museum, Sitka; Anchorage Historical and Fine Arts Museum, University of Alaska Museum, Fairbanks.

PLACES OF INTEREST

Alaska Marine Highway: that part of the Inside Passage between Prince Rupert, B.C., and Skagway; passenger and vehicle ferry.

Bethel: fishing and fur-raising village near mouth of Kuskokwim River.

Cordova: on Prince William Sound; old copper mines; Miles and Childs glaciers; Lake Eyak.

Denali National Park: between Fairbanks and Anchorage; continent's highest peak, 20,320 feet (6,194 meters); large glaciers of the Alaska Range; spectacular wildlife, includes caribou, moose, and grizzly and brown bears.

Dillingham: fishing town on Bristol Bay; sport fishing and hunting; trapping center.

Eklutna Dam: 34 miles (55 kilometers) northeast of Anchorage.

Glacier Bay National Park: surrounds Glacier Bay and Fairweather Range west of Juneau; Muir and other great tidal glaciers.

Haines: near end of Lynn Canal; terminus of Haines Highway; fishing; Chilkat Indian dancers.

Homer: open coal seams; fishing; mining.

Katmai National Park: on Alaska Peninsula; Mount Katmai erupted 1912; Valley of Ten Thousand Smokes; home of world's largest brown bears.

Malaspina Glacier: west of Yakutat Bay; reaches height of 2,500 feet (760 meters).

Matanuska Valley: state's largest farming area.

Mendenhall Glacier: north of Juneau; 12 miles (19 kilometers) long and 1½ miles (2 kilometers) wide; reached by automobile.

Metlakatla: cooperative Tsimshian Indian village near Ketchikan; salmon cannery; sawmill.

Nenana: time of ice breakup in Tanana River guessed in annual Nenana Ice Classic.

Nome: historic gold-rush town; Eskimo crafts.

Palmer: Matanuska Valley civic center; coal mines; moose and bear hunting; sport fishing; state fair.

Point Barrow: northernmost point of Alaska; Eskimo village.

Pribilof Islands: fur-seal breeding ground; bird rookery.

Seward: ice-free port on Resurrection Bay; supply center; gateway to Kenai Peninsula and interior; headquarters for big-game hunters; Silver Salmon Derby.

Sitka National Historical Park: adjoins Sitka; site of stockade where Indians made last stand against Russian settlers; totem poles.

Skagway: port at head of Lynn Canal; terminus of White Pass and Yukon Route.

Taku Valley: glacier, 30 miles (48 kilometers) long; fishing.

Valdez: ice-free port; Columbia Glacier; Keystone Canyon; Bridal Veil Falls; southern terminal of Alaska Pipeline.

BIBLIOGRAPHY FOR ALASKA

Bailey, B. F. Picture Book of Alaska, rev. ed. (Whitman, 1968).

Cheney, Cora. Alaska, Indians, Eskimo, Russians, and the Rest (Dodd, 1980).

Clarke, Tom E. Alaska Challenge (Lothrop, 1959).

Coombs, Charles. Pipeline Across Alaska (Morrow, 1978).

Fradin, Dennis. Alaska in Words and Pictures (Childrens, 1977).

Hunt, W. R. Alaska: a Bicentennial History (Norton, 1976).

McNeer, May. The Alaska Gold Rush (Random, 1960).

McPhee, John. Coming into the Country (Farrar, Straus & Giroux, 1977).

Shumaker, Virginia O. Alaska Pipeline (Messner, 1979).

Stefansson, E. B. Here is Alaska (Scribner, 1973).

Wheeler, Keith. Alaskans (Time-Life, 1977).

All Fact Summary data are based on current government reports.

ALASKA

254

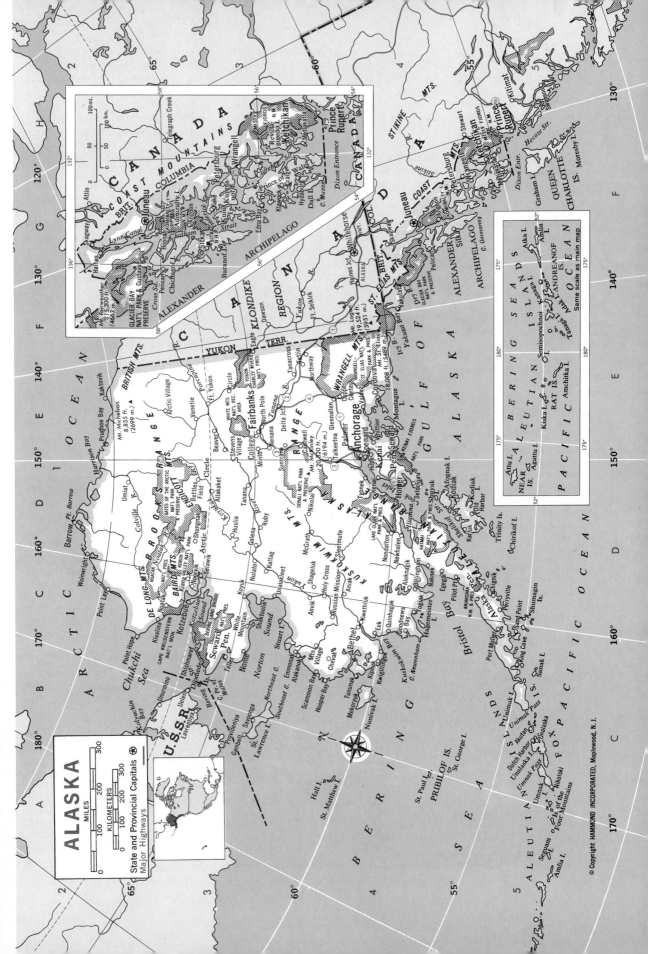

ALASKA BOUNDARY DISPUTE. The discovery of gold in the Canadian Klondike in 1896 led to a disagreement between the United States and Canada over the Alaska-Canada boundary. The treaty of 1867, by which the United States had bought Alaska from Russia, established the boundary of southeast Alaska (the Panhandle) as 30 miles (48 kilometers) from the coast. The entrance to the Klondike was through an inlet called Lynn Canal. The Canadians claimed that the boundary ran across inlets from headland to headland. This would have placed Lynn Canal within Canada. The United States held that the line followed all the windings of the coast.

The problem was referred to a joint arbitration commission of six members. Three were American, two were Canadian, and one was British. The commission met in London in 1903. The United States claim was upheld by a vote of four to two.

ALASKA HIGHWAY. The only land route between Alaska and the rest of the mainland United States is the Alaska Highway. Most of it is in Canada. It begins at Dawson Creek, B.C., stretches north 1,221 miles (1,965 kilometers) through British Columbia and Yukon Territory, then crosses the Alaska border. It runs 207 miles (333 kilometers) to Big Delta, where it connects with the Richardson Highway and extends 95 miles (153 kilometers) to Fairbanks. The total length from Dawson Creek to Fairbanks is 1,523 miles (2,451 kilometers).

United States Army engineers hurriedly constructed the highway for defense purposes during World War II. Originally called the Alcan Highway, it was built with the consent and help of Canada. The route was chosen by the United States War Department to connect airfields and to maintain the Canol pipeline system. Construction began in April 1942, and the preliminary road was completed on November 20. The initial cost was 135 million dollars. The Canadi-

an section was transferred to the Canadian government in 1946 and is maintained by the Canadian Army Northwest Highway System.

For tourists, the Alaska Highway offers one of the most spectacular tours in North America. The highway slashes through almost endless forests of virgin timber, climbs and twists through some of the continent's highest mountains, and skirts great glaciers and clear deep lakes. Portions of the highway have been paved, but most of it is gravel, 26 feet (8 meters) wide. (*See also* Road and Street.)

Summer is the ideal time for vacationers. By mid-June maintenance forces have repaired the damage caused by winter freezing and spring thaws. Daytime temperature may reach a high of about 70° F (21° C), and there are 16 to 20 hours of daylight.

ALASKA RANGE. Mountain climbers are challenged by the lofty peaks and rugged terrain of the Alaska Range. Tourists are attracted to its enormous glaciers and Arctic scenery.

The mountains stretch from the Aleutian Range in south-central Alaska to the Yukon boundary in southern Alaska. They are a northwestward continuation of the Coast Mountains and Rocky Mountains of Canada. Four great mountain masses dominate the range. These are divided by several low passes and river valleys, some of which provide travel routes across the mountains. The Alaska Range separates the interior tundra prairie of Alaska from the Pacific coastal region of the state.

The mountains form an enormous arc for about 600 miles (960 kilometers), and vary in width from 120 miles (190 kilometers) at some points to 30 miles (48 kilometers) near the Canadian border. Mount McKinley, in Denali National Park and near the center of the Alaska Range, reaches 20,320 feet (6,194 meters), which is the highest point in North America (*see* McKinley, Mount). Some other peaks in the

Although much of it is unpaved, the Alaska Highway offers the adventurous vacationer spectacular views of mountains, forests, glaciers, and lakes.

Steve and Dolores McCutcheon

Alaska Range, including Mount Hunter, Mount Hayes, and Mount Foraker, exceed 13,000 feet (3,900 meters). The Alaska Range is crossed at Isabel Pass by the trans-Alaska pipeline en route to its southern terminal at Valdez.

ALBANIA. The People's Socialist Republic of Albania is among the least developed countries of Europe. Since 1946 it has been a Communist state. It is a member of the United Nations but has no strong economic or political ties with other countries. Located on the Balkan Peninsula, it is bordered by Greece on the south and Yugoslavia on the north and east. The Adriatic Sea washes its western shore.

The Land and Climate

Albania is the smallest country on the Balkan Peninsula with an area of only some 11,100 square miles (28,748 square kilometers). The country is largely mountainous with some peaks reaching over 8,000 feet (2,500 meters) in height. The highest mountain is Korab at 9,026 feet (2,751 meters). The only lowland area, which is located along the coast, occupies about a quarter of the total area of the country and contains about half the population.

The country has a Mediterranean climate, with hot dry summers and mild wet winters. The seasonal nature of the rainfall affects the flow of the rivers. In winter they become torrents and cause severe flooding, while in summer they are reduced to mere trick-

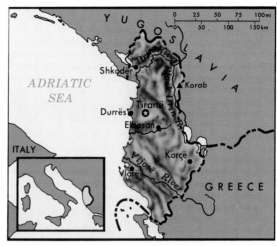

Albania faces Italy across the Adriatic Sea.

les. The longest river is the Drin, which begins in Yugoslavia and flows for 174 miles (280 kilometers) through northern Albania. The major rivers of the south are the Shkumbin, the Mat, and the Vijosë.

Soils in general are poor, and even in the plains they are infertile and poorly drained. Only about 15 percent of the country's area is used for farming.

Plants and Animals

Much of Albania was once forested, but little of the original vegetation remains due to centuries of clearing and livestock grazing; many areas are covered with only bushes and scrub. The remaining forests in the mountains are mainly of oak, beech, and pine. Mountain meadows are found above the timberline. Reforestation is a primary government goal.

Because of the removal of forests and because hunting was unrestricted, few wild animals remain in Albania except in the remote forests. Among the animals are wolves, wild hogs, bears, deer, and a few chamois (small goatlike antelopes). Wild birds are plentiful, however. Hunting laws to preserve the country's wildlife have now been enacted.

The People

The people of Albania belong to two major groups, the Ghegs to the north of the Shkumbin River and the Tosks to the south. Each group speaks its own dialect of the Albanian language. The Tosk dialect is now used as the official language. Minority groups are small and consist mainly of Gypsies, some Greeks in the south, and the Vlachs, a Romanian-speaking people. These groups together make up only about 3 percent of the population.

Under the Communist regime religion has been discouraged and Albania is officially an atheist nation, but religion-based cultural differences remain. Of those professing a faith the most numerous are Muslim, Roman Catholic, and Greek Orthodox.

Albania has the smallest population of the Balkan countries. Only about 2.7 million people live there.

Facts About Albania

Official Name: People's Socialist Republic of Albania.

Capital: Tiranë.

Area: 11,100 square miles (28,748 square kilometers).

Population (1980 estimate): 2,734,000; 246 persons per square mile (95 persons per square kilometer); 38 percent urban, 62 percent rural.

Major Language: Albanian (official).

Major Religion: Atheistic state; no recognized religions.

Literacy: About 75 percent.

Mountain Ranges: North Albanian Alps, Pindus Mountains.

Highest Peak: Korab, 9,026 feet (2,751 meters).

Largest Lakes: Shkodër, 143 square miles (370 square kilometers); Prespa; Ohri.

Major Rivers: Drin, Seman, Vijosë, Shkumbin, Mat, Erzen, Buenë.

Form of Government: People's Republic.

Chief of State: President of the Presidium of the People's Assembly.

Head of Government: Chairman of the Council of Ministers.

Legislature: People's Assembly.

Voting Qualifications: All citizens 18 years of age.

Political Divisions: 26 rethi (provinces).

Major City (1979 estimate): Tiranë (193,000).

Chief Manufactured and Mined Products: Asphalt, cement, chromite, crude petroleum, lignite, petroleum products.

Chief Agricultural Products: *Crops*—corn (maize), grapes, potatoes, rice, sugar beets; wheat. *Livestock*—cattle, goats, poultry, sheep.

Flag: *Colors*—red, black, and gold (*see* Flags).

Monetary Unit: 1 lek = 100 qindars.

257

However, in the early 1980's Albania had the highest rate of population increase of any European country, about 2.2 percent per year. The Albanian people are traditionally divided into clans or tribes, each of which traces its ancestry back to a single individual. Disputes or crimes involving other clans often resulted in blood feuds among males in the clans.

As a result of almost five centuries of Turkish rule the Albanians have adopted a way of life, including clothing, building styles, and art forms, which is similar to that of western Asia. This is especially true of the Muslim population.

About two thirds of the population lives in rural areas, with the rest located in a few cities that lie mainly in the lowlands. The largest city is the capital Tiranë, with more than 190,000 inhabitants in 1979. The other cities are small. Durrës has more than 80,000 inhabitants, while Vlorë, Shkoder, Korçë and Elbasan each has over 50,000 inhabitants. Many of these cities are of ancient origin, and most have architectural features that reveal Turkish influence.

The Economy

The Albanian economy is one of the poorest in Europe. It relies largely on agriculture. When the Communists took control after World War II, they abolished private land ownership. At present about 80 percent of agricultural land is operated by cooperatives and the rest is farmed directly by the state.

The Albanians are traditionally herders who take their herds of sheep and goats to mountain pastures during summer. Herding is still important, but at present crops account for two thirds of the farm products. The chief grain crop is wheat, followed closely by corn (maize). Rice is also grown. These grains occupy about two thirds of the area planted with crops. Other important farm products include cotton, sugar beets, potatoes, vegetables, and fodder crops. The warm summers permit the growing of olives, grapes, tobacco, and citrus fruits.

Albania has substantial reserves of several industrial minerals. There is sufficient oil to meet the country's requirements and permit some export. A pipeline leads from the oil fields at Qytet Stalin to the port of Vlorë, and the nation also has several refineries. Some natural gas is produced. There are scattered deposits of lignite (brown coal) suitable for electric power production. Most of the electric power of the country is, however, obtained from hydroelectric power stations, the largest of which is on the Drin River. Among metallic minerals chromite is the most important and is exported in substantial quantities.

Other exports of Albania include copper, iron ore, asphalt, tobacco, fruit and vegetables, and wine. Imports are restricted generally to the country's equipment requirements.

The development of industry, especially oil and chemicals, is being given the highest priority in Albania. A small iron and steel plant at Elbasan opened in 1976, and there are several small chemical plants. Large textile combines operate at Tiranë and Berat.

Stern—Black Star

The principal church (center) of Berat, Albania, became a museum under the country's Communist government.

Transportation, Communication, and Education

The first railroad line was built in Albania in 1948 linking Tiranë, Durrës, and Elbasan. More recently the construction of highways has received government emphasis. The main ports are Durrës, Vlorë, Shëngjin, and Sarandë.

Albania has a somewhat limited telephone network. There is a fairly extensive broadcasting service, however, and television programming began in 1971. Newspaper circulation is quite limited. There is a state university at Tiranë.

Government

Political power since 1946 has rested entirely in the hands of Albania's Labor (Communist) party. In practice the party acts as a government and decides all political, social, and economic matters. There is a People's Assembly and a Council of Ministers, respectively the highest legislative and executive bodies in the country. The Council of Ministers consists mainly of high party officials. A "socialist" constitution was adopted in 1976.

History

Before the Roman invasion in the 2d century B.C., the present territory of Albania was inhabited by the Illyrians, an Indo-European people. After the collapse of the Roman Empire, Albania first came under the control of the Byzantine Empire and later of Serbia. When the Ottoman Turks invaded the Balkans at the end of the 14th century, Albania became part of the Ottoman Empire. In spite of the fierce resistance of the Albanians, led by their national hero Skanderbeg, the Turks ruled the country for almost

500 years. Albania did not gain its independence from the Turks until 1912. At that time, however, the country was too weak to resist the pressures exerted by the major European powers, which awarded to Serbia a large area with an Albanian population.

During World War I Albania was occupied by the troops of several of the warring powers, including Italy. Although these troops ultimately withdrew, the Italians retained an interest in the country. In 1922 a clan leader named Ahmed Beg Zogu became the premier. He then became president, and in 1928 he declared himself King Zog. After the Italians invaded Albania in April 1939, Zog fled the country.

During World War II the country was occupied by the Germans as well as the Italians. When they retreated in 1944, a leader of the Communist-led resistance movement, Enver Hoxha, became head of the Albanian government. In 1946 a people's republic was declared; private land was confiscated and industry nationalized. Immediately after the war Yugoslavia virtually controlled Albania. When Yugoslavia left the Soviet bloc in 1948, Albania broke its ties with that country and became a close ally of the Soviet Union, joining the Warsaw Pact in 1955. Albania broke with the Soviet Union and became an ally of China in 1961, largely because of Soviet policies after the death of Joseph Stalin. This resulted in the cessation of Soviet aid. Chinese aid ended after Albania's ties with China were terminated in 1978. (*See also* Balkans.)

ALBANY, N.Y. The capital of the state of New York lies on the west bank of the Hudson River. Located 145 miles (233 kilometers) north of New York City, it is an inland seaport and a center of trade, government, and industry. The Port of Albany

handles medium-sized ocean vessels and is connected by river with the New York State Barge Canal.

The advantages of Albany's geographical position were recognized by the early 1600's. In 1609 the English explorer Henry Hudson sailed his ship, the *Half Moon*, up the river to the present site of the city, one of the farthest points within the continent to which an ocean vessel could go.

In the early 1800's the broad Mohawk Valley, which begins just north of Albany, became the route for the Erie Canal (now part of the New York State Barge Canal). Goods were carried on water from New York City, up the Hudson to the Mohawk, and then into the western part of the state. Railroads were built westward through the Mohawk Valley and northward along the level passages of the Hudson.

With its industrial suburb of Rensselaer, across the Hudson, Albany has developed many industries. These include printing and the manufacture of paper, machine tools, felt, and metal products. The city also has large grain elevators.

The business district is dominated by the State Capitol. Its construction took more than 30 years, from 1867 to 1899. Behind the Capitol is the 32-story Alfred E. Smith State Office Building, named for a former governor. South of the Capitol is the Governor Nelson A. Rockefeller Empire State Plaza, a complex of cultural facilities and state offices. The tower of the nearby City Hall houses the municipal carillon, with its 60 bells.

Among Albany's colleges are the law, medical, and pharmacy schools of Union University; the State University of New York at Albany; and College of Saint Rose. Albany Institute of History and Art, the state's oldest museum, was founded in 1791.

Of historical interest are the Schuyler Mansion, home of Philip Schuyler, Revolutionary War general, and the Ten Broeck Mansion, both built in the 18th century. Washington and Lincoln parks and Bleecker Stadium provide public recreation facilities.

In 1614 Dutch fur traders built Fort Nassau on Castle Island near the present site of Albany. In 1624 the first permanent settlers from Holland built Fort Orange, named in honor of the Dutch ruling house.

In 1630 Kiliaen van Rensselaer, with two partners, bought land on both sides of the river, and under the patroon system set up a vast estate. On part of this land Peter Stuyvesant laid out the village of Beverwyck in 1653. In 1664 Fort Orange fell to the English and Beverwyck was renamed Albany for the Duke of York and Albany (later James II). Its city charter was granted in 1686.

In 1754 the Albany Congress met to establish friendly relations with the Indians and to draw up a plan of union. A plan, largely the work of Benjamin Franklin, was adopted but was rejected by the colonists and the king.

In the Revolutionary War Albany was the objective of the British expedition of Gen. John Burgoyne that ended in his surrender at Saratoga. In 1797 the city became New York's permanent capital. It has a mayor-council government. (*See also* New York.) Population (1980 census), 101,727.

ALBANY CONGRESS. From June 19 to July 11, 1754, an intercolonial conference was held at Albany, N.Y. Present were 23 delegates from the English colonies of New York, Pennsylvania, New Hampshire, Connecticut, Massachusetts, Rhode Island, and Maryland, along with 150 members of the Iroquois Indian federation. The Albany Congress had been called by the London Board of Trade to deal with two pressing issues: grievances of the Iroquois against the colonies and the presence of hostile French forces and their Indian allies to the west of the English colonies (*see* French and Indian War).

The Indians complained that land speculators were stealing their lands; that an illegal English-French trade was bypassing them, thus avoiding letting them act as middlemen for profit; and that colonials were trading directly with other Indians supposedly under the rule of the Iroquois. The congress had to placate the Iroquois, because they were needed as allies against the French.

More serious was the French threat. To meet it, the congress drew up a plan of colonial union. Written mainly by Benjamin Franklin, the plan provided for one general government for all the colonies to manage defense and Indian affairs, pass laws, and raise taxes. The chief executive was to be a president general appointed by the king of England. The legislature, or grand council, would consist of representatives appointed by the colonial legislatures.

The Albany plan of colonial union failed because of opposition from both the king and the colonies: each thought it granted the other too much power. It was, nevertheless, a farsighted document. It contained solutions that the colonies would draw upon in forming a union after independence was declared in 1776.

ALBATROSS. Gliding on tireless and apparently motionless wings, the albatross may follow a ship for days. The great ocean bird used to hold a strange spell over sailors who believed that it had unnatural power and that killing one brought bad luck. The famous poem by Coleridge, 'The Rime of the Ancient Mariner', is based on this old superstition.

The wandering albatross (*Diomedea exulans*) has the greatest wingspread of any bird. Though its body is only about 9 inches (23 centimeters) wide, its wings often measure more than 11 feet (3 meters) from tip to tip. It weighs about 25 pounds (11 kilograms). The male's body feathers are white, the tips of its wings quite black. The female has brownish patches on neck and back.

The albatross lives mostly on the wing. It sits down on the water to eat, floating like a cork, and scoops up small squids, fish, or scraps from ships with its yellow hooked beak. At times it skims the surface of the water, then soars so high it is out of sight. It may stand still in the air, balanced with delicate wing motion against the breeze; yet, when taking advantage of a favorable wind, its speed may exceed a hundred miles an hour.

During the nesting season these birds go to barren antarctic islands where the female lays a single egg in a nest of clay and grass.

There are about 17 species of albatrosses, and all prefer the tropic seas. The black-footed species (*D. nigripes)* wanders as far north as Alaska and is often seen on the Pacific coast.

ALBEE, Edward (born 1928). One of the 20th century's best known American dramatists and theatrical producers was Edward Albee. He established a reputation for creating dramatic tension while simultaneously voicing serious social criticism.

Edward Franklin Albee was born on March 12, 1928. He was an adopted child whose place of birth is uncertain, though it was somewhere near Washington, D.C. He was educated at the Choate School in Wallingford, Conn., graduating in 1946. He then spent a year at Trinity College in Hartford, Conn.

Nancy Crampton

Edward Albee

Albee first attempted to write novels and poetry but turned to plays in the late 1950's. During those trying years he supported himself with minor writing jobs for radio. His experimental early one-act plays include 'The Zoo Story' (first performed in 1959), 'The Death of Bessie Smith' (1960), 'The Sandbox' (1960), and 'The American Dream' (1960).

Albee's first three-act play, 'Who's Afraid of Virginia Woolf?' (1962), received numerous awards, as did the motion-picture version (1966). The acting requirements for the four roles in 'Virginia Woolf' were so demanding that two casts were needed if the play was performed twice in the same day. 'Virginia Woolf' was followed by 'Tiny Alice' (1964), 'A Delicate Balance' (1966), 'Box' and 'Quotations from Chairman Mao Tse-tung' (both 1968), 'Seascape' (1975), and 'The Lady from Dubuque' (1980). Both 'A Delicate Balance' and 'Seascape' won Pulitzer prizes. (*See also* Drama.)

ALBERT I (1875–1934). The courage displayed by King Albert of Belgium when Germany invaded his country in 1914 won him the devotion of his people and the admiration of the world. He was well educated in engineering and mechanics and widely traveled. He was a flier in the pioneer days of the airplane, an enthusiastic mountain climber, and a patron of artists, writers, and musicians.

In 1900 he married Elizabeth, duchess of Bavaria. They had three children, Leopold, Charles, and Marie José. He was interested in social and legal reforms and made a personal investigation of conditions in Belgium's African colony in the Congo. When he succeeded his uncle Leopold II as king in 1909, he brought about badly needed reforms there.

His plans for modernization of the army were long delayed by his parliament. When Germany demanded permission to cross Belgium to attack France (Aug. 2, 1914), his forces were only partly reorganized. Nevertheless Albert refused. As commander in chief he fought beside his soldiers.

On Feb. 18, 1934, King Albert was found dead at the foot of a cliff he had been scaling alone. His elder son was named king as Leopold III but abdicated in 1951 in favor of his son Baudouin.

ALBERTA

COAT OF ARMS

SEAL

FLORAL EMBLEM

ALBERTA. The westernmost of Canada's three Prairie Provinces, Alberta is a land of dramatic contrasts. Here the rich black sod of the plains gives way to rolling foothills and then to the rugged Rocky Mountains. Yet Alberta has become increasingly urbanized: two of its cities—Edmonton, the provincial capital, and Calgary—are now ranked among the ten largest cities in Canada. (*See also* Canada.)

Petroleum, natural gas, and coal have brought industry to a land once totally dependent upon agriculture. The vast fields of Alberta supply wheat, one of Canada's most important exports. Cattle and sheep flourish on ranches in the plains and foothills.

Pipelines carrying natural gas and petroleum connect Alberta with the Pacific coast, the eastern provinces, and the United States. All-weather roads, railways, and airlines crisscross the province and bring tourists to Banff, Jasper, and Waterton Lakes national parks. Artists from around the world come to study at the Banff School of Fine Arts and Centre for Continuing Education.

One of the many rivers in the province, the Bow, was named by the Indians who fashioned their weapons from the springy wood found along its banks. The most aggressive Plains Indians, the members of the Blackfeet nation, once hunted thundering herds of buffalo in the province. In 1877, under the leadership of Chief Crowfoot, they ceded their tribal lands to the government.

The Canadian Pacific Railway reached Calgary in 1883 and Edmonton in 1891, opening the fertile lands to settlers. It brought immigrants from eastern Canada, the British Isles, the United States, and northern Europe into the province and carried back the wheat and livestock that they raised. From 1900 to 1910 the population of the province increased by more than 500 percent.

Irrigation has made diversified agriculture possible in southern and eastern Alberta. Industrialization developed rapidly after petroleum was first discovered near Edmonton in 1947. The production of petroleum and natural gas by-products such as sulfur and plastics has brought manufacturing plants into Alberta. Later petroleum discoveries have encouraged settlement in the northern part of the province. The development of the vast petroleum and natural

COAT OF ARMS: On shield, under cross of Saint George, are mountain range, foothills, prairie, and field of wheat.

SEAL: An impression of the provincial seal is used on official papers, such as letters patent.

FLORAL EMBLEM: Wild rose (adopted 1930).

MOTTO: None official.

FLAG: For picture in color, *see* Flags of the World.

Government of the Province of Alberta

In Jasper National Park, Cavell Lake reflects Mount Edith
Cavell. The spectacular scenery of this wilderness area, now
accessible by paved highways, attracts scores of visitors.

gas potential during the 1970's has made Alberta
Canada's leading fuel-producing province. Almost 90
percent of Canada's petroleum and natural gas is
produced in Alberta, and the province contains over
80 percent of the total proven Canadian reserves for
each of these fuels.

With an area of 255,285 square miles (661,185
square kilometers), Alberta is larger than the other
Prairie Provinces—Manitoba and Saskatchewan. It
extends about 760 miles (1,220 kilometers) northward
from the international boundary, which it shares
with Montana, to the Northwest Territories. Its
width, between Saskatchewan on the east and British Columbia on the west, varies from 180 miles (290
kilometers) at the 49th parallel to 400 miles (640 kilometers) near the 54th parallel.

Province of Three Natural Regions

Alberta lies in three natural physiographic regions.
These are the Interior Plains and Lowlands, with
their continuation northward in wooded parklands
and heavy forests; the Rocky Mountain section of
the Cordilleran Region in the southwest; and in the
extreme northeast, the Canadian Shield.

Interior Plains and Lowlands. Most of Alberta
lies in the High Plains subdivision of the Interior
Plains and Lowlands. The High Plains extend into
the United States, where they are known as the
Great Plains. The High Plains are divided into three
areas that vary in elevation, climate, and natural

Population (1981 estimate): 2,135,900—rank, 4th province.
Urban, 75.0%; rural, 25.0%. Persons per square mile, 8.4
(per square kilometer, 3.2)—rank, 6th province.

Extent: Area, 255,285 square miles (661,185 square kilometers), including 6,485 square miles (16,796 square kilometers) of water surface (4th province in size). Greatest
length (north to south), 760 miles (1,220 kilometers);
greatest width (east to west), 400 miles (640 kilometers).

Elevation: Highest, Mount Columbia, 12,294 feet (3,747 meters); lowest, Slave River valley, 573 feet (175 meters);
average, 4,000 feet (1,200 meters).

Temperature: Extremes—lowest, −78° F (−61° C), Fort
Vermilion, Jan. 11, 1911; highest, 108° F (42° C), Medicine
Hat, July 12, 1886. Averages at Edmonton—January,
6.6° F (−14.1° C); July, 63.1° F (17.3° C); annual, 36.9° F
(2.7° C). Averages at Medicine Hat— January, 12.1° F
(−11.1° C); July, 69.1° F (20.6° C); annual, 41.5° F
(5.3° C).

Precipitation: Average annual total—at Edmonton, 13.26
inches (337 millimeters); at Medicine Hat, 9.42 inches (239
millimeters).

Land Use: Agricultural 30%; forest 61%; urban, water, and
other 9%.

For statistical information about Cities, Employment, Government, Population Trends, and Production, see ALBERTA
FACT SUMMARY.

resources: the Southern Plains, the Central Parkland, and the Northern Forests.

In the northeast, the High Plains slope to a lower elevation. Here they meet two other subdivisions of the Interior Plains and Lowlands— the Saskatchewan Plain, which comes in from northwestern Saskatchewan, and the Great Slave Plain, which continues northward into the Northwest Territories.

The Southern Plains, lying in the southeast, are gently sloping treeless plains. They rise in elevation steadily from more than 2,000 feet (600 meters) above sea level in the east to about 3,500 feet (1,100 meters) in the west. The climate is semiarid. Irrigation waters are furnished by the Milk River and by the South Saskatchewan and its tributaries. The area affords good grazing for livestock. In the southwest are rolling grasslands and timber-covered foothills of the Rockies. This area too is considered to be ideal stock-raising country.

In the Red Deer River valley are the badlands of Alberta. This is a vast expanse of eroded, brilliantly colored land containing fossilized remains of many prehistoric animals. Dinosaur Trail and Museum, near Drumheller, draws thousands of visitors yearly.

About 100 miles (160 kilometers) north of Calgary the country becomes a rolling, wooded parkland. This area, called the Central Parkland, is drained by the North Saskatchewan River. The Central Parkland is the most thickly populated area in the province. Edmonton, the provincial capital, is its center. It is a rich agricultural region, with fertile black soil suited to the raising of a variety of field crops. The farmers also engage in mixed farming, which includes dairying, poultry and purebred stock raising, fur farming, and beekeeping. Most of Alberta's great natural gas fields are in the Central Parkland. East of Edmonton is Elk Island National Park, a big-game reserve.

The Northern Forests occupy the northern half of Alberta. The area consists mostly of forests, lakes, and bogs, called muskegs. It was long frequented only by lumbermen, trappers, and hunters. Farmers did not begin to settle in the area until after it was found that certain hardy grains, such as Marquis wheat, could be raised successfully in the Peace River country (see Peace River).

The Athabasca River winds across northern Alberta. It originates in Athabasca Glacier in Jasper National Park and flows northeastward into Lake Athabasca. The largest of the lakes that lie entirely within Alberta are Lesser Slave Lake, Lake Claire, and Lake Bistcho.

The High Plains slope downward in the northeast and merge gradually into the Saskatchewan Plain and the Great Slave Plain. These subdivisions also are a forested wilderness. In this area is Wood Buffalo National Park, home of the only remaining herd of

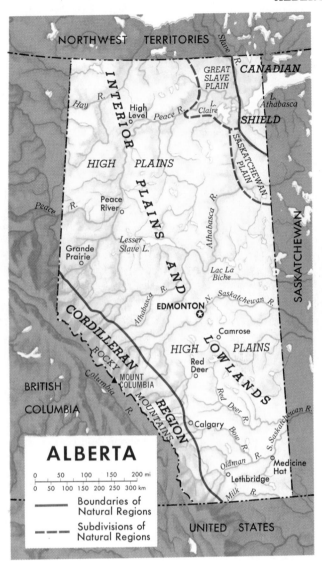

Alberta's diverse physical regions include both lofty Rocky Mountain ranges and extensive plains and lowlands that are crossed by numerous rivers. Land use is related to the physical features of each region.

wood bison in North America and nesting ground of the rare whooping cranes (see Birds).

Canadian Shield. Adjoining the Great Slave Plain and the Saskatchewan Plain, in the extreme northeastern corner of the province, is the Canadian Shield. It is also called the Laurentian Plateau (see Laurentian Plateau). The Slave River marks its western edge, and the west end of Lake Athabasca lies in this region. The lowest point in the province is in the Slave River valley, 573 feet (175 meters) above sea level. This is a land of subarctic forest and tundra. Fort Chipewyan, at the junction of the Peace and Slave rivers, and Fort Fitzgerald, to the north, are the only populated centers in this region.

Cordilleran Region. The Rocky Mountain section of the Cordilleran Region, which straddles the south-

The Great Canadian Oil Sands plant near Fort McMurray has provided employment for many workers since it began operations in 1967. The plant recovers petroleum from deposits of oil-impregnated sands that lie along the Athabasca River in northeastern Alberta. The deposits have been estimated to contain about half the world's petroleum reserves.

eastern border of British Columbia, affords a striking contrast to the low-lying northern wilderness. There are more than 30 peaks over 10,000 feet (3,000 meters) high. The highest is Mount Columbia (12,294 feet; 3,747 meters) in Jasper National Park. From Willmore Wilderness Park in the northwest to Waterton Lakes National Park in the southeast, the Rockies are renowned for their scenic beauty. There are extensive glaciated areas, such as the Columbia Icefield; beautiful waterfalls, such as Athabasca Falls; and mirrorlike lakes, such as Louise and Moraine in Banff National Park and Maligne in Jasper National Park. The entire region serves as a forest conservation area and a wildlife sanctuary for the grizzly bear, mountain goat, mule deer, bighorn sheep, and other animals.

Variable Climate

Alberta has a continental climate, with cold winters and warm summers. In the winter, blizzards are common, with bitterly cold temperatures, high winds, and driving snow. The mean January temperature is 6.6° F (−14.1° C) at Edmonton. The lowest on record is −78° F (−61° C) at Fort Vermilion. The chinook—a dry, westerly wind that is warmed as it descends from the mountains—may blow all winter, bringing almost springlike weather (see Wind).

Temperatures vary less in the summer. The mean July temperature is 63.1° F (17.3° C) at Edmonton. The highest recorded was 108° F (42° C) at Medicine Hat. In the north, temperatures may be almost as high as in the south, owing to the long hours of summer sunlight and the lower altitude.

Rainfall is usually adequate for crops, except in the southeast. There the chinook prevents much snow from falling and carries off summer moisture.

The People and Their Origins

The population of Alberta (1981 estimate) is 2,135,900, and the density is only 8.4 persons to the square mile (3.2 persons to the square kilometer). The population is 25 percent rural and 75 percent urban. About half of Alberta's people are of British origin. Other national groups include Germans, Ukrainians, Scandinavians, French, Dutch, Poles, and Italians. Most came in the early 1900's.

Alberta has about 35,000 Indians, descended from such tribes as the Assiniboin, Chipewyan, Cree, Beaver, Blackfeet, and Slave, who once roamed this region. There are 98 reserves and settlements.

Agriculture and Irrigation

Ranching and farming account for about one eighth of the value of Alberta's production. Cowboys still ride the range and cattle ranches extend from the Southern Plains to the Peace River district. The ranches in the south are also noted for the raising of sheep and horses, and those in the central and northern parts for the raising of hogs.

Irrigation has opened southeastern Alberta for farming. The first large project was begun near Lethbridge in 1883. Since then, some 15 major projects have been completed. Alberta has over one million acres (405,000 hectares) of irrigable land. About 5,300 farms use irrigation water. The St. Mary Dam on the St. Mary-Milk rivers system provides water to irrigate about 293,000 acres (118,600 hectares).

Alberta produces more wheat than any province except Saskatchewan. Other crops are barley, rapeseed (canola), sugar beets, and alfalfa. Potatoes, carrots, peas, and other vegetables are grown.

The Oil Province

Alberta, called the "Oil Province" because it produces almost 90 percent of Canada's crude oil, has about 35,000 producing oil and natural gas wells. Immense petroleum deposits are located in the Leduc-Woodbend and Pembina areas, near Edmonton. The rich reserves of the fields at Redwater, Bonnie Glen, Swan Hills, Fenn-Big Valley, Wizard Lake, and Rainbow Lake have also been tapped.

In the oil sands along the northern Athabasca, Alberta has one of the greatest known oil reserves, yielding more than 37 million barrels (5 million metric tons) of oil per year. Natural gas wells in the Pincher Creek, Viking-Kinsella, and other areas produce almost 90 percent of Canada's natural gas. The petrochemicals industry manufactures chemicals for making plastics, fertilizers, synthetic rubber, and many other products.

Alberta's oil is carried to refineries on the British Columbia and Washington coasts by the Trans-Mountain Pipeline. The Interprovincial Pipeline extends from Edmonton through the United States into eastern Canada. Feeder pipelines connect with the two major lines.

Gas pipelines have been constructed from the province to British Columbia, the United States, and eastern Canada. The longest is the Trans-Canada Pipeline, which terminates in Montreal, Que.

Coal and Other Minerals

At one time the coal mines in the vicinity of Lethbridge and Drumheller yielded 50 percent of the coal produced in Canada. Along with the development of the province's fuel oil and natural gas resources, the production of coal has also increased. Alberta now accounts for approximately 40 percent of the total national production of coal and for about 98 percent of the total production of sulfur. Sand and gravel, clay, cement, lime, stone, and salt are among other important products that are mined in Alberta.

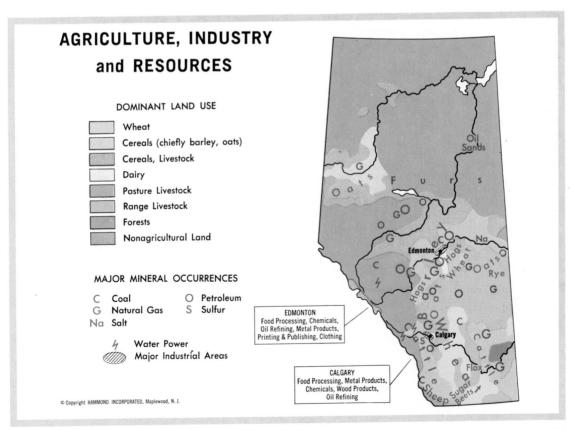

AGRICULTURE, INDUSTRY and RESOURCES

DOMINANT LAND USE

Wheat
Cereals (chiefly barley, oats)
Cereals, Livestock
Dairy
Pasture Livestock
Range Livestock
Forests
Nonagricultural Land

MAJOR MINERAL OCCURRENCES

C Coal   O Petroleum
G Natural Gas   S Sulfur
Na Salt

⚡ Water Power
     Major Industrial Areas

© Copyright HAMMOND INCORPORATED, Maplewood, N. J.

EDMONTON
Food Processing, Chemicals,
Oil Refining, Metal Products,
Printing & Publishing, Clothing

CALGARY
Food Processing, Metal Products,
Chemicals, Wood Products,
Oil Refining

Jagged peaks of the Canadian Rockies overlook cattle grazing peacefully on a ranch in southwestern Alberta. The region has been used for cattle ranching since the 1870's.

The annual Calgary Exhibition and Stampede, known as the world's greatest wild West show, is a tradition dating from 1912. The week-long rodeo is held in early July.

Manufacturing and Cities

Alberta's recent industrial growth has been impressive. It is based on abundant natural resources, ample low-cost fuels, and excellent road, rail, and other transportation facilities. The province's principal manufacturing industries are slaughtering and meatpacking, petroleum refining, dairying, poultry products, industrial chemical production, and flour milling. Other leading manufactures are semifinished wood products, bakery goods, printed materials, and structural metal products.

From forests of spruce, jack pine, balsam fir, and poplar comes the lumber used by furniture factories, sash and door mills, and pulp and paper mills. Important to Alberta's economy are breweries, distilleries, bakeries, sugar refineries, and vegetable canneries. Other industrial plants include textile factories, feed mills, cement plants, potteries, brick and tile works, and printing establishments.

Calgary, Alberta's largest city, is not only important industrially but is also a leading financial and transportation center (*see* Calgary). The second largest city, Edmonton, is the oil center of the province and the distributing point for a rich farming district (*see* Edmonton). Lethbridge and Medicine Hat are marketing and industrial centers. Red Deer is noted for dairy and petroleum products.

Tourism and Transportation

One of Alberta's greatest assets is its spectacular mountain scenery. More than 10 million tourists visit the province each year to enjoy its beauty and to engage in mountain climbing, skiing, golfing, camping, trail riding, fishing, and hunting. All-weather paved highways, including a 282-mile (454-kilometer) segment of the Trans-Canada Highway, provide year-round access to the scenic areas and the population centers (*see* Trans-Canada Highway). The sever-

ity of the winter climate, however, makes road maintenance a continual task.

Alberta has about 6,000 miles (9,670 kilometers) of operating railroad tracks. The Canadian Pacific Railway crosses the southern part of the province; the Canadian National Railway, the central part. The Northern Alberta Railway runs into the north, and branch lines crisscrosses the province.

Educational Opportunities

The elementary and secondary educational system of Alberta is administered by local school authorities, under the general supervision of the Department of Education. It is supported by local taxation and provincial grants. Rural town and village schools are almost completely centralized.

The oldest institution of higher learning is the University of Alberta, in Edmonton, founded in 1906. Its affiliates include St. Joseph's and St. Stephen's colleges, also at Edmonton, and Camrose Lutheran College, at Camrose. The University of Calgary was formerly the Calgary branch of the University of Alberta. Affiliated with it are Mount Royal College, at Calgary, and Medicine Hat College. Other institutions are the University of Lethbridge and Athabasca University, at Edmonton. There are institutes of technology in Calgary, Banff, and Edmonton.

Provincial Government

The government of Alberta is centered in Edmonton. The lieutenant-governor is appointed by the governor-general of Canada for a five-year term. The single-chamber Legislative Assembly of 79 members is elected for up to five years. From it are chosen a premier and an Executive Council (or Cabinet) of ministers, each of whom has charge of one or more government departments. Alberta is represented in the Canadian Parliament by 27 members—21 in the House of Commons and 6 in the Senate.

Judicial power is vested in the Supreme Court, Court of Appeal, and district and county courts. Since 1873 law and order in Alberta has been entrusted to the Royal Canadian Mounted Police.

HISTORY OF ALBERTA

For 200 years the history of Alberta was the history of the fur trade in western Canada (*see* Fur Trade, History of). It was a part of vast Rupert's Land, granted to the Hudson's Bay Company in 1670 by Charles II of England. Alberta was unoccupied, however, until the rival North West Company built forts in the late 18th century. Roderick McKenzie of the North West Company established Fort Chipewyan on Lake Athabasca in 1788. Three years later Alexander Mackenzie explored the Peace River district. He was followed by David Thompson, another fur trader, who explored the Rocky Mountain region. The North West and Hudson's Bay companies built forts near present-day Edmonton in 1794 and 1795. The companies combined in 1821.

In 1869 the Dominion of Canada bought Rupert's Land from the Hudson's Bay Company for £300,000 (about 1½ million dollars) and organized it as the Northwest Territories. The province was named for Princess Louise Caroline Alberta, a daughter of Queen Victoria who visited the prairies in 1881. Ranching and farming attracted settlers, whose numbers increased after the Canadian Pacific Railway reached Calgary in 1883. The preceding year four provincial districts—Alberta, Saskatchewan, Athabaska, and Assiniboia—had been set up south of the 60th parallel. In 1905 the districts were reorganized as the provinces of Alberta and Saskatchewan.

Ever since the Liberals came to power in 1905, political parties in Alberta had been primarily concerned with the province's agricultural interests and with its social services. The party known as the United Farmers of Alberta gained control of the government in 1921. It owed its popularity to the success of wheat pools and cooperative grain marketing. During the depression of the 1930's, it was supplanted by the Social Credit party, led by William Aberhart. Aberhart was premier from 1935 until his death in 1943. He advocated radical changes in the control of money and banking, but his more extreme measures were overruled by the Supreme Court of Canada. Under his successor, Ernest C. Manning, the Social Credit party was victorious in every provincial general election from 1944 to 1971, when it was upset by the Progressive Conservatives. As oil became increasingly important in the province's economy, their majority grew. By 1979 the Conservatives held 74 of the 79 seats in the legislature.

The history of Alberta since World War II has revolved around its oil prosperity. Because the provincial government owns about 90 percent of the mineral rights, it has received vast sums in royalties, rentals, and lease sales, almost eliminating the public debt. Much has been done to improve schools, hospitals, roads, and cultural enterprises.

City of Edmonton Business Development Department

The striking modern buildings of Edmonton rise out of the plains of central Alberta. The capital of the province, Edmonton grew on the site of a fur-trading post built in 1795.

University of Alberta

The University of Alberta was created at Edmonton in 1906 during the first session of the provincial legislature.

The Columbia Icefield, on the British Columbia–Alberta border, is the Rocky Mountains' largest ice field. It lies partly in Jasper National Park and is accessible by highway.

Government of the Province of Alberta

ALBERTA FACT SUMMARY

POPULATION TRENDS

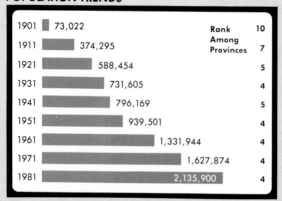

Year	Population	Rank Among Provinces
1901	73,022	10
1911	374,295	7
1921	588,454	5
1931	731,605	4
1941	796,169	5
1951	939,501	4
1961	1,331,944	4
1971	1,627,874	4
1981	2,135,900	4

LARGEST CITIES (1981 census)

Calgary (592,743; metropolitan area 592,743): manufacturing and agricultural center in wheat-growing and livestock-raising district; oil refining; meat-packing; flour milling (*see* Calgary).

Edmonton (532,246; metropolitan area 657,057): provincial capital; manufacturing and trading center in agricultural region; center of Canadian oil and natural gas development; coal mining (*see* Edmonton).

Lethbridge (54,072): city in partly irrigated farm area; ranching; flour, beet sugar, coal; food processing.

Red Deer (46,393): on Red Deer River; oil and natural gas center; dairy products.

Medicine Hat (40,380): in wheat-growing and cattle-raising area; natural gas.

GOVERNMENT

Capital: Edmonton (since 1905).

Admission to Confederation: Parliamentary system established by Alberta Act, effective Sept. 1, 1905.

Representation in Federal Parliament: House of Commons—21; Senate—6.

Lieutenant-Governor: Appointed by Governor General-in-Council; term, 5 years.

Legislative Assembly: 79 elected members; term, 5 years; annual sessions.

Executive Council (Cabinet): Headed by Premier, who is the leader of the majority party in the Legislative Assembly; other ministers are members of the Legislative Assembly appointed to their posts by the Premier.

Judiciary: Justices of the Supreme Court, the Court of Appeal, and the Court of Queen's Bench are appointed by the Governor General-in-Council; judges of the Provincial Courts are appointed by the Lieutenant-Governor.

MAJOR PRODUCTS

Agricultural: Wheat, rapeseed, barley, cattle, hogs, timber.

Manufactured: Meat and poultry products, refined petroleum, chemicals, paper, wood products.

Mined: Crude petroleum, natural gas, sulfur, coal.

EMPLOYMENT

Number of persons employed: 1,068,000.

Per Capita Income: $9,717.

Percentage Employed (by industry): Agriculture 7.8; forestry, fishing, trapping, mining 6.1; manufacturing 9.4; construction 9.8; transportation, communications, utilities 8.8; trade 18.1; finance, insurance, real estate 5.3; services 28.3; government 6.5.

EDUCATION AND CULTURE

Universities and Colleges: University of Alberta, Edmonton; University of Calgary, Calgary.

Libraries: Yellowhead Regional Library, Spruce Grove; Parkland Regional Library, Lacombe; Calgary Public Library; Edmonton Public Library.

Notable Museums: Provincial Museum of Alberta, Edmonton; Edmonton Art Gallery; Glenbow-Alberta Institute (Glenbow Museum, Calgary and Luxton Museum, Banff); Heritage Park, Calgary; John Walter Historical Site, Edmonton; Muttart Conservatory, Edmonton.

PLACES OF INTEREST

Banff National Park: scenic mountain resorts; mineral hot springs; ice fields and glaciers; wildlife; northwest of Calgary.

Columbia Icefield: in Banff and Jasper national parks high in the Rocky Mountains; covers more than 150 square miles (390 square kilometers); glacier meltwater drains to Atlantic, Pacific, and Arctic oceans.

Elk Island National Park: natural preserve east of Edmonton; herd of Plains bison; deer, elk, moose; Astotin Lake.

Jasper National Park: majestic mountain scenery; alpine lakes and valleys; hot springs; big-game sanctuary; west of Edmonton.

Provincial Parks: 53 parks among which are Crimson Lake, Cypress Hills, Dinosaur, Park Lake, and Writing-on-Stone.

Rocky Mountain House National Historic Site: fur-trading post built by the North West Company in 1799; artifact displays and period demonstration sites; west of Red Deer.

Waterton Lakes National Park: adjoins Glacier National Park in Montana to form the Waterton-Glacier International Peace Park; mountain lakes among high Rocky Mountain peaks.

Wood Buffalo National Park: straddles the Alberta-Northwest Territories border; protects only remaining herd of wood bison and summer nesting site of wild whooping cranes.

BIBLIOGRAPHY FOR ALBERTA

Allan, Richard, ed. Man and Nature on the Prairies (Canadian Plains, 1976).

Bercuson, D. J. Opening the Canadian West (Grolier, 1980).

Brebner, J. B. Canada: a Modern History (Univ. of Michigan Press, 1970).

Hocking, Anthony. Alberta (The Canada Series) (McGraw, 1979).

Tomkins, D. M., Tomkins, G. S., and Scarfe, N. V. Alberta: Where the Mountains Meet the Plains (Gage, 1970).

All Fact Summary data are based on current government reports.

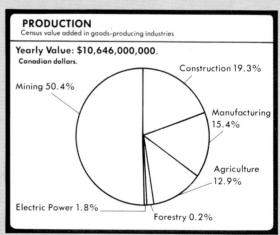

PRODUCTION
Census value added in goods-producing industries

Yearly Value: $10,646,000,000.
Canadian dollars.

- Mining 50.4%
- Construction 19.3%
- Manufacturing 15.4%
- Agriculture 12.9%
- Electric Power 1.8%
- Forestry 0.2%

The chart above shows the province's major product categories and each category's percentage of the total value.

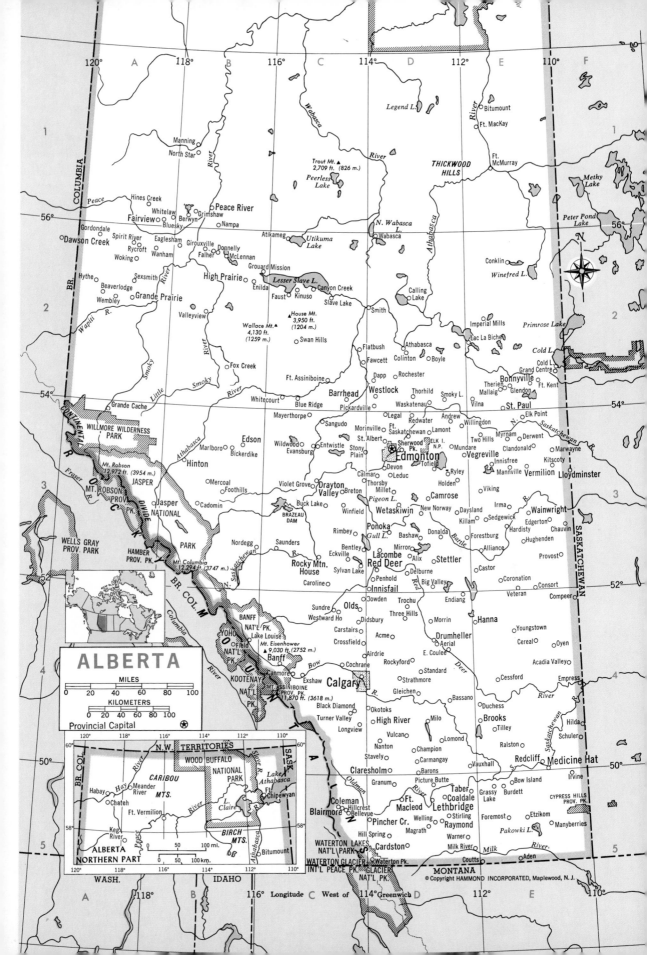

ALBERTA

MILES
0   20   40   60   80   100

KILOMETERS
0   20   40   60   80   100

Provincial Capital ✪

ALBERTA
NORTHERN PART

ALBERTA NORTHERN PART inset:

N.W. TERRITORIES

CARIBOU
MTS.

WOOD BUFFALO
NATIONAL
PARK

Lake
Athabasca

SASK.

BR. COL.

Habay
Meander River
Chateau
Ft. Vermilion
Keg River

CARIBOU
MTS.

Ft.
Chipewyan

L.
Claire

BIRCH
MTS.

Bitumount

Main map labels:

COLUMBIA
BR.

Peace

Dawson Creek
Gordondale
Spirit River
Rycroft
Woking
Hythe
Beaverlodge
Wembley
Grande Prairie

Hines Creek
Fairview
Whitelaw
Bluesky
Berwyn
Grimshaw
Nampa
Peace River
Manning
North Star

Eaglesham
Girouxville
Wanham
Falher
Donnelly
McLennan
Grouard Mission
Enilda
High Prairie
Faust
Kinuso
Canyon Creek
Slave Lake
Lesser Slave L.

Sexsmith
Valleyview
Fox Creek

Wabasca
River
Trout Mt.
2,709 ft. (826 m.)
Peerless
Lake

Legend L.
River
Ft. MacKay
Bitumount
THICKWOOD
HILLS
Ft. McMurray

Athabasca

Methy
Lake

Peter Pond
Lake

N. Wabasca
L.
Wabasca
Atikameg
Utikuma
Lake
Calling
Lake
Smith

Conklin
Winefred L.

Cold L.

House Mt.
3,950 ft.
(1204 m.)
Wallace Mt.
4,130 ft.
(1259 m.)
Swan Hills

Imperial Mills
Lac La Biche
Primrose Lake

Cold L.
Grand Centre
Bonnyville
Ft. Kent

Flatbush
Fawcett
Dapp
Colinton
Athabasca
Boyle
Rochester

Therien
Mallaig
Glendon
St. Paul

Ft. Assiniboine
Barrhead
Westlock
Thorhild
Smoky L.
Vilna

Vilna
Elk Point
Saskatchewan

Whitecourt
Blue Ridge
Pickardville
Waskatenau
Andrew
Willingdon
Two Hills
Myrnam
Derwent

Mayerthorpe
Sangudo
Legal
Redwater
Ft.
Saskatchewan
Lamont
Willingdon
Clandonald
Marwayne

Edson
Marlboro
Bickerdike
Wildwood
Evansburg
Entwistle
Morinville
St. Albert
Stony
Plain
Sherwood
Pk.
ELK I.
N.P.
Mundare
Innisfree
Mannville
Vegreville
Vermilion
Kitscoty
Lloydminster

Hinton
Mercoal
Foothills
Violet Grove
Devon
Leduc
Calmar
Tofield
Ryley
Holden
Viking
Irma

Mt. Robson
12,972 ft. (3954 m.)
MT. ROBSON
PROV. PK.
JASPER
Jasper
NATIONAL
PARK

Edmonton

Cadomin
Drayton
Valley
Breton
Thorsby
Millet
Pigeon L.
Camrose
New Norway
Daysland
Sedgewick
Wainwright
Edgerton
Chauvin

Nordegg
Buck Lake
Winfield
Wetaskiwin
Bashaw
Donalda
Killam
Forestburg
Hardisty
Hughenden

Rimbey
Ponoka
Gull L.
Mirror
Alliance
Provost

Saunders
Bentley
Eckville
Lacombe
Alix
Stettler
Castor
Coronation
Consort

Rocky Mtn.
House
Sylvan Lake
Red Deer
Delburne
Big Valley
Compeer

Caroline
Penhold
Innisfail
Veteran

Sundre
Bowden
Olds
Trochu
Endiang
Hanna
Youngstown

Westward Ho
Didsbury
Three Hills
Morrin
Cereal
Oyen

Carstairs
Acme
Drumheller
Aerial
Acadia Valley

Crossfield
Airdrie
E. Coulee
Standard

BANFF
NAT'L. PK.
Lake Louise
Field
YOHO
NAT'L.
PK.
Mt. Eisenhower
9,030 ft. (2752 m.)
Banff
Canmore
KOOTENAY
NAT'L.
PK.
Exshaw
MT. ASSINIBOINE
PROV. PK.
11,870 ft. (3618 m.)

Cochrane
Rockyford
Calgary
Strathmore
Gleichen
Cessford
Empress

Bow
R.
Black Diamond
Turner Valley
Okotoks
High River
Milo
Brooks
Tilley

Longview
Vulcan
Lomond
Ralston
Hilda
Schuler

Nanton
Champion
Medicine Hat

Stavely
Carmangay
Vauxhall
Redcliff

Claresholm
Barons
Granum
Picture Butte
Bow Island
Irvine

Coleman
Hillcrest
Bellevue
Blairmore
Pincher Cr.
Ft.
Macleod
Taber
Coaldale
Lethbridge
Grassy
Lake
Burdett

CYPRESS HILLS
PROV. PK.

Hill Spring
Welling
Stirling
Raymond
Warner
Foremost
Etzikom
Manyberries

Waterton Lakes
Nat'l Park
Cardston
Milk River
Pakowki L.

WATERTON GLACIER
INT'L PEACE PK.
Waterton Pk.
GLACIER
NAT'L PK.

MONTANA
Coutts
Aden
Milk
River

© Copyright HAMMOND INCORPORATED, Maplewood, N.J.

WASH.   IDAHO   Longitude   West of   Greenwich

COLUMBIA
WELLS GRAY
PROV. PARK
HAMBER
PROV. PK.
MT. COLUMBIA
12,294 ft. (3747 m.)
WILLMORE WILDERNESS
PARK
Grande Cache

CONTINENTAL
DIVIDE
ROCKY
MOUNTAINS
BR. COL.
Fraser
R.
Columbia
River
KANANASKIS
BR. COL.

Peace
River
Hay
River
Meander River

ALBERTA

270

ALBERTI, Leon Battista (1404–1472). Humanist, architect, and principal initiator of Renaissance art theory, the Italian Leon Battista Alberti is considered a typical example of the Renaissance "universal man." He belonged to a wealthy merchant-banker family of Florence and at the age of 10 or 11 was sent to boarding school in Padua. There Alberti was given a classical Latin training, and he emerged as an accomplished writer.

Alberti wrote a Latin comedy at the age of 20 that was acclaimed as the "discovered" work of a Roman playwright—and was still published more than 100 years later as a Roman work. He completed his formal education at the University of Bologna, receiving his doctorate in church law in 1428. Alberti then accepted a position as a secretary rather than pursue a legal career. By 1432 he was a secretary in the Papal Chancery in Rome. He took holy orders, and though he was known to lead an exemplary, and apparently celibate, life, there is almost nothing in his subsequent career indicating that Alberti was a churchman. His interests and activities were wholly secular, and he issued an impressive series of humanistic and technical writings.

The treatise 'Della Famiglia' (On the Family), which he began in Rome in 1432, is the first of several dialogues on which his reputation as a thinker and writer largely rests. He wrote these in the vernacular, the language of the people.

Traveling with the papal court to Florence, Alberti established close associations with the sculptor Donatello and the architect Filippo Brunelleschi. These relationships led to one of his major achievements: the book 'De Pictura' (On Painting), which was published in 1435 and which set forth for the first time the rules for drawing a three-dimensional scene on a flat surface. It had a major effect on Italian painting and relief work, giving rise to the ordered space that became typical of the Renaissance style.

His friendship with the Florentine cosmographer Paolo Toscanelli resulted in a small treatise on geography, the first work of its kind since antiquity. It sets forth the rules for surveying and mapping a land area, and it was probably as influential as his earlier treatise on painting.

At the ducal court of Este in Ferrara, where Alberti was first made welcome in 1438, he was encouraged (and commissioned) to direct his talents toward architecture. Alberti's earliest effort at reviving classical forms of building was a miniature triumphal arch in Ferrara. He began to study the architectural and engineering practices of antiquity and by 1447 was knowledgeable enough to become the architectural adviser to Pope Nicholas V. His collaboration with the pope resulted in the first large-scale building projects of Renaissance Rome, beginning among other works the reconstruction of St. Peter's and the Vatican Palace. His long study of Vitruvius resulted in his 'De re aedificatoria' (Ten Books on Architecture), published in 1452, not a restored text of Vitruvius but a wholly new work that won him a reputa-

The nave of the church of Sant'Andrea in Mantua was designed by Leon Battista Alberti based on the great Roman basilicas, with vaulted chapels between massive piers.

tion as the "Florentine Vitruvius" and that became a bible of Renaissance architecture.

During the final 20 years of his life, Alberti carried out his architectural ideas in several outstanding buildings. The facades of Santa Maria Novella and the Palazzo Rucellai, both in Florence, are noted for their proportions. The new sense of space, which is notable in the majestic church of Sant'Andrea in Mantua, announced the fullness of the High Renaissance style. In addition to being the foremost theorist of Renaissance architecture, Alberti had become one of its great practitioners.

Although Alberti traveled to various cities and courts of Renaissance Italy, Rome and Florence remained his intellectual homes. He produced two highly original works: the first Italian grammar, in which he demonstrated that the Tuscan vernacular was as "regular" a language as Latin and hence worthy of literary use, and a pioneer work in the writing of secret codes. His final and his finest dialogue was written in Florence in Tuscan prose. Called 'De iciarchia' (On the Man of Excellence and Ruler of His Family), it represents in its fullness the public-spirited humanism of the earlier age to which he belonged. Alberti died in Rome "content and tranquil," according to his 16th-century biographer, Giorgio Vasari, leaving behind him "a most honorable name."

ALBINO. People without the ability to form the natural pigment melanin have a condition called albinism and are referred to as albinos. Members of any race can be albinos, and there are approximately 25,000 in the United States. Other creatures can also inherit this inability to manufacture the color pigments normal for their species.

In humans albinism is caused by a recessive gene (*see* Genetics). When two normal people each having a gene for albinism produce children, chances are that one in four of their offspring will be an albino. Such children are born without color in their eyes, hair, or skin. Often the eyes appear to be pink, because the color of blood can be seen through the iris (*see* Eye). Albino hair is a light yellowish to white, and the skin is as white as milk. The result of this lack of pigment is skin that is easily sunburned and eyes that need protection from strong light. Many albinos have problems with their vision and need glasses to see well. An eye condition called strabismus, which causes the eyes to make involuntary movements, is also often found in albinos.

There is no treatment for the correction of albinism. Sunscreen creams can be used to prevent burns, and dark glasses can be worn to protect sensitive eyes from strong light.

Albinism can also affect plants. Such plants cannot produce chlorophyll, which makes plants green. Because this substance is necessary for the manufacture of food, the young albino plant dies when the nourishment of the seed is consumed.

ALBUMIN. The chemical compound known as albumin is an important type of protein that occurs in nearly all animal tissue, bacteria, and certain plant matter, including mold. Serum albumin, for example, is the most abundant protein in human blood, comprising more than 50 percent of the volume of plasma proteins. Other common forms of albumins include ovalbumin found in egg white and lactalbumin contained in milk. The albumins were once thought to be a single substance rather than an entire group of similar but not identical compounds. This single substance, considered the principal component of egg white, was called albumen, a term derived from the Latin *albus*, meaning "white."

Albumins consist largely of long chains of amino acids composed of carbon, hydrogen, nitrogen, oxygen, and sulfur. They also contain small amounts of carbohydrates and phosphoric acid. Albumins characteristically have high molecular weights, the various forms ranging from about 34,000 to more than 70,000. As globular proteins, albumins are soluble in water as well as in most dilute solutions of acids, bases, or salts. If hydrolyzed, or reacted chemically with water, they undergo denaturation, a fundamental change resulting in the irreversible loss of characteristic properties such as solubility. Heating also causes denaturation, as illustrated by the coagulation of egg white when heated. This coagulability and the tendency to collect foreign matter while forming a semisolid mass make albumins, particularly ovalbumins, suitable for certain important industrial applications. Examples are sugar refining and the manufacture of adhesives, varnishes, and inks, where they serve to remove impurities from liquids.

Nutritionally albumins are almost perfect proteins. They contain liberal amounts of the 11 amino acids essential for proper growth in children and the six amino acids needed to maintain good health in adults. Serum albumin performs several important physiological functions in the blood. It plays a key role in maintaining blood viscosity and osmotic pressure. If the concentration of albumin in the bloodstream drops, fluid from the plasma may escape into the surrounding soft tissue and accumulate, producing an abnormal condition known as edema. Serum albumin is also responsible for transporting fatty acids between cells of adipose tissue—that is, fat in the connective tissue throughout the body. An abnormally large amount of albumin discharged in urine is generally symptomatic of a kidney disorder.

ALBUQUERQUE, N. M. One of the fastest-growing cities in the southwestern United States is Albuquerque, New Mexico's largest city. It is situated on the banks of the Rio Grande, 59 miles (96 kilometers) southwest of Santa Fe. To the east are the Sandia and

Manzano mountains. Since the city was founded in 1706 by Francisco Cuervo y Valdés, four flags—those of Spain, Mexico, the United States, and the Confederacy—have flown over the plaza of its Old Town. In early days it was known as San Felipe de Alburquerque. It was named for King Philip V of Spain and the duke of Alburquerque, who was then viceroy of New Spain. Later the name was shortened and changed to Albuquerque.

Albuquerque came under Mexican rule when Mexico gained its independence from Spain in 1821. It became United States property in 1848, at the end of the Mexican War, when Mexico ceded the province of New Mexico. During the Civil War Albuquerque was alternately held by Union and Confederate forces. It acquired its New Town in 1881 when the newly completed Atchison and Topeka Railroad (now The Atchison, Topeka and Santa Fe Railway) passed about two miles (three kilometers) east of the plaza and a huddle of shacks was built around the depot. In 1890 Albuquerque was incorporated as a city.

Today, as a division point on the main line of the railway, Albuquerque is the leading commercial and distributing center of New Mexico. The sheep ranches in the surrounding region have made it an important wool-shipping center, and its packing plants process meat from livestock. Canneries utilize the fruits and vegetables raised by farmers on the irrigated lands of the Rio Grande Valley.

The varied manufactures of Albuquerque's industries include electronic equipment, machine tools, cement, gypsum wallboard, lumber products, furniture, clothing, trailers, and aerospace parts. Large railroad shops are located in the city. Several oil refineries have been erected to accommodate the San Juan Basin oil field in northwestern New Mexico and the city's pipeline connections with Texas oil fields.

A warm, dry climate has made the city a popular health and vacation resort. Jewelry and pottery for the economically important tourist trade are made by Indians in nearby villages and reservations.

Albuquerque has been a noted educational center ever since it was selected as the seat of the University of New Mexico in 1889. The University of Albuquerque, a Roman Catholic institution, is the former College of St. Joseph on the Rio Grande.

During World War II Albuquerque was selected as the site of United States Defense Department installations and Air Force training centers. Later the Sandia and Kirtland bases were converted into atomic and rocket research centers, which have played a vital role in United States space exploration. The city has a mayor-council form of government. (*See also* New Mexico.) Population (1980 census), 331,767.

ALCHEMY. During the Middle Ages there existed a kind of primitive science called alchemy. The objective of alchemy was to discover a substance called the philosophers' stone. This elusive material was thought to transform common metals such as lead into silver or gold. Another objective of the alchemists' researches was the "elixir of life"—a potion that would cure all diseases and prolong life indefinitely. (*See also* Chemistry, History of.)

Historical Basis

Alchemy was based on ideas passed along by older cultures, including Chinese, Egyptian, East Indian, Greek, Syrian, and Islamic. These ancient peoples had learned how to extract metals from ores and knew how to make alloys, soap, glass, leather, alum, dyes, and fermented liquors.

Many alchemists were impostors and fakers who pretended to be able to produce gold. Others, however, were honest. They performed practical experiments in their quest for the philosophers' stone. They never found it, but they made contributions to chemistry and developed laboratory techniques. By heating the compound iron sulfate, for example, they produced "oil of vitriol," which is known today as

'The Alchemist', by the 17th-century Flemish painter David Teniers the Younger, shows an alchemist at work.

Fisher Scientific Co.

sulfuric acid. They made hydrochloric and nitric acid and compounds such as potash and sodium carbonate. They also identified the elements arsenic, antimony, and bismuth.

Theories of Matter

One of the ancient ideas held by the alchemists was that matter was composed of four "elements"— earth, air, fire, and water—which came from one common source. Matter was thought to have a soul, which could be transferred from one element to another by means of the philosophers' stone.

Some alchemists believed that gold was formed when fire and water combined, under planetary influences, in the depths of the Earth. If the resulting product was only slightly impure, it was thought to become silver. If it was markedly impure, a base metal such as lead was believed to result. If, however, fire and water could be brought together in states of superfine quality, the philosophers' stone would at last have been found.

ALCIBIADES (450?–404 B.C.). When the philosopher Socrates was tried and convicted, in 399 B.C., for corrupting the young men of Athens, it is possible that the example of Alcibiades was on the minds of the judges. Intelligent, handsome, and charming, Alcibiades was an outstanding politician and a brilliant general. Unfortunately he was motivated entirely by personal ambition, and his loyalties were determined by expediency. His unscrupulous dealings made him a divisive influence in ancient Greece during most of the Peloponnesian War (431–404 B.C.).

Born in Athens about 450 B.C., Alcibiades was raised by the statesman Pericles. As a youth he seemed inspired by the brilliance and integrity of Socrates. But he soon turned away from this example to pursue his personal goals.

During the course of the Peloponnesian War, he switched his loyalty from Athens to the enemy, Sparta, and back again, as advantage and circumstance dictated. Upset by a peace settlement in 420 B.C., he fomented an anti-Spartan alliance that was defeated at the Battle of Mantineia in 418 B.C. Fortunate enough to escape banishment from Athens, he was given partial command of an expedition to Sicily against Syracuse. But when he was recalled to Athens to stand trial for religious offenses, Alcibiades defected to Sparta. When the Spartans expelled him as a troublemaker in 412 B.C., he fled to Sardis in Asia Minor to enlist the aid of the Persians in overthrowing the government at Athens. Failing in this, he was nevertheless recalled to Athens to help the navy defeat the Spartans between 411 and 408 B.C.

His spectacular success in this conflict made him extremely popular in his native city, and he was given command of the conduct of the war. But a naval defeat in 407 B.C. led to his ostracism. Alcibiades went to Thrace and later to Phrygia in northwestern Asia Minor. There the Spartans induced the Persian governor to have him murdered in 404 B.C.

ALCOHOL. An important chemical substance widely used both in science and in technology is an organic compound known as alcohol (*see* Organic Chemistry). Its name comes from the ancient Arabic word *al-kuhl*, meaning "a powder for painting the eyelids." The term was later applied to all compounds that contain alcoholic spirits. These include beverages such as wine, beer, and whisky. In modern chemistry alcohol usually refers to one type of compound—*ethyl alcohol*. It is also known as *ethanol* or *grain alcohol*.

Man discovered alcohol in early times. He found that certain grains, fruits, and sugars produced an intoxicating liquid when they fermented (*see* Fermentation). Today the manufacture of alcoholic beverages is a major industry. The distillation and sale of beverages containing ethyl alcohol have a direct effect on a nation's economy. The United States derives about 5 billion dollars each year from taxes levied on the manufacture and sale of drinking alcohol. Most other countries impose similar taxes.

Government regulations maintain rigid control over the quality and purity of drinking alcohol. If such beverages do not meet prescribed standards, they cannot be legally sold. In the United States drinking alcohol is sold by "proof," or "degree proof." A 100-degree-proof spirit, for example, contains 50 per cent absolute alcohol at 60° F.

PRODUCTION OF ALCOHOL

KIND	MANUFACTURE	USES
Methyl (wood alcohol, methanol)	By destructive distillation of wood. Also by synthesis from hydrogen and carbon monoxide under high pressure.	Solvent for fats, oils, resins, nitrocellulose. Manufacture of dyes, formaldehyde, antifreeze solutions, special fuels, plastics.
Ethyl (grain alcohol, ethanol)	By fermentation of sugar, starch, or waste sulfite liquor. Synthesis from ethylene or acetylene. Direct hydration of ethylene.	Solvent for products such as lacquers, paints, varnishes, glues, pharmaceuticals, explosives. Also as "building block" in making high-molecular-weight chemicals.
Isopropyl (isopropanol)	By hydration of propylene from cracked gases. Also as by-product of certain fermentation processes.	Solvent for oils, gums, alkaloids, resins. Making acetone, soap, antiseptic solutions.
Normal propyl	As a coproduct of air oxidation of propane and butane mixtures.	Solvent for lacquers, resins, coatings, films, waxes. Also as brake fluid, in manufacture of propionic acid, plasticizers.
Butyl (n-butanol)	By fermentation of starch or sugar. Also by synthesis, using ethyl alcohol or acetylene.	Solvent for nitrocellulose, ethyl cellulose, lacquer, urea-formaldehyde, urea-melamine plastics. Diluent of hydraulic fluids, extractant of drugs.
Isobutyl	By synthesis from carbon monoxide and hydrogen at high pressure, then distillation from products formed.	Solvent for castor-oil-base brake fluids. Substitute for n-butyl alcohol in making urea resins.
Secondary butyl	By hydration of 1-butane, formed in petroleum cracking.	In making other chemicals such as methyl ethyl ketone. Solvent in nitrocellulose lacquers. Production of brake fluids, special greases.
Tertiary butyl	By hydration of isobutylene, derived from petroleum cracking.	In perfume making. As wetting agent in detergents. Solvent for drugs and cleaning compounds.
Amyl (pentyl)	By fractional distillation of fusel oil, a coproduct of ethyl alcohol manufacture by fermentation.	Solvent for many natural and synthetic resins. Diluting brake fluids, printing inks, lacquers. In medicinal products.
Ethylene glycol	By oxidation of ethylene to glycol. Also by hydrogenation of methyl glycolate made from formaldehyde and methanol.	Deicing fluid, antifreeze, brake fluid. In production of explosives. Solvent for stains, oils, resins, enamels, inks, dyes.
Diethylene glycol	As coproduct in manufacture of ethylene glycol.	Solvent for dyes, resins. Antileak agent. In gas drying. Softening agent in adhesive printing inks.
Triethylene glycol	Coproduct in manufacture of ethylene glycol.	Air disinfectant and dehumidifier. Production of resins, plasticizers.
Glycerol (glycerin; 1-, 2-, 3-propanetriol)	From treatment of fats in soapmaking. Synthetically, from propylene. By fermentation.	In alkyd resins, explosives, cellophane. Tobacco humectant.
Pentaerythritol	By condensation of acetaldehyde and formaldehyde.	In synthetic resins. As tetranitrate in explosives. Also as drug for treatment of heart disease.
Sorbitol	By reduction of sugar, usually corn sugar, with hydrogen.	In foods, pharmaceuticals, in chemical manufacture. Conditioning agent in paper, textiles, glue, cosmetics. Source of alcohol in resin manufacture.
Cyclohexanol	By catalytic hydrogenation of phenol. By catalytic air oxidation of cyclohexane.	Intermediate in making chemicals used in nylon manufacture. Stabilizer and homogenizer of soaps, synthetic detergents. Solvent.
Phenyl ethyl	By synthesis from benzene and ethylene oxide.	Principally in perfumes.

Alcohol has certain physiological effects on the body. It acts specifically on the central nervous system. In excess it may become habit-forming. This leads to a condition called alcoholism. Organs such as the brain, liver, and kidneys may be damaged by excessive indulgence in alcohol. Mental impairment may also result. Several private organizations are dedicated to influencing legislation that would outlaw the manufacture and sale of alcoholic beverages (*see* Alcoholism; Prohibition; Temperance).

The main value of alcohol is not as an intoxicating drink. It is important in the making of thousands of products. Many of its uses are listed in the table on the preceding page.

Methyl alcohol, or wood alcohol, was originally made by the destructive distillation of wood. Now it is usually produced synthetically by passing compressed hydrogen and carbon monoxide over catalysts, then condensing the reaction product. It is used chiefly in the manufacture of denatured alcohol.

Denatured alcohol is ethyl alcohol to which other substances have been added to make it unfit to drink. Because it is not sold as a beverage, denatured alcohol is not subject to heavy taxation. It is made under government regulations. Wood alcohol and benzene are the two most common denaturing additives. Substances such as pyridine, diethyl phthalate, and nicotine may be added.

Chemically, alcohol is defined as the hydroxyl derivative of a hydrocarbon. The chemist represents one hydroxyl molecule by the symbol OH. The hydroxyl group is also called a hydroxide, or "a combination of hydrogen and oxygen." When a hydrogen atom that is contained in a hydrocarbon molecule is replaced by a hydroxyl group, a molecule of alcohol is produced.

One molecule of ethane, a hydrocarbon, is written as CH_3CH_3. If one "H" in the second "CH_3" is replaced by an OH, the ethane molecule becomes a molecule of ethyl alcohol, CH_3CH_2OH.

Alcohols may be classified according to the OH groups in each molecule. Ethyl alcohol, with one OH group, is a monohydric alcohol. Ethylene glycol (CH_2OHCH_2OH) has two OH groups and is a dihydric alcohol. A trihydric alcohol such as glycerol, or glycerin ($CH_2OHCHOHCH_2OH$), has three hydroxyl groups. Hexahydric alcohols have four OH groups, and polyhydric alcohols have many.

The manufacture of alcohol for industry is based on the principle of replacing hydrogen atoms with hydroxyl groups. Until 1930 this process was carried out by simple fermentation of grains such as corn, wheat, rice, and barley. Other alcohol was obtained from the fermentation of starches and sugars—principally of blackstrap molasses. Some industrial alcohol is still produced by fermentation.

Most of the industrial alcohol produced in the United States, however, is made synthetically. It is usually synthesized from ethylene gas that comes from natural-gas deposits or from petroleum cracking processes.

ALCOHOLIC BEVERAGES

ALCOHOLIC BEVERAGES. Plants such as corn, rye, barley, potatoes, and grapes contain sugars. Under certain conditions these sugars can be transformed into ethyl alcohol and carbon dioxide gas. This chemical reaction, called fermentation, is the basic process by which alcoholic beverages are made. These drinks include beer, wine, whiskey, gin, vodka, rum, and many more. The term proof is often used to indicate the percentage of ethyl alcohol in the beverage. In the United States each degree of proof represents 0.5 percent alcohol. Thus a liquor having 50 percent alcohol is termed 100 proof. In Great Britain 50 percent alcohol is equivalent to 114.12 United States proof.

After fermentation beer and wine are aged. Other alcoholic beverages undergo a further process called distillation. The fermented liquid is heated until the alcohol and flavorings vaporize and can be drawn off, cooled, and condensed back into a liquid. Water remains behind and is discarded. The concentrated liquid is known as a distilled beverage and includes such types as whiskey, gin, vodka, rum, brandy, and liqueurs, or cordials.

Beer and Wine

Beer is the best-known member of the malt family of alcoholic beverages, which also includes ale, stout, porter, and malt liquor. It is made from malt, corn, rice, and hops. Beers range in alcoholic content from about two percent to about eight percent. (*See also* Beer and Brewing.)

Wine is made by fermenting the juices of grapes or other plants, such as cherries, raspberries, or even dandelions. Winemaking begins with the selection, cultivation, and harvest of grapes or other fruits. The juice of the fruits is fermented in large vats at the winery under rigorous temperature control. Then fermentation is complete, the mixture is filtered, aged, and bottled. Natural, or unfortified, wines generally contain from 8 to 14 percent alcohol; these include burgundy, chianti, and sauterne. Fortified wines, to which alcohol or brandy has been added, contain 18 to 21 percent alcohol. They include sherry, port, and muscatel.

Distilled Beverages

One of the most popular types of distilled alcoholic beverages is whiskey. Whiskies and most other distilled beverages range in their alcoholic content from 40 to 50 percent.

Of the several common whiskies, Scotch—which is made from both malted and unmalted barley, corn, rye, and other small grains—is apparently the oldest. To make it, barley grains are malted, dried over peat fires, mashed with other grains, fermented, triple-distilled, aged in oak casks for up to ten years, and blended with other whiskies.

Rye and bourbon whiskies were originated in the United States by early settlers. Rye is made from a mixture of grains in which malted and unmalted rye predominate. Both bourbon and rye are aged in charred oak containers. Corn predominates in the mash used to make bourbon.

Gin is commonly made from ethyl alcohol and juniper berries that are mashed together and then distilled. Flavors including angelica root, coriander, licorice, lime, and lemon have been added to the gin-making mixture by manufacturers.

Although vodka has been made from molasses, potatoes, and even fruits, it is distilled today from grain and then filtered for purity through layers of activated charcoal. Because it is colorless and flavorless, vodka mixes well with other liquids.

Rum was first mentioned in records from the West Indies in about 1650. Most rum still comes from the Caribbean area, with Jamaica and Puerto Rico the major producers. Venezuela and Mexico also make much rum. Blackstrap molasses, a thick, dark-colored syrup obtained from sugarcane during the refining process, is fermented with yeast, distilled, and aged in wooden casks to make rum.

Brandy can be distilled from the fermented fruit mashes produced during winemaking. Beverage brandies contain about 50 percent alcohol, while brandy used to fortify dessert wines is about 80 to 95 percent alcohol. The term brandy derives from the Dutch *brandewijn*, meaning "burnt wine." The best-known type is Cognac, named for the region of France from which it comes. Made in pot stills on small farms, Cognac is sold to bottlers who age it in oak barrels and then blend it. Other familiar brandies are Armagnac (from another region of France); California grape brandy; blended applejack, distilled from fermented apple juice; Kirschwasser, made in Germany from black cherries; and Slivovitz, or plum brandy, from the Balkans.

Liqueurs, sometimes called cordials in the United States, are mixtures and redistillations of pure alcohol, brandy, gin, and flavorings derived from fruits, flowers, and plants. Some of the best-known kinds today—Benedictine and Chartreuse, for example—bear the names of monasteries, where they were first made. Other familiar liqueurs include Curaçao, flavored by the dried peels of the green oranges of the island of Curaçao; crème de menthe, flavored with peppermint; and anisette, which is derived from aniseed. The alcoholic content of liqueurs ranges from about 25 to 50 percent.

Alcohol and Government

Governments have customarily taken contradictory attitudes toward alcoholic beverages. On one hand the products yield large tax revenues, and so there is good reason to encourage production. On the other hand, governments deal every day with the numerous problems that alcohol creates. Drunk drivers and socially unacceptable, drunken behavior are two common problems. Alcoholism, or alcohol addiction, is a serious disease that takes a toll on both the alcoholic and society in general. Thus, in most places the sale and use of alcohol is strictly controlled. (*See also* Alcoholism; Prohibition.)

ALCOHOLISM. An uncontrolled desire to drink alcohol is a disease called alcoholism. Alcohol is a drug. In the United States alcoholism is the most serious form of drug abuse, affecting at least 10 million persons. Approximately one third of high school students in the United States are thought to be "problem drinkers." Many already may be alcoholics. Alcoholism accounts in part for the 25,000 fatal automobile accidents caused by drunk drivers each year in the United States. It is a leading cause of loss of income and of social and personal problems. Alcoholism also creates many severe physical problems. (*See also* Drugs, section "Drug Abuse.")

More than three drinks a day over even a few weeks causes destructive changes in the liver. (One ounce of hard liquor, 4 ounces of dry wine, or 12 ounces of beer are each considered one drink.) About 15 percent of heavy drinkers develop cirrhosis, which can be fatal. Changes in the brain and nervous system result in hostile behavior, loss of mental sharpness, and poor judgment. One third of the babies born to mothers who drink heavily have birth defects. Some drugs, such as tranquilizers, when taken with alcohol can result in death. Sexual potency and sperm count are greatly reduced in alcoholic men, and alcoholic women often produce no fertile eggs.

It has long been thought that alcoholism resulted from a combination of psychological and social factors. Current scientific research suggests that a tendency to abuse alcohol runs in families and that an inherited chemical defect also plays a role.

A family or individual with an alcoholism problem is in serious trouble. The alcoholic's main goal is to get something alcoholic to drink. The drinking usually continues until the victim is drunk. Family, work, and friends are of little concern compared to the need for alcohol. Drunkenness inhibits the alcoholic's control of normal behavior, and depresses the ability to perform even the simplest functions.

Fighting the Disease

There are many resources to help the alcoholic, but there are two absolute rules that apply to "kicking the habit." An alcoholic must accept the fact that there is a real problem and decide to stop drinking. An alcoholic must also realize that any form or quantity of alcohol is literally poison. When recovered, an alcoholic can never take another drink, for alcoholism is a life-long condition to which the recovered alcoholic must adjust.

It is difficult to break the alcoholic habit, but it is possible. Groups such as Alcoholics Anonymous and psychiatric, psychological, and social services are among the resources that help the alcoholic to become an abstainer. Sometimes a brief stay in a detoxification unit in a hospital may be necessary in order for the body to clean and restore itself.

Researchers are looking into the reasons why many people can drink moderately and alcoholics cannot. Many businesses have programs to help addicted employees become and remain sober.

ALCOTT, Louisa May (1832–88). Louisa May Alcott was born in Germantown, Pa., on Nov. 29, 1832, and grew up in Boston and Concord, Mass. Her father, Amos Bronson Alcott, was a teacher and a transcendental philosopher, a close friend of Ralph Waldo Emerson. Alcott's "conversational" method of teaching was far in advance of his time and won him few pupils. It was, however, very successful with Louisa. She began to write poems and stories. When she was 15, she was writing and producing amateur theatricals. By 1860 her verses and stories were appearing in *The Atlantic Monthly.*

In 1862, during the Civil War, Louisa Alcott served as a nurse in the Union hospital at Georgetown, now part of Washington, D.C. Her letters home telling of her hospital experiences were published in 1863 under the title 'Hospital Sketches' and brought her $2,000. With this money she made her first trip to Europe.

On her return she began 'Little Women'. This book, published in 1868, made her famous and enabled her to pay off all the family debts. Alcott with

Louisa May Alcott
Louisa May Alcott Memorial Association

her sister May also took a long tour of Europe. In Rome she wrote 'Little Men'.

Louisa Alcott took an active part in the temperance and the woman's suffrage movements. She never married. She died on March 6, 1888, two days after her father. Orchard House, in Concord, where she wrote 'Little Women', was made a memorial in 1911.

Alcott's best-known works are 'Little Women' (1868); 'An Old-Fashioned Girl' (1869); 'Little Men' (1871); 'Eight Cousins' (1874); 'Under the Lilacs' (1878); and 'Jo's Boys' (1886).

ALDEN, John (1599?–1687). Among the Pilgrims who arrived in America on the *Mayflower* in 1620 was John Alden, a cooper (barrelmaker). He was successful enough in business in Plymouth to become one of the eight bondsmen who assumed responsibility for the colonial debt. Later he moved to Duxbury and took over a farm near his friend Miles Standish.

Henry Wadsworth Longfellow made Alden famous in his poem 'The Courtship of Miles Standish'. It tells how Alden courted Priscilla Mullins (or Molines) for Standish until she asked, "Why don't you speak for yourself, John?" There is little historical foundation for this story. John did marry Priscilla, however, and they had 11 children.

For many years Alden was assistant to the governor of Plymouth Colony. He died on Sept. 12, 1687, in Duxbury and was buried near Standish. (*See also* 'Mayflower'.)

ALDER. Along stream banks from Saskatchewan and Nebraska eastward, the speckled alder is a familiar tree. It is often a large shrub, but it may grow to a height of 60 feet (18 meters). The leaves are oval, coarse, and irregularly notched. They are dark green above with a whitish down underneath. In late summer male and female catkins form on the same twig. The mature fruit resembles small fir cones. The wood is soft, light, and of little value.

On the Pacific coast the red alder grows to 80 to 130 feet (24 to 40 meters). The wood is used for furniture, veneers, and wooden novelties. It is one of the first trees to appear on burned and logged areas. The European alder has become naturalized.

Alders belong to the birch family, Betulaceae. The scientific name of the speckled alder is *Alnus incana;* red alder, *A. rubra;* European alder, *A. glutinosa.*

ALEPPO, Syria. The principal modern city of northern Syria, Aleppo was the chief marketplace of the Middle East during the 16th century. The city lies at an altitude of 1,279 feet (390 meters) and is about 60 miles (100 kilometers) from both the Mediterranean Sea and the Euphrates River.

Aleppo is an ancient city that played a significant historical role because of its position on important trade routes. As early as the 6th through the 4th century B.C., the city was a key point on the ancient caravan route linking the Mediterranean lands to the East. At this time it was under Persian rule, but it became a part of the Roman province of Syria in the 1st century B.C. In 637 it was conquered by the Arabs; in 1516 it was incorporated into the Ottoman Empire.

The city prospered in the 18th century and flourished under French mandate in the first part of the 20th century. Aleppo's development as an industrial, political, and educational center continued during World War II and after Syria's independence from France. It is the site of a university and the National Museum, noted for its ancient relics. The principal industries are silk weaving and cotton printing (pressing designs onto cotton fabric with dye, oil, or wax). (*See also* Syria.)

Aleppo's limestone buildings gave the city its Arabic name, Halab ash-Shahibah (Aleppo the White). It has long been fascinating because of its varied architectural styles, which include Hellenistic, Byzantine, and modern European. Some of the most striking covered bazaars in the Middle East, dating from the Ottoman period, are found there. The most remarkable monument is the 13th-century citadel, which still stands as it originally appeared. Population (1980 estimate), 962,954.

ALEUTIAN ISLANDS. The chain of small islands that make up the Aleutian Islands separates the Bering Sea from the main part of the Pacific Ocean. They form part of the state of Alaska in the United States. The almost 70 islands form an arc that extends for about 1,100 miles (1,800 kilometers) from the tip of the Alaska Peninsula to Attu Island in the North Pacific. They occupy a land area of 6,821 square miles (17,666 square kilometers). Most of the islands were formed by volcanic eruptions.

The Aleutians were discovered by two explorers sent on a voyage of discovery by the Russians in 1741. Upon learning of the abundance of fur-bearing animals, Siberian hunters flocked to the area, then gradually moved to the mainland. In 1867 the Russians sold the islands, along with the rest of Alaska, to the United States.

The climate of the Aleutians is one of fairly uniform temperatures, high winds, and heavy rainfall. The average mean temperature is 33.4° F (0.8° C) for February and 51.8° F (11.0° C) for August. The shores are rocky and worn by the surf, and the approaches are dangerous. The land rises abruptly from the coasts to steep, bold mountains. There are hardly any trees, but the islands are covered with a rich growth of grasses and many flowering plants. Aleutian wildlife consists mostly of sea otters and seals. By regulating the wildlife population, the Alaska Maritime National Wildlife Refuge has eliminated the threat of starvation for the native islanders (Aleuts), who are related to the Eskimos and who live by fishing and hunting. In one of the largest towns of the Aleutian Islands, Unalaska, there are several dozen crab canning operations.

During World War II, the Aleutian Islands were fought over by the Americans and the Japanese because they have significant strategic importance. Now Aleutian military stations are vital links in the air defense of North America. (*See also* Alaska.) Population (1980 census), 7,768.

ALEXANDER. Three Romanov rulers of Russia were named Alexander.

ALEXANDER I (born 1777, ruled 1801–25) came to the throne after the murder of his father, Paul I, the "mad czar." At the beginning of his reign he carried out many important reforms.

In 1805 Alexander joined with England, Austria, and Prussia in the European coalition against Napoleon I. After the Russian defeat at Friedland in 1807, he deserted his allies, and in the Treaty of Tilsit he and Napoleon agreed to divide the world between them (*see* Napoleon I). Rivalry developed, and Napoleon invaded Russia in 1812. After the winter retreat of the French forces, Alexander carried the war to French soil. At the Congress of Vienna in 1814–15 he was a leading figure (*see* Vienna).

In 1815 Alexander tried to create a world order based on Christian principles. It was called the Holy Alliance, a name later applied to the Grand Alliance, which virtually ruled Europe (*see* Europe). Before he died he undid many of his reforms.

ALEXANDER II (born 1818, ruled 1855–81) was the son of Nicholas I. He was called the "czar liberator" because in 1861 he freed the serfs. He also relaxed the censorship of the press and extended education. Nevertheless attempts were made on his life. In 1880 part of the Winter Palace was blown up. The next year Alexander was killed by a bomb while driving in his carriage.

ALEXANDER III (born 1845, ruled 1881–94) came to the throne after the assassination of his father, Alexander II. Unlike his father, he was a firm believer in autocracy and practically suppressed revolutionary agitation. He was succeeded by his son, Nicholas II, the last of the Russian czars.

ALEXANDER NEVSKI (1220?–63). An outstanding military commander, Alexander Nevski was a Russian prince who stopped Swedish and German expansion into Russia. He also helped the Mongol Empire to consolidate its hold on his country.

At the time of Alexander's birth, Russia was divided into about a dozen principalities. His father, Yaroslav II Vsevolodovich, grand prince of Vladimir, was foremost among Russian rulers. In 1236 Alexander was elected prince of Novgorod. Four years later, Sweden invaded Russia. Alexander defeated the Swedes at the point where the Rivers Izhora and Neva meet. From this battle he earned the name Nevski, or "of the Neva."

Very soon after this battle the Germans invaded Russia, and Nevski, after a number of battles, defeated them in April 1240. He continued to fight both the Swedes and Germans, stopping their expansion.

Prince Yaroslav died in 1246. Alexander's brother, Andrew, was appointed to succeed him. When Andrew began to conspire against the Mongol rulers, Alexander sought the aid of the Mongol khan and had his brother deposed. Alexander became grand prince of Vladimir and continued to govern Novgorod.

In 1257 a rebellion against the Mongols broke out in Novgorod because of a proposed census and tax levy. Alexander succeeded in quelling the revolt, and in so doing he firmly established Mongol rule in northern Russia. Another tax revolt in 1262 was also stopped by Alexander. To avoid reprisals against his people, he traveled to the Mongol capital at Saray on the Volga River. He fulfilled his mission, but on the return trip he died at Gorodets on Nov. 14, 1263.

Although Alexander was a willing collaborator with the Mongols, he was popular both with his people and the Russian church. He was made a saint by the Russian Orthodox church in 1547.

ALEXANDER THE GREAT (356–323 B.C.). More than any other world conqueror, Alexander III of Macedon, or ancient Macedonia, deserves to be called the Great. Although he died before age 33, he conquered almost all the then known world and gave a new direction to history.

Alexander was born in 356 B.C. at Pella, the capital of Macedon, a kingdom north of Hellas (Greece). Under his father, Philip II, Macedon had become strong and united, the first real nation in European history. Greece was reaching the end of its Golden Age. Art, literature, and philosophy were still flourishing, but the small city-states had refused to unite and were exhausted by wars. Philip admired Greek culture. The Greeks despised the Macedonians as barbarians. (*See also* Macedonia; Greece, Ancient.)

Alexander was handsome and had the physique of an athlete. He excelled in hunting and loved riding his horse Bucephalus. When Alexander was 13 years old, the Greek philosopher Aristotle came to Macedon to tutor him. Alexander learned to love Homer's 'Iliad'. He also learned something of ethics and politics and the new sciences of botany, zoology, geography, and medicine. (*See also* Aristotle.) His chief interest was military strategy. He learned this from his father, who had reformed the Greek phalanx into a powerful fighting machine (*see* Warfare).

Philip was bent on the conquest of Persia. First, however, he had to subdue Greece. The decisive battle of Chaeronea (338 B.C.) brought all the Greek city-states except Sparta under Philip's leadership. Young Alexander commanded the Macedonian left wing at Chaeronea and annihilated the famous Sacred Band of the Thebans.

Two years later (336 B.C.) Philip was murdered. Alexander's mother, Olympias, probably plotted his death. Alexander then came to the throne. In the same year he marched south to Corinth, where the Greek city-states (except Sparta) swore allegiance to him. Thebes, however, later revolted, and Alexander destroyed the city. He allowed the other city-states to keep their democratic governments.

With Greece secure Alexander prepared to carry out his father's bold plan and invade Persia. Two centuries earlier the mighty Persian Empire had pushed westward to include the Greek cities of Asia Minor—one third of the entire Greek world (*see* Persian History; Persian Wars).

In the spring of 334 B.C., Alexander crossed the Hellespont (now Dardanelles), the narrow strait between Europe and Asia Minor. He had with him a Greek and Macedonian force of about 30,000 foot soldiers and 5,000 cavalry. The infantry wore armor like the Greek hoplites (*see* Armor) but carried a Macedonian weapon, the long pike. Alexander himself led ·the "companions," the elite of the cavalry. With the army went geographers, botanists, and other men of science who collected information and specimens for Aristotle. A historian kept records of the march, and surveyors made maps that served as the basis for the geography of Asia for centuries.

In Asia Minor Alexander visited ancient Troy to pay homage to Achilles and other heroes of the 'Iliad'. At the Granicus River, in May, he defeated a large body of Persian cavalry, four times the size of his own. Then he marched southward along the coast, freeing the Greek cities from Persian rule and making them his allies. In the winter he turned inland, to subdue the hill tribes.

According to legend, he was shown a curious knot at Gordium in Asia Minor. An oracle had said the man who untied it would rule Asia. Alexander dramatically cut the Gordian knot with his sword.

Alexander the Great
W. A. Mansell & Co.

Alexander's army and a huge force led by Darius III of Persia met at Issus in October 333 B.C. Alexander charged with his cavalry against Darius, who fled. Alexander then marched south along the coast of Phoenicia to cut off the large Persian navy from all its harbors. Tyre, on an island, held out for seven months until Alexander built a causeway to it and battered down its stone walls.

Late in 332 B.C. the conqueror reached Egypt. The Egyptians welcomed him as a deliverer from Persian misrule and accepted him as their pharaoh (king). In Memphis he made sacrifices to Egyptian gods. Near the delta of the Nile River he founded a new city, to be named Alexandria after him (*see* Alexandria). At Ammon, in the Libyan desert, he visited the oracle of the Greek god Zeus, and the priests saluted him as the son of that great god.

Leaving Egypt in the spring of 331 B.C., Alexander went in search of Darius. He met him on a wide plain near the village of Gaugamela, or Camel's House, some miles from the town of Arbela.

Darius had gathered together all his military strength—chariots with scythes on the wheels, elephants, and a great number of cavalry and foot soldiers. Alexander again led his cavalry straight toward Darius, while his phalanx attacked with long pikes. Darius fled once more, and Alexander won a great and decisive victory (July 331 B.C.). After the

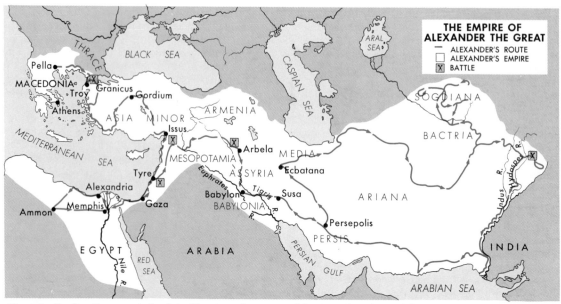

Alexander the Great's conquests freed the West from the menace of Persian rule and spread Greek civilization and culture into Asia and Egypt. His vast empire stretched east into India.

battle he was proclaimed king of Asia. Babylon welcomed the conqueror, and Alexander made sacrifices to the Babylonians' god Marduk. The Persian capital, Susa, also opened its gates. In this city and at Persepolis an immense hoard of royal treasure fell into Alexander's hands. In March (330 B.C.) he set out to pursue Darius. He found him dying, murdered by one of his attendants.

His men now wanted to return home. Alexander, however, was determined to press on to the eastern limit of the world, which he believed was not far beyond the Indus River. He spent the next three years campaigning in the wild country to the east. There he married a chieftain's daughter, Roxane.

In the early summer of 327 B.C. Alexander reached India. At the Hydaspes River (now Jhelum) he defeated the army of King Porus whose soldiers were mounted on elephants. Then he pushed farther east.

Alexander's men had now marched 11,000 miles (18,000 kilometers). Soon they refused to go farther, and Alexander reluctantly turned back. He had already ordered a fleet built on the Hydaspes, and he sailed down the Indus to its mouth. Then he led his army overland, across the desert. Many died of hunger and thirst.

Alexander reached Susa in the spring of 324 B.C. There he rested with his army. The next spring he went to Babylon. Long marches and many wounds had so lowered his vitality that he was unable to recover from a fever. He died at Babylon on June 13, 323 B.C. His body, encased in gold leaf, was later placed in a magnificent tomb at Alexandria, Egypt.

The Hellenistic Age

The three centuries after the death of Alexander are called the Hellenistic Age, from the Greek word

hellenizein, meaning "to act like a Greek." During this period, Greek language and culture spread throughout the eastern Mediterranean world.

The sudden death of Alexander left his generals without any plan whereby the vast territories he had conquered should be administered. Some of his followers, including the rank and file of the Macedonian army, wanted to preserve the empire. But the generals wanted to break up the empire and create realms for themselves. It took more than 40 years of struggles and warfare (323–280 B.C.) before the separate kingdoms were carved out. Finally three major dynasties emerged: the Ptolemies in Egypt, the Seleucids in Asia, Asia Minor, and Palestine, and the Antigonids in Macedonia and Greece. These kingdoms got their names from three generals of Alexander—Ptolemy, Seleucus, and Antigonus.

The richest, most powerful, and longest lasting of these kingdoms was that of the Ptolemies. It reached its height of material and cultural splendor under Ptolemy II Philadelphus, who ruled from 285 to 246. After his death, the kingdom entered a long period of war and internal strife that ended when Egypt became a province of the Roman Empire in 30 B.C.

The Seleucid Empire was the largest of the three kingdoms. The Seleucids were the most active of the kingdoms in establishing Greek settlements throughout their domain. During the more than 200 years of its existence, the empire continually lost territory through war or rebellion, until it was reduced to Palestine, Syria, and Mesopotamia in 129 B.C. It continued to decline until annexed by Rome in 64 B.C.

The Antigonid Kingdom of Macedonia lasted only until 168 B.C. Continually involved in wars with other kingdoms and struggles with the Greek city-states, it was finally overtaken by the military might of Rome.

ALEXANDRIA, Egypt.

More than 2,000 years ago, Alexandria was the capital and the greatest city of Egypt. Today, although it has been surpassed by Cairo in both its size and its importance, Alexandria is Egypt's foremost seaport and its second largest city. Roads, trains, and airlines connect it with Cairo, 110 miles (175 kilometers) up the Nile Delta to the southeast.

Miles of beautiful white sand along the Mediterranean coast provide the setting for this trading city and holiday resort. Summertime brings crowds of people to the beaches that stretch to the suburbs of Agami in the west and Abu Qir in the east. Clear, calm waters make Abu Qir a popular place for fishing and other water sports. Unlike most of Egypt, Alexandria is sometimes chilly and rainy in winter.

The center city is brightened by flowering plants in the Nuzhah, Zoological, and Antoniadis gardens. Seaside gardens decorate the grounds of the Muntazah Palace on a high dune overlooking Muntazah Bay. Muntazah was formerly the summer residence of the Egyptian royal family. After the monarchy was overthrown in 1952, the palace buildings, Haramlek and Salamlek, were put to other uses. The Haramlek contains a casino on the ground floor and a museum of royal family relics on the upper levels. The Salamlek has been converted to a hotel.

Stone structures remain from the time when Alexandria was part of the Roman Empire. The Roman

A magnificent museum located at Alexandria was formerly the summer palace of King Fuad I, who reigned from 1922 to 1936.

Camera Press—Pix

amphitheater of Kawm al Dikka, with its 12 marble galleries, has been unearthed almost intact. Pompey's Pillar (A.D. 297), 82 feet (25 meters) high, commemorates in granite the victories of the Roman emperor Diocletian. The catacombs of Kawm ash Shuqafah are 2d- and 3d- century tombs, carved three tiers deep in the rock. Ancient artifacts are displayed in the Greco-Roman Museum.

A peninsula that was once an island separates two harbors, one to the east and the other to the west. At the entrance to the eastern harbor, at the tip of the peninsula, the three-story Fort of Qa'it Bay houses a naval museum. Not far from the museum is the Marine Life Institute, with specimens of rare animals from the surrounding waters.

Islam is the principal religion of the roughly 2½ million people of Alexandria. The 17th-century Mosque of Abu al'Abbas, with its high minaret and four domes, is a city landmark.

Education is compulsory for children aged 6 to 12. Young people may continue through technical school or university level free of charge. The state-controlled University of Alexandria, founded in 1942, has 13 faculties. It offers instruction in both the Arabic and the English languages.

Ancient Alexandria

Alexander the Great conquered Egypt and founded Alexandria in 332 B.C. The coastal city was designed to handle Mediterranean shipping between Greece, the center of Alexander's empire, and his new Egyptian province. After Alexander's death in 323 B.C., his generals broke up his empire into three major dynasties. One general, Ptolemy, took over the rule of Egypt with Alexandria as his capital.

Under the Ptolemaic dynasty, Alexandria was a busy port and a center of Greek culture. The Pharos of Alexandria, a lighthouse, was built at the entrance to the harbor. Reaching a height of more than 400 feet (120 meters), it was considered one of the Seven Wonders of the World (see Seven Wonders of the World). Euclid wrote his famous geometry text in Alexandria. The library of the university (called the Museum, home of the Muses) held half a million manuscripts. After the suicide of Cleopatra, the last Ptolemaic monarch, in 30 B.C., Alexandria (with the rest of Egypt) became part of the Roman Empire.

In the early Christian era, Alexandria enjoyed the status that came with leadership in the Roman world as a center of Christianity. Tradition says that St. Mark introduced the new religion there in A.D. 45 to 62. Many Christian men moved to the desert to live as hermits. Later these men joined together to form powerful monastic communities. Theological ferment produced the orthodoxy of Athanasius, the heresy of Arius, and the gnosticism of Valentinus. The bishops throughout a wide region answered to the patriarchs of Alexandria.

The greatness of ancient Alexandria ended with the Arab conquest of 642. The Arabs built a new capital at Cairo and neglected the older city. Islam replaced Christianity. The Pharos crumbled. In 1480 Sultan Qa'it Bay built a fort on the lighthouse foundations for defense, but he failed to save Egypt from Turkish conquest in 1517.

In 1798 Napoleon landed French forces at Alexandria and marched inland to drive out the Ottoman Turks. British troops helped the Turks to expel the French from Egypt. By 1805 Mohammed Ali Pasha, a skillful politician from Macedonia, had emerged as viceroy of Egypt. He made Alexandria his summer capital and redeveloped the city as a center of trade and industry. (*See also* Egypt.) Population (1976 census), 2,318,655.

ALFONSO XIII (1886–1941). Thirteen rulers of Spain have borne the name Alfonso. King Alfonso XIII, the last of the line, was the most important. He was born a few months after his father, King Alfonso XII, died. In the first 16 years of the king's life his mother ruled the country for him.

It was a time of violent internal disorders and of the Spanish-American War of 1898, by which Spain lost practically the last of its colonial possessions. Alfonso took personal charge of the government in 1902. Charming and politically adroit, he held the crumbling monarchy together with the aid of a dictatorship until April 1931. Elections at that time demonstrated the overwhelmingly republican sentiment of his people. The "last of the Bourbons" then quit his throne and was forced to leave Spain (*see* Bourbon, House of).

The name Alfonso (or Alphonso) has also been a favorite one in Portugal, where six monarchs have been so called. The last was King Alfonso VI, who reigned from 1656 to 1667.

ALFRED THE GREAT (born 848? ruled 871–899). The course of English history would have been very different had it not been for King Alfred. He won renown both as a statesman and as a warrior and is justly called "the Great."

The England of Alfred's time was a country of four small kingdoms. The strongest was Wessex, in the south. Alfred was the youngest son of Ethelwulf, king of Wessex. Each of Alfred's three older brothers, in turn, ruled the kingdom. Alfred was by temperament a scholar, and his health was never robust. Nevertheless in his early youth he fought with his brother Ethelred against the dreaded Danish invaders. He was 23 when Ethelred died, but he had already won the confidence of the army and was at once acclaimed king (871). By this time the Danes, or Vikings, had penetrated to all parts of the island. Three of the Saxon kingdoms—Northumbria, Mercia, and East Anglia—had one after another fallen to them.

Under Alfred's leadership, the Saxons again took courage. The worst crisis came in the winter of 877, when the Danish king, Guthrum, invaded Wessex with his whole army. In 878 Alfred was defeated at Chippenham, where he was keeping Christmas, and was forced to go into hiding.

A few months later he forced Guthrum to surrender at Chippenham. The Danes agreed to make the Thames River and the old Roman road called Watling Street the boundary between Alfred's kingdom and the Danish lands to the north. The treaty, however, did not mean permanent peace. The Danes harried London and the coast towns repeatedly. Not until about 896 did they admit defeat and cease to struggle for a foothold in southern England.

Alfred was much more than the defender of his country. He took a keen interest in law and order and was much concerned in improving the cultural standards of his people. He encouraged industries of all kinds and rebuilt London, which had been partly destroyed by the Danes. He collected and revised the old laws of the kingdom. He invited learned men from other countries to instruct the people because even the clergy of Wessex had largely ceased to know Latin, the international language of the church. He established a school similar to the Palace School of Charlemagne.

The "books most necessary for all men to know" were translated from Latin into English so that the people might read them. Alfred himself took a part in preparing the translations. The 'Anglo-Saxon Chronicle' was probably begun under his direction.

Alfred died at the age of 51. He was in no sense a true king of England, for he ruled less than half the island. After his death, however, his capable son, Edward the Elder, and his grandsons extended their rule over all of England.

ALFVÉN, Hannes (born 1908). An important Swedish astrophysicist, Hannes Alfvén was the 1970 winner, with Louis Néel of France, of the Nobel prize for physics. Alfvén received the award for his outstanding contributions in founding the field of plasma physics, the study of gaseous mixtures containing positive and negative particles.

Hannes Olof Gösta Alfvén was born May 30, 1908, in the town of Norrköping, Sweden. He was educated at the University of Uppsala in Sweden and received his Ph.D. degree there in 1934.

During the late 1930's and early '40's, Alfvén made remarkable contributions to space physics. He developed a theory that explained how, under certain conditions, a plasma is bound to the magnetic lines of flux that pass through it. He later used this theory to explain the origin of cosmic rays.

In 1939 Alfvén published a theory about magnetic storms. This greatly influenced the modern theory of the magnetosphere (a region of the Earth's magnetic field). He discovered a mathematical approximation that is widely used to facilitate the calculation of the complex spiral motion of a charged particle in a magnetic field. Magnetohydrodynamics (MHD), the study of plasmas in magnetic fields, was largely pioneered by Alfvén. He was a professor at the Royal Institute of Technology in Stockholm from 1940 to 1973 and also a professor at the University of California in San Diego from 1967.

ALGAE. The green stain on damp rocks and tree trunks, the fine scum on quiet ponds, delicate sea plants of many colors and shapes, massive seaweeds of the oceans—these plants and thousands more are algae (Latin for "seaweeds").

In the natural world, algae are the chief food source for fishes and for all other types of organisms that live in the water. They also contribute substantially to the store of oxygen on Earth. There are about 25,000 species of algae.

The simplest alga consists of a single cell of protoplasm, a living jellylike drop. No larger than three microns, the size of a large bacterium, it is visible only under a microscope. The most complex algae are the giant kelps of the ocean that may be 200 feet (60 meters) long.

Algae are found all over the Earth, in oceans, rivers, lakes, streams, ponds, and marshes. They sometimes accumulate on the sides of glass aquariums. Although usually found in water and moist places, some inhabit the soil and can survive dry conditions for a long time. Algae are found on leaves, especially in the tropics and subtropics, and on wood and stones in all parts of the world. Some live in or on higher forms of plants and animals. And some exist in places where few living things are able to survive. One or two species capable of tolerating temperatures of 176° F (80° C) dwell in and around hot springs. A small number live in the snow and ice of the Arctic and Antarctic regions. Although they often bear a striking resemblance to mosses and fungi, algae are neither. (*See also* Fungi; Moss.)

Marine algae, such as the common seaweeds, are most noticeable on rocky coastlines. In northern temperate climes they form an almost continuous film over the rocks. In the tropics they are found on the floors of lagoons. They are associated with coral reefs and island atolls. A few saltwater species of green algae secrete limestone that contributes to reef for-

Osamu Umebayashi

Algae is grown on coconut-fiber nets in Japan where it is harvested as a major food crop for human consumption.

mation. In the Southern Hemisphere, algae are commonly seen near the low-water mark and below the shoreline. In Arctic and Antarctic waters they extend to considerable depths. In fresh water, algae are not conspicuous unless the water is polluted.

All algae contain the green pigment chlorophyll. This substance makes it possible for algae to use the energy of sunlight to manufacture their own food (carbohydrates) out of carbon dioxide and water. This process is called photosynthesis. Other pigments also are present, giving the different algae the distinct colors that are used as a basis of classification. (*See also* Plants, Physiology of.)

Algae are of special interest because they include the most primitive forms of plants. They have no true roots, stems, or leaves, and do not produce flowers or seeds, as higher plants do. Yet all other groups of plants have probably evolved from algae.

The simplest algae—single cells of protoplasm— float about in the water and absorb food through their thin cell walls. They multiply vegetatively; one

A small sample of the thousands of different kinds of algae includes *Rivularia* (right) living amongst barnacles, desmids (far right) magnified 85 times, *Halimeda discoidea* (below left), and *Caulerpa* (below right).

(Right and below left) Douglas P. Wilson; (far right) Winton Patnode—Photo Researchers; (below right) Richard H. Chesher

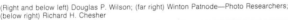

Algae in varying habitats include some turning snow red (top, far left), others forming an algal bloom on a stagnant freshwater pond (top left), those forming an algal red tide in the ocean (above), some coating part of a tree (far left), and others thriving at high temperatures in a hot spring (bottom left).

(Top, far left) Janet R. Stein; (top left) E. R. Degginger; (above) Carlton Ray—Photo Researchers; (far left) Richard C. York; (bottom left) Yellowstone National Park

cell buds from another by simple cell division. Among the larger kinds of algae, methods of reproduction vary greatly. Sometimes a small section breaks away from the main plant to grow into another complete new plant. This is called fragmentation. Or budding cells may remain clinging to the parent cells to form a string of beads, a knot, or a cluster. Sometimes they bud all around the sides and form mats, or flat networks of cells. Some of these nets and mats float onto rocks in quiet places where the motion of the water is not strong enough to float them off again. The cells on the rocks cannot gather much food, so they cling while the floating cells wave in the water, gather the food, bud, and spread into feathery, leaflike fronds. Certain cells collect budding material in little raised dots on the fronds. When the dots ripen, they are washed off. These bud dots are spores (tiny reproductive bodies, usually only a single cell, that can develop into a new plant). Some algae produce spores called gametes. Two gametes of opposite sex must unite to produce the cell that will develop into a new alga. Spores and gametes are simpler than seeds. The cells that cling to the rocks suggest roots, and the cells that spread out and float are hints of leaves.

Since very early in recorded history, some algae were used as food by the Chinese, Japanese, Hawaiians, and inhabitants of some European countries. The growing world population may one day rely upon algae as a plentiful food crop that can be cultivated in water to supplement crops that are cultivated on land. Algae have value as roughage, and their minerals, vitamins, and iodine are necessary nutri-

ents. They have been proposed for use in space travel as a source of food and oxygen.

Many of the most beautiful plants on the seashore are red algae, as are some food plants, especially laver, dulse, and Irish Moss. Various red algae are a source of agar, a gelatinous substance with a wide variety of commercial uses.

Brown algae include common seaweeds. Free-floating masses of Sargasso, or gulf, weed live in warm regions of the oceans. Kelp is eaten as a vegetable in the Orient. It is also used as fertilizer and in the manufacture of algin, the gel used as thickener in ice cream and as a stabilizer-emulsifier in cosmetics and other products. Some kelp has a thick, tough stem that can be used as rope. (*See also* Seaweed.)

Blue-green algae often appear as blue-green, brown, or black stains, cushions, or layers. They may be numerous enough to color a body of water.

Golden or golden brown algae include diatoms, one-celled plants with a tiny shell or exterior skeleton. When diatoms die, their shells fall to the bottom forming deposits that may build up to several meters. These shells are used as abrasive ingredients in some cleansing powders.

Botanically algae are classified among the thallophytes, along with fungi, lichens, and primitive, single-celled plants and bacteria. Thallophytes are plants devoid of true roots, stems, leaves, or flowers. Certain algae have some qualities of plants and some qualities of animals. They are sometimes called protozoan animals, or they may be classified as protists, somewhere between the plant and animal kingdoms.

FUNDAMENTAL CONCEPTS IN ALGEBRA

ALGEBRA. An important branch of mathematics, algebra today is studied not only in high school and college but, increasingly, in the lower grades as well. Taught with insight and understanding of the new mathematics programs, it can be an enjoyable subject. Algebra is as useful as all the other branches of mathematics—to which it is closely related. For some careers, such as those in engineering and science, a knowledge of algebra is indispensable. (*See also* Arithmetic; Geometry; Calculus; Mathematics; Numeration Systems and Numbers.)

Parents are aware of the growing emphasis upon mathematics in present-day school programs. They may not realize, however, that they have many opportunities at home to help their children take the natural step from solving arithmetic problems to solving algebra problems.

For example, suppose a father is asked his age by his eight-year-old son. Instead of answering the boy directly, the father can attempt an experiment by replying that he is 30 years older than the boy. This is a problem that the son is interested in solving. He can quickly perform the addition and find that his father is 38 years old:

$$8 + 30 = 38$$

Suppose the boy then asks the age of his mother. The father might at this point present a more challenging problem. For example, the father may answer that if the boy added six years to his mother's age, the result would be equal to the father's age. The father has thus found an excellent opportunity to help his son understand how an *algebraic equation* may be made up and solved.

The father writes the mother's age on a slip of paper and turns the slip over so the boy cannot see the numeral. He then lays the slip, blank side up, on a tablet. Next to the slip he writes the symbols that will help solve the problem:

$$\blacksquare + 6 = 38$$

The son takes only a moment to guess that his mother is 32 years old. When the father turns the slip of paper over, they see this answer is correct:

$$\boxed{32} + 6 = 38$$

This will have been the boy's first lesson in algebra because he essentially solved the equation

$$x + 6 = 38 \text{ [say "x plus 6 is equal to 38"]}$$

The father did not say anything about a mysterious letter "x" that can stand for any number. Nor did he tell the boy about any rule such as "changing the sign of the six and writing it on the other side of the equation." Instead, the boy's first lesson in algebra evolved in a natural way from a problem in arithmetic.

When the boy studies algebra in school, he will learn more about the relationship between algebra and arithmetic. Some of the fundamental concepts of algebra that are taught in school are explained here. Their applications in solving various types of mathematical problems are discussed in the section "Applying the Fundamental Concepts of Algebra."

OPEN SENTENCES

The open sentence is a commonly used teaching device. It is also often used in giving students examinations. In a test consisting of a list of sentences to be completed, the first three sentences might be, for example:

1. ⬜⬜⬜⬜ is the capital of Pennsylvania.

2. _____ is the capital of California.

3. ⬭⬭⬭⬭ is the capital of Illinois.

The student is expected to fill in the blanks with the correct answers to convert these sentences into **true statements**.

A student taking the test converted the first sentence into a *true statement* as follows:

1. *Harrisburg* is the capital of Pennsylvania.

He converted the second sentence into a *false statement:*

2. *Hollywood* is the capital of California.

He didn't know the name of the city which is the capital of Illinois, so he went on to the other sentences, leaving the third sentence open:

3. ⬭⬭⬭⬭ is the capital of Illinois.

By not filling in the blank in the third sentence, the student did not convert it into a true statement or into a false statement. Sentences which are neither true nor false are called *open sentences*.

The problem of converting open sentences into true

statements is quite common in mathematics. Here are some examples of open sentences that you may easily convert into true statements by filling in each of the blanks or frames with an appropriate numeral:

1. $6 + 32 = \square$
2. $\_\_ + 2 = 5$
3. $5 - 3 = \bigcirc$
4. $5 \times \diamondsuit = 10$

These open sentences may be converted into true statements by writing '38' in the frame in the first sentence, '3' in the blank in the second sentence, '2' in the frame in the third sentence, and '2' in the frame in the fourth sentence:

1. $6 + 32 = \boxed{38}$
2. $\underline{3} + 2 = 5$
3. $5 - 3 = \boxed{2}$
4. $5 \times \boxed{2} = 10$

If, however, you write '10' in the frame in the first sentence, you will convert it into a false statement:

$$6 + 32 = \boxed{10}$$

VARIABLES

Consider the following short composition written by a student:

> Every year many people visit it. It is a famous city. Abraham Lincoln lived in it. It is the capital of Illinois.

Since none of these sentences asserts a definite statement that can be judged to be true or false, each one is an open sentence. The teacher might ask the student to convert each of the sentences into a true statement by replacing the pronoun 'it' with a proper noun—the name of the correct city.

If in each sentence the student had replaced the pronoun 'it' with the proper noun 'Washington', the first three sentences in his composition would have been converted into true statements, but the fourth sentence would have become a false statement. However, if he had used the proper noun 'Springfield', all four of the sentences would have been converted into true statements:

> Every year many people visit Springfield. Springfield is a famous city. Abraham Lincoln lived in Springfield. Springfield is the capital of Illinois.

In mathematics, as in ordinary language, open sentences may be written without using blanks or frames. For example, the open sentence

$$\square + 3 = 5$$

may also be written

$$x + 3 = 5$$

Just as the open sentence

> It is the capital of Illinois.

may be converted into a true statement or a false statement by replacing the mark 'It' with a name, the open sentence

$$x + 3 = 5$$

may be converted into a true statement or a false statement by replacing the mark 'x' with a name. The mark 'It' serves as a *placeholder* for a name of a city; the mark 'x' serves as a placeholder for a name of a number.

We may of course use other marks to serve as placeholders. Letters such as 'a', 'b', 'c', or 'x' which are serving as placeholders are called *variables*.

The sentence

$$m + 3 = 8$$

may be converted into a true statement by replacing the variable 'm' with the numeral '5':

$$\boxed{5} + 3 = 8$$

It may be converted into a false statement by replacing the variable 'm' with the numeral '2':

$$\boxed{2} + 3 = 8$$

Here are some other examples of open sentences which you may easily convert into true statements or false statements:

1. $y - 5 = 4$
2. $3 \times a = 12$
3. $k \div 3 = 4$
4. $\frac{m}{4} = 3$

These sentences may be converted into true statements by replacing 'y' with '9', 'a' with '4', 'k' with '12', and 'm' with '12'.

In mathematics the multiplication sign '$\times$' is often replaced by a dot '·'. Sometimes, as between a numeral and a variable, or between two variables, it is omitted altogether. Thus, for example, the sentence '$3 \times a = 12$' may be written as

$$3 \cdot a = 12 \text{ or } 3a = 12$$

The sentence '$k \div 3 = 4$' may be read as

The result of dividing k by 3 is 4.

The sentence '$k \div 3 = 4$' may also be written

$$\frac{k}{3} = 4$$

NUMBERS, NUMERALS, AND EQUATIONS

The number of eggs in this carton

has many names. For example,

$\frac{1}{2}$ dozen, 6, $3 + 3$, $\frac{18}{3}$, and $3 \cdot 2$

are all different *names* for the number of eggs in the carton.

A name for a *number* is called a *numeral* or a *numerical expression*. The open sentence

$$x - 4 = 2$$

may be converted into a true statement by replacing

'x' with any numeral which names the number of eggs in the carton pictured above. For example,

$$6 - 4 = 2,$$
$$(3 + 3) - 4 = 2, \text{ and}$$
$$(3 \cdot 2) - 4 = 2$$

are true statements. We say that

> the number **6** **satisfies** the open sentence 'x − 4 = 2'.

We may also say that

> the number **3+3** satisfies the open sentence 'x − 4 = 2'.

Since

$$5 - 4 \neq 2 \text{ [say "5 minus 4 is not equal to 2"],}$$

we say that

> the number **5** does not satisfy the open sentence 'x − 4 = 2'.

Although the variable 'x' may be replaced by many numerals to convert the open sentence 'x − 4 = 2' into a true statement, all such numerals are names for the same number because there is one and only one *number* which satisfies this open sentence. It is true that the number 6 satisfies this open sentence, and that the number 3 + 3 also satisfies this open sentence, but '6' and '3 + 3' are just different names for the same number.

The sentence

$$6 - 4 = 2 \quad T$$

is called an *equation*. This equation tells us that 6 − 4 is the same number as 2. It is a true statement because the numerals '6 − 4' and '2' name the same number. The equation

$$5 - 4 = 2 \quad F$$

is a false statement because '5 − 4' and '2' are not names for the same number.

The equation

$$(3 + 3) - 4 = (3 \cdot 2) - 4$$

is a true statement because '(3 + 3) − 4' and '(3 · 2) − 4' are names for the same number. The parentheses in the numeral '(3 + 3) − 4' tell you that you may find another name for the number (3 + 3) − 4 by first adding 3 and 3 and then subtracting 4 from their sum:

$$\left. \begin{array}{l} (3 + 3) - 4 = 6 - 4 \\ \qquad\quad 6 - 4 = 2 \end{array} \right\} \text{ so, } (3 + 3) - 4 = 2$$

The parentheses in the numeral '(3 · 2) − 4' tell you that you may find another name for the number (3 · 2) − 4 by first multiplying 3 by 2 and then subtracting 4 from their product:

$$\left. \begin{array}{l} (3 \cdot 2) - 4 = 6 - 4 \\ \qquad\quad 6 - 4 = 2 \end{array} \right\} \text{ so, } (3 \cdot 2) - 4 = 2$$

The open sentence

$$x - 4 = 2$$

is also called an equation. The set of all numbers which satisfy this equation is called the *solution set* of the equation. The solution set of this equation consists of just the number 6, because 6 is the only number which satisfies this equation.

A shorthand notation for the set of all numbers which satisfy the equation 'x − 4 = 2' is

$$\{x: x - 4 = 2\}$$

We may read this as "the set of all numbers x such that x − 4 = 2."

The sentence

$$\{x: x - 4 = 2\} = \{6\}$$

says that the set of all numbers which satisfy the equation 'x − 4 = 2' consists of just the number 6.

Notice, for example, that the sentences

$$\boxed{3} \cdot 0 = 0 \text{ and } \boxed{7} \cdot 0 = 0$$

are true statements. In fact, if any number is multiplied by 0, the result is 0. Thus the open sentence

$$\boxed{} \cdot 0 = 0$$

is satisfied by every number. In other words, the solution set of 'x · 0 = 0' consists of every number:

$$\{x: x \cdot 0 = 0\} \text{ consists of all numbers.}$$

GENERALIZATIONS

Since the sentence

 is the capital of Illinois.

is a true statement, we may say that

> there is a city which is the capital of Illinois.

Similarly, since the equation

$$\boxed{8} - 5 = 3$$

is a true statement, we may say that

> there is a number with such a property that when 5 is subtracted from it the result is 3.

More briefly, we say that

> there exists a number x such that x − 5 = 3.

This last sentence tells us about a property of numbers, and it is called a *generalization*. Since it tells us that there exists among the numbers one which has a certain property, the sentence is called an *existential generalization*.

Existential generalizations are often written in an abbreviated form by using a turned-around 'E'. The sentence

$$\exists_x \, x - 4 = 2$$

is a shorthand notation which tells you that there exists a number with such a property that when 4 is subtracted from it the result is 2. The sentence '∃ₓ x − 4 = 2' may be read as follows:

> There exists x such that x minus 4 is equal to 2.

Sentences such as

$$\boxed{5} - 4 = 2 \quad \text{F}$$
$$\text{or} \quad \boxed{8} - 4 = 2 \quad \text{F}$$

are called *instances* of the above generalization. These instances are, of course, false statements. The instance

$$\boxed{6} - 4 = 2 \quad \text{T}$$

is, of course, a true statement. The existential generalization

$$\exists_x \, x - 4 = 2$$

is a true statement because it has *at least one true instance*. That is, the existential generalization is true because there exists at least one number with such a property that when 4 is subtracted from it the result is 2.

Recall that the sentences

$$\boxed{3} \cdot 0 = 0 \quad \text{and} \quad \boxed{\tfrac{1}{2}} \cdot 0 = 0$$

are true statements. In fact,

each number has such a property that when it is multiplied by 0 the result is 0.

More briefly, we may say that

for each number x, x · 0 = 0.

This last sentence tells us about a property of numbers, and it too is called a generalization. Since it tells us that each number has a certain property, the sentence is called a *universal generalization*.

Universal generalizations are often written in an abbreviated form by using an upside-down 'A'.

The sentence

$$\forall_x \, x \cdot 0 = 0$$

is a shorthand notation which tells you that each number has such a property that when it is multiplied by 0 the result is 0. The sentence '$\forall_x \, x \cdot 0 = 0$' may be read as follows:

For each x, the product of x by 0 is 0.

Sentences such as

$$\boxed{5} \cdot 0 = 0 \quad \text{T}$$
$$\text{or} \quad \boxed{6} \cdot 0 = 0 \quad \text{T}$$

are instances of the above generalization. This universal generalization is a true statement because *all of its instances are true statements*.

Notice that there is no number which satisfies the open sentence x · 0 = 5. That is, the existential generalization

$$\exists_x \, x \cdot 0 = 5 \quad \text{F}$$

is a false statement. This is equivalent to saying that each number satisfies the open sentence

$$\boxed{} \cdot 0 \neq 5$$

Therefore, the universal generalization

$$\forall_x \, x \cdot 0 \neq 5 \quad \text{T}$$

is a true statement.

288

Notice, for example, that '$2 \cdot \boxed{4} = 6$' is a false statement. Thus it is not the case that each number satisfies the open sentence '$2x = 6$'. That is, the universal generalization

$$\forall_x \, 2 \cdot x = 6 \quad \text{F}$$

is a false statement. This is equivalent to saying that there is a number which satisfies the open sentence

$$2 \cdot \boxed{} \neq 6$$

Therefore the existential generalization

$$\exists_x \, 2 \cdot x \neq 6 \quad \text{T}$$

is a true statement.

The symbol '$\exists$' is called the *existential quantifier*. The symbol '$\forall$' is called the *universal quantifier*.

Here are some other examples of generalizations. Some are true and some are false:

1. $\exists_x \, x + 3 = 8$ 3. $\exists_x \, x \cdot 0 = 0$
2. $\forall_x \, x + 3 = 8$ 4. $\exists_x \, x + 3 = 3$

The first generalization is true because '$\boxed{5} + 3 = 8$' is a true instance of it. The second generalization is false because not all of its instances are true statements. For example, '$\boxed{6} + 3 = 8$' is a false statement. The third generalization is true because, for example, '$\boxed{1} \cdot 0 = 0$' is a true statement. The fourth is true because '$\boxed{0} + 3 = 3$' is a true statement.

PATTERNS AND PRINCIPLES

Let us consider the following question:

Does there exist a number with such a property that the result of adding it to 3 is the same as the result of subtracting it from 15?

This amounts to asking if there is a number which satisfies the open sentence

$$3 + \boxed{} = 15 - \boxed{}$$

The number 2 does not satisfy this open sentence because the sentence

$$3 + \boxed{2} = 15 - \boxed{2} \quad \text{F}$$

is a false statement. The number 6 does satisfy the above open sentence because

$$3 + \boxed{6} = 15 - \boxed{6} \quad \text{T}$$

is a true statement.

Notice that although the equation

$$3 + \boxed{5} = 15 - \boxed{7}$$

is a true statement, it does not follow the *pattern* suggested by the open sentence

$$3 + \boxed{} = 15 - \boxed{}$$

A sentence follows the pattern of this open sentence if and only if the *same* numeral is written in both square frames.

For each frame we may substitute an 'x'. Consider the open sentence

$$3 + x = 15 - x$$

This open sentence may be converted into a true statement by replacing each occurrence of the variable 'x' with the numeral '6'. It may be converted into a false statement by replacing each occurrence of the variable 'x' with the numeral '2'.

Thus we see it is true that

$$\exists_x \; 3 + x = 15 - x \quad \mathcal{T}$$

and it is false that

$$\forall_x \; 3 + x = 15 - x \quad \mathcal{F}$$

Let us now consider a very important fundamental property of numbers. Notice that, for each pair of numbers, the result of adding the second number to the first is the same as that for adding the first number to the second. For example:

$$\boxed{2} + \boxed{3} = \boxed{3} + \boxed{2} \qquad \begin{cases} 2 + 3 = 5 \\ 3 + 2 = 5 \end{cases}$$

$$\boxed{5} + \boxed{15} = \boxed{15} + \boxed{5} \qquad \begin{cases} 5 + 15 = 20 \\ 15 + 5 = 20 \end{cases}$$

Because of this property, each pair of numbers satisfies the open sentence

$$\square + \bigcirc = \bigcirc + \square$$

We agree that we shall be following the pattern suggested by this open sentence if a first numeral is written in each square frame and a second numeral is written in each circular frame.

Using variables instead of frames, we may say that each pair of numbers satisfies the open sentence

$$x + y = y + x$$

We agree that each occurrence of the variable 'x' is to be replaced by a first numeral and that each occurrence of the variable 'y' is to be replaced by a second numeral.

The property of numbers to which we have been referring may be stated as follows:

$$\forall_x \; \forall_y \; x + y = y + x$$

This universal generalization is called *the commutative principle for addition*. It tells you that

for each x and each y, $x + y = y + x$.

This is a true generalization because all of its instances are true statements.

The universal generalization

$$\forall_{x \neq 0} \; x \cdot \frac{1}{x} = 1$$

tells you that each *nonzero* number satisfies the open sentence $\square \cdot \dfrac{1}{\square} = 1$. This generalization is also a true statement because all of its instances are true statements. For example, the following instances are true statements:

$$\boxed{2} \cdot \frac{1}{\boxed{2}} = 1 \qquad\qquad \boxed{4} \cdot \frac{1}{\boxed{4}} = 1$$

The first of these sentences tells you, for example, that two halves of a pie is one pie. The second sentence tells you, for example, that four quarters of a pie is one pie. The number $\frac{1}{2}$ is called 'the *reciprocal* of 2';

the number $\frac{1}{4}$ is the reciprocal of 4.

Another basic property of numbers is suggested by the multiplication tables. For example, consider the following:

$$
\begin{aligned}
1 \cdot 2 &= 2 \\
2 \cdot 2 &= 4 \\
3 \cdot 2 &= 6 \\
4 \cdot 2 &= 8 \\
5 \cdot 2 &= 10 \\
6 \cdot 2 &= 12 \\
7 \cdot 2 &= 14
\end{aligned}
$$

$3 + 4 = 7 \qquad\qquad 6 + 8 = 14$

We see that the following sentence is a true statement:

$$\left(\diamondsuit{3} + \blacktriangle{4} \right) \cdot \boxed{2} = \left(\diamondsuit{3} \cdot \boxed{2} \right) + \left(\blacktriangle{4} \cdot \boxed{2} \right)$$

The open sentence

$$\left(\diamondsuit + \blacktriangle \right) \cdot \square = \left(\diamondsuit \cdot \square \right) + \left(\blacktriangle \cdot \square \right)$$

is converted into a true statement if a first numeral is written in each diamond-shaped frame, a second numeral is written in each triangular frame, and a third numeral is written in each square frame.

The universal generalization

$$\forall_x \forall_y \forall_z \; (x + y) \cdot z = (x \cdot z) + (y \cdot z)$$

tells you that

for each x, each y, and each z, the result of multiplying the sum of x and y by z is the same as the result obtained by multiplying x by z and y by z and then adding the products.

This universal generalization is called the *distributive principle* [technically: the distributive principle for multiplication over addition]. It is a true generalization because all of its instances are true. Thus, for example, the complicated numerical expression

$$(27 \cdot 18) + (73 \cdot 18)$$

may be simplified quite easily by noticing that, by the distributive principle,

$$\left(\diamondsuit{27} \cdot \boxed{18} \right) + \left(\blacktriangle{73} \cdot \boxed{18} \right) = \left(\diamondsuit{27} + \blacktriangle{73} \right) \cdot \boxed{18}$$

$$= 100 \cdot \boxed{18}$$
$$= 1800$$

So, $(27 \cdot 18) + (73 \cdot 18) = 1800$

REAL NUMBERS

Numbers-of-arithmetic are numbers which are used as measures of *magnitude*. For example, we use numbers-of-arithmetic when we speak of a 10-mile trip, a 15-pound package, or a 7-day vacation.

Real numbers are numbers which are used as measures of *directed change*—they measure *direction* as well as *magnitude*. For example, if you gain 10 pounds, the change in your weight is measured by the real number

+10 [say "positive ten"].

If you go on a diet and lose 10 pounds, the change in your weight is measured by the real number

−10 [say "negative ten"].

The set of real numbers consists of all the positive numbers, all the negative numbers, and 0. The real number 0 corresponds to the number-of-arithmetic 0. Corresponding to each nonzero number-of-arithmetic there are exactly two real numbers: one positive number and one negative number. For example, +10 and −10 are the two real numbers corresponding to the number-of-arithmetic 10. The number-of-arithmetic 10 is called the *arithmetic value* of +10 and of −10.

The sum of a pair of real numbers is the real number which is the measure of the *resultant* of the corresponding pair of directed changes. For example, if you gain 10 pounds [a change in weight measured by the real number +10] and then lose 6 pounds [a change in weight measured by −6], the resultant change in weight is a gain of 4 pounds [measured by +4]. For short,

+10 + −6 = +4

If you gain 6 pounds [+6] and then lose 10 pounds [−10], your net change in weight is a loss of 4 pounds:

+6 + −10 = −4

If you gain 10 pounds and then lose 10 pounds, your net change in weight is 0:

+10 + −10 = 0

We say that

the **opposite** of +10 is −10

and that

the **opposite** of −10 is +10.

A short name for the opposite of +10 is − +10,

and a short name for the opposite of −10 is

− −10.

Since   − +10 = −10,

the sum of +10 and its opposite is 0:

+10 + − +10 = +10 + −10

+10 + −10 = 0

So, $\boxed{+10} + − \boxed{+10} = 0$

Similarly, $\boxed{−10} + − \boxed{−10} = 0$

In fact, for each real number the sum of that real number and its opposite is 0. Moreover, if the sum of a pair of real numbers is 0, then each is the opposite of the other. For example,

+10 + −10 = 0,

and +10 and −10 are each the opposite of the other.

Notice that

0 + 0 = 0,

so the opposite of 0 is 0.

The opposite of a given real number is called the *additive inverse* of the real number. For example, the additive inverse of +10 is −10, and the additive inverse of 0 is 0. Each real number has an additive inverse.

Basic Principles for Addition

We shall list certain principles concerning addition of real numbers. These are called *basic principles*. We start our list with three principles mentioned above:

(A0)
- (a) The sum of a pair of real numbers is a real number.
- (b) 0 is a real number.
- (c) The opposite of a real number is a real number.

Notice that a gain of 10 pounds followed by a loss of 6 pounds,

+10 + −6,

results in the same change in weight as a loss of 6 pounds followed by a gain of 10 pounds,

−6 + +10

Thus,

$\boxed{+10} + ⬤−6 = ⬤−6 + \boxed{+10}$

This suggests that addition of real numbers is a commutative operation, and we accept this as another of our basic principles for addition of real numbers:

(A1) $\forall_x \forall_y \; x + y = y + x$

A gain of 10 pounds followed by no further gain or loss of weight results in a gain of 10 pounds:

$\boxed{+10} + 0 = \boxed{+10}$

This suggests our next basic principle:

(A2) $\forall_x \; x + 0 = x$

We mentioned in the last section that the sum of a real number and its opposite is 0. We accept this as another basic principle:

(A3) $\forall_x \; x + − x = 0$

Finally we complete our list of basic principles with the *associative principle* for addition of real numbers. Before stating this principle, let us consider an example.

Suppose that you go on a two-week vacation. If you gain 2 pounds the first week and lose 3 pounds the second week [a resultant change in weight measured by the real number +2 + −3] and then come home and gain 4 pounds [+4], your resultant change in weight is measured by the real number

(+2 + −3) + +4

If, instead, you gained 2 pounds [+2] the week before going on vacation and then lost 3 pounds the first week and gained 4 pounds the second week [−3 + +4] of vacation, your resultant change in weight is measured by the real number

$$+2 + (^-3 + {}^+4)$$

Since

$$(^+2 + {}^-3) + {}^+4 = {}^-1 + {}^+4 = {}^+3$$

and

$$+2 + (^-3 + {}^+4) = {}^+2 + {}^+1 = {}^+3,$$

it follows that

$$(\boxed{{}^+2} + \blacktriangle) + \bullet = \boxed{{}^+2} + (\blacktriangle + \bullet)$$

This suggests that the open sentence

$$(\square + \blacktriangle) + \bullet = \square + (\blacktriangle + \bullet)$$

is converted into a true statement if a first numeral is written in each square frame, a second numeral is written in each diamond-shaped frame, and a third numeral is written in each circular frame.

The universal generalization

(A4) $\forall_x \forall_y \forall_z (x + y) + z = x + (y + z)$

is called the *associative principle* for addition of real numbers. This basic principle tells you that

> for each x, each y, and each z, the result of adding (x + y) and z is the same as the result of adding x and (y + z).

A short way of saying that addition of real numbers satisfies the basic principles (A0) through (A4) is to say that the set of real numbers is a *commutative group under addition*.

Basic Principles for Multiplication

Consideration of real numbers as measures of directed change suggests basic principles for multiplication of real numbers.

Let us first consider some examples. If you gain 3 pounds [a change in weight measured by $^+3$] each week, then 2 weeks from now [a change in time measured by $^+2$] you will be 6 pounds heavier [$^+6$]. We say that the product of $^+3$ and $^+2$ is $^+6$. For short,

$$+3 \cdot {}^+2 = {}^+6$$

If you gained 3 pounds [$^+3$] each week, then 2 weeks ago [$^-2$] you were 6 pounds lighter [$^-6$]:

$$+3 \cdot {}^-2 = {}^-6$$

If you lost 3 pounds [$^-3$] each week, then 2 weeks ago [$^-2$] you were 6 pounds heavier [$^+6$]:

$$-3 \cdot {}^-2 = {}^+6$$

If a given real number is multiplied by the real number $^+1$, the product is the given real number. For example:

$$\boxed{{}^+2} \cdot {}^+1 = \boxed{{}^+2} \qquad \boxed{{}^-2} \cdot {}^+1 = \boxed{{}^-2}$$

We stated earlier that each real number has an additive inverse. It is also the case that each real number [except 0] has a *multiplicative inverse*. It is called the *reciprocal* of the real number. The result of multiplying a real number by its reciprocal is $^+1$; if the product of a pair of real numbers is $^+1$, then each is the reciprocal of the other. So, for example, the

reciprocal of $^+3$ is named by the fraction

$$\frac{+1}{+3}$$

because $\boxed{{}^+3} \cdot \dfrac{+1}{\boxed{+3}} = {}^+1$

Each nonzero real number satisfies the open sentence

$$\square \cdot \frac{+1}{\square} = {}^+1$$

Notice also that multiplication of real numbers satisfies the commutative principle. That is, the open sentence

$$\square \cdot \blacktriangle = \blacktriangle \cdot \square$$

is converted into a true statement if a first numeral is written in each square frame and a second numeral is written in each triangular frame. For example:

$$\boxed{{}^+2} \cdot \blacktriangle_{-3} = {}^-6$$

$$\blacktriangle_{-3} \cdot \boxed{{}^+2} = {}^-6$$

So, $\boxed{{}^+2} \cdot \blacktriangle_{-3} = \blacktriangle_{-3} \cdot \boxed{{}^+2}$

Multiplication of real numbers also satisfies the associative principle. For example:

$$(\boxed{{}^+2} \cdot \blacktriangle_{-3}) \cdot \bullet_{+4} = {}^-6 \cdot {}^+4 = {}^-24$$

$$\boxed{{}^+2} \cdot (\blacktriangle_{-3} \cdot \bullet_{+4}) = {}^+2 \cdot {}^-12 = {}^-24$$

So, $(\boxed{{}^+2} \cdot \blacktriangle_{-3}) \cdot \bullet_{+4} = \boxed{{}^+2} \cdot (\blacktriangle_{-3} \cdot \bullet_{+4})$

These investigations of properties of real numbers suggest a list of basic principles for multiplication of real numbers which are similar to the basic principles for addition of real numbers. Corresponding to the basic principle (A0), we accept the basic principle:

(M0)
(a) The product of a pair of real numbers is a real number.
(b) $^+1$ is a real number, and $^+1 \neq 0$.
(c) The reciprocal of a nonzero real number is a real number.

Corresponding to the basic principles (A1) through (A4), we accept the basic principles:

(M1) $\forall_x \forall_y \; x \cdot y = y \cdot x$

(M2) $\forall_x \; x \cdot {}^+1 = x$

(M3) $\forall_{x \neq 0} \; x \cdot \dfrac{+1}{x} = {}^+1$

(M4) $\forall_x \forall_y \forall_z \; (x \cdot y) \cdot z = x \cdot (y \cdot z)$

The basic principle (M3) tells you that the product of each nonzero real number ($\forall_{x \neq 0}$) and its reciprocal is $^+1$.

Finally we complete our list of basic principles for addition and multiplication of real numbers by adding the distributive principle to the list:

(D1) $\forall_x \forall_y \forall_z \; (x + y) \cdot z = (x \cdot z) + (y \cdot z)$

291

ALGEBRA

A short way of saying that addition and multiplication of real numbers satisfies the basic principles (A0) through (A4), (M0) through (M4), and (D1) is to say that the set of real numbers is a *field*.

In the next section we shall give some examples of how we may use these principles to deduce other properties of addition and multiplication of real numbers.

Using the Basic Principles

Let us use the basic principles to obtain some other principles of addition and multiplication of real numbers. We agree that the basic principles are true statements, and we show that other sentences are true statements by proving that they are logical consequences of the basic principles.

We begin with a very simple example. Notice that the sentence

$$\boxed{+3} + 0 = \boxed{+3}$$

is a true statement because it is an instance of the universal generalization (A2). The sentence

$$0 + \boxed{+3} = \boxed{+3}$$

is not an instance of (A2) because it does not follow the pattern suggested by 'x + 0 = x'. But it is a true statement. Do we need to do any computing to discover that it is true?

No! We can show that the sentence

$$0 + \boxed{+3} = \boxed{+3}$$

is true by showing that it is a consequence of (A1) and (A2). Here is how we might do this. The following sentence is an instance of (A1):

$$0 + \boxed{+3} = \boxed{+3} + 0$$

and this is an instance of (A2):

$$\boxed{+3} + 0 = \boxed{+3}$$

From these two sentences it follows that

$$0 + \boxed{+3} = \boxed{+3}$$

This suggests a pattern which we may follow in order to show that any instance of the universal generalization

$$(*) \quad \forall_x \, 0 + x = x$$

is a consequence of the basic principles (A1) and (A2). In view of this we say that the universal generalization itself is a consequence of (A1) and (A2).

The generalization (*) differs in an important respect from the generalizations listed in the basic principles. We accept the basic principles on the basis of computation with some examples. We accept (*) because it follows *logically* [that is, by reasoning alone] from the accepted basic principles. We *postulate* the basic principles, but we can *prove* (*).

Notice that the sentence

$$\boxed{+3} \cdot {}^+1 = \boxed{+3}$$

is a true statement because it is an instance of the universal generalization (M2). The sentence

$${}^+1 \cdot \boxed{+3} = \boxed{+3}$$

is not an instance of (M2). Can you show that it is a true statement by proving that it is a consequence of (M1) and (M2)? [Try it!]

Notice that none of the basic principles which we have listed says that the product of 0 and each real number is 0. We do not need a basic principle which says this because we can *prove* the universal generalization

$$\forall_x \, 0 \cdot x = 0$$

by showing that it is a consequence of our basic principles. As an example of the argument that may be used, here is a proof of the sentence

$$0 \cdot \boxed{+3} = 0$$

First we notice that the following sentence is an instance of (A2):

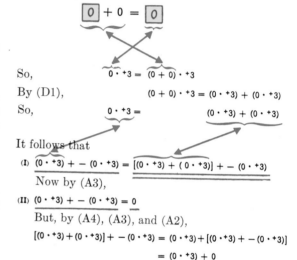

So,

$$0 \cdot {}^+3 = \overbrace{(0 + 0)} \cdot {}^+3$$

By (D1),

$$(0 + 0) \cdot {}^+3 = (0 \cdot {}^+3) + (0 \cdot {}^+3)$$

So,

$$0 \cdot {}^+3 = (0 \cdot {}^+3) + (0 \cdot {}^+3)$$

It follows that

(I) $\overbrace{(0 \cdot {}^+3)} + - (0 \cdot {}^+3) = \overbrace{[(0 \cdot {}^+3) + (0 \cdot {}^+3)]} + - (0 \cdot {}^+3)$

Now by (A3),

(II) $(0 \cdot {}^+3) + - (0 \cdot {}^+3) = 0$

But, by (A4), (A3), and (A2),

$$[(0 \cdot {}^+3) + (0 \cdot {}^+3)] + - (0 \cdot {}^+3) = (0 \cdot {}^+3) + [(0 \cdot {}^+3) + - (0 \cdot {}^+3)]$$
$$= (0 \cdot {}^+3) + 0$$
$$= 0 \cdot {}^+3,$$

and so it follows that

(III) $[(0 \cdot {}^+3) + (0 \cdot {}^+3)] + - (0 \cdot {}^+3) = 0 \cdot {}^+3$

From sentences (I), (II), and (III), it follows that

$$0 \cdot {}^+3 = 0$$

Thus we have shown that '$0 \cdot {}^+3 = 0$' is a consequence of (A2), (D1), (A3), and (A4).

We may follow the pattern of argument to show that *any* instance of the universal generalization

$$\forall_x \, 0 \cdot x = 0$$

is a consequence of our basic principles. In view of this we say that the universal generalization itself is a consequence of our basic principles.

Recall now that our basic principle (M0)(b) tells us that

$${}^+1 \neq 0$$

We therefore know that for each real number, the product of 0 and that real number is not ${}^+1$. That is,

$$\forall_x \, 0 \cdot x \neq {}^+1$$

This explains why 0 has no multiplicative inverse: the

292

result of multiplying a real number by its multiplicative inverse is $^+1$, but the result of multiplying 0 by any real number is not $^+1$.

Many other generalizations concerning addition and multiplication of real numbers may be shown to be consequences of our basic principles.

Subtraction of real numbers may be defined in terms of addition of real numbers. For example:

$$\boxed{+10} - \triangle{+3} = \boxed{+10} + - \triangle{+3}$$

$$\boxed{+10} - \triangle{-3} = {}^+10 + - \triangle{-3}$$

Subtraction of real numbers may be defined by the universal generalization

$$\forall_x \forall_y \; x - y = x + -y.$$

We may show, for example, that the universal generalization

$$\forall_x \forall_y \; (x - y) + y = x$$

is a consequence of our basic principles and the definition of subtraction.

The reader should try to show that a particular instance of this universal generalization is a true statement. For example, try to show that the sentence

$$(^+3 - {}^-4) + {}^-4 = {}^+3$$

is a consequence of the definition of subtraction, (A4), (A1), (A3), and (A2). Here is how you might start:

By the definition of subtraction,

$$(^+3 - {}^-4) + {}^-4 = (^+3 + -{}^-4) + {}^-4$$

By (A4),

$$(^+3 + -{}^-4) + {}^-4 = {}^+3 + (-{}^-4 + {}^-4)\ldots$$

[You complete the argument, using (A1), (A3), and (A2).]

In an analogous manner we may define division of a real number by a nonzero real number in terms of multiplication and reciprocating. For example:

$$\boxed{+10} \div \triangle{+3} = \boxed{+10} \cdot \triangle{{}^{+1}_{+3}}$$

Division of a real number by a nonzero real number may be defined by the universal generalization

$$\forall_x \forall_{y \neq 0} \; x \div y = x \cdot \frac{^+1}{y}$$

We may show, for example, that the universal generalization

$$\forall_x \forall_{y \neq 0} \; (x \div y) \cdot y = x$$

is a consequence of our basic principles and the definition of division.

The reader should try to show, for example, that the sentence

$$(^+3 \div {}^-4) \cdot {}^-4 = {}^+3$$

is a consequence of the definition of division, (M4), (M1), (M3), and (M2). [Start in a manner analogous to the manner in which you started to derive the sentence '$(^+3 - {}^-4) + {}^-4 = {}^+3$'.]

(For a more complete study of the algebra of real numbers, *see* the section "Applying the Fundamental Concepts of Algebra" later in this article. *See also* Numeration Systems and Numbers.)

THE BEGINNINGS OF ALGEBRA

More than 3,500 years ago an Egyptian named Ahmes collected together a set of mathematical problems and their solutions. Included were problems such as finding the number which satisfies the equation

$$x\left(\frac{2}{3} + \frac{1}{2} + \frac{1}{7} + 1\right) = 37$$

About 2,500 years ago the Greek mathematician Pythagoras started a religious-mathematical brotherhood. Its members were called Pythagoreans. Intensely interested in geometry, they classified numbers according to geometrical properties. For example, they studied properties of the triangular numbers

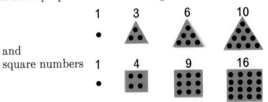

and square numbers

The famous Greek geometer Euclid discovered important properties of numbers through a study of geometry. For example, the truth of the sentence

$$2 \cdot (3 + 4) = (2 \cdot 3) + (2 \cdot 4)$$

is verified geometrically by noting that the area of the following rectangle:

$$\text{area} = 2 \cdot (3 + 4)$$
$$= 2 \cdot 7$$
$$= 14$$

is the same as the sum of the areas of the following rectangles:

$$\text{area} = 2 \cdot 3 \qquad \text{area} = 2 \cdot 4$$
$$= 6 \qquad\qquad\;\; = 8 \qquad [6 + 8 = 14]$$

Diophantus, another famous early Greek mathematician, has been called the "father of algebra." He treated algebra from a purely numerical point of view. He made a special study of certain types of equations which are today called Diophantine equations.

Our modern word "algebra" comes from the Arabic *al-jabr*, which appeared in the title of an algebra text written about A.D. 825 by the Arab astronomer and mathematician al-Khwarizmi. The words "algorism" and "algorithm" are derived from his name.

MODERN ALGEBRA

Our algebra of real numbers developed through the centuries from considerations of problems in arithmetic. The study of the algebra of real numbers and the recent recognition of the fundamental importance of the *basic principles* have led to the development of what is now called *modern algebra* or *abstract algebra*.

One of the earliest pioneers in this direction was the

French genius Évariste Galois (1811–32). Although he lived a tragic life and died in a foolish duel at the age of 20, his work led to the development of the modern *theory of groups and fields.*

The concepts of modern algebra have been found to be extremely useful in other branches of mathematics, as well as in the physical and social sciences. A chemist may use modern algebra in a study of the structure of crystals; a physicist may use modern algebra in designing an electronic computer; a mathematician may use modern algebra in a study of logic.

In the algebra of real numbers we study the properties of addition and multiplication of real numbers which follow as a consequence of certain basic principles. In modern algebra we may work with any set of objects. [We need not work just with real numbers.] We consider certain operations on these objects. [These operations need not be addition and multiplication.] We agree that certain basic principles are satisfied by these operations. [These basic principles need not be the same as our basic principles for addition and multiplication of real numbers.] Then we derive various properties which follow as consequences of the assumed basic principles.

BOOLEAN ALGEBRA

An important branch of mathematics is called *Boolean algebra* for the English mathematician and logician George Boole (1815–64). It combines algebraic methods and logic. Let us consider a simple example.

Suppose that two sources of electric power are connected to a motor which we shall label 'Motor ⊕':

We suppose that Motor ⊕ is operating if at least one of the power sources is in operation but is not operating if neither power source is operating. We now ask a series of three questions, each of which can be answered 'Yes' or 'No', and such that the answers to the first two questions determine the answer to the third question. We list the different possible combinations of answers to the first two questions, and the corresponding answers to the third question:

Is source A in operation?	Is source B in operation?	Is Motor ⊕ in operation?
No	No	No
No	Yes	Yes
Yes	No	Yes
Yes	Yes	Yes

Given the answers to the first two questions, we can determine the answer to the third question. The above list suggests that we may define an operation which we shall denote by the symbol '⊕':

No	⊕	No	= No
No	⊕	Yes	= Yes
Yes	⊕	No	= Yes
Yes	⊕	Yes	= Yes

Suppose now that Motor ⊕ is replaced by a new motor, which we shall label 'Motor ⊗':

We suppose that Motor ⊗ is not operating unless both sources of electricity are in operation. We may ask the same series of three questions, and again the answers to the first two questions determine the answer to the third question:

Is source A in operation?	Is source B in operation?	Is Motor ⊗ in operation?
No	No	No
No	Yes	No
Yes	No	No
Yes	Yes	Yes

This list suggests another operation, which we shall denote by the symbol '⊗':

No	⊗	No	= No
No	⊗	Yes	= No
Yes	⊗	No	= No
Yes	⊗	Yes	= Yes

The operations ⊕ and ⊗ suggest a type of miniature arithmetic in which we work with the objects

No and **Yes**

instead of real numbers. These operations satisfy certain basic principles which qualify the arithmetic to be called a Boolean algebra.

For example, just as in the algebra of real numbers, ⊕ and ⊗ satisfy the commutative principles

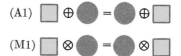

Thus, for example, the sentences

are, by our rules, true statements.

These are only a few of the basic principles of a Boolean algebra. The basic principles of a Boolean algebra are very much like those of the algebra of real numbers. A knowledge of Boolean algebra is very useful in fields requiring the application of mathematics and logic. Electronic-computer programming and the construction of electronic circuits are examples of such fields.

At this point, the student has developed an understanding of the fundamental algebraic concepts and of algebra's relationship to other branches of mathematics. The following section will deepen this understanding by explaining how the fundamental concepts of the algebra of real numbers may be applied in solving various kinds of mathematical problems.

Applying the Fundamental Concepts of Algebra

AN UNDERSTANDING of the fundamental concepts of algebra and of how those fundamental concepts may be applied is necessary in many professional and most technical careers. For engineers and scientists it is an essential requirement.

The fundamental concepts of algebra are described in the preceding section of this article. How these concepts may be applied to aid in the solution of various types of mathematical problems is explained here.

USING REAL NUMBERS

An example of the use of real numbers is in the measurement of temperatures. If it is a very cold day, it may not be enough to tell someone that the temperature is **5** degrees; you may have to indicate whether it is **5** degrees "above zero" or **5** degrees "below zero." You may use the real numbers $^{+}5$ [say "*positive* **5** "] or $^{-}5$ [say "*negative* **5** "] to indicate the temperature. The degree temperatures "above zero" are measured by positive real numbers, and the degree temperatures "below zero" are measured by negative real numbers.

It may be helpful to picture the set of real numbers as the set of points on a line:

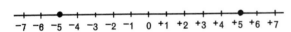

A diagram such as this is often called a *picture of the number line*. The point labeled '0' is called the *origin* (*see* Numeration Systems and Numbers).

The *number-of-arithmetic* **5** is the arithmetic value of the real numbers $^{+}5$ and $^{-}5$. The numbers-of-arithmetic are used as measures of *magnitude;* the real numbers are used as measures of *magnitude and direction*.

As another example of how real numbers are used, consider the measurement of distances above and below sea level. The elevation of Mount McKinley is 20,320 feet *above* sea level, measured by the real number $^{+}20{,}320$. Death Valley has an elevation of 282 feet *below* sea level, measured by the real number $^{-}282$. The elevation at sea level is 0; distances above sea level are measured by positive real numbers, and distances below sea level are measured by negative real numbers.

OPERATIONS ON REAL NUMBERS

In the preceding section of this article, it was mentioned that the *sum* of a pair of real numbers is the real number which is the measure of the *resultant* of the corresponding pair of directed changes. To gain further insight into addition of real numbers it may be convenient to refer to a picture of the number line.

For example:

$$^{+}3 + {}^{+}2 = {}^{+}5$$

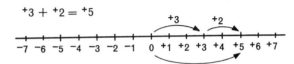

$$^{-}3 + {}^{-}2 = {}^{-}5$$

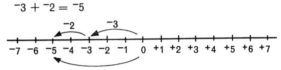

Notice that we may apply our knowledge of addition of numbers-of-arithmetic when we wish to add a pair of positive numbers [or a pair of negative numbers]; for the arithmetic value of the sum of a pair of positive numbers [or of a pair of negative numbers] is the sum of their arithmetic values:

$$3 + 2 = 5$$

If we wish to find the sum of a positive number and a negative number, for example:

$$^{+}3 + {}^{-}2 = {}^{+}1$$

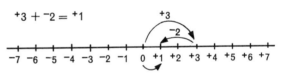

or the sum of a negative number and a positive number, for example:

$$^{-}3 + {}^{+}2 = {}^{-}1$$

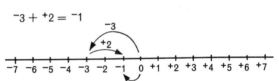

we may apply our knowledge of subtraction of numbers-of-arithmetic:

$$3 - 2 = 1$$

In the preceding section of this article, subtraction of real numbers was defined in terms of addition and oppositing. For example:

$$^{+}3 - {}^{+}2$$

is simply a shorthand notation for

$$^{+}3 + - {}^{+}2$$

Since

$$- {}^{+}2 = {}^{-}2$$

it follows that

$$^{+}3 - {}^{+}2 = {}^{+}3 + - {}^{+}2 = {}^{+}3 + {}^{-}2 = {}^{+}1$$

Thus, the result of subtracting $^{+}2$ from $^{+}3$ is $^{+}1$.

Similarly, the result of subtracting $^+3$ from $^+2$ is $^-1$:

$$^+2 - {}^+3 = {}^+2 + -{}^+3 = {}^+2 + {}^-3 = {}^-1$$

Multiplication of real numbers is similarly related to multiplication of numbers-of-arithmetic:

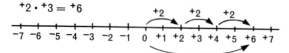

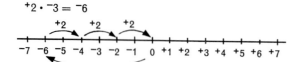

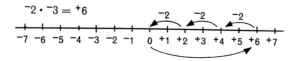

Notice that the arithmetic value of the product of a pair of real numbers is the product of their arithmetic values:

$$2 \cdot 3 = 6$$

Notice also that the product of a positive number by a positive number [or of a negative number by a negative number] is a positive number. The product of a positive number by a negative number [or of a negative number by a positive number] is a negative number.

In the preceding section of this article, division of a real number by a nonzero number was defined in terms of multiplication and reciprocation. For example:

$$^+6 \div {}^+3$$

is simply a shorthand notation for

$$^+6 \cdot \frac{^+1}{^+3}$$

Let us see what it means to divide $^+6$ by $^+3$. We wish to find the real number which satisfies the open sentence

$$^+6 \cdot \frac{^+1}{^+3} = \boxed{}$$

A real number satisfies this open sentence if and only if it satisfies the following open sentence:

$$\left(^+6 \cdot \frac{^+1}{^+3}\right) \cdot {}^+3 = \boxed{} \cdot {}^+3$$

But,

$$\left(^+6 \cdot \frac{^+1}{^+3}\right) \cdot {}^+3 = {}^+6 \cdot \left(\frac{^+1}{^+3} \cdot {}^+3\right)$$

$$= {}^+6 \cdot \left(^+3 \cdot \frac{^+1}{^+3}\right)$$

$$= {}^+6 \cdot {}^+1$$

$$= {}^+6$$

So a real number satisfies the open sentence

$$^+6 \cdot \frac{^+1}{^+3} = \boxed{}$$

if and only if it satisfies the open sentence

$$^+6 = \boxed{} \cdot {}^+3$$

We notice that $^+2$ is the real number which satisfies the last open sentence

$$^+6 = \boxed{^+2} \cdot {}^+3$$

So it follows that

$$^+6 \cdot \frac{^+1}{^+3} = \boxed{^+2}$$

or, equivalently, that

$$^+6 \div {}^+3 = \boxed{^+2}$$

Here are some other examples to illustrate division of real numbers:

$^+15 \div {}^+5 = \boxed{^+3}$ because $^+15 = \boxed{^+3} \cdot {}^+5$

$^+16 \div {}^-2 = \boxed{^-8}$ because $^+16 = \boxed{^-8} \cdot {}^-2$

$^-12 \div {}^+2 = \boxed{^-6}$ because $^-12 = \boxed{^-6} \cdot {}^+2$

$^-9 \div {}^-3 = \boxed{^+3}$ because $^-9 = \boxed{^+3} \cdot {}^-3$

Notice the similarity between division of real numbers and division of numbers-of-arithmetic. For example:

$15 \div 5 = \boxed{3}$ because $15 = \boxed{3} \cdot 5$

$16 \div 2 = \boxed{8}$ because $16 = \boxed{8} \cdot 2$

Notice also that the result of dividing a positive number by a positive number [or of dividing a negative number by a negative number] is a positive number. The result of dividing a positive number by a negative number [or of dividing a negative number by a positive number] is a negative number.

FORMULAS, FUNCTIONS, AND GRAPHS

A fruit dealer sells apples priced at 12 cents each. He may find it convenient to make a list of the cost of various quantities of apples:

Number of apples	Cost
0	$ 0
1	.12
2	.24
3	.36

He may, of course, extend this list as far as necessary.

Notice that to find the cost of any quantity of apples he may use the *formula*

$$C = .12 \cdot N$$

If he substitutes a numeral for 'N', he can find the corresponding cost by using this formula. For example, to find the cost of 17 apples he substitutes '17' for 'N':

$$C = .12 \cdot 17$$

If he multiplies .12 by 17, he finds that the cost of 17 apples is $2.04.

We assume that the dealer is not interested in knowing the cost of fractional parts of an apple. Thus the *values* of 'N' are simply the whole numbers

$$0, 1, 2, 3, \ldots$$

and the values of 'C' are simply the multiples of .12.

It is also useful to consider the set of *ordered pairs:*

$$\{(0, 0), (1, .12), (2, .24), \ldots\}$$

The first member of an ordered pair is called the *first component*, and the second member of an ordered pair is called the *second component*. For example, the first component of the ordered pair (3, .36) is 3, and its second component is .36. Notice that in the set of ordered pairs which we are considering, no two ordered pairs have the same first component. [For example, the two ordered pairs (1, .12) and (2, .24) have different first components.]

A set of ordered pairs which satisfies the condition that no two ordered pairs in the set have the same first component is called a *function*. Thus, the set of ordered pairs given above is a function.

The set of ordered pairs given above may be described as the set of all ordered pairs (n, c), where the first component is a whole number, such that

$$c = n \cdot .12$$

The *domain* of a function is the set of first components of the set of ordered pairs of which the function consists. The *range* of a function is the set of second components. In the example considered above, the domain of the function is the set of whole numbers, and the range of the function is the set of multiples of .12.

Instead of listing the costs of various quantities of apples, the dealer may make a *graph:*

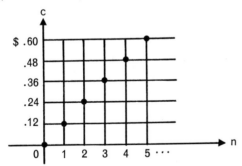

The dot which is above '1' and to the right of '.12' illustrates the point which corresponds to the ordered pair (1, .12). The dot which is above '2' and to the right of '.24' illustrates the point corresponding to the ordered pair (2, .24). By referring to the graph, the dealer can see at a glance that the cost of 4 apples is 48 cents.

The domain of the function whose graph is pictured above consists of only the whole numbers. For this reason, the graph of this function consists of only a sequence of points.

Linear Functions

Consider the set of all ordered pairs of real numbers (x, y) which satisfy the condition that the sum of the first and second components is $^+5$:

$$x + y = {}^+5$$

Some ordered pairs which belong to this function are:

$$({}^+5, 0), \left({}^+3\tfrac{1}{2}, {}^+1\tfrac{1}{2}\right), ({}^+6, {}^-1)$$

This set of ordered pairs may also be described as the set of all ordered pairs of real numbers (x, y) such that

$$y = {}^-1 \cdot x + {}^+5$$

This set of ordered pairs of real numbers is a function whose domain and range is the set of all real numbers. The graph of this function is a line:

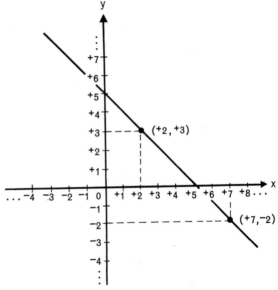

The points on the graph which correspond to the ordered pairs ($^+2$, $^+3$) and ($^+7$, $^-2$) are marked on the graph. You may find it worthwhile to locate the points on the graph which correspond to the following ordered pairs:

$$(0, {}^+5), ({}^+1.5, {}^+3.5), ({}^-1, {}^+6)$$

Since the graph of the function is a line, the function is called a *linear function*, and the equation

$$y = {}^-1 \cdot x + {}^+5$$

is called a *linear equation*.

Since the graph of a linear function is a straight line, many geometric problems which involve lines and line segments may be solved by algebraic methods. The properties of linear functions are studied in analytic geometry and calculus.

Another example of a linear function is the set of all ordered pairs of real numbers (x, y) such that

$$y = x + {}^+1$$

Some ordered pairs which belong to this function are:

$$(0, {}^+1), ({}^-1, 0), ({}^+2.5, {}^+3.5), ({}^-2.5, {}^-1.5)$$

The graph of this function is a line:

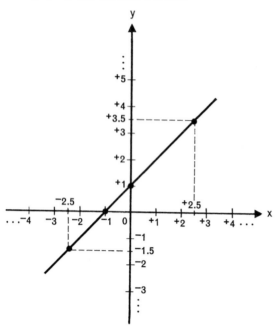

Here are other examples of linear equations:

$$y = x + {}^-6 \qquad y = {}^+5x + {}^-2 \qquad y = {}^-4x + {}^+1$$

In fact, if 'a' and 'b' are real numbers, and 'a' $\neq$ 0,

$$y = ax + b$$

is a linear equation. The corresponding function is a linear function, and its graph is a straight line.

Quadratic Functions

The formula for computing the area of a *rectangle* is

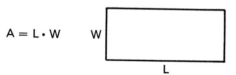

$$A = L \cdot W$$

This formula tells you that the area of a rectangle may be found by multiplying its length by its width. For example, the area of a rectangle 5 inches long and 2 inches wide may be found by substituting '5' for 'L' and '2' for 'W' in the formula and then multiplying:

$$A = 5 \cdot 2 = 10$$

Hence the area of the given rectangle is 10 square inches.

If the rectangle is such that the length is the same as the width, the rectangle is called a *square*, and the formula for its area is

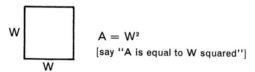

$$A = W^2$$

[say "A is equal to W squared"]

298

The numeral '2' is called an *exponent*. The expression 'W²' is a shorthand notation for

$$W \cdot W$$

The set of all ordered pairs of real numbers (x, y) such that

$$y = x^2$$

is a function. Some ordered pairs which belong to this function are:

$$(0, 0), ({}^+1, {}^+1), ({}^-1, {}^+1), ({}^+2, {}^+4), ({}^-2, {}^+4)$$

The graph of this function is not a line; the function is not a linear function. It is an example of a *quadratic function*. Its graph is a *parabola*:

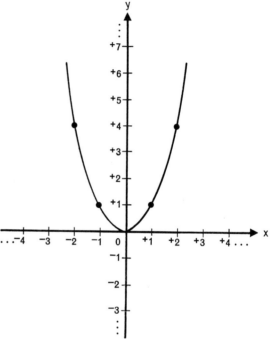

Another example of a quadratic function is the set of all ordered pairs of real numbers (x, y) such that

$$y = {}^+2x^2 + {}^+5x + {}^-1$$

If 'a', 'b', and 'c' are real numbers, and 'a' $\neq$ 0, then the set of all ordered pairs (x, y) such that

$$y = ax^2 + bx + c$$

is called a quadratic function. The properties of quadratic functions are studied in analytic geometry and calculus.

Functions of Higher Degree

Consider the function consisting of all ordered pairs of real numbers (x, y) such that

$$y = x^3 \quad \text{[say "y is equal to x cubed"]}$$

The expression 'x³' is a shorthand notation for

$$x \cdot x \cdot x$$

Some ordered pairs which belong to this function are:

$$(0, 0), ({}^+1, {}^+1), ({}^-1, {}^-1), ({}^+2, {}^+8), ({}^-2, {}^-8)$$

This function is an example of a *third degree* function:

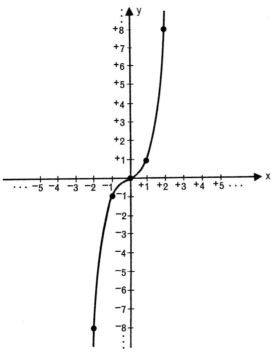

The function consisting of the set of all ordered pairs of real numbers (x, y) such that

y = x⁴ [say "y is equal to x to the fourth"]

is an example of a *fourth degree* function. The expression 'x⁴' is, of course, a shorthand notation for

x • x • x • x

Some ordered pairs which belong to this function are:

(0, 0), (⁺1, ⁺1), (⁻1, ⁺1), (⁺2, ⁺16), (⁻2, ⁺16)

You might find it interesting to draw a graph of this function.

Properties of Exponents

In the preceding section of this article, the basic principles for addition and multiplication of real numbers were listed. From these basic principles, other principles were derived. We now note some properties of exponents which follow easily from the basic principles.

Notice, for example, that
$$2^2 \cdot 2^3 = (2 \cdot 2) \cdot (2 \cdot 2 \cdot 2)$$
$$= 4 \cdot 8$$
$$= 32$$

and that $2^5 = 2 \cdot 2 \cdot 2 \cdot 2 \cdot 2 = 32$

In fact, it is easy to prove the following principle:
$$\forall_x \; x^2 \cdot x^3 = x^5$$

This principle tells you that for each real number 'x', the product of 'x²' by 'x³' is 'x⁵'. [Notice that 2+3=5.]

Note also, for example, that
$$\frac{2^5}{2^2} = \frac{2 \cdot 2 \cdot 2 \cdot 2 \cdot 2}{2 \cdot 2} = \frac{32}{4} = 8 = 2 \cdot 2 \cdot 2 = 2^3$$

and that $\frac{2^2}{2^5} = \frac{2 \cdot 2}{2 \cdot 2 \cdot 2 \cdot 2 \cdot 2} = \frac{4}{32} = \frac{1}{8} = \frac{1}{2 \cdot 2 \cdot 2} = \frac{1}{2^3}$

These examples suggest the following principles which are easily proved to be consequences of the basic principles:
$$\forall_{x \neq 0} \; \frac{x^5}{x^2} = x^3 \qquad \forall_{x \neq 0} \; \frac{x^2}{x^5} = \frac{1}{x^3}$$

[Notice that 5−2=3.]

The principles suggest methods you may use to solve problems like the following without using pencil and paper:

(a) $3^3 \cdot 3^5 = ?$ [Solution: $3^3 \cdot 3^5 = 3^8$]

(b) $\frac{2^6}{2^2} = ?$ [Solution: $\frac{2^6}{2^2} = 2^4$]

(c) $\frac{2^2}{2^6} = ?$ [Solution: $\frac{2^2}{2^6} = \frac{1}{2^4}$]

You may, of course, check the answers by computing. For example, in the last problem we have:
$$\frac{2^2}{2^6} = \frac{2 \cdot 2}{2 \cdot 2 \cdot 2 \cdot 2 \cdot 2 \cdot 2} = \frac{4}{64} = \frac{1}{16} = \frac{1}{2 \cdot 2 \cdot 2 \cdot 2} = \frac{1}{2^4}$$

Products and Factoring

You already know that, for each real number 'a',
$$2 \cdot a + 3 \cdot a = 5 \cdot a$$

This follows from the distributive principle (*see* section on fundamental concepts)
$$2 \cdot a + 3 \cdot a = (2 + 3) \cdot a$$

and the fact that 2+3=5.

Consider now the *indicated product:*
$$(a + 2) \cdot (a + 3)$$

From the basic principles it follows that:
$$(a + 2) \cdot (a + 3) = (a + 2) \cdot a + (a + 2) \cdot 3$$
$$= (a^2 + 2 \cdot a) + (a \cdot 3 + 2 \cdot 3)$$
$$= (a^2 + 2 \cdot a) + (3 \cdot a + 6)$$
$$= a^2 + (2 \cdot a + 3 \cdot a) + 6$$
$$= a^2 + 5 \cdot a + 6$$

Thus,
$$(a + 2) \cdot (a + 3) = a^2 + 5 \cdot a + 6$$

We say that the expression $a^2 + 5 \cdot a + 6$ is the *expanded* form of the indicated product
$$(a + 2) \cdot (a + 3)$$

When we transform an expression into an indicated product, we say that the expression has been *factored*. We see that the expression
$$a^2 + 5 \cdot a + 6$$

may be factored, and that its *factors* are
$$(a + 2) \text{ and } (a + 3)$$

Notice that for each pair of real numbers 'a' and 'b':
$$(a + b) \cdot (a + b) = (a + b) \cdot a + (a + b) \cdot b$$
$$= (a^2 + b \cdot a) + (a \cdot b + b^2)$$
$$= a^2 + (a \cdot b + a \cdot b) + b^2$$
$$= a^2 + 2 \cdot a \cdot b + b^2$$

Thus,
$$(a + b) \cdot (a + b) = a^2 + 2 \cdot a \cdot b + b^2$$

and we see that for each pair of real numbers 'a' and 'b', the expression

$$a^2 + 2 \cdot a \cdot b + b^2$$

may be factored.

For each pair of real numbers 'a' and 'b', the expression

$$a^2 - b^2$$

may also be factored. This is demonstrated as follows:

$$
\begin{aligned}
(a - b) \cdot (a + b) &= (a - b) \cdot a + (a - b) \cdot b \\
&= (a^2 - b \cdot a) + (a \cdot b - b^2) \\
&= (a^2 + - a \cdot b) + (a \cdot b - b^2) \\
&= a^2 + (- a \cdot b + a \cdot b) - b^2 \\
&= a^2 + 0 - b^2 \\
&= a^2 - b^2
\end{aligned}
$$

Thus,

$$(a - b) \cdot (a + b) = a^2 - b^2$$

A knowledge of factoring may be helpful when we wish to simplify a given expression. The following two examples illustrate this:

Example 1: $\dfrac{5 \cdot a + 5 \cdot b}{5} = ?$

Solution:
$$
\begin{aligned}
\frac{5 \cdot a + 5 \cdot b}{5} &= \frac{5 \cdot (a + b)}{5} \\
&= 5 \cdot (a + b) \cdot \frac{1}{5} \\
&= (a + b) \cdot \left(5 \cdot \frac{1}{5}\right) \\
&= (a + b) \cdot 1 \\
&= a + b
\end{aligned}
$$

Example 2: $\dfrac{a^2 - 4}{a - 2} = ?$ $\quad [a \neq 2]$

Solution: $\dfrac{a^2 - 4}{a - 2} = \dfrac{a^2 - 2^2}{a - 2} = \dfrac{(a - 2) \cdot (a + 2)}{a - 2} = a + 2$

A knowledge of factoring may also provide a shortcut in computing. The following example illustrates this:

Example 3: $19 \cdot 21 = ?$

Solution:
$$
\begin{aligned}
19 \cdot 21 &= (20 - 1) \cdot (20 + 1) \\
&= 20^2 - 1^2 \\
&= 400 - 1 \\
&= 399
\end{aligned}
$$

The ability to factor is also important in finding the solutions of quadratic equations. This will be shown under the subhead "Quadratic Equations."

It will be instructive for you to try to factor the following expressions by transforming each expression into an indicated product:

    (a) $3 \cdot 3 + 3 \cdot 4$

    (b) $a^2 - a \cdot b$

    (c) $a^2 - 2 \cdot a \cdot b + b^2$

Answers: (a) $3 \cdot 3 + 3 \cdot 4 = 3 \cdot (3 + 4)$

    (b) $a^2 - a \cdot b = a \cdot (a - b)$

    (c) $a^2 - 2 \cdot a \cdot b + b^2 = (a - b) \cdot (a - b)$

Quadratic Equations

Consider the equation

$$x^2 - {}^{+}25 = 0$$

This equation is an example of a *quadratic equation*. The real numbers $^{+}5$ and $^{-}5$ both *satisfy* the above open sentence:

$$\boxed{{}^{+}5}\,{}^2 - {}^{+}25 = 0$$

$$\boxed{{}^{-}5}\,{}^2 - {}^{+}25 = 0$$

The solution set of the given equation consists of simply the real numbers $^{+}5$ and $^{-}5$. We say that $^{+}5$ and $^{-}5$ are the two *roots* of the given quadratic equation.

When we are trying to find the roots of a quadratic equation, we often make use of an important principle of real numbers. This principle, which is derived from the basic principles listed in the preceding section, states that the product of a pair of real numbers is 0 if and only if one of the numbers is 0. That is,

$$\forall_x \ \forall_y \ xy = 0$$

if and only if

$$x = 0 \text{ or } y = 0$$

Let us see how we may use this principle to find the roots of the quadratic equation

$$x^2 - {}^{+}16 = 0$$

We first notice that the expression

$$x^2 - {}^{+}16$$

may be factored:

$$x^2 - {}^{+}16 = x^2 - {}^{+}4^2 = (x - {}^{+}4) \cdot (x + {}^{+}4)$$

Thus, we may transform the given equation

$$x^2 - {}^{+}16 = 0$$

into the *equivalent* equation

$$(x - {}^{+}4) \cdot (x + {}^{+}4) = 0$$

A real number satisfies the last equation if and only if it satisfies the given equation.

We know that

$$(x - {}^{+}4) \cdot (x + {}^{+}4) = 0$$

if and only if

$$x - {}^{+}4 = 0 \text{ or } x + {}^{+}4 = 0$$

Thus, a real number satisfies the equation

$$(x - {}^{+}4) \cdot (x + {}^{+}4) = 0$$

if and only if the real number satisfies one of the following equations:

$$x - {}^{+}4 = 0 \text{ or } x + {}^{+}4 = 0$$

The solution set of the equation

$$x - {}^{+}4 = 0$$

consists of simply the number $^{+}4$, since

$$\boxed{{}^{+}4} - {}^{+}4 = 0$$

The solution set of the equation

$$x + {}^{+}4 = 0$$

consists of simply the number $^{-}4$, since

$$\boxed{{}^{-}4} + {}^{+}4 = 0$$

Thus, the solution set of the equation

$$(x - {}^{+}4) \cdot (x + {}^{+}4) = 0$$

consists of the numbers $^+4$ and $^-4$. Hence the roots of the given quadratic equation

$$x^2 - {}^+16 = 0$$

are the numbers $^+4$ and $^-4$. We may check this result:

Check: $\boxed{+4}^2 - {}^+16 = 0$ and $\boxed{-4}^2 - {}^+16 = 0$

Here is another example which shows how factoring aids us in finding the roots of a quadratic equation:

Example: Find the roots of the equation

$$x^2 - {}^+3x = 0$$

Solution: The expression $x^2 - {}^+3x$ may be factored

$$x^2 - {}^+3x = (x - {}^+3) \cdot x$$

Hence the given equation may be transformed into the equivalent equation

$$(x - {}^+3) \cdot x = 0$$

A real number satisfies this equation if and only if it satisfies one of the following equations:

$$x - {}^+3 = 0 \text{ or } x = 0$$

The only real number which satisfies the equation

$$x - {}^+3 = 0$$

is $^+3$, and the only real number which satisfies the equation

$$x = 0$$

is 0. Thus, the roots of the given equation are $^+3$ and 0.

Check: $\boxed{+3}^2 - {}^+3 \cdot \boxed{+3} = 0$ and

$\boxed{0}^2 - {}^+3 \cdot \boxed{0} = 0$

SOLVING PROBLEMS

The following are some typical problems which, in a natural way, lead us to algebraic equations. In each problem, the solution to the problem is found by finding the solution set of an equation. When we find the solution set of an equation, we say that we have *solved* the equation.

Example 1: A number has such a property that when 6 is subtracted from twice the number, the result is 16. What is the number?

Solution: The required number must satisfy the open sentence

$$2 \cdot \square - 6 = 16$$

or, equivalently, the required number must satisfy each of the following open sentences:

$$(2 \cdot \square - 6) + 6 = 16 + 6$$
$$2 \cdot \square = 22$$
$$\tfrac{1}{2} \cdot (2 \cdot \square) = \tfrac{1}{2} \cdot 22$$
$$\square = 11$$

Since the only number which satisfies the last equation is 11, 11 is the required number. We may check our result:

Check: $2 \cdot \boxed{11} - 6 = 22 - 6 = 16$

Example 2: A number has such a property that when 10 is subtracted from twice the number, the result is the same as when 6 is added to the number. What is the number?

Solution: A number has the required property if and only if it satisfies the open sentence

$$2 \cdot x - 10 = x + 6$$

or, equivalently, a number has the required property if and only if it satisfies each of the following open sentences:

$$(2 \cdot x - 10) + 10 = (x + 6) + 10$$
$$2x = x + 16$$
$$-x + 2x = -x + (x + 16)$$
$$(-x + x) + x = (-x + x) + 16$$
$$x = 16$$

The only number which satisfies the last open sentence is 16. Therefore, 16 is the required number.

Check: $2 \cdot \boxed{16} - 10 = \boxed{16} + 6$

Example 3: Suppose that Tom has $6.00 more than Bill and that together they have a total of $12.00. How much money does Tom have? How much money does Bill have?

Solution: Suppose that Tom has 't' dollars and that Bill has 'b' dollars. Since Tom has $6.00 more than Bill, then

$$(1) \quad t = 6 + b$$

Since Tom and Bill have together a total of $12.00, then

$$(2) \quad t + b = 12$$

Equation (1) tells us that

$$t \text{ is the same as } 6 + b$$

We may therefore replace 't' by '6+b' in equation (2):

$$(6 + b) + b = 12$$

Thus,

$$6 + 2b = 12$$
$$2b = 6$$
$$b = 3$$

Therefore Bill has $3.00. It follows that

$$t = 6 + b = 6 + 3 = 9$$

and so Tom has $9.00.

Check:

$(1)\quad \boxed{9} = 6 + \triangle{3}$

$(2)\quad \boxed{9} + \triangle{3} = 12$

The Ahaggar is one of several heavily eroded volcanic massifs in the Saharan region of southern Algeria. This dry, barren part of the country is relatively lifeless. There is, however, an oasis on the western edge of the massif that is regularly visited by desert caravans.

J. P. Charbonnier—Photo Researchers

ALGERIA. Situated on the north coast of Africa, Algeria is the second largest country of the continent. It covers more than 900,000 square miles (2,300,000 square kilometers), about four fifths of which is in the Sahara Desert. The country's Mediterranean coastline extends about 620 miles (1,000 kilometers). Algeria is bordered by Tunisia, Libya, Niger, Mali, Mauritania, Western Sahara, and Morocco.

Eighty percent of Algeria's inhabitants live in the agricultural lands and cities of the north, called the Tell. An independent republic since it won freedom from France in 1962, Algeria has links to Europe across the Mediterranean Sea and to southern Africa via the Sahara. History, language, and the Muslim religion make the country a part of the Arab world.

Land and Climate

Northern Algeria is divided into five distinctive physical regions. Three are in the far north: the arable coastal strip, the plains just to the south, and the Tell Atlas Mountains running east and west along the plains. Farther south, the High Plateaus form another east-west barrier. The fifth region is the Saharan Atlas Mountains, which extend into the desert.

The region of the Tell Atlas Mountains is geologically young and unstable, and earthquakes are common. It has a Mediterranean climate, with warm, wet winters and hot, dry summers. Rainfall averages 28 inches (700 millimeters); mean temperatures range from 50° F (10° C) in January to 80° F (27° C) in July. Hot, dry winds from the Sahara intensify summer drought, which may severely damage crops.

The semiarid lands of the High Plateaus area form a wide, almost featureless plain. Annual rainfall ranges from 16 inches (400 millimeters) in the north to 8 inches (200 millimeters) in the south. Temperatures range from 48° F (9° C) in January to 80° F (27° C) in July. The High Plateaus region has no permanent streams.

The Saharan Atlas Mountains are rugged and vegetation is sparse. The northern edge of the mountains receives about 8 inches (200 millimeters) of rain yearly. Farther south, precipitation decreases.

The arid Sahara region consists of several large, saucer-shaped basins, plateaus, and highlands. Some of the basins contain extensive fields of sand, called ergs. To the south are large heavily eroded volcanic massifs (mountain blocks). The Ahaggar is the largest, with Algeria's highest peak, Tahat, at 9,574 feet (2,918 meters). At the desert's northern edge, the annual rainfall is about 7 inches (175 millimeters). Average temperatures range from 45° F (7° C) in January to 85° F (29° C) in July. The central Sahara has less than one inch (25 millimeters) of rainfall annually; average temperatures range from 57° F (14° C) in January to 99° F (37° C) in July.

Plant and Animal Life

Plant and animal life relate to the patterns of rainfall. The amount of rainfall increases from west to east but decreases from north to south. The Saharan Atlas Mountains roughly divide the country into two principal agricultural and vegetation zones. North of the mountains, dry farming is possible, and fine forests and abundant vegetation are found. Cork oaks grow, along with grapes, olives, citrus fruits, grain, tobacco, and cotton. Other trees include Aleppo pines, evergreen oaks, and thugas. To the south, vegetation common to steppe regions, including esparto grass or wormwood, appears. Some plants grow quickly after a rain and disappear almost at once. Grasses, stunted shrubs, athels, acacia, jujube trees, and other plants can survive despite meager rainfalls.

Vegetation on the High Plateaus consists mainly of scattered bushes and clumps of grasses. Seasonal pastures are used for grazing livestock. Depending on the amount of rainfall, the cultivation of grain crops may be possible. In 1975 the government began to plant a belt of trees just south of the Saharan Atlas chain. Some 930 miles (1,500 kilometers) long, it was designed to keep the desert from drifting northward.

Elephants, hippopotamuses, and crocodiles once lived in Algeria. Today, few species are found, mainly because the sparse vegetation will not support diverse animal life. Hyenas and jackals, monkeys, hawks, and desert snakes are native to the region; so are some antelope, gazelles, hares, jerboa, and wild boars. A few types of birds and insects are found.

The People

Two ethnic strains, the Arab and the Berber, predominate in Algeria. Many of the country's inhabitants are of mixed Arab and Berber descent. The Berbers originally lived in the region and today form an important element of the population; the Arabs came later, during the 600's, and today comprise about 90 percent of the population. But no sharp division between the two exists.

Islam, the religion of the Muslims, helps to unify Algeria's peoples. About 99 percent of the population is Muslim; the great majority belongs to the Sunni sect of Islam (see Islam; Mohammed). Most of the others are Roman Catholics of French descent.

Both Berber and Arabic are spoken in Algeria. But most Berbers also speak Arabic, the official language. Even though most of the French residents left after 1962, French continued to be used as a second lan-

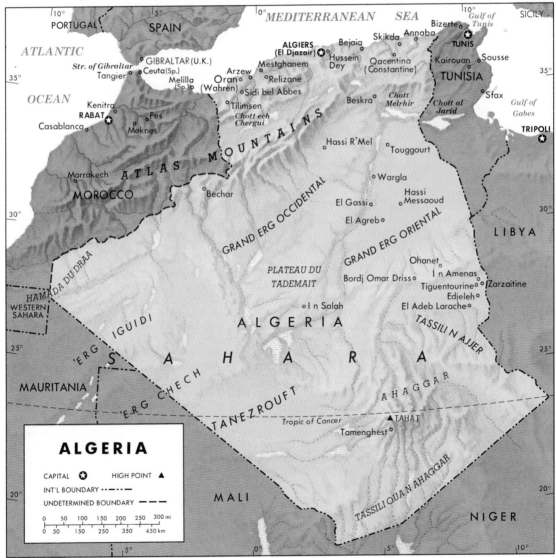

303

guage. Efforts have been made to increase the use of Arabic. At the same time the Berbers have struggled to keep their own language and culture.

Algeria's peoples follow ways of life that vary from region to region. In the capital, Algiers, and other cities many people live in the style of Europeans (*see* Algiers). In the northern plains, farmers lead simple lives while seminomadic and nomadic groups range the highlands and deserts (*see* Nomad).

Working to preserve the traditional Arabic and Muslim culture, the government has at the same time encouraged original artistic and cultural forms. In 1968 the National Institute of Music began programs to encourage traditional music and dances and preserve folklore. Many of these forms developed from Arabian and Spanish Andalusian styles. The Algerian National Theater has presented the Arabic-language works of Algerian playwrights. In painting, the themes of revolution and socialism have been widely used. Craft workers produce inlaid furniture, rugs, earthenware, camel-skin products, jewelry, and a variety of other goods.

Economy

The Algerian government controls the nation's economy. Since independence, Algeria has nationalized most foreign-owned companies and properties. The government also runs all heavy industry and controls the production and distribution of petroleum, natural gas, and minerals.

Most Algerians work in agriculture, but less than 10 percent of the arable land is permanently cultivated. On the coastal plains, cereal grains, grapes, olives, and citrus fruits are the principal crops. Cereals—primarily wheat and barley—and livestock herding are important in the Tell Atlas and the High Plateaus. Permanent meadows and pastures are used by pastoral nomads to support goats, sheep, and camels.

The Algerian government has enacted several land reform programs since independence. In 1971, for example, large farms were redistributed to landless peasants who were organized into agricultural cooperatives. The government also nationalized 6.7 million acres (2.8 million hectares) of pastureland.

Petroleum and natural gas are Algeria's main exports. The major oil fields are located in the northeastern Sahara and on the Libyan border. Algeria has petroleum reserves of 8.2 billion barrels (1981 estimate). Natural gas reserves are the fourth largest in the world (1981 estimate). Most of the reserves are at Hassi R'Mel, 400 miles (640 kilometers) south of Algiers. Gas is piped to the coast in liquefied form. In the early 1980's, the government was investing in new pipelines, liquefaction plants, and tankers.

Algeria also has abundant mineral resources. It mines and exports high-grade iron ore, phosphates, lead, zinc, and antimony. Three fourths of the iron ore is produced at Ouenza.

Manufacturing accounts for only a small part of Algeria's income. The major industries are iron, steel, and petroleum refining. The production of fertilizers and the manufacture of industrial vehicles and farm machinery are also important. The country's growing industries include paper, textiles, electrical goods, and flour milling.

Transportation, Communication, and Education

Two thirds of Algeria's roads and railroad tracks are in the north. Main roads link towns and large cities and extend to the petroleum and natural gas fields. The trans-Saharan "Road of African Unity" has been completed to Tamenghest. Algeria has some 2,450 miles (3,950 kilometers) of railway.

Algiers is the country's main port. Other important ports are Annaba and Oran (Wahren). Houari Boumedienne, near Algiers, is a modern jet airport. Annaba, Qacentina (Constantine), and Oran have smaller modern airports. Air Algérie (Air Algeria) provides domestic and international service.

In the 1970's and early 1980's, Algeria's postal, telephone, and telegraph services were expanding. The official Algerian Press Service reported local and international news for radio, television, and newspapers. Two Arabic-language and two French-language newspapers were being published in Algiers. Founded in 1962, the Algerian Radio and Television System now broadcasts throughout the country. Programs are produced in Arabic and French.

Starting in 1962, the Algerian government tried to open educational opportunities for all citizens. Arabic was to replace French as the language of instruction, but the changeover proceeded slowly. From a literacy rate below 20 percent in 1954, Algeria's population developed a rate between 25 and 30 percent by the middle 1970's. Eighty percent of all school-age children were receiving educations by the early 1980's. Ten major universities serve thousands of students, and more are planned.

Government and History

Algeria is a socialist state that is controlled by the National Liberation Front (*Front de Liberation Nationale*, or FLN) party. The president is the head of state. He must be more than 40 years old and a Muslim. The president is nominated by the FLN party; he is elected by popular vote for a five-year term. He may be reelected for any number of consecutive terms. The president presides over a Council of Ministers, all of whom he appoints. The National Popular Assembly passes all national laws.

Berbers made up the majority of ancient Algeria's population. The country was called Numidia by the Romans. The Berbers were conquered by successive waves of invaders—Phoenicians, Carthaginians, Romans, and Vandals. Arab armies conquered Algeria in the 7th and 8th centuries. Mass Arab migrations to Algeria followed in the 11th century. Although the Berbers converted to Islam, they later resisted Arab rule and joined radical Islamic sects.

The Ottoman Turks gained control of northern Algeria in 1518 (*see* Turkey). By the 17th century, Algiers maintained diplomatic relations with European states and profited by piracy in the Mediterranean Sea. Piracy flourished until 1815, when an American fleet under Stephen Decatur defeated the corsairs, or Barbary coast pirates. The Berbers maintained their independence under Turkish rule.

France conquered Algiers in 1830. The country was not wholly subdued until 1857, when the last Berbers surrendered. The French confiscated most of the best land in the Tell Atlas and the High Plateaus for French colonization. By 1961 1.5 million Europeans, about one half of whom were born in Algiers, were in control of the country's economy, its politics, and its foreign policy.

The Algerian nationalist movement began after World War I. Attempts to improve the position of Algerian Arabs and Berbers were unsuccessful. The promises of the new constitution of 1947 went unfulfilled, and a war of independence began in 1954 under the leadership of the FLN. After Charles de Gaulle came to power in France in 1958, he agreed that Algeria should be independent. A truce was signed in March 1962. After a referendum Algeria was declared independent on July 3, 1962.

Ahmed Ben Bella became premier of the new republic in September (see Ben Bella, Ahmed). One year later, after a new constitution was adopted, Ben Bella became president. Economic reconstruction was the major government goal. More than seven years of war and the departure of the Europeans after 1962 had left Algeria in trouble. Most of the labor force was unemployed and unskilled. In 1965, Col. Houari Boumedienne replaced Ben Bella in a military coup. Boumedienne installed a revolutionary regime dedicated to socialism and political and economic independence. Boumedienne died in December 1978 and Col. Chadli Bendjedid was elected president. Algeria played a major role in the release of American hostages by Iran in January 1981.

BIBLIOGRAPHY FOR ALGERIA

Carpenter, Allan and Balow, John. Enchantment of Africa: Algeria (Childrens, 1978).
Horne, Alistair. A Savage War of Peace: Algeria, 1954–1962 (Viking Press, 1978).
Picles, D. M. Algeria and France (Greenwood, 1976).
Wolf, J. B. The Barbary Coast: Algeria Under the Turks (Norton, 1979).

Algeria Fact Summary

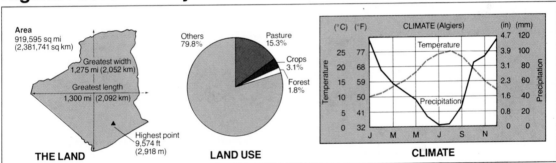

THE LAND — Area 919,595 sq mi (2,381,741 sq km); Greatest width 1,275 mi (2,052 km); Greatest length 1,300 mi (2,092 km); Highest point 9,574 ft (2,918 m)

LAND USE — Others 79.8%; Pasture 15.3%; Crops 3.1%; Forest 1.8%

CLIMATE (Algiers)

Official Name: Democratic and Popular Republic of Algeria.
Capital: Algiers (El Djazair).

NATURAL FEATURES

Mountain Ranges: Atlas Mountains, Ahaggar.
Highest Peak: Tahat, 9,574 feet (2,918 meters).
Principal Physical Features: Sahara Desert, Grand Erg Oriental, Grand Erg Occidental, High Plateaus.
Major Rivers: No navigable rivers.

PEOPLE

Population (1980 estimate): 18,525,000; 20 persons per square mile (8 persons per square kilometer); 61 percent urban, and 39 percent rural.
Major Cities: Algiers (El Djazair, 1,998,000), Oran (Wahren, 500,000), Qacentina (Constantine, 430,000), Annaba (340,000), Tizi Ouzou (230,000), Sidi Bel Abbes (158,000).
Major Religions: Islam (official), Christianity.
Major Languages: Arabic (official), Berber, and French.
Literacy: About 30 percent of the people can read and write.
Leading Universities: University of Algiers (El Djazair); University of Qacentina (Constantine); University of Oran (Wahren); University of Science and Technology of Algiers.

GOVERNMENT

Form of Government: Republic.
Chief of State and Head of Government: President of the Republic nominated by the National Liberation Front party; elected by popular vote for five-year term.

Legislature: National Popular Assembly; elected by vote for five-year term.
Voting Qualifications: Age 19.
Political Divisions: 31 Provinces (Wilayas):
Adrar; Algiers (El Djazair); Annaba; Batna; Bechar; Bejaia; Beskra (Biskra); Bouira; Ech Cheliff (El Asnam); El Boulaida (Blida); El Djeffa (Djeffa); Guelma; Jijel; Laghouat; Lemdiyya (Medea); Mestghanem (Mostaganem); Mouaskar (Mascara); M'Sila; Oran (Wahran); Oum el Bouagui (Oum el Bouaghi); Qacentina (Constantine); Saida; Sidi Bel Abbes; Skikda; Stif (Setif); Tamenghest (Tamanrasset); Tbessa (Tebessa); Tihert (Tiaret); Tilimsen (Tlemcen); Tizi Ouzou; Wargla (Ouargla).
Flag: Rectangular, one green and one white vertical band with red crescent and star in center (see Flags).

ECONOMY

Chief Agricultural Products: *Crops*—barley, dates, grapes, oats, olives, onions, oranges, potatoes, tangerines, tomatoes, watermelons, wheat. *Livestock*—camels, cattle, donkeys, goats, horses, poultry, sheep.
Chief Mined Products: Antimony, crude petroleum, iron ore, lead, natural gas, phosphates, zinc.
Chief Manufactured Products: Cement, crude steel, fertilizer, motor vehicles, petroleum products.
Chief Exports: Crude petroleum, natural gas, petroleum products, wine.
Chief Imports: Chemicals, food, iron and steel, machinery (electrical and nonelectrical), motor vehicles, textile yarn and fabrics.
Monetary Unit: 1 dinar = 100 centimes.

ALGIERS, or **EL DJAZAIR, Algeria.** The capital of Algeria, Algiers is located between the Mediterranean Sea and the Sahara Desert. It lies on the Bay of Algiers and extends along the slopes of the Sahel Hills. Algiers has a distinctly seasonal climate of cool, wet winters and hot, dry summers.

The city was founded in ancient times by the Phoenicians. After being destroyed by a series of invasions, it was revived by the Berbers in the 10th century as a commercial center. Under the Turks in the 17th century it became a flourishing city.

In April 1827, an incident led to the French conquest of Algeria. A claim by two Algerian citizens for payment for wheat delivered to France had been outstanding since the end of the 18th century. While discussing this claim, a Turkish officer struck the French consul with a fly whisk. To avenge this insult, France, under Charles X, instituted a naval blockade. When this had no effect, the French sent a military and naval expedition and took Algiers in 1830. The city became a military and administrative headquarters for France's colonial empire.

During World War II Algiers became the headquarters of Allied forces in North Africa and for a time the provisional capital of France. In the 1950's Algiers was the scene of much fighting and bloodshed during the Algerian struggle for independence from France, which was achieved in 1962.

Contemporary Algiers has grown up around the old Muslim town with its narrow, winding streets. Modern office buildings and apartment houses in southern European style create a white city that gleams next to the blue waters of the bay. Ancient ruins still exist near the city's main square. Two beautiful mosques are also preserved, one that is from the 11th century and one that is from the 17th century. Part of the national library is housed in a 1798 Moorish palace. The old quarter includes the Kasbah, or Casbah, a section that has been romanticized in literature.

The sparkling white, modern city of Algiers lies between the Bay of Algiers and the Sahel Hills.

Dominique Darbois

After independence, about half of the Europeans left and many Algerians migrated to the city. The educational system was reorganized, increasing the number of people being educated. Algiers has two universities, the University of Algiers and the University of Science and Technology of Algiers.

The city has four daily newspapers. There are several weeklies and an army paper that is published in both Arabic and French. One television station operates within the city.

The city's main exports are wine, vegetables, oranges, iron ore, and phosphates. Algiers has an international airport, Houari Boumedienne, which has regular flights to Tunisia, Morocco, and a number of European countries. The airport is also a principal stop on regular air routes between Europe and Africa south of the Sahara, as well as on the routes of eastward-bound flights from the Americas. (*See also* Algeria.) Population (1978 estimate), 1,998,000.

ALHAMBRA *see* SPAIN.

ALI, Muhammad (born 1942). One of the greatest United States heavyweight boxing champions, Muhammad Ali was also one of the nation's most controversial figures. He was almost as renowned for his flamboyant personality as for his boxing ability. His motto was "I am the greatest!" He became the first boxer to win the heavyweight title three times.

Ali was born Cassius Marcellus Clay in Louisville, Ky., on Jan. 17, 1942. His name was changed when he joined the Black Muslim religious sect in later years. Ali began boxing as an amateur at the age of 12. In 1960 he won Amateur Athletic Union, Golden Gloves, and Olympic Games championships. Ali won a share of the world heavyweight championship on Feb. 25, 1964, when he defeated Sonny Liston. On Feb. 6, 1967, Ali outpointed Ernie Terrell, the World Boxing Association champion, and became the undisputed world champion.

After Ali joined the Black Muslims he refused, on religious grounds, to be drafted into the armed forces. He was convicted in 1967 of violating the Selective Service Act, barred from boxing, and stripped of his title. His conviction was reversed by the United States Supreme Court in 1971.

In New York City on March 8, 1971, he lost a 15-round decision to the heavyweight champion, Joe Frazier. Ali won a unanimous decision over Frazier in New York City on Jan. 28, 1974. His eighth-round knockout of George Foreman on Oct. 30, 1974, in Kinshasa, Zaire, regained for Ali the world heavyweight title. After defending his title successfully six times, he lost to Leon Spinks on Feb. 15, 1978. He then won the title for the third time, defeating Spinks in September 1978.

Muhammad Ali retired in 1979. He had lost only 3 decisions in 59 fights. Coming out of retirement, Ali was defeated by champion Larry Holmes in the tenth round of a fight in Las Vegas, Nev., on Oct. 2, 1980. (*See also* Boxing.)

ALIEN AND SEDITION ACTS. The administration of President John Adams drew sharp criticism from newspaper editors and public speakers. To check these attacks Congress passed four measures in 1798 called the Alien and Sedition Acts.

These measures were: (1) a naturalization act, making a residence of 14 years necessary before foreigners could become citizens; (2) an alien act, giving the president power to deport any aliens judged "dangerous to the peace and safety of the United States"; (3) an alien enemies act, still in force, by which subjects of an enemy nation might be deported or imprisoned in wartime; (4) a sedition act, providing heavy penalties for conspiracy against the government or for interfering with its operations.

Public outrage against the acts was voiced throughout the land. Two of the most reasoned responses to them were sets of resolutions passed by the Virginia and Kentucky legislatures. Written respectively by James Madison and Thomas Jefferson, these resolutions affirmed the rights of the states to determine the validity of laws passed by the federal government. Thirty years later John C. Calhoun adopted this notion as the basis for his theory of nullification of federal laws (*see* Calhoun).

ALKALI METALS. The chemical elements that are identified as alkali metals are lithium, sodium, potassium, rubidium, cesium, and the extremely rare radioactive substance called francium. They occupy the first column of the periodic table of the elements. The alkali metals are so called because they form *alkalies*—that is, strong bases capable of neutralizing acids—when they combine with other elements (*see* Acids and Bases).

Alkali metals bear little resemblance to more familiar metals such as iron and tin. They are silver-white in color, malleable, and soft enough to cut with a knife. The alkali metals are the most chemically active of all metals, readily forming ions with a single positive electric charge. This property is a consequence of their atoms having only a single, highly mobile electron in the outermost shell. Alkali metals react rapidly, sometimes violently, with both oxygen and water. Because of their reactivity, they always occur in nature combined with other elements as simple or complex compounds. Pure alkali metals can be extracted from such compounds through the electrolysis of fused (molten) salts or hydroxides (*see* Electrochemistry). Another process, which is called thermal reduction, is also used to obtain lithium and cesium. In the laboratory pure alkali metals are generally stored in oil to prevent them from forming compounds with other elements.

The only members of the alkali metal family that are fairly abundant in the Earth's crust are sodium and potassium. Because these elements and their compounds have many important uses, they are discussed in separate articles (*see* Potassium; Sodium).

Lithium, the lightest known metal, and its alloys are used in treating steel to improve its tensile

THE ALKALI METALS			
Lithium	Li	Rubidium	Rb
Sodium	Na	Cesium	Cs
Potassium	K	Francium	Fr

strength. They also are utilized to remove impurities from copper and certain other metals. Lithium salts are added to glass, porcelain enamels, and ceramic glazes to render them heat-resistant. Some such salts, furthermore, are employed in experimental high-voltage batteries for electrically powered automobiles. Lithium compounds have various other applications, as, for example, the use of lithium carbonate as a medication for a mental disorder called manic depressive psychosis.

Metallic rubidium ionizes extremely rapidly when struck by light and so is used in photocells. Cesium metal has even better photoelectric properties, making it particularly useful for scientific instruments designed to measure very weak electromagnetic radiation emitted by cosmic rays and nuclear particles. Methods of power generation exploiting the ionization of cesium are under investigation, as is the use of the element as a solid fuel for ion-propulsion engines for spacecraft.

Francium closely resembles cesium in its chemical properties but is unstable. A radioactive decay product of actinium, it in turn rapidly breaks down into radium or astatine. Therefore it exists only briefly in nature. Physicists, however, have succeeded in producing francium artificially by bombarding thorium in devices called particle accelerators.

ALKALINE EARTH METALS. The family of chemical elements called the alkaline earth metals consists of beryllium, magnesium, calcium, strontium, barium, and radium. These chemical elements occupy the second column of the periodic table. The designation of earth for these elements comes from the Middle Ages when alchemists referred to many substances that were insoluble in water and unchanged by fire as earths (*see* Alchemy).

Alkaline earth metals are basically grayish white, though they differ somewhat in shade of color. All of them are malleable, but they vary considerably in hardness. Beryllium, for example, is hard enough to cut glass, while barium is as soft as lead. Unlike the alkali metals, many alkaline earth metals are insoluble in water. They are, however, very active chemically, readily combining with most oxides and with many nonmetals; thus they never occur as pure metals in nature. Except for magnesium, the pure metals can be obtained through the electrolysis of fused, or molten, salts (*see* Electrochemistry).

THE ALKALINE EARTH METALS			
Beryllium	Be	Strontium	Sr
Magnesium	Mg	Barium	Ba
Calcium	Ca	Radium	Ra

Magnesium and calcium are the only abundant alkaline earth metals in the Earth's crust. They are also the most commercially important members of the family and so are treated in separate articles (*see* Calcium; Magnesium).

Although the lightest of the rigid metals, beryllium is extremely strong. Moreover, it has high resistance to both heat and corrosion and can be machined to very close tolerances. For these reasons it is valuable for aerospace applications such as in the manufacture of structural components for rockets and spacecraft. In addition, beryllium is added to copper alloys used in cutting tools and in springs to improve their resilience and resistance to fatigue.

Strontium compounds have several uses. Strontium nitrate is utilized in flares and pyrotechnic devices because it burns with an intense red flame. Strontium sulfide has luminescent properties and is used in certain kinds of luminous paints. Two artificially produced isotopes of the element, strontium-89 and strontium-90, are extremely hazardous to health. Found in the fallout of certain nuclear explosions, these long-lived radioactive isotopes damage bone marrow and induce cancer.

Barium metal, like metallic strontium, has few uses. A number of its compounds, however, are important industrially. Barium carbonate, for example, is used in producing fine glassware and optical glass. Barium sulfate, a highly insoluble salt, serves as a pigment in paints and cosmetics and as a filler in paper and rubber goods. It also has an important medical application. Physicians commonly have their patients ingest a solution of barium sulfate before making radiographs (X-ray pictures) of the gastrointestinal, or digestive, tract. The barium compound absorbs X rays, providing an excellent contrasting medium that causes the intestines to stand out distinctly on the radiographs.

Radium, the heaviest of the alkaline earth metals, is highly radioactive and is continuously formed in nature by the decay of uranium-238. For many years radium was used for treating cancerous tumors, but it has largely been supplanted for this purpose by certain less hazardous radioactive isotopes such as cobalt-60. It remains the chief source of the radioactive element radon, which is also employed in certain medical procedures.

ALLEN, Ethan (1738–89). One of the first heroes of the American Revolution was Ethan Allen. He was especially famed for leading a small force against the British at Fort Ticonderoga and winning a bloodless surrender on May 10, 1775.

Ethan Allen was born in Litchfield, Conn., on Jan. 21, 1738. In 1757 he served in the French and Indian War, at Fort William Henry on the New York frontier. In 1762 Allen married Mary Bronson. They had five children. Soon after he was married, he moved to the New Hampshire Grants (now Vermont) and bought farmlands. Both New York and New Hampshire claimed this area under their colonial grants.

Allen was a leader among the New Hampshire claimants, and in 1770 he was made the head of an irregular force that was called the Green Mountain Boys. Their attacks upon the Yorkers led the New York governor to offer a reward of £100 (about $485) for Allen's capture.

When the American Revolution started, Allen and members of the Connecticut assembly raised a small force. He led this band and his Green Mountain Boys against Fort Ticonderoga. They arrived at dawn, and the astonished British commander surrendered. In the autumn Allen was captured while attacking Montreal. In 1778 an exchange of prisoners between the British and Americans brought Allen's release.

During this time the Hampshire Grant settlers had organized a provisional government and asked Congress for statehood (*see* Vermont). This government made Allen a major general. After they failed to win statehood, Allen plotted with the British to make Vermont a separate British province. For his part in this affair, he was accused of treason, but later the charge was dropped. In 1783 his wife died, and about a year later he married Frances Buchanan. They had three children. Allen died on Feb. 12, 1789.

ALLEN, Richard (1760–1831). A pioneer black abolitionist and founder of the African Methodist Episcopal church, Richard Allen was born a slave on Feb. 14, 1760, in Philadelphia. While a child, he was sold with his family to a farmer living near Dover, Del. There Allen grew to manhood and became a Methodist. He succeeded in converting his master, who allowed him to hire out his time. By cutting wood and working in a brickyard, Allen earned the money to purchase his freedom.

After the American Revolution, Allen traveled through the East preaching to blacks and whites alike. In 1784 he was ordained as a Methodist minister. He was called to Philadelphia in 1786 to preach to the racially mixed congregation at St. George's Church. As the number of black worshipers increased, they were eventually denied their customary seats. One day they were restricted to the gallery. When Allen and several others knelt to pray at the front of the gallery, they were forcibly moved back by several whites. Rather than submit to further degradation, they walked out of the church.

Acting on a proposal Allen had made some time earlier, he and his followers raised the money to build their own church. Named Bethel (House of God), it was dedicated in 1794. It was joined by other eastern black congregations in 1816 to form the African Methodist Episcopal church. Chosen its bishop, Allen labored to the end of his life to make the church a unifying force among American blacks.

With the black clergyman Absalom Jones, Allen organized Philadelphia's blacks to nurse and bury yellow-fever victims in 1792 and 1793. In 1830 Allen led the first national black convention in denouncing attempts to colonize American blacks in Africa. Allen died on March 26, 1831.

ALLEN, Woody (born 1935). The "poet of America's emotionally disenfranchised," Woody Allen weaves his fables of urban anxiety in a framework of classic slapstick. But, instead of banana peels, his anxiety-prone characters slip on their hang-ups, their fantasies, and, most of all, their relationships.

Woody's view of life is as a concentration camp from which no one can escape alive. His wry comedies deal with his alter egos' evasion of this reality through unsatisfactory distractions—the games they play and the options they waste. The original title for his most personal film was 'Anhedonia', a psychoanalytic term for the incapacity to experience pleasure.

Woody was born Allen (or Alan) Stewart Konigsberg on Dec. 1, 1935, in Brooklyn, N.Y. His parents, Martin and Nettie Konigsberg, were Orthodox Jews, and he attended Hebrew school for eight years. He loathed and regretted all his schooling, including a few months spent flunking out of two New York colleges: "I like to be taught to read and write and add and then be left alone."

Until he was 18, Woody read nothing but comic books. But he was a natural writer. In between playing baseball and practicing magic tricks and teaching himself jazz clarinet, he began selling one-liners for a dime apiece to gossip columnists. He was only 15 when a public relations firm hired him to produce jokes wholesale—50 jokes a day for $25 a week. Two years later he became a television staff writer, contributing material for most of the top comedy shows during the "Golden Age of Television."

In the early 1960's Woody Allen began performing as a stand-up comic. His wistful appearance, flustered mannerisms, querulous Flatbush accent, and self-deprecating jokes created a "schlemiel image." Because his humor relied on verbal cartoons that were fantasies or exaggerations from his own life, his live concert records were also popular.

The growing Woody cult brought an offer to write and act in a movie, which became the surrealistic farce 'What's New, Pussycat?' (1965). 'What's Up, Tiger Lily?' (1966) was a Japanese spy film that he converted into a comedy by dubbing in his own free-wheeling dialogue. Meanwhile, he had two Broadway hits—'Don't Drink the Water' (1966) and 'Play It Again, Sam' (1969), in which he played a neurotic film critic who enlists the help of Humphrey Bogart's ghost to get a girl. The film version (1972) revealed the first elements of Allen's bent for visual parody. Later films contained homages to such directors as Bergman, Eisenstein, and Fellini.

To maintain control over his material, Allen became a director with 'Take the Money and Run' (1969), a mock documentary about a would-be public enemy. 'Bananas' (1971) depicted life as a television game show. Other cartoon films, in which the bizarre sight gags submerge Allen's anguish, were 'Everything You Wanted to Know About Sex (1972), 'Sleeper' (1973), and 'Love and Death' (1975).

By the time he made the introspective 'Annie Hall' (1977), his definitive chronicle of the flaws and fail-

Diane Keaton (left) appeared in many of Woody Allen's films. As 'Annie Hall', she was a perfect foil for his insecurities.

ures of relationships, Allen was willing to delete scattershot gags that would have damaged its credibility. It brought him three Academy awards—for best picture, best direction, and best screenplay. (Diane Keaton, a longtime companion and the prototype Allen heroine, also won an Oscar for best actress.)

There was no role for Allen in his stark and stylized 'Interiors' (1978). In 'Manhattan' (1979), a paean to the city he "adored," Allen was again the romantic cynic in search of "a decent life amidst all the junk of contemporary culture." Because audiences view his works as autobiographical, they rejected the mordant 'Stardust Memories' (1980), which seemed to reject them in its portrait of a funnyman who wants to make serious movies. Allen's favored refrain of erratic couplings and uncouplings reappeared in a 'A Midsummer Night's Sex Comedy' (1982).

Two brief marriages—to Harlene Rosen, a teacher, and the actress Louise Lasser—ended in divorce. In 'Manhattan' he complained, "I've never had a relationship with a woman that lasted as long as Hitler's with Eva Braun."

Allen has been in psychoanalysis for more than half his life. He regularly plays clarinet with a New Orleans-style jazz group, but he insists that his real ambition is to be a black basketball player. Given his short, frail stature and thick horn-rimmed glasses, he was an ideal character for his own syndicated comic strip. The notes for one of his antic essay collections, 'Side Effects' (1980), conclude that his "one regret in life is that he is not someone else."

ALLERGY. Some people suffer from hay fever when pollen is in the air. Others develop skin rashes when they touch certain substances. Still others experience stomach cramps after eating particular foods. These ailments are all caused by allergic reactions to various substances. In most cases, an allergy causes relatively mild symptoms such as sneezes from breathing dust. A rare and severe allergic reaction can trigger anaphylactic shock that occasionally leads to death. Death from bee stings is an example of this severe type of allergic reaction.

An allergy develops in much the same way as does an immunity against an infectious disease (*see* Disease, section on infectious diseases). Several things happen to cause an allergy. First, a person is exposed to a substance such as pollen. The bodies of most people simply ignore pollen, but others treat pollen as a foreign invader. When this happens, a substance in the blood known as an antigen becomes active. Antigens cause the formation of antibodies whose job it is to fight off the invading substance.

Antibodies are normally in the blood and are activated by the antigen to which each is specifically linked. For instance, if a person who is allergic to shrimp eats the food, an antigen to shrimp will cause the formation of antibodies whose only function is to work against that one antigen.

Antigens that cause allergies are called allergens. The most common of these include dust, pollens, foods, animal danders (bits of dry skin or fur), insect venoms, cosmetics, soap, and drugs. Heat, cold, sunlight, and the emotions can also act as allergens.

Of the two people in ten who have some sort of allergy, many belong to families in which parents and other close relatives also have allergies. An inherited tendency to asthma, for instance, appears to be quite common. Specific allergies, such as those to pollen, are not inherited. A person becomes sensitive, or allergic, to pollen as a result of exposure to it.

How an Allergy Develops

Regardless of differences in the causes of allergies, the process by which they affect the body can be described in a general way. First, a person must be susceptible to some specific substance, or allergen. The first time one is exposed to this allergen, one's body makes antibodies against it. The body readies itself to fight the effects of the substance. The next time one comes in contact with the substance, the antibodies react, causing the release of the chemical histamine from cell tissues. This is the most important factor in producing symptoms of allergy.

Histamine is present in all animal and vegetable tissues. It is neutral, or harmless, while it remains inside the cells. When histamine is released, however, it triggers a series of dramatic actions. The blood vessels become larger, and the speed of the blood flowing through them slows. These changes in size and volume of cells and blood allow fluid to leak through cell walls. This fluid causes swelling, or edema, of the surrounding tissues. The inflamed tissue becomes irritated and swollen. Puffy, red eyelids and a stuffy nose in hay fever are examples.

Histamine also causes smooth muscles to contract. Smooth muscles are also called involuntary, meaning they do not respond to commands to act as do other types of muscle. Smooth muscles are found mostly in the internal organs, the intestines, blood vessels, and breathing passages. The effect of histamine on these muscles can provoke an asthma attack or induce cramps and pain in the stomach.

Treatment

Most people learn quickly the substances to which they are allergic. When possible, one should avoid contact with the pollens, foods, or whatever has previously caused an allergic reaction. Many substances are so widespread, however, that it is difficult to avoid them. These include dust, pollens, and polluted air. Reactions to these can be lessened by taking antihistamines (*see* Antihistamine).

When allergy is severe, it is possible to desensitize the person to the offending allergen. This is done by a physician who injects a small amount of an extract of the allergen under the skin. The dose is gradually increased until a tolerance to the allergen is built up.

ALLIGATOR AND CROCODILE. Humans have always feared large, flesh-eating reptiles, and with good reason. Alligators and crocodiles, in addition to being among the ugliest of all living creatures, can also be among the most dangerous.

The term crocodilian is applied to any of the order Crocodilia—alligators, caimans, and gavials, as well as true crocodiles. There are about 20 species of living crocodilians, all of which are lizardlike, egg-laying meat-eaters. The largest modern reptiles, they constitute the last living link with the dinosaurlike reptiles of prehistoric times. (*See also* Reptiles.)

Crocodiles are tropical reptiles belonging to the family Crocodylidae. They are usually found near swamps, lakes, and rivers in Asia, Australia, Africa, Madagascar, and the Americas. The best known species is the Nile, or African, crocodile (*Crocodylus niloticus*). Like the saltwater, or estuarine, crocodile (*C. porosus*) from the coastal marshes of southern India and Malaysia, it can be a man-eater.

Alligators, which belong to the family Alligatoridae, are found in two freshwater locales. The American alligator (*Alligator mississipiensis*) inhabits the southeastern United States from North Carolina to Florida and west to the lower Rio Grande. The Chinese alligator (*A. sinensis*) is found in the Yangtze River valley of China.

Alligators and crocodiles exhibit several major physical differences. Alligators have broader heads and blunter snouts. Their lower teeth fit inside the edge of the upper jaw and cannot be seen when the lipless mouth is closed. The crocodile's fourth tooth in each side of the lower jaw is always visible. The teeth are used for seizing and holding prey instead of for chewing. They are replaced continuously as new ones grow up, forcing old ones out.

All crocodilians are characterized by a lizardlike shape and a thick skin composed of close-set overlapping bony plates. These animals can grow to very large sizes. Adult crocodiles range from 7 to 30 feet (2 to 9 meters) long. Alligators have been known to reach 20 feet (6 meters), though 6 to 8 feet (1.8 to 2.4 meters) is the average.

Crocodiles and alligators are most at home in the water but are able to travel on land by sliding on their bellies, stepping along with their legs extended, or galloping awkwardly. Large adults can stay underwater for over an hour without breathing. They swim primarily by snakelike movements of their bodies and by powerful strokes of their muscular, oarlike tails, which are also effective weapons.

When alligators and crocodiles float in the water, they leave only their nostrils, eyes, and ears above the surface. Both animals have unusual protective features for these organs. Their eyes can be covered with semitransparent membranes, and the ears and nostrils can be closed over by folds of skin.

Life Cycle

All crocodilians are egg-laying animals. After a period of courtship and mating, which takes place in the water, the eggs are deposited in nests prepared by the mother. She then watches over them until they hatch, in two to three months. The number of eggs in a nest depends on the age and size of the mother, but may range from 30 to 100. The white, hard-shelled eggs are about the same size as chicken eggs, weighing between 1.4 and 3.2 ounces (40 and 90 grams). The eggs are incubated by sun-warmed rotting vegetation placed on them by the mother.

When still in the shell but ready to hatch, the crocodilians utter squeaking sounds. The mother, alerted by these sounds, removes the debris covering the eggs, and the young emerge by puncturing the egg with a horny growth on the tip of the snout. The mother provides little further care for her offspring.

Newborn alligators or crocodiles are about 8 to 10 inches (20 to 25 centimeters) long and are vulnerable to many predators, including fish, birds, and larger crocodilians. They increase in length about one foot (30 centimeters) per year for their first three to four years. Growth then continues more slowly. Sexual maturity occurs at about 10 years of age. Captive crocodilians may live up to 40 years; those in the wild can live much longer—some beyond 100 years.

Behavior

Crocodilians are predators and are nocturnal—that is, active mostly at night. During the day they often lie at the water's edge in large numbers, sunning themselves. At night they retreat to the water, where they live solitary lives and establish individual territories. A resident animal roars loudly at the approach of an intruder.

Young crocodiles and alligators eat worms and insects. As they mature, they add frogs, tadpoles, and fishes to their diets. Older animals eat mammals and occasionally humans.

Crocodilians capture water animals in their jaws. To catch land animals, they knock unsuspecting prey into the water with their long, powerful tails. Animals too large to be swallowed whole are either torn to pieces or are drowned and permitted to decay in burrows. These burrows, which are dug at or just

From 'Mitteilungen aus dem Zoologischen Museum in Berlin'

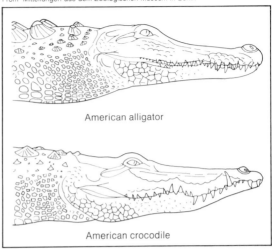

American alligator

American crocodile

The physical difference between the alligator and the crocodile is most noticeable in their snouts.

above the waterline, can extend for many feet and eventually end in a den, or chamber. The alligators hibernate in these burrows during cold weather.

Relationship to Humans

Crocodilians have always drawn strong reactions from their human neighbors, who have worshiped, feared, hunted, and tamed them for thousands of years. The ancient Egyptians considered the crocodile a symbol of the gods, and it is still regarded as sacred by some groups in Pakistan.

Crocodiles and alligators have been hunted for many reasons, including the protection of domestic animals and the safety of humans. Crocodiles are more likely to attack than are alligators, although alligators will attack when cornered. Thousands of crocodilians are killed every year by humans for sport and for commercial ventures. The skins provide leather for handbags, luggage, shoes, belts, and other items. The musk glands of some species are used in perfumes, and the fat has many industrial uses. Alligators and crocodiles have also been collected for use as pets and zoo specimens. If kept in captivity from birth, some species learn to recognize their keepers, to beg for food, and to permit petting.

The unrestricted hunting of crocodilians has severely depleted their population. The Chinese alligator is now considered rare. The disappearance of the crocodiles from parts of Africa has had a clear effect on the ecosystem. It has resulted in an overabundance of the catfish *Clarias*, which in turn has greatly diminished the supply of certain more desirable food fishes. The American alligator, on the verge of extinction in the 1960's, has been on the increase since 1973, when the Endangered Species Act gave it protection. Other governments also have passed laws to prevent the extinction of alligators and crocodiles. To reduce the need for hunting, both alligators and crocodiles have been bred and raised on farms to be harvested like other livestock.

ALLOY. A metal made of two or more mixed and fused pure metals is an alloy. A few alloys are made with a metal and one or more nonmetals. Alloys are used in millions of ways each day: Airplanes, automobiles, building metals, and cooking pots are typical objects made of alloys. We usually speak of metal articles as though they were made of such pure elements as iron, aluminum, or copper, but in fact almost all of them are alloys.

Metals in their pure states do not have a great many uses. A pure aluminum cooking pot would be weak and soft and would wear away quickly. One made of aluminum alloyed with copper or silicon can be used daily year after year. A pure-iron knife blade would become dull with its first use because pure iron is relatively soft. A knife made of iron alloyed with carbon and other elements, however, will cut well and retain its sharp edge.

Internal Structure of Alloys

All alloys, by definition, contain one or more metals. It is the internal structure of the metals in alloys that most directly determines their characteristics.

Atomic Structure. A pure metal consists of identical atoms packed closely together in an orderly (lattice-like) arrangement. The atoms are held in place by electrostatic forces.

When elements are mixed to make an alloy, the metallic element present in the largest amount by weight is called the parent metal and the others are the alloying agents. The alloying agents are dissolved in the parent metal but do not combine chemically with it. Instead, they also arrange themselves in a regular pattern, filling the spaces between the atoms of the parent metal without disturbing its basic atomic structure.

This need for orderly arrangement explains why some elements do not form alloys. Imagine a large box in which many balls are to be stacked. If all the balls are the same or nearly the same size, as basketballs and volleyballs, the job is easy. It is impossible, however, to neatly stack balls that differ widely in size, such as basketballs and golf balls. The same is true for atoms. For alloying to take place, the diameters of the atoms of the parent metal and alloying agents cannot differ by more than 15 percent. Thus, the number of possible alloys is limited.

Crystalline structure. Alloys are made up of regularly shaped crystals, some of which are so large that they can be seen with the naked eye. To study the crystals, scientists use microscopes, spectroscopes, and X rays. They have discovered that alloy crystals are collections of tiny grains between which there is a boundary material.

Some grains are hard and some are soft, because of the different elements mixed in the alloy. The hard grains support loads and resist wear. The soft grains, being more pliable, permit the hard grains to move. Thus, if one attempts to bend a piece of metal that has only hard grains, it breaks. But if hard and soft grains are intermixed, the piece can be bent.

THE ELEMENTS MOST USED IN ALLOYS

Aluminum*	Chromium*	Manganese*	Silver*
Antimony	Cobalt*	Mercury*	Sulfur*†
Beryllium	Copper*	Molybdenum*	Thorium
Bismuth	Gold*	Nickel*	Tin*
Boron†	Iridium	Palladium	Titanium*
Cadmium*	Iron*	Phosphorus*†	Tungsten*
Carbon*†	Lead*	Platinum*	Vanadium*
Cerium	Magnesium*	Silicon*†	Zinc*

There are other alloying elements besides those listed here. Almost all alloys now used, however, are made up of two or more of the elements in this list. *Element is discussed in a separate article. †Nonmetal.

In general, fine-grained metals are tougher than large-grained metals. In large-grained alloys, the boundaries may be continuous. Such a structure is weak because fewer grains interlock. This makes most large-grained alloys brittle, for they will fracture readily along their boundary lines.

Changing Alloy Structure

Heating and cooling can change the sizes and shapes of the grains of an alloy and thus its crystalline structure. An alloy is heated to a certain temperature (always below its melting point) and then cooled in different ways and at different rates to achieve various degrees of hardness and strength.

When high-carbon steel is heated above 760° C (1,400° F) and then cooled suddenly, for example, it becomes hard and brittle. This happens because the crystalline structure does not have time to change gradually as it would during a longer cooling period. It is usually desirable to temper such extreme hardness by the process of annealing. This consists of reheating the alloy and then cooling it slowly.

The Steel Alloys

Iron is the major constituent of the most frequently used alloys, the ferrous alloys, from the Latin *ferrum*, meaning "iron." When carbon is dissolved in iron, the resulting alloy is steel. The simplest such alloy, called plain carbon steel or wrought carbon steel, has varying qualities depending upon its carbon content. It can be given other qualities by including other elements. Steel containing manganese is easier to shape in rolling mills; so most steels contain it. Steels with nickel are rust resistant. Chromium steels are hard and strong. Silicon steels have magnetic properties that make them ideal in electric generators and other electrical devices.

Stainless steels, so called because they resist rust and acid corrosion, are usually alloys of iron with 10 to 20 percent chromium and 5 to 10 percent nickel. They are used to make eating utensils, lighting fixtures, decorative trim for automobiles, and many other articles. Stainless steels are also employed in machinery and vats for processing and storing chemicals that would destroy ordinary steels.

Automotive spring steels, which contain chromium, are elastic and absorb road shocks well. High-

---

SOME SPECIAL-PURPOSE STEEL ALLOYS

Type of Steel	Typical Uses*
Carbon Steels	
Plain (or wrought) carbon†	Sheets for auto bodies, tinplate for cans, structural shapes (for example, I-beams), bars, plates, saw blades, pipe, railroad-car axles
Free cutting‡	Screws, nuts, bolts, heavily machined parts
Alloy Steels§	
Chromium	Auto and truck springs, ball bearings, gears, shafts
Chromium, nickel	High-strength structural shapes; stainless steel
Nickel	Gears, rails, armor plate
Manganese	Wear-resistant parts (for example, rail intersections, excavating equipment, rock-crushing equipment, mining tools)
Tungsten, chromium, vanadium	High-speed tools
Titanium	Stoves, refrigerators, and other enameled products
Silicon	Electric motors, generators

*Only some examples are given. †Plain (or wrought) carbon steels ordinarily contain one percent or less of carbon and limited amounts of manganese, silicon and copper, and oily residues of phosphorus and sulfur. ‡Contain sulfur, selenium, or lead. §These contain small amounts of other elements not listed above.

---

speed tool steels, so named for their use in high-speed cutting tools, retain a cutting edge even when red-hot. They can be made hard enough to cut almost any material, including other very hard steels. High-speed tool steels are made of iron, tungsten, chromium, and vanadium. Tungsten is the most important element in these steels because of its high melting temperature of 3,370° C (6,098° F).

Nonferrous Alloys

Alloys that contain no iron are called nonferrous. Of these, the copper alloys are the largest group. Most copper alloys are brasses and bronzes. Brass is copper alloyed with zinc. Most kinds of brass are easily shaped and have a pleasing appearance. Bronze originally meant copper alloyed mostly with tin. Many different alloys classed as bronzes are now made by substituting other elements (zinc, lead, aluminum, phosphorus, silicon) for part or all of the tin. Most bronzes possess strength, toughness, and elasticity.

Alloys containing aluminum or magnesium are structurally strong and lightweight. They are used in spacecraft, airplanes, kitchenware, and automobiles. Monel metal, a very corrosion-resistant alloy, consists on the average of 67 percent nickel, 28 percent copper, and 5 percent other elements. Copper is often alloyed with precious metals to make coins.

Fusible Alloys

Alloys with a low melting point are called fusible alloys. They are used in solders, electric fuses, safety plugs such as those used in building sprinkler systems, and in other special applications.

Babbitt metal is one of the most important fusible alloys. It is an alloy of tin, antimony, and copper. It is used where a spinning steel shaft in a machine must be supported. In general, less friction develops between dissimilar metals than between metals that resemble one another, and Babbitt metal and steel are very dissimilar. In addition, because Babbitt metal melts at a low temperature, it can be poured into a mold fitted around a steel shaft without harm to the shaft. Once cooled, the metal forms a bearing in which the shaft rotates with little wear.

Most kinds of solders are alloys of lead and from one third to two thirds tin. Alloyed, these metals melt at a lower temperature than either does by itself. Brazing solder, which forms stronger joints than ordinary solder, is made of equal parts of copper and zinc. Silver is added for jewelry work.

Bismuth, lead, tin, and cadmium are combined to make Wood's fusible metal, an alloy that melts at 71° C (160° F). This metal makes a good fuse in an electric circuit, for when it is heated by an excess of current that might damage electrical apparatus or cause a fire, it melts, stopping the flow of current. Safety plugs made of similar alloys are used in boilers, water heaters, and pressure cookers. When the internal heat in such vessels passes the danger point, the plug melts, allowing steam to escape before the vessel explodes. Sprinkler systems hold water under pressure with a safety plug that melts and releases the water when fire causes the room temperature to rise. Some fire alarm systems use a similar safety plug.

Electric Wire Alloys

Alloys that are highly resistant to electric current produce heat and light as current flows through them. Heating units for toasters and electric stoves are made with such alloys composed of nickel and chromium. These alloys are not only highly resistant to electricity but also capable of withstanding great heat. A highly resistant alloy of tungsten and thorium is used in very-high-voltage electronic filaments. Vacuum tubes used in television sets and X-ray devices contain filaments made of an alloy of nickel, cobalt, iron, titanium, and manganese.

Some Other Alloys

Ten percent copper hardens silver coins. Sterling silver contains 7.5 percent copper. Laboratory apparatus that must resist heat and chemical action is usually made of a platinum-iridium alloy.

Small amounts of certain elements are added to some alloys to chemically expel undesired constituents. The added element does not necessarily become a valuable constituent of the alloy. Aluminum, titanium, calcium, zirconium, and lithium are commonly used in this way.

Misch metal, an alloy of 50 percent cerium and several rare-earth metals, is used during manufacture to remove undesired sulfur, gases, and oxides from other alloys. Misch metal also is alloyed with 35 percent iron to make flints for cigarette lighters and

---

SOME NONFERROUS ALLOYS

General Composition*	Name of Alloy	Special Qualities	Typical Uses†
Aluminum and copper	Lynite	Hard, strong	Machinery housings, cooking utensils
Bismuth, lead, tin, and cadmium	Wood's fusible metal	Very low melting point	Safety plugs in water heaters, boilers
Cerium and iron	Ignition pin alloy	Emits hot spark with friction	Lighter flints
Cobalt, tungsten, molybdenum, silicon, and chromium	Stellite	Extreme hardness	Cutting tools
Copper and zinc	Brass	Easily shaped, good appearance	Hardware
Copper and beryllium	Beryllium copper	Very hard, high strength	Nonsparking tools, rifle parts, small castings
Gold and palladium	White gold	Color, durability	Jewelry
Lead, antimony, tin, and copper	Type metal	Low melting point, expansion on cooling	Printing type
Lead and tin	Plumber's solder	Low melting point	Sealing metal joints
Magnesium, aluminum, silicon, manganese, copper, nickel, and zinc	Dowmetal	Lightweight, high strength	Airplane parts, complex die castings
Nickel, copper, iron, manganese, and silicon	Monel metal	Corrosion resistance	Steam valves, turbine blades
Nickel and chromium	Nichrome	Electrical resistance, nonoxidizing	Heating elements in stoves, irons, toasters
Tin, antimony, and copper	Babbitt metal	Low melting point, low friction	Bearings
Tungsten and thorium	Tungsten filament	High melting point, electrical resistance	Very high voltage electronic filaments

*The largest constituent is listed first. †These alloys have many additional uses.

---

miners' lamps. Added to carbon in carbon arc lamps, it gives the intense light required in photography and in motion-picture projection.

Platinite is a useful industrial alloy containing 46 percent nickel and 54 percent iron. When heated, this alloy expands at exactly the same rate as glass. Platinite is used to connect the socket contact and the filament through the glass of a light bulb.

Historical Development

Perhaps as early as 4000 B.C., metalworkers in the Middle East discovered that certain copper ores could be heated in a charcoal fire to produce a metal that was harder than copper, had a lower melting temperature, and was easier to cast. The ores contained tin and the alloy produced was bronze. The Bronze Age, born with this discovery, saw the spread of bronze technology throughout the world.

By 3000 B.C. copper-arsenic, copper-gold, and lead-tin alloys were also in use. Objects made of these included jewelry, mirrors, statuary, and various implements. Brass, made from copper and zinc ores, appeared between 2000 and 1000 B.C., but was not important until the Romans began to use it to make coins about 200 B.C. Great progress in metallurgy occurred under the Roman Empire. Medieval alchemists, attempting without success to transform other metals into gold, found many new alloys.

Beginning in the 6th century A.D., and for the next thousand years, the most important developments in alloying technology centered around iron and steel. In the 16th century *De la pirotechnia*, written by Vannuccio Biringucci, an Italian metalworker, and *De re metallica*, by the German miner and metallurgist Georgius Agricola, were published. In these books knowledge of metallurgy was formalized for the first time. Alloying developed from an art that depended on trial and experience into a blend of art and science based on firm principles of chemistry and physics. Present-day alloying progress is largely a matter of refinement. Occasionally new alloys are created to meet unusual specifications, such as for spacecraft, or as substitutes for materials that are becoming scarce such as tin. (*See also* Metallurgy and the articles on various alloys and metals.)

ALMOND. The almond is a nut-bearing tree of the rose family. It is related to the plum and the peach and reaches a height of 20 to 30 feet (6 to 9 meters).

Early in the spring delicate white or pink flowers bloom on the almond tree. The leaves are oval, pointed, and notched at the edges. The fruit has a soft outer coat enclosing the shell, within which is located the seed, or kernel.

A tree with white blossoms produces bitter almonds. A tree with pink blossoms bears sweet almonds. Bitter almonds are used in the manufacture of flavoring extracts and prussic acid. Sweet almonds are classified as paper-shell, soft-shell, standard-shell, and hard-shell. They may be cooked and salted for eating or processed into paste, butter, and oil.

Almonds are grown extensively in western Asia, in the Mediterranean countries, and in California. The scientific name is *Amygdalus communis*.

ALPACA *see* CAMEL.

ALPHABET

ALPHABET. To write the letters c, a, and t for "cat" seems as natural as pronouncing the word. Each letter stands for one sound in the spoken word. To write the word, the sign for each sound is simply set down in the proper order.

This kind of writing is called *alphabetic*, from the names *alpha* and *beta*—the first two letters in the Greek alphabet. Because the method is so simple, it is hard to imagine anybody writing in any other way. Actually alphabetic writing came late in history, though its prehistory dates to very ancient times.

Origin of the English Alphabet

Most people would designate as "English" the writing which is used to express the English language. This writing might also be termed "Latin," for even in its modern form English writing differs little from the Latin writing of more than 2,000 years ago. The history of Latin writing can be traced backward in a series of steps.

The Latin alphabet is a development from the Greek alphabet. The Greek alphabet, in turn, is an adaptation of a writing which was developed among the Semites of Syria about 1500 B.C. Outwardly, this first Semitic writing seems to be an original and individual creation. Its principles, however, are certainly based on the Egyptian word-syllabic writing, which, together with the Sumerian, Hittite, Chinese, and other writings, belongs to the great family of ancient Oriental systems of writing. The history of the oldest of these writings, Sumerian, can be followed from about 3100 B.C. (*See also* Writing.)

Egyptian Word-Syllabic Writing

Two kinds of signs are found in the Egyptian writing. These are word-signs and syllabic signs. The word-signs are signs which stand for words of the language, as in the English signs + for "plus," $ for "dollar," and ¢ for "cent."

The definition of syllabic signs is more difficult. The word Toledo, for example, has three syllables. In English writing the division in syllables is disregarded and only the single sounds are expressed. The ancients, however, did not know how to write single sounds, and they expressed only syllables. The ancient syllabic signs consisted of one or more consonants. Thus Toledo could be written with three signs, *To-le-do*, or with two signs, *Tole-do* or *To-ledo*. These syllables end in vowels. However, syllables ending in a consonant were written the same way. The name Lester, for example, might be written *Le-s(e)-te-r(e)*, *Les(e)-te-r(e)*, or the like. It would be taken for granted that certain vowels, here put in parentheses, would not be pronounced.

The Semitic Writings

Sometime between 1500 and 1000 B.C. the Semites of Syria and Palestine created their own systems of writing patterned after the Egyptian. They refused, however, to be burdened with the hundreds of different signs contained in the Egyptian system. They discarded all the Egyptian word-signs and all the syllabic signs with more than one consonant. The Semites retained a simple syllabary of about 30 signs, each consisting of one consonant plus any vowel.

The writings of the Phoenicians in Byblos had great influence on the development of the alphabet. The sounds of the letters in the Semitic language (left) did not correspond to those in the Greek language.

	BYBLOS	LATE GREEK		LATIN	
'	Қ	A A	(A)	A A	A
B	𐤟	Ɓ B	(B)	Ɓ B	B
G	↑	Γ ⟨ ⟨	(Γ)	⟨	C
D	△	△ △ D	(△)	Ɗ D	D
H	⋐	F E E	(E)	·· E	E
W	Y	F ⸢ F	···	·· F	F
Z	I	I	··· (Z)	····	
				·· G	G
Ḥ	⯊	B H	(H)	·· H	H
Ṭ	⊕	⊗ Θ	(Θ)	····	
J	⟨	⟨ ⟨ I	(I)	·· I	I
	··				J
K	ψ	Ϙ K	(K)	· K	K
L	⟨	Γ V Λ	(Λ)	↳ L	L
M	⟨	M M	(M)	· M	M
N	⟨	N N	(N)	·· N	N
S	⟊	‡	··· (Ξ)		
C	O	O ···	(O)	·· O	O
P	⟨	Γ Γ ··	·· (Π)	Γ P P	P
Ṣ	⟨	····	····	····	
Q	φ	φ Q		Q Q	Q
R	⟨	P R	(P)	R R	R
Š	W	⟨ ⟨ ⟨	(Σ)	⟨ S	S
T	+X	T ···	(T)	·· T	T
··	··	V Υ	(Υ)	·· V	U
			(Φ)		V
					W
··	··	+ ··	(X)	·· X	X
··	··	··	(Ψ)	·· Y	Y
··	··	··	(Ω)	·· Z	Z

ALPHABETS

	GERMAN			HEBREW			GREEK		RUSSIAN			ARABIC		
A	𝔄 α	(art)	א	ALEPH[2]		A α	ALPHA	А		(art)	١[5]		ALIF[2]	
B	𝔅 b	(bat)	בּ	BETH	(bat)	B β	BETA	Б		(bat)	ب ب ب		BE	(bat)
			ב	(VETH)[3]	(vat)			В		(vat)	ت ت ت ت		TE	(tea)
C	ℭ c	(can, its)	גּ	GIMEL	(go)	Γ γ	GAMMA	Г		(go)	ث ث ث ث		SE	(thin)
D	𝔇 d	(day)	ד	DALETH	(day)	Δ δ	DELTA	Д		(day)	ج ج ج[9]		JIM	(go, jour)
E	𝔈 e	(egg, ate)	ה	HEH	(ha)	E ε	EPSILON	Е		(yell)	ح ح ح[9]		HE	(ah!)
F	𝔉 f	(fat)	פּ	(FEH)[3]	(fat)						خ خ خ[9]		KHE	(hoch)
			ו	VAV	(vat)			Ж		(azure)	د		DAL	(day)
G	𝔊 g	(gay)	ז	ZAYIN	(zeal)	Z ζ	ZETA	З		(zeal)	ذ		ẒAL	(djug)
H	𝔥 h	(ha)[1]	ח	CHETH[4]	(hoch)	H η	ETA	И (I, V)[6]		(eel)	ر		RE	(rod)
			ט	TETH	(tea)	Θ θ	THETA				ز		ZE	(zeal)
I	𝔍 i	(it)	י	YOD	(yet)	I ι	IOTA	Й		(oil)	س س س[9]		SIN[2]	
J	𝔍 j	(yet)									ش ش ش[9]		SHIN	(shop)
K	𝔎 k	(kit)	ךּ	CAPH[5]	(can)	K κ	KAPPA	К		(kit)	ص ص ص[9]		SAD[4]	
			ךּ	CHAPH[3,5]	(hoch)						ض ض ض[9]		DAD[4]	
L	𝔏 l	(let)	ל	LAMEDH	(let)	Λ λ	LAMBDA	Л		(let)	ط		TA[4]	
M	𝔐 m	(man)	ם	MEM[5]	(man)	M μ	MU	М		(man)	ظ		ZA[4]	
N	𝔑 n	(no)	ן	NUN[5]	(no)	N ν	NU	Н		(no)	ع ع ع		AIN[2]	
			ס	SAMEKH	(see)	Ξ ξ	XI				غ غ غ		GHAIN	(gem)
O	𝔒 o	(more)	ע	AYIN[2]		O o	OMICRON	О		(other)	ف ف ف[9]		FE	(fat)
P	𝔓 p	(pay)	ףּ	PEH[5]	(pay)	Π π	PI	П		(pay)	ق ق ق[9]		QAF	(qaow)
			ץ	TSADI[4]							ك ك ك[5]		KEF	(kit)
Q	𝔔 q	(kvass)	ק	KOPH	(kit)						ل ل ل[9]		LAM	(let)
R	𝔑 r	(her)	ר	RESH	(rod)	P ρ	RHO	Р		(her)	م م م		MIM	(man)
S	𝔖 ſß[5]	(see, is)	שׂ	SIN	(see)	Σ σ s[5]	SIGMA	С		(say)	ن ن ن		NUN	(no)
			שׁ	(SHIN)[3]	(shop)						ة		HE	(ha)
T	𝔗 t	(tea)	תּ	TAV	(tea)	T τ	TAU	Т		(tea)	و		WAW	(way)
			ת	(THAV)[4]	(the)						ى ي		YE	(yet)
U	𝔘 u	(boo)				Υ υ	UPSILON	У		(boo)				
V	𝔙 v	(fat)				Φ φ	PHI	Ф (Θ)		(fat)				
W	𝔚 w	(vat)	**VOWEL POINTS**					Х		(hoch)				
X	𝔛 x	(hicks)	ָ	(awe)		X χ	CHI	Ц		(its)				
Y	𝔜 y	(yet)	ָ	(of)		Ψ ψ	PSI	Ч		(church)				
Z	𝔷 z	(its, adze)	ַ	(am)		Ω ω	OMEGA	Ш		(shop)				
			ֵ	(ere)				Щ		(Christian)				
			ֶ	(egg)				Ъ[7]						
			ִ	(it)				Ы		(nymph)				
	Pronounced with		וֹ	(no)				Ь[8]						
	Rounded Lips		וּ	(boo)				Э		(egg)				
	𝔄 ä	(ayee)	ֻ	(full)				Ю		(unit)				
	𝔒 ö	(oeh)						Я		(yard)				
	𝔘 ü	(uee)												

PRONUNCIATIONS are shown by italicized letters in English words, as *g* in (go).

[1] Pronounced at start of word, otherwise silent.

[2] Harsh vowel or silent—used in Hebrew to take vowel points.

[3] A variant of another character with a dot omitted or shifted; not counted in the alphabet.

[4] Sound not used in English.

[5] Second form final—used at ends of words.

[6] First form preferred to others.

[7] Used like ' to indicate division of words.

[8] Indicates that preceding consonant is soft.

[9] First form initial, second within words, third final.

SPECIAL LETTERS IN CERTAIN ALPHABETS

SCANDINAVIAN		POLISH			PORTUGUESE	
Æ, Ä	(care)	C, CZ	(its, itch)	Ó (boo)	Ã	(aa^{ny})
Å	(law)	DŹ, DŻ	(edge)	Ś (shop)	Ç	(cent)
Ø, Ö	(German Ö)	Ł	(wood)	Ź (jour)	Õ	(o^{ny})

In the Semitic writing the same sign stood for the syllables *pa*, *pi*, and *pu*. In other systems these syllables would be represented by three different signs. In Mycenaean and Japanese writings the distinctions in vowels were regularly indicated but not the distinctions in some related consonants. In these syllabaries three different signs would be used to indicate the vowel distinctions in *pa*, *pi*, and *pu*, but the same sign would stand for *pa*, *ba*, and *pha*.

Although the syllabic type of writing was an idea that the Semites borrowed from the Egyptians, they did not borrow the forms of the individual signs from the Egyptians. They created their own. Several early Semitic systems were used within limited areas and for a very short time only. They all died out without leaving any direct descendants.

Phoenician Syllabic Writing

About 1000 B.C. a new syllabic writing originated which was destined to have world-shaking influence upon the subsequent evolution of writing. This writing was created by the Phoenicians at Byblos, the city famous for export of the writing material known as papyrus. From this Phoenician city's name were derived the Greek word *biblia* (books) and the English word Bible. The Phoenician writing consisted of only 22 signs, because the Phoenician language had fewer consonants than the earlier Semitic languages.

After 1000 B.C. the Phoenician writing spread in all directions. The Phoenicians carried it with them on their seafaring activities along the Mediterranean coast. A form of the Phoenician system was used in Palestine by the old Hebrews and their neighbors. Another branch developed among the South Arabs, who lived in an area which corresponds roughly to modern Yemen. From the South Arabs this writing spread to Ethiopia, where it is still in use today.

One of the most important branches of the Phoenician writing is Aramaic. A form of this writing was adopted by the Hebrews. It replaced their older system, which was derived directly from the Phoenician. This new Hebrew writing is still used among the Jews of today. It is called "the square writing," after the square shape of its characters. The North Arabs took over a form of the Aramaic system and, in the course of the centuries after the rise of Islam, spread it to the far corners of the world.

The Greeks Borrow Phoenician Writing

The most important writing derived from the Phoenician is Greek, the forerunner of all the Western alphabets. All indications favor the 9th century B.C. as the time when the Greeks borrowed Phoenician writing, but this is still in some doubt. The Greeks took over from the Phoenicians the forms and names of signs, the order of the signs in the alphabet, and the direction of the writing. They made many changes, however.

The older Greek writing resembles the Phoenician very closely. Anyone who has had practice with the Phoenician writing would have no difficulties in reading correctly the individual signs of the Greek system. The later Greek forms changed considerably. They resemble more the forms of Latin, and consequently English, writing.

The names of the Greek signs were taken over, with very slight changes only, from the Phoenician. For example, the Greek names *alpha*, *beta*, *gamma*, and *delta* correspond to the Phoenician *'aleph*, *beth*, *gimel*, and *daleth*. The orders of the signs in the Phoenician and Greek systems were originally identical. The Phoenician signs *waw*, *sade*, and *qoph* were used by the Greeks under the names *digamma*, *san*, and *koppa* in the earlier periods but were later dropped. The three signs are still used for the numbers 6, 900, and 90 in the scheme of writing numbers by means of the letters of the alphabet.

While the direction of signs and lines in the Phoenician writing was from right to left—as it is in modern Hebrew and Arabic—the direction in the Greek writing varied greatly in the older periods. It could run from right to left; from left to right; or from right to left and from left to right in the same inscription, changing direction alternately from line to line. Only gradually did the method of writing from left to right prevail in the Greek system. This method passed on to the Latins and then to the Western world.

The most radical changes in the Greek system were in regard to the values of the signs. Three signs, as has been noted, were dropped; two changed their original values, namely the Phoenician *ṭ* and *s*, which became *th* and *x*; and five new signs, called *upsilon*, *phi*, *chi*, *psi*, and *ōmega*, were added.

The changes which were to become revolutionary in the history of writing involved the creation of signs for vowels. Phoenician, like other West Semitic writings, consisted of syllabic signs beginning with a consonant and ending in any vowel. In this system the name *Dawid* (in English, David) could have been written by means of three signs, *da-wi-d(i)*. Because the vowels in these signs were not indicated, this writing could stand also for *di-wi-di*, *du-wi-di*, *da-wa-du*, and so on. In most cases people who were familiar with the common words and names of their language had no difficulties in reading such a writing. *Y cn fnd prf fr ths sttmnt n ths sntnc.* In cases where two readings were possible, however, for example, in *Dawid* or *Dawud*, new ways had to be found in order to insure the correct reading. They were found in the use of some weak consonants, such as *y* and *w*. In the writing of *da-wi-yi-d(i)* for *Dawid* the sign *yi* did not stand for an independent syllable; its sole function was to make sure that the preceding syllabic sign, *wi*, would be read as *wi* and not as *wa*, *we*, *wo*, or *wu*.

While the Phoenicians only occasionally employed such full spellings, the Greeks used them systematically after each syllabic sign. They used for this purpose six signs with weak consonants which they inherited from the Phoenicians. Since most of these sounds were used only in the Phoenician, the Greeks had no use for them as consonants. They turned them into the vowels *a*, *e*, *u*, *ē*, *i*, and *o*.

Once the six signs developed their values as vowels in Greek, the natural step was to reduce the remaining syllabic signs to consonants. If, in the writing of *da-'a-wi-yi-d(i)*, the second sign, *'a*, is taken as a vowel *a* to help in the correct reading of the first sign as *da* (not *de, di, do,* or *du*) and if the sign *yi* is taken as *i* to indicate *wi*, then the value of the signs *da* and *wi* must be reduced from syllables *da* and *wi* to consonants *d* and *w*. Once this was done the Greeks developed for the first time a full alphabet, composed of both vowels and consonants.

From the Greeks the alphabet passed on to the Etruscans of Italy; to the Copts of Egypt (where it replaced their old Egyptian hieroglyphic writing); and to the Slavonic peoples of Eastern Europe. The Latin writing of the Romans was derived from that of the Etruscans.

Like the earlier Greek, the Latin writing consisted of 24 signs; but the similarity in number was coincidental, for Latin underwent a different set of changes and replacements. The Greek *digamma* sign of *w* became *f* in Latin, and the Greek *eta* became *h*. The Greek sign *gamma* for *g* was used in older Latin for both *c* and *g*. Later the *g* sign was differentiated from *c* by the addition of a small horizontal bar (recognizable in the English capital letter *G*).

The Greek letters *th, z,* and *x* were dropped altogether in the early Latin writing. The later additions to the Latin writing were placed at the end of the alphabet. The *v* sign developed from the same sign as *f*, which stood for both the sounds *u* and *v* (pronounced as *w* in English). Later the sign *v* developed two forms, *v* for the sound *v* and *u* for the sound *u*. The signs for *x, y,* and *z* were added by the Latins when they became aware of the need to spell the many words and names that they borrowed from the Greek during the imperial Roman period. With the addition of the letters *j* (developed from *i*) and *w* (developed from *v* or *u*) in the Middle Ages, the number of letters of the Latin alphabet increased to 26. This became the basic alphabet of the English language and the languages of Western Europe and of Western civilization. The sounds of different languages are further differentiated by combining letters, as in the English *sh* or the German *sch*, or by diacritic marks, as in the Czech *š*. The sound of all these letters is the same.

The Alphabet Returns to the Semites

The alphabet passed in the course of time from the Greeks back to the Semites, thus repaying the debt of the original borrowing of the Phoenician writing by the Greeks. In the Semitic writings, however, the vowels were generally indicated by means of diacritic marks in the form of small strokes, dots, and circles, placed either above or below or at the side of consonant signs. Thus *ta* would be written as *t* in Hebrew and as *t̄* in Arabic. The development of a full Greek alphabet expressing single sounds of language by means of consonant and vowel signs was the last important step in the history of writing.

Capitals and Small Letters

In English handwriting and print two kinds of letters are used: capitals (called "majuscules") and small letters (called "minuscules"). This is a relatively modern innovation. The Romans, Greeks, and Oriental peoples never distinguished capitals from small letters, as is done in English writing. All these earlier peoples employed two forms—a carefully drawn form of writing with squarish and separate signs on official documents and monuments and a less carefully drawn form of cursive (running) writing with roundish and often joined signs on less official documents, such as letters.

During the Middle Ages a form of capital letters called "uncials" was developed. Uncials (from a Latin word meaning "inch-high") were squarish in shape, with rounded strokes. They were used in Western Europe in handwritten books, side by side with small-letter cursive writing, used in daily life. After the Renaissance and the introduction of printing in Europe, two types of letters were distinguished: the majuscules, which were formed in imitation of the ancient Latin characters, and the minuscules, which continued in the tradition of the medieval cursive writing. Another distinction in printing form developed at the time was between the upright characters of the roman type and the slanting characters of the italic type. (*See also* Book and Bookmaking.)

ALPS, THE. From the French-Italian border region near the Mediterranean Sea, the Alps curve north and northeast as far as Vienna, Austria, forming a giant mountain spine that divides the central part of Western Europe into northern and southern portions. This division has done much to shape the nations, languages, and ways of life of Europe. Occupying roughly 68,000 square miles (175,000 square kilometers), the Alps fill most of Switzerland and Liechtenstein and extend into France, West Germany, Austria, Italy, and Yugoslavia. The Austrian and Italian portions are commonly called the Tyrol.

Physical Character

The most common Alpine rocks are sedimentary. Geologists say the rock was laid down in an ancient sea called Tethys. The Alps were created when convulsion moved the Earth's surface northward, folding the sea bottom rocks against ancient mountains in central France, southern Germany, and Czechoslovakia. Some folding cracked the Earth's crust, letting molten rock well up to form high, rugged mountains, such as Mont Blanc, the Alps's highest peak (15,771 feet; 4,807 meters). Other high peaks formed from the folding include Dufourspitze (15,203 feet; 4,634 meters), the Matterhorn (14,691 feet; 4,478 meters), and Finsteraarhorn (14,022 feet; 4,274 meters). All of these peaks rise on or near the Swiss-Italian border, generally speaking the highest Alpine region.

The Alpine peaks and crests receive snow and rain from moisture-laden westerly winds. Above about

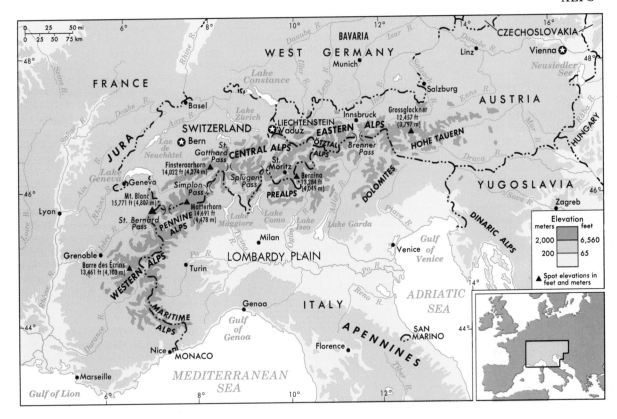

9,500 feet (2,900 meters), snow accumulates, turns to ice, and then flows down the valleys as glaciers. The largest of the glaciers is the Altesch, near the central Alps. On the slope of Mont Blanc in France is another noted glacier, the Mer de Glace, which is highly regarded for its beauty. Sometimes, masses of snow rush uncontrolled down the mountainsides as avalanches, endangering Alpine communities. At lower levels, the ice and snow melt, feeding the great Rhône, Rhine, Danube, and Po rivers.

Plants and Animals

The Alps are divided into an almost treeless high zone and a lower forested area. Mountain meadows, called alps, that spread out beneath the permanent snow line give the range its name. The Alpine turf, which bears grasses, shrubs, and flowers, varies in thickness. The tiny white edelweiss, floral symbol of Switzerland, grows among grasses high in the Alps. Beech trees are found in the lower forest area, spruce and fir at higher levels. Larch and pine grow on the interior mountains. Alpine lakes, set among magnificent mountain landscapes, are noted for their beauty. Among the most prominent are Lakes Geneva, Constance, Como, and Zürich.

Alpine animals include the ibex, a sturdy, nimble goat that survives in preserves. The Alpine marmot, a thick–bodied type of squirrel, lives in colonies. The grouselike mountain ptarmigan and the mountain hare assume protective white coats for winter. Na-

tional parks have been established by Alpine countries to preserve various animal species.

People and Economy

From prehistoric times, the Alps have been the site of human habitation. German cultures generally developed in the eastern Alps, while Roman culture influenced the West. The main language groups that survive today are German (33 percent of the population), French (26 percent), Italian (22 percent), and Slovene (11 percent). Romansh, an ancient Latin language, is spoken in a region of eastern Switzerland.

Some Alpine folk traditions are still preserved and often displayed as part of the tourist-entertainment industry. Alpine music, poetry, dance, wood carving, and embroidery are quite distinctive. Yodeling, a kind of singing, is marked by rapid switching of the voice to falsetto. The alpenhorn, used for signaling between valleys, is a trumpetlike bark instrument up to 12 feet (3.5 meters) long.

During the five centuries following Christ's birth, Rome dominated the Alps. The Romans built roads to promote trade and link their Mediterranean and northern provinces. Economic activity of the period included wine grape culture, iron-ore mining, and pottery manufacture.

Alpine valleys and many mountainsides were cleared of forests during the Middle Ages. Farmers settled the land, planted crops, and developed transhumance, an Alpine practice by which cattle are stall-fed in villages during winter and led to high mountain meadows for summer grazing. While the animals are gone, the farm family tends hay, grain, and other forage crops for use in winter. Milk produced in summer usually is made into cheese; in winter it is sold to dairies. Forestry is practiced in the Alps, and forest conservation programs have been developed.

During the 19th century, hydroelectricity was developed and railroads were constructed, opening up the area. The electric power made by damming Alpine rivers encouraged manufacturing. The region has no coal or oil. Industrial growth caused many people to abandon agriculture for factory jobs. Lighter types of manufacture, including watches and precision machinery, have thrived in the Alps.

Tourism became a major Alpine industry during the 20th century as Europe prospered and air, auto, and rail transportation to the Alps improved. One of the world's longest auto tunnels, passing through Mont Blanc, was opened in 1965. Railroads follow paths through traditional routes such as the Simplon, St. Gotthard, and Brenner passes. Winter sports gained mass popularity as a result of the accessibility of the Alpine region. Today entire villages lodge, feed, and entertain tourists. Resorts such as Innsbruck, Grenoble, and St. Moritz—all of which have hosted the Olympic Games—are world famous.

Historical Character

The location of the Alps has made the Mountains politically significant, for the range is a natural barrier between Germanic Europe to the north and Mediterranean Europe to the south. As a barrier the Alps were pierced in the 3d century B.C. by Hannibal, a Carthaginian general and an enemy of Rome. His was the first major military campaign carried out there. Hannibal led his force from Iberia (now Spain) through the Little St. Bernard Pass to invade the Roman countryside (see Hannibal). Centuries later, in 1800, Napoleon Bonaparte of France crossed the Alps with his army. He descended through the St. Bernard Pass into the Po Valley and defeated the Austrians at Marengo, Italy. Alpine passes were the scene of battles between Italy and Austria during World War I, and Allied troops moved through the region in World War II. (See also Europe; Tyrol; articles on individual Alpine countries.)

ALSACE-LORRAINE. The fortunes of France's two old northeast provinces—Alsace and Lorraine—have filled many pages of history. They lie along the boundary of France and West Germany at a crossroads of trans-European travel. This position helped bring them wealth from commerce, but it also placed them in the path of war and invasion. Their national-

ity shifted repeatedly as the great powers fought for possession of their fertile fields and rich resources. Today they compose one of France's most important industrial areas.

Although the two are often spoken of as a single territory, they are quite distinct regions. Alsace starts as a gentle plain west of the Rhine. It rises to a western boundary in the Vosges. Lorraine lies to the west on a stream-carved plateau that merges with the Paris Basin. The chief rivers of Lorraine are the Moselle and the Meuse. (See also France, section on geographic regions.)

In Alsace the terraces rising from the Rhine bear meadows and fields and vineyards that yield Rhine wines. Higher slopes are clothed in forests and dotted with picturesque old castles and monasteries. Beside the Vosges streams are textile mills, founded when their power came from waterwheels. The old cities near the Rhine and its parallel tributary, the Ill, had their start as medieval trading centers. They grew with the building of canals, railways, highways, and industries in recent centuries.

The chief cities of Alsace are Strasbourg, its historic capital, population 253,384 (1975 census), and Mulhouse, population 117,013 (see Strasbourg). The industries of Alsace are diversified. The leading products are foods, chemicals, textiles, machine tools and equipment, and other engineering products. Potash salts are mined and processed.

The noted iron and steel and chemical industries of Lorraine are based on its iron mines—the largest in Europe—coal reserves, and rock-salt deposits. A vast industrial district reaches south from the Luxembourg and German borders. Here are many mining and manufacturing towns. Nancy, the historic capital of Lorraine, population 107,902 (1975 census), and Metz, 111,869, are the largest cities.

Lorraine took its name from that of Charlemagne's grandson Lothair I. He was given the territory of Lotharingia when Charlemagne's empire was divided at the partition of Verdun in 843. In feudal times the rulers of the duchy of Lorraine were chiefly French nobles. In 1766 Lorraine was joined to France, but it had special privileges until the French Revolution.

Alsace was a part of Germany for several centuries but was given to France in 1648 by the Treaty of Westphalia. In 1681 the French seized and retained Strasbourg, the chief city of the region.

Germany's victory in the Franco-Prussian War brought it all of Alsace and a large part of Lorraine. The area saw some of the bloodiest fighting of World War I. France regained the "lost provinces" through the Allied victory in that war. (See also Franco-Prussian War; World War I; Verdun.)

In World War II the Germans outflanked the fortifications of the Maginot Line in 1940 and occupied Alsace-Lorraine. In 1945, American armies swept across the provinces, driving the Germans out. After the war the French reconstructed and reequipped the damaged and obsolete plants in the area and built modern iron and steel mills.

ALTERNATIVE SCHOOL. A public school that offers an unconventional learning experience, usually characterized by innovative teaching methods and nontraditional curricula, is an alternative school. Such institutions may serve students ranging in age from preschool to young adult. They usually appear when traditional public schools are believed to have failed in some respect or when special needs arise within the community that can only be satisfied with new forms of education.

Alternative schools exist today in Scandinavia, the United Kingdom, and North America. Some of the first, called infant schools, opened in England during the late 1940's to serve children in the primary grades. Their approach to education—characterized by informality, individual attention, and organization around interest centers within the classroom or building—was adopted later by open schools, which serve all grades. In a typical open school, students ranging in age from 6 to 18 years and reflecting a wide cultural diversity meet in an informal atmosphere with their teachers. As they mature, students are encouraged to take more and more responsibility for their own education.

Schools-without-walls extend the classroom into the community as students leave the school building for a broader learning experience. Each school-without-walls is unique in that it reflects the characteristics and resources of the area it serves.

A learning center offers special programs and usually draws its student body from the entire community. Covered by this term are the magnet schools, educational parks, career-education centers, and vocational and technical high schools. Learning centers represent an efficient way to provide instruction in subjects such as aircraft maintenance, auditing, or classical Greek that only attract a small number of students. Centers can provide individualized assistance, including career counseling and job placement.

Continuation schools serve people whose education has been interrupted for some reason. Dropouts often attend such schools. The highly individualized classwork is normally supplemented by a program of counseling that is designed to encourage students to obtain their diplomas. Most continuation schools offer evening and adult classes. Some have special programs for men and women who are planning on reentering the work force.

Schools-within-schools offer an optional alternative within a traditional framework. Inside a regular high school, for example, a small group of students with widely varying backgrounds may volunteer for a special program of upgraded, informal classes.

Multicultural schools serve students from many backgrounds and often have bilingual programs (see Bilingual Education). Free schools are so called because of their exceptional informality: both students and staff operate in an unstructured atmosphere. Private schools are not considered alternative schools, regardless of the reason for which they exist or the manner in which they operate.

ALUMINUM. The chemical element aluminum ranks among the most industrially important metals. Except for magnesium and beryllium, it is the lightest structural metal and is highly ductile, capable of being cast, rolled, stamped, drawn, machined, or extruded. Moreover, it is corrosion resistant, heat reflective, and an excellent conductor of electricity. Although aluminum is soft and has relatively low tensile strength in its pure form, it can be made much harder and stronger if alloyed with copper, magnesium, or zinc. Because of these desirable physical and metallurgical properties, aluminum is more widely used than any other metal except iron and steel.

Pure aluminum metal is utilized in electronic components, reflectors, and fine jewelry. It is also converted into a powder that can be mixed with other substances to produce metallic paints, rocket propellants, flares, and solders. Aluminum alloys have a far wider range of applications. Aluminum-copper alloys, which have mechanical properties superior to those of certain forms of steel, are employed extensively as structural components of aircraft, space satellites, railroad cars, and boats. In addition, the growing emphasis on improved fuel economy has stimulated the widespread use of these high-strength/low-weight alloys in the manufacture of automobiles and other motor vehicles. Aluminum alloyed with boron conducts electricity nearly as well as does copper; but it is much lighter, making it the preferred material for overhead transmission cables. Aluminum-manganese alloys exhibit exceptional resistance to weathering and corrosion and so are commonly used for siding, roofing, window frames, and other construction hardware as well as for storage tanks and highway signs. Aluminum-based magnesium alloys have many of the same properties, plus superior weldability. Tamost important commercial applications include the manufacture of appliances and food and beverage packaging, principally in the form of foil wrappings and cans.

During the late 1970's the annual world production of aluminum totalled more than 16 million tons (14.5 million metric tons). The United States, which is the leading manufacturer of aluminum, produced nearly a third of the world output. Other major aluminum producers were the Soviet Union, Japan, Canada, and West Germany.

Aluminum's Raw Material — Bauxite

Aluminum is the most plentiful metal in the Earth's crust. As a silicate or oxide compound it is found in every clay bank and in most of the common rocks. At present, however, it is not economical to extract the metal from clay. Nearly all aluminum for use in the United States comes from the ore bauxite (a name derived from Les Baux, France, where it was first discovered).

Bauxite contains hydrated alumina, $Al_2O_3 \cdot 2H_2O$, that is usually combined with impurities of iron, silicon, and titanium oxides. The ore itself may be as soft as clay or as hard as rock and may appear in any of

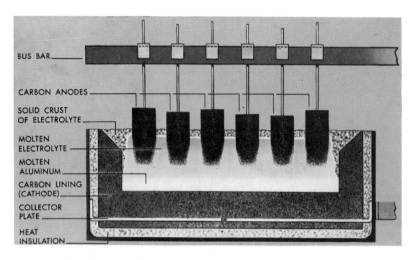

Aluminum is obtained through the process of electrolysis. In the electrolytic cell, a strong electric current goes from the bus bar down through the anodes to the cathode. The alumina in the electrolyte is split into oxygen and aluminum.

several colors. Bauxite deposits are usually near the Earth's surface, where open-pit mining methods are used. For deeper deposits, miners dig shafts and tunnels to reach the ore.

The principal bauxite-producing countries are Australia, Guinea, Jamaica, Surinam, the Soviet Union, and Yugoslavia. Most of the bauxite mined in the United States comes from Arkansas. Canada has no bauxite deposits of its own and imports much of what it uses from Guinea and Jamaica.

At mills near the mines the bauxite is crushed and sometimes dried out before shipment to treatment plants. The first step in treatment is to remove impurities from the ore. This refining process turns bauxite into aluminum oxide, or alumina. Four to six pounds (two to three kilograms) of bauxite yield two pounds (one kilogram) of alumina, making one pound (one half kilogram) of pig aluminum.

One important process for recovering alumina was developed in 1888 by Karl Josef Bayer, an Austrian chemist. In the Bayer method, powdered bauxite is mixed with hot caustic soda (sodium hydroxide). In large pressure tanks, called digesters, the hydrated aluminum oxide of bauxite forms a solution of sodium aluminate. The impurities remain in solid form and are filtered out as "red mud." The hot solution is then pumped into tall precipitating tanks. As it cools, crystals of aluminum hydroxide appear. Kilns heat the crystals white hot and drive off the chemically combined water, leaving pure alumina.

Alumina is reduced to pure aluminum by electrolysis (see Electrochemistry). In the electrolytic cell used in making aluminum, the alumina is dissolved in a bath, or electrolyte. Then a strong electric current is passed through the solution. The action reduces the alumina (takes out the oxygen) and deposits nearly pure aluminum on the bottom of the bath. When enough has accumulated, the molten aluminum is tapped, or siphoned off, and cast into pigs.

The electrolytic cell is a rectangular steel shell lined with carbon. The carbon lining serves as the cathode. Carbon anodes hanging in the bath from overhead bus bars lead in the current. Oxygen given up by the alumina and carbon from the anodes forms carbon dioxide gas, which bubbles out of the bath. Six to eight kilowatt-hours of electricity are required to produce one pound of aluminum.

The bath consists of a melted mineral called cryolite, a fluoride of aluminum and sodium (Na_3AlF_6). Large deposits of natural cryolite are found only in Greenland. Synthetic cryolite is also used.

Pig aluminum contains some impurities as it comes from the bath. These are removed by remelting it before the aluminum is made into useful objects. "Commercially pure" aluminum is actually more than 99 percent pure. During the remelting process, aluminum can be alloyed with other metals. The remelted metal is cast into ingots of various sizes and shapes.

Early Work with Aluminum

Ever since Biblical times, people have been using alum, one of the aluminum compounds found in nature. Its chemical identity was not discovered until 1746, when the German chemist Andreas Marggraf proved that alum has as its base an unknown metal that is now called aluminum. For decades scientists tried to isolate aluminum. The Danish scientist Hans Christian Oersted succeeded in 1825, but he could not repeat his effort. Friedrich Wöhler, a German chemist, continued the search for a method to produce pure aluminum. In 1845 he isolated a small quantity of the metal by decomposing anhydrous aluminum chloride with potassium.

A few years later the French chemist Henri Sainte-Claire Deville substituted the less expensive sodium

PROPERTIES OF ALUMINUM

Symbol......................................Al	Density at 32° F (0° C) 2.699
Atomic Number......................13	Boiling Point
Atomic Weight..............26.9815	....................3,272° F (2,467° C)
Group in Periodic	Melting Point
Table................................IIIA	............1,219.46° F (660.37° C)

for potassium and exhibited an aluminum ingot at the Paris Exposition in 1855. Emperor Napoleon III realized that the new metal could lighten his army's equipment and permit more mobility. He commissioned Sainte-Claire Deville to find a way to make large amounts of aluminum cheaply. The French chemist was not able to produce more than a few tons yearly, but it was enough to acquaint scientists and manufacturers with aluminum and its possibilities.

In 1886 Charles Martin Hall of the United States and Paul-Louis-Toussaint Héroult of France developed almost simultaneously, but independently, a method of reducing alumina in which alumina is dissolved in molten cryolite and decomposed electrolytically. This method, commonly known as the Hall-Héroult process, remains the basis of commercial aluminum production. (*See also* Hall.)

ALVAREZ, Luis W. (born 1911). An experimental physicist who was the winner of the 1968 Nobel prize for physics, Luis W. Alvarez was awarded the coveted prize for work that included the discovery of resonance particles (subatomic particles that have very short lifetimes and that occur only in high-energy nuclear collisions).

Luis Walter Alvarez was born in San Francisco on June 13, 1911. He was educated at the University of Chicago, where he received his B.S. degree in 1932 and his Ph.D. in 1936. That same year he joined the faculty of the University of California at Berkeley, where he became professor of physics in 1945 and later associate director (1954–59, 1975–78) of the Lawrence Radiation Laboratory (now Lawrence Berkeley Laboratory).

Alvarez worked on microwave radar research at the Massachusetts Institute of Technology from 1940 to 1943 and at the Los Alamos (N.M.) Scientific Laboratory from 1944 to 1945. He helped to develop microwave beacons, linear radar antennas, the ground-controlled landing approach system, and a method for aerial bombing that used radar to locate targets. He also suggested the technique for detonating the implosion type of atomic bomb.

After World War II Alvarez helped construct the first proton linear accelerator. He also developed the liquid hydrogen bubble chamber in which subatomic particles and their reactions are detected.

AMARILLO, Tex. Once the scene of wild buffalo hunts and thundering cattle drives, Amarillo is now the chief city of the Texas Panhandle. Tall buildings rise beside busy streets. The surrounding treeless prairie is a checkerboard of pastures and fields of grain.

Amarillo is an airline, highway, and railroad junction. It is a marketing center for the petroleum, natural gas, cattle, and grain of the area. Pipelines transport natural gas and oil from the Amarillo area to northern and eastern parts of the United States. The city is also an industrial hub. Oil refining, flour milling, meat-packing, and copper refining are among its industries. The manufactured products of Amarillo include farm equipment, metal products, petrochemicals, leather goods, and Western-style apparel. The city also has helicopter factories and is the site of a major United States government helium plant and atomic research project.

Amarillo has a theater company and a symphony orchestra. Each September the city is host to the Tri-State Fair. There is also an annual rodeo and a music festival. Amarillo College is a junior college operated by the city. To the south, in Canyon, is West Texas State University. Nearby, along a headstream of the Red River, is a trench, 1,100 feet (340 meters) deep, in Palo Duro Canyon State Park.

The Spanish conquistador Francisco Vázquez de Coronado, in his fruitless search for the Seven Cities of Cibola, visited the area in 1541 (*see* Coronado). Amarillo began in 1887 as a collection of buffalo-hide huts near a railway construction camp. Then called Ragtown, it was a supply center and shipping point for cattle ranchers and buffalo hunters. The city was renamed Amarillo, which is the Spanish word for yellow, the color of nearby clay deposits. It soon grew into a cow town crowded with hotels, cafés, saloons, and gambling houses. The community had no local government. For years it was run by county officials and the Texas Rangers, stationed there to curb cattle rustling. Amarillo was incorporated in 1892. After the discovery of nearby natural-gas and oil fields in the 1920's, industry began to develop.

The city has a council-manager form of government. Population (1980 census), 149,230.

AMAZON. In Greek mythology the Amazons were a nation of female warriors ruled by a queen. No man was permitted to dwell in their country, located on the south coast of the Black Sea. Male infants were sent to their fathers, the Gargareans, in a neighboring land. The girls were trained in agriculture, hunting, and the art of war.

The Amazons were fearsome warriors. Usually they fought on horseback. Their weapons were the bow, spear, ax, and a shield. According to the myths, they invaded Greece, Syria, the Arabian peninsula, Egypt, Libya, and the islands of the Aegean. Legends tell of the adventures of Hercules and Theseus in the land of the Amazons.

In various parts of the globe anthropologists have found peoples among whom the rights of the mother exceed those of the father and where women have an importance that elsewhere belongs to men. Such a society is called a matriarchate. It is thought that the Amazon myths arose from tales of such societies.

History records many instances of women warriors. In modern times the king of Dahomey (now Benin), had an army of women. A female "battalion of death" fought in the Russian Revolution of 1917. Women soldiers served with Soviet troops in World

War II, and the South Korean army had women fighters in 1950. Women also were active in the Israeli army's conflicts with the Arabs. The Amazon River gained its name from the fact that an early explorer there was attacked by a savage tribe among whom the women fought alongside the men.

AMAZON RIVER. The greatest river of South America, the Amazon is also the world's largest river in water volume and the area of its drainage basin. Together with its tributaries the river drains an area of 2,270,000 square miles (5,870,000 square kilometers)—roughly one third of the continent. It empties into the Atlantic Ocean at a rate of about 58 billion gallons (220,000 cubic meters) per second.

Location and Physical Description

Beginning in the high Andes Mountains in Peru, the Amazon and its tributaries flow 4,087 miles (6,577 kilometers) to the Atlantic through Venezuela, Ecuador, Colombia, Bolivia, and Brazil; by far the largest portion is in Brazil. Among the more than a thousand known tributaries, there are seven (Japurá, Juruá, Madeira, Negro, Purus, Tocantins, and Xingu) whose individual lengths exceed 1,000 miles (1,600 kilometers). The Madeira is more than 2,000 miles (3,200 kilometers) from source to mouth.

The Amazon varies in width from 2 to 9 miles (3 to 14 kilometers); its mouth is more than 125 miles (200 kilometers) wide. The largest oceangoing steamers

can ascend the river 1,000 miles (1,600 kilometers) to Manaus, a Brazilian inland port.

For most of its course the river flows just south of the Equator, and so the Amazonian climate is hot and humid. Annual rainfall amounts to about 50 inches (130 centimeters), while the average temperature over a year is about 85° F (30° C). Most of the Amazon Basin is a lowland forest of hardwoods and palms. The northeastern portion has extensive savannas, or grasslands, with occasional trees and shrubs.

Plants and Animals

The remarkably rich and diverse Amazon Basin plant and animal life is a resource of world importance. Of the 22,767 species of plants known in the world, 16,619—almost three fourths—live in the Amazon Basin. There are only 150 kinds of fish in all of Europe, but about 1,500 species are known to exist in the Amazon waters, and there may be as many as 2,000. The basin also has an immense variety of insect, bird, reptile, and mammal life.

The vegetation of the Amazon jungle grows rapidly, soon covering cleared areas unless it is cut back constantly. Again and again the jungle has defeated settlement efforts. At the same time, conservationists are concerned about the overcutting of valuable plants such as hardwood trees and also the destruction of rare plant species when the jungle is burned over for clearing. The many Amazonian plants are a valuable source for development of new hybrids.

E. Aubert de la Rue

Near Manaus, Brazil, the milky white waters of the Amazon River are joined by the black waters of the Negro River, one of the chief tributaries of the Amazon. A 1929 treaty between Colombia and Brazil guaranteed perpetual free navigation of the world's largest river.

Mammals include the capybara, a rodent weighing up to 110 pounds (50 kilograms) whose flesh is eaten; the tapir, an edible kind of pig; the nutria, a tropical otter whose pelt is traded; the great anteater; and many kinds of monkeys. Markets along the river sell a variety of fish, including the pirarucu, which weighs up to 325 pounds (150 kilograms), and the giant catfish. Silver carp, neon tetras, and the flesh-eating piranhas are shipped to tropical fish stores throughout the world. The electric eel is a dangerous fish capable of discharging up to 500 volts.

The wide range of vividly colored Amazonian birds includes hummingbirds, toucans, and parrots. Among the reptiles are the anaconda, a huge snake that crushes its victims; the poisonous coral snake; and alligators. Giant butterflies are among the most spectacular of the insects.

The People

Prior to European colonization, the Indian population in the basin was about 6,800,000. The Indians lived by hunting and fishing, gathering fruits and nuts, and planting small gardens. A typical house consisted of a frame of poles, walls woven of branches, and a roof thatched with palm leaves. For several reasons the Indian population had declined to less than one million by the early 1980's.

In the 17th century many Indians were enslaved and taken from Brazil. As Europeans attempted to settle the Amazon Basin and to establish mines and farms there, they killed many Indians and took their land. Also during construction of the Trans-Amazon and the Manaus-Boa Vista highways, the Brazilian government seized Indian reservation land. At that time the Indians obtained weapons, fought govern-ment troops, and either died or were displaced in great numbers. Most now live in remote reservations.

The Economy

Plant products such as rubber, hardwoods, Brazil nuts, rosewood and vegetable oils, and jute and other fibers are major Amazon Basin exports. Manganese ore, diamonds, gold, and petroleum are extracted and sold. Fish are marketed locally but also are frozen and sent to other countries.

The 3,000-mile (4,800-kilometer) Trans-Amazon highway traverses the basin, linking the road system of northeastern Brazil with others of countries to the north; it continues to Brazil's border with Colombia and Peru. This highway together with connecting roads in the network has improved trade within the basin, greatly lowering transportation costs and opening up large new areas for development. All highways were designed to connect to the existing water transportation network.

History

The Amazon River was discovered by Francisco de Orellana, a Spanish explorer, in 1541. After descending the river from Quito, Ecuador, to the Atlantic, Orellana claimed to have seen women tribal warriors, and he named the river *Amazonas* for the women warriors of Greek mythology. In 1637 Pedro Teixeira, a Portuguese explorer, ascended the Amazon with 2,000 men in 47 canoes.

About 1751 Charles Marie de la Condamine, a French scientist, made the first geographical survey of the basin and brought the deadly Indian arrow poison curare to Europe. At the beginning of the 19th century the German explorer Alexander von Humboldt and the French botanist Aimé Bompland mapped portions of the area.

In the 1980's the Amazon Basin was undergoing one of its many periods of rapid economic development. There have been several such booms in the past. In most cases the jungle and the climate defeated all but the hardiest settlers. However, modern technology seems to have made permanent large-scale settlement of the region possible. (*See also* Brazil; South America.)

AMBER. Millions of years ago in the Oligocene epoch of the earth's history, clear resin seeped from pine trees growing in the Baltic Sea basin. As centuries passed, lumps of this resin were covered by layers of soil. The Ice Age glaciers poured over it. The resin was hardened by time and pressure into a fossil called amber. It is a brittle, yellow-to-brown, translucent substance. It is hard enough to be carved though it is not as hard as marble or glass.

When the resin was fresh, soft, and sticky, sometimes leaves, flowers, or live insects were trapped in it. They may be seen in the amber today.

The ancient Phoenicians, Greeks, and Romans valued amber highly. They believed that it had the ability to cure certain diseases. Amber takes a charge of static electricity when it is rubbed, so the Greeks called it *elektron.* The word "electricity" is derived from the Greek term.

The amber-producing pines grew chiefly on the site of the Baltic and North seas where the land was later submerged. When violent storms disturb the seas, pieces of amber may be washed up on the shores. Most amber, however, is obtained by mining. Lumps weighing up to 18 pounds (8 kilograms) have been discovered. Small amounts are found in Great Britain, Sicily, Siberia, Greenland, and the United States, but the chief source is the Baltic region.

Other fossil resins include *burmite, copalite,* and *retinite.* Pressed amber, or *ambroid,* is made by heating and compressing amber fragments. Amber has been used for jewelry and ornaments since prehistoric times. Its use for such items as the mouthpieces of pipes has declined since plastics have been manufactured (*see* Plastics).

AMBLER, Eric (born 1909). A highly distinguished writer of spy and crime fiction, Eric Ambler was credited with being an originator of the espionage genre that became popular in the 1970's. Some critics have described Ambler's stories as fables for our times, in which the pervading sense of fear symbolizes the confusion and uncertainty of the modern world.

Eric Ambler was born on June 28, 1909, in London. He was a student of engineering and, from 1926 to 1935, an advertising copywriter before turning to literature. Between 1936 and 1940 he wrote six novels, the best known of which was 'The Mask of Dimitrios' (American title, 'A Coffin for Dimitrios'), published in 1939. After serving in World War II, he also wrote screenplays in Hollywood.

Ambler's books create a terrifying, though credible, world of unseen danger. The central characters were usually normal men involved by circumstance in a web of violence and intrigue from which escape seems impossible. Beginning in the mid-1960's, the Ambler hero-narrator was often a battered soldier of fortune. Other novels include 'Judgment on Deltchev' (1951) and 'The Care of Time' (1981). Several of his books were made into movies.

AMBULANCE. A vehicle used to transport people who are ill or injured is called an ambulance, from the Greek word *ambulare,* "to move about." The usual use of an ambulance is to carry an accident victim or a person with a serious illness to a hospital. Formerly used only for transport, the modern ambulance can be outfitted with sophisticated equipment and staffed by people trained in emergency medical service (Emergency Medical Technicians, or EMTs).

In the United States ambulances are required by law to carry specific items of equipment that are necessary for the care of patients. Kits for use in emergency care for breathing failure, heart disorders, broken bones, and burns are standard. The ground vehicles may be provided with everything found in the critical and intensive care units of hospitals, including equipment for intravenous procedures and for heart monitoring, oxygen and other gases, traction devices, and incubators for newborn infants.

Airplanes and helicopters, as well as ground vehicles, may be used as ambulances, and they are similarly equipped. Airplanes are used to reach settlements in remote areas such as the Australian outback, where the Royal Flying Doctor Service has operated for many years. Helicopters are often used for emergency rescue work, when other means of transport cannot reach the victims or transport them quickly enough (*see* Helicopter).

To be effective, an ambulance service must be able to respond to a call for assistance in less than 20 minutes. One ambulance for every 10,000 people is necessary for adequate emergency service.

Emergency treatment given immediately following an accident or heart attack can save a life. A cadre of men and women have been trained to deliver treatment in such areas as cardiopulmonary resuscitation, splinting of fractures, and control of bleeding. Basic EMT training is taught in about 80 to 150 hours. Advanced training in special areas, such as that for cardiac technicians, requires as much as 500 hours of training and often more. Much of this is paid for by the United States Public Health Service.

Probably the earliest formal use of an ambulance service was during the Crusades in the 11th and 12th centuries, when men wounded in battle were transported by horse-drawn carts back into their own lines for treatment instead of being left to die on the battlefield. Out of this grew the Order of the Hospital of St. John of Jerusalem, or Hospitallers, which still operates worldwide in many areas of charitable medicine as the St. John's Ambulance Corps.

Christopher Columbus is traditionally honored as
the discoverer of America. His voyages were sponsored
by the Spanish crown. This is an early artist's conception
of his first landing in the New World.

DISCOVERY AND
COLONIZATION OF AMERICA

AMERICA, DISCOVERY AND COLONIZATION OF. During the 15th century, the European nations of Spain and Portugal began a series of explorations to find trade routes to the Far East. An accidental outcome of this search was the discovery by Christopher Columbus in 1492 of land in the Western Hemisphere. Although he and his immediate successors failed to recognize it, he had found another world.

The New World contained all the natural wealth for which 15th-century people longed—and far more. Here were great deposits of the gold which they sought so eagerly. Here also were vast reserves of other minerals. Mile upon mile of plains, valleys, and mountains held fertile farmlands and pastures.

The New World was scantily settled by its people, the American Indians. Large areas where the Indians lived by hunting, fishing, or gathering had no permanent settlements. The tribes that lived by farming had, however, domesticated many valuable plants. Corn (maize), potatoes, pumpkins and squash, peanuts, and other new crops from America were to play a big role in nourishing mankind. (For map of crops raised by the Indians, *see* Indians, American.)

America or the Americas is the name given the two continents of the Western Hemisphere, with their adjacent islands. They lie between the Atlantic Ocean on the east and the Pacific on the west. North America and South America together contain some 16,230,000 square miles (42,040,000 square kilometers). This area is about four times as large as Europe. The two continents are about three fourths as large as Europe and Asia together.

The New World is scarcely comparable with the Old in population. The estimated total population of the Americas is about 615,000,000, compared with the 750,000,000 of Europe alone.

North and South America together have the greatest north-south extent of any landmass on earth. With Greenland, usually considered as part of North America, the two Americas extend from 83° 39′ North latitude to 55° 59′ South—or nearly 140 degrees. This is more than 9,600 miles (15,500 kilometers). North America's greatest width is some 3,000 miles (4,800 kilometers); South America's, about 3,200 miles (5,150 kilometers). (*See also* North America and South America.)

327

National Gallery

Storms drove Leif Ericson's Viking ship to Vinland almost 500 years before Columbus discovered America. Norse settlements there were abandoned and forgotten for centuries. This painting of Leif's voyage to the North American coast is by Christian Krohg.

America's Shape and Structure

The two continents are similar in physical structure. Each forms a rough triangle, with the base in the north. They are joined by the Isthmus of Panama —part of Central America, a division of North America. South America lies southeast of North America. Between them in the Caribbean Sea stretch the West Indies islands, geographically part of North America. (For map, see World.)

Near the west coast of both continents rise the Cordilleras. This is a great system of young fold mountains which in places encircles plateaus and basins. It is made up of a number of parallel ranges. They are fringed by a narrow Pacific coastal plain. Both North and South America contain broad interior plains. From them the land rises again to lower, older highlands in the east.

Rivers of America

These vast continents are drained by some of the world's greatest rivers. The rivers of North America fall mainly into two groups—those which drain the western mountain system and flow into the Pacific and those which drain the Interior Plains and send their waters directly or indirectly into the Atlantic. Those flowing into the Pacific include the Yukon, Fraser, Columbia, and Colorado. The waters of the Great Lakes reach the Atlantic through the St. Lawrence. The Mississippi River flows southward to the Gulf of Mexico, carrying the waters of its huge tributaries—the Missouri, Arkansas, Red, Ohio, and Tennessee. East coast rivers are shorter, but they are important for the gaps they have cut through the Appalachian Highlands and for the fine harbors at the drowned mouths of the Hudson, Delaware, and Po-

tomac. (For map of river drainage in the United States, see United States.)

South America's greatest streams drain the basins that make up its central plains. They flow into the Atlantic. They are the Amazon, the Orinoco, and the Paraná-Paraguay.

Broad Range of Climate

America affords every type of climate on earth and almost every class of vegetation. Temperature, rainfall, growing season, and wet and dry seasons are affected by the physical features of the continents as well as by the wide range of latitude.

North America is broadest in the high and middle latitudes. Three quarters of its area lies in the middle latitudes so favorable to human activity and to the growth of many of the most useful crops. Three quarters of South America lies in the tropics. Its greatest width is near the equator. Heat and humidity have delayed development here. South America's middle latitude lands are in the narrower south. (See also Climate; Rainfall; Grasslands.)

Varied Natural Resources

America's great natural wealth is widely distributed. The resources of one region contribute to the development of another through trade. Bolivia's tin, Chile's copper, Argentina's wool, Brazil's manganese, Venezuela's iron, and Canada's nickel are used by industries in the United States. Canada's wood pulp and paper, grain, and fish are traded for the coffee, bananas, cacao, sugar, and cotton of the tropical and semitropical sections. Manufactured wares from the United States include machinery for the industrial development of all America.

When the Northmen Sailed to America

The first European to land in America was Leif Ericson, a Viking seaman from Greenland (see Ericson). The ancient sagas give different accounts of this voyage made in the year 1000. Leif landed on a forested shore which he called Vinland. He did not realize he had found a new continent, and Europe heard nothing of his discovery. In 1963 archaeologists uncovered the remains of a Viking settlement on the northern tip of Newfoundland. According to radiocarbon dating it was occupied about A.D. 1000. This was the first proof that white men had lived in North America before Columbus.

Most medieval Europeans were ignorant of other places in the world. Maps of the time showed only

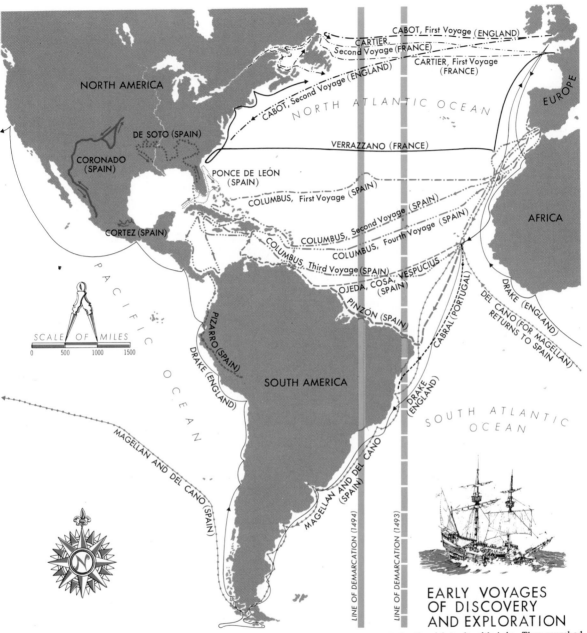

NORTH AMERICA

DE SOTO (SPAIN)

CORONADO
(SPAIN)

CORTEZ (SPAIN)

PONCE DE LEÓN
(SPAIN)

COLUMBUS, First Voyage (SPAIN)

COLUMBUS, Second Voyage (SPAIN)

COLUMBUS, Fourth Voyage (SPAIN)

COLUMBUS, Third Voyage (SPAIN)

OJEDA, COSA, VESPUCIUS
(SPAIN)

PINZÓN (SPAIN)

PIZARRO (SPAIN)

DRAKE (ENGLAND)

SOUTH AMERICA

MAGELLAN AND DEL CANO (SPAIN)

MAGELLAN AND DEL CANO
(SPAIN)

DRAKE
(ENGLAND)

CABRAL (PORTUGAL)

DEL CANO (FOR MAGELLAN)
RETURNS TO SPAIN

DRAKE (ENGLAND)

CABOT, First Voyage (ENGLAND)

CARTIER,
Second Voyage (FRANCE)

CARTIER, First Voyage
(FRANCE)

CABOT, Second Voyage (ENGLAND)

NORTH ATLANTIC OCEAN

VERRAZZANO (FRANCE)

EUROPE

AFRICA

PACIFIC OCEAN

SCALE OF MILES

0   500   1000   1500

SOUTH ATLANTIC
OCEAN

LINE OF DEMARCATION (1494)

LINE OF DEMARCATION (1493)

N

EARLY VOYAGES
OF DISCOVERY
AND EXPLORATION

Europe's great powers of the 15th and 16th centuries—Spain, Portugal, England, and France—rivaled one another in sending expeditions of discovery across the Atlantic. They sought a direct water route for the rich trade with Asia. They searched for gold and for land to build overseas empires. The general outlines of America emerged and colonization advanced.

a broad strip of land and water reaching from Greenland south to the Mediterranean coasts of Europe and Africa and far eastward to China's Pacific shore.

Events and developments in the next 500 years had served to make Europeans curious about the world by the time Columbus rediscovered America in 1492. Christian knights from Europe had been fighting in wars, called Crusades, in western Asia (see Crusades). The crusaders had brought wonderful products home from Asia. There were cloves, pepper, and other spices to make food taste good and keep it from spoil-

ing. There were sheer, colorful silken cloths, rich carpets, and sparkling jewelry. Europeans wanted these luxuries so much that Venice and Genoa, in Italy, grew rich trading in them. People were excited by the story of Marco Polo, which told of a trip to China and the greater wonders there (see Polo, Marco).

Discoveries in the science of the stars—astronomy—now helped seamen navigate their ships better. Some men believed that the earth was round. Part of the new knowledge came from the long-forgotten writings of great thinkers of ancient Greece and Rome. This

329

rebirth of interest in ancient learning was called the Renaissance (*see* Renaissance).

The magnetic compass had reached Europe in the 1100's. Within a hundred years or so sea captains learned to rely on it. Men began to make better maps. Little by little it became safer for sailors to venture into unknown seas.

Trade Routes Enlarge the World

At first the wealth of the East trickled into Western Europe mainly by overland routes. Goods changed hands many times before they reached the consumer, and at each exchange the cost increased. Shipping costs were also high. Goods were transported by camel or horse caravans, each animal carrying only a comparatively small load. After 1453 the Moslem Turks controlled Constantinople, which was the crossroads of important trade routes. They permitted cargoes from the East to pass through the city only on their own terms.

Western European merchants thought that if they could find sea routes to the Orient they could import goods directly to their own cities. Soon they were prepared to outfit ships for sea captains sailing in search of new routes. Each contributed only a portion of the expense, so that no one would be completely ruined if the venture failed. They also secured the king's approval of their enterprises and his promise to defend their claims to lands discovered along the way. The king of Spain always demanded a fifth of the gold and silver found by his explorers.

The Italian port cities were satisfied with their monopoly of the old routes. The Scandinavian countries were far removed. Germany was split into many small states. Thus the work of discovery fell to Portugal, Spain, England, and France.

Portuguese Exploration Around Africa

Under the sponsorship of Prince Henry the Navigator, Portugal took the lead in the 1400's (*see* Henry the Navigator). Portuguese sea captains made ever-

lengthening voyages along the western coast of Africa. Bartholomew Diaz first saw the cliffs of the Cape of Good Hope at Africa's southern tip in 1488 (*see* Diaz, Bartholomew). In 1497–98 Vasco da Gama rounded the Cape and reached India by sea. He brought back a cargo of spices that netted a huge profit (*see* Gama). Portugal occupied key cities on the sea lanes between China and the Red Sea. Its wealth became the envy of Western Europe.

Others before Vasco da Gama had planned new sea routes to the Orient, and some had guessed that such a route might be found by sailing west. Few men could agree on how *far* west Asia lay from Europe by sea, and no one dreamed that the American continents stood in the way.

Columbus Sails West

One of the most optimistic advocates of the western route was Christopher Columbus (*see* Columbus, Christopher). For years he begged the courts of Portugal, England, France, and Spain for a grant of ships and men to prove that Asia lay only a few thousand miles west of Europe. Finally in 1492 Queen Isabella of Castile provided the money, and Columbus sailed with three ships. Pressing onward over the growing objections of his captains and crews, he finally sighted one of the Bahamas and shortly thereafter discovered Cuba and Hispaniola.

On three later voyages he found the mainlands of Central and South America. Until his death, in 1506, Columbus never swerved from his belief that the lands he discovered were actually part of Asia.

Spain and Portugal Divide the New World

When Columbus first returned to Spain, the Portuguese claimed that he had merely visited a part of their dominion of Guinea in Africa. Spain and Portugal accordingly asked Pope Alexander VI to settle the dispute. He complied by drawing a north-south Line of Demarcation in 1493. If Spain discovered lands west of this line, the Spanish king was to have them if they were not already owned by a Christian ruler. In 1494 the line was drawn through a point 370 leagues west of the Cape Verde Islands.

In 1500 a Portuguese mariner, Pedro Alvarez Cabral, sailing along Africa en route to India, was carried by a storm to Brazil. He claimed the land for Portugal since it lay east of the line. When the Portuguese king heard of Cabral's discovery, he sent out an expedition which sailed hundreds of miles along the South American coast.

New Land Named for Vespucius

An Italian merchant, Americus Vespucius, asserted he was a member of exploring parties to the New World and wrote a letter telling of what he had seen. Martin Waldseemüller, a German

Brown Brothers

The *Golden Hind* was the only ship from the fleet of Sir Francis Drake that passed through the stormy Strait of Magellan. With it he captured Spanish treasure ships off Peru and sailed around the world to England.

Jean Nicolet was one of the explorers Samuel de Champlain sent into the Great Lakes region of New France. This painting shows Nicolet at Green Bay in 1634. He was the first white man to set foot in what is now Wisconsin.

scholar, included the letter in a popular geography and suggested that the new land be called America. The name caught on and brought Vespucius an honor he did not deserve (*see* Vespucius).

By 1510 men realized that the new land was not part of the Orient, but they still thought that China and India were just beyond. In 1513 Vasco Nuñez de Balboa, the Spanish adventurer, crossed the Isthmus of Darien and became the first European to see the Pacific Ocean from American shores (*see* Balboa).

By this time Spain claimed that the Line of Demarcation extended around the globe, but no one knew where it fell in the Eastern Hemisphere. A Portuguese captain, Ferdinand Magellan, believed there might be a water passage through the New World that would lead to the Orient. He convinced the king of Spain that the richest lands in the Far East lay in the region reserved for Spain by the papal line. The king commissioned Magellan to find a western route.

Magellan's Ship Circles the Globe

In 1519 Magellan sailed from Spain to Brazil. Then he proceeded south along the coast to the tip of the continent and passed through the strait that now bears his name. He sailed into the ocean which he named the Pacific. Magellan was killed in the Philippine Islands, but one of his ships went on to India and finally in 1522 to Spain by way of the Indian Ocean and the Cape of Good Hope (*see* Magellan).

The voyage established Magellan as the foremost navigator in history. For the first time the globe was circled and the vast expanse of the Pacific was revealed. No longer could America be regarded as an outlying part of Asia.

Spain and Portugal each claimed that the rich Spice Islands of the East lay within its allotted territory. Spain's westward route was so much longer than Portugal's eastern route that Spain could not profit from the trade. In 1529 Spain surrendered to Portugal its claims in Asia and received the Philippine Islands in return. Magellan's voyage thus failed to break Portugal's supremacy in the Orient.

The Spanish Penetrate America

The Spanish took the lead in exploring and colonizing the New World. The earliest settlements were in the West Indies. Hispaniola had the first towns. Santo Domingo, established in 1496, became the first capital of New Spain. Other settlements rose in Cuba, Puerto Rico, and Jamaica. From island harbors sailed expeditions to explore the coasts and penetrate the continents. They found gold, silver, and precious stones and enslaved the Indians. Ambitious men became governors of conquered lands. Missionaries brought a new religion to the Indians.

One adventurer, Juan Ponce de León, sailed from Puerto Rico in 1513. He landed on a new shore that he called Florida. He was interested in exploration and slave trading. He also wanted to find a fabled fountain whose waters made men perpetually young. He returned to Florida in 1521 to build a settlement, but he was slain by Indians (*see* Ponce de León).

Riches for Spain from Mexico and Peru

The Spanish dream of finding great riches in America was realized when Hernando Cortez conquered the empire of the Aztecs in Mexico in 1519–21 (*see* Cortez). A few years later Francisco Pizarro with a small force vanquished the Inca empire and seized the treasure of Peru in South America (*see* Pizarro). Gold and silver from these lands poured into the Spanish king's treasury, rousing the envy of other rulers. The treasure ships attracted bloodthirsty pirates and privateers (*see* Pirates and Piracy).

Spanish and Portuguese in North America

Other Spanish conquerors (called in Spanish *conquistadores*) turned north to the lands now forming the southern part of the United States. In 1539 Hernando de Soto came from Spain by way of Cuba to the east coast of Florida. From there he trekked overland to the Mississippi. He wandered into what is now Arkansas and Oklahoma and later floated down the Arkansas River to its mouth. In 1542 he died and was buried in the Mississippi (*see* De Soto).

Indian traditions and stories of Spanish wanderers told that somewhere north of Mexico the golden towers of the Seven Cities of Cibola gleamed in the sun. Francisco de Coronado, governor of a province in western Mexico, set out in 1540 to find them. He crossed the deserts and plains between what is now western New Mexico and central Kansas, but he found only poor Indian towns (pueblos). Coronado returned to Mexico without gold and jewels. Although Coronado had traveled well into the heart of North America, the Spaniards did not care to explore further the disappointing lands he had seen (*see* Coronado; Southwest, American).

Earlier, in 1524–25, a Portuguese sea captain, Estevan Gómez, serving the king of Spain, explored the coast of North America from Maine to New Jersey. His descriptions led the Spaniards to consider this region far less valuable than the lands they had in the south. Thus they ignored the greater part of the east coast of North America.

The Portuguese made one important discovery in this northern region. In 1501 Gaspar Corte-Real reached Newfoundland. His voyages were not followed up, for Portugal soon needed all its resources to develop its East India empire and its colony in Brazil.

The English Seamen

England's first port for mariners sailing west was the city of Bristol. Bristol merchants hoped that if a new route to the Orient lay directly west across the Atlantic, their city would become the principal trade center. In 1497 they sent John Cabot, a Genoese sea captain, in search of this new passage. Cabot touched land between Newfoundland and Nova Scotia and returned believing that he had visited the outlying parts of Asia. His voyage gave England its later claim to North America (*see* Cabot).

After realizing that Cabot had not reached Asia, England tried to open a route to the Orient around northern Europe—the "Northeast Passage." In 1576 Sir Humphrey Gilbert wrote his 'Discourse of a Northwest Passage', in which he reasoned that a water route led around North America to Asia. A few years later Gilbert sailed to establish a base in Newfoundland but died on the way home. Two other captains, Martin Frobisher and John Davis, each made three voyages between 1575 and 1589 to the network of

El Morro mesa, now a national monument in New Mexico, was for 170 years a camping place for Spanish explorers. Here is the record of an encampment by Juan de Oñate in 1605.

straits and inlets north of the St. Lawrence River, but neither could find a way to the Pacific.

Search for Northwest Passage

To give England a foothold in the Far East, Queen Elizabeth I chartered the East India Company in 1600. In 1602 the company sent George Weymouth to find a passage through the continent to the Pacific, but he did not sail beyond Labrador. Another expedition the same year, under Bartholomew Gosnold, explored the New England coast. When the Virginia Colony was founded in 1607, John Smith and other settlers hoped to find a waterway across the country that would lead them to the Pacific.

England had another motive for entering the competition: to weaken Spain as a European power. In the 1500's England had established a national Protestant church. Spain wished to restore the pope's authority over England. The Spanish military might was largely supported by the gold and silver from Mexico and Peru. Another source of revenue was the high duty levied on the Spanish traders, who held a monopoly on importing Negro slaves into Spanish colonies. John Hawkins, an English sea rover, began smuggling Negroes from Africa into the Spanish West Indies. He made three such voyages and reaped huge profits. On his third voyage he was attacked by a Spanish fleet and lost all but two ships (*see* Hawkins).

The Adventures of Drake

Hawkins escaped the Spaniards, taking with him his daring partner and cousin, Francis Drake (*see* Drake). Drake realized that England could gain more by seizing Spanish treasure in the West Indies than by smuggling slaves. He sailed to the Caribbean on a raiding expedition, but the Spaniards were well guarded and he won little spoil. Then he planned a bolder move. Knowing that the Spanish ships and ports on the Pacific were unprotected, he sailed from England, passed through the Strait of Magellan, and fell upon the Spaniards off Chile and Peru. He took so much plunder that he used silver for ballast. He sailed north, seeking an eastward passage through North America. Failing in this, he sailed across the Pacific and followed the route of Magellan's party back to Europe.

The English raids on the Spaniards in America helped plunge the two nations into open war. In 1588 the great Spanish Armada preparing to invade England was completely crushed (*see* Armada, Spanish). Spain's sea power swiftly declined and with it Spain's strength to keep England from the opportunities of the New World.

The riches of Spanish America prompted many Englishmen to search for gold in their own holdings in North America. In 1576 Martin Frobisher found samples of a "black earth" that he thought was a gold ore. He was wrong, but for a time England thought it was on the track of great wealth. Walter Raleigh sent out parties between 1584 and 1587 to explore and colonize the area named Virginia, but his ventures failed (*see* Raleigh, Sir Walter).

The French in Canada

While the conquistadores were busy in Central America, Spain and France were at war at home. Francis I, king of France, wanted a share of the Oriental trade to finance his armies. He commissioned a Florentine navigator, Giovanni da Verrazzano, to find a passage to Asia. In 1524 Verrazzano touched the American coast at North Carolina and then sailed north to Newfoundland. His report to the king contained the first description of the northeastern coast of North America and gave France its claim to American lands.

The next French explorer was Jacques Cartier. He made three voyages between 1534 and 1541 in quest of the Asia route. He ascended the St. Lawrence as far as the site of Montreal (see Cartier). After Cartier's voyages, a series of religious wars at home stopped France from sending out other parties. France made attempts, however, to establish two colonies as refuges for the Huguenots (French Protestants). One colony, in Brazil (1555–58), was destroyed by the Portuguese. The other, in Florida (1562–65), was wiped out by the Spaniards. Starting about 1540, French fishermen annually fished off the Newfoundland coast and in the Gulf of St. Lawrence.

Under the vigorous rule of Henry IV (1589–1610) France was again united and at peace. Once more French explorers began to seek a strait to the Pacific.

The Dutch Come Last

The Netherlands was the last to begin exploration in the New World. For years the Dutch struggled to win their independence from Spain. During this struggle, Spain in 1580 annexed Portugal and gained control of the Oriental trade. The Dutch realized that Spain might be weakened by striking at its trade. They formed the Dutch East India Company and dispatched Henry Hudson, an English sea captain, to find a shortcut to the Orient. Hudson entered the Hudson River in 1609 and ascended it to the site of Albany (see Hudson).

THE ERA OF COLONIZATION

The period of exploration and discovery that began with Columbus in 1492 soon became an international race to plant colonies around the world. The major European states—England, France, Spain, Portugal, and Holland—vied with one another for nearly four centuries to gain economic advantages in overseas territories. Colonies were founded in Africa, India, the Far East, Oceania, and in the Western Hemisphere.

The New World, consisting of North and South America and the islands of the Caribbean Sea, was viewed as an enormous wilderness area with great economic potential. The native Americans, called Indians, were not considered to be owners of the new lands; they were looked upon, rather, as primitives or savages who could benefit from the introduction of European civilization and religion.

Spain and Portugal were the first to enter the New World competition. Spain claimed and settled most of Central and South America, Florida, the Southwestern region of the present United States, and several islands in the Caribbean. France colonized Canada; the valleys of the St. Lawrence, Ohio, Mississippi, and Alabama rivers; French Guiana (now part of Guyana) on the northeast coast of South America; and a few Caribbean islands. Portugal gained control of Brazil. The Dutch settled in the Hudson Valley of North America and in Guiana, as well as in some island territories in the Caribbean. Sweden laid claim to the Delaware River valley in North America. England eventually planted 13 colonies on the Atlantic coast of North America, settled British Honduras (now Belize) in Central America, and took possession of several Caribbean islands.

Many of these colonies were financed by European-based trading companies. These companies sought riches in the crops, furs, and minerals of the New World. Trading groups were granted large areas of land by European governments, which expected in return some of the riches of the Americas, as well as secure settlements to uphold their territorial claims. The managers of the colonies worked their lands with servants, slaves, or tenant farmers.

Colonizing nations fought among themselves and against native Indian peoples for control of the land and its trading possibilities. Wars in Europe had their counterparts in nationalistic rivalries among American colonists. Cutthroat pirates and buccaneers hid out in the Caribbean, threatening shipments of gold and other riches from the New World to the Old. It was not until the 19th century that most colonial disputes were ended by treaty or by national independence movements.

The European colonists developed untamed wilderness lands into farms, villages, and cities. They established governments, legislatures, schools, colleges, churches, and businesses. Above all, they braved a hostile environment to lay the foundations of the many nations of the Western Hemisphere.

Spain's American Empire

In land area, Spain's was the largest of the colonial empires in the New World. It comprised the largest of the Caribbean islands—Cuba, Hispaniola, and Puerto Rico—as well as The Bahamas and other smaller islands; all of Mexico and most of Central America; large sections of east-coastal South America except for Brazil; Florida; and the Southwestern quarter of what is now the United States.

Spain was the first of the European nations to colonize the New World. People from France, England, Holland, and Sweden did not settle in the Americas until after 1600. Spain had the advantage of nearly a full century to stake its claims. By 1512 the larger Caribbean islands had been occupied. The rich finds of gold and silver Cortez found in Mexico prompted expeditions north and south of the region. Five years after Pizarro set out to conquer the Inca kingdom of Peru, in 1531, the conquest of the Chibcha Indians of Colombia was undertaken.

In 1562 a group of French Protestants settled in northern Florida. This seeming threat to Spanish interests prompted an expedition led by Pedro Menéndez de Áviles to get rid of the intruders. His expedition arrived in Florida in 1565, destroyed the French settlement, and built a fort on the site of what is now St. Augustine (*see* St. Augustine).

Colonization of the region north of Mexico did not begin until very late in the 16th century. In 1598 a group of settlers arrived in the New Mexico–Arizona area. Most of them, finding the climate and Indians inhospitable, returned to Mexico by 1605; but at least a small start had been made in the colonization of New Mexico. The city of Santa Fe was founded in 1610 (*see* Santa Fe).

Spain's other outposts in North America, Texas and California, were not colonized until the 1700's. By 1800 Texas was little more than a collection of small missions and the towns of San Antonio and

Nacogdoches. The settlement of California was more successful. More than 20 missions were founded between 1769 and 1800, augmented by a number of presidios, or army posts.

To regulate its American empire, Spain created two organizations, the House of Trade to deal with commerce and the Council of the Indies to make laws. The system of colonization was called the viceroyalty, a system begun in 1535 when Antonio de Mendoza was sent to govern Mexico. The viceroys, responsible to the king, were the chief colonial officials. Under them were the proprietors, charged with the direct administration of the colonies.

There were four major viceroyalties. New Spain, including all of Mexico, Central America, and the Caribbean islands, had been set up as an administrative region in 1518. New Castile, established in 1542, comprised the west coast of South America (except for the southernmost section) and much of present-day Argentina. New Granada, the northern area of South America, was organized in 1739. The last vice-

The map shows the colonial empires of Spain, Portugal, France, England, and Holland in the Americas at the end of the 17th century. With a 100-year start over the other European powers, Spain obtained the largest New World holdings. The largest privately held area was Rupert's Land, a property of Hudson's Bay Company. The period of Russian colonization of the Americas did not begin until the 18th century.

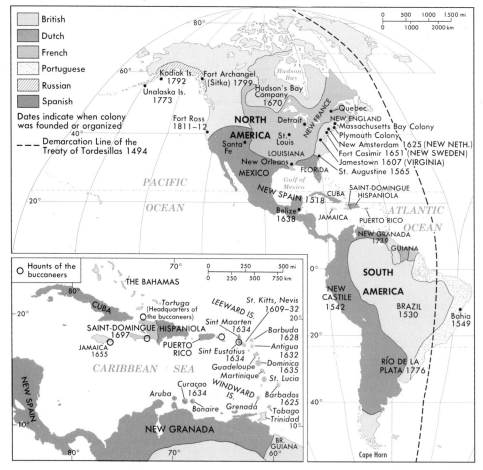

royalty, Río de la Plata (present-day Paraguay), was not organized until 1776.

A controversial aspect of Spanish colonialism was the encomienda system, an arrangement under which the Spanish landholders had "commended" to them the care of the Indians on their lands. It was in fact a system for enslaving the Indians. Indians were regarded as subject to the proprietors of New Spain, who, theoretically at least, cared for their physical and spiritual needs in return for the right to their labor. In practice, Indians were often abused and exploited. While some Spanish friars and priests condemned such slavery as early as 1515, landowners resisted the movement to abolish the encomienda.

Indians living in areas controlled by the Spanish died in great numbers from exploitation and diseases, such as smallpox, from which they had no immunity. The Indians of the Caribbean virtually disappeared; the estimated 50 million aborigines living in mainland New Spain at the time of its colonization had dwindled by the 17th century to only 4 million.

Another feature of Spanish colonialism was the influence of the "black robes"—as the Jesuit priests were called among the native peoples they hoped to convert to Christianity. These priests often led the movement into frontier areas. There they established educational institutions and religious missions while bringing the culture of European Spain into the wilds of California, Florida, and Mexico. In Florida alone, some 38 missions were founded by 1655.

Spain's colonies north of the Rio Grande were lost to the United States in the 19th century. Florida was given up in 1819, and war with Mexico brought the Southwest territories into the hands of the United States government in 1848 (*see* Mexican War).

Spain's holdings in Mexico, Central America, and South America were lost between 1810 and 1825 through a series of revolutionary movements. Only the islands of Puerto Rico and Cuba remained as colonies, and these were lost in the Spanish-American War in 1898 (*see* Spanish-American War).

The end to colonialism was prompted by a variety of factors. The American and French revolutions in the late 18th century inspired other peoples to strive for self-determination. The immediate impetus to decolonization came in the Napoleonic Wars in Europe between 1803 and 1814. French occupation of Spain and Portugal in 1807 served to isolate the American colonies from the mother countries. This isolation, coupled with long-smoldering discontent in Latin America, led to the formation of nationalist and revolutionary movements. Spain and Portugal, on the other hand, were too weakened by war at home to respond forcefully to troubles in the Americas. They could not count on help from Great Britain in retaining their colonies. British merchants were eager to trade with the newly independent nations of Latin America, which would not have colonial trade restrictions.

In 1823, during the presidency of James Monroe, the United States promulgated the Monroe Doctrine declaring against any further colonization or interference by Europe in the affairs of the Americas. With the help of the British navy, this doctrine forestalled any new colonial enterprises for several decades (*see* Monroe Doctrine).

Portugal in America

Although the Portuguese were among the earliest and most prominent world explorers, their efforts in the New World centered entirely on Brazil. After the first discoveries of Spain and Portugal of the Western Hemisphere, a conflict arose between the two countries concerning colonization rights to the New World. In 1494 a north-south Line of Demarcation was established at 370 leagues west of the Cape Verde Islands: all territory east of the line fell to Portugal, all territory west of it went to Spain. This agreement was called the Treaty of Tordesillas. Although the signers of the pact were not yet aware of the extent of the Western Hemisphere, by chance it happened that the region of coastal Brazil in South America became the possession of Portugal.

Brazil was discovered by Pedro Alvarez Cabral in 1500. The new land was of little interest to Portugal until 1530 when the threat of a French or Spanish incursion prompted King John III to order the surveying and settling of the Brazilian coastal region.

Brazil was divided into capitanias, strips of land individually colonized by a proprietor called a donatario. He, in turn, granted land to farmers. In 1549 these capitanias were united into one colony under a governor-general at Bahia (now Salvador).

The Portuguese farmers grew sugarcane for export to Europe. Sugar was first cultivated in Brazil in 1620, using Indian slave labor. This practice continued until 1755, when the Indians began to be replaced by African slaves.

In 1580 Philip II of Spain seized the throne of Portugal. Brazil came under the control of Spain until 1640, when Portugal's independence was restored. Brazil remained a colony until 1822, when a bloodless revolution set up an independent monarchy.

New Netherland

The settlement of the Dutch in the New World was led by commercial traders under the sponsorship of the Dutch West India Company, a joint stock company founded in 1621. Three years later New Netherland was founded in what is now New York State. The city of New Amsterdam was founded on Manhattan Island in 1625. The following year, Peter Minuit of the Dutch West India Company purchased the island from local Indians with trinkets worth 60 guilders (24 dollars). The Dutch built 30 houses on Manhattan that year.

The first colonists from The Netherlands were either free citizens who could own their own homesteads and receive two years of free provisions, or they were indentured husbandmen (*bouwlieden*), who had to work under contract for a term of service on Dutch West India Company farms.

In 1629 the Dutch established the patroon system. Patroons were colonists given large grants of land by the Dutch government; they held such rights as the privilege of holding court hearings in their areas. There were five large patroon land grants settled along the Hudson River from New Amsterdam to Fort Orange (present-day Albany, N.Y.). The Dutch government hoped that this arrangement would promote self-sufficient and profitable settlement of their part of the New World.

Dutch colonists faced violent conflict with local Indians. In 1644 the Dutch built a wall across lower Manhattan Island to defend their city. This is the wall for which Wall Street—the financial center of New York City—is named. Even more devastating were their conflicts with the English. In 1664, English military forces captured New Amsterdam, renaming it New York in honor of the Duke of York. Although temporarily retaken by the Dutch, New York became permanently English under the terms of the Treaty of Westminster in 1674.

The Dutch tried and failed to colonize Brazil between 1624 and 1654. They did succeed in planting colonies in the Caribbean. They settled six islands there: the Leeward Islands of Curaçao (taken from Spain in 1634), Aruba, and Bonaire; and the Windward Islands of Sint Eustatius, Sint Maarten, and Saba. The Netherlands Antilles are presently self-governing territories of The Netherlands.

England's Colonies

Although the English colonized areas throughout the New World, their most significant establishment proved to be the 13 colonies along North America's Atlantic coastline. These communities, weak and struggling at first, grew and developed to become the 13 original states of the United States of America.

An earlier British colony had been established at Roanoke Island, presently part of North Carolina, in 1584 by Sir Walter Raleigh. This colony of over 100 people mysteriously disappeared by 1591, leaving behind only the word "Croatoan" (the name of a nearby island) carved on a tree.

Of the 17th-century colonies on the Atlantic coast of North America, England founded all but two. The first settlement was established at Jamestown in 1607 (see Jamestown, Va.). The second settlement was at Plymouth in 1620; the colony was absorbed by Massachusetts in 1691 (see Plymouth, Mass.). The British colonies, in order of their founding, were Virginia (1607); Massachusetts (1630); Maryland (1634); Connecticut (1635); Rhode Island (1636); the Carolinas (1663); New Hampshire (1679); Pennsylvania (1682); New Jersey (1702); and Georgia (1732). North and South Carolina became separate colonies in 1730. The four most northerly English colonies—Massachusetts, Rhode Island, Connecticut, and New Hampshire—received the collective name New England, after the name Capt. John Smith had given the region when he first explored it in 1614. Today New England also includes Maine and Vermont.

New York (1624) was originally settled by the Dutch as New Netherland. The Swedes established Delaware as a colony (1638). These areas were eventually taken over by the English. All of the 13 colonies thus became English in speech and customs within a couple of generations.

English reign over the colonies barely served to conceal the great ethnic diversity of the settlers. The 17th century saw the arrival of Germans, Bohemians, Irish, Poles, Scots, Jews, Dutch, French, Finns, Italians, Swedes, Danes, south Slavs, and other nationalities. Slave ships brought blacks from the west coast of Africa. Of the non-British colonists, the Germans who settled heavily in Pennsylvania and Georgia were probably the most numerous.

Economic opportunity drew settlers from the Old World to the New. The sparsely populated colonies, not burdened with European traditions and class systems, were a wilderness waiting to be developed.

Throughout the whole colonial era there was a persistent labor shortage. The need for an adequate work force led to the development of the systems of indentured, redemptioner, and slave labor. Indentured servants were immigrants too poor to come to America on their own. They sold themselves under contract into specific periods of servitude, usually from three to seven years. After the time was up, a servant was freed from his obligation, given whatever money was due to him, and invested with the rights of citizenship.

Redemptioners were also immigrants too poor to get to the colonies on their own, but they arrived without labor contracts. If no relative or friend paid for their passage, the ship's captain sold them to the highest bidders for unspecified periods of service. If they managed to earn enough money, in a few years they could "redeem" themselves and be free. Otherwise they were likely to become and remain slaves.

The indenture and redemptioner systems were legally sanctioned arrangements that slowly disappeared because of disuse and public disapproval. The slave system was to persist in the Americas until the 19th century. The development of the slave trade from Africa and the exploration of the New World were almost simultaneous events. The Portuguese introduced slaves from Africa into Europe in the 15th century. After the Americas were discovered and settlements had begun, the Spaniards introduced slave labor into their colonies. Before long the great ship companies of Europe were competing for this very profitable trade. The English, in the 18th century, became the chief suppliers of African slaves to the New World. Most of the slaves went to the Caribbean islands at first, but after the economies of the English colonies of North America began to prosper, slaves were introduced there. The first slaves were brought to Virginia in 1619. (See also Slavery.)

The earliest English colonies—Virginia, Plymouth, and Massachusetts—were founded by joint stock companies. The other New England colonies were offshoots of Massachusetts Bay. Maryland and

Pennsylvania were founded as proprietary colonies: grants of land were given by the king of England to individual entrepreneurs to start a colony. Maryland was founded by Cecilius Calvert (Lord Baltimore), and Pennsylvania was founded by William Penn (*see* Baltimore, Lords; Penn). Settlers of these colonies were tenants of the proprietor, rather than landowners. Eventually all of the other colonies except Rhode Island and Connecticut came under the jurisdiction of the English crown.

The Carolinas were founded as a proprietary colony, but later came under the king's control. Georgia was started as a philanthropic enterprise, a haven for debtors and other underprivileged Englishmen. It too became part of the king's domain.

Whether royal or proprietary, all of the 13 colonies eventually had their own representative assemblies and local institutions of government. Self-rule flourished in the Atlantic colonies for a variety of reasons: they were remote from England and communication was slow; they were not so highly valued for their economic potential as were colonies in the Caribbean, India, and the Far East; the English Civil War and other troubles in Europe kept the mother country too occupied to bother with the distant colonies for long periods of time.

Theoretically, the only bond of union common to the colonies was their loyalty to the king. It was the king who appointed colonial governors, and these officials were expected to carry out royal policy. As the decades passed, however, the colonies found themselves drawn together by stronger ties than the monarchy. Their representative assemblies were quite similar in character. All of the colonies had similar agricultural economies, hence similar problems. Improved roads and shipping made communication easier. To the west, all the colonies faced the common enemy of New France and its Indian allies.

This variety of common interests eventually provided the basis of common action when English policies became oppressive. Until the end of the Seven Years' War, settled by the Treaty of Paris in 1763, England had not overly interfered in colonial life. After 1763 it began enforcing restrictions on manufacturing and trade. Parliament levied direct taxes on the colonies to help it pay its military budget. These new policies led to revolution in 1775 and to independence in 1776 (*see* Revolution, American).

Besides the 13 colonies of North America, England settled other parts of the New World. In the Caribbean, the Leeward Islands of Antigua, St. Kitts, Nevis, and Barbados were colonized between 1609 and 1632. Jamaica was seized from the Spanish in 1655. Belize was settled in 1638. Scattered settlements on the north coast of South America were united into the colony of British Guiana in 1831.

Of all the settlements in the Caribbean basin, Barbados was most successful commercially. By 1651 it was a leading producer of sugar. This commodity, much in demand by Europeans, was introduced into the island about 1637. By 1676 the sugar trade had promoted Barbados to a first-rank colony in the eyes of England. Its population was larger than that of New England, and it was far more prosperous.

Barbados was typical of the colonized Caribbean because it was not so much settled entirely by Europeans as captured by them and settled with slaves and servants to work the fields. Millions of slaves were forced into labor on the islands during the three centuries from 1500 to 1800. The first English slave-trading voyage was made by John Hawkins in 1562. After the British slave trade ended in 1807, plantation owners imported coolie (unskilled) labor from China, India, and Java. (*See also* Barbados.)

The French Colonies

The French colonized vast areas of the New World. They tried and failed to settle Brazil, the Carolinas, and Florida. They had greater success in the Caribbean and Canada.

By 1664 France controlled 14 islands in the Caribbean basin. The principal possessions were Saint-Domingue (now Haiti), Martinique, Guadeloupe, and Dominica. The economies were based largely on sugar. The labor system was African slavery. The island societies had a rigid class structure headed by white officials and planters (*gros blancs*) who governed the merchants, buccaneers, and small farmers, white laborers (*engagés*), and the slaves.

On the northeast coast of South America, the colony of French Guiana was founded about 1637. One hundred years later it was still a struggling, commercially unsuccessful colony, with a population of only about 600 whites. Not until the 19th century did the colony achieve any real prosperity. French Guiana is probably best known for Devil's Island, the former penal colony off the coast. (*See also* Guiana.)

The largest French colony in the New World was New France. This region comprised most of eastern Canada and the portion of the present United States from the Appalachians in the east to the Missouri River in the west and from the Great Lakes in the north to the Gulf of Mexico in the south. To the

Black Africans attempt to escape from 18th-century English slave traders.

337

north of New France was the large territory controlled by the Hudson's Bay Company, an English trading association (see Hudson's Bay Company).

The first colonization efforts were led by Samuel de Champlain, the "Father of New France." His first expedition sailed for America in 1603. Port Royal, Acadia (now Annapolis, N. S.), was established in 1605 as a fur trading post and fishing village. Champlain founded Quebec in 1608 and explored as far west as Lake Huron by 1615 (see Champlain).

For all the vast area the French laid claim to in North America, New France was never effectively colonized. Many permanent communities were founded, but the main interest of the mother country was commercial exploitation. The fur trade, far more lucrative than farming or fishing, became the basis of the economy. This led the French to explore widely in the region, to forge strong alliances with the native Indians, and to set up forts and trading posts. But the population of New France never grew to the same extent as that of the English colonies. By 1754, on the eve of the French and Indian War, the population of New France was only about 55,000.

What the French did very well was explore. During the 17th century a vast number of Frenchmen—traders, missionaries, and soldiers—traversed the wilderness from eastern Canada to New Orleans. They ventured throughout the whole Great Lakes region and the Mississippi Valley, claiming the territory for the king of France. Some of the most notable explorers were Père Jacques Marquette, Jean Nicolet, Pierre Radisson, Louis Jolliet, Père Louis Hennepin, and Daniel Greysolon, sieur du Lhut. The most famous of all the explorers was René-Robert Cavelier, sieur de La Salle. In 1682 his expedition made the first descent of the Mississippi, from the Illinois Territory to the Gulf of Mexico (see La Salle; Marquette).

Within this vast midsection of North America, many permanent settlements were founded, including Detroit, St. Louis, Baton Rouge, and New Orleans. Under French rule all of these settlements remained frontier outposts. Only after 1800, when citizens of the United States began trekking westward in search of plentiful, inexpensive land, did they experience real growth.

In a vain attempt to encourage emigration to North America, France instituted a colonization policy based on seigneuries, grants of land that were to be parceled out to farmers or other inhabitants. In Canada there was some increase in immigration during the second half of the 17th century, but after 1700 most French Canadians were native-born. Since the seigneurial estates could not compete with the allure of the fur trade, particularly for young men, agriculture was crippled in the French colony.

During the 17th, 18th, and early 19th centuries, France and England were frequently at war. The wars they fought in Europe generally had counterparts in the colonies—King William's War (1689–97), Queen Anne's War (1702–13), King George's War (1740–48), and the French and Indian War, a phase of Europe's Seven Years' War (1754–63).

These wars were generally detrimental to France's colonial holdings. After Queen Anne's War, the British acquired French Acadia, renaming it Nova Scotia. The French and Indian War was the most costly for France. By 1760 the British had conquered all of Canada and the French settlements on the Great Lakes. The Treaty of Paris, which ended the conflict, ceded all of New France east of the Mississippi River, except for New Orleans, to England. New France ceased to exist in 1803 when the United States purchased the territories west of the Mississippi from France (see Louisiana Purchase).

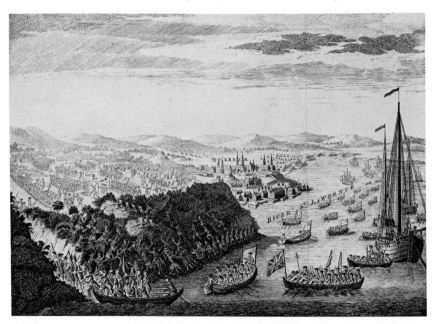

In 1759, during the French and Indian War, British troops landed upstream from Quebec and defeated the French troops on the Plains of Abraham.

Library of Congress

New Sweden

Sweden entered the race for the colonization of the New World in 1633 with the formation of the New Sweden Company. Peter Minuit, who had switched his loyalties from the Dutch to the Swedes, helped this trading organization to found Fort Christina (now Wilmington, Del.) on the Delaware River in 1638. In 1643 the Swedes expanded to a settlement of log cabins at Tinicum Island, on the Schuylkill River. They also established Fort Krisholm in 1647 and Fort Casimir (now New Castle, Del.) in 1651. Fort Casimir was especially critical because it protected the route to the rest of the Swedish colonies. In 1655 the governor of New Netherland, Peter Stuyvesant, seized Fort Casimir, making New Sweden a part of New Netherland.

Russia in North America

The expansion of Russia into North America began during the reign of Czar Peter the Great, who ruled from 1689 to 1725. He was determined to compete with other European nations in getting a foothold in the New World. The expansion of the Siberian fur trade motivated the explorations that eventually resulted in the discovery of Alaska.

Shortly before his death, Peter commissioned Capt. Vitus Bering, a Dane serving in the Russian navy, to investigate the possible land connection from Siberia to North America. Bering's first voyage, in 1728, did not succeed in locating any connection. On his voyage of 1741 he did arrive at the southern coast of Alaska; but his ship was wrecked, and he died there. Survivors returned to Russia with pelts of sea otter fur. For the next several decades the Russians exploited the fur trade of the region.

Communities and fur trading posts were established at Captain's Harbor on Unalaska Island (1773), Kodiak (1792), and New Archangel (now Sitka; 1799). As the Russians moved into Alaska, other European trading groups and colonial powers began converging on the area. To fend off competition, the Russian merchants formed a trading monopoly, the Russian-American Company, in 1799. New Archangel became the center of all commercial activity. Besides the trading post, there were a shipbuilding industry, a foundry, a sawmill, and a machine shop.

Because the Russians in Alaska were unable to make themselves self-sufficient in agriculture, they founded a new colony, Fort Ross, in northern California in 1811–12. It was hoped that the farms in this area would be able to supply enough food for the residents of Alaska. This venture never became profitable, and Fort Ross was abandoned in 1841.

In spite of repeated attempts by the Russian government to maintain a fur monopoly in Alaska and to control the waters surrounding the colony, Europeans and Americans began to move into the region during the first half of the 19th century. By 1850 hundreds of non-Russian whaling vessels were operating near Alaska. The great distance of Alaska from the Russian capital at St. Petersburg made it virtually impossible for the czar to enforce any regulations or prohibitions in his American colony.

With the outbreak of the Crimean War in 1854, Russian forces had to be concentrated in Europe. This meant that Alaska, so far away, could not be securely held and defended. In 1857 the Russian minister to the United States suggested that Alaska might be for sale. The United States Civil War prevented any transaction from taking place immediately. Finally, in 1867, a treaty was negotiated by Secretary of State William H. Seward by which the United States purchased Alaska for $7,200,000.

The End of Colonialism

For the most part, the nations of the Western Hemisphere became independent from Europe in the 50-year period from 1775 to 1825. Some vestiges of colonialism remained in the Caribbean Sea; for example, Cuba and Puerto Rico did not become free of Spain until 1898, and Barbados did not gain independence from Great Britain until 1966. Since World War II, there has been a general movement throughout the world to decolonize overseas possessions. Most of the European colonial powers lost their remaining holdings in the decades after 1945. Martinique and Guadeloupe remain departments of France, as does French Guiana. Curaçao, Aruba, and Bonaire remain part of The Netherlands overseas territories. Great Britain and the United States divide control of the Virgin Islands. Although a self-governing commonwealth, Puerto Rico is a territory of the United States. (See also West Indies.)

Canada became a self-governing dominion within the British Empire in 1867 under the terms of the British North America Act. In 1926 Canada, along with the other nations of the imperial Commonwealth, was recognized as an autonomous community within the empire. Not until 1982 did Canada promulgate its own constitution, thus freeing it to implement its own laws without the supervision of the British Parliament. Canada remained a member of the Commonwealth. (For more information on the colonial era, see the histories of Canada; Mexico; United States; South America. For the colonial wars, see French and Indian War; King George's War; King William's War; Queen Anne's War.)

BIBLIOGRAPHY FOR DISCOVERY AND COLONIZATION OF AMERICA

Babcock, W. H. Early Norse Visits to America (Gordon Press, 1976).
Buehr, Walter. French Explorers in America (Putnam, 1961).
Franklin, Wayne. Discoverers, Explorers, Settlers (Univ. of Chicago Press, 1979).
Honour, Hugh. The New Golden Land (Pantheon, 1976).
Horgan, Paul. Conquistadors in North America (Farrar, Straus & Giroux, 1963).
Horgan, Paul. Great River (Holt, Rinehart & Winston, 1954).
Morison, S. E. European Discovery of America: the Northern Voyages (Oxford, 1971).
Morison, S. E. European Discovery of America: the Southern Voyages (Oxford, 1974).
Parkman, Francis. Pioneers of France in the New World, reprint of 1865 ed. (Corner House, 1970).

AMERICAN LITERATURE

In Herman Melville's 'Moby-Dick', one of the greatest books in American literature, Ahab scans the sea for the white whale. This illustration is by Rockwell Kent.

AMERICAN LITERATURE. Wherever there are people there will be a literature. A literature is the record of human experience, and people have always been impelled to write down their impressions of life. They do so in diaries and letters, in pamphlets and books, and in essays, poems, plays, and stories. In this respect American literature is like any other. There are, however, many characteristics of American writing that make it different from all others. This has not always been true.

American literature began with the first English colonies in Virginia and New England. Colonists came to the New World to find religious freedom and prosperity. They came, however, in no spirit of revolution. They came as Englishmen, bringing with them the literary wealth of English legends, ballads, and poems and the richness of the English language. They were loyal to the Crown. These settlers did not even call themselves Americans.

How the English colonists slowly came to think and act as "Americans" is a familiar and proud story. How their literature slowly grew to be "American" writing is less well known. The growth of American literature, however, follows closely the history of the nation from its beginning to the present time.

American authors have written countless essays and songs, poems and plays, novels and short stories. There is space here to discuss only the most important and the best. Even a short summary, however, shows something of the splendid accomplishment of American literature since it emerged from its crude colonial beginnings more than 300 years ago.

Colonial Times in America

THE MAN SOMETIMES called the first American writer was Capt. John Smith (1580–1631). He was a soldier-adventurer who came to Virginia in 1607 and wrote pamphlets describing the new land. His first, 'A True Relation of Virginia' (1608), aimed at attracting settlers and winning financial support for the colony.

His 'General History of Virginia' (1624) elaborates on his experiences. In it he tells how his life was saved by Pocahontas. Smith was an able leader and an interesting reporter. His books are valued because he was the first person to write about the English settlements. (*See also* Smith.)

340

Colonial life in Virginia was best described by William Byrd (1674–1744), owner of Westover, an estate of almost 180,000 acres on the James River. The beautiful house is a showplace today. Educated in England, Byrd returned home to lead the life of a country gentleman. He worked hard managing his affairs. His most notable public act was to survey the boundary between Virginia and Carolina, fighting his way through the great Dismal Swamp. He described this adventure of 1728–29 in 'History of the Dividing Line', published in 1841. He told, often amusingly, of settlement life in the backcountry. Byrd's 'Secret Diary', discovered in 1940, gives intimate glimpses of colonial times and helps bring to life this refined and witty colonial gentleman.

Plantation life in Virginia was civilized, even elegant. The people were not intellectual, however, and they produced little writing. The inhabitants, descended from the Royalist, or "Cavalier," group in England, were faithful members of the Church of England. They accepted religion as a matter of course and felt no need to write about it. In addition, the system of plantation life produced a number of isolated communities, as did the feudalism of the Middle Ages. This kept people from gathering in cities.

People in the Southern Colonies therefore had little need to write, and social conditions did not encourage them to do so. The South's great contributions, both to statecraft and to literature, came later. The significant writing of colonial times was done in New England, where American literature may properly be said to have begun.

Colonial life began in New England with the landing of the Pilgrims at Cape Cod in 1620. Before going ashore they signed the Mayflower Compact, an agreement to live together in harmony under law (see 'Mayflower'). It is found in 'History of Plimoth Plantation'. This moving account of the early struggles of the colonists was written by William Brad-

Cotton Mather, the leading Boston clergyman in the early 1700's, was one of the most influential Puritans.

ford (1590–1657), who was governor for 30 years. A similar journal was kept by Governor John Winthrop (1588–1649) of the Massachusetts Bay Colony, founded ten years after Plymouth (see Winthrop). Present-day knowledge of Thanksgiving, the Pilgrims' dealings with Indians, and other experiences of the first settlers comes from these two narratives of the colonization.

The Influence of Puritanism

For more than 100 years after the Pilgrim landing in 1620, life and writing in New England were dominated by the religious attitude known as Puritanism. To un-

In colonial times in America many women were believed to be witches in league with the devil. Cotton Mather wrote extensively of them. These old woodcuts are from his 'On Witchcraft', published by the Peter Pauper Press.

Nathaniel Hawthorne's 'Scarlet Letter', from which this illustration is taken, well portrays the stern ideas of the Puritans.

Religious Quality of Puritan Writing

New Englanders have always been industrious writers. Most of what they wrote in colonial times was prompted by their religious feeling. Many sermons were published and widely read. Cotton Mather (1663–1728), the leading clergyman in Boston in the early 1700's, wrote more than 400 separate works. The most ambitious was his 'Magnalia Christi Americana' (Christ's Great Achievements in America), published in 1702.

Clergymen encouraged some people to keep personal diaries or journals. The most readable of these today is the diary of Samuel Sewall (1652–1730). The 'Diary of Samuel Sewall 1674–1729' (published 1878–82) is lively and often amusing, as when the author wrote of his courtship of Madame Winthrop: "Asked her to acquit me of rudeness if I drew off her glove. Enquiring the reason, I told her 'twas great odds between handling a dead goat and a living lady."

Sewall was a courageous man. A judge during the witchcraft trials in 1692, he concurred in the decision to hang 19 persons condemned as witches. After the hysteria had died down, however, he alone among the judges stood up in meeting and publicly asked "to take the blame and shame" for his part in the executions. He was also an early foe of slavery. His 'Selling of Joseph' (1700) was perhaps the earliest antislavery pamphlet in America.

The Puritans wrote little imaginative literature. The theater was not welcomed by them any more than it was by the Puritans who closed the London theaters in 1642. Fiction writing (stories and novels) was in its infancy in England, and it probably did not occur to men and women in the New World to write stories. The only imaginative Puritan literature was poetry; and that, like everything else in Puritan life, was prompted by religion.

The first book in English to be published in the New World was the 'Bay Psalm Book' (1640). The new translations of the Biblical psalms were plain; the meter and rhyme were regular, as in Psalm xxiii, which begins as follows:

The Lord to me a shepherd is, want therefore shall not I.
He in the folds of tender-grass doth cause me down to lie.

This familiar rhythm was used by Michael Wigglesworth (1631–1705) in 'The Day of Doom' (1662), a 224-stanza account in verse of the Last Judgment. Based on the Puritan religious belief in Calvinism, the poem presents in dramatic terms the divine judgment of those condemned to eternal torment in hell and also of those who, by God's grace, are elected to gain eternal salvation in the world to come. Many Puri-

derstand colonial life and literature one must understand Puritanism, one of the major influences in American life.

The early settlers in New England were Protestants. England had become a Protestant country when Henry VIII broke away from the Roman Catholic church. Some Englishmen, however, felt that the break was not complete. They wanted to "purify" the church of Catholic features; they were therefore known as Puritans. Another group, the Separatists, wanted to separate, or break away entirely, from the Church of England. These were the Pilgrims. Both groups came to the New World in order to worship God in their own way. They felt they had a divine mission to fulfill. It was the will of God, they believed, that they establish a religious society in the wilderness. This belief must have helped them endure the hard life they faced as colonists.

In the Puritan view, God was supreme. The Puritans held that He revealed His will through the Bible, which they believed literally. Clergymen interpreted the Bible in sermons, but each man and woman was obliged to study it for himself too. The people had to be educated in order to read the Bible, to discuss it, and to write about it. Harvard College was founded in 1636 partly to meet this demand for an educated populace. Other colleges and public schools followed. Indeed, the intellectual quality of New England life, which later influenced other parts of the country, is traceable to the Puritans' need for a trained and literate population.

tans, both young and old, committed 'The Day of Doom' to memory.

More interesting, because it is better poetry, are the religious verses of Edward Taylor (1642–1729). These were first published in 1939. Taylor was a devout clergyman, but his poems are not harsh and gloomy. Instead, they express his feeling of joy and delight in the Christian life. For instance, in one poem he pictured the church members as passengers in a coach, Christ's coach, singing as they rattle along to salvation in the next world:

For in Christ's coach they sweetly sing,
As they to Glory ride therein.

Taylor's verse is full of such vivid and exciting metaphors. His is the most interesting American poetry of colonial times.

Jonathan Edwards—The Last Puritan

Puritanism could not maintain its authority forever. As the seaboard settlements grew and people became prosperous, as more political power was given to the people, and as a more scientific attitude challenged the old religious way of thinking, men and women in New England came to be more worldly and to take their religion for granted. It was to combat this worldliness that Jonathan Edwards (1703–58),

the last and the greatest Puritan, taught and preached and wrote. Puritanism was fated to die out, but not before Edwards made heroic efforts to keep it alive.

Edwards believed that the people were too matter-of-fact about religion. To be religious, one must feel deeply, he thought. He therefore joined with others in preaching emotional sermons. These produced a wave of religious revivals. After the enthusiasm had passed, however, Edwards was dismissed from his congregation and became a missionary to the Indians. He was a brilliant theologian and philosopher, and most of his writings are difficult to read. His 'Personal Narrative', however, which tells the story of his youthful religious experiences, is an honest and moving revelation. It was written about 1740.

The nation owes a great debt to Puritanism. It is true that in several ways Puritan life was harsh and unlovely, as one learns from reading 'The Scarlet Letter', Nathaniel Hawthorne's great novel. Nevertheless one must admire the Puritans for their zeal, their courage, and their strong moral nature. They recognized that man is often guilty of evil actions. Their hardheaded view of human nature has much truth in it. The 20th century has seen enough cruelty and depravity for one to believe that the Puritan view of human beings was valid in some respects.

The Shaping of a New Nation

AMERICAN WRITING in colonial days, as has been seen, dealt largely with religion. In the last 30 years of the 18th century, however, men turned their attention from religion to the subject of government. These were the years when the colonies broke away from England and declared themselves a new and independent nation. It was a great decision for Americans to make. Feeling ran high, and people expressed their opinions in a body of writing which, if not literature in the narrow sense, is certainly literature in the sense of its being great writing.

Since World War II moves for national independence have been numerous throughout the world. Historically, however, the first people to throw off a colonial yoke were those of the American Colonies. The literary record of their struggle thus is a fascinating and inspiring story to people everywhere.

Franklin—Spokesman for a Nation

The birth of the United States was witnessed by Benjamin Franklin (1706–90) in his last years. His career began in colonial days. At 17 he ran away from his home in Boston and went to Philadelphia. How he took up printing, made enough money to retire at 42, and educated himself is the subject of his 'Autobiography', first published in book form in English in 1793. This is the first and most celebrated story of the American self-made man. Many of his rules for self-improvement ("Early to bed, early to rise," and so forth) appeared in his 'Poor Richard's Almanack', first published in 1732.

Franklin was simple in manners and tastes. When

The fiery pamphlets of Thomas Paine inspired the American people to declare their independence from Great Britain.

he represented the colonies in the European courts, he insisted on wearing the simple homespun of colonial dress. He used the plain speech of the provincial people. He displayed the practical turn of mind of a people who had shrewdly conquered a wilderness. (*See also* Franklin, Benjamin.)

Franklin embodied the American idea. That idea was defined by Michel Guillaume St. Jean de Crèvecoeur (1735–1813), a Frenchman who lived in America for many years before the Revolution. In his 'Letters from an American Farmer' (1782) he described the colonists as happy compared with the suffering people of Europe. In one letter he asked, "What then is the American, this new man?" This is a challenging question even today, nearly 200 years later. Crèvecoeur's answer then was:

"*He* is an American, who, leaving behind him all his ancient prejudices and manners, receives new ones from the new mode of life he has embraced, the new government he obeys, and the new rank he holds. He becomes an American by being received in the broad lap of our great *Alma Mater* (nourishing mother). Here individuals of all nations are melted into a new race of men, whose labours and posterity will one day cause great changes in the world . . . The American is a new man, who acts upon new principles; he must therefore entertain new ideas and form new opinions . . . This is an American."

The immigrant prospered in America, and he became fiercely loyal to the system that made possible his prosperity. That system, which included a large measure of personal freedom, was threatened by the British. Americans tried to preserve it by peaceful means. When this became impossible, they chose to become a separate nation.

Thomas Paine Arouses the Patriots

The power of words to affect the course of history is clearly seen in the writings of Thomas Paine (1737–1809). The shooting had started at Lexington and Concord in April 1775, but for months there was no move to break away from England. Then, in January 1776, appeared Paine's pamphlet 'Common Sense'. In brilliant language, logical and passionate, yet so simple that all could understand, Paine argued in favor

Perhaps no man has so greatly influenced the "American" language as Webster. Because of him Americans spell many words differently from the English.

of declaring independence from Britain. The effect was electric.

By June the Continental Congress resolved to break away; and on July 4, 1776, the Declaration of Independence appeared. Paine continued his pamphleteering during the war in 'The Crisis', a series of 16 papers. The first one begins, "These are the times that try men's souls." George Washington said that without Paine's bold encouragement the American cause might have been lost. (*See also* Paine.)

The famous Declaration of Independence was largely the work of Thomas Jefferson (1743–1826). In justifying the American Revolution to the world he stated the political axioms on which the revolution was based, among them the proposition that "all men are created equal." This phrase is at the very heart of democracy. (*See also* Jefferson.)

After the war Americans, having rejected their rulers, were faced with the job of governing themselves. They attempted "to form a more perfect Union." The result was the Constitution. Although the United States has flourished under the system of government outlined in the Constitution, not all Americans favored adopting the new plan when it was proposed. In the great debate over adopting it, Alexander Hamilton (1755?–1804) and others wrote 85 essays, known as 'The Federalist' (1787–88), in support of the Constitution. These are models of clear and forceful writing.

Poets during these years wrote patriotic verses on political themes. Some of the poems of John Trumbull (1750–1831) and Joel Barlow (1754–1812) are interesting, but in style they were imitative of English poetry. Novels too resembled those written of England. Susanna (Haswell) Rowson (1762–1824) wrote 'Charlotte Temple' (1791), a sentimental tale of a betrayed heroine. 'Wieland' (1798), by Charles Brockden Brown (1771–1810), is patterned after an English novel. This imitativeness is not surprising: writers were in the habit of writing like Englishmen.

More and more, however, authors wanted to write as Americans. They had won political independence; they now wanted literary independence. The poet Philip Freneau (1752–1832) pleaded for a native literature. So did Noah Webster (1758–1843). "Customs, habits, and language," he wrote, "should be national." He did his part by compiling 'The American Spelling Book' (1783) and his 'American Dictionary of the English Language' (1828). "Center," instead of "centre," and "honor," instead of "honour," are typical of Webster's "Americanized" spelling. (*See also* Webster, Noah.)

Literature of the Early Republic

IT WAS ONE thing for writers to want to create a native American literature; it was quite another thing to know how to do it. For 50 years after the founding of the nation, authors patterned their work after the writings of Englishmen. William Cullen Bryant was known as the American Wordsworth; Washington Irving's essays resemble those of Addison and Steele; James Fenimore Cooper wrote novels like those of Scott. Although the form and style of these Americans were English, the content—character and especially setting—was American. Every American region was described by at least one prominent writer.

Frontier life in western Pennsylvania is pictured in 'Modern Chivalry' (1792–1815), written by a friend of James Madison and Philip Freneau, Hugh Henry Brackenridge (1748–1816). This episodic narrative, modeled on Miguel de Cervantes' 'Don Quixote', shows how people in the backcountry behaved politically under the new Constitution. Henry Adams called 'Modern Chivalry' a "more thoroughly American book than any written before 1833." American it is, in character, setting, and theme.

The beauties of New England's hills and forests were sung by William Cullen Bryant (1794–1878). 'Thanatopsis' (1817) and 'A Forest Hymn' (1825) show a reverence for nature. The English critic Matthew Arnold thought 'To a Waterfowl' (1818) the best short poem in the English language. (*See also* Bryant.)

New York City and its environs were the province of Washington Irving (1783–1859). 'Salmagundi' (1807–8), which he coauthored, describes the city's fashionable life. 'A History of New York . . . by Diedrich Knickerbocker' (1809), an imaginary Dutch historian, is an amusing account of its history under Dutch rule.

Irving's masterpieces were his sketches 'The Legend of Sleepy Hollow' and 'Rip Van Winkle', both published in 1820. These tales—the first of Icha-

This is one of the thrilling episodes in 'The Deerslayer', by Cooper. The picture (originally in color) is by N. C. Wyeth (copyright by Charles Scribner's Sons).

Here the Headless Horseman (in reality the reckless horseman Brom Bones) chases luckless Ichabod Crane in 'The Legend of Sleepy Hollow', by Washington Irving. This picture by F. O. C. Darley was drawn for an early edition of the story.

Another of Irving's well-known characters, Rip Van Winkle, left his shrewish wife to seek peace in the Catskills. He returned after his 20-year nap to find his world entirely altered. His wife was dead, and even his faithful dog did not recognize him.

bod Crane, a superstitious schoolmaster, the second of Rip, who sought refuge in the Catskills from his shrewish wife and slept for 20 years—are among the best-loved American stories. Irving's literary skill was appreciated in England too. There he was recognized as the first important American writer. (See also Irving.)

James Fenimore Cooper

James Fenimore Cooper (1789–1851) wrote more than 30 novels and many other works. He was an enormously popular writer, in Europe as well as at home. Of interest to readers today are his opinions on democracy. Reared on an estate near Cooperstown, N. Y., the writer had a patrician upbringing. When he criticized democracy, as in 'The American Democrat' (1838), he criticized the crudity he saw in the United States of Andrew Jackson. Yet he defended the American democratic system against attacks by European aristocrats.

In his day Cooper was best known as the author of the 'Leatherstocking Tales', five novels of frontier life. These stories of stirring adventure, such as 'The Last of the Mohicans' (1826) and 'The Deerslayer' (1841), feature Cooper's hero Natty Bumppo, the skillful, courageous, and valorous woodsman. This character embodied American traits and so to Europeans seemed to represent the New World. (See also Cooper.)

The South too was portrayed in fiction in these years. 'Swallow Barn' (1832), by John Pendleton Kennedy (1795–1870), pictures life on a Virginia plantation. Later portrayals of life in the Old Dominion, in fiction and in motion pictures, often follow the idealized picture of Virginia given in 'Swallow Barn'. In South Carolina many adventure novels of frontier life, such as 'The Yemassee' (1835), came from the pen of William Gilmore Simms (1806–70), sometimes called the Cooper of the South.

Thus by 1835 American writers had made a notable start toward creating a new and independent national literature. In Scotland in 1820 Sydney Smith, a famous critic who wrote for the *Edinburgh Review*, had asked: "In the four quarters of the globe, who reads an American book?" Sensitive Americans, conscious of their cultural inferiority, winced at this slighting remark. More and more, however, they had reason to be proud of their writers. In the next 20 years American literature would come to the full flowering which had been hoped for since the Revolution.

The Flowering of American Literature

THE MIDDLE of the 19th century saw the beginning of a truly independent American literature. This period, especially the years 1850–55, has been called the American Renaissance.

More masterpieces were written at this time than in any other equal span of years in American history. New England was the center of intellectual activity in these years, and Ralph Waldo Emerson (1803–82) was the most prominent writer.

Emerson and Thoreau

Emerson began his career as a clergyman. He came to feel, however, that he could better do his work outside the church. Thus he became an independent essayist and lecturer, a lay preacher to Americans. He preached one message—that the individual human being, because he is God's creature, has a spark of divinity in him which gives him great power. "Trust thyself," Emerson said in his essay 'Self-Reliance' (1841). He believed it made no difference what one's work is or where one lives. Emerson himself lived in the village of Concord. There, as oracle and as prophet, he wrote the stirring prose that inspired an entire nation. (*See also* Emerson.)

One person who took Emerson's teaching to heart and lived by it was his Concord neighbor Henry David Thoreau (1817–62). Thoreau lived a life of independence. He was a student of wildlife and the great outdoors. He was also a student of literature, who himself wrote fresh, vigorous prose. His masterpiece is 'Walden, or Life in the Woods' (1854), an account of his two-year sojourn at Walden Pond. "I went to the woods," he wrote, "because I wished to live deliberately"—that is, to decide what is important in life and then to pursue it.

The simplicity of Thoreau's life makes a strong appeal to modern readers. They are impressed too by his essay 'Civil Disobedience' (1849), which converted Emersonian self-reliance into a workable formula for opposing the power of government. He advocated passive resistance, including, if necessary, going to jail, as he himself did. Mahatma Gandhi, who was jailed so many times in his fight to free India from British rule, was strongly influenced by

the ideas contained in this essay of Thoreau's. (*See also* Thoreau.)

Popular New England Poets

More conventional and less challenging than the Concord writers were the popular poets of New England. Oliver Wendell Holmes (1809–94) won early renown with 'Old Ironsides' (1830), which told the story of the *Constitution* in such stirring words that people rallied and saved it from destruction. His 'Last Leaf' (1833) and 'Chambered Nautilus' (1858) were also favorites. Holmes took time from his medical practice to write 'The Autocrat of the Breakfast-Table' (1858), which first appeared in the newly founded *Atlantic Monthly*. The autocrat is a thin

In Longfellow's well-known poem 'The Courtship of Miles Standish', John Alden intends to speak for Miles Standish but actually wins Priscilla for himself. This painting is by W. L. Taylor.

disguise for Holmes himself. Holmes was a witty conversationalist; and through his mouthpiece, the autocrat, he gave lively expression to a variety of opinions (*see* Holmes, Oliver Wendell).

The poems of James Russell Lowell (1819–91) were admired in his day. This wellborn Bostonian was versatile. He was editor of the *Atlantic Monthly*, a professor at Harvard, United States minister to Spain and then to England, a literary critic, and a poet.

Lowell's 'Vision of Sir Launfal' (1848) has long been popular. Fresher and more native is his 'Biglow Papers' (1848–67), rhymed verse in Yankee dialect used for humor and satire. Hosea Biglow, the pre-

tended author, is blessed with common sense and a strong New England conscience. By capturing the thought and speech of the American rustic, Lowell showed one way in which American literature could be truly national. (*See also* Lowell, James Russell.)

The favorite American poet in the 19th century was Henry Wadsworth Longfellow (1807–82). He was a storyteller in verse. 'The Courtship of Miles Standish' (1858), 'Evangeline' (1847), and 'The Song of Hiawatha' (1855) use native incident and character. Longfellow was trying to give the United States legends like those of Europe. His lyrics too were admired. 'A Psalm of Life' (1839) was memorized by generations of school children. (*See also* Longfellow.)

Nearly as popular as Longfellow was John Greenleaf Whittier (1807–92), author of such well-known ballads as 'Barbara Frietchie' (1863). Whittier was a Quaker and thus a foe of slavery, which he attacked in both verse and prose. After the Civil War he wrote 'Snow-Bound' (1866). This homely poem, based on the poet's childhood experiences, pictures farm life in an earlier day. It must have reminded many readers of their own rural childhoods. (*See also* Whittier.)

Poe and Hawthorne

The major writer in the South during these years was Edgar Allan Poe (1809–49). Instead of American characters, themes, and settings, Poe wrote of timeless places and people. He did brilliant work in three areas: poetry, short fiction, and criticism. Poems such as 'The Raven' (1845), 'The Bells' (1849), and 'Ulalume' (1847) are vague in thought but hauntingly beautiful in sound.

Poe's short stories are of two kinds: (1) tales of detection, such as 'Murders in the Rue Morgue' (1843) and 'The Purloined Letter' (1845) (Poe's Dupin being the forerunner of Sherlock Holmes and other later fictional detectives); and (2) psychological tales of terror, such as 'The Fall of the House of Usher' (1839) and 'The Masque of the Red Death' (1842). Both types of stories observe the principles he outlined in his critical writing— that a story should be short, that it should aim at a definite effect, and that all its parts should contribute to the effect, thus making for unity. Modern short-story

In a quiet meadow near Walden Pond, Thoreau found time to analyze life's essentials. The result of his thoughts was the famous 'Walden'. This picture is by Rudolph Ruzicka (copyright by R. R. Donnelley & Sons Co.).

RALPH WALDO EMERSON
The New England essayist Ralph Waldo Emerson preached that man has a spark of divinity in him which gives him power.

OLIVER WENDELL HOLMES
This popular poet won early fame with 'Old Ironsides', a poem which saved the ship *Constitution* from destruction.

writers owe much to Poe's critical ideas. (*See also* Poe.)

Although Poe disliked most New England writing because it was too obviously moral in intention, he greatly admired the stories of Nathaniel Hawthorne (1804–64), The son of a sea captain from Salem, Mass., Hawthorne grew up in that old port city rich in legends of the past. He steeped himself in the history of Puritan times and laid many of his stories in that period. The earlier settings made his tales shadowy and, because the Puritans were conscious of sin, gave the author a chance to explore the sinful human heart in his fiction. He did so in the stories 'Young Goodman Brown' (1835) and 'The Minister's Black Veil' (1837), as well as in his full-length masterpiece, 'The Scarlet Letter' (1850). His fiction, seemingly simple, is rich and subtle. It is also often profound in its treatment of life's darker side, the side which the Puritans had freely acknowledged but which Hawthorne's contemporaries often chose to ignore. (*See also* Hawthorne.)

Herman Melville

Modern readers are warm in their praise of Hawthorne. They have come to admire also the work of his neighbor and spiritual ally, Herman Melville (1819–91). All but forgotten by the public in his later years, Melville in modern times is regarded as one of the great writers in American literature. He was the first to treat the South Seas in fiction;

'Typee' (1846) and 'Omoo' (1847) give fascinating pictures of this exotic region.

These books and the three that soon followed them prepared Melville to write 'Moby-Dick' (1851), considered by some as the greatest contribution of American letters to world literature. This work is many books in one: an epic, a tragedy, a novel, a treatise on the whaling industry, and a spiritual autobiography. At the story's center is Captain Ahab, who obsessively searches the seven seas to kill the white whale which bit off his leg. Melville's later works, short pieces such as 'Benito Cereno' (1856) and 'Billy Budd' (written shortly before his death), are artfully done and full of meaning. Few writers wrestled more heroically with the basic problems of existence than did Herman Melville. (*See also* Melville.)

Whitman—Poet of the People

The other major writer at mid-century, Walt Whitman (1819–92), was unique. His 'Leaves of Grass' (1855) was new in form and in content. Whitman wrote about his country in a way never done before. At first the little book of strange verse seemed a failure. Emerson, however, recognized its greatness; and now most people agree that it was the first book of truly American poetry.

Here, at last, was the fresh, distinguished bard destined to create an art wholly American. Through

Whitman's poetry the new nation is caught in its largeness, its variety, and its great energy. 'One's-Self I Sing' and his major poem, 'Song of Myself', are brilliant and complex utterances of the human spirit freed in the New World.

Walt Whitman's poems are a love letter to his country. To accomplish his purpose of singing the praise of the untrammeled American spirit, Whitman forsook the confining poetic forms of his day. His poems are melodic chants, suited to the ear.

Readers of American literature around the world have turned to Whitman as the spokesman for the new democratic society. No poet has celebrated that society with more enthusiasm or more poetic genius than Walt Whitman. His verses are charged with the energetic American spirit. They are a striking contrast to the neat meters and rhymes of conventional poetry previously written. Since Whitman's death, his writing has influenced many other American poets. (*See also* Whitman, Walt.)

Edgar Allan Poe's famous story 'The Purloined Letter' turns on the fact that a completely obvious hiding place will be overlooked. This picture is by W. A. Dwiggins (copyright by R. R. Donnelley & Sons Co.).

Transition to the Modern Age

THE CIVIL WAR sharply interrupted American literary activity. Although seven of the ten major authors of the American Renaissance continued to write after the war years, most of these had done their best work by 1860. Literary leadership passed to a new generation of writers. Their work is interesting in itself. It is interesting also because it prepared the way for the excellent writing which followed in the 20th century.

The Civil War was a harsh experience. In addition to enduring the pain and sorrow of war, Americans were shocked by the threat to the nation itself. They realized that democracy was not an inevitable system of government; it could fail, though it had survived the test of civil war. It was subject to further strains, however, from corruption in Washington, D. C.; from growing industrialism, which moved people from farms to cities and led to bitter quarrels between workers and employers; and from immigration and westward expansion.

These problems and disappointments were perplexing. No longer could men look to the future with complete optimism. In place of the exuberant chants to democracy he had written in 1855, Whitman, in 'Democratic Vistas' (1871), was urging Americans to look critically at their society and work hard to keep it healthy. In short, postwar conditions prompted the people to view their world directly and honestly.

Writing in the War Years

The most memorable writing of the war years came from the pen of Abraham Lincoln (1809–65). The prairie president had earlier shown his mastery of the art of cogent and compelling argument. In his wartime utterances he rose to new heights. The Gettysburg Address and his second inaugural address are prose of haunting beauty.

The Confederacy is represented in verse by Henry Timrod (1828–67) and Paul Hamilton Hayne (1830–86). Had not the war shaken their health and devastated their region, they might have achieved more. Timrod's 'Ode' (1873) on the graves of the Confederate dead in a Charleston cemetery is an excellent poem.

Sidney Lanier (1842–81) is the most interesting Southern poet of the period. He is best known for his musical verse, such as 'The Song of the Chattahoochee' (1883), and for poems of vague mysticism, such as 'The Marshes of Glynn' (1878). (*See also* Lanier.)

Whitman wrote some of his best verse after the war. 'Drum-Taps' (1865) contains brilliant and moving war vignettes; and the excellent long poem 'Passage to India' (1871) voices his hope for world unity and his belief in the oneness of creation.

The outstanding poet of these years, however, wrote works as different from Whitman's as they could possibly be. The lyrics of Emily Dickinson (1830–86) are short, compressed, rhymed, and metrical; whereas Whitman's lines, in free verse, are loose, unrhymed and somewhat diffuse. There is another difference as well: whereas Whitman had his poetic fingers on the nation's pulse, Emily Dickinson lived in a world not much larger than the garden of her father's house in Amherst, Mass. The world of her imagination, however, was as vast as the universe. In tight, rhyming hymn meters she wrote of the nature she knew intimately, of love, and of the ultimate questions of death and immortality.

The works of Emily Dickinson were hardly known during her lifetime beyond a small circle of friends, for they were not published until after her death. Modern readers have come to value her as one of the truly great American poets. (*See also* Dickinson.)

Regional Prose After the Civil War

The postwar years seemed better suited to prose than to verse. The regional story or novel became popular. Bret Harte (1836–1902) acquainted the country with the Western miner in such stories as 'The Luck of Roaring Camp' (1868) (*see* Harte). Joel Chandler Harris (1848–1908), through his character Uncle Remus, depicted plantation life in the Deep South (*see* Harris). George Washington Cable (1844–1925) wrote of Creoles and the bayou country near New Orleans. Indiana was the province of Edward Eggleston (1837–1902), whose 'Hoosier Schoolmaster' (1871) became a favorite.

Harriet Beecher Stowe (1811–96) is best known for her novel about slavery, 'Uncle Tom's Cabin' (1852); but her 'Oldtown Folks' (1869) is a fine portrayal of life in New England (*see* Stowe). New England is also pictured in the stories of Sarah Orne Jewett (1849–1909) and Mary E. Wilkins Freeman (1852–1930).

Every section of the country was represented in these local-color stories. The customs, manners, and especially the speech ways of the locality were carefully portrayed. Such elements made the stories realistic. However, because the authors usually depicted their regions as they were in their own youth, they often flavored their stories with sentiment. The mixture of realism and sentiment was appealing, and local-color stories filled the pages of the leading magazines until the end of the century.

Three Major Novelists

The three major novelists in this period stand in an interesting relationship to one another. At one extreme is Mark Twain (1835–1910), self-educated, a product and a depicter of the frontier. At the other extreme is Henry James (1843–1916), wealthy, educated by tutors, a resident in Europe, a man of cosmopolitan tastes. His novels portray Americans traveling or living in Europe and so confronting an old, rigid, and traditional society. Twain and James were not personally acquainted, but each was a good friend of William Dean Howells (1837–1920), who in several ways embodied both the provincial and the cosmopolitan interests of his two friends.

Mark Twain's works are of several kinds. 'The Innocents Abroad' (1869) and 'Roughing It' (1872) are books of travel which combine personal anecdotes, description, and humorous comment in a delightful mixture. Twain's interest in the past is seen in 'The Prince and the Pauper' (1882); in the

The poet Walt Whitman sprawls on a high point above the shore of Long Island Sound and contemplates the grass that gave him the title for his most famous work—'Leaves of Grass'. This picture is by Lewis C. Daniel.

351

No boy in fiction is more beloved than Huck Finn. His adventures on the Mississippi River have been relived by generations of readers. This picture is by E. W. Kemble (drawn in 1884 for the first edition).

hilarious 'A Connecticut Yankee in King Arthur's Court' (1889); and in 'Personal Recollections of Joan of Arc' (1896), which Twain thought his best work.

Favorites with most readers are his Mississippi River books: 'The Adventures of Tom Sawyer' (1876), a delightful treatment of a boy's life in a small town; 'Life on the Mississippi' (1883), which re-creates vividly the colorful days of steamboating on the great river; and 'The Adventures of Huckleberry Finn' (1884), Twain's masterpiece.

The adventures of Huck, the boy, and Jim, the runaway slave, as they float downstream on a raft, appeal to all readers. It is Huck who tells the story throughout, and his language, so limited yet so expressive, is a literary achievement of the first order (see Writing, Creative). One of the great novels of the world, Mark Twain's story set a new style in fiction by showing the literary possibilities in common, everyday American speech. (See also Twain.)

Henry James studied the American character in his stories and novels but by a method quite different from Twain's. James's usual way was to depict Americans in the process of experiencing Europe, thereby contrasting two cultures, the old and the new. In this contrast the manners of Americans sometimes suffer by comparison with those of Old World aristocrats. Morally, however, James's Americans compare favorably with Europeans. The author saw good in both groups and was less interested in taking sides than in exploring, in an elaborate and elegant style, the many differences between them. 'The American' (1877), 'The Portrait of a Lady' (1881), and 'The Ambassadors' (1903) all develop the international theme. James's fiction is not always easy to read, but it is as rich and subtle as any in American literature.

William Dean Howells was a champion of realism. Novels, he believed, should present life as it is, not as it might be. Accordingly his books study types of persons prominent in American life of the time: women in the professions, in 'Dr. Breen's Practice' (1881); the self-made man, in 'The Rise of Silas Lapham' (1885); factory workers and summer resort people, in 'Annie Kilburn' (1889). His books also discuss serious social questions honestly: divorce, in 'A Modern Instance' (1882); and social justice, in 'A Hazard of New Fortunes' (1889). Taken together, Howells' novels give a full, clear picture of American life in the last years of the 19th century. (See also Howells.)

The Birth of Naturalism

The novels of Howells and James presented life truthfully as the authors saw it. In the opinion of a later generation, however, their fiction omitted great areas of life: Howells was too polite, too proper; and James was too exclusively concerned with the leisure classes. Several novelists at the turn of the century therefore undertook to portray those sides of life, often ugly, which they felt had not been fully recognized in literature.

Stephen Crane (1871–1900) depicted life in New York City slums in 'Maggie: A Girl of the Streets' (1893); and in the excellent 'The Red Badge of Courage' (1895) he wrote of how the Civil War, in all its horror, impinged on the consciousness of a youthful recruit. Frank Norris (1870–1902) showed the ugly violence in economic life in 'The Octopus' (1901), which depicts the struggle between railroads and wheat ranchers in California, and in 'The Pit' (1903), a story of speculation on the Chicago wheat exchange. The vigorous, often ruthless, activities of men in the business world were also the province of Theodore Dreiser (1871–1945). His 'Sister Carrie' (1900), 'The Financier' (1912), and 'The Titan' (1914) show men and women caught up in the cruel, raw forces of commercial life. In his best work, 'An

American Tragedy' (1925), youthful Clyde Griffiths is victimized by these forces.

All these novels were written in the mode of literary naturalism, which invited writers to examine human beings objectively, as a scientist studies nature. In portraying ugliness and cruelty, the authors refrained from preaching about them; rather they left readers to draw their own conclusions about the life so presented. Naturalistic fiction shocked many readers; but in revealing hitherto neglected areas of life, it greatly broadened the scope of fiction.

The 19th century closed with the Gay Nineties. In the opinion of many, however, the times were more somber than gay. Political corruption, violent conflicts between capital and labor, loss of religious certitude, concern over the developments of science —these causes, among others, gave to literature a darker cast than it had had in earlier times. The writer who best caught this mood was Henry Adams (1838–1918), historian and descendant of two presidents of the United States. In 'The Education of Henry Adams' (1918) he depicts himself as a misfit and, he would have readers believe, a failure. A failure he certainly was not, but the book shows why he thought he was. Unlike his forbears, Adams felt powerless to affect the course of history. Men were at the mercy of great social and economic forces, which worked for the disintegration of society. This view seemed sound to many. For them the 'Education' summed up an era. (*See also* Adams, Henry.)

Modern American Literature

AMERICAN LITERATURE of the 20th century is different from earlier literature in significant ways. It is possible to list several of its characteristics which are implied in the term *modern:*

1. The scope of modern literature is broad. For example, writers are able to treat ugliness and violence freely.

2. The meanings of modern literature are deeper and more complex than in earlier writing because life itself has become more complex. Present-day writers have learned much about economics, sociology, anthropology, and especially psychology; and their works often embody ideas drawn from these new areas of thought.

3. Modern writing is technically sophisticated. To write about the life of today, authors have discovered new ways to express their ideas. These ways are fresh and stimulating, but they sometimes make severe demands on readers.

4. If technique is complicated, the language of modern writing is simpler than that of earlier times. In place of the old formal language, thought proper for literature, contemporary writers have substituted language much closer to that of everyday speech.

5. Modern literature exhibits more variety than that of earlier periods. Because life today is varied, so is the writing that reflects it varied—in subject, in region portrayed, in philosophical outlook, in scope (broad and sociological or concentrated and psychological), and in form and technique.

In a short space, only some of the outstanding writers and their works can be noted. The following discussion groups the chief modern writers by literary field—poetry, drama, and fiction.

This 1920 scene shows Main Street in Sauk Centre, Minn., from which Sinclair Lewis took the name for his novel 'Main Street'.

A satirical novelist, Lewis wrote of small-town life during the years following World War I.

Poetry in the Middle West

In the years following the Civil War, poetry, except for the work of Whitman and Emily Dickinson and two or three minor poets, was at low ebb. The age was one of prose. Early in this century, however, poetry once again came into its own.

In 1912 Harriet Monroe (1860–1936) founded the little magazine *Poetry: a Magazine of Verse*, in Chicago. She sought to encourage struggling poets everywhere and to train readers in the art of reading verse. The first issue of *Poetry* quoted Whitman for its motto: "To have great poets there must be great audiences too." The founding of *Poetry* was a timely act, for, as Harriet Monroe soon found out, there were a number of unknown poets who needed just such an outlet for their work. *Poetry* published the first or early work of nearly every distinguished modern American poet. (*See also* Monroe, Harriet.)

Poetry magazine discovered excellent new writers in its own backyard, the Middle West, never until then known for its poets. One such discovery was Edgar

Lee Masters (1869–1950), known primarily for 'Spoon River Anthology' (1915). It is a series of poems in free verse (that is, unrhymed and not in strict meters). Each poem is a report on his own life by a character now buried in the village graveyard. As each person reveals himself he helps build up the picture of an entire Illinois village. More than 200 people are there: "The weak of will, the strong of arm, the clown, the boozer, the fighter." Not all the poems are good, but some are excellent, and the total effect of the book is strong.

Vachel Lindsay (1879–1931) was another *Poetry* discovery. 'The Congo and Other Poems' (1914) secured him fame, especially the title poem, with its jazz rhythms and its strong refrain:

Then I saw the Congo, creeping through the black,
Cutting through the Jungle with a golden track.

Almost as popular are 'General William Booth Enters into Heaven' (1913) and the more stately poem 'Abraham Lincoln Walks at Midnight' (1914).

The third striking discovery by *Poetry* was Carl Sandburg (1878–1967). Like Masters and Lindsay, Sandburg made poetry out of the materials of the Midwest. He first won a prize with 'Chicago' (1914), still his best-known poem, which begins:

Hog-butcher for the World,
Tool-maker, Stacker of Wheat,
Player with Railroads and the
      Nation's Freight-handler;
Stormy, husky, brawling,
City of the Big Shoulders.

The importance of Whitman's influence on modern American poetry is unmistakably shown in Sandburg's lines. Sandburg also used the sprawling unmetered and unrhymed line, and he too was the spokesman for all the American people. Like the martyred Lincoln, whom he portrayed in a great biography, Sandburg affirmed a faith in the democratic process and in the people for whom it operates. "The people will live on," the poet asserted confidently in 'The People, Yes' (1936), his book of democratic chants. (*See also* Sandburg.)

Poets of Modern New England

. About the time that *Poetry* was first published in the Middle West, two Eastern poets attracted favorable attention. The first, Edwin Arlington Robinson (1869–1935), had for years been writing poems ignored by all but a few. After 1912, with the newly awakened interest in poetry, Americans began to read his verse. Today he is ac-

'Look Homeward, Angel', the first of Wolfe's long, passionate novels, is in many ways his best. This scene was taken from the stage version of the book.

Robert Frost (left), a New Englander, and Carl Sandburg, a Midwesterner, wrote poetry which was universally loved.

T. S. Eliot, shown here receiving an honorary degree in Great Britain, his adopted country, influenced many modern poets.

knowledged to be one of the most important American poets of the 20th century.

Robinson wrote about defeated people, those who found the complexities of life baffling and wearing. Everything he wrote, however, had a dry humor and wit as well as a profound sense of pity for men's suffering. Although most of his best poetry concerned New England, Robinson wrote several long poems about King Arthur's knights. 'Tristram' (1927) was a best seller. (*See also* Robinson.)

The second New England poet to win both popularity and fame was Robert Frost (1874–1963). His poems, such as 'Mending Wall' (1914) and 'Birches' (1916), deal lovingly with the country Frost knew as a New Hampshire farmer. As Emily Dickinson described her own poetry, he wrote "New Englandly," particularly in his early poems. His writing treats of simple, enduring experiences, with a delightful humor and tenderness. Simple his poems are, but at the same time they are deep and provocative. Some poets appeal to masses of readers; others appeal chiefly to persons of sophisticated taste. Frost is admired by both groups. (*See also* Frost, Robert.)

T. S. Eliot and New Techniques

The Middle West and New England both appear in the poetry of T. S. Eliot (1888–1965). Born and educated in the United States, Eliot later became a British subject. Nonetheless the sights and memories of his earlier years make up the substance of his best poetry, with a few exceptions.

Although Eliot has published few poems, they have had a tremendous influence on modern poetic technique. 'The Love Song of J. Alfred Prufrock' (1915) was the first poem of Eliot's to be widely read. 'Prufrock' describes the thoughts of a timid, well-educated man on his way to an elegant party. He fears what the people there will say about his clothes, his figure, his thinning hair—"in short, I am afraid." Prufrock stands for the fearful people of the world, who, though outwardly prosperous, are inwardly defeated.

Eliot's second important poem was 'The Waste Land' (1922). Here modern life is portrayed as a land of desert and rocks, lacking water upon which life depends. The rich, heroic stories of the past are referred to repeatedly, as a contrast to the sterile, empty present. The poem is an immediate reflection of the disillusionment which many artists felt after World War I, when life seemed meaningless and trivial. 'The Waste Land' at first puzzled critics with its technique of placing splintered fragments of thought against one another in striking combinations.

Eliot's later poetry, as complicated in technique as 'The Waste Land', is more affirmative than disillusioned. 'Four Quartets' (1943) is a reasoned discussion of the foundations of the Christian faith. The influence of Eliot's ideas and his technique has been very great. Other modern poets have followed his lead. (*See also* Eliot, Thomas Stearns.)

E. E. Cummings (1894-1962) satirized modern pettiness and emptiness, as Eliot had done, but Cum-

355

© Houghton-Mifflin Co.

Ántonia Shimerda longs for a better life in Willa Cather's 'My Antonia', a story of an immigrant Nebraskan farm family. This picture is by W. T. Benda.

mings also wrote lyrics of tenderness and beauty. His technique is arresting, because his verse usually omits punctuation marks and capitalization (he signed his name "e e cummings").

Another exciting modern poet is Hart Crane (1899–1932), whose early death cut short a promising career. His poem 'To Brooklyn Bridge', a portion of the longer work 'The Bridge' (1930), is reminiscent of Whitman's 'Crossing Brooklyn Ferry'. As in the Whitman poem, the scene of New York Harbor is used symbolically to say things about man and human relations.

The poetry of Wallace Stevens (1879–1955) is also distinguished modern verse. An insurance executive in Hartford, Conn., Stevens in a sense was a poetic amateur, yet his verse is brilliant. Like all true poets, he was in love with the medium of language. In his verse every word counts, for it is made to carry subtle shades of meaning and to affect the reader through its sound as well. 'Peter Quince at the Clavier' (1923) is one of his best-known poems. Marianne Moore (1887–1972) also used poetic symbols extensively in her work.

The old traditional appeals of poetry were not forgotten with increased use of new techniques. Edna St. Vincent Millay (1892–1950) used the sonnet form to express age-old concepts of romantic love. Archibald MacLeish (1892–1982) wrote stirringly of the Spanish conquest of Mexico in 'Conquistador' (1932), and Stephen Vincent Benét (1898–1943) re-created the American past in 'John Brown's Body' (1928), a

book-length epic of the Civil War. Elinor Wylie (1885–1928) and Sara Teasdale (1884–1933) wrote poetry of delicate perception.

Mention should be made also of popular light verse. Although not "great," such verse, when skillfully written, is enjoyed by many. Ogden Nash (1902–71) was noted for his playful satires, deliberately rendered in bad versification which includes outrageous rhymes (*see* Nash). The verse of Phyllis McGinley (1905–78), which often appeared in *The New Yorker* magazine, is more conventional in form. In her verse she captured the details of modern living and implicitly commented on life satirically or with affection; yet feeling is subdued because of the detachment afforded by her clever versifications.

Modern American Drama

Thus far no mention has been made of the drama. The reason is that although the theater was active during the 19th century, the American plays produced were mostly sensational melodrama and hence of small literary importance. The case is different with drama of the 20th century, however. As the country has matured culturally, audiences have encouraged serious playwrights to write plays which, if not so great as those of Sophocles and Shakespeare, are interesting and important as literature.

The first step in creating a serious drama was to abandon the improbable situations of melodrama and to adopt the realistic approach of the Norwegian dramatist Henrik Ibsen. 'Street Scene' (1929), by Elmer Rice (1892–1967), and 'Dead End' (1935), by Sidney Kingsley (born 1906), show life as it is lived, using realistic scenery and authentic dialogue.

Realism on the stage was an improvement over melodrama, but too frequently it was unable to get beneath the surfaces of life. For this reason dramatists experimented with new techniques. 'Beggar on Horseback' (1924), by George S. Kaufman (1889–1961) and Marc Connelly (1890–1980), and 'The Adding Machine' (1923), by Rice, use the technique of expressionism, in which realism is clearly abandoned in favor of fantasy and other representational devices in an effort to show meanings beneath appearances.

'Our Town' (1938), by Thornton Wilder (1897–1975), was also experimental. No scenery is used, and actors are planted in the audience. With such unconventional methods the playwright presented a sympathetic picture of life in a small American town.

Another technical experiment in the modern theater was drama in verse. Sophocles and Shakespeare used verse in their plays, and some modern dramatists have sought to follow their example in an effort to achieve emotional intensity. Several of the plays of Maxwell Anderson (1888–1959), such as 'Winterset' (1935), are written in blank verse (*see* Anderson, Maxwell). The same is true of T. S. Eliot's 'Murder in the Cathedral' (1935), a dramatization of the martyrdom of Thomas Becket, archbishop of Canterbury. These experiments in verse drama were interesting but have had no lasting influence on dramatic construction in the modern theater.

Eugene O'Neill—Leading American Playwright

It is generally agreed that the leading American dramatist is Eugene O'Neill (1888–1953). He tried bold experiments in dramatic technique. In such plays as 'The Emperor Jones' (1920) and 'The Hairy Ape' (1922) all the attention is concentrated on the central character, the other characters being unimportant. In 'The Great God Brown' (1926) the actors use masks to distinguish between the real thoughts and the assumed thoughts of the characters. In 'Strange Interlude' (1928) the characters reveal their true opinions by uttering two kinds of remarks: one to the other characters, the other to the audience, as a dramatic aside.

O'Neill's most ambitious work was 'Mourning Becomes Electra' (1931), a trilogy that presents in American terms Aeschylus' drama of Agamemnon's return from the Trojan War. It is a somber work, as are most of O'Neill's plays. He was versatile enough, however, to achieve many different kinds of dramatic success. 'Ah, Wilderness!' (1933), a study of adolescence, is an amusing and refreshing folk comedy of New England life. In quantity, variety, profundity, and technical boldness, O'Neill is clearly the leading figure in modern American drama. (*See also* O'Neill.)

Williams and Miller

The most important playwrights since O'Neill were Tennessee Williams (1911–83) and Arthur Miller (born 1915). Williams portrayed a decadent Southland with tarnished or frustrated belles in 'A Streetcar Named Desire' (1947) and 'Cat on a Hot Tin Roof' (1955). 'The Glass Menagerie' (1944) also portrays faded grandeur, but more tenderly.

'Death of a Salesman' (1949), written by Miller, reveals the aloneness of an ordinary, undistinguished man. Undeniably poignant, the play approaches true tragedy. 'The Crucible' (1953), based on the witchcraft persecutions in colonial New England, reminds modern audiences that fear of the unknown, mass hysteria, and perversions of justice infect life in the 20th century as they did in the 17th.

© 1939 Metro-Goldwyn-Mayer, Inc.

Margaret Mitchell's 'Gone with the Wind' is a good example of the historical novel. The book, dealing with the Civil War, became an all-time best seller. This scene is from the movie made from the novel.

New York Public Library

'Mourning Becomes Electra' by Eugene O'Neill is an American version of Aeschylus' tragedy 'Oresteia'.

Modern American Fiction

Poetry has enjoyed a rebirth, and drama has come of age artistically. It is prose fiction, however, that is the major form of literary expression in the 20th century.

Writers of important modern fiction are numerous, the level of their achievement is high, and the variety of their work is remarkable. Grouping of some of the more significant writers reveals their variety.

Historical Novelists

The historical novel has appealed to Americans eager to discover their cultural roots. Although the form has been popular since the days of James Fenimore Cooper, the massive best seller 'Anthony Adverse' (1933), by Hervey Allen (1889–1949), gave a new vogue to the historical novel. 'Gone with the Wind' (1936), by Margaret Mitchell (1900–49)—about the Civil War and also a big book—was an all-time best seller. The times of the American Revolu-

tion formed the background for 'Drums Along the Mohawk' (1936), by Walter Edmonds (born 1903), and for 'Northwest Passage' (1937), by Kenneth Roberts (1885–1957).

The American frontier West has been a favorite subject for historical romancers. Standing considerably above most Westerns is 'The Big Sky' (1947), by A. B. Guthrie (born 1901). His narrative skill did justice to the great epic theme of the West.

Regional Novelists

A number of modern novelists have sought to picture the region of the country that they knew best. As a rule these "regionalists" are more authentic than their predecessors, the post-Civil War local-color writers. Willa Cather (1875–1947) is best remembered for depicting Nebraska of frontier days. 'O Pioneers!' (1913) and 'My Ántonia' (1918) are heartwarming stories of settlement on the prairie. (*See also* Cather.)

The Norwegian-born novelist O. E. Rölvaag (1876–1931) wrote a moving story of Norwegian settlers, 'Giants in the Earth' (translated 1927), which can be claimed for American literature. The Midwest in more recent times is the subject of 'The Folks' (1934) and 'Iowa Interiors' (1926), by Ruth Suckow (1892–1960).

The list of Southern regionalists is long, for the American South has produced an impressive number of fine writers in recent years—Eudora Welty (born 1909), Carson McCullers (1917–1967), Jesse Stuart (1907–1984), and, most notable, William Faulkner (1897–1962).

The works of Robert Penn Warren (born 1905) are laid in his native Southland. The best is perhaps his study of a political demagogue in Louisiana, 'All the King's Men' (1946). One of the outstanding novelists of recent years, Warren was also a skillful poet and critic.

The metropolitan sections of the East have formed the settings of several distinguished novelists. Edith Wharton (1862–1937), a disciple of Henry James, wrote of the well-to-do classes of New York City, as in 'The House of Mirth' (1905). Equally gifted was Ellen Glasgow (1874–1945), who studied changing attitudes and social behavior in and near Richmond, Va., in 'Barren Ground' (1925) and 'Vein of Iron' (1935). New England aristocrats, genteel and rather stuffy, were the special concern of John P. Marquand (1893–1960). The best of his kindly satires is perhaps 'The Late George Apley' (1937), the story of a vigorous Boston aristocrat who succumbs to the pressures of social convention, until his life is stunted and meaningless.

Although Pearl S. Buck (1892–1973) did not deal with American themes, she ranks high among modern American writers. She portrayed Chinese peasants sympathetically in 'The Good Earth' (1931) and other novels. (*See also* Buck.)

Depicters of Their Eras

Just as some novelists are associated with the regions of which they write, others are associated with the times of which they seem to be the spokesmen. F. Scott Fitzgerald (1896–1940) caught the mood of the Roaring Twenties in 'This Side of Paradise' (1920) and 'The Great Gatsby' (1925). A volume of his stories was appropriately titled 'Tales of the Jazz Age' (1922). (*See also* Fitzgerald.)

Small-town life in the postwar years is the theme of 'Main Street' (1920), by Sinclair Lewis (1885–1951). His 'Babbitt' (1922) satirizes the dull, unimaginative life of a middle-class businessman. (*See also* Lewis, Sinclair.)

In the following decade, the years of the big depression, novelists concerned themselves with problems of a people caught in hard times. 'The Grapes of Wrath' (1939), by John Steinbeck (1902–68), tells of the Joads, a family of Oklahoma farmers who are driven from their drought-stricken land and make a heroic trek West in an old jalopy. It is a memorable and moving tale. John Dos Passos (1896–1970) is also associated with the depression years. His anger toward the system that permitted wholesale misery fired several novels openly critical of abuses of the economic system. His major work is the trilogy 'U.S.A.' (1937), which chronicles the lives of several persons over a 30-year period. It is not a flattering picture of American life; but the portrait is vivid, made so by the unique way in which the story is told. (*See also* Steinbeck; Dos Passos.)

The novels of Thomas Wolfe (1900–38) have moved many readers. A physical giant of colossal appetites, Wolfe wrote novels proportionately huge. They tell of a young man finding his place in the world and so are full of the passion, ecstasy, anger, and frustration of youth. The first to be written, 'Look Homeward, Angel' (1929), is in many ways the best; but almost equally powerful is the last, 'You Can't Go Home Again' (1940). (*See also* Wolfe, Thomas.)

Hemingway and Faulkner

The two greatest American novelists of recent times are Ernest Hemingway (1899–1961) and William

Wide World

Laura and a "gentleman caller" admire one of her glass animals in Tennessee Williams' play 'The Glass Menagerie'.

Faulkner. Both are representative of the modern world, yet in several important ways they are quite different. Hemingway's novels are about man alone, uprooted and facing the Great Enemy (which takes several forms) as bravely as he can. Faulkner, on the other hand, presented a society, a variety of persons of differing colors and classes, in his native Mississippi. His work is a saga of the South, and the same characters reappear in his successive novels.

Both writers were concerned with moral values. For Hemingway courage was the paramount virtue. Man cannot win in the struggles in which he engages, but the important thing is how he behaves. If he meets his defeat without flinching, then he achieves "grace under pressure," which is a triumph of sorts, that gives meaning and dignity to his struggle. Faulkner's moral values were social rather than personal. The South was cursed with slavery, which bred countless problems before, but especially since, the Civil War. The good people, white and black, do what they can to solve the problems; but they are

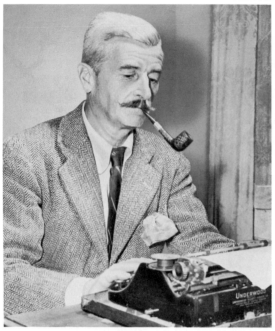

The novels of William Faulkner constitute a saga of the American South. His characters reappear in successive books.

A Nobel laureate, as was Faulkner, Ernest Hemingway wrote of man alone facing life without flinching at danger.

often helpless before the conniving, unscrupulous people who dominate their lives.

Finally, the writing styles of the two men are markedly different. Faulkner's prose is ornate and complex; his sentences are long and complicated; and many nouns and adjectives are used. Hemingway's style is quite the opposite. His sentences are short and pointed; adjectives are used sparingly. The effect is one of great power and compression.

The level of performance of these two writers is high. The outstanding works by Hemingway include 'The Sun Also Rises' (1926); 'A Farewell to Arms' (1929); 'For Whom the Bell Tolls' (1940); and the minor masterpiece 'The Old Man and the Sea' (1952). Among Faulkner's best known books are 'The Sound and the Fury' (1929), 'Light in August' (1932), 'Absalom, Absalom!' (1936), and 'The Town' (1957). (*See also* Faulkner; Hemingway.)

The Modern Short Story

Although the novel seems to be the dominant form of prose fiction in modern times, at least equally impressive is the short story. It is a form to which American literature has some claim. The features of the short story were first defined by Poe, and many Americans practiced in the form to fill the newly founded magazines after the Civil War. Most of the important 20th-century authors have written at least a few excellent stories. In former years authors spoke of trying to write the "great American novel," envisioning, apparently, a gigantic work of fiction that somehow would capture the entire American experience. Such an intention has come to seem more and more like a fond dream, as the country has grown and

as modern life has become more varied. In place of the broad canvas, many writers prefer the vignette; they feel that fiction can best explore and reveal life if it does so in small, manageable units.

Some outstanding short-story writers, many of whom are also important novelists, are: Ring Lardner (1885–1933), Sherwood Anderson (1876–1941), Katherine Anne Porter (1894–1980), Irwin Shaw (1913–84), James Thurber (1894–1961), Eudora Welty (born 1909), William Saroyan (1908–81), John O'Hara (1905–70), John Cheever (1912–82), and J. D. Salinger (born 1919). (*See also* Anderson, Sherwood.)

AMERICAN LITERATURE SINCE THE 1950's

A foreshortened time perspective and the enormous amount of literature published since the 1950's has made it virtually impossible to distinguish between the enduring and the merely successful. Another hindrance to assessment has been the profusion of various types of fiction, drama, and poetry. In addition to the fairly traditional literary forms, there was much experimental writing that sought new modes of expression in both structure and content.

Fiction

In recent decades thousands of novels, representing a wide range of fiction types, have been published. There were epic historical novels, spy fiction, war novels, science fiction, novels growing out of the civil rights and the women's rights movements, and regional novels, as well as more standard fiction depicting all facets of life in the United States.

Some of the best-selling fiction works have been the historical novels by James Clavell (born 1924),

James Michener (born 1907), and Herman Wouk (born 1915). Clavell's novels are set in the Far East. His first book, 'King Rat' (1962), was the story of a Japanese prison camp in Singapore. This was followed by 'Tai-Pan' (1966), an account of late 19th-century Hong Kong; 'Shogun' (1975), a fictional retelling of the founding of the Tokugawa shogunate in medieval Japan; and 'Noble House' (1981), a story of modern China. Michener's long historical novel 'Hawaii' (1959) was followed by 'Centennial' (1974), set in 19th-century Colorado; 'Chesapeake' (1978), a story of the Eastern Seaboard of the United States; and 'Covenant' (1980), a novel based on the history of South Africa. Two of Wouk's novels—'Winds of War' (1971) and 'War and Remembrance' (1978)—comprised one story about World War II.

Similar to the historical novel, but representing a distinct style, was the so-called New Journalism as practiced by such writers as Alex Haley (born 1921), Truman Capote (1924–84), Norman Mailer (born 1923), and Tom Wolfe (born 1930). Such writers often used the novel as a device to relate history or to report on the changing American scene. Haley's 'Roots' (1976) is concerned with a black man's search for his family background. Capote's 'In Cold Blood' (1966) is based on a true murder story. Mailer's first novel was a World War II epic, 'The Naked and the Dead' (1948). In addition to writing several other novels, he used the journalistic approach in 'The Armies of the Night' (1967), about the anti-Vietnam demonstration against the Pentagon; 'Miami and the Siege of Chicago' (1968), on the Republican and Democratic conventions of 1968; and 'Of a Fire on the Moon' (1971), about the United States space program. Tom Wolfe portrayed the counterculture of the 1960's in 'The Electric Kool-Aid Acid Test' (1968), and in 'The Right Stuff' (1979) he depicted the development of the American astronauts.

Much experimental fiction was written in the 1960's and 1970's. The term experimental is a broad one in this case since it includes some authors who used the traditional novel structure to make a point quite beyond the story line itself, and other writers who devised new ways to tell a story in their attempts to make sense of 20th-century existence. Among the experimentalists were Vladimir Nabokov (1899–1977), Kurt Vonnegut (born 1922), Joseph Heller (born 1923), Thomas Pynchon (born 1937), and John Barth (born 1930). The Russian-born Nabokov used a fairly traditional structure in 'Lolita' (1955), whose antihero Humbert Humbert is possessed by an overpowering desire for young girls. But his 'Pale Fire' (1962), a novel comprising a long poem and a commentary on it, demonstrated his mastery of unorthodox structure. (*See also* Nabokov.)

Vonnegut has frequently combined traditional and unorthodox forms in one novel. In his best known book, 'Slaughterhouse Five' (1969), he recreates his experience in World War II during the firebombing of Dresden, Germany. In 'The Sirens of Titan' (1959) he simulates science fiction in a story that suggests that the history of the human race is an accident that occurred because of an alien planet's search for a spare part for a spaceship. His work is generally critical of scientific and technological progress that detracts from mankind's nobler human qualities.

Heller used a war novel, 'Catch-22' (1961), to create a biting satire on war itself. His second novel, 'Something Happened' (1974), was written as a man's inner dialogue, as he tries to understand the meaning of his life. In 'Good as Gold' (1979) Heller combined a plot about a comic Jewish family with an assault on governmental stupidity and confusion.

Like Vonnegut and Heller, Pynchon used the comic and the bizarre to explore the malaise of the 20th century. His 'Gravity's Rainbow' (1973), one of the major novels of the 1970's, has as its central character a man who can predict where German missiles will fall during World War II. The novel has been described as a dramatization of paranoia and the imagery of impending destruction. History is viewed as having been set on an irreversible course by modern bureaucracy and technology.

Barth is a novelist who combines philosophical complexity with strong satire and occasional bawdy humor. In 'The Sot-Weed Factor' (1960) Barth explores his philosophical concerns in a novel that is both a burlesque of the early history of Maryland and a parody of the 18th-century English novel. 'Giles Goat Boy' (1966) is a tale of a mythic hero set in a world of great, computer-run universities.

The success of experimental writing did not diminish efforts in traditional fiction. Popular novels were often oriented toward regionalism, ethnic groups, social criticism, or the women's movement.

Regional writers from the South and Southwest were especially noteworthy. From writers like Faulk-

Most of Truman Capote's works reveal a craftsmanlike style and an interest in eccentric and bizarre characters.

Nicholas Sapieha—Camera Press/Photo Trends

Nancy Crampton

The first novel of experimental fiction writer Joseph Heller, 'Catch 22', is an ironic work of protest literature.

ner, Welty, and Warren, a new generation of writers learned how to paint vivid pictures of a place and a time. Larry McMurtry (born 1936) showed himself to be a brilliant creator of intense and highly personal fiction in such Texas-based works as 'Horseman, Pass By' (1961), 'The Last Picture Show' (1966), and 'All My Friends Are Going to Be Strangers' (1972). William Styron (born 1925) stated that his 'Confessions of Nat Turner' (1967), a novel about a 19th-century slave revolt, was a meditation on history. Reynolds Price (born 1933) explored the history of two families in the Carolina Piedmont region in 'The Surface of the Earth' (1975). Flannery O'Connor (1925–64), a Catholic, used Southern settings and strange violent incidents to query religious faith.

John Cheever and John Updike (born 1932) both lived in the Northeast. Their short stories and novels were regional in a more limited sense than the works of Southern writers. They both wrote of life in the suburbs, of affluent people deeply dissatisfied with their lives. In 'The Wapshot Chronicle' (1957) and 'The Wapshot Scandal' (1964) Cheever focused on a family in suburban St. Botolphs, Mass. His satirical 'Bullet Park' (1969) also deals with suburbanites. One of the most ambitious chronicles of suburbia was Updike's series of novels about the life of Harry "Rabbit" Angstrom: 'Rabbit, Run' (1960), 'Rabbit Redux' (1971), and 'Rabbit Is Rich' (1981).

Fiction by black Americans attained considerable literary stature. 'Invisible Man' (1952), by Ralph Ellison (born 1914), and many of the books by James Baldwin (born 1924)—for example, 'Go Tell It on the Mountain' (1953), 'Another Country' (1962), and 'If Beale Street Could Talk' (1974)—were all vivid por-

trayals of the plight of blacks in a white society. Ishmael Reed (born 1938), in books like 'The Free-Lance Pallbearers' (1967) and 'Nineteen Necromancers from Now' (1970), created an avant-garde comedy of black-influenced language. Toni Morrison (born 1931) used elements of folklore to tell a contemporary story in her novel 'Song of Solomon' (1977). (*See also* Baldwin.)

Some of the eminent Jewish-American writers in recent decades were Nobel prizewinners Saul Bellow (born 1915) and Isaac Bashevis Singer (born 1904), Philip Roth (born 1933), and Bernard Malamud (born 1914). Bellow was adept at creating characterizations of modern urbanites, alienated from society but unbroken in spirit. His first great success came with 'The Adventures of Augie March' (1953), the story of a poor Jewish boy from Chicago trying to make sense of his life in the 20th century. The heroes of 'Herzog' (1964), 'Mr. Sammler's Planet' (1970), and 'Humboldt's Gift' (1976) are Jewish intellectuals whose interior monologues are set against the realities of the outside world. (*See also* Bellow.)

Singer, who was born in Poland, wrote in Yiddish. His novels and short stories are moving presentations of Jewish life in Poland and the United States. Among his major novels are 'The Family Moskat' (1950), 'The Magician of Lublin' (1960), 'The Slave' (1962), and 'Enemies, a Love Story' (1972).

Roth uses a confessional approach in his writing. In more or less autobiographical novels such as 'Goodbye Columbus' (1959), 'Portnoy's Complaint' (1966), and 'My Life as a Man' (1974), he turns the pains and frustrations of his own life into brilliant and often vulgar comedy.

Malamud is a teller of religious and cultural fables with strong moral lessons. His Brooklyn, N.Y., childhood environment is the setting for most of his books. His first novel, 'The Natural' (1952), is the story of a baseball hero. 'The Assistant' (1957) and 'The Fixer' (1966) also use themes from his background. But in 'God's Grace' (1982) he contrived an original scenario about the life of one Calvin Cohn, the sole human survivor of a nuclear war; it is a book filled with Biblical allusions and religious symbolism.

The growth of the women's movement and a strong but failing struggle for passage of the Equal Rights Amendment to the Constitution motivated a profusion of feminist literature. One of the most prominent authors was Mary McCarthy (born 1912), already an established novelist by the time the women's movement gained momentum in the 1960's. Some of her works were satirical commentaries on marriage, sex, and the role of the emancipated woman in society. In 'The Group' (1963) she followed the lives of eight Vassar graduates as they resist or succumb to the intellectual fads of the 1930's and 1940's.

Other feminist writers included Joan Didion (born 1934), author of 'Play It As It Lays' (1970) and 'A Book of Common Prayer' (1977); Sandra Hochman (born 1936), author of 'Endangered Species' (1977); Cynthia Buchanan (born 1937), author of 'Maiden'

(1972); Marilyn French (born 1929), author of 'The Women's Room' (1977) and 'The Bleeding Heart' (1980); Erica Jong (born 1942), author of 'Fear of Flying' (1974); Lois Gould (born 1938), author of 'Final Analysis' (1974); Sue Kaufman (1926–77), author of 'Diary of a Mad Housewife' (1967) and 'Falling Bodies' (1974); Judith Rossner (born 1935), author of 'Looking for Mr. Goodbar' (1975) and 'Emmeline' (1980); Alix Kates Shulman (born 1932), author of 'Burning Questions' (1978); Gail Godwin (born 1937), author of 'Violet Clay' (1978); and Mary Gordon (born 1949), author of 'Final Payments' (1978) and 'The Company of Women' (1981).

Drama

The experimental theater movement of the 1960's tried to break down the barriers between life and art, actor and writer, actor and audience. An example is 'The Connection', by Jack Gelber (born 1932), which was first produced at New York City's Living Theatre in 1959. Before the play begins, a group of heroin addicts are assembled onstage, occasionally improvising some jazz while waiting for their supplier. A "producer" and "author" explain to the audience that they are making a documentary film about these men. To further destroy the illusion of the play, addict-actor-musicians panhandle in the lobby during intermission. The play compares addiction to other shortcuts to happiness.

All the members of these experimental groups worked together to create and perform plays. Groups like La Mama Experimental Theatre Club (1961), The Company Theatre (1967), and The Negro Ensemble Company (1966) created opportunities for playwrights such as Sam Shepard (born 1943), Lonne Elder (born 1931), Megan Terry (born 1932), and Lanford Wilson (born 1937) to develop new works.

In 1959 'Raisin in the Sun', by Lorraine Hansberry (1930–65), a realistic drama about a black Chicago family, opened the way for other plays by and about American blacks. Under his original name, LeRoi Jones, the playwright Imamu Baraka (born 1934) wrote 'The Dutchman', which was a great critical success in 1964. The one-act play was set in the subways of New York City. Baraka's message, that blacks must free themselves from hostile white culture, was stated in a more and more violent and radical way in his later plays. Ed Bullins (born 1935) was another playwright whose many works were written for the black community. Plays such as 'In the Wine Time' (1968) and 'The Duplex' (1970) used common situations—problems of growing up or finding love—to show the vitality of black characters and the ways they acquiesce in their own cultural destruction. Both Bullins and Baraka used theater to create a new sense of awareness, pride, and community among American blacks. (*See also* Baraka.)

Two of the best known playwrights of the 1960's and 1970's were Edward Albee (born 1928) and Sam Shepard (born 1943). Albee's plays present characters who are uncomfortable in their isolation but are often unable to love. In his most famous play, 'Who's Afraid of Virginia Woolf?' (1962), a couple's turbulent marriage is centered on the fantasy child they have created. In a nightlong confrontation, they give up their illusion in favor of a more genuine relationship. Albee used complex and rich dialogue to reveal the characters and gradually expose their fantasy world. A later experimental play, 'Quotations from Chairman Mao Tse-Tung' (1968), blended Albee's dialogue with readings from Mao's 'Quotations' and from a 19th-century poem. (*See also* Albee.)

Shepard began writing for the off-off-Broadway theaters in New York City's Greenwich Village in 1964. His plays often drew characters, images, and themes from popular culture; for example, Mae West, Jesse James, and Marlene Dietrich are characters in 'Mad Dog Blues' (1971). Shepard stated: "I'm pulled toward images that shine in the middle of junk. Like cracked headlights shining on a deer's eyes." His plays include: 'La Turista' (1966), 'The Tooth of Crime' (1972), and 'The Buried Child' (1978).

David Rabe (born 1940) used army life as an image for the meaningless ways most men waste their lives in 'The Basic Training of Pavlo Hummel' (1971) and 'Streamers' (1976). 'Sexual Perversity in Chicago' (1974) and 'American Buffalo' (1975), by David Mamet (born 1947), show his ear for dialogue and an awareness of the complexities of relationships.

Popular plays included a series of domestic comedies by Neil Simon (born 1927)—for example, 'Barefoot in the Park' (1962), 'The Odd Couple' (1965), and 'The Sunshine Boys' (1972). Cartoonist Jules Feiffer (born 1929) wrote 'Little Murders' (1966).

Poetry

American poets of the 1960's and 1970's were divided into many schools of thought about the function of poetry. Some, like Allen Ginsberg (born 1926) and Adrienne Rich (born 1929), believed that poetry can transform reality. Others, like John Ashbery (born 1927), felt that we live in an absurd world where

The works of black playwrights, such as Ed Bullins, have helped instill a new sense of pride among American blacks.

Nancy Crampton

363

©1982 Layle Silbert

Robert Bly led a movement that called for images, written in the American idiom, to express the poet's feelings.

man's thoughts and feelings have only an arbitrary and illogical connection with exterior reality. In general, poets of these decades were striving against traditional poetic forms—they experimented with line length, rhythm, diction, and syntax. All of these experiments in poetry aimed at creating a more direct expression of personal experience.

In the 1950's poets like Robert Lowell (1917–77) and John Berryman (1914–72) began to replace the detached, formal speaker of traditional poetry with their own frank, sometimes anguished, voices. The poet himself became the center and the subject of his poems. The poems in Lowell's 'Life Studies' (1959) deal with his adolescent rebellion and later bouts with mental illness. This poetry of self-revelation is called confessional poetry. In the process of searching for psychological truth, the confessional poets—including Anne Sexton (1928–74), W. D. Snodgrass (born 1926), and Sylvia Plath (1932–63)—needed forms flexible enough to reflect their changes of emotion. Berryman uses this approach in 'Dream Songs' (1969), in which he adopted a six-line stanza with changing line lengths and irregular rhyme.

At its best, the free investigation of feeling in confessional poetry recorded the poet's private experience in a way that seems familiar or significant for everyone. In her poems, Plath was able to control and express her frightening and self-destructive feelings. Much of her poetry was published after her suicide in 1963.

Rich has been called an autobiographical rather than a confessional poet. Like Plath's works, her poems were an examination of her feelings, but her material had a wider political purpose. She wrote about motherhood, marriage, divorce, and lesbianism, so that, by voicing her experience, she might make it possible for women to understand themselves. In 'Diving Into the Wreck' (1973), Rich investigated how conventional ways of thinking and feeling destroy equality and mutual understanding.

In the 1950's Ginsberg used poems of self-revelation to attack a society that defined him as an outsider and a madman. In works like 'Howl' (1956) and 'Planet News' (1968), Ginsberg piled up images in long lines to jar the reader into seeing American culture in a new way. His openness of feeling and free association had some influence on the confessional poets. His conviction that the war in Vietnam was a logical extension of a violent, self-righteous society that denied its members both truth and love made him a spokesman for the protest movement of the 1960's and early 1970's.

Denise Levertov (born 1923) was one of the Black Mountain poets. The group—which included Robert Creeley (born 1926), Robert Duncan (born 1919), and the playwright Baraka—formed in the 1950's around Charles Olson (1910–70). For Olson, a poem was a process of perceiving and feeling. Levertov used sound and rhythm to imitate, as precisely and immediately as she could, how an experience felt. Because each experience was different, each poem took on a new form and each was an improvisation.

For Robert Bly (born 1926), "The poem expresses what we are just beginning to think, thoughts we have not yet thought." Bly thought it impossible for the poet to describe his feelings, relying on images, the language of dreams, to express what he feels. With images, Bly tried to reach truths that are beyond his consciousness.

In this search for inner, unconscious truth, Bly, like W. S. Merwin (born 1927), and Ashbery were influenced by the European surrealists. Merwin's fragmented and disconnected sentences resisted giving experience a logical order. Objects and images in his poems took on new richer meanings, as he wrote in "Second Sight,"

> It's the old story.
> Every morning something different is real.

Ashbery's poems were even more detached from external reality. His grammatical sentences were often nonsense statements. His poetry followed a flow of free associations without claiming to provide a new source of order or a new way to understand the outside world. Ashbery, Frank O'Hara (1926–66), and Kenneth Koch (born 1925) were poets of the New York School, a movement that emphasized the separation of reality from perception of it.

Several excellent poets cannot be classified in any school. James Merrill (born 1926) wrote highly polished poetry, much of it in traditional meters. Merrill's 'The Book of Ephraim' (1976) is a long poem in which a spirit speaks to Merrill and a friend through the Ouija board. The poem's structure allowed Merrill freedom in introducing a variety of themes and characters into the poem.

A. R. Ammons (born 1926) focused on the natural world in his poetry. In 'Sphere: the Form of Motion' (1974), astronomy, botany, and biology provided materials for a long meditation.

Representative American Writers

COLONIAL TIMES IN AMERICA

BETWEEN the founding of Jamestown (1607) and the signing of the Declaration of Independence (1776), scattered English settlements grew into a group of colonies ready to declare themselves a nation. The colonists changed from thinking and acting as Englishmen to full awareness of themselves as Americans.

During this time almost all writing was devoted to spiritual concerns and to practical matters of politics and promotion of settlements. In New England, fiction was considered sinful and little poetry was written. A few interesting personal journals and diaries survive.

Bradford, William (1590–1657), historian—'History of Plimoth Plantation'.

Byrd, William (1674–1744), historian and diarist—'History of the Dividing Line'; 'Secret Diary'.

Edwards, Jonathan (1703–58), theologian—'Personal Narrative'; 'The Freedom of the Will'.

Mather, Cotton (1663–1728), theologian—'Wonders of the Invisible World'; 'Magnalia Christi Americana'.

Sewall, Samuel (1652–1730), diarist—'Diary of Samuel Sewall 1674–1729'; 'The Selling of Joseph'.

Taylor, Edward (1642–1729), poet—'God's Determinations'; 'Sacramental Meditations'.

Ward, Nathaniel (1578?–1652), essayist—'The Simple Cobler of Aggawam'.

Wigglesworth, Michael (1631–1705), poet—'The Day of Doom'.

THE SHAPING OF A NEW NATION

THE GREAT questions in the last years of the 18th century were political ones. Should the colonists declare independence from England? Once they had done so, how, they asked, should they govern themselves? The literature of political discussion and

debate in these years is of high quality. Immediately following independence, writers also made efforts to develop a native literature. This is the period of beginning for poetry, fiction, and drama in the United States.

Barlow, Joel (1754–1812), poet—'The Vision of Columbus' ('The Columbiad'); 'The Hasty Pudding'.

Brown, Charles Brockden (1771–1810), novelist—'Wieland'; 'Edgar Huntly'; 'Jane Talbot'.

Crèvecoeur, Michel Guillaume St. Jean de (1735–1813), essayist—'Letters from an American Farmer'.

Franklin, Benjamin (1706–90), prose writer—'Autobiography'; 'Poor Richard's Almanack'.

Freneau, Philip (1752–1832), poet—'The Indian Burying-Ground'; 'The British Prison Ship'.

Hamilton, Alexander (1755?–1804), essayist—'The Federalist' (coauthor).

Hopkinson, Francis (1737–91), poet—'The Battle of the Kegs'.

Jefferson, Thomas (1743–1826), historian—'Notes on the State of Virginia'.

Paine, Thomas (1737–1809), political philosopher—'Common Sense'; 'The Crisis'; 'The Rights of Man'.

Payne, John Howard (1791–1852), playwright—'Clari, or the Maid of Milan' (with song 'Home, Sweet Home').

Rowson, Susanna (Haswell) (1762–1824), novelist—'Charlotte Temple'; 'Rebecca'.

Trumbull, John (1750–1831), poetic satirist—'M'Fingal'; 'Progress of Dullness'.

Webster, Noah (1758–1843), lexicographer—'Spelling Book'; 'American Dictionary of the English Language'.

Weems, Mason Locke (1759–1825), biographer—'The Life and Memorable Actions of George Washington'.

LITERATURE OF THE EARLY REPUBLIC

IN THE EARLY years of the 19th century several full-fledged American writers developed. The most notable among them were Bryant, Cooper, and Irving.

These writers were recognized even in England. In different ways each of them tried to make his works American.

Bird, Robert M. (1806–54), novelist and playwright—'Nick of the Woods'; 'The Gladiator'.

Brackenridge, Hugh Henry (1748–1816), novelist—'Modern Chivalry'.

Bryant, William Cullen (1794–1878), poet—'Thanatopsis'; 'To a Waterfowl'; 'A Forest Hymn'.

Cooper, James Fenimore (1789–1851), novelist—'The Pilot'; 'The Last of the Mohicans'; 'The Spy'; 'The Deerslayer'; 'The Pathfinder'; 'The Pioneers'.

Irving, Washington (1783–1859), essayist and short-story writer—'A History of New York, by Diedrich Knickerbocker'; 'The Alhambra'; 'The Sketch Book'.

Kennedy, John Pendleton (1795–1870), novelist—'Swallow Barn'; 'Horse-Shoe Robinson'.

Simms, William Gilmore (1806–70), novelist and poet—'The Yemassee'; 'Atalantis'.

Thompson, Daniel Pierce (1795–1868), novelist—'The Green Mountain Boys'; 'The Rangers'.

THE FLOWERING OF AMERICAN LITERATURE

FROM 1836 to the Civil War was a period of rapid growth in the United States. The nation was self-sufficient in agriculture, and the Eastern cities buzzed with commerce. War with Mexico brought California into the Union just when gold was discovered there. This event and the opening of Oregon sent thousands of pioneers westward. However, slavery in the South and in new Western territories became a fighting issue.

In the East the period was a golden age. Essays by Emerson and Thoreau vied with tales by Poe. Novels were popular, and Longfellow's poems were best sellers. Historians such as Parkman and Prescott added knowledge of the American past.

Bancroft, George (1800–91), historian—'History of the United States'.

Dana, Richard Henry, Jr. (1815–82), autobiographer—'Two Years Before the Mast'.

Emerson, Ralph Waldo (1803–82), poet and essayist—'Self-Reliance'; 'Compensation'; 'Nature'; 'Poems'.

Fuller, Margaret (1810–50), sociological writer and critic—'Woman in the Nineteenth Century'; 'Papers on Literature and Art'.

Hawthorne, Nathaniel (1804–64), novelist and short-story writer—'The Scarlet Letter'; 'The House of the Seven Gables'; 'Tanglewood Tales'.

Holmes, Oliver Wendell (1809–94), poet, essayist, novelist—'Old Ironsides'; 'The Chambered Nautilus'; 'The Autocrat of the Breakfast-Table'.

Longfellow, Henry Wadsworth (1807–82), poet—'The Song of Hiawatha'; 'Paul Revere's Ride'; 'Evangeline'; 'The Courtship of Miles Standish'.

Longstreet, Augustus Baldwin (1790–1870), novelist—'Georgia Scenes'.

Lowell, James Russell (1819–91), poet, critic, essayist—'The Vision of Sir Launfal'; 'Biglow Papers'; 'Among My Books'; 'My Study Windows'.

Melville, Herman (1819–91), novelist—'Moby-Dick'; 'Typee'; 'Omoo'; 'White-Jacket'; 'Billy Budd'.

Motley, John Lothrop (1814–77), historian—'The Rise of the Dutch Republic'.

Parkman, Francis (1823–93), historian—'The Oregon Trail'; 'A Half-Century of Conflict'.

Poe, Edgar Allan (1809–49), poet, critic, short-story writer—'The Raven'; 'The Poetic Principle'; 'Tales of the Grotesque and Arabesque'; 'The Bells'.

Prescott, William Hickling (1796–1859), historian—'Conquest of Mexico'; 'Conquest of Peru'.

Thoreau, Henry David (1817–62), essayist—'Walden; or, Life in the Woods'; 'Excursions'; 'Cape Cod'.

Whitman, Walt (1819–92), poet—'Leaves of Grass'; 'November Boughs'; 'Drum-Taps'; 'Democratic Vistas'.

Whittier, John Greenleaf (1807–92), poet—'Snow-Bound'; 'The Barefoot Boy'; 'Barbara Frietchie'.

TRANSITION TO THE MODERN AGE

THE CIVIL WAR scarred the United States for four bloody years. The North was quick to recover; the South less so. As the nation revived, however, the pulse of expansion and growth quickened. Cities boomed; industries expanded; and rail lines stretched from coast to coast. The conquest of the wilderness was nearly complete. Great fortunes were made, by a few individuals, and many social and economic injustices arose from the ruthless competition of getting ahead.

Writers reacted in various ways. Some wrote of the lawless West, others of the culture of the East. Many found subjects for fiction and poetry among their surroundings; these were the first *regional*, or *local-color*, writers. A few protested against what they considered the evils of the age.

Adams, Henry (1838–1918), historian—'The Education of Henry Adams'; 'Mont-Saint-Michel and Chartres'.

Alcott, Louisa May (1832–88), novelist and short-story writer—'Little Women'; 'Little Men'; 'Moods'.

Bierce, Ambrose (1842–1914?), short-story writer—'In the Midst of Life'; 'Can Such Things Be?'.

Cable, George Washington (1844–1925), novelist and short-story writer—'The Grandissimes'; 'Old Creole Days'.

Crane, Stephen (1871–1900), novelist—'The Red Badge of Courage'; 'The Little Regiment'; 'Maggie: A Girl of the Streets'.

De Forest, John William (1826–1906), novelist—'Miss Ravenel's Conversion from Secession to Loyalty'.

Dickinson, Emily (1830–86), poet—'Poems'; 'Letters'.

Dreiser, Theodore (1871–1945), novelist—'Sister Carrie'; 'An American Tragedy'; 'The Genius'.

Eggleston, Edward (1837–1902), novelist and historian—'The Hoosier Schoolboy'; 'The Hoosier Schoolmaster'; 'The Circuit Rider'.

Frederic, Harold (1856–98), novelist—'The Damnation of Theron Ware'; 'The Copperhead'.

Freeman, Mary E. Wilkins (1852–1930), novelist and short-story writer—'A New England Nun'; 'Madelon'.

Garland, Hamlin (1860–1940), novelist and short-story writer—'Main-Travelled Roads'; 'A Son of the Middle Border'; 'Prairie Folks'.

Hale, Edward Everett (1822–1909), novelist—'The Man Without a Country'.

Harris, Joel Chandler (1848–1908), short-story writer—'Uncle Remus' stories; 'On the Plantation'.

Harte, (Francis) Bret(t) (1836–1902), short-story writer—'The Luck of Roaring Camp'; 'The Outcasts of Poker Flat'; 'The Twins of Table Mountain'.

Hayne, Paul Hamilton (1830–86), poet—'Legends and Lyrics'; 'The Broken Battalions'.

Hearn, Lafcadio (1850–1904), essayist—'In Ghostly Japan'; 'Creole Sketches'; 'Chita'.

Howe, E(dgar) W(atson) (1853–1937), novelist, journalist—'The Story of a Country Town'; 'Plain People'.

Howells, William Dean (1837–1920), novelist—'A Modern Instance'; 'The Rise of Silas Lapham'.

James, Henry (1843–1916), novelist—'Daisy Miller'; 'The American'; 'The Portrait of a Lady'.

James, William (1842–1910), psychologist and philosopher — 'Principles of Psychology'; 'Pragmatism'; 'Varieties of Religious Experience'.

Jewett, Sarah Orne (1849–1909), novelist and short-story writer—'Tales of New England'.

Kilmer, (Alfred) Joyce (1886–1918), poet—'Trees and Other Poems'; 'Rouge Bouquet'.

Lanier, Sidney (1842–81), poet—'The Marshes of Glynn'; 'The Song of the Chattahoochee'.

London, Jack (1876–1916), novelist—'The Call of the Wild'; 'The Sea Wolf'; 'Martin Eden'.

Miller, Joaquin (Cincinnatus Hiner Miller) (1841?–1913), poet—'Songs of the Sierras'.

Moody, William Vaughn (1869–1910), playwright and poet—'Gloucester Moors'; 'Ode in Time of Hesitation'.

Norris, Frank (1870–1902), novelist—'The Octopus'; 'The Pit'; 'McTeague'.

O. Henry (William Sydney Porter) (1862–1910), short-story writer—'The Four Million'.

Page, Thomas Nelson (1853–1922), novelist and short-story writer—'In Ole Virginia'.

Riley, James Whitcomb (1849–1916), poet—'Rhymes of Childhood'; 'The Old Swimmin' Hole'.

Stowe, Harriet Beecher (1811–96), novelist—'Uncle Tom's Cabin'; 'Oldtown Folks'.

Twain, Mark (Samuel Langhorne Clemens) (1835–1910), novelist and humorist—'The Adventures of Tom Sawyer'; 'The Adventures of Huckleberry Finn'; 'Life on the Mississippi'.

Wister, Owen (1860–1938), novelist—'The Virginian'.

MODERN AMERICAN LITERATURE

THE 20th century began quietly, but soon new forces brought profound changes. Although science and technology enriched material life, two World Wars and the prospect of a third raised grave concern about the future. The federal government intervened increasingly in the activities of the people. The nation also learned that it was involved in the problems of peoples around the globe.

Literature reflected various reactions to the new circumstances. Some writers were deeply pessimistic; others viewed the same realities with hope for the future. One literary school surveyed the American past in an attempt to find meaning for the present. The writing that seemed most likely to survive emphasized enduring human values and the unquenchable vitality of man's spirit.

Agee, James (1909–55), poet, novelist, critic—'Let Us Now Praise Famous Men'; 'A Death in the Family'; 'Agee on Film'.

Albee, Edward (Franklin) (born 1928), playwright—'Who's Afraid of Virginia Woolf'; 'The Death of Bessie Smith'; 'A Delicate Balance'; 'Tiny Alice'.

Algren, Nelson (1909–81), novelist and short-story writer—'The Man with the Golden Arm'.

Anderson, Maxwell (1888–1959), playwright—'Mary of Scotland'; 'Valley Forge'; 'Winterset'; 'Key Largo'.

Anderson, Sherwood (1876–1941), novelist and short-story writer—'Poor White'; 'Dark Laughter'; 'Winesburg, Ohio'; 'The Triumph of the Egg'.

Baldwin, James (born 1924), novelist, essayist, playwright—'Go Tell It on the Mountain'; 'Notes of a Native Son'; 'The Fire Next Time'; 'Giovanni's Room'; 'Blues for Mister Charlie'.

Baraka, Imamu (LeRoi Jones) (born 1934), playwright, poet, essayist—'Dutchman'; 'Preface to a Twenty Volume Suicide Note'; 'Blues People'; 'The Slave'.

Barry, Philip (1896–1949), playwright—'Holiday'; 'The Philadelphia Story'; 'The Animal Kingdom'.

Barth, John (born 1930), novelist—'The Sot-Weed Factor'; 'Giles Goat-Boy'; 'Lost in the Funhouse'.

Barthelme, Donald (born 1931), short-story writer and novelist—'Snow White'; 'Come Back, Dr. Caligari'.

Bellow, Saul (born 1915), novelist—'The Adventures of Augie March'; 'Herzog'; 'Mr. Sammler's Planet'.

Benét, Stephen Vincent (1898–1943), poet, novelist, short-story writer—'Five Men and Pompey'; 'John Brown's Body'; 'The Devil and Daniel Webster'.

Bradbury, Ray (Douglas) (born 1920), short-story writer and novelist—'The Martian Chronicles'; 'Fahrenheit 451'; 'The Illustrated Man'.

Bradford, Roark (1896–1948), novelist—'Ol' Man Adam an' His Chillun'; 'John Henry'.

Brooks, Van Wyck (1886–1963), critic—'America's Coming-of-Age'; 'The Flowering of New England'.

Brown, Claude (born 1937), essayist—'Manchild in the Promised Land'.

Buck, Pearl S(ydenstricker) (1892–1973), novelist—'The Good Earth'; 'The Mother'; 'The Patriot'.

Burroughs, William (born 1914), novelist—'The Ticket that Exploded'; 'Naked Lunch'; 'Nova Express'.

Caldwell, Erskine (born 1903), novelist, short-story writer, essayist—'Tobacco Road'; 'God's Little Acre'; 'Jackpot'; 'You Have Seen Their Faces'.

Capote, Truman (1924–84), novelist, short-story writer, playwright—'Other Voices, Other Rooms'; 'In Cold Blood'; 'Breakfast at Tiffany's'.

Cather, Willa (1873–1947), novelist and short-story writer—'O Pioneers!'; 'My Antonia'; 'A Lost Lady'; 'Death Comes for the Archbishop'.

Cheever, John (1912–82), novelist and short-story writer—'The Wapshot Chronicle'; 'Falconer'; 'The Wapshot Scandal'; 'Bullet Park'.

Coffin, Robert P(eter) Tristram (1892–1955), poet, novelist, essayist—'Strange Holiness'; 'An Attic Room'.

Connelly, Marc(us) (1890–1980), playwright—'The Green Pastures'; 'Beggar on Horseback' (coauthor).

Crane, (Harold) Hart (1899–1932), poet—'White Buildings'; 'The Bridge'.

Cullen, Countee (1903–46), poet—'Color'; 'Copper Sun'.

Cummings, E(dward) E(stlin) (1894–1962), poet and novelist—'No Thanks'; 'The Enormous Room'.

De Vries, Peter (born 1910), novelist and short-story writer—'The Blood of the Lamb'; 'I Hear America Swinging'; 'Reuben, Reuben'; 'Madder Music'.

Dos Passos, John (1896–1970), novelist—'Manhattan Transfer'; 'U.S.A.' (trilogy).

Dunne, Finley Peter (1867–1936), humorist—'Mr. Dooley in Peace and in War'; 'Mr. Dooley's Philosophy'.

Durant, Will(iam James) (1885–1981), historian—'The Story of Philosophy'; 'The Story of Civilization'.

Edmonds, Walter D(umaux) (born 1903), novelist—'Drums Along the Mohawk'; 'The Night Raider'.

Eliot, T(homas) S(tearns) (1888–1965), poet, critic, playwright—'Prufrock and Other Observations'; 'The Waste Land'; 'Murder in the Cathedral'.

Ellison, Ralph (Waldo) (born 1914), novelist—'Invisible Man'.

Farrell, James T(homas) (1904–79), novelist—'Studs Lonigan' (trilogy); 'A World I Never Made'.

Faulkner, William (1897–1962), novelist—'The Sound and the Fury'; 'Light in August'; 'Sanctuary'; 'Absalom, Absalom!'; 'The Town'; 'Intruder in the Dust'.

Ferber, Edna (1887–1968), short-story writer and novelist—'So Big'; 'Show Boat'; 'Cimarron'; 'Giant'.

Field, Rachel (1894–1942), novelist—'All This, and Heaven Too'; 'Time Out of Mind'.

Fitzgerald, F(rancis) Scott (1896–1940), novelist and short-story writer—'The Great Gatsby'; 'This Side of Paradise'; 'Tender Is The Night'; 'The Last Tycoon'; 'Tales of the Jazz Age'; 'The Crack-up'.

Freeman, Douglas Southall (1886–1953), biographer—'R. E. Lee'; 'George Washington'.

Friedman, Bruce Jay (born 1930), novelist and playwright—'Stern'; 'Scuba Duba'.

Frost, Robert (1874–1963), poet—'A Boy's Will'; 'North of Boston'; 'In the Clearing'.

Gale, Zona (1874–1938), novelist and short-story writer—'Miss Lulu Bett'; 'Friendship Village'.

Ginsberg, Allen (born 1926), poet—'Howl'.

Giovanni, Nikki (born 1943), poet—'Black Feeling, Black Talk'; 'Black Judgement'; 'Gemini'.

Glasgow, Ellen (1874–1945), novelist—'Barren Ground'; 'The Romantic Comedians'; 'Vein of Iron'.

Green, Paul Eliot (1894–1981), playwright—'In Abraham's Bosom'; 'Johnny Johnson'.

Guthrie, A(lfred) B(ertram) (born 1901), novelist—'The Big Sky'; 'The Way West'.

Hart, Moss (1904–61), playwright—'You Can't Take It with You' (coauthor); 'Act One' (autobiography).

H. D. (Hilda Doolittle) (1886–1961), poet—'Sea Garden'; 'Red Roses for Bronze'.

Heinlein, Robert A(nson) (born 1907), novelist—'Rocket Ship Galileo'; 'Stranger in a Strange Land'.

Heller, Joseph (born 1923), novelist—'Catch-22'.

Hellman, Lillian (1905–84), playwright and essayist—'The Little Foxes'; 'Watch on the Rhine'; 'Pentimento'; 'An Unfinished Woman'; 'Scoundrel Time'.

Hemingway, Ernest (1899–1961), novelist and short-story writer—'A Farewell to Arms'; 'For Whom the Bell Tolls'; 'The Old Man and the Sea'.

Hersey, John (Richard) (born 1914), novelist and essayist—'Hiroshima'; 'The Algiers Motel Incident'; 'A Bell for Adano'; 'The Child Buyer'.

Howard, Sidney (Coe) (1891–1939), playwright—'They Knew What They Wanted'; 'The Silver Cord'.

Hughes, (James) Langston (1902–67), poet—'The Negro Mother'; 'A New Song'.

Inge, William (Motter) (1913–73), playwright—'Picnic'; 'The Dark at the Top of the Stairs'.

Irving, John (born 1942), novelist—'The World According to Garp'; 'The Hotel New Hampshire'.

Jeffers, Robinson (1887–1962), poet—'Roan Stallion'.

Jones, James (1921–77), novelist—'From Here to Eternity'.

Kaplan, Justin (born 1925), biographer—'Lincoln Steffens'; 'Mister Clemens and Mark Twain'; 'Walt Whitman'.

Kaufman, George S(imon) (1889–1961), playwright—'You Can't Take It with You' (coauthor).

Kelley, William Melvin (born 1937), novelist—'dem'; 'A Different Drummer'; 'Drop of Patience'.

Kerouac, Jack (Jean-Louis) (1922–69), novelist and poet—'On the Road'; 'The Dharma Bums'; 'The Subterraneans'.

Kingsley, Sidney (born 1906), playwright—'Dead End'.

Kopit, Arthur (born 1937), playwright—'Oh Dad, Poor Dad, Mama's Hung You in the Closet and I'm Feelin' So Sad'.

Lardner, Ring(gold Wilmer) (1885–1933), humorist and short-story writer—'You Know Me, Al'.

Lash, Joseph P. (born 1909), biographer—'Eleanor and Franklin'; 'Helen and Teacher'.

Lewis, Sinclair (1885–1951), novelist—'Main Street'; 'Babbitt'; 'Arrowsmith'; 'Dodsworth'.

Lindsay, (Nicholas) Vachel (1879–1931), poet—'The Congo'; 'General William Booth Enters into Heaven'.

Lowell, Amy (1874–1925), poet and critic—'Sword Blades and Poppy Seeds'; 'John Keats'.

Lowell, Robert (Traill Spence, Jr.) (1917–77), poet—'Lord Weary's Castle'; 'Life Studies'.

McCarthy, Mary (Therese) (born 1912), novelist and critic—'The Group'; 'The Groves of Academe'; 'Birds of America'.

McCullers, Carson (1917–67), novelist—'The Heart Is a Lonely Hunter'; 'Member of the Wedding'.

McGinley, Phyllis (1905–78), poet—'Times Three'.

MacLeish, Archibald (1892–1982), poet and playwright—'Conquistador'; 'Land of the Free'; 'J. B.'.

Mailer, Norman (born 1923), novelist and essayist—'The Naked and the Dead'; 'The Deer Park'; 'The Presidential Papers'; 'Armies of the Night'; 'An American Dream'.

Malamud, Bernard (born 1914), novelist and short-story writer—'The Assistant'; 'The Fixer'; 'The Magic Barrel'; 'Pictures of Fidelman'.

Mamet, David (born 1947), playwright—'Sexual Perversity in Chicago'; 'American Buffalo'.

Markham, Edwin (1852–1940), poet—'The Man with the Hoe, and Other Poems'.

Marquand, John P(hillips) (1893–1960), novelist—'The Late George Apley'; 'Wickford Point'.

Masters, Edgar Lee (1869–1950), poet and novelist—'Spoon River Anthology'; 'Domesday Book'.

Mencken, H(enry) L(ouis) (1880–1956), essayist and critic—'Prejudices'; 'The American Language'.

Michener, James A(lbert) (born 1907), novelist, short-story writer, essayist—'Tales of the South Pacific'; 'Hawaii'; 'Kent State'; 'Sports in America'.

Millay, Edna St. Vincent (1892–1950), poet—'Renascence'; 'Second April'; 'Conversation at Midnight'.

Miller, Arthur (born 1915), playwright—'All My Sons'; 'Death of a Salesman'; 'The Crucible'.

Miller, Henry (1891–1980), novelist and essayist—'Tropic of Cancer'; 'Tropic of Capricorn'.

Miller, Merle (born 1919), novelist and biographer—'Reunion'; 'Plain Speaking'; 'Lyndon'.

Mitchell, Margaret (1900–49), novelist—'Gone with the Wind'.

Moore, Marianne (1887–1972), poet—'Poems'; 'Collected Poems'; 'What Are Years'.

Morrison, Toni (born 1931), novelist—'Song of Solomon'.

Oates, Joyce Carol (born 1938), novelist and short-story writer—'them'; 'Do With Me What You Will'.

O'Connor, Flannery (1925–64), short-story writer—'Wise Blood'; 'Everything that Rises Must Converge'.

O'Hara, John (Henry) (1905–70), novelist and short-story writer—'Appointment in Samarra'; 'Butterfield 8'; 'Pal Joey'; 'Sermons and Soda-Water'; 'A Rage to Live'.

O'Neill, Eugene (Gladstone) (1888–1953), playwright—'The Iceman Cometh'; 'Mourning Becomes Electra'.

Parker, Dorothy (1893–1967), short-story writer and poet — 'Not So Deep as a Well'; 'Laments for the Living'; 'Here Lies: the Collected Stories'.

Plath, Sylvia (1932–63), poet and novelist — 'Ariel'; 'The Bell Jar'.

Porter, Katherine Anne (1894–1980), short-story writer and novelist — 'Flowering Judas'; 'Ship of Fools'; 'Pale Horse, Pale Rider'.

Pynchon, Thomas (born 1937), novelist — 'V'; 'The Crying of Lot 49'; 'Gravity's Rainbow'.

Rabe, David (born 1940), playwright — 'Sticks and Bones'; 'The Basic Training of Pavlo Hummel'; 'Streamers'.

Ransom, John Crowe (1888–1974), poet — 'Chills and Fever'.

Rice, Elmer (1892–1967), playwright — 'Street Scene'.

Roberts, Kenneth (Lewis) (1885–1957), novelist and essayist — 'Northwest Passage'; 'Oliver Wiswell'.

Robinson, Edwin Arlington (1869–1935), poet — 'The Man Who Died Twice'; 'Tristram'; 'Merlin'.

Roethke, Theodore (1908–63), poet — 'The Waking'; 'Words for the Wind'.

Roth, Philip (Milton) (born 1933), novelist and short-story writer — 'Goodbye, Columbus'; 'Letting Go'; 'When She Was Good'; 'Portnoy's Complaint'; 'My Life as a Man'.

Salinger, J(erome) D(avid) (born 1919), short-story writer and novelist — 'Nine Stories'; 'The Catcher in the Rye'; 'Franny and Zooey'.

Sandburg, Carl (1879–1967), poet and biographer — 'The People, Yes'; 'Abraham Lincoln: the Prairie Years'; 'Abraham Lincoln: the War Years'.

Saroyan, William (1908–81), short-story writer, novelist, playwright — 'The Time of Your Life'; 'The Human Comedy'; 'Places Where I've Done Time'.

Sexton, Anne (Harvey) (1928–74), poet — 'Live or Die'; 'To Bedlam and Part Way Back'; 'The Death Notebooks'.

Shapiro, Karl (Jay) (born 1913), poet — 'V-Letter'.

Shaw, Irwin (1913–84), playwright, short-story writer, novelist — 'Bury the Dead'; 'The Young Lions'.

Sherwood, Robert E(mmet) (1896–1955), playwright — 'Abe Lincoln in Illinois'; 'The Petrified Forest'.

Simpson, Louis (Aston Marantz) (born 1923), poet and essayist — 'Caviare at the Funeral'; 'A Revolution in Taste'.

Sinclair, Upton (1878–1968), novelist — 'The Jungle'.

Sontag, Susan (born 1933), novelist and essayist — 'Against Interpretation'; 'Illness as a Metaphor'.

Steinbeck, John (1902–68), novelist and short-story writer — 'Of Mice and Men'; 'The Grapes of Wrath'.

Stribling, T(homas) S(igismund) (1881–1965), novelist — 'The Forge'; 'The Store'; 'Unfinished Cathedral'.

Stuart, Jesse (Hilton) (1907–84), novelist and poet — 'Taps for Private Tussie'; 'Beyond Dark Hills'.

Styron, William (born 1925), novelist — 'The Confessions of Nat Turner'; 'Lie Down in Darkness'; 'Sophie's Choice'.

Teasdale, Sara (1884–1933), poet — 'Rivers to the Sea'.

Thurber, James (Grover) (1894–1961), humorist and essayist — 'My Life and Hard Times'.

Tuchman, Barbara W(ertheim) (born 1912), historian — 'The Guns of August'; 'A Distant Mirror'.

Updike, John (Hoyer) (born 1932), novelist and short-story writer — 'Rabbit Run'; 'Rabbit is Rich'; 'Rabbit Redux'; 'The Centaur'; 'Couples'; 'Bech: a Book'.

Van Doren, Carl (1885–1950), critic and biographer — 'American Literature'; 'Benjamin Franklin'.

Vidal, Gore (born 1925), novelist and playwright — 'Julian'; 'Burr'; 'The Best Man'; 'Washington, D.C.'.

Vonnegut, Kurt, Jr. (born 1922), novelist — 'Cat's Cradle'; 'Slaughterhouse-Five'; 'Breakfast of Champions'.

Warren, Robert Penn (born 1905), poet and novelist — 'All the King's Men'; 'Night Rider'; 'Being Here'.

Welty, Eudora (born 1909), short-story writer and novelist — 'A Curtain of Green'; 'The Ponder Heart'.

West, Nathanael (Nathan Weinstein) (1903–40), novelist — 'Miss Lonelyhearts'; 'The Day of the Locust'.

Wharton, Edith (1862–1937), novelist and short-story writer — 'Ethan Frome'; 'The House of Mirth'.

Wilder, Thornton (Niven) (1897–1975), playwright and novelist — 'The Bridge of San Luis Rey'; 'Our Town'.

Williams, Tennessee (Thomas Lanier Williams) (1911–83), playwright — 'The Glass Menagerie'; 'A Streetcar Named Desire'; 'Cat on a Hot Tin Roof'.

Williams, William Carlos (1883–1963), poet and novelist — 'The White Mule'; 'Paterson'.

Wilson, Lanford (born 1937), playwright — 'Lemon Sky'; 'The Hot l Baltimore'.

Wolfe, Thomas (Clayton) (1900–38), novelist — 'Look Homeward, Angel'; 'You Can't Go Home Again'.

Wolfe, Tom (Thomas Kennedy Wolfe, Jr.) (born 1931), essayist — 'The Kandy-Kolored Tangerine Flake Streamline Baby'; 'The Electric Kool-Aid Acid Test'; 'Radical Chic and Mau-Mauing the Flak Catchers'; 'The Right Stuff'.

Wright, Richard (1908–60), novelist and short-story writer — 'Native Son'; 'Black Boy'.

Wylie, Elinor (1885–1928), poet and novelist — 'Nets to Catch the Wind'; 'The Orphan Angel'.

BIBLIOGRAPHY FOR AMERICAN LITERATURE

History and Criticism

Barnett, L. K. Ignoble Savage: American Literary Racism, 1790–1890 (Greenwood, 1975).

Bateson, F. W. and others. A Guide to English and American Literature, rev. ed. (Longman, 1976).

Blackman, Murray. A Guide to Jewish Themes in American Fiction, 1940–80 (Scarecrow, 1981).

Brooks, Cleanth and others. American Literature, 4 vols. (St. Martin's, 1974).

Brooks, Van Wyck and Bettmann, Otto. Our Literary Heritage. (Paddington, 1977).

Gayle, Addison, Jr. The Way of the New World: the Black Novel in America (Doubleday, 1976).

Hart, J. D. The Oxford Companion to American Literature, 4th ed. (Oxford, 1965).

Hendin, Josephine. Vulnerable People: a View of American Fiction Since 1945 (Oxford, 1978).

Parrington, V. L. Main Currents in American Thought, 3 vols. (Harcourt, 1955–63).

Spacks, P. M. Contemporary Women Novelists (Prentice, 1977).

Spiller, R. E. and others. Literary History of the United States, 4th ed. rev. (Macmillan, 1974).

Trent, W. P. and others, eds. The Cambridge History of American Literature, 3 vols. in 1 (Macmillan, 1943).

West, R. B. The Short Story in America, 1900–1950 (Arno, 1952).

Anthologies

Adams, William and others, eds. Afro-American Literature, 4 vols. (Houghton, 1970).

Angoff, Charles and Levin, Meyer, eds. The Rise of American Jewish Literature (Simon & Schuster, 1970) o.p.

Foerster, Norman. American Prose and Poetry, 2 vols., rev. ed. (Century, 1977).

Foley, Martha, ed. The Best American Short Stories (Houghton, annual).

Gassner, John, ed. Best American Plays, 5 vols. (Crown, 1947–67).

Hatch, J. V. and Shine, Ted, eds. Black Theater, U.S.A. (Free Press, 1974).

Hughes, Langston and Bontemps, Arna, eds. Poetry of the Negro, 1746–1970 (Doubleday, 1970).

Untermeyer, Louis, ed. A Treasury of Great Poems, 2 vols., rev. ed. (Simon & Schuster, 1964).

Williams, Oscar, ed. Master Poems of the English Language (Trident, 1966).

AMERICAN REVOLUTION *see* REVOLUTION, AMERICAN.

AMIENS, France. The ancient cathedral city of Amiens lies on the Somme River in northern France some 80 miles (130 kilometers) north of Paris. The river valley is a natural route both for trade and for invading armies. Hence its largest city is an important  center of commerce and has been the scene of a number of decisive battles. Since the Middle Ages it has also been a center of the textile-weaving industry. Amiens, which was the ancient capital of Picardy, is now the capital of the French department of Somme.

Amiens is noted above all for its magnificent Cathedral of Notre Dame. Celebrated as one of the most splendid monuments of Gothic architecture, the cathedral dates from the 13th century. Begun in 1220 by the architect Robert de Luzarches it was enlarged from time to time and completed about 1270. The interior is unusually spacious. At its highest point the ceiling is nearly 140 feet (43 meters) above the floor. The choir stalls are adorned with more than 3,500 wood figures carved in the 16th century.

Invasions and bombardments of the city have several times threatened the cathedral with destruction. In the Franco-Prussian War (1870) Amiens fell to Germany, and early in World War I it was stormed and held briefly by German troops. Because of its importance as a railway center and its commanding position on the Somme River, it became a British army base in that war. In 1918 it withstood another German attack. The cathedral, damaged by bombs and artillery shells, was repaired after the war. During the German conquest of France in 1940, Amiens was heavily bombed before it fell, but the cathedral remained practically intact.

Early in its history the city was captured by Caesar and became a stronghold of the Roman Empire. A momentous event associated with its name was the signing of the Treaty of Amiens between Napoleon and Great Britain on March 27, 1802. The treaty gave the British the only breathing spell they had during the wars following the French Revolution. It was the rupture of this treaty, in 1803, that enabled the United States to purchase from Napoleon the Louisiana Territory, a possession that the French regarded as too remote to be defended.

Amiens has several interesting structures. The town hall, built in the 17th century and almost entirely rebuilt in the 19th century, stands in the center of the old section of town. North of the hall is the 15th-century church of St. Germain and south is the Picardy museum containing collections of archaeological finds, paintings, and sculpture. An ancient theater has a Louis XVI façade.

Amiens today is an important railroad junction and a commercial and industrial center. Its manufactures include silk, woolen and cotton cloths, velvet,

and carpets. Also produced there are machinery, chemicals, and tires. Truck farmers from the adjacent heavily watered bottom lands market their products in the city from small boats. Amiens also trades in grain, sugar, wool, oilseeds, and duck pasties (pies) and macaroons, for which it is famous. (*See also* France.) Population (1975 census), 131,476.

AMIN, Idi (born 1925). The African country of Uganda was in a shambles, both politically and economically, by the time its dictator, Idi Amin, was ousted on April 13, 1979. He had ruled Uganda as a tyrant for nearly a decade and was reported to have ordered the execution of up to 300,000 Ugandans.

Idi Amin Dada Oumee was born in Koboko, Uganda, in 1925, a member of the Bakeva tribe. With only a limited education, he found a career in the British colonial army. He was the heavyweight boxing champion of the army for almost ten years.

As an army officer, Amin was a close associate of President Milton Obote when Uganda became independent of Great Britain in 1962. In 1971, after a conflict with Obote, he staged a successful military coup and made himself president and commander-in-chief. In 1976 he appointed himself president for life.

An extreme nationalist, Amin expelled all foreign residents, mostly Asians, from Uganda in 1972. This move effectively destroyed the prosperous middle class, leading to a breakdown of the economy. He ordered the persecution of many tribal groups. Also in 1972, he defeated an attempt to reinstate Obote.

In October 1978 Uganda was invaded by a force of Ugandan nationalists and Tanzanian soldiers. Seven months later Amin fled and went into hiding.

AMINO ACIDS *See* BIOCHEMISTRY; ORGANIC CHEMISTRY.

AMMAN, Jordan. Capital of the kingdom of Jordan and by far its largest city, Amman is also the country's only modern urban area. It is built on rolling hills in the northwestern part of the country, about 50 miles (80 kilometers) from the Jordan River.

Amman is an ancient city. Called Rabbath Ammon in Biblical times, it was the capital of the Ammonite settlers. When the city was conquered by Egyptian King Ptolemy II Philadelphus, who ruled 285–246 B.C., he renamed it Philadelphia. This name was kept during Roman and Byzantine times. The Romans rebuilt much of the city, and extensive ruins from their rule still stand in modern Amman.

After coming under Arab control in the 7th century, the city declined. By 1300 it had disappeared. (Historians still do not know the cause of this.) In 1878 Ottoman Turks resettled the site with Russian refugees. The settlement remained a small village until after World War I.

Amman's modern development began in 1921 when it became the capital of Jordan, at that time called Transjordan. After 1946, when Jordan gained independence from Britain, Amman grew rapidly. It was severely damaged in 1970 when political conflict between the government and rebellious Palestinian guerrillas erupted into open civil war in the streets.

Amman is Jordan's chief commercial, financial, transportation, and international trade center. It has an international airport. Industries include food and tobacco processing and manufacture of textiles, paper products, plastics, and aluminum utensils. Factories on the outskirts produce electrical batteries and related products and cement. The University of Jordan, founded in 1962, is located in Amman.

Sites of interest include the remains of the ancient citadel, the adjoining archaeological museum, and a large finely preserved Roman amphitheater. The royal palaces are in the eastern part of the city; the parliament building is in the western section. (*See also* Jordan.) Population (1979 census), 648,587.

AMMUNITION. In the broadest sense, ammunition includes any device used to carry a destructive force. Bullets, artillery shells, bombs, torpedoes, grenades, and explosive mines are all forms of ammunition. Rockets and guided missiles, particularly the small types, are sometimes considered ammunition.

The earliest ammunition probably consisted of thrown rocks. Prehistoric warriors later developed the bow and arrow and used slings to hurl rocks at an enemy. The first arrows were thin wooden shafts with stone arrowheads, and later ones had metal arrowheads. The first slings were used to shoot small, smooth stones. The ancient Phoenicians loaded their slings with molded lead pellets for greater range and deadlier force. Such military machines as the catapult and the ballista used huge rocks and large arrows or javelins as ammunition.

The Development of Ammunition

Most forms of ammunition require a propellant—that is, a means of propulsion to shoot the projectile at a target. Before the invention of gunpowder, propulsion came from the muscle power of one or more people. A bow stored muscle power until the string was released to shoot an arrow. Catapults and ballistas stored the muscle power of several people to propel rocks. Gunpowder is a propellant that explodes when ignited by a primer (*see* Gunpowder).

Early cannons fired projectiles made of stone, lead, iron, or bronze. The largest cannons shot stone projectiles because their barrels could not withstand the high internal pressure produced by firing heavy metal cannon balls. Through the years, other kinds of projectiles were developed for artillery. These included canister and grapeshot, which were cases of small metal balls that could be loaded into a cannon as a single unit. The balls scattered after being fired, with lethal effect on enemy troops.

Crude explosive shells were developed by the 16th century. They consisted of hollow cannon balls filled with gunpowder plus a slow-burning fuse. A shell was fired after its fuse had been lit. During the 19th century, cast lead balls were replaced by bullet-shaped projectiles that provided greater range and accuracy.

In early firearms, the gunpowder was ignited by fire. Gunsmiths later modified small arms and some cannons to use the sparks from flint or steel to ignite the powder. In the early 19th century, the development of primers in the form of percussion caps provided a more reliable method of igniting gunpowder. These caps consisted of a chemical, such as mercury fulminate or potassium chlorate, that exploded when struck by a gun hammer. The chemical was contained in capsules of metal, foil, or paper, similar to the paper caps used in modern toy pistols.

The next development was the self-contained cartridge, usually made of soft brass. The projectile of the cartridge was at one end, in front of the propellant, and the rear held the primer, where the firing pin could strike it. All small-arms ammunition soon used this design, which later was incorporated into shells for small and medium artillery. The self-contained cartridge made possible the invention of breech-loading, repeating firearms, and of rapid-firing weapons, such as the machine gun.

PRINCIPAL PARTS OF A FIXED ROUND OF ARTILLERY AMMUNITION

shell
bursting charge
fuze
cartridge case
propellant
primer

Source: United States Department of the Army

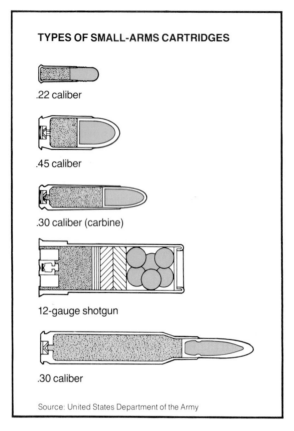

TYPES OF SMALL-ARMS CARTRIDGES

.22 caliber

.45 caliber

.30 caliber (carbine)

12-gauge shotgun

.30 caliber

Source: United States Department of the Army

The final step in the development of modern ammunition was the invention of smokeless powder. The word smokeless can be misleading because modern gunpowder produces some smoke. However, it causes much less smoke than the old kind of powder, now often called black powder. It also creates a much greater explosive force and does not leave nearly as much solid residue in gun barrels.

Ammunition manufacturers have developed modern propellants from smokeless powder and have further reduced the amount of smoke and flash. Gunpowder has also been improved so that it keeps its explosive strength if unused and so that it does not explode unexpectedly.

Small-Arms Ammunition

Ammunition size for small arms—pistols, rifles, shotguns, and machine guns—is usually expressed in caliber, or the diameter of the projectile in millimeters or inches. The various types of small-arms ammunition are usually called bullets or cartridges. In much of this ammunition, the projectile is made of a lead alloy and encased in a thin jacket of a copper alloy or copper-coated steel. Some small-arms projectiles have cores made of a steel alloy.

Military forces use certain kinds of small-arms ammunition for special purposes. Armor-piercing bullets have cores of hardened steel or tungsten carbide to penetrate armor. Tracer bullets have a chemical in

the base of the projectile that ignites when the shell is fired. The chemical leaves a visible trail by burning while the projectile is in flight. Incendiary bullets contain a chemical in the nose of the projectile that ignites inflammable materials.

Shotgun shells are made of plastic, and most contain more than one projectile, usually round lead pellets. Shells used to shoot birds and small game have tiny pellets measuring 2 to 4 millimeters (0.08 to 0.16 inch) wide. Shells for deer and other large game use buckshot up to 8.5 millimeters (0.34 inch) wide. Some shotgun shells contain solid slugs. (*See also* Firearms.)

Artillery Ammunition

Most modern artillery ammunition resembles small-arms ammunition, but many types contain a major additional component—the fuze, which is used to detonate explosive warheads. Small and medium artillery generally use fixed rounds, in which the projectile, propellant, and primer are in one container, as in the case of small-arms cartridges. In larger artillery, the projectile is loaded separately from the propellant and primer. A fixed round for large artillery would be too large and cumbersome for efficient loading. Loading the projectile separately has other advantages as well. The type of projectile can be chosen from a variety on hand, and the quantity of propellant can be varied according to the intended use.

Artillery shells with nuclear warheads were developed in 1953. The first projectiles had a caliber of 280 millimeters (11 inches) and weighed about 85 tons (77,000 kilograms). Smaller ones were subsequently developed for the United States Army, including one with a 155-millimeter (6-inch) caliber shell.

High-explosive artillery projectiles are designed for use against enemy troops. Their usefulness depends on the number, size, and velocity of the fragments produced when the shells explode. One type of projectile, developed by a 19th-century British officer named Henry Shrapnel, contains a number of small projectiles that are propelled by an explosive charge. The term shrapnel has come to be used for fragments of any kind from artillery shells or bombs.

A modern type of shrapnel shell uses thousands of small steel darts called flechettes. One form of flechette projectile includes an explosive charge that bursts, driving the flechettes in all directions. Another form of flechette projectile resembles a grapeshot or canister and releases the flechettes as the projectile leaves the cannon. (*See also* Artillery.)

The fuzes in modern ammunition are not armed, or activated, until the projectile, bomb, or missile has been launched. This feature makes fuzed ammunition safe to transport and use. Fuzes are armed in a variety of ways. Many types of artillery projectiles are armed by the force of acceleration when hurled from the cannon, or by the spinning created by the rifled barrel of the weapon. In many bombs, the fuzes are armed after they are dropped by the force of rushing air. The fuzes of explosive mines are usually armed manually. With many guided missiles, the fuzes are armed electronically after the missiles have traveled a safe distance from the launch site.

Various kinds of fuzes detonate in different ways. Impact fuzes, also called contact fuzes, detonate upon striking a solid object. Time fuzes detonate after a preset time has passed. Proximity fuzes detonate when an internal mechanism, such as a small radio transmitter, determines that the target is close enough to be damaged or destroyed. Such fuzes are most commonly used for antiaircraft shells because it is much more difficult for the projectile itself to hit an enemy plane than for exploding fragments to do so. Command fuzes detonate when they receive an electronic signal. More than one fuze may be used in a projectile or missile to assure detonation.

Rockets and Guided Missiles

Many rockets and guided missiles use explosive projectiles similar to those in artillery. Propellants for rockets and guided missiles may be liquid or solid. Solid propellants were first used by the ancient Chinese in fireworks. All rockets had solid propellants until the 20th-century invention of liquid types. Liquid propellants were developed for early guided missiles, and they provided much more propulsive force than any solid propellants known at that time.

New types of solid propellants have been introduced since World War II. They not only equal many liquid propellants in power but also are better for numerous purposes because their greater stability makes them easier to handle. Most kinds of guided missiles now have solid propellants, but some continue to use liquids. (*See also* Ballistics; Bomb; Guided Missile; Rocket.)

AMNESIA. The loss of the ability to remember is called amnesia. Although commonly thought of as relating to someone who has completely forgotten who and where he or she is, amnesia can apply to the loss of old or new memories; it can be partial or total; and it can be permanent or last only a short time. The causes of amnesia vary.

Memory appears to be stored in several parts of the limbic system of the brain (*see* Brain), and any condition that interferes with the function of this system can cause amnesia. Aging is a frequent cause. As humans advance in age, the heart's action, as well as the walls of blood vessels, change. It is thought that too little blood reaching brain cells, and sometimes the lack of certain nutrients, causes the death of small portions of the brain. Old memories and new ones are kept in different portions of the brain, and many older people can recall events that took place years before while being unable to remember what they ate at their last meal. An inability to store or learn new information may also occur with advanced age. Several degenerative diseases of old age can cause profound amnesia. Primarily in older men, transient global amnesia causes severe loss of memory for minutes or hours. This is a progressive condition about which little can be done.

Alcoholism is another leading cause of amnesia. Many heavy drinkers cannot recall the events of the time when they were intoxicated. In alcoholism of long duration (*see* Alcoholism), the gradual deterioration of brain cells takes place, and memory can become permanently confused.

Injuries to the head often result in amnesia for the time just before and just after an accident. As the injury heals, memory gradually returns. Tumors or other growths in the brain that affect the limbic system can also cause amnesia. When treatment of the growth is successful, the amnesia is cured.

Other Types of Amnesia

Classic amnesia may be described as the condition of an otherwise healthy person who "wakes up" in a strange place unable to recall his name, where he came from, or where he is going. It is interesting to note that such a person, however, retains knowledge of language and social customs. This kind of amnesia is probably due to emotional stress and is called hysterical amnesia. It occurs when some event is seen as so shameful or when problems become so overwhelming that the person concerned is unable to face reality. Instead, complete amnesia develops. Hysterical amnesia is treated through psychotherapy and sometimes the administration of drugs such as sodium amibarbital, which causes a person to talk freely. Clues to the past may appear under the sedation, and the psychotherapist can use these to prod the memory of the patient.

There can also be partial amnesia from brain damage. In auditory amnesia no memory for words remains. Tactile amnesia is the inability to identify objects by touch, and visual amnesia is the inability to recognize objects and, often, printed words.

AMNESTY. The legal term amnesty is related to the word amnesia—loss of memory. Amnesty means forgetting past deeds, consigning them to oblivion so that they may not become an issue in the future.

Amnesty has often been used as a means of healing animosities and divisions caused by war. After the American Civil War, President Andrew Johnson granted amnesty to most Southerners who had fought against the Union. His General Amnesty Proclamation, issued in 1865, granted amnesty to many supporters of the Southern Confederacy; and his Universal Amnesty in 1868 did the same for all but 300 Confederates.

Amnesty is closely related to another legal term, the pardon; in fact they are often used interchangeably. They are not quite the same, however. The pardon is normally used for a person who has been convicted of a crime. The chief executive officer of a country or state, such as the president or a governor, may pardon a criminal or may prevent an offender from being prosecuted. The most famous pardon in United States history occurred on Sept. 8, 1974, when President Gerald R. Ford pardoned former President Richard M. Nixon "for all offenses which he, Richard

Nixon, has committed or may have committed or taken part in" during his terms of office (*see* Nixon). Because there has been no strict distinction made between amnesty and pardon in the United States, both the president and the Congress have the power of amnesty, but only the president has the power to grant a pardon.

For hundreds of years amnesty has been used after wars and periods of civil strife. Twelve years after the English Civil War (1642–48), when Charles II was restored to the throne, he proclaimed a general amnesty, excepting only those who had taken part in the execution of his father, Charles I. After the Boer War in South Africa (1899–1902), the British granted amnesty to Boers who accepted British nationality, with the exception of some army officers who were said to be in violation of the laws of war.

In more recent history, President Jimmy Carter, in 1977, extended amnesty to draft resisters—men who had chosen to leave the country or be jailed rather than fight in the Vietnam conflict (1964–75). Later in the same year the president established a system of review for Vietnam-era deserters and veterans with a less-than-honorable discharge from the service. Veterans could apply to have their discharges upgraded and deserters could apply for less-than-honorable discharges and then seek to have the discharges upgraded. President Carter was hoping to end the divisions and bad feelings caused by a war that was unpopular among many segments of the population.

The Soviet Union, Switzerland, Sweden, France, and The Netherlands are some of the countries that make a practice of destroying criminal records after a specific period—usually 10 to 20 years—provided the offender has committed no more crimes. In Italy criminal amnesties are sometimes given to celebrate the inauguration of a new president or simply to empty crowded prisons.

Political Amnesty

With the emergence of a number of totalitarian regimes in the 20th century, amnesty for political prisoners has become a significant issue. In the Soviet Union, China, North Korea, South Korea, Taiwan, Iran, Argentina, Chile, the nations of Eastern Europe, and in several other countries, political dissent and the exercise of civil liberties have been severely curtailed. Millions of individuals were put into concentration camps and prisons.

To bring the problem of political prisoners to the attention of the world, an English lawyer named Peter Benenson founded an organization called Amnesty International in 1960. Its aims were to work for the release of persons imprisoned for political or religious opinions, to seek fair and public trials for such prisoners, to help refugees who had been forced to leave a country by finding them asylum and work, and to work for effective international means of guaranteeing freedom of opinion and conscience. Amnesty International, which was awarded the Nobel peace prize in 1977, formed 2,500 "adopting groups"

in 40 countries. Each group was responsible for maintaining contact with specific prisoners and pleading their cases with the government concerned.

Political history in the 20th century has demonstrated that a policy of amnesty is effective as a legal protection in nations with truly constitutional governments, where the rule of law is impartially applied. These nations have independent court systems that are able to enforce the principle of amnesty. In totalitarian regimes the courts are more likely to carry out the policies and dictates of the executive power, the rights of the state taking precedence over the rights of individuals.

AMOEBA. A tiny blob of colorless jelly with a dark speck inside it—this is what an amoeba looks like when seen through a microscope. The colorless jelly is cytoplasm, and the dark speck the nucleus. Together they make up a single cell of protoplasm, the basic material of all living things (*see* Cell).

Amoebas are usually considered the lowest and most primitive form of animal life. But simple as they may seem, these tiny one-celled organisms carry out their activities competently and efficiently. They are often studied in zoological and other research laboratories.

When the amoeba is stained with dye, its nucleus takes up more color than the cytoplasm. The interior cytoplasm takes up more color than the outer portion, which is clear. The interior can be seen as a dense and grainy mass, containing crystalline bodies, tiny drops of fluids, fat, and food in the process of being digested.

The amoeba has two kinds of cytoplasm: at the surface, a stiff, gellike cytoplasm forms a semisolid layer that acts as a membrane. It holds the inner, more watery cytoplasm and its contents together. The membrane is flexible, taking on the shape of the more watery cytoplasm inside, which is continually moving and changing the body shape of the amoeba. The name amoeba comes from a Greek word that means "change."

It is by changing its body shape that the amoeba travels. First it extends a lobelike portion called a pseudopod, meaning "false foot." Then it slowly pours the rest of its body into the pseudopod, which enlarges and finally becomes the whole body. New pseudopods form as old ones disappear. Their shapes range from broad and blunt to long, thin, sometimes

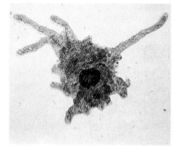

Fingerlike extensions from the amoeba's single cell are called pseudopods, or false feet. Fluid cytoplasm forms and flows into these ever-changing lobes, enabling the animal to move.
Russ Kinne—
Photo Researchers

branching structures. Often many pseudopods form at the same time in an uncoordinated way, as though the amoeba were starting off in all directions at once. But most pseudopods exist only for a short time, then flow back into the main body.

The amoeba feeds mainly on other microscopic, one-celled plants and animals including algae, bacteria, and tiny protozoa in the surrounding water. It has no mouth or other body parts for taking in or digesting food. If it finds itself near something edible, it may put out pseudopods to surround the food and flow over it. In this way, the food, along with a tiny drop of water around it, is completely enclosed in a bubblelike chamber in the amoeba's body. The chamber is called a food vacuole, and an amoeba may have several in its body at the same time. Once the food is digested, the vacuole disappears.

The outer membrane prevents any nutrients—fats, proteins, carbohydrates, and salts—from escaping. At the same time, it allows liquid wastes to flow out into the surrounding water. The membrane also allows the surrounding water to pass into the amoeba's cell. This process of water absorption is called osmosis. The amoeba must work to keep its cytoplasm from becoming too watery: it gets rid of the excess water by pumping it out through a tiny pore. Its pump is a clear vacuole inside its body called the contractile vacuole. The amoeba "breathes" through its membrane. Oxygen from the surrounding water passes in and carbon dioxide passes out.

If an amoeba is cut apart, it instantly forms a new membrane over the cut surfaces. The part containing the nucleus may survive, but the other part cannot digest food and eventually dies.

The nucleus is necessary for reproduction, which is asexual. The nucleus simply pinches in two in the middle; the two halves pull apart; each takes half the cytoplasm; and one amoeba has become two. The process, called fission, takes less than one hour.

Although the amoeba has no nerves, it reacts to its surroundings. With its whole body it responds by moving toward or away from stimuli. It retreats from strong light, or from water that is too hot or too cold. If touched or shaken, it rolls into a ball. An amoeba may survive extremely unfavorable circumstances such as a dry spell by rolling into a ball, losing most of its water, and secreting a protective coat called a cyst membrane. Once the surroundings are again suitable, the coat opens and the amoeba comes out.

Various kinds of amoebas dwell in fresh and salt waters, in moist soils, and in moist body parts of other animals. Common species are found in the debris of stagnant ponds and puddles. The very common *Amoeba proteus* is found on decaying vegetation at the bottom of freshwater streams and ponds. One ordinary, harmless species, *Entamoeba coli*, is found in the human intestine. There are numerous parasitic amoebas, most of which are harmless. But some amoebas are responsible for serious diseases: *Entamoeba histolytica*, for instance, is the cause of amoebic dysentery. Frequently found in unsanitary areas, these amoebas are carried by sewage, polluted water, and unwashed food. They settle in the large intestine where they eat cells and tissues (*see* Parasites). The amoeba is classified as a member of the subphylum *Sarcodina* of the phylum *Protozoa* (*see* Protozoa).

AMPÈRE, André-Marie (1775–1836). While Jean-Jacques Ampère was awaiting execution during the French Revolution, he wrote that his greatest expense had been for books and scientific instruments for his son, André-Marie, whom he had tutored. The investment proved to be worthwhile. André-Marie Ampère became known as the father of the theory of electromagnetism.

André-Marie Ampère was born on Jan. 22, 1775, in the village of Polémieux, near Lyons, France. His father was a justice of the peace. André-Marie was recognized as a prodigy in his early years. In 1793, the year his father was guillotined, he devised an international language intended to unite mankind and promote peace.

From about the age of 21, Ampère gave private lessons at Lyons in chemistry, mathematics, and language. In 1799 he married his childhood sweetheart, Julie Carron, and the following year their son, Jean-Jacques, was born. In 1801 Ampère became professor of physics and chemistry at Bourg. His sick wife and infant son remained in Lyons, where Julie Ampère died of tuberculosis three years later. This was a tragedy from which Ampère never wholly recovered; but he dedicated himself with greater zeal to his experiments. A second marriage, in 1807, was a failure, lasting only two years. There was one child, a daughter. In 1809 he was appointed professor of mathematics at the École Polytechnique in Paris.

In 1820 Ampère heard of the work of the Danish physicist Hans Christian Oersted, who had observed that an electric current deflects a magnetic needle. The news of this phenomenon stimulated Ampère, and he quickly formulated a theoretical explanation of electromagnetism and related phenomena. His paper on the subject was presented to the Académie des Sciences one week after he first heard of Oersted's work. Ampère applied mathematical formulas to the reactions between magnets and electric currents (Ampère's Law). (*See also* Electricity.) His theories formed the basis for the science of electrodynamics.

Ampère also invented the astatic needle, which led to the development of the galvanometer (*see* Galvanometer). In 1824 Ampère became a professor of physics at the Collège de France in Paris. His son, a lecturer and literary historian, also taught there.

Ampère later wrote a remarkable work on the philosophy of science in an attempt to classify all human knowledge. He also wrote on differential and integral calculus; the theory of probability; optics; animal physiology; and other scientific subjects. The intimate details of his life were carefully recorded in his journals and in his letters. He died in Marseilles on June 10, 1836. The ampere, or unit of flow of an electric current, was named for him.

AMPHIBIAN. Four hundred million years ago the most advanced forms of life on Earth, the fishes, lived in the water. Plants and insects alone occupied the land until the appearance of the amphibians about 350 million years ago. Almost all amphibians have features that fall between those of fishes and those of reptiles. The most commonly known of these animals are frogs, toads, and salamanders. Although most have changed very little since they first began to breathe on land, some of the early amphibians were the ancestors of today's reptiles, birds, and mammals.

The word amphibian comes from the Greek *amphi*, meaning "both," and *bios*, meaning "life." It describes those cold-blooded animals with backbones that pass their lives both in fresh water and on land. Because amphibians live in water and on land, their natural environments are shores, ponds, marshes, swamps, and low meadows.

Kinds of Amphibians

There are approximately 2,500 existing species of amphibians. They are divided into three orders: Anura, or Salientia (about 2,100 species); Urodela, or Caudata (about 300 species); and Apoda, or Gymnophiona (about 75 species). Amphibians are distributed throughout the world, except in regions covered with snow all year long.

The anurans include true frogs, tree frogs, and toads. True frogs have long hind legs and well-developed swimming and leaping powers. Tree frogs have suction pads on their fingers and toes so that they can hold on to smooth surfaces. Toads have shorter legs than frogs, and their skin has a warty appearance. The skin of the toad is usually dry to the touch, while the frog's skin is moist and smooth. The toad is brownish olive, usually with some darker spots, and with a yellowish streak down the middle of the back. Most frogs are drab green, brown, and yellow; but some are brightly colored and able to change their appearance somewhat so as to blend in with their environment as a form of camouflage.

Anurans live as far north as the swamplands of northwestern Canada. They are found on all the major landmasses of the world except Antarctica, New Zealand, and Greenland.

All anurans begin life as tadpoles, tiny fishlike larvae with tails and gills. As they become adults, they lose their tails and gills and develop hind legs suitable for jumping. There are more frogs than any other kind of amphibian. (*See also* Frog, Anatomy of.)

The urodeles are the tailed amphibians. All of them resemble the most numerous members of this order—the salamanders. Basically animals of the Northern Hemisphere, urodeles live in or near streams, and are sometimes found under rocks and logs. They have long tails, poorly developed legs, and smooth, moist skin. They were probably the first vertebrates (animals with backbones) to exist for any length of time on land. The giant salamander of Japan is the largest of all amphibians. It grows to a length of about 5 feet (1.5 meters).

In the table opposite, the lengths are average lengths, not extremes. The table represents a small selection of some species of amphibians and is not intended to be inclusive.

The gymnophions are the least understood and most rarely seen amphibians. They are blind and limbless, with long, slender bodies, like worms or snakes. Between the mouth and the useless eye is a slit with a protruding tentacle. The animal uses this organ to feel its way about. Gymnophions range in size from 4 inches (10 centimeters) to 53 inches (135 centimeters). They burrow in the moist earth, feeding mostly on earthworms. Some eat dead animals as well. They are found throughout the tropics, mostly in South America, Africa, and islands of the Indian Ocean. Their scales are buried in their skin, unlike those of other amphibians.

Physical Characteristics

Some of the physical features of amphibians, like the scales of gymnophions, suggest their fish ancestry. Other characteristics are more clearly related to those of their descendants—the reptiles, birds, and mammals. Amphibians are unlike fishes in that most types have limbs instead of fins and generally breathe through lungs and skin instead of through gills. Unlike reptiles, they lack a scaly or armored covering and take in water and oxygen through their skin. Amphibians have developed in many different ways in order to survive in areas with widely varying climates, dangers, and food sources.

Most amphibians are relatively small animals. Except for the salamander of Japan, the giants among them became extinct long ago. They vary in length from less than $\frac{2}{5}$ inch (1 centimeter) to over 60 inches (150 centimeters). There is a West African giant frog that grows to more than 1 foot (30 centimeters) in length and may weigh as much as a full grown house cat. Most of the species have four limbs. The hands generally end in four fingers, and the feet in five toes. Although the limbless gymnophions crawl like worms or snakes, most amphibians with legs move by jumping, climbing, or running.

The skulls are usually flat and wide, and the teeth, which grow in the jawbones and roof of the mouth, lack roots and are replaced intermittently. Amphibians do not chew with these teeth. They use their long, flexible tongues to capture their prey, which they then swallow whole.

The moist, supple skin of most amphibians provides protection and absorbs water and oxygen. The upper skin layer is regularly shed in a process called molting. The skin usually comes off in one piece and is then eaten by the animal.

The lower skin layer, called the dermis, often includes mucous and poison glands. The mucous glands help provide essential moisture to the body. The poison glands are found in different places on different

Common Toad
(Bufo bufo)
Length: up to 15 cm (5.9 in)

American Bullfrog
(Rana catesbeiana)
Length: 8.9–15.2 cm (3.5–6 in)

South American Escuerzo
(Ceratophrys ornata)
Length: up to 15.2 cm (6 in)

Leopard Frog
(Rana pipiens)
Length: 5.1–8.9 cm (2–3.5 in)

Ornate Chorus Frog
(Pseudacris ornata)
Length: 2.5–3.2 cm (1–1.25 in)

Southern Cricket Frog
(Acris gryllus)
Length: 1.5–3.2 cm (.6–1.25 in)

Midwife Toad
(Alytes obstetricans)
Length: 5.1–7.6 cm (2–3 in)

Japanese Giant Salamander
(Megalobatrachus japonicus)
Length:.9–1.5 m (3–5 ft)

Hellbender
(Cryptobranchus alleganiensis)
Length: 50.8–73.7 cm (20-29 in)

Slender Dwarf Siren
(Pseudobranchus striatus spheniscus)
Length: 10.2–15.2 cm (4–6 in)

Mud Puppy
(Necturus maculosus)
Length: 30.5–45.7 cm (12–18 in)

Red-spotted Newt
(Diemictylus viridenscens)
Length: 7.6–11.4 cm (3–4.5 in)

Two-toed Amphiuma
(Amphiuma means)
Length: 61–76.2 cm (24-30 in)

Red-backed Salamander
(Plethodon cinereus)
Length: .9–1.4 m (3–4.5 ft)

Siphonops
(Siphonops annulatus)
Length: 17.8–30.5 cm (7–12 in)

The eggs of a leopard frog (A) develop into tadpoles (B, C) in about a month. The tadpoles gradually develop limbs and begin to lose their tails (D, E) in the next month or two. The adult (F) is two to four inches (five to ten centimeters) long.

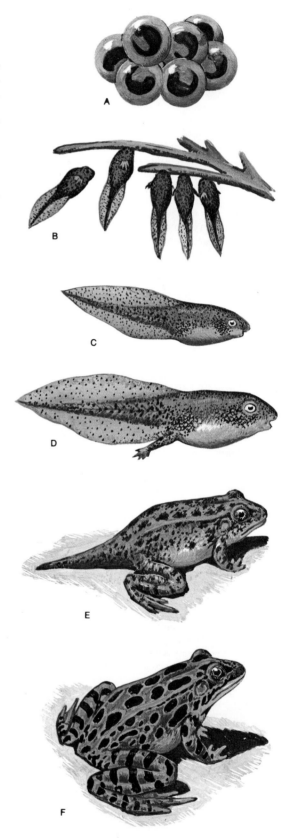

A

B

C

D

E

F

species—by the ears in certain toads, and behind the eyes of salamanders. These glands produce poisons that are toxic to natural enemies, such as birds and small mammals, but that rarely harm humans.

These glandular secretions give some amphibians distinct odors. The spotted salamander and the common toad smell of vanilla. Some frogs smell of onion, and the fire-bellied toad smells of garlic.

The skin's protective properties include the ability to change color so that the animal can hide when an enemy is nearby. Certain cells under the skin alter the color so that the amphibian can blend into its surroundings. Sometimes parts of the skin become brightly colored. The amphibian displays these colors to enemies to warn them to keep away.

The sense organs vary greatly, depending on the order and the species. The eyes are virtually useless in underground amphibians but are well-developed in other species. The sense of smell is generally good. Hearing ability varies according to the species. Some amphibians also have pores on their bodies, called lateral line organs, that are sensitive to vibrations in the water.

Life Cycle

Most amphibians begin their lives in the water as tadpoles, or larvae, which breathe by means of external gills instead of lungs. At first the tadpole has no definite shape, and no tail can be seen. The mouth is a V-shaped sucker on the underside of the body. As the head grows, a round mouth with a horny rim develops. At the same time, the tadpole grows a flat, finlike tail. The tiny creature later changes to adult form and breathes at least partly through lungs. This transformation process is called metamorphosis (from the Greek *meta*, meaning "change," and *morphē*, meaning "form"). The larval stage lasts from several weeks to one year, depending on the particular species and upon environmental factors such as temperature and humidity. Certain species of amphibians, particularly among the salamanders, remain in larval form all their lives. This phenomenon is called neoteny.

The larvae of the three orders differ from one another in several ways. The urodele larvae are long and slender, with limbs, three pairs of gills, and large mouths. The anurans, with short trunks and small mouth openings, lack lungs, eyelids, jaws, and legs. They look much more like fishes than like frogs or toads. The gymnophion larvae are limbless and slender and have distinctive gills.

Although a female amphibian is capable of producing thousands of offspring during the course of a lifetime, the general population of amphibians remains about the same. This is because during the process of metamorphosis many die and others are destroyed by predators.

Metamorphosis alters the feeding and breathing habits of an animal as well as its physical shape. Amphibians change from gill breathers to lung breathers. They also change from plant eaters to meat eaters. Adults eat insects or small animals, especially mollusks, worms, and other amphibians. Some frogs also eat small mammals and birds.

Most amphibians reach maturity at three or four years. They breed for the first time about one year after metamorphosis.

Although some amphibians carry their eggs within their bodies until hatching takes place, most lay eggs in moist places to allow their offspring to develop at least to the larval stage before hatching. The eggs vary from 1/25 of an inch (1 millimeter) to 1/6 of an inch (4 millimeters) in diameter, depending on the species. Some species abandon their eggs in a pool, a stream, or some other moist place, but others watch over their eggs until they hatch.

The life span of an amphibian depends on its species and on its environment. Amphibians in captivity have been known to live up to 20 years. The general life span probably ranges from 10 to 40 years.

Behavior

All amphibians must live near water because their soft skin provides little protection against dehydration. If their skin dries up, they soon die. Most live in the areas between fresh water and dry land or in regions that have plenty of dew and moisture.

Some species of amphibians are active by day, while others move about at night. Their activity is also influenced by temperature and humidity.

Amphibians are cold-blooded animals, meaning they are about the same temperature as their environment. When the temperature drops or rises or the humidity falls, they change habitats in order to become more comfortable. This is necessary because their body temperature influences such processes as growth and egg formation.

Where temperature becomes high and humidity low, or where dry and rainy seasons alternate, some amphibians become inactive until conditions are again favorable. This is called aestivation.

In cold or temperate regions, some amphibians go into hibernation. They seek out mud, trees, or caverns in which they remain in a state of inactivity for periods ranging from two to eight months, until the environment is again warm enough (see Hibernation).

Some amphibians are considered moderately intelligent. They are known to communicate with each other by calls or croaks that indicate mating, distress, or territorial concerns. Sounds, which vary greatly among the species, are made by the passage of air across the vocal cords. Male frogs have vocal sacs on either side of the throat. These act to amplify sounds. Some frogs and toads even sing in chorus.

Frogs and toads have a strong sense of location. When taken from their territories or breeding grounds, they can find their way back by smell and instinctively by the position of the stars. Many migratory species tend to return to the same breeding grounds year after year.

Amphibians respond to danger in several ways. Some dive in the water or hide in dens. Others pretend to be dead or camouflage themselves by changing color. Others protect themselves with poisonous skin secretions, or puff up to look large and frightening. The enemies of amphibians include foxes, hedgehogs, storks, herons, snakes, and large spiders.

Humans are the most serious threat to amphibians. Although amphibians help keep insect populations under control, they are often destroyed when people drain marshes to kill mosquitos and other insect pests. Amphibians are eaten in some countries; frog legs are a delicacy. Many amphibians are used in scientific experiments. Some are also frequently kept in aquariums and terrariums as pets.

The Evolutionary Record

Amphibians are studied by scientists because of their role in the evolution of life. Fossil remains of the earliest known amphibians indicate they probably developed from fishes called crossopterygians. These fishes possessed an early form of lungs. Although they also had gills, their lungs allowed them to absorb the oxygen necessary to live when they were on land. These fishes also developed moveable, paired fins to help them move on dry land.

About 350 million years ago, during a time of alternating dry and wet periods called the Devonian period, the early amphibians could cross land to find other bodies of water if the ones they inhabited dried up. They became the first four-footed animals (tetrapods). (See also Animals, Prehistoric.)

The earliest known amphibians are believed to be the ichthyostegalians. These creatures had short stubby legs with five toes and a tail fin. They had scales on their bellies and tails.

Most early amphibians were much larger than the species that exist today. Some of them were as long as 15 feet (4.6 meters). They fed on large insects. There were no other land animals. They were the dominant land animals for at least 75 million years.

After the Devonian period came the Coal, or Carboniferous, period during which many land areas were under water. This environment was hospitable to the amphibians. At the end of this period the land became dryer. Those species that best adapted to the new conditions evolved into the early reptiles.

AMSTERDAM, The Netherlands. Bustling Amsterdam, capital of The Netherlands, is famous for its scenic canals, countless bridges, and stately old houses. Some 63 miles (101 kilometers) of canals lace the inner city, so that one is never more than a few blocks from the nearest waterway. Ships sailing out of Amsterdam's harbor to conduct lucrative trade across the

Netherlands Information Service

According to tradition, Montelbaan Tower is one of the towers from which Dutch seamen's wives waved good-bye to their husbands centuries ago.

oceans made Amsterdam a great commercial and financial center.

Low and flat, Amsterdam lies about 12 feet (4 meters) below sea level, on the Amstel and IJ (pronounced "eye") rivers. An elaborate system of dams, dikes, pumps, and canals keeps the water from rushing in over the city and the surrounding countryside. The inland lake called the IJsselmeer, near Amsterdam, was formerly a bay of the Atlantic Ocean called the Zuider Zee. Now a causeway 20 miles (32 kilometers) long separates the IJsselmeer from the ocean, and Amsterdam has become an inland city.

Canals extend in a cobweb pattern through every part of old Amsterdam. They were dug first as moats around the city walls and later as a system of waterways that made it possible for people to travel about by boat. The main canals form concentric rings around the inner city. Using these and the smaller canals that crisscross them, a boat can move easily between parts of the city. Streets crowded with cars, bicycles, and pedestrians weave among the waterways by means of more than a thousand bridges.

Architecture of Amsterdam

Between the canals the underlying soil is soft and wet. The older buildings stand on timber piles driven into the soft earth for support. It is estimated that 5 million such piles support the old city. Modern architecture has not changed the need for such supports. The Harbor Building, a glass and concrete tower built in 1960, rises on hundreds of concrete columns sunk 80 feet (24 meters) into the earth.

Most buildings in the central city date from the 17th and 18th centuries, when rich merchants dominated it. Brick and stone townhouses, warehouses, and churches line the canals. The Royal Palace faces Dam Square in the heart of the city. More than 7,000 structures are registered as historic monuments; no changes are allowed in their appearance.

Urban renewal (by repair or replacement) has been designated as Amsterdam's top priority. Outside the center city, many 19th- and early 20th-century buildings were cheaply erected and poorly maintained. The city council decided in 1978 that the goal of urban renewal should be to benefit the present inhabitants. The aim was to create new apartments with modest rents, enabling people to stay in the neighborhoods where they already lived.

Culture and Commerce

Amsterdam has earned a reputation for tolerance and individualism. People of differing religions and life-styles have long been welcome there. Many na-

The domes of Sint Nicolaas Kerk, a Catholic church built about 1885, rise by the inner harbor of Amsterdam. The port is in the left background. The harbor is an embarkation point for sight-seeing cruises of the city's canals.

Louis Goldman—Rapho/Photo Researchers

tionalities are represented in the cosmopolitan city, ranging from Indonesians (whose country was once a Dutch possession) to migrant workers from Morocco and Kurdish refugees from Iran.

The arts flourish in the city. More than 40 museums display the work of Dutch artists, old and new. The Rijksmuseum (National Museum) contains paintings by such masters as Rembrandt (who lived in Amsterdam), Vermeer, and Frans Hals. The Vincent van Gogh Museum features more than 500 paintings and drawings by Van Gogh. Contemporary artists and craftspeople display their products in shops and galleries. The Concertgebouw (Concert Building) is notable for its acoustics as well as for its world-famous orchestra.

Educational institutions include the University of Amsterdam (1632) and the Free (Protestant) University (1880). There are fewer political institutions than one might expect in a national capital, for the actual seat of government of The Netherlands is in The Hague. Certain ceremonial functions involving the royal family are still held in Amsterdam, however. In 1980 Queen Beatrix was invested as monarch in the 17th-century Nieuwe Kerk (New Church). The city itself is governed by a 45-member city council.

Commerce, banking, and industry are the basis of Amsterdam's prosperity. Deep canals connect its inland port with the North Sea and the rivers of central Europe. Diamonds, mined in South Africa and elsewhere, are brought to Amsterdam for cutting and polishing in the city's diamond factories.

History

Amsterdam started as a small fishing village called Amsteldam. Its name referred to its site by a dam built across the Amstel River sometime before 1275 by the lord of Amstel to protect his castle from being flooded by the Zuider Zee.

During the religious wars of the 16th century, Jews and members of many Protestant sects fled from other parts of Europe to Amsterdam in search of freedom. The 17th century was the city's golden age. Merchants sent ships out through the Zuider Zee into the North Sea and the Baltic for herring, grain, fur, and timber. Trade spread to other parts of the globe, and the spices of the East Indies, especially, brought great wealth to Amsterdam merchants. A banking system was developed to facilitate complex business transactions.

Later the city faced a series of setbacks. Trade slowed as the Zuider Zee filled with silt, reviving only after the construction of the North Sea Canal in 1865–76. The German occupation during World War II brought hunger and suffering to the entire city and death to most of its Jewish citizens—among them Anne Frank, whose famous diary was published after the war and whose hiding place is preserved as a museum. After the war Amsterdam recovered and continued in its position as the leading cultural and industrial center of The Netherlands. (*See also* Netherlands, The.) Population (1981 estimate), 712,294.

AMU DARYA. The longest river in Soviet Central Asia, the Amu Darya stretches from its headwaters in the eastern Pamirs (mountains in central Asia) to its mouth on the southern shore of the Aral Sea in the Soviet Union. The river is 1,578 miles (2,540 kilometers) long. Its basin extends for 600 miles (970 kilometers) from north to south and for more than 900 miles (1,450 kilometers) east to west. (*See also* Aral Sea.)

The mountainous area of the Amu Darya is characterized by heavy rainfall in winter and spring and by sharp variations in air temperature. Juniper and poplar trees grow down to the river's edge, and there is an abundance of sweetbrier and blackberries. At the river's reed-covered delta, willow, oleaster, and poplar trees form a tangled mass.

Fish found in the Amu Darya include varieties of sturgeon, carp, barbel, and trout. Boars, wildcats, jackals, foxes, and hares live near the riverbanks. More than 200 species of birds also inhabit the area.

Because of its unstable riverbed and sandbars, there is little navigation on the Amu Darya. A complicated dam system has been constructed to provide water for irrigation and to protect the nearby cultivated fields from floods. Further dams and reservoirs have been planned.

Systematic research of the river was not begun until the end of the 19th century. At the end of the 1920's, a map of the entire river basin was published in Tashkent, Uzbek S.S.R. Detailed studies by Soviet scientists are continually undertaken.

AMUNDSEN, Roald (1872–1928). One of the most important men in the history of polar exploration was Roald Amundsen. He was the first man to reach the South Pole, the first to sail around the world via the Northwest and Northeast passages, and the first to fly over the North Pole in a dirigible.

Roald Amundsen was born in Borge, Norway, on July 16, 1872. His father, a shipowner, died when the boy was 14. In school young Amundsen read stories about Sir John Franklin and other polar explorers and set his heart on becoming one himself.

Young Amundsen's mother, however, wanted him to become a physician. To please her, he studied medicine for two years at the University of Christiania (now Oslo). When his mother died, Amundsen dropped his studies at the university and went to sea.

At the age of 25 Amundsen became the first mate of the ship *Belgica* on a Belgian expedition to the Antarctic. After he returned to Norway, he prepared for his first independent venture.

In 1903 Amundsen set sail in the ship *Gjöa*, hoping to locate the north magnetic pole. For 19 months he remained at King Wilhelm Land, in the northeastern part of Greenland, making observations. His studies indicated that the magnetic pole has no stationary position but is in continual movement.

While on this expedition, he also traversed, in 1905, what explorers had been seeking for more than 300 years—the Northwest Passage from the Atlantic to the Pacific. He sailed through bays, straits, and

Three years after Roald Amundsen began a voyage of exploration on the *Gjöa*, the sea captain (far left, front row) posed with his crew in Nome, Alaska. They had been the first men to successfully navigate the Northwest Passage.

Library of Congress

sounds to the north of Canada. Thus Amundsen justified the search for a shorter route to the Orient which had challenged countless navigators.

Amundsen had planned next to drift across the North Pole in Fridtjof Nansen's ship *Fram*. When he learned that the American explorer Robert E. Peary had reached the North Pole in April 1909, he decided to seek the South Pole instead. He arrived there Dec. 14, 1911—just 35 days before the arrival of Robert F. Scott (*see* Scott, Robert F.).

In the summer of 1918 Amundsen once again set sail for the Arctic, in the newly built ship *Maud*. He planned to drift across the North Pole from Asia to North America, but he failed in this purpose because the ship was unable to penetrate the polar ice pack. Two years later, however, when Amundsen reached Alaska, he had sailed also through the Northeast Passage, by way of Siberian coastal waters connecting the Atlantic with the Pacific.

After he had sent the *Maud* back to the Arctic to continue observations, Amundsen turned to the project of flying over the North Pole. His efforts were crowned with success on May 11–13, 1926. In the dirigible *Norge*, piloted by Col. Umberto Nobile, an Italian aviator, he flew over the pole on a 2,700-mile (4,300-kilometer) flight between Spitsbergen and Teller, Alaska. He was accompanied by Lincoln Ellsworth, an American explorer.

Two years later Amundsen embarked on his last adventure. In June 1928 he left Norway to fly to the aid of Nobile, whose dirigible had crashed on a second Arctic flight. Amundsen's plane vanished, though Nobile was later rescued. Months afterward the discovery of floating wreckage told the tragic story of how Amundsen met his death. (*See also* Polar Exploration.) Amundsen's books include 'The South Pole' (1912) and, with Ellsworth, 'First Crossing of the Polar Sea' (1927).

AMUR RIVER. The most important waterway in the far-eastern part of the Soviet Union is the Amur River. It is formed by the union of the Argun and Shilka rivers. For 1,100

miles (1,800 kilometers) the river provides a natural boundary between the Soviet Union to the north and the People's Republic of China to the south. It then flows some 650 miles (1,050 kilometers) northeastward across the Soviet Union to the Tatar Strait, an arm of the Pacific Ocean. To the north the Amur's principal tributaries are the Zeya, the Bureya, and the Amgun rivers; to the south its main tributaries are the Sungari and the Ussuri, which constitutes another portion of the border between the Soviet Union and China. Including its headstreams, the length of the Amur River is about 2,700 miles (4,300 kilometers).

Known to the Chinese as the "River of the Black Dragon," the Amur reaches its high point in midsummer during the monsoon rains. From May to November, when the river is free of ice, the Amur is navigable for its entire length.

Russia first became interested in the Amur River region about 1640, when explorers penetrated westward to the Sea of Okhotsk. Chinese troops, however, resisted Russian efforts to settle the region, and the Treaty of Nerchinsk, signed in 1689, gave the territory to China. In 1849 Capt. Gennadi Nevelskoy of the Russian navy explored the Amur's mouth and realized that the river could be of great commercial value. The Treaty of Aigun, signed in 1858, gave the left bank of the Amur to Russia. Today the Amur River provides an important waterway for several industrial centers of the Soviet Union, including Khabarovsk, Blagoveshchensk, and Komsomol'sk.

AMUSEMENT PARK. Permanent commercial outdoor resorts began in Europe almost 350 years ago, but the amusement park, with its Ferris wheel and hot dogs, its midway and fireworks, is really an American creation. In the United States amusement parks have become a huge industry.

There are famous examples in Europe such as the Prater in Vienna. Originally a royal animal park, it was opened to the public in 1766. The 1873 Vienna World's Fair was held there. The Viennese had a fine view of their city from the top of the *Riesenrad* ("giant wheel"), a Ferris wheel that was 210 feet (64 meters) high, installed in 1897. The Prater was almost totally destroyed by bombing during World War II but was afterward rebuilt.

Aside from the Prater, there are few contemporary examples of predominantly commercial amusement parks in Europe. Temporary fairs and elaborate public gardens, such as the Tivoli Gardens in Copenhagen or Gorki Park in Moscow, provide public recreation. The American type of park, however, has become popular in Japan. Notable examples are Toshimaen, Korakuen, and Yomiuri Land—all in the Tokyo area; one at the Sagami Bay beach resort of Oiso (southwest of the Tokyo-Yokohama metropolitan area), known as the Coney Island of the East; Takarazuka in the Osaka-Kobe region; and Dreamland at Nara.

Attractions

The types of attractions, as the amusements are called, are the rides, concession booths, and games of the midway. There are often exhibits, displays, and theatrical presentations, too. The rides have traditionally been the most popular type of attraction. The most venerable of these is the merry-go-round, or carousel (called a roundabout in England). It had its beginnings in medieval jousting tournaments, specifically in the sport of ring-spearing. Knights demonstrated their horsemanship and skill with a lance by riding full speed at a suspended ring and attempting to spear it. Noble children were trained in this sport on a rotating device with suspended wooden horses that was pushed around by servants. With miniature lances they would try to spear rings. This crude carousel became a popular European folk entertainment, and by the 19th century carousels had become quite elaborate. Powered by steam and later by electricity, they featured mechanical organs.

The roller coaster is an adaptation of the ice slides built for public amusement in Russia as early as 1650. Up to 70 feet (21 meters) high, these were timber frames supporting a 40- to 50-degree incline covered with frozen water. A French traveler saw one of these in the early years of the 19th century and took the idea to Paris. Instead of ice, he laid an inclined carriage track. The earliest of these roller coasters, built in 1804, was called the Russian Mountains.

In the United States such gravity pleasure rides began to appear in the 1870's, inspired by the switch-back gravity railway at Mauch Chunk (now Jim

The giant Ferris wheel called the *Riesenrad* looms over the Prater, an amusement park in Vienna, Austria. From the top, riders can see all of Vienna and much of the countryside.

Thorpe), Pa. Formerly used for transporting coal down a mountain, it became a pleasure ride and was in operation until 1939.

The sensation of great speed and danger on a modern roller coaster is mostly an illusion. In the United States roller coasters seldom go faster than about 40 miles (64 kilometers) per hour. Accidents are almost unknown because of the combination of safety devices used.

The Ferris wheel is another popular ride. It is a modern version of the European-Oriental "pleasure wheel." Its present form originated with the enormous wheel built by George Washington Gale Ferris for the World's Columbian Exposition at Chicago in 1893. Its popularity resulted from the spectacular view at the top of the wheel, 264 feet (80 meters) above the ground. Ferris built his wheel to meet the challenge of the Eiffel Tower, an engineering marvel when it was built for the Paris Exposition of 1889.

The various "sky rides" are derived from Swiss Alpine ski lifts and aerial tramways. Examples are the Delta Flyer and the Southern Cross at Marriott's Great America just outside Chicago.

In addition to these large rides, there are many others. The principal types include water rides such as the shoot-the-chutes, consisting of an incline down which water flows and boats slide into a pool at the

Nathan's refreshment stand became a landmark at Coney Island, New York City's famous amusement park in Brooklyn. Nathan's was founded in 1916. This photograph was taken in 1922.

bottom. There are circle swings that typically carry the rider around in a seat suspended from a revolving frame. "Flat rides" are the most common type, and they include all the many devices that carry riders around a flat or undulating track. Among these are the Whip, invented in 1914, which spins riders around while centrifugal force keeps them in their seats, and the Dodg'em, or bumper cars, in which the riders guide themselves.

Illusion rides, or "dark rides," attempt to produce the sensation of going to strange or exotic places. In a fun house the visitor walks, or tries to walk, while being bounced around and disoriented by optical illusions and mirrors. The effects of an illusion ride and a fun house can be combined—for example, in a "haunted house" attraction.

The concession booths on a midway offer many attractions. The oldest are games of chance such as the vertical Wheel of Fortune, which often offers stuffed animals as prizes. Cheating customers in midway games, or gaffing, is now considered bad business, but it once was common.

Other typical midway concessions offer games of skill such as the milk bottle pitch and shooting galleries. The oddest concession may be the bozo joint. The bozo's job is to insult the passersby. He sits on a board above a tub of water. Customers pay for balls and throw them at a target, which, if hit, will unlock the board and dump the bozo into the water.

Food is just as popular as games on the midway. Refreshment stands are called grab joints because the customer is supposed to take the food and eat it elsewhere. The best-known refreshment stand in the United States is probably Nathan's at Coney Island on New York City's Brooklyn seashore. Started by Nathan Handwerker in 1916, it is now a chain operation. The hot dog on a roll supposedly was introduced at Nathan's original concession.

The types of shows or displays that may be seen at amusement parks have always included brilliant lighting effects and fireworks. Before the widespread use of electric light, bright outdoor illumination at night was a novelty.

Beginning with Luna Park on Coney Island at the turn of the 20th century, ambitious amusement park operators have installed displays and features imitating those at world's fairs and expositions. Various kinds of animal shows were also introduced, such as the sea lion attraction featured in Coney Island's first park and the performing whales, dolphins, and sea lions at Sea World, which opened in 1964 in San Diego, Calif.

History

The origins of amusement parks lie in ancient and medieval religious festivals and trade fairs. Merchants, entertainers, and food sellers gathered to take advantage of the large temporary crowds. Permanent outdoor amusement areas also date from antiquity, but public resorts for individual relaxation and recreation did not appear in Europe until the Renaissance. They were called pleasure gardens.

The first one with an international reputation was Vauxhall Gardens in London, which opened in 1661. It covered 12 acres (5 hectares) and admission was free. Entertainment included music, acrobatic acts, and fireworks. Mozart as an eight-year-old prodigy performed there in 1764.

English pleasure gardens developed from resort grounds run by proprietors of inns and taverns. In France they were created by professional showmen such as the Ruggieri family, who opened the Ruggieri Gardens in Paris in 1766. As in London, fireworks were a popular attraction. Balloon and parachute acts were introduced at the end of the 18th century.

United States parks typically started as picnic grounds where organizations of working people went for outings. The largest of these early parks was Jones's Wood, located along the East River between what are now 70th and 75th streets in New York City. Lake Compounce, in Bristol, Conn., began as a bathing beach and concert grove and is now the oldest amusement park in continuous operation in the United States. Beer was the most popular refreshment at these 19th-century resorts, and they were called beer gardens.

The growth of public transportation has been a decisive factor in the development of the amusement park as an industry in the United States. In the 1880's, excursion boats took visitors to such early resorts as Parker's Island along the Ohio River near Cincinnati. Today, more acreage at California's Disneyland is devoted to car parking than to the park itself. Railroads deserve most of the credit for making an industry out of fun. When a rail line reached Coney Island in the 1870's, daily attendance jumped to more than 50,000. Traction companies, responsible for building the first streetcar lines, began in the 1890's to construct amusement parks at the end of the lines. They used the parks as a way to lure riders out of the city on weekends. Whalom Park in Lunenburg, Mass., began in this way.

Traction companies soon quit the business, leaving it in the hands of such people as circus and carnival operators. Safety problems arose. There were complaints about fraudulent advertising and about cheating by midway amusement operators. Some parks even sold franchises to professional pickpockets. Cities and towns found it difficult to regulate the parks, but they could not close them because of their popularity. A few towns actually bought parks, while other parks were taken over by civic-minded organizations.

By the early 20th century amusement parks had become profitable enough to attract the attention of big business. Forest Park in St. Louis, Mo., was built by a brewery, and so was Pabst Park in Milwaukee, Wis. The Hershey Chocolate Company built a now-famous park in Hershey, Pa. Real estate heir William Schmidt saw Copenhagen's Tivoli Gardens while on a European trip and erected Riverview Park in Chicago when he returned.

The single most important inspiration for United States amusement parks was the 19th-century world's fair, or exposition. These fairs were enormous events, combining trade exhibits, educational installations, and (not always officially) entertainment of every sort. A miniature railway four miles (six kilometers) long was shown at the Philadelphia Centennial Exposition of 1876 and thereafter copied by amusement parks everywhere. The Ferris wheel first appeared in 1893 at the World's Columbian Exposition in Chicago. Forty years later, at Chicago's Century of Progress fair, the sky ride was first seen.

The influence of these large temporary spectacles goes far beyond the introduction of specific rides. They provided a model for the layout of amusement parks, and they pioneered the peculiar combination of entertainment with educational, or instructive, exhibits that led to the modern "theme" parks such as Disneyland. The trade fairs spread information about foreign places, new commercial products, "primitive" peoples, technological developments, and scientific discoveries. The amusement parks transformed the information into entertainment.

Coney Island, called the Empire of the Nickel, is one of the best-known amusement resorts in the United States and was the home of several well-known parks. The earliest was Sea Lion Park founded by "Captain" Billy Boyton in 1895. Elmer Dundy, a former politician, and Frederick W. Thompson, an engineer and inventor, took over Boyton's operation in 1902. Inspired in part by the Columbian Exposition of 1893, Thompson created Luna Park, which may be considered the first modern amusement park. The Chicago fair's influence is evident in the names of many of Luna Park's attractions: Canals of Venice, Eskimo Village, Electric Tower, and Trip to the North Pole. There was even an infant incubator where newborn children could be viewed. Dreamland

The Matterhorn is one of the attractions at Disneyland in Anaheim, Calif. It offers visitors bobsled rides with glimpses of the Abominable Snowman.

© Walt Disney Productions 1981

Park, even larger than Luna Park, opened on Coney Island in 1904. There was a Lilliputian Village, where 300 midgets lived, and Fighting Flames, a show in which a six-story building was set on fire and fire fighters made dramatic rescues.

Second only to Coney Island is Atlantic City, N.J., which features amusement piers. Steel Pier is the best known, extending 2,000 feet (610 meters) into the ocean. There are many other well-known parks in the United States. Kennywood Park, outside Pittsburgh, pioneered the creation of "kiddielands." A portion of the park was set aside for children. Parks were sometimes built around specific attractions such as Geauga Lake Park in Aurora, Ohio, that had one of the longest roller coasters ever built.

Traditional parks began to decline during and after World War II. They did not suffer much from competition with other amusements, but visitors began to demand more sophisticated entertainment. Some parks went out of business. A startlingly high number burned; fire had always been a serious hazard for the flimsily built park structures. Older operations lacked sufficient parking space as more and more people began to drive automobiles. The rising value of urban real estate led to some parks being sold for more profitable types of development. And finally, vandalism became a far more serious problem than it had previously been.

In 1955 a revolution occurred in the United States amusement industry. Disneyland, a creation of cartoonist Walt Disney, opened in Anaheim, Calif. (*see* Disney). This was the first of a new type of park, the theme park. There was no Ferris wheel and no roller coaster. Instead the Disney designers, drawing on their experience with film-set design and cartoons, planned a series of "lands" with themes borrowed from popular motion pictures. There are seven theme lands at Disneyland, including Adventureland (based on exotic foreign scenes), Frontierland (a re-creation of the Old West), and Tomorrowland.

The spectacular success of Disneyland has been imitated by other theme parks, though many are traditional parks with a theme disguise. An unusual exception is Opryland in Nashville, Tenn., whose theme is the country music business based there. Walt Disney World, opened in 1971 at Lake Buena Vista, Fla., is the largest theme park yet built. In addition to many theme lands, it contains recreation facilities, hotels, and campgrounds. The entire resort covers an area the size of San Francisco. Epcot Center, a futuristic showplace with world's fair pavillions, opened nearby in 1982.

Social Influence

The economic and social importance of a park on the scale of Walt Disney World cannot be overstated. During the first ten years of its existence, Disney World guests spent an estimated 14 billion dollars in central Florida. The effect of traditional amusement parks cannot be so easily measured, for they provide more than information and amusement.

'Showboat' is a production at the Opryland U.S.A. musical entertainment theme park in Nashville, Tenn.

Amusement parks were originally built not for children but for adults. They were usually located at the edge of large cities. Easily accessible by public transportation, the parks provided a safety valve for inner-city dwellers to let off steam. They provided a safe channel for aggressive or destructive impulses that could not be satisfied elsewhere in socially acceptable ways. One park ran a concession where patrons could go into a room and smash dishes. The need to experience danger, even if it is largely an illusion, is satisfied by roller-coaster rides.

The great world's fairs and expositions have presented new technology and scientific discoveries and have exposed patrons to exotic people and places. Such exposure to the new and unusual has helped to replace fear with curiosity. Yet the fear may never completely fade. Amusement parks may have helped to lessen fear by taking the new and the strange and informing while entertaining on a grand scale. J. J. Stock invented a fun house in the mid-1920's called the Katzenjammer Castle. He put a sign in front of it that read, "If you can't laugh, you must be sick."

Good books about amusement parks include 'Step Right Up, Folks!' by Al Griffin, published in 1974, and 'The Great American Amusement Parks' by Gary Kyriazi, published in 1976.

ANACONDA *see* SNAKE.

ANAHEIM, Calif. One of the fastest-growing cities in the Los Angeles area is Anaheim. The largest city in prosperous Orange County, it is situated some 20 miles (32 kilometers) southeast of Los Angeles.

The diversified industries of the Anaheim area produce electrical machinery and electronic components, aircraft parts, communications equipment, fabricated metal products, paper goods, plastics, and chemicals. The processing of citrus fruits and walnuts grown in the Anaheim vicinity is also important.

The tourist industry is a major source of income for Anaheim. Disneyland, a world-famous amusement park, brings millions of visitors to the city each year. Other attractions include a theater-in-the-round and the annual Halloween Festival. A modern convention center was completed in Anaheim in 1967. Anaheim Stadium, which opened in 1966, is the home of the California Angels baseball team and the Los Angeles Rams football team.

Anaheim is known as the "mother colony" of southern California. It was founded in 1857 by German settlers from San Francisco as an experiment in communal living. The city was named after the nearby Santa Ana River, which provides water for irrigation in the area. The German word *heim* ("home") was added as a suffix.

Originally, the main crop of the area was grapes, raised for making wine. However, the vines were destroyed by blight in the 1880's, and attempts to restore the vineyards failed. Valencia oranges, other citrus fruits, and walnuts were then introduced.

Since the late 1920's Anaheim has undergone rapid industrial development. The city was incorporated in 1870 and has a council-manager form of government. Population (1980 census), 221,847.

ANALGESIC. A drug with the main effect of reducing or eliminating pain without causing loss of consciousness is called an analgesic. The effect on pain is referred to as analgesia. Analgesics are also called painkillers. Animals and human beings produce in their bodies several natural analgesics called enkephalins. The roles of these substances are unclear.

Analgesic drugs generally can be divided into two categories, depending on the way they act to produce their pain-relieving actions. Local, or minor, analgesics such as aspirin, acetaminophen, and propoxyphene hydrochloride (Darvon) act on the chemical receptors that play a part in causing pain. These receptors are specialized cellular or tissue elements with which a drug interacts to produce its effects. On the other hand, central analgesics affect the central nervous system and in this way interfere with the perception of pain. Some analgesics may act in both ways. In many cases the ways in which these drugs function are not known.

Local Analgesics

Aspirin is the best example of a locally acting analgesic. Aspirin is thought to prevent the manufacture of prostaglandins, chemicals known to play a role in the process by which pain is caused. Because of its ability to lessen inflammation of tissue, often a major cause of pain, aspirin is used to treat chronic conditions such as rheumatoid arthritis. It is also effective in reducing fever. Taken in large quantities over long periods of time, however, aspirin often causes bleeding in the stomach.

Aspirin and related analgesics have a limited but definite effect on minor pain. Aspirin has been used for many hundreds of years in its natural form from the spirea bush from which its active chemical, acetylsalicylic acid, may be extracted by boiling. It was not until the 20th century that aspirin was first synthetically duplicated.

Central Analgesics

Centrally acting analgesics are thought to affect the opiate receptors in the brain and perhaps also those in the spinal cord. The most widely used and effective of these narcotic analgesics are derived from opium alkaloids. Morphine is one typical example. The abuse of such narcotics is a major social and medical problem.

Although the exact mechanisms by which opiate drugs work against pain is poorly understood, it is thought that an important action of, for example, morphine is its ability to cause euphoria. A person in this state, while still able to feel pain, is not concerned with it as long as the effects of the drug are active. These drugs, which include heroin and codeine, are effective analgesics but may cause a number of unwanted side effects such as depressing the respiratory system and the cough reflex. Because they can cause physical and psychological addiction, their use must be carefully controlled. To prevent addiction, they cannot be given to people with chronic or permanent pain conditions. Their use is limited largely to the relief of acute pain of a temporary nature such as the pain following surgery.

Tranquilizers and amphetamines are often combined with opiate drugs whose effects they increase. Thus, a smaller dose of morphine is effective when taken in combination with the tranquilizer diazepam.

Other Types and Conditions

Nonanalgesic drugs may also have an analgesic effect. Alcohol, for example, has this effect, and people who are intoxicated often injure themselves without feeling immediate pain. Analgesia can also result from diseases affecting the sensory nervous system. This can endanger the lives of those afflicted, as pain is a vital warning system both of injury and of illness.

Nerve blocks, in which a local anesthetic is injected directly into the nerves along which a pain signal travels, are sometimes used as analgesics (*see* Anesthesia). In some conditions, such as causalgia (severe pain from unknown causes), a series of nerve blocks can sometimes permanently stop the pain.

The most sophisticated use of analgesics is in the treatment of patients with severe, intractable pain such as the pain accompanying types of cancer. Combinations of various analgesics with other drugs have been formulated to relieve pain while allowing the patient to retain a reasonable functional level.

ANALYTICAL CHEMISTRY *see* CHEMISTRY.

ANARCHISM. The word anarchism derives from a Greek term meaning "without government." Along with socialism and communism, anarchism was one of the leading political philosophies to develop in Europe in the 19th century. The chief tenet of anarchism was that government and private property should be abolished. Also part of anarchism was the concept that the people should be allowed to live in free associations, sharing work and its products.

Although a 19th-century movement, anarchism had theoretical roots in the writings of two English social reformers of the two previous centuries: Gerrard Winstanley and William Godwin. Winstanley was a 17th-century agrarian reformer who believed that land should be divided up among all the people. Godwin, in a book entitled 'Political Justice' (1793), argued that authority is unnatural and that social evils arise and exist because people are not free to live their lives according to the dictates of reason. He predicted that, in the future, technology would free people from long hours of work and would enable them to enjoy abundance without the restraints that are imposed by government.

The work of Winstanley and Godwin was little noticed during their time. It was the French political writer Pierre Joseph Proudhon who coined the term anarchism and laid the theoretical foundations of the movement in his books 'What is Property' and 'Economic Contradictions'. In many ways Proudhon's thought was similar to socialism (*see* Socialism). He urged the abolition of private property and the control of the means of production by the workers. Instead of government, Proudhon desired a federal system of agricultural and industrial associations.

The theories of Proudhon attracted many followers, among them the Russians Mikhail Bakunin, Peter Kropotkin, and Emma Goldman; the German Johann Most; the Italian Enrico Malatesta; the Frenchman Georges Sorel; and the American Paul Goodman. These individuals all elaborated theories of anarchism based on Proudhon's work, theories that often aligned anarchism with other political theories such as socialism, communism, and democracy. For some anarchists, the only means to change society was terrorism. Malatesta, for example, advocated "propaganda by the deed," a point of view that led to a number of political assassinations (*see* Assassination). Sorel tried to merge anarchism with the labor syndicates (unions) of France in a movement called anarcho-syndicalism, the idea being that the workers

of France would help in restructuring society by leading in the destruction of capitalism and the state.

It was the economic and social change wrought by the Industrial Revolution that led to the proliferation of political theories such as anarchism, communism, and socialism. These movements vied for followers and power from the middle of the 19th century until after World War II. Anarchism never gained the popularity of the other two political philosophies. In the United States its successes were negligible, supported basically by immigrants such as Most and Goldman. There was a brief revival of interest in anarchism during the civil rights and antiwar movements of the 1950s and 1960s.

Anarchism persists primarily as an ideal, a warning against the dangers of concentrating power in the hands of governmental or economic institutions. (*See also* Bakunin; Communism.)

PROFILES OF LEADING ANARCHISTS

Some prominent persons are not included below because they are covered in the main text of this article or in other articles in Compton's Encyclopedia (*see* Fact-Index).

Goldman, Emma (1869–1940). Born in Kovno, Lithuania. Emigrated to the United States in 1883. Carried on anarchist propaganda and activities until 1917, when she was arrested for obstructing the war effort. After two years in prison, she was deported to Russia. Active in Spanish Civil War. Died in Toronto, Ont.

Goodman, Paul (1911–72). Born in New York City. Writer and lecturer who espoused anarchism in the 1930s. Urged educational decentralization in his book 'Growing Up Absurd', which made him popular with protesters of the 1960s. Also an author of poems, plays, and short stories.

Malatesta, Enrico (1850–1930). Italian anarchist who promoted "the insurrectionary deed," an act of terrorism done to change society. Exiled from Italy, he lived in France and the United States as a publisher of anarchist journals.

Most, Johann (1846–1906). German publisher of Socialist and anarchist newspapers. Imprisoned in both Germany and France for his views, he emigrated to the United States in the early 1880s. After several imprisonments there, he abandoned the anarchist philosophy.

Proudhon, Pierre J. (1809–65). Born at Besançon, France. Self-educated theorist of anarchism. He urged the division of property among owner-producers who would band together in mutual-benefit associations. Called for an economy in which money was based upon productivity rather than specie (gold). A vehement opponent of Karl Marx and Communism.

Sorel, Georges (1847–1922). Born at Cherbourg, France. Social philosopher and author. He became a convert to Marxism in 1893, but by 1902 had turned altogether against government, even under Communism. Adopted revolutionary syndicalism as the means of social change. Author of 'Reflections on Violence'. Died at Boulogne-sur-Seine, France.

Stirner, Max (1806–56). Real name was Johann Kaspar Schmidt. Born at Bayreuth, Bavaria (now in West Germany). A student of the philosopher Hegel at the University of Berlin. Friend of the revolutionaries Marx and Engels. Published 'The Ego and His Own' in 1845 under the name Stirner. The book was an attack on all philosophical systems and an exaltation of the absolute individual. He asserted that the person has no obligations except to himself. He saw the state as the enemy of the people and proposed a rebellion of all individuals instead of a political revolution which would only establish another state.

DIGESTIVE SYSTEMS COMPARED

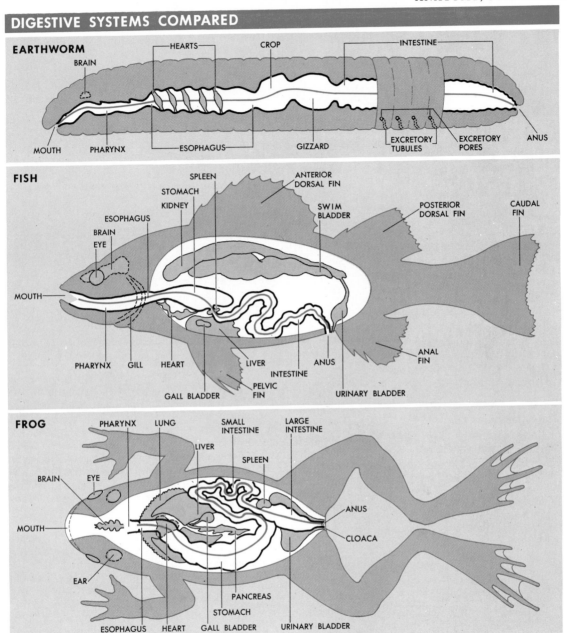

EARTHWORM

BRAIN — HEARTS — CROP — INTESTINE —

MOUTH — PHARYNX — ESOPHAGUS — GIZZARD — EXCRETORY TUBULES — EXCRETORY PORES — ANUS

FISH

SPLEEN — STOMACH — KIDNEY — ESOPHAGUS — BRAIN — EYE — ANTERIOR DORSAL FIN — SWIM BLADDER — POSTERIOR DORSAL FIN — CAUDAL FIN

MOUTH — PHARYNX — GILL — HEART — LIVER — INTESTINE — ANUS — ANAL FIN — GALL BLADDER — PELVIC FIN — URINARY BLADDER

FROG

PHARYNX — LUNG — SMALL INTESTINE — LARGE INTESTINE — LIVER — SPLEEN — BRAIN — EYE

MOUTH — ANUS — CLOACA

EAR — PANCREAS — STOMACH — URINARY BLADDER

ESOPHAGUS — HEART — GALL BLADDER

ANATOMY, COMPARATIVE. The job any machine can do depends upon its parts and their arrangement. A saw is able to cut wood because it has teeth. A sewing machine can pierce cloth because it has a needle. Every kind of animal and every kind of plant also has its own peculiar structure. How and where it can live depends upon its structure.

In comparative anatomy the structures of various animals are studied and compared. The drawings on this page show the digestive systems of the earthworm, the fish, and the frog. The colored lines trace the animals' digestive tracts. As can be seen, the systems are alike in many ways. Each animal has a

mouth, a pharynx, an esophagus, an intestine, and an anus. There are also differences. For example, the frog and the fish have livers whereas the earthworm has a gizzard. The differences enable each animal to digest the food found where it lives.

The drawings show other organs that equip each animal for its way of life. The fish, which lives in water, has gills through which it breathes. It has no lungs. The frog, which lives on land as well as in water, is equipped with lungs for air breathing. The earthworm has neither lungs nor gills. It breathes through its skin. (*See also* Animal; Earthworm; Fish; Frog, Anatomy of.)

HUMAN ANATOMY

An understanding of the human body is important to everyone. These students are using special models to compare the structures of a human and an animal skeleton.

ANATOMY, HUMAN. It is common practice to divide the human body into eight systems. The principal parts of each of these systems and their relationships are shown in the drawings in this article.

The Skeleton

The skeleton consists of the bones, joints, and cartilages that make up the framework of the body. There are between 200 and 212 bones in the body, depending upon how many small accessory bones there are around certain joints. Bones are of two principal types—the long and the flat. The long bones are those in the arms, legs, hands, and feet. The flat bones are the breastbone and ribs, the face bones, and the cranial, or skull, bones. Some of these are curved, and some are more massive than flat. Small bones in the wrist and ankle have various shapes, neither round nor flat.

Joints are formed where two bones come together. In the skull these are simple irregular lines where the bones join without moving. Joints that have movement are of three principal kinds. In the shoulders and hips there are joints in which a ball fits into a socket, giving a wide range of circular motion. In the elbows, knees, jaw, fingers, and toes, there are hinged joints. They permit back-and-forth motion, which is largely limited to one plane. In the ankles, wrists, and between the bones in the spine, sliding motion is limited.

Joints are made of the adjacent surfaces of bones which are covered with cartilage, or gristle. Large strips of cartilage connect the ribs to the breastbone. The joints are further secured in place by heavy sheets of fibrous connecting tissue known as joint capsules or ligaments. In each joint is a small amount of slippery lubricating fluid.

The spine gives strength with flexibility to the back through small bones called vertebrae. There are 7 of these in the neck (cervical), 12 in the chest (thoracic), and 5 in the back (lumbar). The hipbones are attached to a united mass of 5 more (sacrum). The spine ends with 4 small bones fused together (coccyx). The long and the flat bones have cavities filled with marrow. The marrow makes the red and certain kinds of white blood cells. (*See also* Skeleton; Bone.)

The Muscles

Muscles in the body are of three kinds. These are voluntary, or striped; involuntary, or smooth; and heart muscles, which are striped and branched.

The voluntary muscles move parts of the body and help hold the head and body upright. Each of these muscles is attached by a fibrous cord (ligament) to a bone. The voluntary muscles are composed of fibers which can contract. Thus they pull on the bones and move the limb or other body part.

Most smooth muscles act automatically under control of the nervous system. They are found in the lungs, the intestines, and the bladder.

Heart muscle fibers are branched and striped. The heart has a bundle of fibers which combines the qualities of muscles and nerves. This originates and regulates the automatic heartbeat. (*See also* Muscles.)

Circulation and Respiration

All parts of the body depend upon the circulation of blood and a fluid called lymph for nourishment, oxygen supply, and the removal of waste products. Circulation is maintained by the heart, the blood-vessel system, and the lymph circulation. The lungs

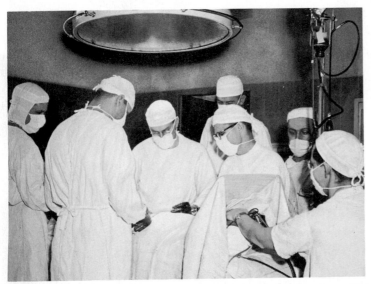

Doctors, particularly surgeons, must have a thorough knowledge of anatomy. The patient's life depends upon the skill of these men.

The Digestive System

The digestive system is a modified tube (*see* Digestion). Food enters the body and is digested; useful food is absorbed, and waste is expelled.

In the mouth are the tongue, the teeth, and the glands which produce saliva. Food is chewed and mixed with saliva in the mouth. Sugar digestion begins. When it is swallowed through the long, elastic esophagus, the food enters the stomach. There it is mixed with acid and two principal digestive ferments. One of these curdles milk. The other begins the digestion of protein.

The stomach mixes the food before passing it into the small intestine. There bile from the liver and digestive ferments from the pancreas are added. The liver is the body's largest internal organ. (*See also* Stomach; Liver.)

The small intestine is about 21 feet long and is packed into the abdominal cavity in coils. Its inner lining provides more digestive juices and the means of absorbing food substances into the blood. The muscular coat moves the liquified contents onward by stages. Finally they reach the large intestine. Here they encounter a valvelike barrier which relaxes from time to time to allow liquid to enter the large intestine. Attached to the large intestine near its junction with the small intestine is the appendix.

The large intestine is a six-foot-long muscular structure. Its main function is to reduce its almost liquid contents to a semisolid form by the absorption of moisture. It then expels waste materials.

The Urinary System

The body automatically maintains its water balance through a complicated system centering about the kidneys. These two organs are each about the size of a human fist and shaped like a bean.

The kidneys are complicated filters. In addition to regulating the amount of water in the body, they control the concentration of many substances in the blood. The final secretion of the kidneys is urine. It trickles through long tubes which pass from each kidney to the bladder. The bladder is an elastic and muscular vessel that holds the urine until it can be voided. (*See also* Kidneys.)

The Glandular System

The actions of the body are controlled in part by a system of interrelated organs known as endocrine glands, or glands of internal secretion. Their products, known as hormones, are absorbed directly into the blood. (*See also* Gland; Hormones.)

The chief gland is the pituitary, located under the brain. The gland is in two parts. Its hormones

may be regarded as part of the circulatory system also. (*See also* Blood; Lungs; Respiration.)

The heart is a muscular pump. Its beat circulates the blood through the body. Its two parts are nearly identical. The heart's system of valves permits the blood to flow in at the top and flow out through the principal arteries only. The left side of the heart receives blood from the lungs, where it has taken up oxygen. The blood is then pumped through the arteries to all parts of the body. The arteries branch into smaller and smaller tubes and finally end in a network of microscopic thin-walled capillaries. (*See also* Heart and Circulation.)

The lymph is a fluid closely allied to blood. It is circulated toward the heart by the pressure of blood in the capillaries and other body activity.

Portal circulation consists of the capillaries in the digestive system. These unite into veins and finally form a large vein which carries the blood to the liver.

The lungs fill the entire chest that is not taken up by the heart and the great blood vessels. They are a spongy structure consisting of fibrous tubes leading to air sacs. These small tubes merge into larger ones that unite to form the windpipe. At the upper end of the windpipe is the larynx, or voice box, which opens into the throat. The larynx admits air from the nose or the mouth. It is protected from inhaling food particles by a valvelike structure, the epiglottis.

The diaphragm is a sheet of muscular tissue dividing the chest from the abdomen. When one breathes in, the chest is raised by the ribs and the diaphragm is drawn downward, thus increasing the chest cavity. (*See also* Diaphragm.)

The spleen is an accessory organ to the circulatory system. It is located on the left side of the abdomen, under the liver. The spleen destroys red blood cells when they are no longer useful.

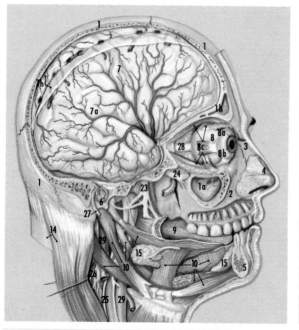

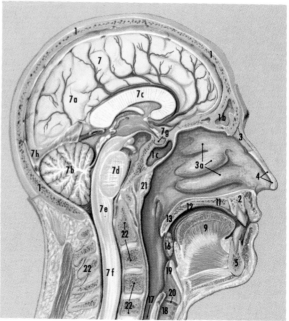

KEY TO HEAD DRAWINGS

1. Skull bones	7. Brain	8c. Muscles that move eyeball	19. Epiglottis
1a. Maxillary sinus	7a. Cerebrum	9. Tongue	20. Vocal cords of larynx
1b. Frontal sinus	7b. Cerebellum	10. Throat muscles	21. Adenoid
1c. Sphenoid sinus	7c. Corpus callosum	11. Hard palate	22. Neck bones
2. Upper jawbone (maxilla)	7d. Pons	12. Soft palate	(cervical vertebrae)
3. Nose bone	7e. Medulla oblongata	13. Soft palate muscles	23. Mandibular nerve
3a. Turbinates	7f. Spinal cord	14. Muscles that move head	24. Maxillary nerve
covered by mucosa	7g. Pituitary gland	15. Salivary glands	25. Vagus nerve
4. Nose cartilages	7h. Covering membranes	16. Tonsil	26. Cervical nerves
5. Lower jawbone	8. Eyeball	17. Esophagus	27. Facial nerve
(mandible)	8a. Iris	18. Trachea	28. Optic nerve
6. Ear canal	8b. Pupil		29. Arteries and veins

govern growth and development (in conjunction with the thyroid and the sex glands); water balance (in conjunction with the kidneys); and the action of involuntary muscles.

At the base of the neck is the thyroid gland. This controls the speed of body chemistry, known as metabolism. The thyroid is closely related to the pituitary and the sex glands. The sex glands make hormones and reproductive cells.

Near the thyroid and sometimes buried in it are the parathyroid glands. These are concerned with the use of calcium in the body and with muscular action.

Perched like a cap on each kidney is a gland known as the adrenal. It produces cortisone and epinephrine, popularly called adrenalin.

The pancreas is located in the upper abdomen. It secretes a hormone known as insulin. This controls the body's ability to use sugars and starches.

The Nervous System

The brain is in the head protected by the skull. It is the control center for the nervous system, which regulates body movement. The lower portions of the brain are concerned mainly with automatic functions.

Here are the nervous centers that control balance and breathing and, in conjunction with the glands and internal secretions, regulate body functions.

In the higher brain are the centers for vision, touch, hearing, taste, and smell and the functions of memory and thought. Here too are the centers which control the speech and the voluntary muscular actions. Nerve fibers run to all portions of the body through a channel in the spinal column. These fibers make up the spinal cord, which is a two-way nerve pathway with many intermediate nerve connections to body parts such as arms and legs. (*See also* Brain and Spinal Cord; Nerves.)

The Skin

The skin protects the structures underneath. Through its network of blood vessels, it helps control body temperature with the aid of sweat glands. These glands pour sweat onto the surface, where it cools by evaporation. Coloring matter guards the skin against too much sunlight. The skin contains the nerve endings, which give sensations such as heat, itching, and pain. Oil glands waterproof the skin. It absorbs almost nothing, thus protecting the body from harmful contacts. (*See also* Skin.)

KEY TO ANATOMICAL DRAWINGS*

1. Muscle that
   wrinkles neck skin

2a, 2b, 2c. Network
of veins under skin

3. Connection with
   deeper veins

4. Underlayer of skin

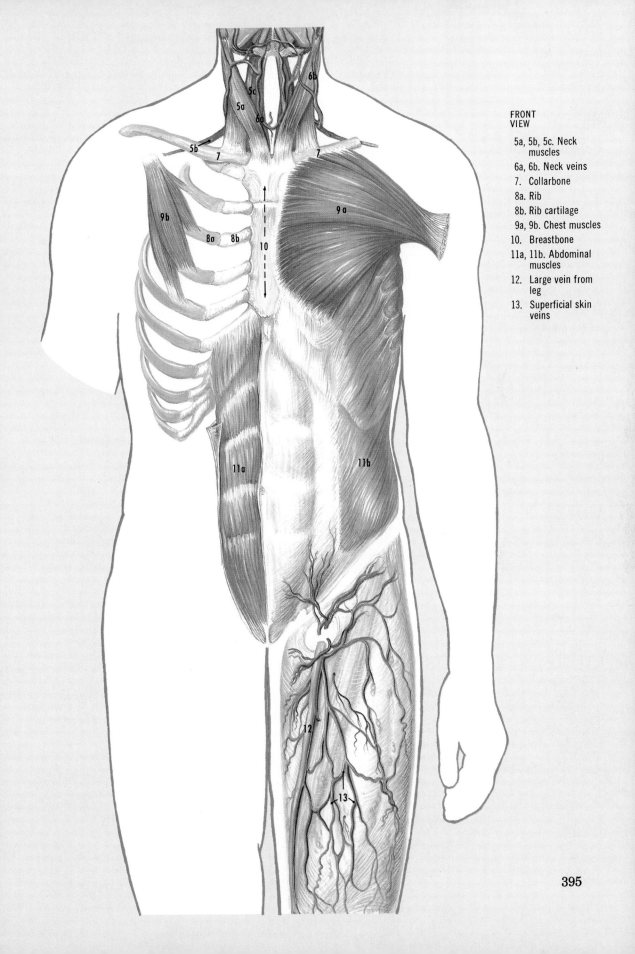

FRONT
VIEW

5a, 5b, 5c. Neck
muscles

6a, 6b. Neck veins

7. Collarbone

8a. Rib

8b. Rib cartilage

9a, 9b. Chest muscles

10. Breastbone

11a, 11b. Abdominal
muscles

12. Large vein from
leg

13. Superficial skin
veins

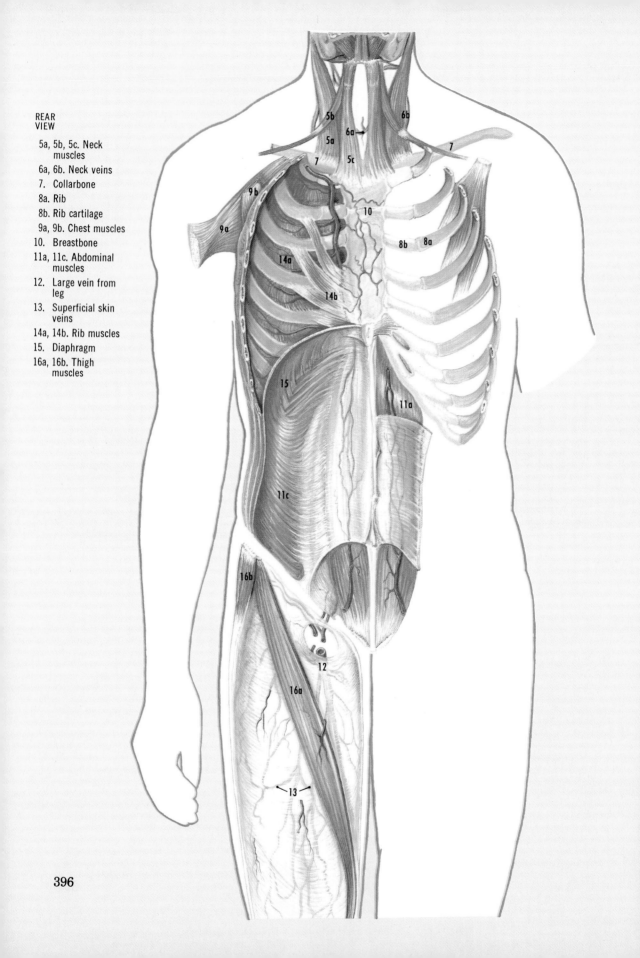

REAR
VIEW

5a, 5b, 5c. Neck
muscles
6a, 6b. Neck veins
7. Collarbone
8a. Rib
8b. Rib cartilage
9a, 9b. Chest muscles
10. Breastbone
11a, 11c. Abdominal
muscles
12. Large vein from
leg
13. Superficial skin
veins
14a, 14b. Rib muscles
15. Diaphragm
16a, 16b. Thigh
muscles

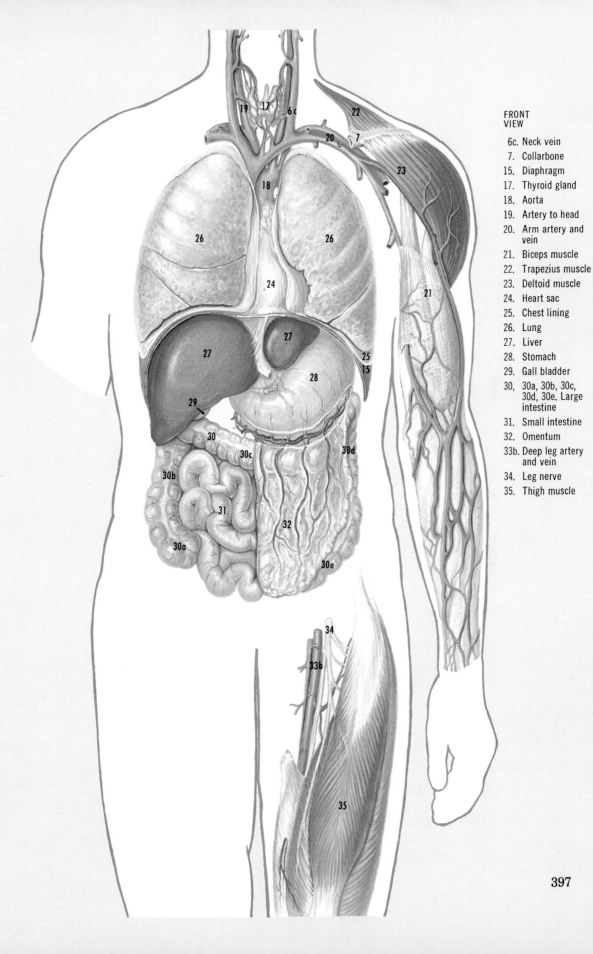

6c. Neck vein

 7. Collarbone

15. Diaphragm

17. Thyroid gland

18. Aorta

19. Artery to head

20. Arm artery and vein

21. Biceps muscle

22. Trapezius muscle

23. Deltoid muscle

24. Heart sac

25. Chest lining

26. Lung

27. Liver

28. Stomach

29. Gall bladder

30, 30a, 30b, 30c, 30d, 30e. Large intestine

31. Small intestine

32. Omentum

33b. Deep leg artery and vein

34. Leg nerve

35. Thigh muscle

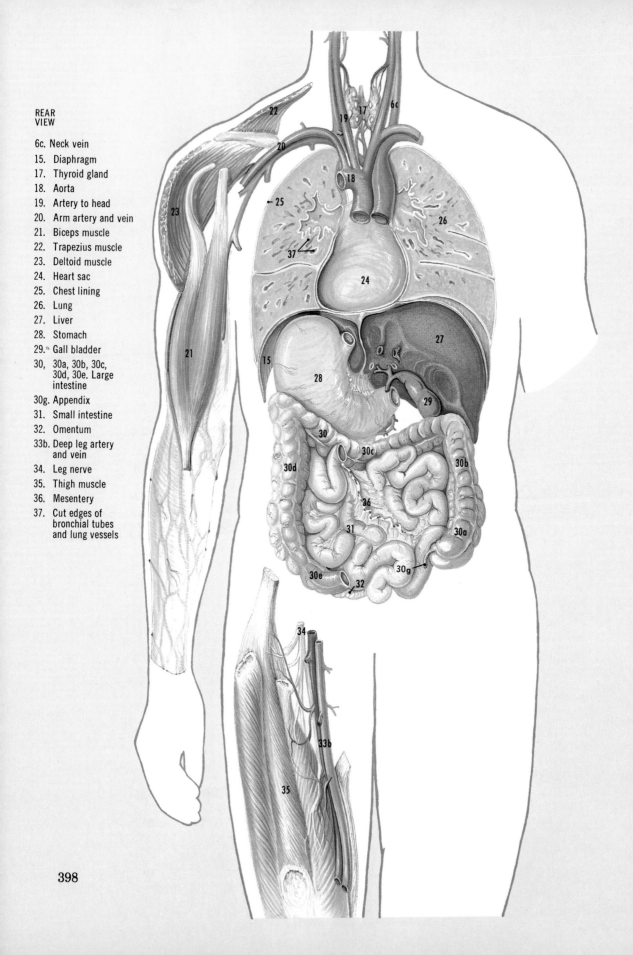

6c. Neck vein

15. Diaphragm

17. Thyroid gland

18. Aorta

19. Artery to head

20. Arm artery and vein

21. Biceps muscle

22. Trapezius muscle

23. Deltoid muscle

24. Heart sac

25. Chest lining

26. Lung

27. Liver

28. Stomach

29. Gall bladder

30, 30a, 30b, 30c, 30d, 30e. Large intestine

30g. Appendix

31. Small intestine

32. Omentum

33b. Deep leg artery and vein

34. Leg nerve

35. Thigh muscle

36. Mesentery

37. Cut edges of bronchial tubes and lung vessels

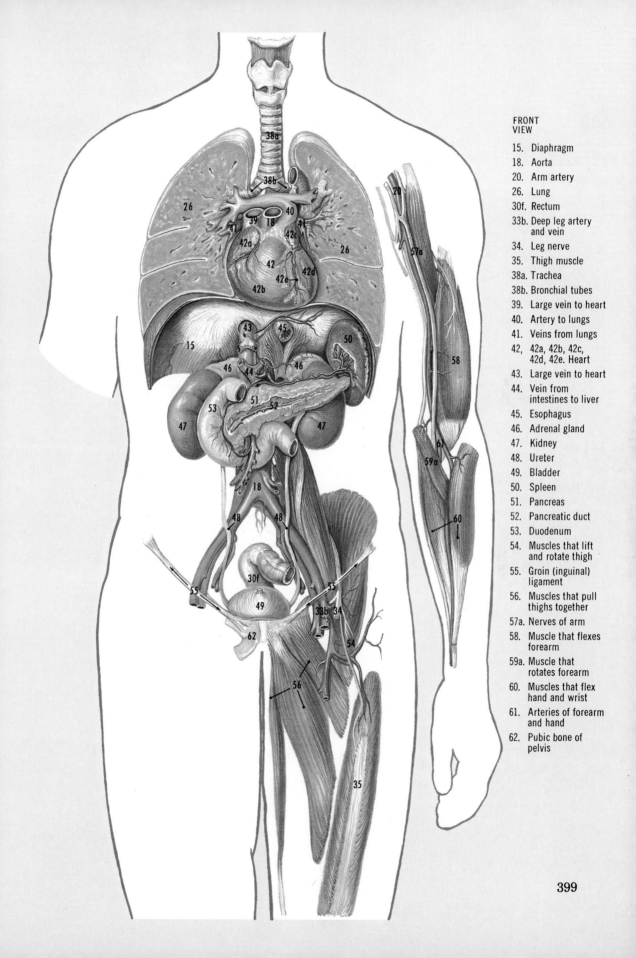

FRONT
VIEW

15. Diaphragm
18. Aorta
20. Arm artery
26. Lung
30f. Rectum
33b. Deep leg artery
and vein
34. Leg nerve
35. Thigh muscle
38a. Trachea
38b. Bronchial tubes
39. Large vein to heart
40. Artery to lungs
41. Veins from lungs
42, 42a, 42b, 42c,
42d, 42e. Heart
43. Large vein to heart
44. Vein from
intestines to liver
45. Esophagus
46. Adrenal gland
47. Kidney
48. Ureter
49. Bladder
50. Spleen
51. Pancreas
52. Pancreatic duct
53. Duodenum
54. Muscles that lift
and rotate thigh
55. Groin (inguinal)
ligament
56. Muscles that pull
thighs together
57a. Nerves of arm
58. Muscle that flexes
forearm
59a. Muscle that
rotates forearm
60. Muscles that flex
hand and wrist
61. Arteries of forearm
and hand
62. Pubic bone of
pelvis

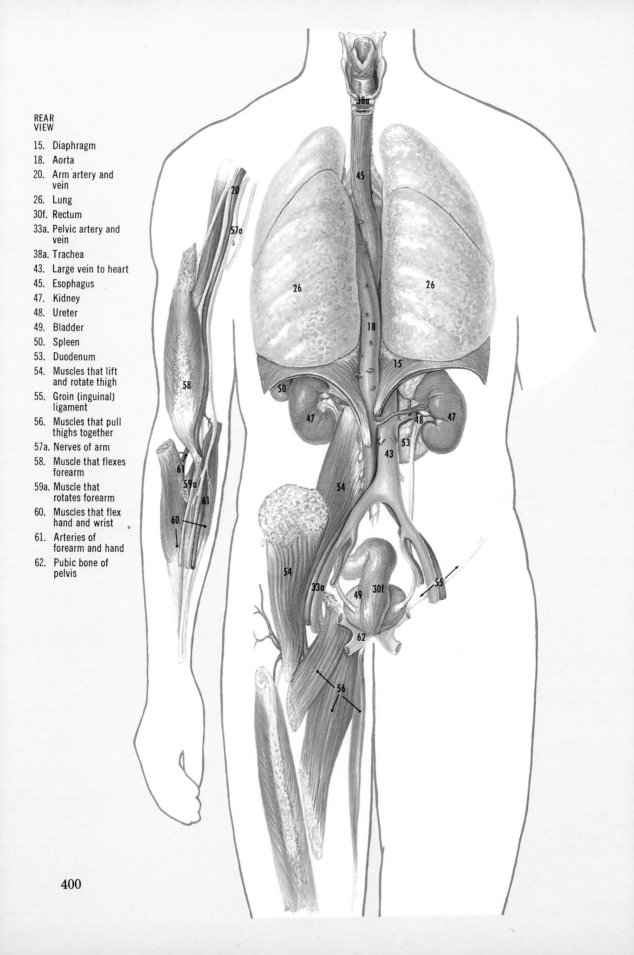

400

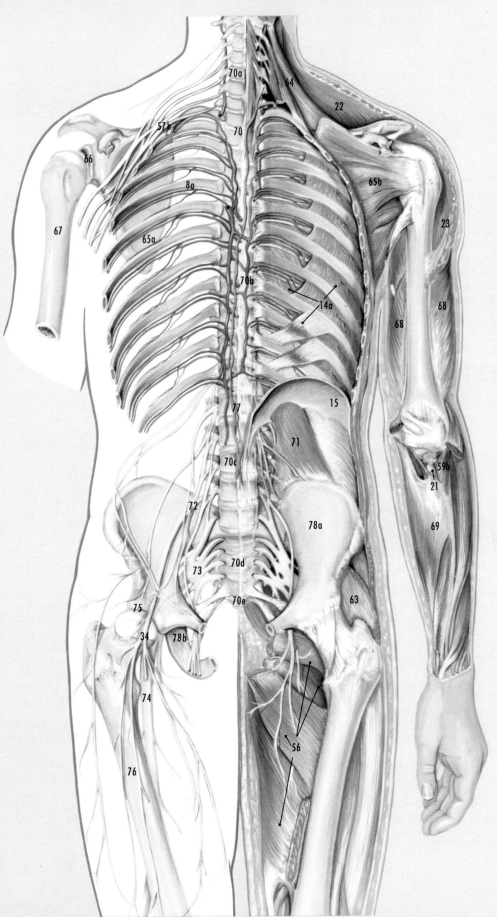

8a. Rib
14a. Rib muscle
15. Diaphragm
21. Biceps muscle
22. Trapezius muscle
23. Deltoid muscle
34. Leg nerve
56. Muscles that pull thighs together
57b. Nerves of neck and shoulder
59b. Muscle that rotates forearm
63. Hip muscle
64. Deep neck muscles
65a. Shoulder blade
65b. Shoulder blade muscles
66. Shoulder joint
67. Upper arm bone
68. Triceps muscle
69. Deep muscles of forearm
70. Backbone
70a. Neck vertebrae
70b. Rib vertebrae
70c. Lumbar vertebrae
70d. Sacrum
70e. Coccyx
71. Main lower back muscle
72. Lumbar nerve network
73. Sacral nerve network
74. Sciatic nerve
75. Hip joint
76. Long thighbone
77. Principal lymph vessel
78a, 78b. Hipbones

401

ANCESTOR WORSHIP. The veneration and respect shown to the dead in many cultures and societies is called ancestor worship. It is one of the oldest and most basic religious beliefs of man. It is believed that when family members die, they join the spirit world and are closer to God or the gods than the living are. Spirits, no longer burdened with bodies, are thought to be very powerful—possessing the ability to help or to harm people in the living world. They may even be powerful enough to be reborn into the community. The living who believe these things therefore view ancestors with a mixture of awe, fear, and respect. They feel they are dependent on the goodwill of ancestors for prosperity and survival. Under such beliefs, the family link does not end with the physical death of the individual.

The dead are thought by those who practice ancestor worship to have many of the same needs and wants as they did when they were alive. Thus, the living believe that they should bestow on them respect, attention, love, food and drink, and music and entertainment. This veneration of ancestors may be carried out either by individuals alone or by the whole community. Community worship would normally center on some great leader or hero, as was the case with the cult of the emperors in ancient Rome. Special days of the year have often been set aside for such commemoration.

In some countries devotion to the ancestors and their needs is still a part of everyday life. In China, for example, ancestor worship has long been a key religious belief and practice. In Hong Kong, where ancient Chinese religious rituals continue, the spirits of the ancestors are still offered food, drink, incense, and prayers. They are asked to bless family events because they are still considered to be part of the family. This belief in the continuity of the life force is expressed in the Chinese saying, "Birth is not a beginning, and death is not an end."

Ancestor worship is prevalent throughout Africa, Asia, and the Pacific area, even among those who have converted to Islam or Christianity. These believers see no conflict in continuing to respect their own family saints. Such worship can also be found in India, Indochina, and Japan.

"Ancestor worship," first coined in 1885 by the British anthropologist Herbert Spencer, is now thought to be a misleading term. "Ancestor respect" might be a more accurate phrase. This broadens the concept considerably but not illogically. Jewish people light candles and say special prayers on the anniversary of the death of a close family member. Christians celebrate All Souls' Day. Putting gifts and flowers on the graves of the family dead is probably the oldest universal human religious gesture and is still a sign of ancestor respect.

These practices, which are followed even in many of the most modern cultures, indicate a belief that at some level people continue to exist after they have died. This is the link between ancestor worship and ancestor respect.

ANCHORAGE, Alaska. In the early evening of Good Friday, March 27, 1964, a devastating earthquake struck southern Alaska. A major portion of downtown Anchorage was demolished. Hundreds of homes, apartment buildings, and places of business were  ruined, and many lives were lost. There was also widespread damage in some nearby residential areas, especially Turnagain, and in surrounding cities and towns. In a surprisingly short time, however, Anchorage had dug out from under the rubble and had begun the giant task of reconstruction.

Anchorage was founded in 1914 as a construction port for the Alaska Railroad. In 1915 the first sales of town lots were held. Five years later the United States government relinquished control of Anchorage affairs and a municipal election was held. The city was incorporated in 1920.

This fast-growing city is farther north than Helsinki, Finland, and 355 miles (571 kilometers) south of the Arctic Circle. However, Anchorage has a surprisingly pleasant climate, with comparatively moderate winters and mild summers.

Unlike most Alaska cities, Anchorage has wide, regular streets. The Z. J. Loussac Public Library and the Anchorage Municipal Auditorium are in the heart of the city. The downtown district also contains restaurants, hotels, theaters, the Federal Building, the City Hall, and the Post Office.

The economy of the Anchorage area depends largely upon government and military activities. The construction of Elmendorf Air Force Base and Fort Richardson during World War II made Anchorage a defense center and spurred the city's growth.

The strategic location of Anchorage has made it a key spot in world aviation. Anchorage International Airport serves several domestic and foreign airlines. The city has a large concentration of seaplane activity, and bush pilots take passengers from Anchorage to remote areas. Anchorage is the headquarters of the Alaska Railroad. The Port of Anchorage opened in 1961, and it has become south-central Alaska's busiest seaport. Trucking is important to Anchorage's economy, with direct roads leading to other major Alaska cities and the Alaska Highway (see Alaska Highway). As a distribution, trade, and financial center, Anchorage serves the important and growing petroleum industry of the area.

Anchorage has an excellent education system with modern elementary and high-school buildings. Institutions of higher education are the University of Alaska, Anchorage campus; Anchorage Community College; and Alaska Business College. The major entertainment event is the annual Anchorage Fur Rendezvous in February. This winter carnival includes Eskimo dances, art exhibitions, parades, and the World Championship Sled Dog Races. (See also Alaska.) Population (1980 census), 174,431.

ANCIENT CIVILIZATION. The term civilization basically means the level of development at which people live together peacefully in communities. Ancient civilization refers specifically to the first settled and stable communities that became the basis for later states, nations, and empires.

The study of ancient civilization is concerned with the earliest segments of the much broader subject called ancient history. The span of ancient history began with the invention of writing about 3100 B.C. and lasted more than 35 centuries. Mankind existed long before the written word, but writing made the keeping of a historical record possible (*see* Man).

The first ancient societies arose in Mesopotamia and Egypt in the Middle East, in the Indus Valley region of modern Pakistan, in the Yellow River valley of China, on the island of Crete in the Aegean Sea, and in Central America. All of these civilizations had certain features in common. They built cities, invented forms of writing, learned to make pottery and use metals, domesticated animals, and created fairly complex social structures with class systems and diverse types of work.

Apart from written records and carved inscriptions, the knowledge about ancient peoples is derived from the work of archaeologists. Most of the significant archaeological findings have been made in the past 200 years. The Sumerian culture of Mesopotamia was discovered in the 1890's, and some of the most important archaeological digs in China were made after the late 1970's. (*See also* Archaeology.)

Agriculture – The Basis of Civilization

The single, decisive factor that made it possible for mankind to settle down in permanent communities was agriculture. After farming was developed in the Middle East about 6500 B.C., people living in tribes or family units did not have to be on the move continually searching for food or herding their animals. Once man could control the production of food and be assured of a reliable annual supply of it, his life was completely changed.

People began to found permanent communities in fertile river valleys. Settlers learned to use the water supply to irrigate the land. Being settled in one place made it possible to domesticate animals to provide other sources of food and clothing.

Farming was a revolutionary discovery. It not only made settlements possible—and ultimately the building of cities—but also made available a reliable food supply. With more food available, more people could be fed. Populations therefore increased. The growing number of people available for more kinds of work led to the development of more complex social structures. With a food surplus, a community could support a variety of workers who were not farmers.

Farming the world over has always relied upon a dependable water supply. For the earliest societies this meant rivers and streams or regular rainfall. The first great civilizations grew up along rivers. Rainy seasons helped develop later communities.

All of the ancient civilizations probably developed in much the same way, in spite of regional and climatic differences. As villages grew, the accumulation of more and heavier goods became possible. Heavier pottery replaced animal skin gourds as containers for food and liquids. Cloth could be woven from wool and flax. Permanent structures made of wood, brick, and stone could be erected. Monuments, city walls, and temples could be built. The diversity of tools increased as the jobs they were needed for multiplied.

The science of mathematics was an early outgrowth of agriculture. Men studied the movements of the moon, sun, and planets to calculate seasons. In so doing they created the first calendars. With a calendar it was possible to calculate the arrival of each growing season. Measurement of land areas was necessary if property was to be accurately divided. Measurements of amounts—for example, of seeds, liquids, or grains—was also a factor in farming and housekeeping. Later came measures of value as commodity and money exchange became common.

The use of various ways of measuring led naturally to record keeping, and for this some form of writing was necessary. The earliest civilizations all seem to have used picture-writing, pictures representing both sounds and objects to the reader. The best known of the ancient writing systems is probably Egyptian hieroglyphics, a term meaning "sacred carvings," since many of the earliest writings were inscribed on stone.

All of the major ancient civilizations—in Mesopotamia, Egypt, the Indus Valley, and China—emerged in the 4th millenium B.C. Which one was first remains a matter of debate among historians. It may well

Fact Finder for Ancient Civilization Articles

The subject of ancient civilization is a broad one. Readers will find additional information on the subject in the articles listed here.

Aegean Civilization	Mayas
Babylonia and	Medes
Assyria	Mesopotamia
Egypt, Ancient	Persian History
Etruscans	Persian Wars
Greece, Ancient	Phoenicians
Hittites	Roman History
Incas	Seven Wonders
Macedonia	of the World

Other related articles in the encyclopedia are:

Acropolis	Pompeii and
Athens, Greece	Herculaneum
Babylon	Pyramids
Carthage	Salamis, Battle of
Corinth, Greece	Salonika, Greece
Delphi	Sparta, Greece
Gladiator	Sphinx
Kish	Thebes, Egypt
Marathon	Thebes, Greece
Mummy	Thermopylae

have been the Middle East, in an area called the Fertile Crescent. This region stretches from the Nile River in Egypt northward along the coast of former Palestine, then eastward into Asia to include Mesopotamia. In this area people settled along the riverbanks and practiced field agriculture. This kind of farming depended on the reproduction of seed, normally from grain crops.

Mesopotamia

Mesopotamia (from a Greek term meaning "between rivers") lies between the Tigris and Euphrates rivers, a region that is part of modern Iraq (*see* Mesopotamia). By about 5000 B.C., small tribes of farmers had made their way to the river valleys. On the floodplains they raised wheat, barley, and peas. They cut through the riverbanks so that water for their crops could flow to lower lying soil.

These early irrigation systems were more fully developed by the Sumerians in Mesopotamia, who drained marshes and dug canals, dikes, and ditches. The need for cooperation on these large irrigation projects led to the growth of government and law. The Sumerians are thus credited with forming the earliest of the ancient civilizations.

The land of the Sumerians was called Sumer (Shinar in the Bible). Their origins are shrouded in the past. They were not Semites, like most of the peoples of the region; they spoke a language unrelated to other known tongues. They may have come to southern Mesopotamia from Persia before 4000 B.C.

Sumerian towns and cities included Eridu, Nippur, Lagash, Kish, and Ur. The cities differed from primitive farming settlements. They were not composed of family-owned farms, but were ringed by large tracts of land. These tracts were thought to be "owned" by a local god. A priest organized work groups of farm-

The Fertile Crescent includes the river valleys of the Nile and of the Tigris and Euphrates.

ers to tend the land and provide barley, beans, wheat, olives, grapes, and flax for the community.

These early cities, which existed by 3500 B.C., were called temple towns because they were built around the temple of the local god. The temples were eventually built up on towers called ziggurats (holy mountains), which had ramps or staircases winding up around the exterior. Public buildings and marketplaces were built around these shrines.

The temple towns grew into city-states, which are considered the basis of the first true civilizations. At a time when only the most rudimentary forms of transportation and communication were available, the city-state was the most governable type of human settlement. City-states were ruled by leaders, called ensis, who were probably authorized to control the local irrigation systems. The food surplus provided by the farmers supported these leaders, as well as priests, artists, craftsmen, and others.

The Sumerians contributed to the development of metalworking, wheeled carts, and potter's wheels. They may have invented the first form of writing. They engraved pictures on clay tablets in a form of writing known as cuneiform (wedge-shaped). The tablets were used to keep the accounts of the temple food storehouses. By about 2500 B.C. these picture-signs were being refined into an alphabet. (*See also* Alphabet; Writing.)

The Sumerians developed the first calendar, which they adjusted to the phases of the moon. The lunar calendar was adopted by the Semites, Egyptians, and Greeks. An increase in trade between Sumerian cities and between Sumeria and other, more distant regions led to the growth of a merchant class.

The Sumerians organized a complex mythology based on the relationships among the various local gods of the temple towns. In Sumerian religion, the most important gods were seen as human forms of natural forces—sky, sun, earth, water, and storm. These gods, each originally associated with a particular city, were worshipped not only in the great temples but also in small shrines in family homes.

Warfare between cities eventually led to the rise of kings, called lugals, whose authority replaced that of city-state rulers. Sumeria became a more unified state, with a common culture and a centralized government. This led to the establishment of a bureaucracy and an army. By 2375 B.C., most of Sumer was united under one king, Lugalzaggisi of Umma.

Babylon

The Sumerians were conquered by their Semitic neighbors. But their civilization was carried on by their successors—the Akkadians, Babylonians, Assyrians, and Chaldeans.

The Babylonians made distinct contributions to the growth of civilization. They added to the knowledge of astronomy, advanced the knowledge of mathematics, and built the first great capital city, Babylon. The Babylonian King Hammurabi set forth the Code of Hammurabi about 1800 B.C. This was the most complete compilation of Babylonian law and one of the first great law codes in the world.)

Egypt

Egyptian farmers had settled in the long and narrow valley of the Nile River by 5000 B.C. Within 2,000 years they had invented writing, built massive irrigation works, and established a culture that bequeathed the pyramids and other magnificent monuments to posterity.

The primitive farming settlements of Egypt were concerned with the raising of vegetables, grains, and animals. These settlements slowly gave way to larger groupings of people. Probably the need to control the Nile floodwaters through dams and canals eventually led to the rise of government in the region.

By the end of the predynastic period (before 3100 B.C.), Egypt was divided into two kingdoms. Lower Egypt had its capital at Buto, while Upper Egypt was centered at Hierakonpolis. In this period, travelers brought in ideas from Sumeria, including the concepts of writing and the pottery wheel.

Egyptian civilization began with the unification in 3100 B.C. of the upper and lower regions by King Menes. He established a new capital at Memphis. In this era the Egyptians developed the first 365-day calendar, discovered the use of the plow, made use of copper, developed hieroglyphic writing, and began to build with stone. Trade and exploration flourished.

The Egyptians were ruled by kings known as pharaohs who claimed to be descended from the god Horus. These kings, supported by a priestly class, lived in splendor; and they saw to it that after their deaths they would be buried in splendor. The tombs built for them were designed as storehouses to hold all the things that the kings would need in the afterlife.

The earliest royal tombs foreshadowed the later great monuments, the pyramids. By about 2700 B.C. the first pyramid was built, in Sakkara. The three great pyramids still standing near Cairo were built between 2650 and 2500 B.C.

Early Egyptian history is divided into three major eras: the Old Kingdom (2700–2200 B.C.), the Middle Kingdom (2050–1800 B.C.), and the New Kingdom (1500–1090 B.C.). By the dawn of the Old Kingdom, the characteristics of Egyptian civilization had already been firmly established. The periods not accounted for by the dates are believed to be times of decline known as the "intermediate period."

India

The valley of the Indus River is considered to be the birthplace of Indian civilization. Located on the Indian subcontinent in modern Pakistan, the Indus civilization was not discovered by archaeologists until 1924. The ancient history of this region is obscured by legend. It appears, however, that by 4000 B.C. primitive farmers were raising vegetables, grains, and animals along the riverbank. By 2700 B.C. two major cities had emerged, Harappā and Mohenjo-daro, and numerous smaller towns.

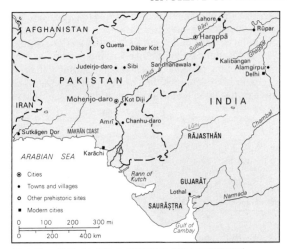

Adapted from Sir Mortimer Wheeler, 'Civilizations of the Indus Valley and Beyond' (1966), Thames and Hudson, Ltd., London, and McGraw-Hill Book Company, New York; original map by Shalom Schotten

The principal sites of the Indus civilization were Mohenjo-daro and Harappā.

There is some evidence that Mesopotamian traders reached the early Indian people by sailing from Sumeria to the Indus Valley. While the Indians shared some developments, such as complex irrigation and drainage systems and the art of writing, with the people of Sumeria, they also developed a unique cultural style of their own.

What little is known of the Indus civilization suggests that it had large, well laid-out cities that were well fortified. There were public buildings, palaces, baths, and large granaries to hold agricultural produce. The many artifacts and artworks found by archaeologists indicate that the residents of the Indus had reached a fairly high level of culture before their civilization was destroyed.

According to the Rig Veda, the ancient Hindu scriptures written about 1500 B.C., Aryan invaders conquered the earliest Indian civilization. The Aryans—nomads from the Eurasian steppes—imposed on Indian society a caste system, which persists to the present day in Hindu law. The caste system, which divides all people into social classes with differing rights and obligations, was a formal expression of the interdependent labor division seen in all civilizations (see Hinduism). By the 6th century B.C., 16 Aryan states had been established on the Indian subcontinent.

Crete

By about 2500 B.C., a civilization had emerged on the island of Crete in the Aegean Sea. Excavations in 1900 at the site of Knossos revealed the existence of a culture named by archaeologists as Minoan after a mythic king, Minos. Minoans probably settled in Crete before 3000 B.C.

There is evidence of outside influence in Crete; apparently Egyptian traders reached the Aegean Sea soon after the Minoans did. Nevertheless, Minoan

405

civilization developed its own unique features, and by about 2000 B.C., great cities with elaborate and luxurious palaces were built, and sea trade was flourishing.

The Minoans had a picture-writing system, as had other ancient peoples. This system has not yet been deciphered by scholars. The Minoan religion seems to have centered on a mother goddess and on the figures

Adapted from A. Herrmann, 'An Historical Atlas of China' (1966); Aldine Publishing Company

The principal settlements of ancient China were located along the country's major rivers, the Yangtze and the Huang Ho.

China

The Chinese had settled in the Hwang Ho, or Yellow River, valley of northern China by 3000 B.C. By then they had pottery, wheels, farms, and silk, but had not yet discovered writing or the uses of metals.

The Shang Dynasty (1523?–1027 B.C.) is the first documented era of ancient China. The highly developed hierarchy consisted of a king, nobles, commoners, and slaves. The capital city was Great Shang, in north Honan. Some scholars have suggested that travelers from Mesopotamia and from Southeast Asia brought agricultural methods to China, which stimulated the growth of ancient Chinese civilization. The Shang people were known for their use of jade, bronze, horse-drawn chariots, ancestor worship, and highly organized armies.

Like other ancient peoples, the Chinese developed unique attributes. Their form of writing, developed by 2000 B.C., was a complex system of picture-writing using forms called ideograms, pictograms, and phonograms. Such early forms of Chinese became known through the discovery by archaeologists of "oracle bones," which were bones with writings inscribed on them. They were used for fortune-telling and record keeping in ancient China.

The Chou Dynasty (1027–250 B.C.) saw the full flowering of ancient civilization in China. During this period the empire was unified, a middle class arose, and iron was introduced. The sage Confucius (551–478 B.C.) developed the code of ethics that dominated Chinese thought and culture for the next 25 centuries (see Confucius).

Meso-America

Meso-America is the term used to describe the ancient settlements of Mexico and Central America. Civilization arose in the Americas much later than in the Middle East. Whether native Americans reinvented the tools of civilization, such as farming and writing, or whether they were brought from older societies is a topic of debate among scholars.

The earliest known of the American civilizations is that of the Olmecs of central Mexico. The Olmecs lived in the humid lowlands of Veracruz and Tobasco from about 1200 B.C. They have left artifacts ranging from tiny jade carvings to huge monuments such as the volcanic rock statues at San Lorenzo, which are nine feet (three meters) high. These monuments suggest the existence of an organized and diverse society with leaders who could command the work of artisans and laborers. Other early civilizations in the Americas include the Chavins of Peru, the Mayas of the Yucatán Peninsula, and the Incas of Peru (see Aztecs; Incas; Mayas).

Only four ancient civilizations—Mesopotamia, Egypt, the Indus Valley, and China—provided the basis for continuous cultural developments in the same location. After the Minoan society on Crete was destroyed, its cultural traditions and legends passed into the life of mainland Greece. As for Meso-America, its cultures were submerged by the Spanish conquerors of the 16th century.

BIBLIOGRAPHY FOR ANCIENT CIVILIZATION

Aldred, Cyril. Egypt to the End of the Old Kingdom (McGraw, 1965).
Budge, E. W. Dwellers on the Nile: the Life, History, Religion and Literature of the Ancient Egyptians (Dover, 1977).
Clark, Grahame. World Pre-history (Cambridge, 1969).
Cotterell, Arthur. The Minoan World (Scribner, 1980).
Darlington, C. D. The Evolution of Man and Society (Simon & Schuster, 1969).
Fairbank, J. K., Reischauer, E. O., and Craig, A. M. East Asia (Houghton Mifflin, 1973).
Hollister, C. W. Roots of the Western Tradition (Wiley, 1977).
Knox, Robert. Ancient China (Watts, 1979).
McNeill, A. H. The Rise of the West (University of Chicago, 1970).
Schwantes, Siegfried. Short History of the Ancient Near East (Baker, 1965).
Thomas, Hugh. History of the World (Harper & Row, 1979).
Wheeler, Sir Mortimer. The Indus Civilization (Cambridge, 1953).

of the bull and the snake. The Minoans are known for their beautiful and colorful wall paintings and fine pottery. About 1400 B.C. Minoan civilization began to decline. The end was hastened by invasions from mainland Greece.

ANDERSEN, Hans Christian (1805–1875). A native of Denmark, Hans Christian Andersen is one of the immortals of world literature. The fairy tales he wrote are like no others written before or since. 'The Steadfast Tin Soldier', 'The Snow Queen', 'The Swineherd', 'The Nightingale' — these are stories that have been translated into almost every language. All over the world people know what it means to be an ugly duckling. Andersen's story of the swan who came from among the ducks is a story in which each person recognizes something of himself.

On the island of Fyn (Fünen), off the coast of Denmark, stands a bleak, windswept fishing village called Odense. Here, in a one-room house, on April 2, 1805, Hans Christian Andersen was born. During the early years of his childhood his grandmother told him old Danish folk tales and legends, and he acted out plays in a homemade puppet theater.

When Hans Christian was 11, his father died. The boy was left virtually alone because his mother and grandmother were hard at work. He went to school only at intervals and spent most of his time imagining stories rather than reading lessons. He could memorize very easily and learned some of his lessons by listening to a neighborhood boy who was in the habit of studying aloud. He memorized and recited plays to anyone who would listen. He haunted the theater in Odense and startled his mother by imitating everything he saw or heard — ballet dancers, acrobats, or pantomimists.

To put an end to this, his mother apprenticed him first to a weaver, then to a tobacconist, and finally to a tailor. Hans Christian knew these occupations were not for him. The only things that held his interest were the theater, books, and stories. When he was 14, he decided to go to Copenhagen, the capital of Denmark, and seek his fortune.

A printer in Odense, who had published handbills for the theater, had given Hans Christian a letter of introduction to a dancer. The boy presented himself to her and sang and danced in his stocking feet before her astonished guests. They laughed uproariously at his absurd manner and brash behavior.

There followed three bitter years of poverty. Hans Christian earned a little money singing in a boys' choir until his voice changed. He tried to act and to join the ballet, but his awkwardness made these careers impossible. He attempted to work with his hands but could not do this either. It never occurred to him to return home and admit defeat.

At last, when he was 17, Andersen came to the attention of Chancellor Jonas Collin, a director of the Royal Theater. Collin had read a play by Andersen and saw that the youth had talent, though he lacked education. He procured money from the king for Andersen's education and sent him to a school at Slagelse, near Copenhagen. Here the young man suffered the humiliation of being in classes with students younger than he. His teacher, a bitter man, treated him harshly and took delight in taunting him about his ambition to become a writer. Andersen was sensi-

Hans Christian Andersen
Brown Brothers

tive and suffered intensely, but he studied hard, encouraged by the kindness of Collin.

Finally Collin, convinced that the teacher was actually persecuting Andersen, took the youth from the school and arranged for him to study under a private tutor in Copenhagen. In 1828, when he was 23, Andersen passed his entrance examinations to the university in Copenhagen.

Andersen's writings began to be published in Danish in 1829. In 1833 the king gave him a grant of money for travel, and he spent 16 months wandering through Germany, France, Switzerland, and his beloved Italy. His first works were poems, plays, novels, and impressions of his travels. He was slow to discover that he especially excelled in explaining the essential character of children.

In 1835 Andersen published 'Fairy Tales for Children' — four short stories he wrote for a little girl, Ida Thiele, who was the daughter of the secretary of the Academy of Art. The stories were 'Little Ida's Flowers', 'The Tinderbox', 'Little Claus and Big Claus', and 'The Princess and the Pea'. He seems to have sent them into the world with little appreciation of their worth and returned to the writing of novels and poems. However, people who read the stories — adults as well as children — wanted more.

Andersen published in all 156 fairy tales. He wrote the stories just as he would have told them. "The real ones come of themselves," he said. "They knock at my forehead and say, 'Here I am'." Although he never married and had no children of his own, he was at his best as an interpreter of child nature.

It was his fairy tales that brought Andersen the affection of the world as well as the friendship of great men and women, such as Jenny Lind, the Swedish singer. The famous writer Charles Dickens was also his friend, and Andersen paid him a long visit in England. Andersen died on Aug. 4, 1875.

ANDERSON, Marian (born 1902). The American contralto Marian Anderson was a pioneer in overcoming racial discrimination. After being prohibited from singing in Constitution Hall in Washington, D.C., because of her race, she performed (1939) instead on the steps of the Lincoln Memorial to an audience of more than 75,000, thereby increasing public awareness of existing prejudice. She was the first black to sing at the Metropolitan Opera in New

Marian Anderson sings from the steps of the Lincoln Memorial in Washington, D.C.

York City (1955), where she portrayed Ulrica in a performance of Verdi's 'Un ballo in maschera'.

Marian Anderson was born on Feb. 17, 1902, in Philadelphia. She began singing in a Baptist church at the age of six. In 1925 she was selected from among 300 contestants to appear as soloist with the New York Philharmonic Orchestra, after which she spent ten years studying and singing in Europe.

Principally a recitalist, Anderson did not sing any other operatic roles. Her voice was that rare thing, a genuine deep contralto, and her repertoire included oratorios, lieder (German art songs), and especially the music of Bach, Handel, Mahler, Sibelius, and spirituals. Her autobiography, 'My Lord, What a Morning', appeared in 1956.

ANDERSON, Maxwell (1888-1959). The American playwright Maxwell Anderson believed in the dignity of man and the importance of democracy. Many of his plays express his ideas of liberty and justice. An expert writer of blank verse, he popularized the use of poetry in modern drama.

Maxwell Anderson was born on Dec. 15, 1888, in Atlantic, Pa. His father was a Baptist minister. Because the Andersons, along with their four children, moved frequently, Maxwell attended a great number of different schools.

The writer received an A.B. degree at the University of North Dakota in 1911. While attending the university he played football and first became interested in the theater. He earned an M.A. degree at Stanford University while he taught English in a San Francisco high school. Three years later he turned from teaching to newspaper work, first in Grand Forks, N. D., then in San Francisco.

In 1918 he went to New York City. While working on the *New York World*, Anderson met Laurence Stallings, a book reviewer, who helped him get his first play, 'The White Desert', produced. With Stallings, Anderson wrote his first really successful drama, 'What Price Glory?', a profane view of a soldier's life. It was produced in 1924.

Anderson later resigned from the *World* and devoted himself exclusively to writing plays. For more than 30 years he turned out a play nearly every season, with varied but generally great success.

The shy, serious author chose to write in solitude on his farm, shunning the busy life of New York and refusing to attend the opening nights of his plays. He wrote very quickly, composing in longhand in a large ledger.

Anderson won the Pulitzer prize in 1933 for his drama 'Both Your Houses', a study of corrupt politics. He received the New York Drama Critics' Circle Award in 1935 for 'Winterset', a social protest play, and again in 1936 for 'High Tor', a comic fantasy.

Other plays by Anderson include 'Elizabeth the Queen' (1930); 'Mary of Scotland' (1933); 'Knickerbocker Holiday' (1938); 'Key Largo' (1939); 'Joan of Lorraine' (1946); and, with composer Kurt Weill, 'Lost in the Stars' (1949).

Anderson was married three times. He died on Feb. 28, 1959, in Stamford, Conn.

ANDERSON, Sherwood (1876-1941). In his short stories and novels, the American writer Sherwood Anderson protested against the frustrations of ordinary people and against what he believed to be the narrow-minded conventions of his time. He was a master of colloquial speech. His concern with the unfulfilled lives of "little" people probably came from his early observations of life.

Sherwood Anderson was born in Camden, Ohio, on Sept. 13, 1876, the third child of a family of five boys and two girls. His father was an irresponsible man who could not hold a job long, but he was a colorful talker and storyteller.

Most of Anderson's boyhood was spent in the small town of Clyde, Ohio, where he attended school irregularly. When he was only 14, his mother died and Anderson ended his formal education.

The young man drifted from one job to another, finally welcoming the chance to serve in the Spanish-American War. When the war was over, he returned to Ohio and eventually became manager of a paint factory in Elyria. It was at this time that Anderson began to write. He became more and more absorbed in writing. One day he walked out of the factory, apparently on a sudden impulse, never to return.

Sherwood joined his brother Karl, a magazine illustrator, in Chicago and took a job with an advertising agency. He became acquainted with the "Chicago group" of writers, which included Theodore Dreiser, Carl Sandburg, Ben Hecht, and Floyd Dell. Dreiser and Dell helped get Anderson's first novel, 'Windy McPherson's Son', published in 1916. It was a story of factory life, based on his own experiences.

His next books were 'Marching Men' (1917), a novel about mines, and 'Mid-American Chants' (1918), a book of poetry. Anderson was best as a short-story writer, and his most successful book was 'Winesburg, Ohio', published in 1919. The book is made up of short stories about small-town people.

After going abroad in 1921, Anderson returned to live in New Orleans and, later, New York. He finally settled in Marion, Va., where he edited two newspapers and continued to write. His autobiographical books are 'A Story Teller's Story' (1924); 'Tar: a Midwest Childhood' (1926); and 'Sherwood Anderson's Memoirs' (1942). Anderson was married four times. He died in Colón, Panama, on March 8, 1941.

ANDES. Ages ago geologic forces pushed the bed of the Pacific Ocean against landmasses in both North and South America. The rocks between the rising Pacific bed and the old lands were squeezed and forced into a towering mountain system called the Cordilleras, from a Spanish term meaning "little ropes." The South American Cordilleras are called the Andes, from an Indian word of uncertain origin.

Physical Features

The giant Andean system, which is the longest mountain chain in the world, stretches along the entire western side of South America, a distance of about 5,500 miles (8,900 kilometers). In elevation it is exceeded only by the Himalayas in central Asia. The tallest peak is Mount Aconcagua, 22,831 feet (6,959 meters) (*see* Aconcagua). Located on the border between Chile and Argentina, Aconcagua is the highest mountain in the Western Hemisphere. Many other Andean peaks rise above 20,000 feet (6,000 meters).

The width of the Andean chain is about 200 miles (320 kilometers) or less, except in Bolivia, where it broadens to about 400 miles (640 kilometers). Bolivia shares with Peru the lofty central plateau, called the altiplano (high plain), between the eastern and western ranges. This is one of the highest inhabited regions in the world.

Throughout much of their length the Andes rise close to the Pacific coast and descend abruptly to low plains on the east. As the main watershed of the continent, the system is the source of short streams flowing to the Pacific and also of most of the headstreams of South American rivers flowing east and north. It is a formidable barrier to transportation. The only railroad crossings are those connecting Chile with neighboring Argentina and Bolivia.

The Andes are rich in nonferrous metals but have no coal. Many deposits are inaccessible. The chief minerals obtained are gold, silver, copper, tin, platinum, antimony, lead, zinc, bismuth, and vanadium.

The natural pastures of the central plateau are suitable for cattle raising. Colombia exports cattle, and Peru has milk-canning and livestock industries. Sheep, goat, llama, and alpaca raising are widespread in Peru and Bolivia. Both countries export sheep and alpaca wool. Other products exported from the Andes

Carl Frank

The Cauca River flows through the Andes Mountains in western Colombia.

include coffee (especially from Colombia), cacao, coca, tobacco, and cotton.

When the Andes were formed, sedimentary rocks were folded and bent into long ridges, called sierras. In some places huge cracks allowed molten granite and other igneous rock to well up from the depths. Wherever this rock reached the surface, it built volcanic cones. Most of the highest peaks in the Andes, including Aconcagua, are volcanoes. Some are active; hundreds are dormant or extinct. The mountains are still settling. Severe earthquakes occur, and volcanoes occasionally erupt, with much destruction.

Climate

The Andes affect the climate by influencing precipitation. In northern Colombia three ranges spread out to catch and hold the moisture of the northeastern trade winds, making this a region of heavy rainfall. On the Pacific side, from the Isthmus of Panama to the equator, the Colombian Andes catch the southwesterly winds, and rains fall almost daily.

From the Gulf of Guayaquil through northern Chile the west coast is extremely dry. This stretch lies in the trade wind belt. Winds tend to come from the east and southeast, and they drop their moisture on the eastern slopes. In summer they have moisture enough to give rain on the western slopes also.

In northern Chile cool trade winds from the Pacific become warmed as they reach the hot coast and hold their moisture as fog. The great desert of Chile is one of the driest places in the world.

In the latitude of Valparaiso the coast has a Mediterranean-type climate, with drying trade winds in the summer and moisture-laden westerly winds in the winter. Farther south the winds come from the west all through the year, and the Chilean slopes of the Andes catch their moisture as drenching rain or heavy snow. The eastern slopes in Argentina are relatively dry. (*See also* South America; and articles on the countries named.)

ANDORRA. One of the smallest countries in the world, Andorra has been independent for more than 1,000 years and an autonomous coprincipality for more than seven centuries. Despite the transformations that neighboring European countries have undergone over the centuries, Andorra has managed to preserve its mountain tranquillity and medieval traditions as well as a stable political system.

Landscape

Andorra's 179 square miles (464 square kilometers) comprise an alpine landscape of high peaks and deep valleys on the southern slopes of the Pyrenees, bounded on the south and west by Spain and on the north and east by France. The physical setting prohibits air transportation. No railway system exists, but good roads link Andorra with France and Spain and permit access by car to the most secluded spots.

The climate is generally dry, with heavy rainfall in spring and autumn and abundant snow that remains for several months in the highlands. Temperature varies greatly, depending on altitude. In the highlands are typical small Andorran villages, with their houses of granite, wood, and slate. In the valleys are the larger villages, where economic growth has brought modern buildings that contrast sharply with the traditional architecture.

The largest villages are Andorra la Vella, the capital, and Escaldes, which has a hydroelectric station and sulfur springs. The Andorrans, mostly of Spanish origin, are predominantly Roman Catholic. Catalan is the official language.

Public Services

The French and Spanish governments, which share jurisdiction over the coprincipality, provide some public services, including postal, telegraph, and schools. Catalan-speaking children are taught in both foreign languages. No national monetary unit exists; however, the French franc and the Spanish peseta currencies are used.

In 1969 mandatory social insurance went into effect, covering illness, disability, and old-age pensions. Poverty is relatively unknown in Andorra. Property taxes are low, and there is no income tax.

Economy

Andorra's principal agricultural products are potatoes, cereal, and tobacco. Minerals include iron, lead, and alum. Sheep and other livestock are raised.

Since the 1950's the country has been affected greatly by a profound change from the traditional pastoral and farming economy to one of commerce and year-round tourism. With the economic expansion, several banks have been established in association with French and Spanish investment firms. The population has increased dramatically and the face of

Andorra's communities and countryside has been altered to accommodate the surge of tourism.

History and Government

Andorra has survived as an independent state since the earliest period of European history. In the year 819 Louis the Pious, a son of the emperor Charlemagne, gave the land belonging to the counts of Urgel, in Spain, to the bishop of Urgel. Andorra's independence has been traditionally attributed to this grant of the lands of the counts.

In 1278 the principality was placed under joint control of the French count of Foix and the Spanish bishop of the See of Urgel. This dual allegiance was interrupted only during the French Revolution in the late 18th century. Since the late 13th century, though Andorra has been governed jointly by the Spanish bishop of Urgel and the president of France, the original status of neutrality has continued. The co-princes alternately receive annual payments of a token tribute from the coprincipality and represent the country internationally. They oversee all legislative, executive, and judicial functions.

The government is administered by the General Council of the Valleys, which has no legislative powers. Its 28 members are elected every four years. In 1970 women received the right to vote. Population (1980 census), 33,861.

ANDRADA E SILVA, José Bonifácio de (1763–1838).

Along with his accomplishments as a statesman, José Andrada e Silva, the father of Brazilian independence, was also a geologist and natural scientist of international repute. His childhood was spent in his birthplace of Santos, Brazil. As a young man he went to Portugal for an education and did not return to his homeland until he was 56 years old. He spent his adult career as a professor at the University of Coimbra and the permanent secretary of the Lisbon Academy in Portugal.

When Andrada e Silva returned to Brazil in 1819, he found all of Latin America in political ferment. The Spanish and Portuguese colonies were attempting to break away from their European masters.

The ruler of Brazil was Dom Pedro, son of the king of Portugal. The Cortes (legislature) at Lisbon, fearful that he might lead a movement for independence, ordered him to return to Portugal. Dom Pedro defied

José Bonifácio de Andrada e Silva
Arquivo Nacional do Brasil

the Portuguese government and, in January 1822, formed his own government with Andrada at its head. On September 7 Dom Pedro proclaimed independence from Portugal. He was named emperor of Brazil on Dec. 1, 1822, and Andrada became the country's first prime minister.

A cruel and unfair ruler, Dom Pedro dissolved the constituent assembly when it proved unmanageable. He found Andrada too radical and forced him into exile from 1823 to 1829. By 1830 Andrada was back in the good graces of the king, and in 1831, when Dom Pedro was forced to abdicate, Andrada became tutor to the new young king, Dom Pedro II.

Accusations of political intrigue led to Andrada's arrest and imprisonment in 1833. Although eventually released, he was never again active in public life. He died at Niterói, Brazil, on April 6, 1838.

ANDROPOV, Yuri (1914–84).

On Nov. 12, 1982, two days following the death of President Leonid Brezhnev, Yuri Vladimirovich Andropov was elected the new leader of the Soviet Union. Far less was known about Andropov than about the five men who led the country before him. His sudden rise to eminence was unusual in that from May 1967 until May 1982 he had headed the KGB, the Soviet intelligence agency. This powerful position had proven to be a political dead end for some of his predecessors.

Andropov was born on June 15, 1914, in the village of Nagutskaya in the Stavropol region, the son of working-class parents. Of his early education little is known, but he began his association with the Communist party at age 16, when he joined Komsomol, the Young Communist League. For a time he worked as a boatman on the Volga River, and in 1936 he graduated from the Inland Waterways Transport College at Rybinsk. Three years later, at 25, he joined the Communist party itself, and in 1940 he was appointed first secretary of Komsomol in the Karelo-Finnish Autonomous Republic. Four years later he was appointed second secretary of the party's Central Committee at Petrozavodsk.

The turning point in Andropov's career was his transfer to Moscow in about 1951 and an assignment to the party's Central Committee there. Appointed ambassador to Hungary in 1953, he helped put down the Hungarian uprising of 1956. He was recalled to Moscow in 1957 to become party secretary in charge of relations with East European countries. In this post he aided Hungarian leaders in their program of reform. By 1973 he had become a full member of the party's Politburo. In contrast with his reputation for relentlessly putting down dissident political opinions within the Soviet Union while head of the KGB, Andropov was often perceived as a leader open to new ideas. General Secretary Andropov was elected to the Soviet presidency on June 16, 1983. He was not seen in public for several months before his death in Moscow on Feb. 9, 1984.

ANEMIA see BLOOD.

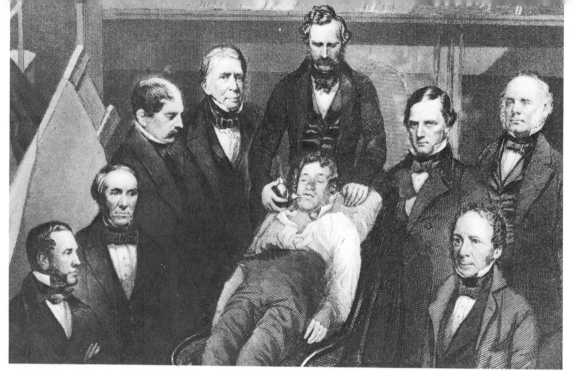

Dr. William Morton, a dentist who had first successfully used ether in extracting a tooth in September 1846, gives the first public demonstration of the use of this anesthetic on Oct. 16, 1846. Surrounded by the medical staff at Massachussetts General Hospital, Dr. Morton administers ether to a patient being prepared to undergo a serious tumor operation.

ANESTHESIA. Certain drugs called anesthetics are able to cause complete or partial loss of feeling. The loss of feeling they produce is called anesthesia. Before their discovery in the late 19th century, surgery was performed only in extreme emergencies and usually resulted in death from shock. The use of effective anesthetics can produce many hours of pain-free unconsciousness, which allows a surgeon to perform complex and delicate operations.

The Pain Pathway

To understand the action of anesthesia, it is necessary to understand the way pain is felt. Pain is experienced by the brain. When a toe is stubbed, for example, the injury affects tiny nerves. These pass a signal to other, larger nerves. In this manner, moving as if from a twig on a tree through the branches to the trunk and into the root, pain travels from the toe to the nerves of the spinal column and into the brain. In the brain the signal is instantly decoded, and the message "hurt" is transmitted to the toe. Because of the shorter distance to the brain, a cut finger, for example, hurts more quickly than a similar injury to one's foot or to a toe.

At any point along this branching nerve system, the pain message can be blocked. This is what all anesthetics do—they block or interfere with the signal for pain. There are two broad types of anesthetics—general and local. General anesthetics produce unconsciousness—a deep, controlled sleep. Local anesthetics cause a loss of feeling in one limited part of the body and are given while the patient is awake. Sometimes hypnosis and acupuncture are used to produce

a painless state (*see* Hypnotism; Acupuncture), but these are beyond the scope of this article, which deals only with chemical anesthetics.

General Anesthetics

A general anesthetic produces unconsciousness by depressing the activities of the central nervous system (*see* Brain). The most commonly used methods of administering general anesthetics are inhalation, in which the patient breathes a gas or vapor into the lungs, from which the anesthetic can enter the bloodstream; and injection with a hypodermic needle, usually into a vein. The exact way in which general anesthetics produce their effects is not completely understood. It is known, however, that a general anesthetic is absorbed by blood cells and transported by the circulating blood to the nervous system.

In the nervous system a general anesthetic changes the nerve cells so that normal communication among many of them is closed off for a time. Sensations of all kinds are temporarily blocked from reaching the brain. At the same time, the person under anesthesia cannot move parts of the body. The muscles are completely relaxed, making surgery easier.

During the administration of a general anesthetic, the patient's breathing and heart rate are constantly monitored to make sure that these functions of the autonomic nervous system have not been depressed too far. The effects of a general anesthetic gradually wear off, usually within 12 to 24 hours after administration of the drug ceases.

Different types of anesthesia are used for different kinds of surgical needs. A state of semiconsciousness,

412

called twilight sleep, is often used during the last stage of delivering a baby. Surgical anesthesia produces total unconsciousness.

The oldest inhalation anesthetic, which was accidentally discovered in 1842 by the United States physician Crawford W. Long (*see* Long, Crawford), is ether. Ether is a colorless, highly volatile (easily turned to vapor) liquid. Like many vapor anesthetics, ether is extremely flammable and explosive. Care is taken to keep any source of flame from ether vapor in the operating room. Ether has an unpleasant odor. Because of this and the fact that it produces unconsciousness slowly it is often used after the patient has been put to sleep by another, faster-acting anesthetic. Cyclopropane, halothane, nitrous oxide (laughing gas), and methoxyflurane are other inhalation anesthetics. Many of these are used in combination with other drugs such as narcotics and muscle relaxants.

Barbiturates are drugs that act largely on the sleep center of the brain and that depress the central nervous system. Of several types of barbiturates, thiopentone and hexobarbital are often used to produce anesthesia, usually in combination with an inhalation anesthetic. Pentothal Sodium is known as "truth serum" because it causes the anesthetized patient to talk freely. When used as anesthetics, barbiturates are administered into a vein.

Local Anesthetics

Local anesthetics do not interfere with consciousness. They simply stop sensations from going beyond the area injected with the anesthetic. The most common use of a local anesthetic is by dentists to deaden a part of the mouth while treating teeth.

Injection of a local anesthetic directly into the tissue to be treated is known as infiltration. When the drug is injected around main nerves that lead to the area to be treated, it is called block anesthesia. Novocain, Pontocaine, and Xylocaine are commonly used local anesthetics.

Local anesthetics may be injected into the space around the spinal cord. This produces a complete loss of feeling in the portion of the body below the site of the injection. Spinal anesthesia is limited to below the level of the cord where nerves controlling breathing and heart action are located and therefore is used mostly for surgery below the waist.

Anesthesiology

From 1846, when Boston dentist William Morton first used ether to pull a tooth, to 1937 anesthesia was given by a physician or nurse with little special training in its use. In 1937 a new, special branch of medical practice was established with medical doctors receiving an additional four to five years of training in anesthesia. This specialty is called anesthesiology. The physician with this specialty training is called an anesthesiologist and is an expert in administering the various anesthetics as well as in resuscitation, which is sometimes necessary for patients who develop life-threatening complications under deep anesthesia. The anesthesiologist becomes familiar with the patient's history before surgery in order to be prepared for any problems that may develop during surgery. The use of anesthesia in surgery always incurs a risk, and the extensive knowledge of the anesthesiologist helps to minimize it. The anesthesiologist selects the drugs to be used, decides how they are to be administered, and constantly monitors the patient's condition during the operation, adjusting the anesthetic and oxygen quantities accordingly. Sometimes anesthesia is administered by a nurse or physician called an anesthetist, who is trained to administer certain types of anesthetics. (*See also* Surgery).

An anesthesiologist (below, left) induces a state of unconsciousness by administering an anesthetic through a plastic tube that leads to a vein in the patient's arm. A type of machine (below, right) commonly used to administer gas anesthetics is readied for the next patient.

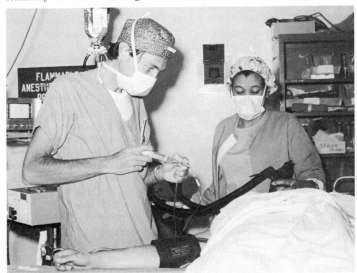

Albert Einstein College of Medicine

Lee Balterman—EB Inc.

ANGEL AND DEMON. The Western religions of Judaism, Christianity, and Islam have all accepted the belief that there is, between God and mankind, a class of intermediary beings called angels. The word angel comes from the Greek word *angelos*, meaning "messenger." Angels are considered to be bodiless minds or spirits who perform various services for God or for people on God's behalf.

Angels are good spirits. They have their counterpart in demons, or evil spirits. The word demon is derived from the Greek word *daimon*, meaning basically any supernatural being or spirit. Belief in spirits of all kinds was quite prevalent in the ancient world. But when Christianity appeared, nearly 2,000 years ago, it condemned belief in such spirits and assigned them the name demon. Ever since, demons have been thought of as evil spirits.

The origins of belief in angels and demons can be traced to the ancient Persian religion of Zoroastrianism. Followers of the prophet Zoroaster believed that there were two supreme beings, one good and the other evil. The good one, Ahura Mazda, was served by angels; the evil one, Ahriman, had demon helpers. Zoroastrians referred to demons as *daevas*, hence the word devil. Belief in good and evil spirits worked its way into Judaism and later into the religions of Christianity and Islam.

Angels are frequently mentioned in the Bible, mostly in the role of messengers from God to man-

The illumination entitled 'Lucifer's Descent into Hell' illustrates the concept of angel and demon.

kind. Their appearances on Earth seem to have been in human form. In the Old Testament books of Job, Ezekiel, and Daniel, as well as in the Apocryphal book of Tobit, angels play significant roles. In the Book of Job the leading demon, Satan, is also introduced. But it is not until the New Testament that Satan is portrayed, under the name Lucifer, as the first of the fallen angels—the angels that rebelled against God.

In the New Testament, angels are present at all the important events in the life of Jesus, from his birth to the Resurrection. In the very dramatic Book of Revelation, angels are portrayed as the agents of God in bringing judgment upon the world. Other New Testament writers also speak of angels. St. Paul especially takes note of them by assigning them ranks. He lists seven groups: angels, archangels, principalities, powers, virtues, dominions, and thrones. The Old Testament had spoken of only two orders: cherubim and seraphim. Early Christianity accepted all nine ranks and in the course of time developed extensive doctrines about both angels and demons. The latter were conceived of as Satan's legions, sent out to lure mankind away from belief in God. Angels and demons play similar roles in Islam and are often mentioned in its holy book, the Koran.

Belief in supernatural spirits has not been limited to the major Western religions. In the preliterate societies of Africa, Oceania, Asia, and the Americas, spirits were thought to inhabit the whole natural world (*see* Animism). These spirits could act either for good or for evil, and so there was no division between them as there has been between angels and demons. The power of these spirits is called *mana*, which can be either helpful or hurtful to people.

Fascination with angels and demons has led to their frequent depiction in works of art and literature. The paintings, stained glass, mosaics, and sculptures of the Middle Ages and Renaissance are especially replete with figures of both. In John Milton's long poem 'Paradise Lost' (1667), Satan himself is a main character; and the angels Raphael, Gabriel, and Michael play prominent roles. In Dante's 'Divine Comedy' (1321?) angels appear as both messengers and guardians, and Satan is vividly portrayed frozen in a block of ice.

ANGEL FALLS. The highest waterfall in the world, Angel Falls barely makes contact with the cliff over which it flows. About 20 times higher than Niagara Falls, it plunges 3,212 feet (979 meters) and is about 500 feet (150 meters) wide at its base.

Angel Falls is on the Churun River, located in the Guiana Highlands in southeastern Venezuela. This area was unknown to Venezuelans until the early 1930's. Overland access is blocked by a huge escarpment (a type of steep slope). However, Venezuelans were able to survey the region with aircraft, and they discovered the falls in 1935. Because of the dense jungle surrounding it, the waterfall is still best observed from the air.

'The Annunciation', a fresco by Fra Angelico, was painted during the years 1438 to 1445. The painting is in the Museum of San Marco in Florence, Italy.

Alinari/E.P.A., Inc.

Angel Falls was named for James Angel, an American adventurer who crash-landed his plane on a nearby mesa two years after the falls had been discovered. The water, which actually seems to be leaping, falls from a flat-topped plateau called Auyán-Tepuí, which means "Devils Mountain." The height of the longest uninterrupted drop is 2,648 feet (807 meters).

Although Angel Falls is difficult to visit, tourists may go there with guides on prearranged tours. In 1971 three Americans and an Englishman climbed the sheer rock face of the falls in an adventure that took ten days. (*See also* Waterfall.)

ANGELICO, Fra (1400?–1455). Called *angelico* (angelic) because of his moral virtues, the monk Fra Angelico was also a great painter who combined the best of the austere Gothic tradition with the spontaneity and brightness of the Italian Renaissance. His works have been praised both for their religious qualities and their artistic excellence.

Born Guido di Pietro at Vicchio near Florence, Italy, he had already gained a reputation as a painter by 1417. He was probably trained by Lorenzo Monaco, the greatest painter and miniaturist of the Gothic tradition. About 1421 he entered the Dominican monastery at Fiesole, taking the name Fra (brother) Giovanni da Fiesole. Most of his life was spent there and in Florence at the monastery of San Marco. He also lived briefly in Cortona and in Rome.

Among the works he executed in Florence are 'Deposition' in the church of the Holy Trinity; the 'Last Judgment' and 'The Coronation of the Virgin' now in the Uffizi Museum; the 'Lamentation' altarpiece for the Brotherhood of Santa Maria della Croce al Tempio; and the 'Annunciation' altarpiece now at a museum in Cortona. During the period 1439 to 1445, while at San Marco, Fra Angelico did most of his mural work and the magnificent altarpiece for the church of San Marco. His murals for the walls of the monastery were the high point in his career. In the chapter hall he executed a large Crucifixion scene, and in one corridor he painted a large 'Annunciation' based on a similar work in Cortona. In 20 of the cells at the monastery, he and his students painted smaller Crucifixion scenes on the walls.

From 1445 to 1450 Fra Angelico worked in Rome, under the sponsorship of popes Eugene IV and Nicholas V, doing frescoes in St. Peter's basilica and in the chapel of the Sacrament in the Vatican. These works have all been destroyed, but his paintings for the chapel of Nicholas V are still extant. In the summer of 1447 Angelico took time out to go to Orvieto to decorate the chapel of Saint Brizio in the cathedral. This work was only partly completed by him. It was continued 50 years later by Luca Signorelli.

Angelico returned to Florence about 1450 to take on his responsibilities as prior of the monastery of San Domenico in nearby Fiesole. His most important work in this period was a cycle of 35 paintings of scenes from the life of Christ. His authorship of most of these paintings is in dispute. Many of them were probably done by his students. But three of them, 'Massacre of the Innocents', 'Flight into Egypt', and 'Presentation in the Temple', are probably his work. For the monastery of Bosco ai Frati he did an altarpiece, now in the Museum of San Marco in Florence, that was his last major work.

Angelico died in Rome on Feb. 18, 1455, in the Dominican monastery. He was buried in the church of Santa Maria della Minerva.

ANGKOR WAT. Angkor means "capital," and a wat is a monastery. The city of Angkor in northwestern Cambodia (now Kampuchea) was for more than 500 years the capital of the Khmer Empire, a kingdom that once ruled most of the Indochinese peninsula. From the end of the 9th century until early in the 13th century, numerous large construction projects

Guy Nafilyan

The 12th-century Angkor Wat still stands as one of Cambodia's most magnificent shrines.

made Angkor one of the most impressive complexes of buildings in the world. After 1431, when armies from Thailand captured and sacked Angkor, the city was abandoned.

The largest and most famous of the buildings in the Angkor complex was Angkor Wat. It was built by King Suryavarman II (ruled 1113–50?) as a temple and administrative center for his empire. All of the religious motifs in the original construction derived from Hinduism. The temple was dedicated to the gods Siva, Brahma, and Vishnu. In 1177 the Cham people of Indochina invaded and sacked Angkor. After this event King Jayavarman VII (ruled 1181–1215?) decided that the gods of Hinduism had failed him. When he built a new capital nearby, Angkor Thom, he dedicated it to Buddhism. Thereafter Angkor Wat became a Buddhist shrine, and many of the carvings and statues of Hindu deities that decorated the temple were replaced by Buddhist art.

The whole Angkor complex, of which Angkor Wat is the largest component, extends 15 miles (25 kilometers) from east to west and 8 miles (13 kilometers) north to south. Besides the buildings, there is a vast system of reservoirs, canals, and moats that were used for water control and irrigation. Together they symbolized the ocean that in Hindu thought surrounded a central mountain, Mount Meru, dwelling place of the gods. In Angkor Wat the five central towers symbolize the peaks of the mountain. The wat is surrounded by an enormous moat, suggesting the oceans at the edge of the world. To reach the wall outside the temple one crosses a 617-foot (188-meter) bridge. Through the gateway the temple is reached by passing through three galleries, each separated by a paved walkway. The temple walls are covered with bas-relief sculptures of very high quality, representing Hindu gods and ancient Khmer scenes.

From the early 15th century, when the Angkor complex was abandoned, until the late 19th century, Angkor Wat was kept intact by Theravada Buddhist monks. It became one of the most important pilgrimage shrines in Southeast Asia. After 1863, when the French colonial system was established in Indochina, the Angkor site became the object of scholarly interest by Westerners. Sponsored by the École Française d'Extrême Orient, teams of archaeologists and other scholars began a program of research that yielded much information about the religious and political system behind the building of Angkor Wat. Archaeologists have also carried out a painstaking program of reconstruction. Many of the original sculptures have been taken to museums to prevent their being stolen. New concrete foundations were put under the buildings to stabilize the walls. New interior walls of concrete were erected behind sandstone blocks. After the 1960's, work on Angkor Wat had to be halted because of the civil war in Cambodia and the subsequent terrorist regime of Pol Pot.

ANGLICAN COMMUNION. In 1534 the Christian church in England separated itself from the jurisdiction of the pope at Rome, and Parliament named King Henry VIII "the only supreme head of the Church of England." This change established a new denomination that became the mother church for many other regional and national church bodies. Together, these church bodies make up what is called the Anglican Communion.

Although the British monarch remains the head of the Church of England, the spiritual and administrative leader is the archbishop of Canterbury. The other church bodies making up the Anglican Communion are autonomous and independent churches with their own bishops and organizational structures. The

Anglican Communion is thus a family of churches that emerged from the same historical background and remains bound together by mutual loyalty and similar beliefs and practices.

The churches of the Anglican Communion are episcopal (from the Greek word *episkopos* meaning "overseer" or "bishop"). The basic geographical unit in a church is the diocese, and each diocese is administered by one bishop. There are approximately 400 dioceses throughout the world.

The diocese belongs to a larger geographical unit called the province. Both the diocese and the province may vary considerably in size. The Church of England has two provinces, while the churches in Australia and Canada have four each. The Protestant Episcopal Church in the United States has nine provinces. Some provinces may include a whole country, as in the cases of Japan and Tanzania. In the cases of Zambia and Polynesia, however, one diocese includes the whole country or area.

The member churches of the Anglican Communion, besides the Church of England, are: the Anglican Church of Australia; the Episcopal Church of Brazil; the Church of the Province of Burma; the Church of the Province of Burundi, Rwanda, and Zaire; the Anglican Church of Canada; the Church of the Province of Central Africa; the Holy Catholic Church of China; the Church of the Province of the Indian Ocean; the Church of Ireland; the Holy Catholic Church in Japan; the Episcopal Church in Jerusalem and the Middle East; the Church of the Province of Kenya; the Church of the Province of Melanesia; the Church of the Province of New Zealand; the Church of the Province of Nigeria; the Anglican Church of Papua New Guinea; the Scottish Episcopal church; the Church of the Province of South Africa; the Anglican Council of South America; the Church of the Province of the Sudan; the Church of the Province of Tanzania; the Church of the Province of Uganda; the Protestant Episcopal Church in the United States; the Church in Wales; the Church of the Province of West Africa; the Church of the Province in the West Indies. There are also smaller churches and diocesan units in such places as Bermuda, the Falkland Islands, Korea, Hong Kong, and Singapore. The worldwide membership was more than 64,000,000 in the early 1980's.

Beliefs and Practices

The separation of the Church of England from the Roman Catholic church in 1534 was intended to be only a break with the authority of the pope, not a departure in faith and practice. Once the separation had taken place, however, the new denomination found itself pushed in different directions by its membership. There were those who wanted to reunite with the Church of Rome; and if they could not attain this goal, they desired to pattern themselves after Catholicism in every respect. Other members were drawn in the direction of the German Reformation, which had taken place only a few years earlier

(*see* Reformation). They wanted a church much more like the one Martin Luther had founded in Germany. This would have meant rejecting all Catholic traditions and practices that could not be specifically verified in the Bible. Still others wanted a more reformed church, one that rejected all similarity to the Roman church. They preferred a church that more closely resembled the simplicity of belief and practice in the earliest centuries of Christianity. The movement they supported eventually came to be called Puritanism (*see* Puritans).

The churches within the Anglican Communion have not attempted to prescribe with exactness what their members are to believe. There are, however, certain foundations of belief and practice commonly accepted by Anglicans. These are: the Bible as the basis of the Christian message; the three ancient creeds of the church—the Apostles' Creed, the Nicene Creed, and the Athanasian Creed; the doctrinal statements propounded by the four Councils of the early church—Nicaea, Ephesus, Constantinople, and Chalcedon; the Thirty-nine Articles; and the Book of Common Prayer.

The Thirty-nine Articles and the Book of Common Prayer were produced by the Church of England in the 16th century. Although they are used by the churches of the Anglican Communion, they are binding only for the Church of England. They are statements of belief that distinguish the Church of England from the positions of the Roman church, on the one hand, and the extreme Protestants on the other.

The Book of Common Prayer is the liturgical service book for Anglicans. First composed in 1549 by Archbishop Thomas Cranmer, it was adopted as the only service book for the Church of England in 1662. In the 20th century it has undergone revisions, and varying versions of it are used by the churches throughout the world. The book allows for a measure of flexibility in the conduct of worship services.

At the Lambeth Conference in 1888, a meeting of Anglican bishops from around the world, a statement called the Chicago-Lambeth Quadrilateral was issued by common consent of all the bishops. Intended as a formulation that could serve as a basis for reconciliation with other Christian denominations, it delineated four positions that are considered essential by Anglicans for all Christians to hold: the primacy of the Bible in the church; acceptance of the sacraments of Baptism and the Lord's Supper; belief in the three historic creeds; and the continuity of the historic ministry of the church.

The idea of the continuity of the church is important to Anglicans. They emphatically deny that Henry VIII was the founder of the Church of England. The church, they maintain, had existed for centuries in England and was an outgrowth and extension of the earliest Christian churches. This historical succession of the ministry of the church is visibly attested to by the office of bishop. The order of bishops traces its descent from the time of Jesus' apostles to the present.

417

The ministry of Anglican churches is divided into three parts: deacons, priests, and bishops. The clergy are allowed to marry. While in some churches the ordination of women is practiced, since the 1970's this has become a divisive issue within the church.

History

In its first decades the Church of England was in great turmoil owing to its internal divisions: the basic problem was whether the church would remain Catholic in essence or whether it would become Protestant. Henry VIII was determined to keep the church Catholic in every way except in allegiance to the pope. After his death, his son Edward VI, who ruled from 1547 to 1553, allowed the Protestant viewpoint to prevail. Queen Mary, who ruled from 1553 to 1558, made a vigorous attempt to return the church to the jurisdiction of the pope.

After Mary's death, her successor, Elizabeth I, was determined to keep the Church of England separate from Rome. Elizabeth disliked the extremes of both Puritanism and Catholicism, and she attempted to work out a tolerant compromise whereby all factions could live together in one national church. She was not allowed to succeed, however. In 1570 Pope Pius V published an interdict, or order, releasing the English people from allegiance to Elizabeth. This act drove the English church toward Protestantism and put English Catholics temporarily in the position of seeming to be traitors to the crown. Nevertheless, the diversity of factions persisted within the English church. The pro-Catholic and pro-Reformed parties continued working toward a mutual accommodation.

In the 17th century the controversy between the pro-Catholic and pro-Reformed parties in the Church of England became more heated. The Puritan cause, or the Reformed group, triumphed temporarily in the English Civil War (1642–48), when the Book of Common Prayer was proscribed and the episcopal structure abolished. After the restoration of the monarchy in 1660, the episcopacy was reestablished and the Book of Common Prayer revised in keeping with the wishes of the pro-Catholic party.

In 1685 James II, a Roman Catholic, came to the throne and attempted to move the church in the direction of unity with Rome. In 1688 a bloodless revolution toppled James from the throne and brought in a Protestant king, William III. In 1689 the English Bill of Rights was passed; it required the monarch to be a Protestant. In 1701 the Act of Settlement required that the monarch also be a member of the Church of England. These statutes remain in effect and keep the church within the Protestant fold.

From the 17th through the 19th century, English explorers founded colonies in the Americas, Africa, India, and the Far East. The Church of England followed the colonists. Through the efforts of its missionary societies—the Society for the Propagation of the Gospel, the Society for the Promotion of Christian Knowledge, and the Church Missionary Society—missionaries founded churches in all of the English colonies. From these missionary efforts grew the separate church bodies that came to form the Anglican Communion.

Because the Anglican Communion is made up of many independent churches, it has developed only the loosest international structure. The first international meeting was the Lambeth Conference of 1867 (named after the London residence of the archbishop of Canterbury). Lambeth conferences convene every ten years, but they do not constitute a governing body for the member churches. They are informal gatherings of representatives from the various Anglican churches.

In addition to the conferences there is a Lambeth Consultative Body that meets every two years to evaluate the work of the conferences and give some cohesion to the work of the churches. In 1948 an Advisory Council on Missionary Strategy was set up to aid in carrying out the missionary activities of the churches. It has no supervisory authority or powers binding on the churches.

In 1968 one additional international organization was formed: the Anglican Consultative Council. Meeting every two years, it represents all areas and interests of world Anglicanism. With slightly more than 50 members, it includes bishops, priests, and lay people. The council has no more authority than the Lambeth Conference, but it reflects and guides the current trends of the Anglican Communion.

THREE ANGLICAN CHURCHES

Anglican Church of Australia. Late in the 18th century, when Australia was still an English penal colony, the first chaplain sent to work with the former convicts was a clergyman from the Church of England. The first bishop of Australia, William Grant Broughton, was consecrated in 1836. The Church of England in Australia, as it was then known, was the established, or state, church until 1890. Since then it has not been supported by public funds. The church became independent from the Church of England in 1962. Membership in the early 1980's was about 4,229,000.

Anglican Church of Canada. Services of the Church of England were first held in Canada at Port Royal, Nova Scotia, in 1710. In 1758 the Church of England became the legally established church. A substantial increase in membership occurred during the American Revolution, when Loyalists from the United States emigrated to Canada. The first bishop, Charles Inglis, was consecrated in 1787. In 1893 the church became independent of the Church of England and elected its own primate, or presiding bishop. Membership in the early 1980's was about 2,567,000.

Protestant Episcopal Church in the United States. The Church of England was the first Protestant denomination in the British colonies of North America. There was a chaplain at the Jamestown settlement as early as 1607. The church became independent of the Church of England after the American Revolution, and Samuel Seabury was its first presiding bishop. The first general convention of the church was held in 1785. There was a temporary split into North-South factions during the Civil War, but they were reunited in 1865. The General Convention of the Episcopal Church, composed of a House of Bishops and a House of Deputies, meets every three years. The House of Deputies has clergy and lay delegates from every diocese. Membership of the church in the early 1980's was about 5,628,000.

ANGOLA. After almost 500 years of Portuguese rule, Angola became an independent nation in 1975. Angola, which is the seventh largest country in Africa, has an area of 481,351 square miles (1,246,700 square kilometers). The nation's estimated population is more than 7 million. Angola was Portugal's largest and richest African colony and was the last of the colonies to gain independence.

Angola lies on the southwestern coast of Africa, and most of the country consists of a plateau covered by open grasslands and small bushes. It also has lowlands along the coast and in the north near the Congo River. In the north, a small area of Angola called Cabinda is separated from the main part of the country by the Congo River and the nation of Zaire. Angola has a tropical climate, with a rainy season of about seven months, from October to mid-May.

Bantu peoples make up most of Angola's native population. Several tribes of Bushmen live in the southeast. Angolan farmers raise sugarcane and cotton on lowland plantations and also grow beans, rice, and corn (maize). On the central plateau of Angola coffee, sisal, and beeswax are produced for export. Some cattle are raised in the plateau areas, where disease-carrying tsetse flies do not threaten them. Angola has valuable diamond deposits and also produces petroleum and natural gas.

History and Government

Before Europeans gained control of Africa during the colonial period, various societies in the Angola area established powerful kingdoms that traded iron and other products. Their economies were based on farming with iron hoes, raising cattle, hunting and fishing, and producing tools and other household goods and crafts.

The Angolan coast was one of the first areas in Africa settled by Portuguese traders after their ships sailed the coastal waters near the end of the 15th century. Angola's capital, Luanda, was founded in 1575, and many buildings and other features of the city's central area resemble those of old Portuguese cities.

Until the end of the 19th century, Portugal actual-

ly ruled only parts of the coastal area and a small section of the interior of Angola. But through the slave trade, military penetration into the interior, and trading in textiles, guns, and other imported goods, the Portuguese had an impact on the entire region. They took about 7 million people from the Congo-Angola area away into slavery, and the area prospered through its slave trade with Brazil, another Portuguese possession. Wars provoked by white and black slave traders sometimes damaged crops, villages, and farms in many parts of Angola.

Some Angolan leaders, such as King Afonso I, who had converted to Christianity in the 16th century, tried to stop the slave trade, but could not. Others, including Queen Nzinga in the 17th century, fought the Portuguese. She ruled her own territory inland from Luanda. Other Angolans cooperated with the Portuguese settlers or officials sent from Portugal.

By the time World War I began in 1914, Portugal had finally conquered all of Angola through a series

Petroleum is shipped from a loading dock at Cabinda, an Angolan port. Crude oil from the tanks on the bluff flows down the pipes, center of photograph, and is loaded into tankers for export.

of bloody wars. The Portuguese officially abolished slavery, but many Africans continued in forced labor on plantations, road construction, and other work.

Under colonial rule Portuguese farmers and businessmen controlled the Angolan economy, which depended largely on coffee, cotton, and other crops. Large companies from South Africa, Europe, and the United States administered Angola's diamond mines and iron mines and the production of its oil, which was discovered in the 1950's. Most of Angola's oil comes from wells in Cabinda.

Many African colonies became self-governing nations during the 1960's, but the Portuguese dictator, Antonio Salazar, did not grant Angola independence. Angola went to war against Portugal in 1961 to gain freedom from colonial rule, and violent guerrilla fighting lasted 14 years. Such organizations as the Popular Movement for the Liberation of Angola (MPLA) fought for independence with the help of several African countries and the United Nations. However, South Africa did not want the MPLA to rule Angola. During the long war South African military forces invaded Angola and destroyed villages and farms. The United States also opposed rule by the MPLA. But with the help of Cuban troops and arms from the Soviet Union the MPLA won the war, and Angola became independent on Nov. 11, 1975. The MPLA leader, Agostinho Neto, took office as Angola's first president. Following his death in 1979, he was succeeded by José Eduardo dos Santos. By the early 1980's almost all countries had recognized the MPLA government; the United States, South Africa, China, and Senegal had not.

The independent Angolan government has expanded the number of schools, hospitals, medical clinics, and community centers, as well as many social services. The government supplies water in some rural areas where wells have been dug, and new irrigation projects also provide water for farmers. Roads have been built to remote parts of the country. Elementary school enrollment has risen dramatically.

During the war against Portugal all but 30,000 of the 335,000 Portuguese left the country. Many were mechanics, doctors, chemists, and others with important skills. Few trained technicians remained to run the economy. This problem, combined with repeated South African military attacks and local political difficulties, has kept the economy in crisis. Only oil production, about 160,000 barrels (21,800 metric tons) a day in the early 1980's, has prevented economic collapse in the potentially wealthy nation. (*See also* Africa.) Population (1980 estimate), 7,078,000.

ANHUI, or ANHWEI. One of the smallest of the 21 provinces of the People's Republic of China, Anhui covers an area of 54,000 square miles (139,900 square kilometers). The province stretches for 400 miles (640 kilometers) from north to south. It

is surrounded by the provinces of Jiangsu to the northeast, Zhejiang to the southeast, Jiangxi to the south, and Hubei and Henan to the west. Hefei, its capital, is located in the heart of the province.

Although its climate is variable, Anhui shares with the rest of mainland China the seasonal monsoon climate of hot, wet summers and cooler, dry winters. Wheat is the predominant winter crop. Summer crops include rice, sweet potatoes, sorghum, soybeans, peanuts, and sesame.

Anhui's main industrial crops are vegetable oilseeds, cotton, fibers, and tobacco. The province has been famous for its tea since the 7th century. Other industries include coal, iron ore, textiles, and chemical fertilizers. Pigs and sheep are raised, and there are nearly 3 million acres (1.2 million hectares) of rivers and lakes that abound in fishes. Fish farms are common all along the Yangtze River (*see* Yangtze). Waterways are the main means of transportation, but there are two rail lines and one highway system.

Throughout its long history Anhui experienced much devastation due to wars, peasant uprisings, and disastrous floods. After World War II, the province was controlled by the Chinese Nationalist party forces. Anhui formed part of the East China Administrative Area from 1949 to 1954, when it became a province of the People's Republic. (*See also* China.) Population (1981 estimate), 48,930,000.

Facts About Angola

Official Name: People's Republic of Angola.

Capital: Luanda.

Area: 481,351 square miles (1,246,700 square kilometers).

Population (1980 estimate): 7,078,000; 15 persons per square mile (6 persons per square kilometer); 21 percent urban, 79 percent rural.

Major Language: Portuguese (official).

Major Religion: Roman Catholicism.

Literacy: 15 percent.

Mountain Ranges: Bié Plateau, Lunda Divide, Melanje Plateau, Serra da Chela.

Highest Peak: Mount Môco, 8,596 feet (2,620 meters).

Major Rivers: Kubango, Kwanza, Kunene, Kwango, Kasai.

Form of Government: People's Republic.

Chief of State and Head of Government: President.

Legislature: People's Assembly.

Voting Qualifications: Loyal citizens over 18 years of age.

Political Divisions: 17 provinces including the coastal enclave of Cabinda.

Major Cities (1970 census): Luanda (480,613), Huambo (61,885), Lobito (59,528), Benguela (40,996).

Chief Manufactured and Mined Products: Beer, cement, cigarettes, crude petroleum, diamonds, natural gas, petroleum products, refined sugar.

Chief Agricultural Products: *Crops*—bananas, beans, cassava, coffee, corn (maize), cotton, palm oil, sisal, sugarcane, tobacco. *Livestock*—cattle, goats, pigs.

Flag: *Colors*—red, black, and gold (*see* Flags).

Monetary Unit: 1 kwanza = 100 lwei.

The letter A

probably started as a picture sign of an oxhead, as in Egyptian hiero-glyphic writing (1) and in a very early Semitic writing used about 1500 B.C. on the Sinai Peninsula (2). About 1000 B.C., in Byblos and other Phoenician and Canaanite centers, the sign was given a linear form (3), the source of all later forms. In the Semitic languages this sign was called *aleph,* meaning "ox."

The Greeks had no use for the *aleph* sound, the glottal stop, so they used the sign for the vowel "a." They also changed its name to *alpha.* They used several forms of the sign, including the ancestor of the English capital A (4). The Romans took this sign over into Latin, and it is the source of the English form. The English small "a" first took shape in Greek handwriting in a form (5) similar to the present English capital letter. In about the 4th century A.D. this was given a circular shape with a projection (6). This shape was the parent of both the English hand-written character (7) and the printed small "a" (8).

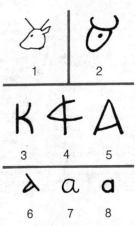

A-1, artificial satellite, *table* S-344

Aa, lava L-90

AA. *see in index* Alcoholics Anonymous

AAA. *see in index* Agricultural Adjustment Agency

AAC. *see in index* Alaskan Air Command

A.& P. Company. *see in index* Great Atlantic and Pacific Tea Company, The

Aachen (or Aix-la-Chapelle), West Germany, city near Belgian border; pop. 307,654 A-2, *map* W-252
Charlemagne C-274
treaty (1748) M-107
World War II W-289

Aalborg, Denmark, chief port of n. Jutland; pop. 114,159.

Aalto, Alvar (1898–1976), Finnish architect A-2
architecture A-568
Finlandia Hall, *picture* F-91
furniture F-462

AAP. *see in index* Association of American Publishers

Aardvark (or African ant bear, or ant bear, or earth pig), mammal *Orycteropusafer* of the family Orycteropodidae A-3
Mammalia, *picture* A-436

Aardwolf, hyena-like mammal A-3

Aare (or Aar), largest river (180 mi; 290 km) entirely within Switzerland B-174, *map* S-537

Aarhus, Denmark, seaport and 2nd largest city; pop. 181,518
Denmark D-97, *map* D-100

Aaron, first high priest of Israelites, brother of Moses; with Moses led Israelite exodus from Egypt M-495
breastpiece J-112

Aaron, Hank (or Henry Louis Aaron; born 1934), outfielder, a right-handed hitter, born in Mobile, Ala.; with Milwaukee Braves 1954–65, Atlanta Braves 1966–74, and Milwaukee Brewers 1975–76; led in home runs in National League 1957, 1966, 1967, tied for lead 1963; on May 17, 1970, had 3,000th major-league hit (a single) and 570th home run; in April 1974 made 715th home run, breaking Babe Ruth's record B-95

AAU. *see in index* Amateur Athletic Union of the United States

AAVSO. *see in index* American Association of Variable Star Observers

ABA. *see in index* American Basketball Association

ABA (or American Book Awards), U.S. L-241

Aba (or abayah), sleeveless outer garment worn by Arabs N-295

Abaca (or Manila hemp) H-133, R-291, P-256, 260, *picture* H-133, *table* F-76

Abacus, calculating device A-4, A-591, S-497

Abadan, Iran, city on island of same name in the Shatt-el-Arab; pop. 306,000 A-4
Iran, *picture* I-307, *map* I-312

Abaft (or aft), direction aboard a boat, *diagram* B-326

Abalone, shellfish, *picture* S-151

Abana, river. *see in index* Pharpar

Abbai River. *see in index* Blue Nile River

'Abbas, al-, Islamic leader C-55

Abbas I the Great (1557–1628), ruler of Persia P-214

'Abbasids (750–1258), Islamic dynasty I-365
caliphate C-55

Abbe, Cleveland (1838–1916), meteorologist and astronomer, born New York, N.Y. W-856

Abbess, head of a convent M-448

Abbeville, France, town on Somme, 12 mi (19 km) above English Channel; pop. 23,770
prehistoric relics M-74

Abbeville, La., town 65 mi (105 km) s.w. of Baton Rouge; pop. 12,391.

Abbevillians, a prehistoric people, *picture* M-77
hand axes M-74

Abbey, monastic house M-445, *pictures* M-444

Abbey Theatre, on Abbey Street, Dublin, Ireland; center for Irish literary revival Y-339
Irish literature I-327

Abbot, head of a monastery M-446, *picture* M-447

Abbot, Anthony. *see in index* Oursler, Charles Fulton

'Abbot, The', historical novel by Scott (1820) S-74

Abbotsford, baronial home of Sir Walter Scott on Tweed River, Scotland S-73, *picture* S-74

Abbott, John (1821–93), Canadian jurist and statesman A-5

Abbreviation A-5

ABC .*see in index* American Bowling Congress

ABC. *see in index* American Broadcasting Company

'Abd ar-Rahman (fl. 750–788), Umayyad caliph of Spain C-55

Abdication, renunciation of an office, usually by a ruler. *see table following*

'Abd ol-Baha' (1844–1921), Baha'i leader B-19

Abdomen
human body
muscles, *pictures* A-395
nerves N-129, *diagram* N-130
insects I-217

'Abdor Rahman Khan (1880–1901), Afghan ruler A-91

'Abduction from the Seraglio, The', comic opera by Mozart O-463, *picture* O-464a

Abdülhamid II (1842–1918), sultan of Turkey; came to throne in 1876; deposed 1909 T-323

Abdul-Jabbar, Kareem (born 1947), U.S. basketball player A-8

Abdullah (1882–1951), Jordanian leader J-142

Abdullah ibn-Hussein (1882–1951), king of Jordan 1946–51, born Mecca, Arabia; 2d son of Hussein ibn-Ali; assassinated July 1951, *list* A-704

Abe, Akira (born 1934), Japanese writer J-83

Abe, Kobo (born 1924), Japanese writer J-83

Abel, Niels Henrik (1802–29), Norwegian mathematician A-8

Abel, Rudolf (1902–72), Soviet spy
espionage E-303

Abelard, Peter (1079–1142), French scholar and philosopher A-8
educational contribution E-84
Latin literature L-78
philosophy P-265

Abelmosk, species of hibiscus H-153

Abelson, Philip Hauge (born 1913), physicist, born in Tacoma, Wash.; director of Geophysical Laboratory, Carnegie Institution of Washington, 1953–71, president 1971–78; with E. McMillan, discovered element neptunium 1940 P-394

Aberdare, Wales, urban district in s.e.; pop. 38,210; coal mining; refractories (firebrick), electric cable, television and radio sets, record players.

Aberdare National Park, Kenya N-23

Aberdeen, Md., residential town 22 mi (35 km) n.e. of Overlea; pop. 11,533; Aberdeen Proving Grounds nearby; incorporated 1892, *map* M-139

Aberdeen, Scotland, city on e. coast; pop. 203,612 A-9, *map* S-67

Aberdeen, S.D., city in n.e.; pop. 25,956; railroad center and wholesale distribution point; food processing, machinery; Northern State College; home of Fischer quintuplets, *maps* S-335, 323, U-40
climate, *list* S-321

Aberdeen, Wash., port city on Grays Harbor, adjacent to Hoquiam and about 45 mi (70 km) w. of Olympia; pop. 18,739; lumber products; fishing; canneries, *maps* W-52, U-40

Aberdeen, University of, Scotland A-9

Aberdeen Angus. *see in index* Angus

Aberdeen Proving Ground, Md.; U.S. reservation; pop. 7,403; for testing ordnance; *map* M-139

Aberdeenshire, county of n.e. Scotland; 1,971 sq mi (5,105 sq km); pop. 321,783; stock raising, agriculture, granite quarrying, fishing A-9

Aberhart, William (1878–1943), Canadian political leader, born in Seaforth, Ont.; an organizer of Social Credit party in Alberta; premier of Alberta 1935–43 A-267

Aberration, physics
lenses P-284
chromatic and spherical S-371
telescope T-66

Aberystwyth, Wales, municipal borough, resort on Cardigan Bay; pop. 10,420; seat of one of colleges of University of Wales and of National Library of Wales.

Abidjan, Ivory Coast, capital and port, on lagoon connected with Atlantic Ocean; pop. 685,800 A-9
Ivory Coast I-406, *picture* I-407

Abilene, Kan., city on Smoky Hill River about 85 mi (140 km) n. of Wichita; pop. 6,572; shipping point for farm produce; Old Abilene Town, restored village
Eisenhower E-134
Hickok, Wild Bill H-153

Abilene, Tex., city about 140 mi (225 km) s.w. of Fort Worth; pop. 98,315; trade and shipping center for farming and ranching region; petroleum products, packed meats, cottonseed products, clothing, candy, faucets, watches; Hardin-Simmons University, Abilene Christian University, McMurry College; military installations nearby, *map* U-40

Abington, Mass., community 4 mi (6 km) n.e. of Brockton; pop. of township 12,334; settled 1668, incorporated 1713, *map* M-161

Abington, Pa., urban township n. of Philadelphia; pop. 59,084; chiefly residential; area turned over to William Penn 1683 by Tammany, Delaware chief, *map* P-185

Abiogenesis (or spontaneous generation)
evolution E-364

Abitibi, Lake, on Ontario-Quebec boundary, Canada; 2 lakes joined by narrows; total area 356 sq mi (922 sq km), most of it located in Ontario; source of Abitibi River, *maps* O-456b, Q-9a

Abitibi River, Ontario, Canada, flows 340 mi (550 km) n. from Lake Abitibi in e. Ontario to Moose River near James Bay; site of large hydroelectric power plant O-456c

Ablation, in aerospace, *table* A-70

Abnaki, people M-53, N-171, *tables* I-136, 138

Abnormal psychology P-522

Åbo, Finland. *see in index* Turku

Abolitionist movement, antislavery movement in United States A-9
Allen A-308
Brown B-465
Civil War issue C-471
Douglass D-234
Dred Scott decision D-259
Garrison G-36
Greeley G-279
Grimke sisters G-286
Liberty and Free-Soil parties P-433, *table* P-495a
Phillips P-263
Stevens S-445
Sumner S-511
Truth T-302
Tubman T-303
Whittier W-158
women's rights movement W-215

Abolition Society, in England A-10

Abominable snowman A-503, M-443

Abominations, Tariff of A-37

Aborigines (or aboriginals), original, or earliest known, inhabitants of a country or area A-10. *see also in index* Pygmy
Australia A-794, *pictures* A-795, A-816
boomerang B-364
India
racial classification, *chart* R-26

Abortion A-11, B-214, B-284
adoption availability A-49
criminal law C-769
United States Supreme Court decision U-196b
women's rights W-215

Aboukir Bay (or Abukir Bay), on n. coast of Egypt, w. of Rosetta mouth of Nile; here Nelson destroyed French fleet (1798), N-127, N-11

Abraham, founder of Hebrew nation A-12, I-360, J-148
Arab origins A-526
Koran stories K-268
Moslem beliefs M-195

Abraham, Plains of. *see in index* Plains of Abraham

'Abraham and the Archangel Michael', mid-12th century tapestry, *picture* T-25

Abraham Lincoln Birthplace National Historic Site, in Kentucky N-29, *picture* K-213

'Abraham Lincoln Walks at Midnight', work by Lindsay A-534

Abrahams, Peter (born 1985), African novelist A-123

Abramovitz, Max (born 1908), architect, born in Chicago, Ill.; partner of Wallace K. Harrison 1940–; designed Corning Glass Center and Philharmonic Hall, Lincoln Center, *picture* U-112

Abrasive, substances used for grinding or polishing, for sharpening tools, etc., as emery wheels and sandpaper A-13

carborundum S-195b
diamond M-332
grinding tools T-224
grindstone O-416
sandblast S-38, P-399

Abruzzi and Molise, historical region in central Italy; divided into separate regions 1965; 5,881 sq mi (15,232 sq km); pop. 1,564,318; includes highest point of Apennines, Gran Sasso d'Italia ("great rock of Italy"), culminating in Mt. Corno (9,560 ft; 2,914 m)
tomb, *map* J-101

Absalom, handsome, unscrupulous son of David; rebelled against his father; caught by his long hair in tree when riding, and slain by Joab; deeply mourned by David (II Sam. xiv-xviii) D-41

'Absalom, Absalom', work by Faulkner A-360

Absaroka Range, n.w. Wyoming R-234a, *maps* W-315, 326, U-80, Y-343

Absent-mindedness H-290

Absolute magnitude, astronomy A-721

Absolute temperature scale H-111. *see also in index* Kelvin scale; Rankine scale

Absolute zero H-111, C-793, *table* W-96
Kelvin, Lord K-196
thermodynamics E-221

Absorption
energy R-34, S-373, *diagrams* R-35
ink I-207
light S-371
refrigeration R-136
spectrum S-371

Abstinence B-307

Abstract art P-58
mobiles and stabiles S-93
Mondrian M-425a
tapestry design T-27

'Abstract Composition', painting by Riopelle P-67a

Abstract expressionism (or action painting) P-64, *picture* P-440
De Kooning's contribution D-68
Kandinsky's influence K-171

Abstraction, writing W-309

Abu, Mount, Rajasthan, India; 5,650 ft (1,720 m); in s.w., 110 mi (180 km) n. of Ahmadabad; tombs, temples, and shrines cover mountainside where Jain pilgrims have gathered for more than 2,000 years.

Abu Bakr (or Abu Bekr; 573-634), first Muslim caliph, born in Mecca, Arabia; initiated spread of Islam as world religion M-421
caliphate C-54

Abuja, Federal Capital Territory, Lagos, Nigeria L-22

Abukir Bay, Egypt. *see in index* Aboukir Bay

'Abundance', drawing by Botticelli D-253

Abu Simbel, Egypt, two temples of Rameses II hewn in rock near 2d cataract of Nile; first discovered in 1812 A-732, *picture* S-79

Abutment, in architecture, *diagram* M-205

Abydus (or Abydos), Asia Minor, ancient city at narrowest point of Hellespont.

Abydus (or Abydos), Egypt, ancient city on Nile, once second only to Thebes; held sacred as burial place of Osiris.

Abyla, in ancient geography, one of the Pillars of Hercules; on African coast opposite modern Gibraltar; now called Apes' Hill.

Abyssal hill, of the ocean floor O-398d, *map* O-395c

Abyssal plain O-398d, O-395a, *map* O-395c-d
earth E-14

Abyssal zone. *see in index* Deep-sea life

Abyssinia. *see in index* Ethiopia

A.C. *see in index* Alternating current

A. C. Nielsen Company, United States
television ratings T-73

Acacia (or wattle), genus of shrubs and trees A-783

Académie, educational district, France F-351

Academy A-14
ancient Athens P-384
ballet training B-32
French R-204
Russian R-332h

Academy award, motion picture industry M-528, *pictures* M-503, 516, *table* M-516. *see also in index* Oscar winning director, *picture* M-510

Academy of Motion Picture Arts and Sciences M-528
award M-528, *pictures* M-503, 516, *table* M-516. *see also in index* Oscar winning director, *picture* M-510

Academy of Natural Sciences, Philadelphia, Pa.; established 1812; noted for extensive historical collections in all the natural sciences; displays several million specimens P-251c, *map* P-251b

Academy of St. Luke, Rome, Italy R-254

Academy of Sciences, France
Lavoisier's role L-90
metric system W-95, M-236

Academy of Sciences, U.S.S.R. R-332h

Academy of Television Arts and Sciences, Hollywood, Calif., established 1946 for the advancement of television; first president, Edgar Bergen. *see also in index* Emmy

Acadia, former French colony in North America A-14, A-338, N-373f, N-162f, M-55, P-497
Canada C-91

Acadia National Park, Maine N-29, *map* N-30, *pictures* N-29, M-59

A cappella, in music M-556, *table* M-566a

Acapulco, Mexico, seaport on Pacific, 180 mi (290 km) s.w. of Mexico City; pop. 456,655 A-15, M-240, *maps* M-241, 260e, *picture* M-252
historic trade with Manila M-87

Acarina, order of arthropod animals; includes the mites and ticks S-388

Acarnania, district of ancient Greece on w. coast, n. of Gulf of Patras; inhabitants, hunters and herdsmen, lingered behind rest of Greece in culture; now forms, with Aetolia, a prefecture of modern Greece (2,137 sq mi; 5,535 sq km); pop. 228,989

Accault, Michel. *see in index* Aco, Michel

Accelerando, in music, *table* M-566a

Acceleration, physics
aerospace hazards A-82
energy, *table* E-217
gravitational acceleration P-160
mass relationship M-168
mechanics M-209
Newton calculation A-714
space travel S-342a, 345, 346, 348b

Accelerator, in business B-517

Accent, in music M-554, *table* M-566a

Accent, in pronunciation, stress or emphasis placed on certain syllables in pronouncing a word. If a word has more than one accent, the most important is called the primary, the less important, the secondary; many foreign languages have definite rules of accent; English has no definite rules, but usually stresses the first syllable in short words
spelling clues S-376

Accessibility, in housing H-244

Acciaccatura, in music, *table* M-566a

Accident
automobile A-862
causes S-3, *chart* S-4, *pictures* S-9
disability D-163
first aid. *see in index* First aid
insurance I-233
lifesaving. *see in index* Lifesaving
police role P-426, 428, *picture* P-425
prevention. *see in index* Safety

Accidental, in music M-564

Accipiter, genus of hawks H-74
falconry F-13

Accipitridae, a family of carnivorous birds, including the kites, hawks, and ospreys; characterized by long legs, rounded wings, and unnotched beaks B-278

Accolade, in knighthood K-258

Accommodation (or focusing), ability of the eye lens to adjust from a distant to a near focus E-388, B-205

Accommodation, intellectual process P-390b

Accordion M-568
reed used R-121

Accounting A-15
financial report, *table* B-59a
vocation V-367

Account manager, in advertising A-60

Accra, Ghana, capital and railroad terminus; pop. 998,772; made capital of British Gold Coast Colony 1876 A-17, *map* A-94
Ghana G-139

Accretion, of land I-256

Acer, tree of maple genus M-92

Acesines River, in Kashmir and the Punjab. *see in index* Chenab

Acetaminophen, in medicine A-387

Acetate, a salt of acetic acid; made by mixing acetic acid with a base; its many forms have a wide scope of industrial uses
man-made fibers F-72
rayon R-98
photographic film P-291
use of generic name F-103

Acetic acid, an organic acid; gives vinegar its characteristic taste; important to industry in making of various acetates O-503. *see also in index* Acetate
photographic stop-bath solution uses P-292
vinegar V-326
white lead manufacture P-73

Acetobacter, genus of bacteria B-15

Acetone, an organic compound, $(CH_3)_2CO$, used as a solvent
bacteria produce B-17
formula O-502
gas G-38

ABDICATIONS OF IMPORTANCE
(For biographical information, *see in index* names below)

Name	Title	Country	Date	Cause
Diocletian (245-313)	Emperor	Roman Empire	305	Wearied of rule
Romulus Augustulus (born 461?)	Emperor	Roman Empire	476	Revolt of German mercenary troops
Richard II (1367-1400)	King	England	1399	Insurrection
Charles V (1500-1558)	Emperor	Holy Roman Empire	1556	Wearied of rule
Mary Stuart (1542-87)	Queen	Scotland	1567	Insurrection
Christina (1626-89)	Queen	Sweden	1654	Distaste for rule
James II (1633-1701)	King	England	1688	Insurrection
Napoleon I (1769-1821)	Emperor	France	1814 1815	Defeat by foreign powers
Pedro II (1825-91)	Emperor	Brazil	1889	Revolution
Manuel II (1889-1932)	King	Portugal	1910	Revolution
Pu-yi (Hsuan T'ung) (1906-67)	Emperor	China	1912	Revolution
Nicholas II (1868-1918)	Czar	Russia	1917	Revolution
Ferdinand I (1861-1948)	Czar	Bulgaria	1918	Defeat in World War I
William II (1859-1941)	Emperor	Germany	1918	Revolution
Charles I (1887-1922)	Emperor	Austria-Hungary	1918	Revolution
Mohammed VI (1861-1926)	Sultan	Turkey	1922	Revolution
Edward VIII (1894-1972)	King	Great Britain	1936	Clash over marriage
Carol II (1893-1953)	King	Rumania	1940	Ousted by dictator
Victor Emmanuel III (1869-1947)	King	Italy	1946	Gave crown to son Humbert
Michael I (born 1921)	King	Rumania	1947	Communists dominated government
Wilhelmina (1880-1962)	Queen	Netherlands	1948	Gave crown to daughter Juliana
Leopold III (1901-83)	King	Belgium	1951	Gave crown to son Baudouin
Farouk I (1920-65)	King	Egypt	1952	Forced to abdicate
Charlotte (1896-1985)	Grand Duchess	Luxembourg	1964	Gave crown to son Jean
Juliana (born 1909)	Queen	Netherlands	1980	Gave crown to daughter Beatrix

Adana, Turkey, city in s.e.; pop. 574,515; situated on old Roman road; once rival of Tarsus; has castle of Harun al-Rashid T-320

Adapa, in Mesopotamian mythology B-7

Adaptation, in biology, fitness of organisms for their different lives; ability to change with environment A-39. *see also in index* Aestivation; Animal migration; Ecology; Hibernation; Protective coloration; Struggle for existence
anthropology A-483
insects I-212
living things L-267
man. *see in index* Man, *subhead* adaptation to environment
plants. *see also in index* Plants, *subhead* adaptation
prehistoric animals A-459

Addams, Charles (Samuel) (born 1912), cartoonist, born Westfield, N.J.; well known for his macabre style; contributor to 'The New Yorker' since 1935.

Addams, Jane (1860–1935), U.S. social reformer A-40
Hall of Fame, *table* H-11
immigrant aid W-215c
Woman's Peace party W-215d

Addax (or addas), an antelope of n. Africa and Arabian peninsula S-16

Adder, the common viper V-328

Adderley, Herbert (nicknamed Herb Adderley; born 1939), football player, born Philadelphia, Pa.; corner back; Green Bay Packers 1961–69, Dallas Cowboys 1970–72.

Adder's-tongue. *see in index* Dogtooth violet

Addiction, habitual or compulsive devotion to something
drug. *see in index* Drug abuse
gambling G-9

'Adding Machine, The', work by Rice A-356

Addis Ababa, Ethiopia, capital; pop. 1,277,159 A-40, E-313, *picture* E-314

Addis Ababa, University College of, Addis Ababa; first university in Ethiopia; founded 1950; opened 1951, *picture* A-104

Addison, Joseph (1672–1719), English poet and essayist A-41
literary contribution E-270
Swift S-531

Addison, Ill., village 19 mi (31 km) w. of Chicago; pop. 28,836; foundries; industrial heating equipment.

Addison's disease H-227–8

Addition, in mathematics A-590
binary system N-379a
fractions F-338
magic square M-164b, *diagram* M-164c
subtraction S-497

'Addition' (or 'Proslogium'), work by St. Anselm A-467

Additive color mixing, color process C-558

Additive inverse. *see in index* Negative numbers

Additives, chemical substances in foods F-274
food processing F-281

Additive system of numeration N-379

Address, forms of, *table* E-317

Adelaide, South Australia, capital and trade center; 7 mi (11 km) from sea on Torrens River; pop. 933,300 A-41, A-767

Adelard of Bath (fl. early 12th century), English scholastic philosopher
translation of 'Elements' E-325

Adelboden, a picturesque valley and village in Switzerland, about 25 mi (40 km) from Lake of Thun; mineral springs; pop. 3,276.

Adélie penguin P-162, *pictures* A-426, P-161

Adelphean (or Alpha Delta Pi), sorority
fraternities and sororities F-389

Aden, People's Democratic Republic of Yemen, national capital in s.w.; on Gulf of Aden; pop. 343,000; formerly in Aden Colony and Protectorate A-42, Y-341. *see also in index* Yemen, People's Democratic Republic of

Adenauer, Konrad (1876–1967), German political leader A-42, G-125
Kennedy, *picture* K-202

Adenine, a purine base that codes hereditary information in the genetic code in DNA and RNA
genetics G-56

Adenoids, a pharyngeal tonsil, *diagram* N-371

Adenosine, in biochemistry P-273. *see also in index* Adenosine diphosphate; Adenosine triphosphate

Adenosine deaminase, enzyme, *table* E-290

Adenosine diphosphate (ADP), in biochemistry B-201, P-273

Adenosine triphosphate (ATP), in biochemistry B-200, B-238, P-273, *diagram* B-202
fatigue F-45

Ader, Clement F. (1841–1926), French aircraft designer; flew his airplanes secretly on grounds of Château d'Armainvillier, near Paris A-201

Adhesive A-43
cement C-243
gum G-318
plastics P-381
plywood P-397

Adige River, n. Italy, rises in Tyrolean Alps and empties into Gulf of Venice; about 230 mi (370 km) long; 170 mi (270 km) navigable; changed its course in AD 587 A-50

Adirondack Forest Preserve, New York N-49, A-44, *picture* N-49

Adirondack Mountains, in n.e. New York A-44, N-237, *maps* E-25, N-239, 261, U-36, 50, *pictures* N-238, 255

Adjective, a word, phrase, or clause that serves to modify, or make more exact, the meaning of a noun or pronoun; may be placed before the noun, after the noun, or after a linking verb; three degrees of comparison: the positive (tall), comparative (taller), and superlative (tallest)
grammar G-209
pronoun usage P-508

Adjustment, social M-173, S-61h, *picture* M-175

Adjutant General's Corps, U.S. Army
insignia, *picture* U-10

Adjutant stork of Africa. *see in index* Marabou

Adjutant stork of India, large East Indian bird *Leptoptilus dubius* S-456

Adler, Alfred (1870–1937), Austrian psychologist A-45
individual psychology P-519

Adler, Felix (died 1962), U.S. clown; wore white-face makeup (grotesque); noted for pantomime; performed until year he died C-437

Adler, Mortimer J. (born 1902), U.S. educator and author A-45

Adler Planetarium and Astronomical Museum, Chicago, Ill., in Grant Park; established 1930; given to city by Max Adler; noted for Zeiss optical projector and collection of astronomical instruments.

Ad libitum, in music, *table* M-566a

Administration, Office of, United States U-157

Administration of Justice Act, U.S. history
Continental Congress C-692

Administrative law, government A-46, B-506

Administrator, law
legal definition, *table* L-92

Admiral, U.S. Navy N-94, *table* N-96
fleet admiral. *see in index* Fleet admiral
insignia, *pictures* U-8

'Admiral Graf Spee', German armored cruiser W-267
'Exeter' model, *picture* S-177

Admiralty Islands, group of small islands in Bismarck Archipelago; 800 sq mi (2,100 sq km); pop. 15,765; coconuts, pearls N-168, *map* P-4

Adobe, sun-dried brick, or a clay for bricks A-46
brick B-436
housing
American Indians I-128, *pictures* A-600, I-113, S-35
Mexico M-244, *picture* M-245
shelter S-159
oven, *picture* S-338
village. *see in index* Pueblo
watchtower, *picture* N-33

Adoff, Mrs. Arnold. *see in index* Hamilton, Virginia

Adolescence, transition period from childhood to adult life A-47
acne A-20
adopted children A-50
anorexia nervosa A-467
bibliography P-525
bone injury B-342
change of voice V-377
child abuse C-319
draft
Russia R-332a
juvenile delinquency J-162
maturity M-173, *pictures* M-174
Philippines P-254
play P-385
psychology P-522
reproductive organs mature R-151c
venereal disease V-274
youth organizations. *see in index* Youth organizations
youth suffrage approved N-293f
26th Amendment U-154

'Adonais', elegy by Shelley on death of Keats S-154

Adonis, in Greek and Phoenician mythology A-49

Adonis, asteroid A-716

Adoption A-49
family law F-21

'Adoration of the Shepherds', medieval mystery play, *picture* M-298

'Adoration of the Shepherds, The', panel painting by Giorgione, *picture* G-146

Adoula, Cyrille (1921–78), Congolese public official, born Léopoldville; premier of Democratic Republic of the Congo (now Zaire) 1961–64 Z-353a

ADP. *see in index* Adenosine diphosphate

Adrenal gland (or suprarenal gland) G-153
anatomy A-392
hormone H-227, *diagram* H-225, *table* H-226

Adrenaline (or epinephrine), hormone H-228, *table* H-226

Adrenocorticotropic hormone (ACTH) H-225, *list* M-192, *table* H-226
gland G-153

Adria, ancient town, Italy A-50

Adrian IV (full name Nicholas Breakspear; 1100?–1159), only English pope; elected 1154; quarreled with Emperor Frederick Barbarossa, initiating long contest between papacy and house of Hohenstaufen P-445, *table* P-99

Adrian VI (1459–1523), pope 1522–23; born Utrecht, Netherlands; became pope through influence of his ex-pupil Emperor Charles V
popes, *table* P-99
Utrecht U-236

Adrian, Edgar Douglas (1889–1977), English physiologist, born in London; with Sir Charles Scott Sherrington discovered function of neuron; at Cambridge University after 1937, professor of physiology 1937–51, Master of Trinity College 1951–65. *see also in index* Nobel Prizewinners, *table*

Adrian, Gilbert (1903–59), U.S. dress designer, created glamorous images for movie stars D-271

Adrian, Mich., city on Raisin River 30 mi (50 km) s.w. of Toledo, Ohio; pop. 21,186; aluminum products, automobile parts and chrome plating, cable controls and linkage, laboratory and hospital furniture, concrete and metal products; Siena Heights College and Adrian College, *map* M-285

Adrianople (Turkish Edirne), Turkey, historic city on Maritsa River, 135 mi (220 km) n.w. of Istanbul; pop. 39,410; grapes, wine, silk, cotton; leather products; named Adrianople for Roman Emperor Hadrian; battle of Adrianople (378), in which Visigoths defeated Roman Emperor Valens, marked beginning of Rome's decline; city fell to Turks 1361 and for nearly a century was their capital; awarded to Greece 1920; regained by Turkey 1923
siege (1912–13), *table* W-8d
treaty (1829), *table* T-274

Adriatic Sea, an arm of the Mediterranean, e. of Italy A-50. *see also in index* Ocean, *table*

Adua. *see in index* Adwa

Adult education A-50
citizenship training N-53
population P-449
Mexico M-247, *picture* M-250
United States U-113
YMCA Y-345
YWCA Y-346

Adulteration, food. *see in index* Food adulteration

Adultery M-117

Adult teeth (or permanent teeth, or secondary teeth), human T-51, *picture* T-52

Ad valorem duty, export tariff T-29

'Advancement of Learning, The', work by Bacon B-11

Advection fog F-246

Advent Christian Church, Adventist church organized in 1860 A-53

Adventists, various religious denominations believing in second coming of Christ A-53. *see also in index* Seventh-day Adventists

Adventitious cyst C-811

'Adventures of Augie March, The', novel by Saul Bellow; winner of 1954 National Book Award A-362, B-157

'Adventures of Huckleberry Finn, The', work by Twain A-352

'Adventures of Tom Sawyer, The', work by Twain A-352

'Adventures While Preaching the Gospel of Beauty', work by Lindsay L-228

'Adventure to the Western Ocean', book by Lo Mou-teng C-390

Adverb, a word, phrase, or clause that modifies, or makes more exact, the meaning of a verb, adjective, or another adverb; used to show comparison, or degree; can usually be shifted to another position in sentence without changing meaning
grammar G-209

Advertising A-54
cigarette T-200
communication C-611
consumerism C-687
cosmetics C-728
economics E-63
'Lusitania' warning, *picture* S-177e
magazine M-33
methods U-109
newspaper N-230
propaganda. *see in index* Propaganda
publicity. *see in index* Publicity
radio R-48, 55
television R-48, T-73
vocational opportunities V-365

Advertising agency A-60

Advisory Council on Missionary Strategies A-418

Adwa (or Adua), Ethiopia, town in n.; pop. 6,000; Italians defeated (1896); captured by Italians (1936); freed from Italy in World War II.

AE. *see in index* Russell, George William

AEC. *see in index* Atomic Energy Commission (United Nations); Atomic Energy Commission (United States)

Aëdes aegypti, new name for Stegomyia mosquito M-497, 500, P-93, *picture* M-498

A.E.F. *see in index* American Expeditionary Force

Aegean civilization, flourished (3000–1200 BC) in Crete and neighboring islands and mainland A-61, A-538, G-263
dress D-260
history, *chart* H-161
Homer's poems H-211
shelter S-157

Aegean Islands, the multitude of Greek islands in the Aegean Sea between Greece and Turkey; principle islands Northern Sporades, Cyclades, and Dodecanese G-254

Aegean Sea, arm of Mediterranean between Greece and Asia Minor A-63, A-61, G-263. *see also in index* Ocean, *table*
mythology T-168

Aegeus, mythical king of Athens; father of the great Athenian hero Theseus and husband of the sorceress Medea who tried to poison Theseus A-63, T-168

Akiba / Alberta

Akiba Ben Joseph (c. 50–136?), Palestinian father of rabbinic Judaism A-221
Akihito (born 1933), crown prince of Japan; married commoner Michiko Shoda 1959; son Naruhito Hironomiya born 1960; visited U.S. 1960, *picture* J-35
Akimiski Island, District of Keewatin, N.W.T., largest island in James Bay; measures 60 mi (96 km) long and 25 mi (40 km) wide; area 898 sq mi (2,326 sq km), *map* O-456b
Akita, Japan, city on n.w. Honshu at mouth of Omono River; pop. 235,873; petroleum products, woodenware, silk textiles; university.
Akkad, Mesopotamian kingdom C-461
Akko, Israel. *see in index* Acre
Aklavik, N.W.T., village on left bank of Mackenzie River; pop. 721; trading post in agricultural and cattle raising region.
Akosombo Dam, dam, Ghana, on Volta River A-106, *picture* A-109
  Ghana G-139
Akritas, Digenis (died 788?), Byzantine author G-279
Akron, Ohio, city 35 mi (55 km) s.e. of Cleveland; pop. 237,177 A-221, *maps* O-420, U-41
  tire manufacture R-303, *picture* O-415
'Akron', U.S. Navy airship B-43, *picture* B-40
Akron, University of, Akron, Ohio, U.S.; founded in 1913 A-221
Ak-Sar-Ben, civic organization in Neb. O-454
Akureyri, Iceland, town in n. on Eyja Fjord; good harbor; pop. 9,943; second town in importance and size; incorporated in 1786 I-11, *picture* I-13
Akutagawa, Ryunosuke (1892–1927), Japanese writer J-82
ALA. *see in index* American Library Association
Alabama, state, U.S.; 51,609 sq mi (133,615 sq km); cap. Montgomery; pop. 3,890,061 A-222, *maps* U-41, 58
  cities. *see also in index* cities listed below and other cities by name
    Birmingham B-222
    Mobile M-417
    Montgomery M-475
  geographic region
    South, the U-56, *map* U-58
  history
    Civil War C-472
      Confederate States of America C-642
    early settlement M-417
  King, Martin Luther, Jr. K-244
  parks, monuments, and other areas
    Battleship Alabama Memorial Park M-417
    Horseshoe Bend N. Mil. P. N-39
    Russell Cave N. Mon. N-44, *map* N-30
  petroleum P-230
  state symbols
    bird W-223
    flag, *picture* F-159
    tree P-328, *table* W-218
  Statuary Hall, *table* S-437a
  taxation, *tables* T-37, 39
  Tennessee Valley Authority T-100, *map* T-101
'Alabama', British built steam cruiser in U.S. Civil War A-238, C-643
  Civil War incident C-477, G-218
'Alabama', music by Coltrane C-587
'Alabama', U.S. battleship M-417
Alabama, University of, university, near Tuscaloosa, and at Birmingham and Huntsville, Ala.; state control; opened 1831; at University: arts and sciences, commerce and business administration, education, engineering, home economics, law, and social work; at Birmingham: general studies, dentistry, medicine, nursing, and optometry; at Huntsville: humanities, engineering, natural science and mathematics, and social and behavioral science; graduate studies at all three locations A-226
Alabama Agricultural and Mechanical University, university Normal, Ala.; state control; opened 1875; arts and sciences, agriculture, applied science, business, education, home economics; graduate studies A-227
'Alabama' claims A-238
  Grant's role G-218
  Russell blamed R-319
Alabama River, river, Alabama, 312 mi (502 km) long; navigable to Montgomery; used for shipment of sand, gravel, logs, pulpwood, cotton, gasoline U-58
Alabaster A-238
Aladdin, character in 'Arabian Nights' A-525
Alamance Creek, Battle of (1771) N-327
Alameda, Calif., city on island in San Francisco Bay, nearly touching Oakland; pop. 70,968; shipbuilding; shipping terminals; U.S. naval air station, *maps* U-40
Alameda County State College. *see in index* California State University, Hayward
Alamein. *see in index* El Alamein
Alamo, fortified Franciscan mission in San Antonio, Tex. A-238, S-35, T-119, 124, *picture* T-115
  Davy Crockett's defense C-779
  flag F-154, *picture* F-155
Alamo Canal. *see in index* Imperial Canal
Alamogordo, N.M., town 90 mi (145 km) s.w. of Roswell; pop. 23,035; diversified industry; farming, ranching, lumbering; lumber processing; state school for blind; nearby are Holloman Air Force Base, White Sands National Monument, Indian reservation, Lincoln National Forest N-211
  atom bomb test N-377h, *picture* N-213
Aland Islands (Finnish Ahvenanmaa), archipelago off Finland at Gulf of Bothnia; area 1,481 sq mi (572 sq km); pop. 20,981; ceded to Russia by Sweden (1809); awarded by League of Nations to Finland (1921) S-524
Alaric (370?–410), king of Visigoths (West Goths), born on island in Danube; under Theodosius, commanded Gothic auxiliaries 394; was elected king of Visigoths 395.
  Goths G-197
Alaska, state, U.S.; 586,412 sq mi (1,518,791 sq km); pop. 400,481; cap. Juneau A-239, *maps* U-39, 94, 117, N-308, P-417
  agriculture U-34, *picture* U-93
  Aleutian Islands A-278
  American Indians I-156
  animals
    bear B-116
    reindeer R-139
    seals S-99, *picture* S-100
    state bird G-292
  Arctic regions A-571
  bibliography U-138
  cemetery, national N-20
  cities. *see also in index* cities listed below and other cities by name
    Anchorage A-402
    Fairbanks F-11
    Juneau J-152
  climatic regions, *map* U-119
  coastline, *map* U-117
  conservation P-441e
  elevation, *map* U-117
  fisheries, *picture* U-93
  glaciers N-38, *pictures* U-38, I-4, N-28f
  history
    boundary dispute A-256, R-286
    Johnson J-128
    statehood S-429a
      Eisenhower's administration E-141
  minerals
    petroleum P-230, *pictures* P-234, U-196b
  mosquitoes M-496
  mountains
    Rockies R-234, *map* R-234a
  northernmost point, *map* U-117
  parks and monuments N-38, *maps* U-94, N-30
    Mount McKinley N.P. M-22, *pictures* N-28f
  people
    Eskimo E-301, *pictures* U-95, 230
  pipelines, *picture* T-265
  rivers Y-352
  Russian exploration A-339
  state symbols
    bird, *picture* N-58
    tree S-398, *table* W-218
  Statuary Hall, *table* S-437a
  taxation, *tables* T-37, 39
  transportation
    Alaska Highway. *see in index* Alaska Highway
  tundra, *picture* B-217
Alaska, Gulf of, along s. coast of Alaska between Alaska Peninsula and Alexander Archipelago U-94, 39
Alaska, University of, near Fairbanks, Alaska; state control; incorporated 1917, opened 1922; arts and letters, behavioral sciences and education, biological sciences and renewable resources; earth sciences and mineral industry, economics and government; engineering, physical sciences; graduate study; senior college campuses including graduate studies at Anchorage and Juneau; community colleges at Anchorage, Auke Bay (Juneau-Douglas), Bethel, Kenai, Ketchikan, Kodiak, Palmer, Sitka A-245, *picture* A-249
Alaska boundary dispute A-256, R-286
Alaska cedar, evergreen tree *Chamaecyparis nootkatensis* of pine family, sometimes called yellow cedar or yellow cypress; average height 80 ft (20 m); tapering trunk, conical crown; lives over 500 years; wood clear yellow; also known in lumber trade as cedar, Sitka cypress, yellow cypress, Nootka cypress and Alaska cypress, *table* W-218
Alaska Claims Settlement Act (1971) I-156
Alaska Federation of Natives (AFN) I-156
Alaska Highway, (first called Alaska-Canada Highway, or Alcan Highway) A-256, A-244, B-455, R-217
Alaska moose M-486
Alaskan Air Command (AAC), U.S. Air Force A-164
Alaska Native Claims Settlement Act (1971) A-245
Alaskan Boundary Arbitration treaty (1903), *table* T-274
Alaskan brown bear B-116, *picture* B-117
Alaskan malamute, dog, *picture* D-200
Alaska Peninsula, s.w. extension of Alaska, *maps* U-39, 94
Alaska Purchase Treaty (1867), *table* T-274
Alaska Range, part of the coast range system, s. of the Yukon drainage system, Alaska; includes Mt. McKinley M-22, A-256, A-402, *maps* U-94, 39
Alaska seal S-100
Alaska time T-189, *map* U-40
Alava Cape, n.w. Washington, s. of Cape Flattery; westernmost point of United States, not including Alaska and Hawaii, *maps* W-52, U-117
Alba, Duke of. *see in index* Alva
Alba Longa, Italy, city of ancient Latium, birthplace of Romulus and Remus; founded, according to tradition, by Ascanius, son of Aeneas R-241, R-258
Albania, country along e. coast of Adriatic Sea; 11,100 sq mi (28,700 sq km); cap. Tiranë; pop. 2,800,000 A-257, *map* W-253
  Balkan states B-25
  Church of Albania E-42
  Communism C-620, *map* C-619
  flag, *picture* F-162
  founding B-31
  money, *table* M-428
  national anthem, *table* N-52
  railroad mileage, *table* R-85
  Tiranë T-192
  totalitarianism T-234
Albania, Church of, Eastern Orthodox church E-42
Albany, Calif., residential city on San Francisco Bay, 4 mi (6 km) n. of Oakland; pop. 15,130; U.S. Department of Agriculture Western Regional Laboratory; incorporated 1908 as Ocean View, present name 1909.
Albany, Ga., city on Flint River in s.w.; pop. 74,059; textile industries, meat-packing, peanut and pecan processing, lumber, farm implements; Albany State College; military installations and Radium Springs resort nearby.
Albany, N.Y., capital of state, on Hudson River; pop. 101,727 A-259, *maps* N-261, 239, 250, U-41
  Capitol building, *picture* N-253
  Erie Canal N-244
  New York State Library N-246
Albany, Ore., city about 22 mi (35 km) s. of Salem, on Willamette River; pop. 26,678; farming, logging; lumber and paper products, metals; meat, poultry; vegetable processing, *maps* O-492, U-40
  timber carnival, *picture* O-488
Albany, State University at, Albany, N.Y., part of State University of New York; chartered 1844; arts and sciences, business, education, library science; graduate study, *picture* N-253
Albany Congress, convention of American colonists (1754) A-259, N-249, R-162
Albany-New York Highway (or Albany Post Road) R-220
Albany Regency, group of Democratic 'bosses' who controlled state of New York under Van Buren's leadership (1820–54) V-261
Albany River, river, Ont., 610 mi (880 km) long; rises in w. lake region and flows e. 400 mi (640 km) into James Bay at Fort Albany, *map* O-456b
Albatross, seabird A-260, *picture* P-14
  animal migration A-450
Albay, Philippines. *see in index* Legaspi
Albedo, astronomy S-52
Albee, Edward (born 1928), U.S. playwright A-260, A-363
  drama D-249
  McCullers M-5
Albemarle, N.C., city about 38 mi (61 km) n.e. of Charlotte; pop. 11,126; grain, poultry products, textiles, hosiery, knit goods, furniture, brick and tile; aluminum plant in vicinity; Morrow Mountain State Park nearby, *map* N-336
Albemarle Island (or Isabela Island), largest of Galápagos Islands; area 2,249 sq mi (5,825 sq km); pop. 446; formed from volcanic activity; many craters; sparsely settled; potatoes, cattle, wild hogs, reptile hides, fish G-3
Albemarle Sound, shallow inlet 60 mi (100 km) long indenting coast of North Carolina; just e. of the sound in Kitty Hawk, N.C., near the scene of Wright brothers' first airplane flight N-322, *maps* N-323, 337
Albéniz, Isaac (1860–1909), Spanish pianist and composer, born in Camprodon, near Olot, Spain; child prodigy, later became court pianist to king of Spain; called first Spanish impressionist; operas and piano works M-560
Albert (1819–61), prince of Saxe-Coburg-Gotha, prince consort of Queen Victoria of England; fostered interest in the arts and sciences; died of typhoid fever V-312
  United Kingdom E-253
Albert I (1255–1308), Holy Roman emperor and king of Germany B-344
Albert I (1875–1934), king of Belgium A-260, B-149
Albert II (1397–1439), Holy Roman emperor; was duke of Austria as Albert V; also crowned king of Hungary and Bohemia A-828
Albert Honoré Charles, (1848–1922), prince of Monaco, ruler of the principality of Monaco and oceanographer; succeeded his father, Charles III 1889.
Albert, Lake (or Albert Nyanza), situated in Zaire and Uganda; area 2,064 sq mi (5,346 sq km); named for British prince consort Albert U-1, S-411, Z-353a
Alberta, province in w. Canada; 255,285 sq mi (661,183 sq km); cap. Edmonton; pop. 1,627,874 A-261, C-75, 80
  cities. *see also in index* cities listed below and other cities by name
    Calgary C-30
    Edmonton E-76
  climate P-145
  flag, *picture* F-172
  government agencies G-202
  history C-102
  mountains
    Rockies R-234, *map* R-234a, *pictures* N-299, 24a
  parks N-24b, *maps* N-24b

Alexander, Lloyd (born 1924), author of books for children, born Philadelphia, Pa.; won 1969 Newbery medal for 'The High King' and 1971 National Book Award for 'The Marvelous Misadventures of Sebastian' R-111

Alexander, Sir William (1567?–1640), Scottish statesman A-14

Alexander Archipelago, group of more than 1,100 islands along coast of s.e. Alaska A-241, maps U-39, 94

Alexander Nevski (1220–63), Russian hero and saint A-278 'Alexander Nevsky', film M-524

Alexanderplatz, Berlin, East Germany B-168, pictures B-169, G-116

Alexander the Great (356–323 BC), king of Macedon, son of Philip of Macedon A-279
Alexandria A-281
artillery development A-658
battle formation, picture A-636
Egyptian conquest E-126
exploration E-373
Greek literature G-276
international relations I-259
Isthmian Games of 336 BC C-716
Nebuchadnezzar's palace B-3
Persian campaigns P-212, I-308
Dardanelles crossed D-35
route of army, map M-7
rule of Greek city-states C-461, G-267
Thebes T-163
Turkestan's conquest T-317

Alexandra Feodorovna (1872–1918), empress of Russia, wife of Nicholas II; born Princess Alix of Hesse, granddaughter of Queen Victoria N-284

Alexandria, Egypt, chief seaport; pop. 2,318,655; center of ancient Hellenic culture A-281, E-115
Alexander the Great A-279, picture A-280
ancient Greece G-268
literature G-277
banner, medieval, picture M-294
Cairo C-16
caravan stop, picture S-381
library L-170
Macedonia, map M-7
medical center, ancient M-215
Pharos (lighthouse) S-116, picture S-116

Alexandria, La., city on Red River, near center of state; pop. 51,565; in timber, agricultural, oil, and salt region; railroad center; lumber and cotton products, chemicals; England Air Force Base nearby, map U-41

Alexandria, Minn., city 120 mi (200 km) n.w. of Minneapolis; pop. 7,608; summer resort in lake area; farm trade; museum exhibiting Kensington Runestone, replica of stone once believed to have been left by Norsemen, map M-363

Alexandria, Va., historic city on Potomac River 6 mi (10 km) s. of Washington, D.C.; pop. 103,217; railroad shops; electronic equipment, metal products, chemicals, dairy products, maps U-41, V-331, 349
Christ Church, picture V-334

Alexandria, Church of, Eastern Orthodox church in Egypt E-42

Alexandria Conference (1785) U-139

Alexandrian rite, Eastern rite tradition E-44. see also Coptic church

Alexandrite, variety of chrysoberyl discovered in Russia J-114

Alexandroúpolis (formerly Dede Agach), Greece, seaport on Aegean Sea, near Turkey, 10 mi (16 km) n.w. of estuary of Maritsa River; pop. 22,995; exports grain; belonged to Turkey till 1913–14, to Bulgaria till 1919.

Alexandrov, Alexander (born 1951), Bulgarian cosmonaut, born in Omourtag, Bulgaria, table S-348

Alexis (1690–1718), Russian czarevitch, eldest son of Peter the Great by his first wife, Eudoxia; ruled briefly (1727–30) as Peter II P-226

Alexius I Comnenus (1048–1118), Byzantine emperor, born Constantinople; succeeded 1081; brilliant soldier, efficient administrator; inspired First Crusade C-786
Byzantine Empire B-536

Alfa plant. see in index Esparto grass

Alfalfa (or lucerne), plant
honey H-214
legume L-120
nitrogen gatherer N-291
root, picture R-291

Alfalfa weevil, insect I-225

Alfama, medieval quarter, Lisbon, Portugal L-238

Alfa Romeo, automobile corporation A-512

Al Fatah, Palestinian guerrilla organization A-527

Al Fayyūm, Egypt. see in index El Faiyûm

Alfieri, Vittorio, Count (1749–1803), Italian tragic dramatist, born Asti, Piedmont, Italy; adhered to classic rules; loved the heroic; tried to revive national spirit in Italy; his eventful life recounted in autobiography
Italian literature I-376

Alföld, large fertile plain of central Hungary; irrigation and drainage projects have increased the farm areas; livestock; wheat, corn, alfalfa, hemp, flax H-274

Alfonsín, Raúl (born 1926), president of Argentina; elected in 1983
Argentina A-583

Alfonso IX (1171–1230), king of Leon from 1188–1230; granted rights to assembly of nobles C-469

Alfonso XII (1857–85), king of Spain, born Madrid; succeeded mother (Isabella II) to throne after collapse of first Spanish republic (1874); defeated the Carlists; suppressed Cuban rebellions; reduced national debt; father of Alfonso XIII S-359

Alfonso XIII (1886–1941), king of Spain A-282, S-359
son and grandson S-361, B-384

Alfonso d'Este. see in index Este, House of

Alfred the Great (848?–99), king of Wessex A-282
England
history E-239
literature E-263

Alfred University, Alfred, N.Y.; private control; chartered 1857; liberal arts, education, nursing; graduate school; college of ceramics branch of State University of New York.

Alfvén, Hannes (born 1908), Swedish physicist A-282. See also in index Nobel prizewinners, table

Algae, type of plants, including seaweed A-283, P-370
amoeba feeds A-375
circadian rhythm B-224
coral interaction C-715
diatoms D-132, O-398b, picture M-291
earth E-16
lichens L-191
seaweed S-104
sloths S-218
water pollution P-441c, diagram P-441d

Algebra, branch of mathematics A-285
Boolean system B-364
new-math methods M-164d–e
powers and roots P-484–5, table P-484

Algeciras, Spain, seaport 10 km (6 mi) across bay from Gibraltar; pop. 51,096; present city built 1760 on site of Moorish town destroyed by Spanish 1704
conference (1906) R-286

Alger, Horatio, Jr. (1832–99), U.S. author, born Revere, Mass.; Harvard University graduate; Unitarian minister; books show triumph of poor boys in face of great obstacles; name used as synonym for "rags to riches" success ('Luck and Pluck'; 'Ragged Dick' series).

Alger, Algeria. see in index Algiers

Algeria, nation in n. Africa; 919,353 sq mi (2,381,113 sq km); cap. Algiers; pop. 18,525,000 A-302
Algiers A-306
Atlas Mountains A-746
date palm, picture P-82
flag, picture F-162
history
African independence A-111
Ben Bella B-159
Boumedienne B-383
French conflict F-365
Morocco agreement M-490
money, table M-428
railroad mileage, table R-85
Sahara S-14, map S-15

Algiers (or El Djazair), Algeria, capital and seaport; pop. of greater city 1,800,000; established by Arabs 935 A-306, A-304, W-287

Algin, obtained from seaweed A-284, P-378

Algol, a variable star S-414, charts S-415, 420-2

Algonquian language, I-137, tables I-138, 139

Algonquian group (or Algonkian), group of North American people who lived from Labrador Peninsula to Rocky Mountains and s. to Pamlico Sound and Cumberland River N-162e

Algonquin, people of Algonquian stock living in Ontario and Quebec
American Indians, map I-136, table I-138
flood story M-574
fur trade F-468
Iroquois N-242

Algonquin Provincial Park, s.e. Ont., about 100 mi (160 km) w. of Ottawa; area 2,910 sq mi (7,537 sq km); famous summer resort O-456c, map O-456

Algorithm, problem-solving logic C-635

Algren, Nelson (1909–81), U.S. novelist and short-story writer, born Detroit, Mich.; went on the road through the Midwest and South, talking with the down-and-out whom he later portrayed in his short stories ('The Neon Wilderness') and novels ('The Man With the Golden Arm', 'A Walk on the Wild Side'); elected to

the American Academy and Institute of Arts and Letters 1981 A-367

Alhambra, Calif., city 8 mi (13 km) e. of Los Angeles; pop. 64,615; petroleum refinery; aircraft equipment, iron and steel products; San Gabriel Mission nearby.

Alhambra, palace at Granada, Spain, picture A-358
legends S-481c

Alhambra, International Order of the, Catholic society F-387

'Alhambra, The', work by Irving I-358

'Ali (600?–661), 4th Muslim caliph; one of Mohammed's first followers; reign characterized by unrest and civil strife; died at hand of assassin M-421, C-54
Islam I-359
Islamic literature I-365

Ali, Muhammad (formerly Cassius Marcellus Clay; born 1942), U.S. boxer A-306
championship B-392, picture B-391

Aliákamon River, river, Greece G-255

Alias, legal term
legal definition, table L-92

'Ali Baba and the Forty Thieves', 'Arabian Nights' story A-525

Alibates Flint Quarries and Texas Panhandle Pueblo Culture National Monument, Texas N-29, map N-30

Alibi, legal term
legal definition, table L-92

Alicante, Spain, seaport on e. coast, 77 mi (124 km) s. of Valencia; pop. 103,289; exports wine, fruit, oil; in ancient times Greek colony, then became Roman city, map S-350

Alice, Tex., city 40 mi (65 km) w. of Corpus Christi; pop. 20,961; oil-field supply center; livestock market; cotton processing.

'Alice's Adventures in Wonderland', work by Lewis Carroll C-176, R-111
children's literature L-247, picture L-246
English literature E-278, picture E-279
marionette production, picture P-537

Alidade, a ruler with simple or telescopic sights; also a graduated circle with a sight for taking bearings
navigation N-86, 92
petroleum prospecting P-234–5
surveying device S-520

Alien, person living outside land of birth or adoption without citizenship in country where he or she resides
citizenship C-440
immigration. see in index Immigration
laws. see in index Alien and Sedition Acts
legal definition, table L-92
naturalization. see in index Naturalization

Alien and Sedition Acts (1798), United States A-307
Adams' opposition A-34
Jefferson's opposition J-93
states' rights affected S-429d

Alien Contract Labor Law M-313

Alighieri, Dante. see in index Dante

Alimentary canal (or digestive tract), anatomy
digestion D-142, diagram S-454

Aliphatic hydrocarbons, chemistry. see in index Paraffin series

Aliquippa, Pa., borough on Ohio River, 18 mi (29 km) n.w. of Pittsburgh; pop. 17,094; steel, concrete, map P-184

Al Ittihad, People's Democratic Republic of Yemen. see in index Madinat ash Sha'b

Alkali, compound of hydroxyl with an alkali metal or ammonium A-307
bases A-19
caustic potash P-465
caustic soda S-247. see also in index Caustic soda
electrochemistry E-171
soapmaking uses S-229, 231

Alkali metals A-307. see also in index Cesium; Lithium; Potassium; Rubidium; Sodium
francium, table P-207
photosensitivity P-274

Alkaline earth metals, those forming hydroxides like alkalies A-307. see also in index Barium; Beryllium; Calcium; Magnesium; Radium; Strontium
acids and bases A-19
periodic table, table P-207

Alkali soil, soil containing unusual amount of salts of potassium, sodium, magnesium, or calcium S-251

Alkaloids, nitrogen-containing organic compounds of plant origin; they are bases, that is, they react with acids to form salts; may occur oily or crystalline
antidotes P-411
atropine N-289
caffeine P-248a
cocaine N-15, P-222
colchicine P-368
morphine B-298
quinine Q-18
strychnine S-490
tobacco T-198

Alkekengia. see in index Chinese lantern plant

Al-Khwarizmi (780?–840?), Arab astronomer and mathematician A-293

Alkyd P-228, table P-382

Alkylation P-241a

Allah, Arabic proper name for God, in Islam M-419, K-268, I-359

Allahabad (translation City of God), India, city at junction of Ganges and Jumna rivers; pop. 490,622; cotton, grain; University of Allahabad

Allama Iqbal Open University. see in index People's Open University

All-American Canal, s.e. Calif.
California C-36
Colorado River C-586
Imperial Valley water supply I-59
irrigation I-356

Allantois, endodermal sac E-201

Allard, Harry Ardell (1880–1963), botanist, born Oxford, Mass.; with Bureau of Plant Industry, U.S. Department of Agriculture, 1906–46 P-373

Allegheny Mountains, Appalachian system U-37, maps U-50, 59
Maryland M-125
New York N-238, map N-239
Ohio O-412, map O-413
Pennsylvania P-164, map P-165
Virginia, maps V-330, 348
West Virginia W-111, map W-112

Allegheny Plateau, U.S. A-508

Allegheny Portage Railroad National Historic Site, near Johnstown, Pa. N-29

THE AMERICA'S CUP COMPETITIONS

Year	Races	Winner	Loser
1851	1	America (United States)	Royal Yacht Squadron fleet (Great Britain)
1870	1	N.Y. Yacht Club (U.S.)	Cambria (Brit.)
1871	5	Columbia, Sappho (U.S.)	Livonia (Brit.)
1876	2	Madeleine (U.S.)	Countess of Dufferin (Canada)
1881	2	Mischief (U.S.)	Atalanta (Canada)
1885	2	Puritan (U.S.)	Genesta (Brit.)
1886	2	Mayflower (U.S.)	Galatea (Brit.)
1887	2	Volunteer (U.S.)	Thistle (Brit.)
1893	3	Vigilant (U.S.)	Valkyrie II (Brit.)
1895	3	Defender (U.S.)	Valkyrie III (Brit.)
1899	3	Columbia (U.S.)	Shamrock (Brit.)
1901	3	Columbia (U.S.)	Shamrock II (Brit.)
1903	3	Reliance (U.S.)	Shamrock III (Brit.)
1920	5	Resolute (U.S.)	Shamrock IV (Brit.)
1930	4	Enterprise (U.S.)	Shamrock V (Brit.)
1934	6	Rainbow (U.S.)	Endeavour (Brit.)
1937	4	Ranger (U.S.)	Endeavour II (Brit.)
1958	4	Columbia (U.S.)	Sceptre (Brit.)
1962	5	Weatherly (U.S.)	Gretel (Australia)
1964	4	Constellation (U.S.)	Sovereign (Brit.)
1967	4	Intrepid (U.S.)	Dame Pattie (Aust.)
1970	5	Intrepid (U.S.)	Gretel II (Aust.)
1974	4	Courageous (U.S.)	Southern Cross (Aust.)
1977	4	Courageous (U.S.)	Australia (Aust.)
1980	5	Freedom (U.S.)	Australia (Aust.)
1983	7	Australia II (Aust.)	Liberty (U.S.)

Amino acids, group of organic acids containing amine radical NH_2; obtained by breakdown of protein in digestion, re-formed as proteins in body cells B-199, B-237, P-514, N-292, O-503, M-190
- albumin composition A-272
- embryology E-202
- enzymes E-290
- evolution E-365
- glycine O-503
- hormone manufacture H-229
- immune system I-56
  - disease D-167
- liver L-261
- milk contains M-322
- PKU H-145
- synthetic fibers F-72

Aminobenzene. see in index Aniline

Aminoglycoside, drug A-489

Amir (or emir), title used in Muslim countries, corresponding roughly to British title of lord; used to denote ruling power or distinct office; also title of honor given to descendants of Mohammed through his daughter Fatima
Kuwait K-311

Amir Khosrow (1253-1325), Persian poet
- Indian literature I-107
- Islamic literature I-367

Amis, Kingsley (born 1922), British writer
- literary contribution E-282, picture E-283

Amish, a branch of the Mennonite church, named from Jacob Ammon, or Amen, who founded it in Switzerland and s. Germany 1698, insisting on strict interpretation of Mennonite principles; many members migrated to Pennsylvania 1730–40, later to Ohio, Indiana, and other states, picture P-170
- family structure F-16

'Amistad', ship in slave revolt, picture B-290

Amistad Dam, dam, Rio Grande, between Texas and state of Coahuila, Mexico R-209, map M-260d

Amistad National Recreation Area, Texas N-29, map N-30

Amitosis, biology, direct cell division, in which the nucleus and the rest of the cell are squeezed into two parts by constriction. see also in index Mitosis

Amman, (Biblical Rabbath Ammon, ancient Philadelphia), modern capital of Jordan; pop. 648,587 A-370, Jordan J-141

Ammann, Othmar Hermann (1879–1965), U.S. bridge designer, born in Schaffhausen, Switzerland; to U.S. 1904, became citizen 1924; chief engineer 1930–37, director of engineering 1937–39 of Port of New York Authority (now Port Authority of New York and New Jersey) B-447

Ammeter, instrument for measuring electric current in amperes G-7. see also in index Galvanometer

Ammonia
- fertilizer F-32, F-58
- inorganic chemistry solvent I-210
- manufacture
  - calcium cyanamide C-19
  - catalytic methods N-292
  - nitric-acid production N-291
  - comet contains A-716
- refrigerating systems R-136
- stimulant for poisoning cases P-411

Ammonite, extinct type of mollusk belonging to the class Cephalopoda; had a flat spiral shell like the modern nautilus; a common fossil
- animal life record, table E-24
- prehistoric animals 461, A-459

Ammonium, chemical radical
- chloride, or sal ammoniac
  - electric dry cell B-108
  - soda production S-247
- diuranate N-378c
- sulfate
  - fertilizer N-292

Ammonium chloride (or sal ammoniac)
- Solvay process produces S-247

Ammonium nitrate, chemical compound
- inorganic chemistry I-211

Ammons, A.R. (born 1926), U.S. poet A-364

Ammunition A-371, A-658
- firearms F-96
- Krupp family K-306
- machine gun M-9, diagrams M-11, table M-9
- shell. see in index Shell

Amnesia A-373

Amnesty, a pardon A-373
- criminals P-505b
- draft resisters P-144
  - Carter grants C-184
  - Ford grants F-303
- pirates P-342a

Amnesty International, organization working to free prisoners jailed for political or religious reasons; founded 1961; members in 107 nations; chairman 1961–75, Sean MacBride A-374. see also in index Nobel Prizewinners, table

Amnesty and Reconstruction, Proclamation of (1863), Lincoln's offer of pardon to all citizens of the seceded states (except certain prominent leaders) who would lay down their arms and take an oath to support the Constitution R-114

Amniocentesis, medical technique B-215
- genetic disorder detection G-48

Amnion, membrane forming a closed sac
- embryology E-201
- human fetus, diagram M-542a

Amoeba, single-celled organism A-374
- breathing R-159
- cells C-238
- classified Protozoa P-515
- evolution E-366
- foot motion F-288
- living things L-265

Amoebic dysentery (or amebic dysentery), disease causes A-375, picture D-170

Amon. see in index Amen

'Amore dei Tre Re, L' ' ('The Love of the Three Kings'), opera by Italo Montemezzi; first produced at La Scala, Milan, Italy, in 1913
- Garden as Fiora, picture O-462

Amorphous carbon C-157

Amorphous substances S-254g, M-167

Amorphous sulfur S-510

Amos, Hebrew prophet (8th century BC) P-508, 509, picture P-509

Amoy. see in index Xiamen

Ampère, André Marie (1775–1836), French mathematician and physicist A-375
- electricity E-155, picture E-161

Ampere and amperage, electricity E-152
- metric system M-236

Ampere meter. see in index Galvanometer

Ampère's Law, in physics A-375

Amphetamines (street names: upper, pep, speed, bennies, whites), drug D-276
- analgesic A-387
- narcotic N-15

Amphiarthrosis, type of joint J-136

Amphibian, class of vertebrate animals including frogs, toads, and salamanders A-376, Reference-Outline Z-368. see also in index Frog; Salamander; Toad
- animal groups, chart Z-366
- bibliography Z-369, S-64g
- breathing R-159
  - gill slits in young V-304
- embryology E-200
- endangered species E-212
- evolution A-461, E-366, R-152
- first appearance P-487, pictures P-487
- fish compared F-123
- heart R-152
- migratory habits A-452

Amphibian plane
- airplane, picture A-173

Amphibious warfare N-94, 99, 101, 106
- landing craft, pictures N-97, 100, M-110, W-10

Amphibole, silicate mineral M-336

Amphibrach, poetic foot P-405

Amphimacer, poetic foot P-405

Amphineura, class of mollusks M-424

Amphion, in Greek mythology, a son of Zeus; by playing a magic lyre which he had received from Hermes, Amphion charmed stones so that they built themselves into walls of the city Thebes.

Amphioxus (or lancelet), a fish-shaped sea animal; about 2 in. long; pinkish white; several species known; classed in the phylum Chordata, subphylum Leptocardia A-435, picture A-434
- animal groups, chart Z-366
- invertebrate group I-286, picture I-285

Amphipoda, crustacean order C-790

Ampisbaenid, legless reptile group
- lizard comparison L-272

Amphitheater, building in which the spectators' seats surround the place used by the performers. see also in index Stadium
- Colosseum at Rome R-257, map R-250, pictures R-256, 254
- Melbourne music bowl, map M-217a, picture M-217b
- Verona, Italy, picture I-393

Amphora, a large, earthenware container used by ancient peoples to hold oil, honey, or wine and as an ornament; commonly had an oval body, narrow neck, and two handles
- glass G-161

Amplification, electric circuits

Amplification, electric circuits
- instrumentation I-228
- laser and maser L-54
- phonograph P-269, diagram P-268d
- photoelectric devices P-274
- radio R-60, diagrams R-46, 57
- transistor T-249

Amplitude, physics; measure of strength of a wave, similar to height from trough to crest of a water wave
- radio waves R-46, 47
- sound waves S-260

Amplitude modulation
- radio R-46, diagram R-50

Amr canal, built in early Christian era, still used to carry fresh water from the Nile River to the city of Suez, Egypt
- canals C-127

Amr ibn-al-As (or Amru; AD 594?–664), Arab general and statesman, born in Mecca; opposed Mohammed until conversion in 629; known as conqueror of Egypt
- foundation of Cairo C-16

Amritsar, India, city in Punjab state; pop. 407,628; silks, shawls, carpets, chemicals; center of Sikh faith.

Amsterdam, The Netherlands, capital, on Amstel River; pop. 712,294 A-381, map N-133, picture N-137
- climate, graphs N-141
- international trade I-271
- Rijksmuseum (State Museum). see also in index Rijksmuseum

Amsterdam, N.Y., city on Mohawk River and New York State Barge Canal, 30 mi (50 km) n.w. of Albany; pop. 21,872; carpet company headquarters; paper boxes, clothing, plastics, boats, fiber glass, electronics, map N-261

Amtrak (or National Railroad Passenger Corporation) R-87
- transportation T-255

Amu Darya (ancient name Oxus), river of w. Asia, rises on Pamir Plateau; flows 1,500 mi (2,400 km) n.w. to Aral Sea A-88, maps R-322, P-212, M-7
- Afghanistan A-381
- Aral Sea A-527
- Tadzhik S.S.R. T-5
- Turkmen S.S.R. T-326

Amulet, a small object worn as a charm to ward off evil or to bring good luck; may be natural, as a precious stone or a tooth, or man-made, as a medallion M-38, 40
- jewelry and superstition J-112

Amundsen, Roald (1872–1928), Norwegian navigator and explorer A-381, A-474
- discovers South Pole P-421
- Gjöa in San Francisco S-41a
- Northwest Passage P-420, map P-417

Amundsen Sea, sea, in South Pacific Ocean, off Marie Byrd Land, Antarctica; discovered 1928–29 by Nils Larsen, a Norwegian, and named for Roald Amundsen, map W-242

Amurath I. see in index Murad I

Amurath II. see in index Murad II

Amurath III. see in index Murad III

Amurath IV. see in index Murad IV

Amur River, great navigable river of n.e. Asia; 1,755 mi (2,824 km) long A-382, C-338, maps R-322, M-84
- Komsomol'sk, picture S-188
- length, comparative. see in index River, table

Amusement park A-383, P-126
- Anaheim tourism A-387
- Disney's accomplishments D-185

Andover / Anguilla

km); pop. 33,861; cap. Andorra la Vella A-410, *map* S-350
flag, *picture* F-162

Andover, Mass., about 22 mi (35 km) n. of Boston; pop. of township 26,370; rubber products, woolens, plastics; electronics; Phillips Academy; incorporated 1646, *map* M-161
Ryder's 'Toilers of the Sea', in gallery at Phillips Academy P-54, *picture* P-55

Andrada e Silva, José Bonifácio de (1763–1838), Brazilian statesman, geologist, and author, A-411

Andrade, Mario de (born 1928), African poet A-122

Andrade, Olegario Víctor (1841–82), Argentine poet, born in Gualeguaychú, near Paraná; career as journalist but famed for poems.

'Andrea Chenier', opera by Umberto Giordano
Tebaldi as Maddalena, *picture* O-466

Andrea del Sarto. *see in index* Sarto, Andrea del

Andreanof Islands, islands, Aleutian group, *map* U-39

Andrée, Salomon August (1854–97), Swedish scientist and aeronaut, born in Gränna, near Jönköping; made first attempt by air to explore the Arctic P-420
wreck of balloon, *picture* P-423

Andreev, Leonid (or Leonid Andreyev; 1871–1919), brilliant Russian writer, mystic, and fatalist, born in Orel; also lawyer, crime reporter, and editor; died in Finland in poverty
chief works R-361

Andrew, Saint, one of the Twelve Apostles; brother of Simon Peter; a fisherman from Capernaum; patron of Scotland and Russia; festival Nov. 30, A-506

Andrew, Prince (or Andrew Albert Christian Edward; born 1960), son of Queen Elizabeth II of England.

Andrew Johnson National Historic Site, site, Tennessee N-29, *picture* J-126

Andrews, Roy Chapman (1884–1960), explorer and naturalist, born in Beloit, Wis.; director American Museum of Natural History, New York, N.Y., 1935–41; explored Alaska, East Indies, Korea, China, Mongolia, central Asia; discovered huge fossil fields in The Gobi; found first dinosaur eggs ever discovered, about 10,000,000 years old, and skeleton of largest land mammal (natural history: 'This Amazing Planet', 'Nature's Ways'; autobiography: 'An Explorer Comes Home'; for younger readers: 'Quest in the Desert', 'All About Dinosaurs', 'All About Whales', 'Quest of the Snow Leopard', 'In the Days of the Dinosaurs'), *picture* W-131
Gobi M-432

Andrews, Tex., city 40 mi (60 km) n.w. of Midland; pop. 11,061; trade and shipping center for oil-producing and cattle-raising region; cotton, sorghum.

Andreyev, Leonid. *see in index* Andreev, Leonid

Andrianov, Nikolai (born 1952), Soviet gymnast G-325

Andric, Ivo (1892–1975), Yugoslav diplomat and writer, born near Sarajevo, Bosnia, now Yugoslavia ('The Bridge on the Drina'; 'Devil's Yard'; 'The Woman from Sarajevo'). *see also in index* Nobel Prizewinners, *table*

Androgen, male hormone A-47

Android, type of robot R-226

Andromache, Greek mythology; wife of Hector H-122

Andromeda, Greek mythology; daughter of King Cepheus and Queen Cassiopeia of Ethiopia; offered to sea monster to appease Poseidon and sea nymphs, who had been angered by Cassiopeia's boasting of her own beauty
Perseus saves P-210

Andromeda, constellation, *charts* S-415, 420, 423, C-681
galaxy U-199, 201, *list* E-8, *picture* M-232

'Andromeda Strain, The', work by Michael Crichton R-112e, *picture* R-111j

Andronicus III Palaeologus (1296–1341), Byzantine emperor B-536

Andropov, Yuri (1914–84), Soviet premier; former head of KGB A-411
Russian history R-358

Andros, Sir Edmund (1637–1714), English colonial governor of New York 1674–81, New England 1686–89, and Virginia 1692–98, born in London; tyrannical and unpopular R-185
flag F-153, *picture* F-155

Andros, Greece, fertile mountainous island in Cyclades group; in Aegean Sea; area 145 sq mi (380 sq km); pop. 10,457; important ancient naval base.

Androscoggin, river in New Hampshire and Maine; flows 180 mi (290 km) to Merrymeeting Bay; abrupt descent gives immense waterpower U-44
Maine, *map* M-53, 65
N.H., *map* N-170, 182

Andros Island, largest island in Bahama archipelago, 125 mi (200 km) s.e. of Miami Beach, Fla.; area 1,600 sq mi (4,150 sq km); pop. 9576; pine, mahogany, hardwood; fish, sponges; pineapples; oil wells B-20, *map* W-104

'And They Shall Walk', work by Kenny K-207

'Andy and the Lion', work by James Henry Daugherty R-107

Anecdote, literary form
folklore F-260

Anemia, or **anaemia,** term meaning "bloodless" for various forms of a blood disease B-316, B-224a, H-85
folic acid prevents V-355
food and nutrition F-279
iron deficiency I-329
sickle-cell H-145, B-237
vitamin B_{12} V-356

Anemone, sea. *see in index* Sea anemone

Anemophilous flower, wind pollinated F-219

Aneroid barometer B-82

Anesthesia A-412, H-240
antihistamine uses A-492
produced by hypnosis H-290
spinal A-398

Anesthesiologist, specialist in anesthesiology S-519b

Anesthesiology, science of anesthesia and anesthetics A-398, S-61g, *table* M-212c

Anesthetics H-240
body temperature B-207
cocaine N-15
chloroform C-393
first uses M-215c, *picture* M-215d
Long's discovery L-295
opiates O-471

Aneto, Pico de, (French Pic de Néthou), highest mountain 11,168 ft (3,404 m) of Pyrenees, in Spain, about 50 mi (80 km) w. of Andorra

Aneurysm, localized abnormal dilation of an artery D-174

Anfa, Berber village on site of present-day Casablanca, Morocco C-194

Anfinsen, Christian Boehmer (born 1916), biochemist, born in Monessen, Pa.; laboratory chief National Institute of Arthritis and Metabolic Diseases 1963–. *see also in index* Nobel Prizewinners, *table*

ANG. *see in index* Reserves

Angara River, river, Siberia; outlet of Lake Baikal (Baykal); flows 1,150 mi (1,850 km) to Yenisey River; also called Upper Tunguska in lower course, *map* R-345

Angel, James, U.S. adventurer A-415

Angel, John (1881–1960), U.S. sculptor, born in Newton Abbot, Devon, England; to U.S. 1925, became citizen 1936; known for religious figures and war memorials S-85
statues for Cathedral of St. John the Divine, *picture* S-84

Angel and demon, supernatural spirits of intermediary being between God and mankind A-414, *picture* M-447
Bosch's 'Vision of Tondalys', *picture* P-33
Cimabue's 'Madonna of the Angels', *picture* P-29
El Greco's 'Assumption of the Virgin', *picture* P-40
Giotto's 'Descent from the Cross', *picture* P-29
'Jonah and the Whale', Persian miniature P-67e, *picture* P-67e
Memling's 'Madonna and Child with Angels', *picture* P-32

Angel Falls A-414
Guiana Highlands G-302
Venezuela, *map* V-275, *picture* V-276
waterfalls W-73, *table* W-73c

Angelfish, popular name of several freshwater and saltwater fishes, including the scalare, a popular aquarium fish, silver with gray or black bars, under 6 in. (15 cm), native to the Amazon and Guiana; also some types of bright-colored coral-reef dwellers, especially the *Angelichthys,* edible fish weighing up to 4 lbs (2 kg). *see also in index* Spadefish
angel shark or monk fish S-144

Angelico, Fra, title given to Giovanni da Fiesole (1387–1455), Italian religious painter A-415

Angel Island, largest island in San Francisco Bay; seat of U.S. immigration and quarantine stations; Fort McDowell military reservation, established 1865 as Camp Reynolds, abandoned by Army 1946; under Spanish occupation a rendezvous of pirates, *map* S-41b

Angell, James Rowland (1869–1949), educator, born in Burlington, Vt.; son of James Burrill Angell; professor of psychology and dean of faculty University of Chicago 1911–20; president of Yale University 1921–37 P-520

Angell, Sir Norman (or Ralph Norman Angell Lane; 1874–1967), English writer and lecturer, born in Holbeach; at various times resident of U.S.; in early career Paris correspondent for U.S. newspapers; general manager *Paris Daily Mail;* lecturer U.S. universities; ('The Great Illusion'; 'The Fruits of Victory'; 'Let the People Know'; 'After All', autobiography). *see also in index* Nobel Prizewinners, *table*

Angel Mounds, extensive group of prehistoric mounds near Evansville, Ind.

Angelo, Valenti (born 1897), U.S. artist and children's author, born in Massarosa, Tuscany, Italy; to U.S. 1905, became citizen 1923; wrote and illustrated 'Nino', 'Golden Gate', 'Paradise Valley', 'Hill of Little Miracles', 'Marble Fountain', 'Acorn Tree', and 'Honey Boat' R-111a

Angel shark (or monk fish), fish of the family Squatinidae
shark S-144

Angel wings *Barnea costata,* mollusk shell, *picture* S-149

Angers, Félicité. *see in index* Conan, Laure

Angers, France, historic city on Mayenne River, 165 mi (270 km) s.w. of Paris; pop. 127,415; varied manufactures; slate quarry nearby.

Angina pectoris, brief paroxysm of severe chest pain with feeling of suffocation D-173

Angiography, blood vessel X-Rays used in medical diagnosis
disease D-173
diagnosis D-127

Angiosperms (or angiospermae), class of flowering, vascular plants of the division Magnoliophyta having seeds in an enclosed ovary F-220, *Reference-Outline* B-279b
classification of plants P-371
seeds, *picture* S-106
trees T-282

Angkor, group of ruins in Kampuchea built by a cultured ancient people called Khmers; most notable are the temple of Angkor and the old city of Angkor Thom; found in 1861 by the French A-415

Angkor Wat, A-415, A-546
stonecarvings, *picture* I-107

Angle, mathematics
geometry G-73, *diagram* G-73
trigonometry T-285, *table* T-287

Angle milling, a machine tool operation T-221

Angle of incidence
mirror M-371

Angle of reflection
mirror M-371

Angler fish, marine fishes of the order Lophiiformes with lure-like appendages for baiting prey
deep-sea form D-60, *picture* D-59
feeding behavior F-124
use of luminescence F-131

Angles, Teutonic people who invaded Britain E-238. *see also in index* Anglo-Saxon

Anglesey, Wales, island in Irish Sea, connected with mainland by two bridges; pop. 39,155; with nearby Holy Island, constitutes the county of Anglesey; area 276 sq mi (715 sq km); pop. 51,705; cattle, sheep, grain; megalithic remains W-3

Angleworm. *see in index* Earthworm

Anglia, East. *see in index* East Anglia

Anglican Cathedral, Liverpool, England L-262

Anglican church. *see in index* England, Church of

Anglican Church of Australia A-418

Anglican Church of Canada A-418

Anglican Communion, family of churches A-416
canon law C-142

Anglican Consultive Council A-418

Anglicans, members of Church of England and of other churches in communion with it. *see in index* England, Church of

Anglo-Egyptian Sudan. *see in index* Sudan, Democratic Republic of the

Anglo-Japanese Alliance (1902) R-362, *table* T-274

Anglo-Saxon, term applied to Teutonic peoples who conquered Britain in 5th and 6th centuries and by the time of Alfred the Great had become one people; also applied to people of English descent, wherever found, as in Europe, America. *see also in index* Angles; Jutes; Saxons
enamel, *picture* E-208
English literature E-264

'Anglo-Saxon Chronicle' A-282
English literature E-263
quotation W-163

Anglo-Saxon language. *see in index* Old English language

Anglo-Saxon literature. *see in index* Old English literature

Angola, formerly **Portuguese West Africa,** nation on s.w. coast of Africa; area 481,350 sq mi (1,246,690 sq km); pop. 7,200,000; cap. Luanda A-419, A-105
communist world, *map* C-619
Cuban support C-804
flag, *picture* F-162
Luanda L-327
money, *table* M-428
railroad mileage, *table* R-85

Angola, University of, university, Luanda L-327

Angora, Turkey. *see in index* Ankara

Angora goat, mammal from whose hair mohair cloth is made G-171

Angora rabbit
furs F-463

Angoulême, France, city 65 mi (105 km) n.e. of Bordeaux, on Charente River; pop. 46,584; paper, brandy, linen; cathedral begun 11th century; birthplace of Margaret of Navarre.

Angra do Heroismo, city, Azores; pop. 17,476, A-890

Angry Young Men movement, movement in English literature and motion pictures of the 1950s; characterized by disdain for the establishment and its class distinctions and mannerisms M-525
English literature E-282

Angstrom unit (or Å, or A.U.), ten-millionth of a millimeter, used to describe length of light waves; named to honor Jonas Angström S-372, *table* R-34
cell membrane B-237

Anguilla, island of West Indies, in St. Kitts-Nevis group, Leeward Islands; 34 sq mi (88 sq km); withdrew from island federation and declared independence 1967, a move not recognized by United Kingdom; reverted to colonial status 1971; became self-governing British